A
TOUR
in
SCOTLAND
and
VOYAGE TO THE HEBRIDES
1772

A
TOUR
in
SCOTLAND
and
VOYAGE TO THE HEBRIDES
1772

by

THOMAS PENNANT

Introduction by
Charles W.J. Withers

ORIGIN

This edition first published in 2019 by
Birlinn Origin, an imprint of
Birlinn Limited
West Newington House
10 Newington Road
Edinburgh EH9 1QS

www.birlinn.co.uk

First published by John Monk, Chester, in
1774 (Volume 1) and 1776 (Volume 2)

First published by Birlinn Ltd in 1998

Introduction © Charles W.J. Withers 1998

ISBN 978 191247 60 15

Typeset by Initial Typesetting Services, Edinburgh
Printed and bound by Gutenberg Press Ltd, Malta

CONTENTS

———➤●◄———

INTRODUCTION

by Charles W. J. Withers

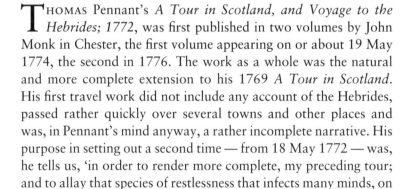

THOMAS Pennant's *A Tour in Scotland, and Voyage to the Hebrides; 1772,* was first published in two volumes by John Monk in Chester, the first volume appearing on or about 19 May 1774, the second in 1776. The work as a whole was the natural and more complete extension to his 1769 *A Tour in Scotland.* His first travel work did not include any account of the Hebrides, passed rather quickly over several towns and other places and was, in Pennant's mind anyway, a rather incomplete narrative. His purpose in setting out a second time — from 18 May 1772 — was, he tells us, 'in order to render more complete, my preceding tour; and to allay that species of restlessness that infects many minds, on leaving any attempt unfinished'. And he admitted too, that some of the things earlier discussed 'merited a little further attention than I at that time paid them'.

Pennant's 1772 *Tour* is not so much a single work, then, as the culmination of a longer individual enterprise designed to describe and to understand Scotland, many parts of which — the Highlands especially — were almost unknown to outside audiences. It is for two principal reasons — which are explored further below — one of the most interesting travel accounts of the late eighteenth century: it represents the mature work of a keenly observant commentator upon the state of Scotland and upon the economic and moral condition of the Highlands in particular, and it illustrates something of the ways in which reliable natural knowledge about other places was then undertaken.

Pennant's contemporaries certainly recognised its worth: reviewers were much more taken with it than with his 1769 tour. The *Critical Review* of July 1774 praised Pennant's accuracy of observation and his 'great attention to the commercial state of the country'. The *London Magazine* in the same month commented upon Pennant's skills in 'communicating to the world, the knowledge of their country in its present state, as well as of several ancient customs and manners, and various antiquities, scarcely known before', and remarked upon his innately sympathetic accounts of Hebridean life which 'cannot fail of inciting both pity and indignation in the human breast'.

Samuel Johnson was taken with Pennant's works. The first volume of Pennant's 1772 *Tour* influenced Johnson then engaged in writing his own *Journey*, just as the 1769 work had been one prompt to his Hebridean travels with Boswell. Boswell also notes Johnson's defence of Pennant whose earlier account of Alnwick and the Percy estates in Northumberland was the subject of criticism by Bishop Percy who felt slighted that Pennant had called his gardens 'trim'. Johnson, in the course of debate with the bishop, termed Pennant 'a Whig, Sir; a sad dog', yet at the same moment remarked, 'But he's the best traveller I ever read; he observes more things than anyone else does'. Boswell, reflecting upon his own experiences and upon Johnson's work, could not agree: 'I could not help thinking that this was too high praise of a writer who traversed a wide extent of country in such haste, that he could put together only curt frittered fragments of his own, and afterwards procured supplemental intelligence from parochial ministers, and others not the best qualified or most impartial narrators ...; a writer, who at best treats merely of superficial objects, and shews no philosophical investigation of character and manners, such as Johnson has exhibited in his masterly 'Journey', over part of the same ground'.

Boswell may here be being loyal to his friend and travelling companion, but he certainly undervalues Pennant's work. Most others appreciated Pennant's work for its factual emphasis, praised the means by which it was undertaken and understood the wider context in which it was set. For the modern reader to understand these things and in order to read Pennant's 1772 *Tour* with interest, we need to know a little more about Pennant himself.

Thomas Pennant was born at Downing in Whitford parish, Flintshire, on 14 June 1726 and educated in Wrexham and, later, The Queen's College, Oxford (although he took no degree). The Pennant family was long established in this area and, with the time afforded by virtue of family wealth, Thomas Pennant began to develop a career as topographer and naturalist even as a young man: he later noted how the gift of a copy of Willoughby's *Ornithology* whilst a boy of 12 stirred his interest in the natural world. In 1746–47, Pennant undertook a tour of Cornwall where he was encouraged by the mineralogist Borlase, and, in 1754, he toured Ireland. His first publication was a short essay on earthquakes, prompted by one felt at Downing in April 1750, but his principal early publication was his four-volume *British Zoology*, the first volume of which was published in 1766. In 1765, Pennant visited mainland Europe and met leading naturalists such as the Comte de Buffon and Peter Pallas, and the philosopher Voltaire. He had by then been corresponding for a decade with Linnaeus, the Swedish botanist and founder of modern plant taxonomy and, arguably, Europe's greatest naturalist in the eighteenth century, and it was through the Swede's support that Pennant was elected a member of the Royal Society of Uppsala in 1757. Pennant was elected a fellow of the Society of Antiquaries in 1754 (but resigned in 1760), and of the Royal Society in London in 1767. In the same year, he began that lengthy correspondence with Gilbert White, then curate at Faringdon in Hampshire, which formed a major part of White's influential text, the *Natural History of Selborne* (1789). At the same time as Pennant was pursuing intellectual interests, he was occupied with the practical demands of estate management and the concerns of a country gentleman. He married, in 1759, Elizabeth Falconer from Chester (she died in 1764). By 1761, Pennant was High Sheriff of Flintshire and, from 1763 and his succession to the family estates at Downing, he expended much effort there in improving the estate.

Pennant's 1772 *Tour* should not be seen, then, either as the work of an unknowing eye or of an untutored mind observing unthinkingly a country undergoing change. To be sure, Pennant was motivated by a concern for completeness arising from his own earlier shortcomings. More importantly, his work and the style he brought to it were influenced by his involvement with Europe's leading naturalists, whose own narratives favoured factual accounts of nature, rooted in direct observation and expressed in clear prose. He was a member of those wider institutionalised networks through which natural knowledge was both undertaken and reported in the eighteenth century, and not just in Europe. Pennant was not some sort of travelling journalist, commenting as he moved upon the scenes before him. He was a more than competent natural philosopher, someone whose scientific contacts and learning and political and domestic responsibilities almost disposed him, as it were, to see and write about things in certain ways.

His first tour had been an impromptu event. But his 1772 tour included travelling companions, each with particular skills: the Rev. John Lightfoot, a botanist, author in 1777 of *Flora Scotica*, a study of Scotland's native flora based on the Linnaean system, and rector of Shalden in Hampshire; the Rev. John Stuart, a Gaelic scholar; and not least, Moses Griffiths, his servant and an 'able artist' who produced the many sketches later published as engravings. Stuart was especially useful, as Pennant acknowledged, 'for a variety of hints, relating to customs of the natives of the Highlands, and of the islands, which by reason of my ignorance of the Erse or Gaelic language, must have escaped my notice'. These social and intellectual connections behind Pennant's 1772 *Tour* and the particular skills of his fellow travellers — botanist-taxonomist, artist and local translator — thus reflect in a smaller way the wider European networks of which he was part and the larger expeditions of the men like Cook, Banks and Bougainville then charting the equally unknown southern hemisphere. And like those counterparts elsewhere, Pennant knew he had, as a 'foreign' observer, to secure the cooperation of the 'natives'. The Rev. Stuart was useful in this respect on a daily basis, and in translating Gaelic plant names for Pennant and Lightfoot. Alerting the locals as to what was wanted would make travelling more effective, both because it presented the opportunity of accumulating natural knowledge systematically, and, if local informants could provide him with much of what he wanted, because he need not stay long in any one place.

It is for these reasons that Pennant advertised his intentions to re-visit Scotland in the *Scots Magazine* in May 1772. In so doing, Pennant was also signalling to the wider community of gentlemanly natural philosophers in Scotland, many of them ministers and gentry, that his enquiries depended upon collective knowledge: 'The great civility and hospitality I experienced in my Journey through part of North Britain in 1769' [declared Pennant], 'encourage me to make a visit to the places I have not yet seen. Permit me to prepare you for my coming, by sending this notice of my intention of being in your neighbourhood the ensuing summer, and paying my respects to you. As my stay can be but very short, I am desirous of being at once directed to the objects most worthy the observation of a traveller ... As my sole objects are my own improvement and the true knowledge of your country, hitherto misrepresented, I have no doubt of your complying with my wishes, which are included in the following queries and requests'. What followed listed questions about topography, commerce, agriculture and local antiquities, together with requests to 'observe and collect against my coming' a variety of natural specimens. Such planning did not endear him to all contemporaries — Horace Walpole as well as Boswell thought his work diminished by such reliance upon others.

Pennant's methods in preparing for his 1772 travels were symptomatic of that growing emphasis upon systematic enquiry characteristic of Europe's natural historians and overseas explorers and, in a Scottish context, they importantly foreshadow Sir John Sinclair's *Statistical Account of Scotland*, completed by parochial ministers working to a pre-circulated brief and published in 21 volumes between 1791 and 1799. Pennant's acknowledged place within and reliance upon the wider scientific community is apparent as early as the *Dedication* in his 1772 *Tour*, which is to Joseph Banks, whose own study in London's Soho Square was the 'centre of calculation' for much late eighteenth-century natural knowledge. Pennant even borrowed Bank's account of the island of Staffa rather than write his own. Pennant was neither lazy nor a plagiarist: he was, simply, prepared to trust what gentlemen of authority and those in position of local knowledge told him, even if his own narrative tends to silence the voices of those who so assisted him.

Pennant's style is that of the factual commentator. He does not embellish his descriptions. His rather deadpan style in the opening sections of his *Tour* may betray a sense of familiarity with the countryside of north-west England, but there is an appealing 'matter-of-factness' about much of his prose. He makes little of the rigours involved in travelling throughout Scotland: of getting to Rum, for example, he almost casually notes; 'Land again: walk five miles up the sides of the island, chiefly over heath and moory ground: cross two deep gullies ... After a long ascent reach Loch-nan-Grun, ... return excessively wet with constant rain.' What was important to Pennant then, and it is one of the reasons, of course, why he is of interest to us now, is his concern for accuracy. Documenting the hardships endured in getting there would not have been regarded as essential to his purpose. Whilst this is, in one sense, laudable, it also has the effect of making his *Tour* and the constant movement on which it was based seem rather uneventful, even timeless.

The structure of his *Tour* is, then, a chronological narrative constructed around description of place — towns, battlefields, natural features and country seats (one later commentator termed it a 'portal-by-portal account'). But it is not one in which we learn much about Pennant actually travelling between places or of attitudes towards the practical difficulties involved in recording one's observations in the field: wearing damp clothes, storing indeterminate specimens, charting 'Rotten, leaky boats' (as he did to get to Gigha), and dining at uncertain hours. Only occasionally are we afforded a glimpse of the companionship, even humour, that must sometimes have marked their travels: 'I shall never forget' [writes Pennant of the MacLeods of Arnisdale] 'the hospitality of the house: before I could utter a denial, three glasses of rum cordialized with jelly of bilberries, were poured into me by the irresistible hand of good Madam Macleod. Messrs Lightfoot and Stuart sallied out in high spirits to botanize: I descended to my boat to make the voyage of the lake.'

Pennant's style, whilst chiefly direct and descriptive, is neither dull nor particularly moral. He only occasionally takes the opportunity to offer personal comments about a place or, even, the state of the nation. His brief account of Nithsdale, for example, as he moved northwards in June 1772, wonderfully evokes something of the pastoral scene: 'Travel over small hills, either covered with corn, or with herds of cattle, flocks of black-faced sheep, attended by little pastors, wrapped in their maides [a sort of long cloak], and setting the seasons at defiance.' His description of Glasgow is of a bustling commercial centre: the prosperity of the tobacco lords, trade with Ireland and with the Americas, a well-to-do population. St Andrew's Church, then only recently completed, is, however, used to cast aspersions about the state of Scotland's churches more generally: 'It is one of the very few exceptions to the slovenly and indecent manner in which the houses of God, in Scotland, are kept: ... for in many parts of North Britain our Lord seems still to be worshipped in a stable, and often in a very wretched one.'

But such remarks are generally few and far between. This is partly, one feels, because of Pennant's own disposition to accurate description rather than to personal comment. Partly, too, it stems from his concern to document the history of particular places or features in which context he sometimes resorts to the work of earlier authorities. He does so both to provide a legitimacy for his own views but also, where Pennant feels it necessary, to correct others' opinions. During his stay at Kirkcaldy, for example, he sent Moses Griffiths out to sketch a nearby stone column earlier 'most erroneously figured by Sir Robert Sibbald' (the natural historian and antiquarian and Scotland's Geographer Royal in the late seventeenth century). In some ways, Pennant's interest in antiquities and in the tales told about certain historical features reflects earlier descriptive traditions in which the emphasis lay with the *local*, with the remarkable, the curious. But Pennant is distinctively of his own age, too, and he is concerned more with the topography of the present than with the historical past.

What Pennant offers us is both a topographical account and a 'prospect'. This latter term had two inter-related meanings in the eighteenth century. It was understood to mean a view outwards and beyond one's point of view, and was, in this sense, principally an aesthetic term. It was also held to have utilitarian meaning, but, importantly, one of *future* utility. Thus, the prospect that lay before Pennant as he stood on the summit of one of the Paps of Jura was, literally, a visual one — the southern Hebrides spread out before him almost like a map, he tells us. But it was also figurative: of a new and future prospect for Scotland, a Scotland then embracing change in the wake of the defeat of the Jacobites at Culloden on 16 April 1746. Further, his view of Scotland's changing economy, particularly in the countryside, presents the modern reader both with a vivid description — vivid because *he* has seen it as well as being told about it by others — and with geographical differences in the nature and rate of change.

Pennant was certainly aware of Scotland's visual grandeur, but it is not a central theme of his *Tour*, even though he knew of recent shifts in cultural attitudes in this respect: 'It is but of late that the North Britons became sensible of the beauties of their scenery; but their search is at present amply rewarded.' His comment upon the bare mountains of Wester Ross and west Sutherland, for example, is more typical of the natural scientist than of the artist: 'I never saw a country that seemed to have been so torn and convulsed: the shock, whenever it happened, shook off all that vegetates.'

Much more important to him is the state of the rural economy and the native inhabitants. Different parts of Scotland are shown as improving, others not and with few signs of doing so. Of Campbeltown in Kintyre, for example, we are told 'rural economy is but at a low ebb here', and, for the island of Rum as a whole, 'In the present economy of the island, there is little prospect of any improvement'. In parts of Sutherland, in Islay and in Skye, Pennant could discern the first instances of emigration, as the familial bonds of the clan system were beginning to break and as the pressure of too many people upon too few resources was building up. On Skye, climate and Nature conditions peoples' lives: there, as more generally throughout the western Highlands, 'the produce of the crops very rarely are in any degree proportioned to the wants of the inhabitants'. Rents were rising, chiefs altering their perspectives to become landlords. Rural life in such places was no arcadian existence: even on Arran 'no time can be spared for amusement of any kind; the whole being given over for procuring the means of paying their rent, of laying in their fuel, or getting a scanty pittance of meat and clothing'. Moses Griffiths captures something of the harsh conditions of existence in his illustrations of house interiors in Islay, for example (Figure XVI p. 216). Yet in parts of central Perthshire, by contrast, the tenantry were engaged in rural manufactures, 'none have yet emigrated', and, in rural east Scotland generally, a 'great spirit of improvement' was apparent. Pennant's account of the changes underway on Robert Barclay's farm at Urie near Stonehaven should not necessarily be regarded as 'typical' precisely because there was so much variability within the rural economy of late eighteenth-century Scotland, but it is a wonderful *vignette* nevertheless of an 'improving' landowner at work, looking to new rotative practices and crops and, of course, to economic betterment in the future.

One gets the sense, indeed, that 'beauty' as a category of visual meaning for Pennant lay in just such scenes — a well-run farm, a working landscape — much more than it did with the picturesque and rugged Highlands. What is certainly true is that Pennant's descriptions of this regional variability have been supported by later work on the transformation of Scotland's rural economy. He is, then, both accurate and reliable. We can, as modern readers, with reasonable confidence accept our position as 'virtual witness' to Scotland's past, in part because of Pennant's own capacities, and, in part, too, because of his use of local informants. Pennant is both commentator and *rapporteur*, allowing Scots, or some of them at least, to represent themselves.

At the same time, however, he could be dismissive of local knowledge and of the ordinary people, and terse when we would rather he were speculative. 'In this island,' he notes of Islay, 'several ancient diversions and superstitions are still preserved: the last indeed are almost extinct, or at most lurk only amongst the very meanest of the people.' 'Miracles,' he notes dismissively when in Kintyre, 'are now ceased.' Such claims reflect, of course, the rationalist in Pennant rather more than the true state of affairs about customary practices and beliefs. For him, such elements of the marvellous and metaphysical did not permit description or measurement, and whilst the lingering presence of 'folklore' (which lingered long after

Pennant, of course) might have permitted speculation as to why such ideas were held by the common folk, such matters would have been a digression. It is precisely his rationalism of tone that makes what we might call his 'dream commentary' so unusual.

At the close of the first volume, Pennant offers a commentary upon the past and present state of the Highlands. Unlike many later travel writers keen to assert their moral authority over the object of their enquiries, however, he does not do so directly. Rather, he uses the literary device of a ghost — of an eponymous Highland chief — who reflects upon the changed nature of Highland life. 'Stranger,' says the figure, 'thy purpose is not unknown to me.' Pennant, it appears, has been watched during his travels by this figure. Having seen Pennant to be trustworthy and thorough, the spectre recounts the former ways of life in the Highlands, the demise of the essentially moral bonds that held people together — 'the ties of affection are no more ... Interest alone creates the preference of man to man' — and advises upon the best means to economic improvement in the future. Pennant is, of course, using the ghost to re-emphasise his own credentials as reliable and credible in order to be able to speak with authority, through the ghost, on Highland affairs. As both a foreigner and, as he earlier described himself, a 'transient visitor', Pennant knew his views might not carry the same weight as those of a native. It is a remarkable imaginative commentary, one that simultaneously allowed Pennant to both offer and distance himself from moral prescriptions for Scotland's future prospects.

While it is easy to see a link between his second tour and that of 1769, it is difficult to know if the critical reception of his 1772 *Tour* and its practical successes influenced Pennant's later travels. He toured the northern counties of England in 1773, Northamptonshire in 1774, several counties north of London in 1776, Kent in 1777 and Wales in 1778, with a shorter trip to Cornwall in 1787. Most of these tours were published. Other books include his 1771 *Synopsis of Quadrupeds* (which, enlarged, was the basis to his 1781 *History of Quadrupeds*), *Indian Zoology* (1781), his *Arctic Zoology*, published in two volumes between 1784–1787 in which he was again reliant upon his fellow naturalists such as George Low, the Orcadian naturalist who had been a guide to Sir Joseph

Banks during Bank's time on Orkney in returning from Iceland, and who had earlier sent Pennant information for his 1772 *Tour*, an essay on the Patagonians, and a topography of the capital, *Of London* (1790), which, in contrast to his earlier works, did find favour with Boswell.

Travel writing and the accurate understanding of the natural world was, then, a major part of his life. In his *Literary Life of Thomas Pennant Esq., Written by Himself* and published in 1793, Pennant reflected upon his life and work. 'I am astonished' [he notes], 'at the multitude of my publications, especially when I reflect on the various duties it has fallen to my lot to discharge. As a father of a family, landlord of a small but very numerous tenantry, and a not inactive magistrate, I had a great share of health during the literary part of my days, much of this was owing to the riding exercise of my extensive tours, to my manner of living and to my temperance.' Even old age did not restrict him. One of his last works was the four-volume *Outlines of the Globe* (1798–1800) — the last two parts were brought to the press by his son, David — in which he constructed imaginative tours of foreign countries, partly from his own fertile mind, partly by drawing upon others' real accounts. Late eighteenth-century Scotland is no less a foreign and distant country. But Pennant makes a splendid guide.

EDITORIAL NOTE

⸻⊰●⊱⸻

THIS edition has been prepared from that brought out by the London publisher Benjamin White in 1774 and 1776. The underlying editorial principle has been to make Pennant's text more accessible to the modern reader, whilst preserving as much as possible of the period flavour. Accordingly, changes have been kept to a minimum. Pennant's syntax has not been modified, and only minor adjustments to punctuation have been made. Spelling has been modernised, except for place-names and personal names, where the original spelling (and inconsistencies) have been retained. Inscriptions and quotations from other sources which occur within the main body of the text have also been left unaltered.

Pennant's *Tour* is presented in White's edition as a continuous text with margin notes. These notes have not been reproduced here. However, place-names which originally occurred as margin notes are included below chapter headings in the new edition to give an outline of Pennant's journey. The chapter headings themselves indicate the regions through which Pennant travelled. The form and spelling of county names has been taken directly from the 1776 edition (see, for example Lanerkshire rather than Lanarkshire in chapter IV). County boundaries are as they were understood by Pennant in 1772.

DEDICATION
TO
JOSEPH BANKS, Esq.

Dear Sir,

I THINK myself so much indebted to you, for making me the vehicle for conveying to the public the rich discovery of your last voyage, that I cannot dispense with this address the usual tribute of such occasions. You took me from all temptation of envying your superior good fortune, by the liberal declaration you made that the Hebrides were my ground, and yourself, as you pleasantly expressed it, but an interloper. May I meet with such, in all my adventures!

Without lessening your merit, let me say that no one has less reason to be sparing of his stores of knowledge. Few possess so large a share: you enjoy it without ostentation; and with a facility of communication, the result of natural endowments joined with an immensity of observation, collected in parts of the world, before, either of doubtful existence, or totally unknown. You have enriched yourself with the treasures of the globe, by a circumnavigation, founded on the most liberal and scientific principles. The sixteenth century received lustre from the numbers of generous volunteers of rank and fortune, who distinguishing themselves by the contempt of riches, ease, and luxury, made the most hazardous voyages, like yourself, animated by the love of true glory.

In reward, the name of Banks will ever exist with those of Clifford, Raleigh and Willughby, on the rolls of fame, celebrated instances of great and enterprising spirits: and the Arctic Solander must remain a fine proof that no climate can prevent the seeds of knowledge from vegetating in the breast of innate ability.

You have had justly a full triumph decreed to you by your country. May your laurels for ever remain unblighted, and if she has deigned to twine for me a civic wreath, return to me the same good wish.

I am, with every due acknowledgement,
Dear Sir,
Your obliged, and
most obedient humble servant,
THOMAS PENNANT.

Downing,
March 1, 1774

A
TOUR
in
SCOTLAND
and
VOYAGE TO THE HEBRIDES
1772

Part 1

ADVERTISEMENT

———⟫⟪———

THIS journey was undertaken in the summer of 1772, in order to render more complete, my preceding tour; and to allay that species of restlessness that infects many minds, on leaving any attempt unfinished. Conscious of my deficiency in several respects, I prevailed on two gentlemen to favour me with their company, and to supply by their knowledge what I found wanting in myself.

To the Rev Mr John Lightfoot, lecturer of Uxbridge, I am obliged for all the botanical remarks scattered over the following pages. But it gives me great pleasure to say that he means to extend his favours, by soon giving to the public a *Flora Scotica*, an ample enumeration and history of the plants observed by him in the several places we visited. To Mr Lightfoot, I must join in my acknowledgements, the Rev Mr John Stuart of Killin, for a variety of hints, relating to customs of the natives of the Highlands, and of the islands, which by reason of my ignorance of the Erse or Gaelic language, must have escaped my notice. To both I was indebted for all the comforts that arise from the society of agreeable and worthy companions.

I must not omit my thanks to the several gentlemen who favoured me at different times with accounts and little histories of the places of their residence, or their environs. To begin with the most southern, my best acknowledgements are due to

Mr Aikin, surgeon, for the account of Warrington.

Mr Thomas West favoured me with several things relating to the north of Lancashire.

Dr Brownrigg, the Rev Dr Burn, Joseph Nicholson, Esq., of Hawksbery, and the Rev Mr Farish of Carlisle, afforded me large supplies relating to their counties of Westmoreland and Cumberland.

In Scotland, John Maxwell, Esq., of Broomholme, and Mr Little of Langholme favoured me with several remarks relating to Eskdale.

The Rev Mr Jaffray, minister of Ruthwell, with a history of his parish.

Sir William Maxwell, Bart., of Springkeld, with variety of drawings, found at the Roman station at Burrens.*

John Goldie, Esq., of Dumfries, supplied me with numbers of observations on that town and county.

The Rev Mr Duncan MacFarlane of Drummond, with an account of his parish.

Mr John Golborn, engineer, with an account of Glasgow, and various miscellaneous remarks.

For the excellent account of Paisley, I am indebted to Mr Francis Douglas.

The Rev Mr Gersbom Stuart sent me materials for an account of the isle of Arran.

Alexander Campbel, Esq., of Ballole, and Charles Freebain, Esq., communicated several observations relating to the isle of Ilay.

Joseph Banks, Esq., communicated to me his description of Staffa; and permitted my artist to copy as many of the beautiful drawings in his collection, as would be of use in the present work.

I must acknowledge myself in a particular manner indebted to the Rev Mr Donald MacQuin of Kilmuir, in the isle of Skie, for a most instructive correspondence relating to the ancient customs of the place, and to its various antiquities. A small part I have mingled with my own account: but the greater share, in justice to the merit of the writer, I have delivered unmutilated in the Appendix to the third volume.

The Rev Mr Dounie, minister of Gairloch, obliged me with various remarks on his neighbourhood.

---

* I must not omit my thanks to the Rev Mr Cordiner, minister of the Episcopal chapel at Banff, for an elegant drawing of the urn in the preceding volume.

The Rev Mr Donald MacLeod of Glenelg, the same, respecting his.

To Dr Ramsay of Edinburgh, I must return thanks, for a variety of services: to Mr George Paton of the same place, for an indefatigable and unparalleled assiduity in procuring from all parts any intelligence that would be of use to the work in view.

Downing,
March 1, 1776

THOMAS PENNANT.

I

CHESHIRE,
LANCASHIRE

———⟫●⟪———

Chester—Hoole Heath—Hellesby Tor—Frodesham—Rocksavage—
Dutton Lodge—Halton Castle—Norton—Warrington—Orford Hall
—Winwick—Wiggan—Haigh Hall—Standish—Holland—Preston—
Garstang—Lancaster—Cartmel—Holker—Ulverston—Peel Castle—
Furness—Black Coomb—Swartzmoor Hall—Coninston—Urswick

O N Monday the 18th of May, for a second time, take my
departure for the north, from Chester; a city without parallel
for the singular structure of the four principal streets, which are as
if excavated out of the earth, and sunk many feet beneath the
surface; the carriages drive far below the level of the kitchens, on a
line with ranges of shops; and over them, on each side the streets,
passengers walk from end to end, secure from wet or heat, in galleries
purloined from the first floor of each house, open and balustraded in
front. The back courts of all these houses are level with the ground,
but to go into any of the four streets it is necessary to descend a
flight of several steps.

   The streets were once considerably deeper, as is apparent from the
shops, whose floors lie far below the present pavement. The lesser
streets and alleys that run into the greater streets, were sloped to the
level of the bottoms of the latter, as is particularly visible in Bridge
Street. It is difficult to assign a reason for these hollowed ways: I can

only suppose them to have been the void left after the destruction of
the ancient vaults mentioned by an ancient historical: 'In this cyte', says
the Polychronicon,[1] 'ben ways under erthe with vowtes and stone-
werke wonderly wrought thre chambred werkes: I grave with olde
mennes names therein. There is also Julius Cezars name wonderly in
stones grave, and other noble mennes also, with the wrytynge about':
meaning the altar and monumental inscriptions of the Romans.

The cathedral (till the Reformation the church of the rich
monastery of St Werburgh) is an ancient structure, very ragged on
the outside, from the nature of the friable red stone[2] with which it
is built; but still may boast of a most elegant western front; and the
tabernacle work in the choir is very neat: St Werburgh's shrine is now
the bishop's throne, decorated with the figures of Mercian monarchs
and saints; to whom the fair patroness was a bright example, living
immaculate with her husband Ceolredus, copying her aunt the great
Ethelreda, who lived for three years, with not less purity, with her
good man Tonberctus, and for twelve with her second husband,
the pious Prince Egfrid. History relates, that this religious house
was originally a nunnery, founded AD 660, by Wulpherus, king of
the Mercians, in favour of his daughter's indisposition. The nuns,
in process of time, gave way to canons secular; and they again were
displaced by Hugh Lupus, nephew to the Conqueror, 1095, and
their room supplied by Benedictines.

The beauty and elegant simplicity of a very antique Gothic chapter
house, and its fine vestibule, merits a visit from every traveller. The
date of the foundation is uncertain, but it seems, from the similitude
of roof and pilasters in a chapel in the square tower in the castle, to
have been the work of contemporary architects, and these architects
were probably Norman; for the mode of square towers, with squared
angles, was introduced immediately on the conquest.

The cloisters, the great refectory, now the free school, and a
gateway of most singular structure, are at present the sole remains
of this monastery. The ruins near St John's church are fine relics of

---

[1] Higden's *Polychronicon*, or rather that by Roger Cestrensis, a Benedictine
monk of St Werburgh's; from whom Higden is said to have stolen the whole work.
This Roger was contemporary with Trivet, who died AD 1328.
[2] Vale-Royal, 19.

the piety of the times; and the massy columns, and round arches within the church, most curious specimens of the clumsy strength of Saxon architecture. The former are probably the remains of the monastery of St Mary, founded by Randal, second Earl of Chester, for Benedictine nuns. The church was founded by King Ethelred, in 689: an uncouth inscription on the walls informs us, that *King Ethelred minding more the bliss of heaven, edified a college church notable and famous in the suburbs of Chester pleasant and beauteous in the honour of God and the Baptist St John with the help of bishop Wulfrice and good Excillion.*[3] It was rebuilt in 906, by Ethelred, Earl of Mercia, after he had expelled the Danes out of the city. This was also the cathedral, until supplanted in 1551, by the church of the abbey of St Werburgh.

The castle is a decaying pile, rebuilt by one of the Norman earls, on the site of the more ancient fortress. The walls of the city (only complete specimen of old fortifications) are one mile three-quarters and a hundred and one yards in circumference, and, being the principal walk of the inhabitants, are kept in excellent order. The views from the several parts are very fine: the mountains of Flintshire, the hills of Broxton, and the insulated rock of Beeston, form the ruder part of the scenery; a rich flat gives us a softer view, and the prospect up the river towards Boughton, recalls in some degree the idea of the Thames and Richmond Hill.

The hypocaust, near the Feathers Inn, is one of the remains of the Romans, it being well known that this place was a principal station. Among many antiquities found here, none is more singular than the rude sculpture of the *Dea Armigera Minerva*, with her bird and altar, on the face of a rock in a small field near the Welsh end of the bridge.

Chester has been, at different times, a *place d'armes*, a great thoroughfare between the two kingdoms, and the residence of a numerous and polished gentry. Trade, till of late years, was but little attended to, but at present efforts are making to enter into that of Guinea, the plantations, and the Baltic; and from the Phoenix Tower is a good Pisgah view of an internal commerce by means of a canal now cutting beneath the walls.

---

[3] So translated from *Bono Auxilio*.

Since the year 1736, and not before, great quantities of linen cloth have been imported from Ireland to each of the annual fairs: in that year 449, 654 yards; and at present about a million of yards are brought to each fair. Hops are another great article of trade, for above ten thousand pockets are sold here annually, much of which is forwarded to the neighbouring island. But the only staple trade of the city is in skins, multitudes of which are imported, dressed here, but sent out again to be manufactured. Here is a well-regulated poorhouse, and an infirmary; the last supported by contributions from the city, its county, and the adjacent counties of North Wales. The first has happily the least use of this pious foundation; for, whether from the dryness of the situation, the clearness of the air, or the purity of the water, the proportion of deaths to the inhabitants has been only as 1 to 31; whereas in London 1 in 20, and three quarters; in Leeds 1 in 21, and three-fifths; and in Northampton and Shrewsbury, 1 in 26, annually pay the great tribute of nature.[4] Might I be permitted to moralize, I should call this the reward of the benevolent and charitable disposition, that is the characteristic of this city; for such is the sacrifice that is pleasing to the Almighty.

About two miles from Chester, pass over Hoole Heath, noted for having been one of the places of reception for strangers established by Hugh Lupus, in order to people his new dominions. This in particular was the asylum allotted for the fugitives of Wales.

Ride through the small town of Trafford: this, with the lordship of Newton, was, as Daniel King observes, one of the sweet morsels that the Abbot of St Werburgh and his convent kept for their own wholesome provision. Get into a tract of sandy country, and pass beneath Hellesby Tor, a high and bluff termination of Delamere Forest, composed of the same friable stone as that near Chester, but veined with yellow. Hence a view of the junction of the Weever and the Mersey, and an extensive tract of marshy meadow, with some good and much rushy grass; and beyond is the beginning of the wide estuary that flows by Liverpool.

[4] Vide the observations on this subject of that humane physician, my worthy friend, Dr Haygarth.

Cross a little brook, called Llewyn, and reach Frodesham; a town of one long street, which, with its castle, was allotted by Edward I to David, brother to Lewelyn, last Prince of Wales, as a retainer in his double perfidy against his own blood, and his own country. Not a vestige is left of the castle, which stood at the west end of the town; was latterly used as a house by the Savages, and was burnt down in 1652, when one of that name, an earl Rivers, lay dead in it.

This, as well as most other towns and villages in Cheshire, stands on an eminence of sandstone, and by that means enjoys a situation dry, wholesome and beautiful.

The church stands at a vast height above the town. In the register are these two remarkable instances of longevity: March the 13th, 1592, was buried, Thomas Hough, aged 141; and the very next day was committed to the earth, Randle Wall, aged 103. I observed also, that in the winter of 1574, the pestilence reached this sequestered place, for four are then recorded to have died of it. In early times that avenging angel spread destruction through all parts of the land; but her power is now ceased by the providential cessation of the natural causes that gave rise to that most dreadful of calamities.

Above the church is Beacon Hill, with a beautiful walk cut along its side. At the foot are four butts (archery being still practised here) for an exercise in which the warriors of this country were of old eminent. The butts lie at four, eight, twelve, and sixteen roods distance from each other: the last are now disused; probably as the present race of archers prefer what is called short-shooting.[5]

Cross the Weever, on a good stone bridge: from a neighbouring warehouse much cheese is shipped off, brought down the river in boats from the rich grazing grounds, that extend as far as Nantwich. The river, by means of locks, is navigable for barges as high as Winslow Bridge; but below this admits vessels of sixty tons. The channel above and below is deep and clayey, and at low water very disagreeable.

---

[5] I think myself indebted to Mr Robertson, librarian to the Royal Society, an old archer, for the correction of this passage.

On the north banks are the ruins of Rocksavage, suffered, within memory, to fall to decay; once that seat of a family of the same name; and not far remote, on the same range, is Aston, a good house, finely situated, but rendered too naked through the rage of modern taste.

About two miles farther, on the right, is Dutton Lodge, once the seat of the Duttons; a family in possession of a singular grant, having *'Magisterium omnium Leccatorum et meretricum totius Cestreshire'*. This privilege came originally from Randal, sixth Earl of Chester, to Roger Lacy, constable of that city, who, when the earl was closely besieged by the Welsh in Rudland Castle, collected hastily for his relief a band of minstrels, and other idle people, and with them succeeded in the attempt; after which his son John assigned it to the Duttons, one of that name being assistant in the affair.

Reach Halton Castle, seated on an eminence, and given by Hugh Lupus to Nigellus, one of his officers, and founded by one of the two. Nigel held it by his honourable and spirited service, that whenever the earl made an expedition into Wales, the Baron of Haldon should be the foremost in entering the country, and the last in coming out.[6] It became afterwards the property of the house of Lancaster, and was a favourite hunting seat of John of Gaunt. The castle is a ruin, except a part kept as a prison. It belongs to the Duchy of Lancaster, and has still a court of record, and other privileges.

From the castle is the most beautiful view in Cheshire; a rich prospect of the meanders of the Mersey, through a fertile bottom; a pretty wooded peninsula jutting into it opposite to Runcorn; the great country of Lancashire, filled with hedgerow trees; and beyond soar the hills of Yorkshire and Lancashire; and on the other side appears Cheshire, the still loftier Cambrian mountains; but close beneath, near the church, is still a more pleasing view; that of a row of neat almshouses, for the reception of the superannuated servants of the house of Norton, founded by the late Pusey Brook, Esq., my friend, and the friend of mankind.

---

[6] Blunt's *Ancient Tenures.*

Descend the hill, and pass by Norton, a good modern house, on the site of a priory of canons regular of St Augustine, founded by William, son of Nigellus, AD 1135, who did not live to complete his design; for Eustace de Burgaville granted to Hugh de Catherik pasture for a hundred sheep, in case he finished the church in all respects conformable to the intent of the founder. It was granted at the Dissolution to Richard Brook, Esq.

Continue my way along a flat dull country, reach the banks of the Mersey, ride over a long causeway, having before me a perfect wood of lofty poplar, that speaks the soil; and Warrington as if in the midst of it. Enter Lancashire, after crossing a handsome stone bridge of four arches, which leads into the town, and was built by the fifth Earl of Derby, to accommodate Henry VIII, then on his road on a visit to his Lordship, probably to soothe the earl after the ungrateful execution of his brother, Sir William Stanly. It was at first a toll-bridge, but his lordship generously released the country from that tax, at a loss of as many marks as was equivalent to the portion of one of his daughters.

The prior of the hermit friars of Augustine, founded before 1379, stood near the bridge, but not a relic exists. The entrance into the town is unpromising, the streets long, narrow, ill built, and crowded with carts and passengers; but farther on are airy, and of a good width, but afford a striking mixture of mean buildings and handsome houses, as is the case with most trading towns that experience a sudden rise; not that this place wants antiquity, for Leland speaks of its having a better market than Manchester upwards of 200 years ago. At that time the principal part of the town was near the church, remote from the bridge, and was accessible only by a ford, but the conveniency of a safer transit soon drew the buildings to that end.

The church has of late undergone much alteration, but two of the ancient side chapels still remain: one belonging to the Masseys contains nothing but a small mural monument, with a very amiable character of Frances Massey, Esq., Lord of the manors of Rixton and Glasbrook, last of the ancient family, which was extinct with him in 1748; but in an opposite chapel is a magnificent tomb of Sir Thomas Boteler and his lady, in alabaster: their effigies lie at top, hand in hand, he in armour, she in a remarkable mitre-shaped cap; round the sides are various figures, such as St Christopher, St George, and other superstitious sculptures. The Botelers were of great antiquity in this place; the first took his name from being butler to Ranulf de Gernons, or Meschines, Earl of Chester. His posterity acquired great possessions in this county,[7] and one of them obtained the charters for markets and fairs at Warrington, from his prince, Edward I. Tradition says, that Sir Thomas, then resident at Beauly House, near this town was, with his lady, murdered in the night by assassins, who crossed the moat in leathern boats to perpetuate their villainy.

Beneath an arch in the wall near this tomb is another, containing a figure in a long robe, muffled up to the chin; a head wrapped in a sort of cap, and bound with a neat fillet.

Besides this church is a neat chapel of ease, lately rebuilt, and many places of worship for Presbyterians, Anabaptists, Quakers, Methodists and Roman Catholics: for in manufacturing places it often falls out that the common people happily have a disposition to seek the Lord, but as unhappily disagree in the means of rendering themselves acceptable to him.

Here is a free school, very considerably endowed, and made very respectable by the merits of the present master. An academy has of late years been established in this town, with a view of giving an education to youth on the plan of a university.

The manufactures of this place are very considerable; formerly a great quantity of checks and coarse linens were made here, but of late years these have given way to that of polldavies, or sailcloth, now carried on with such spirit (in the town and country) as to supply near one half of the navy of Great Britain. The late war gave a great rise to this branch, and a sudden improvement to the town.

The making of pins is another considerable article of commerce; locks, hinges, cast iron, and other branches of hardware, are fabricated here to a great amount: very large works for the refining of copper, are carried on near the town; and the glass and sugar

---

[7] Dugdale's *Baronage* I, 653.

houses employ many hands. By means of all these advantages the town has been doubled within these twenty years; and is supposed to contain at present between eight and nine thousand inhabitants. The manufactures of this place are most readily conveyed down to Leverpool, by means of the Mersey. The springtides rise at the bridge to the height of nine feet, and vessels of seventy or eighty tons can lie at Bank Quay, the port of the town; where warehouses, cranes, and other conveniences for shipping of goods are erected. I must not omit that thirty or forty thousand bushels of potatoes are annually exported out of the rich land of the environs of Warrington, into the Mediterranean, at the medium price of 14d per bushel. This is the root which honest Gerard, about two hundred and forty years ago, speaks of as a food, as also 'a meet for pleasure being either rosted in the embers or boiled and eaten with oile vinegar and pepper or dressed some other way by the hand of a skilful cooke'.[8]

The salmon fishery is very considerable, but the opportunity of sending them to London, and other places, at the beginning of the season, keeps up the price to about 8d per pound, which gradually sinks to 3d or 2d halfpenny, to the great aid of the poor manufacturers. Smelts, or as they are called in all the north, sparlings, migrate in the spring up this river in amazing shoals, and of a size superior to those of other parts, some having been taken that weighed half a pound, and measured thirteen inches.

In this river is found a small fish called the graining, in some respects resembling the dace, yet is a distinct and perhaps new species; the usual length is seven inches and a half; it is rather more slender than the dace, the body is almost straight, that of the other incurvated; the colour of the scales in this is silvery, with a bluish cast; those of the dace have a yellowish or greenish tinge; the eyes, the ventral and the anal fins in the graining are of a pale colour.[9]

Make a visit to John Blackburne, Esq., at his seat of Orford, a mile from Warrington; dine and lie there. This gentleman from his

[8] *Herbal*, 928.
[9] Ray's in P. D. 8. P. P. 15. V. 9. A. 10. C. 32.

earliest life, like another Evelyn, has made his garden the employ and amusement of his leisure hours; and been most successful in every part he has attempted; in fact he has a universal knowledge in the culture of plants. He was the second in these kingdoms that cultivated the pineapple: has the best fruit and the best kitchen garden: his collection of hardy exotics is exceedingly numerous; and his collection of hothouse plants is at least equal to that at Kew. He neglects no branch of botany, has the aquatic plants in their proper elements; the rock plants on artificial rocks; and you may be here betrayed into a bog by attempting to gather those of the morass.

Mrs Blackburne, his daughter, extends her researches still farther, and adds to her empire another kingdom: not content with the botanic, she causes North America to be explored for its animals, and has formed a museum from the other side of the Atlantic, as pleasing as it is instructive.

In this house is a large family picture of the Ashtons of Chadderton, consisting of a gentleman, his lady, eleven children living at that time, and three infants who died in their birth: it was painted in the reign of James I by Tobias Ratcliff; but has so little merit, that I should not have mentioned it, but to add one more to Mr Walpole's list of painters.

May 19th. Pass through Winwick, a small village remarkable for being the richest rectory in England; the living is worth £2,300 per annum; the rector is lord of the manor, and has a glebe of £1,300 annual rent: it is singular that this county, the seventh in size in England, has only sixty-one parishes, whereas Norfolk, the next in dimensions has no fewer than six hundred and sixty.

In the wall of an old porch before the rector of Winwick's house, is safely lodged a bible, placed there by a zealous incumbent, who lived in the days of Oliver Cromwell, in order that at least one authentic book might be found, should the fanatics corrupt the text, and destroy all the orthodox copies.

On the outside of the church is this inscription, cut in old letters:

Hic locus, Oswalde, quondam tibi placuit valde;
Northannumbrorum fueras Rex, nuncque polorum

Regna tenes, Prato passus Marcelde[10] *vocato.*
Anno milleno quingentenoque triceno,
Sclator post Christum murum renovaverat istum:
Nenricus Johnston curatus erat simul hic tunc.

Oswald was King of Northumberland; the most pious prince of his time; and the restorer of the Christian religion in his dominions: at length, AD 640, receiving a defeat near Oswestry, by Penda, pagan King of Mercia, was there slain, his body cut in pieces, and stuck on poles by way of trophies.

At Redbank between this place and Newton the Scots in August 1648, after their retreat from Preston, made a resolute stand for many hours against the victorious Cromwell, who, with great losses on both sides, beat them from their ground; and the next day made himself master of all their remaining infantry, which, with their commander Lieutenant-General Bayly, surrendered on the bare condition of quarter.[11]

Pass through Newton, a small borough town: the country flat and fertile. On approaching Wiggan, observe several fields quite white with thread, bleaching for the manufacture of strong checks and coarse linen, carried on in that town and neighbourhood.

Wiggan is a pretty large town and a borough. It has long been noted for manufactures in brass and pewter, which now give way to that of checks: an ingenious fellow here turns canal coal into vases, obelisks, and snuff-boxes, and forms excellent blackamoor's heads out of the same material.

The best crossbows are also made in this town by a person, who succeeded his father in the business; the last coming there from Rippon about a century ago.

In the church is an inscription in memory of Sir Roger Bradshaigh of Haigh, an eminent loyalist in the time of the civil wars: and a tomb much defaced of a Sir William Bradshaigh, and his lady Mabel, who lived in the reigns of Edward II and III. A remarkable history attends this pair: in the time of the first monarch, he set out for the holy land in quest of adventures, and left his fair spouse at home to

[10] Muserfield near Oswestry.
[11] Whitelock, 332. Clarendon V, 162.

pray for his success: but after some years absence, the lady thinking he made rather too long a stay, gave her hand to Sir Osmund Nevil, a Welsh knight. At length Sir William returns in the garb of a pilgrim; makes himself known to his Mabel, is acknowledged by her, and she returns to her allegiance; Sir William pursues the innocent invader of his bed, overtakes him at Newton Park, where my unfortunate countryman is slain. The poor lady being considered as an accessary to his death, is condemned to a weekly penance of walking barefoot from the chapel in Haigh Hall, three miles distant, to expiate her crime, to a cross near Wiggan, at this day called Mabel's Cross.

Not far from the town is the little River Douglas, immortalized by the victories of our Arthur over the Saxons on its banks.[12] This stream in 1727 was widened, deepened and made navigable by locks, almost to the mouth of the Ribble: and was among the first of those projects which have since been pursued with so much utility to the inland parts of the kingdom. This canal conveys coal to supply the north of the country, and even part of Westmoreland, and in return brings from thence limestone.

On an eminence about a mile from Wiggan, is Haigh, the seat of the Bradshaighs, an ancient house, built at different times, the chapel supposed to be as old as the time of Edward II; in the front are the Stanly arms, and beneath them those of the family; which in all civil commotions had united with the former, even as early as the battle of Bosworth Field.

In this house are some excellent pictures; our Saviour with his disciples at Emmaus, by Titian, with the landlord and waiter; a fine attention and respect is expressed in the countenances of the disciples.

A very fine head of Sir Lionel Tolmach, by Fr Zucchero, on wood; short grey hair, a forked beard, rosy complexion; a beautiful *virdis senectus*.

Elizabeth, Lady Dacres, daughter of Paul, Viscount Bayning, relict of Francis, Lord Dacres, created Countess of Sheppy for life, by Charles II in 1680; a head on wood: a blooming countenance.

---

[12] Henry of Huntingdon, 313.

A head by Riley, of Sir John Guise, great grandfather to the present baronet: and another of Lady Guise, by Kneller.

Charles I in his robes.

George Villiers, Duke of Buckingham, in the robes of the garter, assassinated by the gloomy Felton.

A large equestrian picture of Charles I. A copy after Van Dyck.

His daughter, Mary, Princess of Orange, mother to King William.

Henry Murray, Esq., gentleman of the bedchamber to Charles II. His daughter was married to Sir Roger Bradshaigh, the second baronet.

This neighbourhood abounds with that fine species of coal called 'canal', perhaps 'candle coal', from its serving as cheap light for the poor to spin by during the long winter evenings: it is found in beds of about three feet in thickness; the veins dip one yard in twenty; are found at great depths, with a black bass above and below; and are subject to the same damps fiery and suffocating as the common coal. It makes the sweetest of fires, and the most cheerful: is very inflammable; and so clean, that at Haigh Hall a summer-house is built with it, which may be entered without dread of soiling the lightest clothes.

Leaving Wiggan observe on the roadside near the north end of the town, a monument, erected by Alexander Rigby, Esq., in memory of his gallant commander Sir Thomas Tildesty, who was killed on this spot in the engagement with Lamber, in 1650: a faithful domestic, supporting his dying master, was shot in that situation by a rebel trooper, who was instantly pistoled by his generous officer, who abhorred the barbarity even to an enemy.

Reach Standish, a village with a very handsome church and spire steeple: the pillars within show an attempt of the Tuscan order; it was rebuilt in 1584, and chiefly by the assistance of Richard Moodie, rector of the place, who maintained the workmen with meat, at his own cost, during the time. He was the first Protestant pastor, conformed and procured the living by the cession of the tythes of Standish, probably thinking it better to lose part than all. He lies in effigy on his tomb, dressed in his Franciscan habit, with an inscription declarative of his munificence towards the church. In front of the tomb are two small pillars with Ionic capitals, the dawning of the introduction of Grecian architecture.

Here is a handsome tomb of Sir Edward Wrightington, Knight, King's Council: he died 1658, and lies in alabaster recumbent in his gown. A curious memorial of Edward Chisnal, Esq., of Chisnal, who was, during the civil wars, colonel of a regiment of horse, and another of foot; and lest there should be any doubt, the commissions are given in full length upon wood. This gentleman had the honour of defending Latham House under the command of the heroine the Countess of Derby.

At Mrs Townley's, at Standish Hall, are some few relics of the Arundel collection, particularly eight pieces of glass, with the labours of Hercules most exquisitely cut on them. A large silver square, perhaps the panel of an altar, with a most beautiful relief of the resurrection on it, by *P.V., 1605*. Two trinkets, one a lion, the other a dragon, whose bodies are formed of two vast irregular pearls.

Make an excursion four miles on the west, to Holland, a village where formerly had been a priory of Benedictines, founded by Robert de Holland, in 1319, out of the collegiate chapel, before served by canons regular. Nothing remains at present but the church, and a few walls. The posterity of the founder rose to the greatest honours during several of the following turbulent reigns; but those honours were attended with the greatest calamities. Robert himself, first secretary to Thomas of Woodstock, Earl of Lancaster, after betraying his master, lost his head, by the rage of the people, in the beginning of the reign of Edward III. His posterity, many at least of them, were equally unfortunate: Thomas de Holland, Duke of Surry, and Earl of Kent, fell in the same manner at Cirencester, by the hands of the townsmen, after a rash insurrection, in order to restore his master, Richard II. His half brother, John, Duke of Exeter, and Earl of Huntingdon, underwent the same fate, from the hands of the populace at Plessy, in Essex, for being engaged in the same design. And his grandson Henry, Duke of Exeter, experienced a fortune as various at it was calamitous. He was the greatest subject in power under Henry VI and was brother in law to Edward IV. Yet, as Comines relates, during the first depression of his unhappy master, he was seen a fugitive in Flanders, running barefoot after the Duke of Burgandy's coach, to beg an alms: on the last attempt to replace Henry on the throne, he again appeared in arms at the battle of Barnet, fought manfully, and was left for dead in the field: a faithful domestic gave him assistance, and conveyed him into sanctuary; he escaped, and was never heard of till his corpse was found, by some unknown accident, floating in the sea between Dover and Calais;[13] and thus closed the eventful history of this ill-fated line.

Return through this deep tract into the road at Standish: the country from hence to Preston very good; on the last a long valley runs parallel. At a place called Pincock Bridge cross the Yarrow, a pretty stream, watering a narrow romantic glen, wooded on both sides.

Ride through Walton, a very populous village, near the Ribble, a fine river, extending through a range of very rich meadows, as far as the picturesque vale of Cuerden. Cross the river on a bridge of five arches, ascend a hill, through lanes once deep, narrow, and of difficult approach; where, in 1715, the rebels made some resistance to the king's forces in the ill-concerted affair of that year.

On the top lies Preston, a neat and handsome town, quiet and entirely free from the noise of manufactures; and is supported by passengers, or the money spent by the numerous gentry that inhabit it. It derives its name (according to Camden) from the priests or religious that were in old times the principal inhabitants. Here was a convent of Grey Friars or Franciscans founded by Edmund, Earl of Lancaster, son of Henry III. Robert de Holland abovementioned, was a considerable benefactor to the place, and was buried here. A gentleman of the name of Preston gave the ground.[14] Might not the town take its name from him? Here was also an ancient hospital dedicated to Mary Magdalene, mentioned in 1291 in the Lincoln taxation.[15]

This place was taken by storm in 1643 by the Parliament forces under Sir John Seaton, after a most gallant defence: it was at that time fortified with brick walls.[16]

---

[13] Stow, 426.
[14] Steven's *Monast*. I, 154.
[15] Tanner, 234.
[16] Parliament Chronicle, 268.

North of this town began the action between that gallant officer Sir Marmaduke Langdale, and the Parliament forces under Cromwell. The former commanded the English army that was to act in conjunction with the Duke of Hamilton in his unfortunate invasion in July 1648. Langdale gave the infatuated Scot notice of approach of Cromwell, and in vain advised the assembling of the whole force, his council was lost. He alone made a stand in the fields near Preston for six hours, unassisted by the duke, who pushed the march of his troops over the bridge, leaving Sir Marmaduke to be overpowered with numbers.

The walks on the banks above the Ribble command a most beautiful view of meadows, bounded by delicious risings; the river meandering between till the prospect closes with its estuary. Continue here the whole night, and lie at the Black Bull.

The Spectator has long since pointed out the knowledge that may be collected from signs: it is impossible not to remark the propriety of the reigning ones of this county: The Triple Legs, and The Eagle and Child, denote the great possessions of the Stanleys in these parts; The Bull, the just pre-eminence of its cattle over other counties; and The Royal Oak, its distinguished loyalty to its sovereign. I am amazed they do not add The Graces, for nowhere can be seen a more numerous race of beauties among that order, who want every advantage to set off their native charms.

Go over a flat country, with rushy fields on each side; cross the Broke and the Calder; see on the one side Blazedale Fells, and on the other Pelling Moss, which some years ago made an eruption similar to that of Solway. Cross the Wier, near Garstang, on a bridge of two arches; about twelve miles lower it swells into a fine harbour, whence the provincial proverb, 'as safe as Wier'. Vessels put into it for the sail cloth made at Kirkham.

Breakfast at Garstang; a small town, remarkable for the fine cattle produced in its neighbourhood: a gentleman has refused thirty guineas for a three-year-old cow; has sold a calf of a month's age for ten guineas, and bulls for a hundred; and has killed an ox weighing 21 score per quarter, exclusive of hide, entrails, etc. Bulls also have been let out at the rate of thirty guineas the season; so that well might Honest Barnaby[17] celebrate the cattle of this place, notwithstanding the misfortune he met with in one of its great fairs:

> *Veni Garstang, ubi nata*
> *Sunt armenta fronte lata;*
> *Veni Garstang, ubi male*
> *Intrans forum bestiale,*
> *Forte vacillando vico*
> *Huc et illuc cum amico,*
> *In Juvencae dorsum rui,*
> *Cujus cornu laesus sui*

Abundance of potatoes are raised about the place, and sent to London, Ireland and Scotland.

Sir Edward Walpole is lord of this manor, his father having obtained a grant of it from the crown.

Near the town, on a knowl, is a single tower, the poor remains of Greenhaugh Castle: it was built by the first Stanley, Earl of Derby, to secure himself in his new possessions, the forfeited estates of the Yorkists, who did not bear, without resentment, this usurption on their property. Among the attained lands, which were vested in his lordship, are reckoned those of Pilkington, Broughton, and Wotton.[18]

Soon after leaving Garstang the country grows more barren, uneven, or slightly hilly. From a common called The Grave have a fine view of Lancaster, built of stone, and lying on the side of a hill: the castle built by Edward III,[19] forms one great object, the church another; and far beyond is an arm of the sea, and the lofty mountains of Furness and Cumberland. The town is not regular, but is well built, and contains numbers of very handsome houses. Every stranger must admire the front of Mr Noble's faced with stone, naturally figured with views, rivers and mountains, in the same nature with the *pietra imboscata* and *ruinata* of the Italians. The

---

[17] Better known by the name of 'Drunken Barnaby', who lived at the beginning of the last century, and published his four itineraries in Latin rhyme.

[18] Leland's *Itin.* VI, 35.

[19] *Vetusta Monumenta, etc.*, published by the Society of Antiquarians, no. 41.

inhabitants are also fortunate in having some very ingenious cabinet-makers settled here; who fabricate most excellent and neat goods at remarkably cheap rates, which they export to London and the plantations. Mr Gillow's warehouse of these manufactures merits a visit.

It is a town of much commerce: has fine quays on the River Lune, which brings up ships of 250 tons burden close to the place. Forty or fifty ships trade from hence directly to Guinea and the West Indies: others to Norway. Besides the cabinet goods, some sail cloth is manufactured here; and great numbers of candles are exported to the West Indies. Much wheat and barley is imported.

The custom-house is a small but elegant building, with a portico supported by four Ionic pillars, with a beautiful plain pediment: each pillar is fifteen feet and a half high, and consists of a single stone. There is a double flight of steps, a rustic surbase and coins; a work that does much credit to Mr Gillow, the architect.

The castle is very entire; has a most magnificent front, consisting of two angular towers, and a gateway between; and within is a great square tower: the courts of justice are held here; and here are kept the prisoners of the county, in a safe yet airy confinement.

The church is seated on an eminence near the castle, and commands an extensive, but not a pleasing view. Within is a mural monument in memory of Sir Samuel Eyres, one of the judges of the king's bench in the time of King William; and a very pompous inscription on the gravestone of Covell, six times mayor of the town, forty-eight years keeper of the castle, forty-six years one of the coroners of the county, captain of the freehold land of the hundred of Lonsdale on this side of the sands, etc. Died Aug 1, 1639:

> *Cease, cease to mourn, all tears are vain and void,*
> *He's fled, not dead, dissolved, not destroyed:*
> *In Heav'n his soul doth rest, his body here*
> *Sleeps in this dust, and his fame everywhere*
> *Triumphs: the town, the country, farther forth,*
> *The land throughout proclaim his noble worth.*
> > *Speak to a man so courteous,*
> > *So free and every way magnanimous;*
> > *That story told at large here do you see*
> > *Epitomized in brief, COVELL was he.*

This is given as a specimen of an epitaph so very extravagant, that the living must laugh to read; and the deceased, was he capable, must blush to hear.

On the north side of the churchyard are the remains of an old wall, called the Wery Wall. Camden conjectures it to have taken its name from Caerwerid, or 'the green fortress', the British name of Lancaster: and that it was part of a Roman wall. For my part, with Leland, I suspect it to have been part of the enclosure of the Priory, a cell of Benedictine monks of St Martin, at Sees in France, suppressed by Henry V and given to Sion Abbey.

The shambles of this town must not be omitted: they are built in form of a street, at the public expense; every butcher has his shop; and his name painted over the door.

Cross the Lune, on a handsome bridge of four arches. Turn to the left, and after four miles riding, reach Hessbank, and at low water cross the arm of the sea, the Moricambe of Ptolemy, that divides this part of the country from the hundred of Furness, a detached tract peninsulated by the sea, lake, or river, a melancholy ride of eleven miles; the prospect on all sides quite savage, high barren hills indented by the sea, or drear wet sands, rendered more horrible by the approach of night, and a tempestuous evening, obscured by the driving of black clouds. Beneath the shade, discerned Arnside Tower, the property of the Stanleys for some centuries. Before us was an extensive, but shallow ford, formed by the Kent and other rivers, now passed with trouble by the beating of the waves.

At the entrance into this water am met by a guide, called here the carter, who is maintained by the public, and obliged in all weathers to attend here from sunrise to sunset, to conduct passengers over.

Three miles from the shore is Cartmel, a small town with most irregular streets, lying in a vale surrounded by high hills. The gateway of the monastery of regular canons of St Austin, founded in 1188, by William Mareshcal, Earl of Pembroke, is still standing. But this had long been holy ground, having about the year 677, been given to St Cuthbert, by Egfrid, King of Northumberland, with all its inhabitants, at that time, entirely British.

The church is large, and in form of a cross; the length is 157 feet: the transept 110: the height fifty-seven. The steeple is most singular, the tower being a square within a square; the upper part being set diagonally within the lower. The inside of the church is handsome and spacious: the centre supported by four large and fine clustered pillars: the west part more modern than the rest, and the pillars octagonal. The choir beautiful, surrounded with stalls; whose tops and pillars are finely carved with foliage; and with the instruments of the passion above.

On one side is the tombstone of William de Walton, with a cross on it. He was either first or second prior of this place. The inscription is only *Hic Jacet Frater Wilelmus de Walton Prior de Cartmel.*

On the other is a magnificent tomb of a Harrington and his lady, both lie recumbent beneath a fine carved and open work arch, decorated with variety of superstitious figures; and on the surface are grotesque forms of chanting monks. He lies with his legs across, a sign that he had obtained that privilege by the merits of a pilgrimage to the Holy Land, or a crusade. He is said to have been one of the Harringtons of Wrasholm Tower, his lady a Huddleston of Millum Castle. It is probably the effigies of Sir John de Harrington, who in 1035, was summoned by Edward I with numbers of other gallant gentlemen, to meet him at Carlile, and attend him on his expedition into Scotland; and was then knighted along with Prince Edward, with bathing, and other sacred ceremonies.[20]

The monument erected by Christopher Rawlinson, of Carkhall, in Cartmel, deserves mention, being in memory of his grandfather, father, and mother. The last a monk, descended from a Thomas Monk of Devonshire, by Frances Plantagenet, daughter and coheir of Arthur Viscount Lisle, son of Edward IV, and this Christopher dying without issue was the last male by the mother's side of that great line.

In a side chapel is the burial place of the Lowthers; among other monuments is a neat but small one of the late Sir William.

---

[20] Dugdale's *Baronage* II, 99.

Pass through some fields, a strange mixture of pasture, rock and small groves. Descend a hill to Holker, once the seat of the family of the Prestons, since the property of the Lowthers, and lately that of Lord George Cavendish: a large irregular house, seated in a pretty park, well wooded; and on the side of the house is a range of low rocky hills, directing the eye to an immense chain of lofty mountains.

At Holker are several good pictures: among the portraits, the beautiful, abandoned, vindictive, violent Duchess of Cleveland, mistress to Charles II, by Lely.

A Mrs Lowther, by the same.

Admiral Penn, dressed in black, with a cravat and sash, long hair, and of a good honest countenance. He rose very early in life to the highest naval commands; was a captain at twenty-one, Rear Admiral of Ireland at twenty-three, general in the first Dutch war at thirty-two; disgraced and imprisoned by Cromwell for his unsuccessful attempt on St Domingo, though he added, in that very expedition, Jamaica to the kingdom of Great Britain: on the Restoration, commanded under the Duke of York in the same ship, at the great sea fight of 1665, when the laurels of the first day were blasted by the mystic inactivity of the second; for where princes are concerned, the truth of miscarriage seldom appears. He soon after retired from the service, and died at the early age of forty-nine.

The late Sir James Lowther; a character too well known to be dwelt on.

The head of Thomas Wriothesly, Earl of Southampton, the friend of Clarendon, and virtuous treasurer of the first years after the Restoration.

His lady, leaning on a globe.

A very fine head of a Preston [?] in black, a ruff, short grey hair, round beard.

A head called that of an Earl Douglas, with his inscription: *Novit paucos secura quies, aet. suae xxii. A.M.D. xi.* On the head a black bonnet, countenance good, beard brown, dress black.

A fine head of Van Dyck, when young, leaning: by himself.

An old man reading, and a boy, on wood, marked *j.w. Stap.*

Two boys at dice, and a woman looking on: a fine piece by Morillio.

St Francis d'Assize, kneeling, very fine. And variety of other good paintings.

Cross another tract of sands, three miles in breadth, and am conducted through the ford by another Carter. This officer was originally maintained by the priory of Conished; but at the Dissolution the king charged himself and his successors with the payment: since that time it is held by patent of the Duchy of Lancaster, and the salary is paid by the receiver-general. Reach Ulverston, a town of about three thousand souls, seated near the waterside, and is approachable at high water by vessels of a hundred and fifty tons; has a good trade in iron ore, pig and bar iron, bark, limestone, oats and barley, and much beans, which last are sent to Leverpool, for the food of the poor enslaved Negroes in the Guinea trade. Numbers of cattle are also sold out of the neighbourhood, but the commerce in general declines; at present there are not above sixty vessels belonging to the place; formerly about a hundred and fifty mostly let out to freight; but both master and sailors go now to Leverpool for employ.

Quantities of potatoes are raised here; and such is the increase that 450 bushels have been got from a single acre of ground. Some wheat is raised in low Furness, near the sea, and in the isle of Walney: but the inhabitants of these parts have but recently applied themselves to husbandry. Among the manures sea-sand and live mussels are frequently used; but till within these twenty years even the use of dung was scarcely known to them.

Make an excursion of four miles to the west, to visit the great iron mines at Whitrigs: the ore is found in immense beds beneath two strata, one of pinnel or coarse gravel, about fifteen yards thick; the next is limestone of twenty yards: the stratum of ore is rather uncertain in extent, but is from ten to fifteen yards thick, and forty in extent; and sometimes two hundred tons have been taken up in a week. A cubic yard of ore weighs three tons and a half: the common produce of metal is one ton from thirty-five to forty hundred of ore; but some has been so rich as to yield a ton of iron from twenty seven hundred of the mineral.

The ore lies in vast heaps about the mines, so as to form perfect mountains; is of that species called by mineralogists haematites and kidney ore; is red, very greasy, and defiling. The iron race that inhabit the mining villages exhibit a strange appearance: men, women and children are perfectly dyed with it, and even innocent babes do quickly assume the bloody complexion of the soil.

The ore is carried on board ships for 12s per ton, each ton 21 hundred; and the adventurers pay 1s 6d per ton farm for liberty of raising it. It is entirely smelted with wood charcoal, but is got in such quantities that wood in these parts is sometimes wanting; so that charcoal is sometimes procured from the poor woods of Mull, and other of the Hebrides.

These mines have been worked above four hundred years ago, as appears by the grant of William of Lancaster, Lord of Kendal, to the priory of Conished, in this neighbourhood, of the mine of Plumpton, probably part of the present vein; which he conveys '*libero introitu et exitu ad duos equos cum hominibus minam cariandam*', etc.[21]

The vestiges of the ancient workings are very frequent, and apparent enough, from the vast hollows in the earth wherever they have sunk in.

From one of the banks have a great view of the lower Furness, as far as appears, a woodless tract, and of the isle of Walney, stretching along the coast, and forming to it a secure counterscarp from the rage of the sea. At the south end is Peel Castle, originally built, and supported by the abbey of Furness, and garrisoned with sixty men, as a protection against the Scots.

The abbey lies opposite, and the very ruins evince its former magnificence.[22] It was founded in 1127, by Stephen, Earl of Moriton and Bologne, afterwards King of England, or rather removed by him from Tulket in Aundirness. The monks were originally of the order of Tironensians, of the rule of St Benedict, but afterwards became Cistercians.[23]

---

[21] Dugdale II, 425.

[22] Finely engraven among the views published by the Society of Antiquaries.

[23] Dugdale I, 704. An excellent and full account of this abbey has been lately published, by Mr Thomas West.

The little tarn, or water called Standing Tarn, is within sight; it is of considerable depth, and abounds with pike, roach and eels; also with large trout; and is remarkable for having no visible outlet, but discharges its waters by some subterraneous passage.

See, towards the north, at a small distance, the hill of Black Coomb, in Cumberland, often visible from Flintshire, and an infallible presage to us of bad weather. I found from the report of the inhabitants of these parts, that the appearance of our country is equally ominous to them, and equally unacceptable.

See Swartzmoor Hall, near which Martin Swartz and his Germans encamped in 1487, with Lambert Simnel, in order to collect forces in these parts, before his attempt to wrest the crown from Henry VII. He was supported by Sir Thomas Broughton, a gentleman of this neighbourhood, who, escaping afterwards from the battle of Stoke, like our Owen Glendwr lived many years (when he was supposed to have been slain) in great obscurity, supported by his faithful tenants in Westmoreland.

And in aftertimes the melancholy spirit of George Fox, the founder of Quakerism, took possession of Swartzmoor Hall, first captivating the heart of a widow, the relict of Judge Fell, the then inhabitant, moving her congenial soul to resign herself to him in the bonds of matrimony. From thence he sallied forth, and I trust, unintentionally, gave rise to a crowd of spiritual Quixotes (disowned indeed by his admirers, as his genuine followers) who for a period disturbed mankind with all the extravagances that enthusiasm could invent.

Return to Ulverston, and dine with Mr Kendal of that place, who showed me every civility. In his possession saw a singular tripodal jug, found in the neighbourhood: it was wide at the bottom, and narrow at the top, with a spout and handle made of a mixed metal; the height of the vessel was eight inches three quarters, of the feet two three-quarters. One of the same kind was found in the county of Down,[24] in Ireland; yet probably both might be Roman, the last brought by accident into that kingdom; for Mr Gordon, tab. 42, has given the figure of one carved on the side of an altar.

---

[24] *Ancient and Present State of the County of Down*, 55.

Proceed by Newland iron furnace; ascend a high hill, whose very top, as well as others adjacent, appears well peopled. Descend to Pennybridge, or Crakeford, where a ship of 150 tons was then building. Furnaces abound in these parts, and various sorts of implements of husbandry are made here.

Keep along a narrow glen on excellent roads, amidst thick coppices, or brush woods of various sorts of trees, many of them planted expressly for the use of the furnaces or bloomeries. They consist chiefly of birch and hazel: not many years ago shiploads of nuts have been exported from hence. The woods are great ornaments to the country, for they creep high up the hills. The owners cut them down in equal portions, in the rotation of sixteen years, and raise regular revenues out of them; and often superior to the rent of their land, for freeholders of fifteen or twenty-five pounds per annum, are known to make constantly sixty pounds a year from their woods. The furnaces for these last sixty years have brought a great deal of wealth into this country.

Observe that the tops of all the ash trees were lopped; and was informed that it was done to feed the cattle in autumn, when the grass was on the decline; the cattle peeling off the bark as a food. In Queen Elizabeth's time, the inhabitants of Colton and Hawkshead Fells remonstrated against the number of bloomeries then in the country, because they consumed all the loppings and croppings, the sole winter food for their cattle. The people agreed to pay to the Queen the rent she received from these works, on condition they were suppressed. These rents now called 'bloom smithy', are paid to the crown to this day, notwithstanding the improved state of the country has rendered the use of the former indulgence needless.

Keep by the side of the River Crake: near its discharge from Coninston Mere, at a place called Waterfoot, lay abundance of slate brought down by water from the quarries in the fells: observed also great heaps of birch besoms, which are also articles for exportation.

Reach Coninston or Thurstain Water, a beautiful lake, about seven measured miles long; and the greatest breadth three quarters: the greatest depth from thirty to forty fathoms. At the south end it is narrowed by the projection of several little headlands running far into the water, and forming between them several pretty bays. A little higher up the widest part commences: from thence it runs quite straight to the end, not incurvated as the maps make it. The fish of this water are char and pike: a few years ago the first were sold for 3s 6d per dozen, but, thanks to the luxury of the times, are now raised to eight or nine shillings. The scenery about this lake, which is scarcely mentioned, is extremely noble. The east and west sides are bounded by high hills often wooded; but in general composed of grey rock, and coarse vegetation; much juniper creeps along the surface, and some beautiful hollies are finely intermixed. At the north western extremity the vast mountains called Coninston Fells, form a magnificent mass. In the midst is a great bosom, retiring inward, which affords great quantities of fine slate. The trade in this article has of late been greatly improved, and the value of the quarries highly increased: a work that twenty years ago did not produce to the landlord forty shillings, at present brings in annually as many pounds: and the whole quantity at this time exported yearly from these mountains, is about two thousand tons. At their feet is a small cultivated tract, filled with good farmhouses, and near the water edge is the village and church of Coninston. Formerly these mountains yielded copper; but of late the works have been neglected on account of the poverty of the ore.

Leave the sides of the lake, and ascend a steep hill, surrounded with woods. From the summit have a fine view of the lake, the stupendous fells, and a winding chasm beneath some black and serrated mountains.

The fields in those parts are often fenced with rows of great slates; which no horses will attempt leaping. See at a distance a piece of Winandermere, and that of Eastthwaite; descend the hill, and soon reach the small town of Hawkshead, seated in a fertile bottom. In the church is an altar tomb, with the effigies of William Sandys, and Margaret his wife, most rudely cut in stone, and done by order of his son Edwin, Archbishop of York, who was born in a small house in this neighbourhood. Round the tomb is this inscription:

> *Conditur hoc tumulo, Guilielmus Sandes et uxor,*
> *Cui Margareta nomen et omen erat.*

Armiger ille fuit percharus regibus olim,
Illa sed exemplar religionis erat.
Conjugii fuerant aequali sorte beati,
Felices opibus, stemmate, prole, side.
Quos amor et pietas laeto conjunxit eodem:
Hos sub spe vitae continet iste lapis.

Leave Hawkshead, and ride by the side of Urswickmere, about two miles long, and three-quarters broad; on each side ornamented with a pretty elevated peninsula, jutting far into the water. Its fish are perch, called here bass, pike, eels, but no trout. The eels descend in multitudes through the river that flows from this mere into Winander, beginning their migration with the first floods after midsummer; and cease on the first snows. The inhabitants of the country take great numbers in wheels at that season; when it is their opinion that the eels are going into the salt water; and that they return in spring.

The roads are excellent amidst fine woods, with grey rocks patched with moss rising above. In one place observed a holly park, a tract preserved entirely for sheep, who are fed in winter with the croppings. Wild cats inhabit in too great plenty these woods and rocks.

The *Lichen tartareus*, or 'stone rag', as it is called here, encrusts most of the stones: is gathered for the use of dyers by the peasants, who sell it at a penny per pound, and can collect two stone weight of it in a day.

Reach Graithwaite, the seat of Mr Sandys; and from the Cats Craig, an eminence near the house, have an extensive view up and down the water of Winander, for several miles. The variety of beautiful bays that indent the shore; the fine wooded risings that bound each side; and the northern termination of lofty fells patched with snow, compose a scene the most picturesque that can be imagined.

See on the plain part of these hills numbers of springes for woodcocks, laid between tufts of heath, with avenues of small stones on each side, to direct these foolish birds into the snares, for they will not hop over the pebbles. Multitudes are taken in this manner in the open weather; and sold on the spot for sixteen pence or twenty pence a couple (about twenty years ago at six pence of seven pence) and sent to the all-devouring capital, by the Kendal stage.

After breakfast, take boat at a little neighbouring creek, and have a most advantageous view of this beautiful lake, being favoured with a calm day and fine sky. The length of this water is about twelve miles; the breadth about a mile; for the width is unequal from the multitude of pretty bays, that give such an elegant sinuosity to its shores, especially those on the east, or the Westmoreland side. The horns of these little ports project far, and are finely wooded; as are all the lesser hills that skirt the water.

At a distance is another series of hills, lofty, rude, grey and mossy; and above them soar the immense heights of the fells of Coninston, the mountains of Wrynose and Hardknot, and the conic points of Langden Fells; all except the first in Cumberland.

The waters are discharged out of the south end, at Newby Bridge, with a rapid precipitous current, then assume the name of Leven, and after a course of two miles fall into the estuary called the Leven Sands. The depth of this lake is various, from four yards and a half to seventy-four, and, excepting near the sides, the bottom is entirely rocky: in some places are vast subaqueous precipices, the rock falling at once perpendicular, for the depth of twenty yards, within forty of the shore; and the same depth is preserved across the channel. The fall of the Leven, from the lake to high water mark, is ninety feet; the deepest part of the lake a hundred and thirty-two beneath that point.

The boatmen directed their course northward, and brought us by the heathy isle of Lingholm, and the far projecting cape of Rawlinson's Nab. On the left hand observe the termination of Lancashire, just south of the Stor, a great promontory in Westmoreland, all the remaining western side is claimed by the first; but Westmoreland bounds the rest, so has the fairest claim to call itself owner of this superb water.

On doubling the Stor a new expanse opened before us; left the little isle of Crowholme on the right; traversed the lake towards the horse ferry, and a little beyond, the great holme of thirty acres crosses the water, and conceals the rest. This delicious isle is blessed with a rich pasturage, is adored with a pretty grove, and has on it a good house.

It has been the fortune of this beautiful retreat often to change matters: the flattering hopes of the charms of retirement have misled several to purchase it from the last cheated owner, who after a little time discovered, that a constant enjoyment of the same objects, delightful as they were, soon satiated. There must be something more than external charms to make a retreat from the world long endurable; the qualifications requisite fall to the share of a very few; without them disgust and weariness will soon invade their privacy, notwithstanding they courted it with all the passion and all the romance with which the poet did his mistress:

> *Sic ego secretis possum bene vivere sylvis,*
> *Qua nulla humano sit via trita pede.*
> *Tu mihi currarum requies, tu nocte vel atra*
> *Lumen, et in solis tu mihi turba locis.*[25]

From this island began a new and broader extent of water, bounded on the west by the bold and lofty face of a steep hill, patched with the deep green of vast yews and hollies, that embellished its naked slope. This example is varied with several very pretty isles, some bare, others just appear above water, tufted with trees: on the north-east side is the appearance of much cultivation; a tract near the village of Boulness falls gently to the water edge, and rises again far up a high and large mountain, beyond which is a grand screen of others, the pointed heads of Troutbeck Fells, the vast rounded mass of Fairfield, and the still higher summit of Rydal.

---

[25] Tibullus IV, 13, 9.

II

WESTMORELAND, CUMBERLAND

⸺⸺>●<⸺⸺

Boulness—Ambleside—Rydal Hall—Thirlwater—Keswick Vale—
Derwentwater—Crossthwaite Church—Bassenthwaite Water—
Cockermouth—Whitehaven—Moresby—Workington—Maryport—
Wigton—Carlile—Warwick Church—Wetherel Cells—Constantine's
Cells—Corbie Caste—Arthuret—Netherby—Liddel's Strength

L AND, and dine in Westmoreland, at Boulness, anciently called
Winander, giving name to the lake; and am here treated with
most delicate trout and perch, the fish of this water. The char is
found here in great plenty, and of a size superior to those in Wales.
They spawn about Michaelmas, in the River Brathay, which, with
the Rowthay are the great feeds of the lake, preferring the rocky
bottom of the former to the gravelly bottom of the other. The
fishermen distinguish two varieties, the case-char and the gelt-char
i.e. a fish which had not spawned the last season, and esteemed by
them the more delicate; this spawns from the beginning of January
to the end of March, and never ascends the river, but selects for that
purpose the most gravelly parts of the lake, and that which abounds
most with springs. It is taken in greatest plenty from the end of
September to the end of November, but at other times is very rarely
met with.

The monks of the abbey of Furness had a grant from William of
Lancaster, privileging them to fish on this water with one boat and

twenty nets; but in case any of the servants belonging to the abbey, and so employed, misbehaved themselves, they were to be chastised by the lord of the water; and in case they refused to submit, the abbot was bound to discharge them, and make them forfeit their wages for their delinquency.[1]

Remount my horse, and continue my journey along the sides of the lake, and from an eminence about half a mile north of the village of Boulness, have a fine view of the water and all its windings; and observe that the last bend points very far to the west.

On advancing towards the end have an august prospect of the whole range of these northern Appenines, exhibiting all the variety of grandeur in the uniform immense mass, the conic summit, the broken ridge, and the overhanging crag, with the deep chasm-like passages far winding along their bases, rendered more horrible by the blackening shade of the rocks.

Among the birds which possess this exalted tract, the eagles are the first in rank: they breed in many places. If one is killed, the other gets a new mate, and retains its ancient eyrie. Those who take their nests find in them remains of great numbers of moor game: they are besides very pernicious to the heronries: it is remarked, in the laying season of the herons, when the eagles terrify them from their nests, that crows, watching the opportunity, will steal away their eggs.

The red deer which still run wild in Martindale Forest, sometimes straggled into those parts.

Reach Ambleside, a small town above the extremity of the lake: the inhabitants of these parts are very industrious; are much employed in knitting stockings for Kendal market; in spinning woollen yarn, and in making thread to weave their linsies. The countenances of the people begin to alter; especially in the tender sex; the face begins to square, and the cheek bone begins to rise, as if symptomatic of my approaching towards North Britain.

---

[1] Dugdale, *Monast.* I, 706.

Below Ambleside, in a meadow near the River Brathay, is a Roman camp, the supposed Dictis of the Notitia, where coins, bricks, etc. have been often found. The outline of the work is still visible, and its extent is four hundred feet one way, and three hundred the other: it was the station of part of the cohort of the *Numerus Nerviorum Dictensium*, and placed very conveniently to command several passes.

At a small distance from Ambleside, see Rydal, the house of Sir Michael le Fleming, placed in a most magnificent situation; having the lake full in front, a rich intervening foreground; and on each side a stupendous guard of mountains. This family have been fixed in the north ever since the conquest, and became owners of Rydal Hall by a marriage with one of the coheiresses, daughter of Sir John de Lancaster, in the time of Henry IV.

Near the house is a lofty rocky brae, clothed with multitudes of gigantic yews and hollies, that from their size and antiquity, give it a most venerable appearance; and not far from its foot is Rydal Water, about a mile long, beautified with little isles.

Go through Rydal Pass, or, in the dialect of the country, Rydal Haws, or 'Gullet'. Ride through Grassmere, a fertile vale with a lake clothed at the end by a noble pyramidal mountain.

On a high pass between the hills, observe a large carnedd called Dummail Wrays Stones, collected in memory of a defeat, AD 946 given to a petty king of Cumberland, of that name, by Edmund I, who with the usual barbarity of the times, put out the eyes of his two sons, and gave his country to Malcolm, King of Scotland, on condition he preserved in peace the northern parts of England.

The descent from hence to the vale of Keswick, nine miles. Near this place enter Cumberland, having on the left the long extended front of Helvellin Fells. Most of the hills in these parts are fine sheepwalks, smooth and well turfed. The sheep are small, but the mutton exquisitely tasted, being seldom killed before it is six or seven years old. The wool is coarse, but manufactured into ordinary carpets and blankets. No goats are kept here on account of the damage they would do to the woods.

Arrive within sight of Thirlwater, a most beautiful but narrow lake, filling the bottom of a long dale for near four miles. From an eminence near Dalehead House, have a picturesque view over great part of its extent. About the middle, the land for above a hundred yards, approaches and contracts the water to the size of a little river, over which is a true Alpine bridge; and behind that the water instantly resumes the former breadth.

Regaining the road, have a strange and horrible view downwards, into a deep and misty vale, at this time appearing bottomless, and winding far amidst the mountains, darkened by their height, and the thick clouds that hung on their summits.

In the course of the descent, visit, under the guidance of Dr Brownrigg (the first discoverer) a fine piece of antiquity of that kind which is attributed to the Druids. An arrangement of great stones tending to an oval figure, is to be seen near the road side, about a mile and a half from Keswick, on the summit of a pretty broad and high hill, in an arable field called Castle. The area is thirty-four yards from north to south, and near thirty from east to west; but many of the stones are fallen down, some inward, others outward: according to the plan, they are at present forty in number. At the north end, are two much larger than the rest, standing five feet and a half above the soil: between these may be supposed to have been the principal entrance; opposite to it, on the south side, are others of nearly the same height; and on the east is one near seven feet high. But what distinguishes this from all other druidical remains of this nature, is a rectangular recess on the east side of the area, formed of great stones, like those of the oval. These structures are considered in general to have been temples, or places of worship; the recess here mentioned seems to have been allotted for the Druids, the priests of the place, a sort of holy of holies, where they met separated from the vulgar, to perform their rites, their divinations, or to sit in council, to determine on controversies, to compromise all differences about limits of land, or about inheritances, or for the trial of the greater criminals;[2] the Druids possessing both the office of priest and judge. The cause that this recess was placed on the east side, seems to arise from the respect paid by the ancient natives of this isle to that beneficent luminary the sun, not originally

---

[2] Caes., *De Bello Gal.* VI.

I

IV. II III.

SALVTE
MX MAC
CAES

I.

ANTIQUITIES.

an idolatrous respect, but merely as a symbol of the Glorious All-seeing Being, its great Creator.

In the same plate with these Druidical remains, is engraven a species of fibula cut out of a flat piece of silver, of a form better to be expressed by the figure than words. Its breadth is, from one exterior side to the other, four inches. This was discovered lodged in the mud, on deepening a fish pond in Brayton Park in Cumberland, the seat of Sir Wilfrid Lawson, and communicated to me by Dr Brownrigg. With it was found a large silver hook of two ounces weight. The length of the shank from the top to the curvature at bottom, four inches and three eights. The hook not so long.

Arrive near the Elysium of the north, the Vale of Keswick, a circuit between land and water of about twenty miles. From an eminence above, command a fine bird's eye view of the whole of the broad fertile plain, the town of Keswick, the white church of Crossthwaite, the boasted lake of Derwentwater, and the beginning of that of Bassenthwaite, with a full sight of the vast circumjacent mountains that guard this delicious spot.

Dine at Keswick, a small market town: where, and in the neighbourhood, are manufacturers of carpets, flannels, linsies and yarn: the last sold to people from Cockermouth, who come for it every market day.

Take boat on the celebrated lake of Derwentwater. The form is irregular, extending from north to south, about three miles and a half; the breadth one and a half. The greatest depth is twenty feet in a channel, running from end to end, probably formed by the River Derwent, which passes through, and gives name to the lake.

The views on every side are very different: here all the possible variety of Alpine scenery is exhibited, with all the horror of precipice, broken crag, or overhanging rock; or insulated pyramidal hills, contrasted with others whose smooth and verdant sides, swelling into aerial heights, at once please and surprise the eye.

The two extremities of the lake afford most discordant prospects: the southern is a composition of all that is horrible; an immense chasm opens in the midst whose entrance is divided by a rude conic hill, once topped with a castle, the habitation of the tyrant of the rocks; beyond, a series of broken mountainous crags, now patched with snow, soar one above the other, overshadowing the dark winding deeps of Borrowdale. In these black recesses are lodged variety of minerals, the origin of evil by their abuse, and placed by nature, not remote from the fountain of it:

> *Itum est in viscera terrae,*
> *Quasque recondiderat stygiisque removerat umbris,*
> *Effodiuntur opes.*

But the opposite or northern view is in all respects a strong and beautiful contrast: Skiddaw shows its vast base, and bounding all that part of the vale, rises gently to a height that sinks the neighbouring hills; opens a pleasing front, smooth and verdant, smiling over the country like a gentle generous lord, while the fells of Borrowdale frown on it like a hardened tyrant.

Each boundary of the lake seems to take part with the extremities, and emulates their appearance: the southern varies in rocks of different forms, from the tremendous precipices of the Lady's Leap, the broken front of the Falcon's Nest, to the more distant concave curvature of Lowdore, an extent of precipitous rock, with trees vegetating from the numerous fissures, and the foam of a cataract precipitating amidst.

The entrance into Borrowdale divides the scene, and the northern side alters into milder forms: a salt spring, once the property of the monks of Furness, trickles along the shore; hills (the resort of shepherds) with downy fronts, and lofty summits, succeed; with woods clothing their bases, even to the water's edge.

Not far from hence the environs appear to the navigator of the lake to the greatest advantage, for on every side mountains close the prospect, and form an amphitheatre almost matchless.

Loch Lomond in Scotland, and Lough Lene in Ireland, are powerful rivals to the lake in question: was a native of either of those kingdoms to demand my opinion of their respective beauties, I must answer as the subtle Melvil did the vain Elizabeth: that she was 'the fairest person in England; and mine the fairest in Scotland'.

The isles that decorate this water are few, but finely disposed, and very distinct; rise with gentle and regular curvatures above the surface, consist of verdant turf, or are planted with various

II

t Henry Griffiths del.

R. Woodhouse sc.

VIEW OF SKIDDAW.

trees. The principal is the lord's island, about five acres, where the Ratcliff family had some time its residence; and from this lake took the title of Derwentwater. The last ill-fated earl lost his life and fortune by the rebellion of 1715; and his estate, now amounting to twenty thousand pounds per annum (the mines included) is vested in trustees for the support of Greenwich hospital.

St Herbert's Isle was noted for the residence of that saint, the bosom friend of St Cuthbert, who wished, and obtained his wish of departing this life on the same day, hour and minute, with that holy man.

The water of Derwentwater is subject to violent agitations, and often without any apparent cause, as was the case this day; the weather was calm, yet the waves ran a great height, and the boat was tossed violently with what is called a 'bottom wind'.

Went to Crossthwaite Church; observed a monument of Sir John Radcliff and dame Alice his wife, with their effigies on small brass plates. The inscription is in the style of the times:

> *Of your charity pray for the soule of Sir John Radcliff, knight, and for the soule of dame Alice his wife, which Sir John died the 2d day of February, ad 1527, on whose soule the Lord have mercy.*

Here are also two recumbent alabaster figures of a man and a woman; he in a gown, with a purse at his girdle.

This is the church to Keswick, and has five chapels belonging to it. The livings of this county have been of late years much improved by Queen Anne's bounty, and there are none of less value than thirty pounds a year. It is not very long since the minister's stipend was five pounds per annum, a 'goose-grass', or the right of commoning his goose; a 'whittle-gait', or the valuable privilege of using his knife for a week at a time at any table in the parish; and lastly, a 'hardened sark', i.e. a shirt of coarse linen.

Saw, at Dr Brownrigg's, of Ormathwaite, whose hospitality I experienced for two days, great variety of the ores of Borrowdale, such as lead, common and fibrous, black-jack, and black-lead or wad. The last is found in greater quantities and purity in those mountains than in other parts of the world. Is the property of a few gentlemen, who, least the markets should be glutted, open the mine only once in seven years, then cause it to be filled and otherwise secured from the depredations of the neighbouring miners, who will run any risk to procure so valuable an article, for the best sells from eight to twelve shillings a pound. The legislature hath also guarded their property by making the robbery, felony.

It is of great use in making pencils, black lead crucibles for fusing of metals, for casting of bombs and cannon-balls, cleaning arms, for glazing of earthenware; and some assert that it may be used medicinally to ease the pains of gravel, stone, stranguary, and colic: it has been supposed, but without foundation, to have been the *melanteria* and *pnigitis* of Dioscorides: Dr Merret calls it *Nigrica farbrilis*, and the people of the country, 'killow' and 'wad', from the colouring quality; 'killow', or 'collow', signifying the dirt of coal, and 'wad' seems derived from 'woad', a deep dying plant.[3]

Till of late years the superstition of the Beltane was kept up in these parts, and in this rural sacrifice it was customary for the performers to bring with them boughs of the mountain ash.

Continue my journey; pass along the vale of Keswick and keep above Bassenthwaite Water, at a small cultivated distance from it: this lake is a fine example of four miles in length, bounded on one side by high hills, wooded in many places to their bottoms; on the other side by fields and the skirts of Skiddaw.

Marks of the plough appear on the tops of many of the hills. Tradition says, that in the reign of King John, the pope cursed all the lower grounds, and thus obliged the inhabitants to make the hills arable: but I rather believe that John himself drove them to this cruel necessity, for out of resentment of their declining to follow his standards to the borders of Scotland, he cut down their hedges, levelled the ditches, and gave all the cultivated tracts of the north to the beasts of chase, on his return from his expedition.

From Mr Spedyn's of Armethwaite, at the lower extremity of the lake, have a fine view of the whole. Near this place the Derwent quits the lake, passing under Ouze Bridge, consisting of three arches. Salmons come up the river from the sea about Michaelmas, and

---

[3] MS Letter of Bishop Nicholson to Dr Woodward, Aug. 5, 1713.

force their way through both lakes as far as Borrowdale. They had lately been on their return, but the water near the bridge proving too shallow to permit them to proceed, they were taken by dozens, in very bad order, in the nets that were drawing for trout at the end of the lake.

On a hill near this spot is a circular British entrenchment; and I was told of others of a square form, at a few miles distance, at the foot of Caermote, I suppose Roman.

The country now begins to lower, ceases to be mountainous, but swells into extensive risings. Ride near the Derwent, and pass through the hamlets of Isel, Blincraik and Redmain; in a few places wooded, but generally naked, badly cultivated, and enclosed with stone walls. Reach Bridekirk, a village with a small church, noted for an ancient font, found at Papcastle, with an inscription explained by the learned prelate Nicholson, in Camden's *Britannia*, and engraven in the second volume of the works of the Society of Antiquaries. The height is two feet and an inch; the form square; on each side are different sculptures; on one a cross, on another a two-headed monster, with a triple flower falling from one common stem, hanging from its mouth: beneath is a person, St John the Baptist, performing the office of baptism by the immersion of a child, our Saviour; and above the child is a (now) imperfect dove; on a third side is a sort of centaur, attacked by a bird and some animal; and under them the angel driving our first father out of Eden, while Eve clings close to the tree of life, as if exclaiming:

> *Oh! Unexpected stroke, worse than of death!*
> *Must I then leave thee, Paradise? Thus leave*
> *Thee, native soil!*

And on the fourth side two birds, with some ornaments and figures beneath; and the inscription in runic characters thus deciphered by the bishop: *Er Erkard han men egrocten, and to dis men red wer Taner men Brogten.* That is to say, 'here Ekard was converted, and to this man's example were the Danes brought.'

It is certain that the inscription was cut in memory of this remarkable event; but whether the font was made expressly on the occasion, or whether it was not of much more ancient date (as the antiquary supposes) and the inscription put on at the time of this conversion, appears to me at this period very uncertain.

Pass, not far from Bridekirk, through the village of Papcastle, once a Roman station, conjectured by Mr Horsley to have been the Derventione of the geographer of Ravenna; where many monuments of antiquity have been found. In a field on the left, on descending into the village, are the remains of some dikes. Reach Cockermouth, a large town with broad streets, irregularly built, washed by the Derwent on the western side, and divided in two by the Cocker, and the parts connected by a bridge of a single arch. The number of inhabitants are between three and four thousand: the manufacturers are shalloons, worsted stockings and hats; the last exported from Glasgow to the West Indies. It is a borough town, and the right of voting is vested by burgess tenure in certain houses: this is also the town where the county elections are made.

The castle is seated on an artificial mount, on a bank above the Derwent: is square, and is strengthened with several square towers: on each side of the inner gate are two deep dungeons, capable of holding fifty persons in either; are vaulted at top, and have only a small opening in order to lower through it the unhappy prisoners into this dire prison; and on the outside of each is a narrow slit with a slope from it; and down this were shot the provisions allotted to the wretched inhabitants. In the feudal times death and captivity were almost synonymous; but the first was certainly preferable; which may be one cause why the battles of ancient days were so bloody.

This castle was founded by Waldof, first Lord of Allderdale, and son of Gospatrick, Earl of Northumberland, contemporary with William the Conqueror; Waldof resided first at Papcastle, which he afterwards demolished, and with the materials built that at Cockermouth, where he and his posterity long resided; but several arms over the gateway, which Camden says are those of the Multons, Humfranvilles, Luceys and Perceys, evince it to have been in later times in those families. It appears that it was first granted by Edward II to Anthony de Lucie, son of Thomas de Multon, who had assumed that name by reason that his mother was daughter and coheiress to Richard de Lucie; and afterwards, by marriages, this castle and its honours descended to the Humfranvilles, and finally to the Perceys.[4] In 1648 it was garrisoned for the king; and being besieged and taken by the rebels, was burnt, and never afterwards repaired.

Pursue my journey for about four or five miles along a tolerably fertile country; and then arrive amidst the collieries: cross some barren heaths, with enclosed land on each side, destitute both of hedges and woods. Pass through Dissinton, a long and dirty town, and soon after, from a great height, at once come in sight of Whitehaven, and see the whole at a single glance, seated in a hollow, open to the sea on the north. It lies in the parish of St Bees, whose vast promontory, noted for the great resort of birds, appears four miles to the south; and in days of old, still more noted for its patroness St Bega, who tamed fierce bulls, and brought down deep snows at midsummer.

The town is in a manner a new creation, for the old editions of Camden make no mention of it; yet the name is in Saxton's maps, its white cliffs being known to seamen. The rise of the place is owing to the collieries, improved and encouraged by the family of the Lowthers to their great emolument. About a hundred years ago there was not one house here, except Sir John Lowther's, and two others, and only three small vessels: and for the next forty years, the number of houses increased to about twenty. At this time the town may boast of being one of the handsomest in the north of England, built of stone, and the streets pointing straight to the harbour, with others crossing them at right angles. It is as populous as it is elegant, containing twelve thousand inhabitants, and has a hundred and ninety great ships belonging to it, mostly employed in the coal trade.

The tobacco trade is much declined: formerly about twenty thousand hogsheads were annually imported from Virginia; now scarce a fourth of that number; Glasgow having stolen that branch: but to make amends, another is carried on to the West Indies, where hats, printed linens, hams, etc. are sent. The last week was a melancholy and pernicious exportation of a hundred and fifty

[4] Dugdale's *Baronage* I, 564, etc.

natives of Great Britain, forced from their natal soil, the Lowlands of Scotland, by the raise of rents, to seek an asylum on the other side of the Atlantic.

The improvements in the adjacent lands keep pace with those in the town: the Brainsty estate forty years ago was set for as many pounds; at present, by dint of good husbandry, especially liming, is increased to five hundred and seventy-one.

In the town are three churches or chapels: St James's is elegantly fitted up, and has a handsome gallery, which, with the roof, is supported by most beautiful ranges of pillars. Besides is a Presbyterian meeting, one of Seceders, of Anabaptists, and Quakers.

The workhouse is thinly inhabited; for few of the poor choose to enter. Those whom necessity compels, are most usefully employed: with pleasure I observed old age, idiocy, and even infants of three years of age, contributing to their own support, by pulling of oakum.

The harbour is artificial, but a fine and expensive work, on the south end, guarded by a long pier, where the ships may lie in great security. Another is placed farther out, to break the force of the sea; and within these are two long straight tongues, or quays, where the vessels are lodged: close to the shore, on the south side, is another, covered with what is called here a steer, having in the lower part a range of smiths' shops, and above an extensive floor, capable of containing six thousand wagon loads of coal, of 4,200 lb each. But this is only used as a sort of magazine: for above this are covered galleries with rail roads, terminating in large flues, or hurries, placed sloping over the quay, and through these the coal is discharged out of the wagons into the holds of the ships, rattling down with a noise like thunder. Commonly eight ships, from a hundred and twenty to a hundred tons each, have been loaded in one tide; and on extraordinary occasions twelve. Each load is put on board for ten shillings: and the wagons, after being emptied, are brought round into the road by a turn frame, and drawn back by a single horse. The greater part of the way from the pits, which lie about three or four miles distant from the hurries is down hill; the wagon is steered by one man, with a sort of rudder to direct it; so that he can retard or accelerate the motion by the pressure he gives by it on the wheel.

Many other works are projected to secure the port, particularly another pier on the north side, which when complete, will render this haven quite land-locked. It is to be observed, that in coming in vessels should carry a full sail till they pass the pier head, otherwise they will not be carried far enough in. The greatest part of the coal is sent to Ireland, where about two hundred and eighteen thousand tons are annually exported.

Springtides rise here twenty-four feet. Neaptides thirteen.

Visit the collieries, entering at the foot of a hill, not distant from the town, attended by the agent: the entrance was a narrow passage, bricked and vaulted, sloping down with an easy descent. Reach the first beds of coal which had been worked about a century ago: the roofs are smooth and spacious, the pillars of sufficient strength to support the great superstructure, being fifteen yards square, or sixty in circumference; not above a third of the coal having been worked in this place; so that to me the very columns seemed left as resources for fuel in future times. The immense caverns that lay between the pillars, exhibited a most gloomy appearance: I could not help enquiring here after the imaginary inhabitant, the creation of the labourers fancy, 'the swart fairy of the mine', and was seriously answered by a black fellow at my elbow, that he really had never met with any; but that his grandfather had found the little implements and tools belonging to this diminutive race of subterraneous spirits.[5]

The beds of coal are nine or ten feet thick: and dip to the west one yard in eight. In various parts are great bars of stone, which cut off the coal: if they bend one way, they influence the coal to rise above one's head; if another, to sink beneath the feet. Operations of nature past my skill to unfold.

---

[5] The Germans believed in two species; one fierce and malevolent, the other a gentle race, appearing like little old men, dressed like the miners, and not much above two feet high: these wander about the drifts and chambers of the works, seem perpetually employed, yet do nothing; some seem to cut the ore, or fling what is cut into vessels, or turn the windlass; but never do any harm to the miners, except provoked: as the sensible Agricola, in this point credulous, relates in his book, *De Animantibus Subterraneis*.

Reach a place where there is a very deep descent; the colliers call this Hardknot, from the mountain of that name; and another Wrynose. At about eighty fathoms depth began to see the workings of the rods of the fire engine, and the present operations of the colliers, who work now in security, for the firedamps, formerly so dangerous, are almost overcome; at present they are prevented by boarded partitions, placed a foot distant from the sides, which causes a free circulation of air throughout: but as still there are some places not capable of such conveniences, the colliers, who dare not venture with a candle in spots where firedamps are supposed to lurk, have invented a curious machine to serve the purpose of lights: it is what they call a 'steel mill', consisting of a small wheel and a handle; this they turn with vast rapidity against a flint, and the great quantity of sparks emitted, not only serves for a candle, but has been found of such a nature as not to set fire to the horrid vapour.

Formerly the damp of fiery vapour was conveyed through pipes to the open air, and formed a terrible illumination during night, like the eruptions of a volcano; and by its heat water could be boiled: the men who worked in it inhaled inflammable air, and, if they breathed against a candle, puffed out a fiery stream; so that I make no doubt, was the experiment made, the same phenomenon would appear as John Brugg attributed to my illustrious countryman Pendragon, chief of Britons.[6]

Reached the extremity of this black journey to a place near two miles from the entrance, beneath the sea, where probably ships were then sailing over us. Returned up the laborious ascent, and was happy once more to emerge into daylight.

The property of these works, as well as the whole town, is in Sir James Lowther, who draws from them and his rents of the buildings sixteen thousand pounds a year; whereas his grandfather only made fifteen hundred. The present baronet has instituted here a charity of the most beautiful nature, useful, humane and unostentatious. He always keeps filled a great granary of oats, which he buys from all parts; but never disposes of, while the markets are low; but the

---

[6] Dr Percy's *Ancient Songs*, 2nd ed. III, 313.

moment they rise above five shillings the Cumberland bushel, or three Winchester measures, he instantly opens his stores to the poor colliers and artificers, and sells it to them at five shillings, notwithstanding it might have cost him seven: thus happily disappointing the rapacity of the vulturine monopolizer.

Leave Whitehaven, and return about two miles on the same road I came. See under the cliffs a neat village called Parton, and a pier, intended for shipping of coal; a new creation by Sir James Lowther.

Leave Moresby on the left; a place near the shore, mentioned by Camden, as of great antiquity, a fort of the Romans, and where several inscriptions have been found: he also speaks of certain caverns, called 'Picts' holes', but the lateness of the evening prevented me from descending to visit them. Ride through the village of Herrington, pass over a very naked barren country, and have from some parts of this evening's journey a full view of the Isle of Man, appearing high and mountainous. Reach Workington; the place where the imprudent Mary Stuart landed, after her flight from Dundrannan, in Galloway, credulously trusting to the protection of the insidious Elizabeth. The town extends from the castle, the seat of Mr Curwen, to the sea: it consists of two clusters, one the more ancient near the castle, the other nearer the church and pier; and both contain about four or five thousand inhabitants. They subsist by the coal trade, which is here considerable. The Derwent washes the skirts of the town, and discharges itself into the sea about a mile west: on each bank near the mouth are piers where the ships lie, and the coals are conveyed into them from frames occasionally dropping into them from the rail roads. Ninety seven vessels of different burdens, some even of two hundred and fifty tons, belong to this port.

Observe to the south, on an eminence near the sea, a small tower, called Holme Chapel; said to have been built as a watch-tower to mark the motions of the Scots in their naval inroads.

Near the town is an iron furnace and foundry; the ore is brought from Furness, and the iron stone dug near Harrington. A fine water-wheel and its rods, extending near a mile, are very well worth visiting.

Keep along the seashore to Maryport, another new creation, the property of Humphrey Senhouse, Esq., and so named by him in honour of his lady: the second house was built in only 1750. Now there are above a hundred, peopled by thirteen hundred souls, all collected together by the opening of a coal trade on this estate. For the conveniency of shipping (there being above seventy of different sizes, from thirty to three hundred tons burden, belonging to the harbour) are wooden piers, with quays, on the River Ellen, where ships lie and receive their lading. Beside the coal trade is some skinning business, and a rope-yard.

At the south end of the town is an eminence called the Motehill, and on it a great artificial mount, whose base is a hundred and sixty yards round, protected by a deep ditch, almost surrounding it, ceasing only where the steepness of the hill rendered such a defence unnecessary: this mount is a little hollowed on the top, has been probed in different places to the depth of four or five feet, but was discovered to consist of no other materials than the common soil which had been flung out of the fosse.

On a hill at the north end of the town are the remains of a large Roman station square, surrounded with double ditches, and furnished with four entrances, commanding a view to Scotland, and round the neighbouring country. Antiquaries differ about the ancient name: one styles it Olenacum, another Virosidum, and Camden, Volantium, from the wish inscribed on a beautiful altar found here, *volenti vivas*.[7] It had been a considerable place, and had its military roads leading from it to Moresby, to old Carlile, and towards Ambleside; and has been a perfect magazine of Roman antiquities.

Not far from this station is a tumulus, singular in its composition; it is of a rounded form, and was found, on the section made of it by the late Mr Senhouse, to consist of, first the sod of common turf, then a regular layer of crumbly earth; which at the beginning was thin, encreasing in thickness as it reached the top. This was at first brittle, but soon after being exposed to the air acquired a great hardness, and a ferruginous look. Beneath this was a bed of strong blue clay, mixed with fern roots, placed on two or three layers of turf, with their grassy sides together; and under these, as

---

[7] Vide Camden 1011, Horsely, 281, tab. no. lxvii. *Cumberland.*

the present Mr Senhouse informed me, were found the bones of a heifer and of a colt, with some wood ashes near them.

Took the liberty of walking to Netherhall, formerly Alneburgh Hall: where I soon discovered Mr Senhouse to be possessed of the politeness hereditary in his family towards travellers of curiosity.[8] He pointed out to me the several antiquities that had been long preserved in his house and gardens; engraven by Camden, Mr Horsley, and Mr Gordon; and permitted one of my servants to make drawings of others that had been discovered since.

Among the latter is the altar found in the rubbish of a quarry, which seems to have been worked by the Romans, in a very extensive matter: it has no inscription, and appears to have been left unfinished; perhaps the workmen were prevented from executing the whole by the upper part of the hill slipping down over the lower: a circumstance that still frequently happens in quarries worked beneath the cliffs. On one side of the altar is a broad dagger, on another a patera.

A fragment of a stone, with a boar rudely carved, and the letters O R D.

A large wooden pin, with a curious polygonal head.

The spout of a brazen vessel. Mr Senhouse also favoured me with the sight of some thin gold plate, found in the same place: and showed me, near his house, in Hall-close, an entrenchment of a rectangular form, forty-five yards by thirty-five: probably the defence of some ancient mansion, so necessary in this border county.

It gave me great pleasure to review the sculptures engraven in Mr Horsley's antiquities, and preserved in the walls of this place. The following were fixed in the walls of the house, by the ancestor of Mr Senhouse, coeval with Camden. On no. 65, an altar, appears Hercules with his club, and in one hand the Hesperian apples that he had conveyed 'ab insomni male custodita dradone'. What is singular, is an upright conic bonnet on his head, of the same kind with that, in which the goddess, on whom he bestowed the fruit

---

[8] Vide Camden 1012; and Gordon's *Itin.* Boreal, 100.

is dressed.[9] On another side of the altar is a man armed with a helmet and clothed with a *sagum clausum*, or closed frock reaching only to his knees. In one hand is a thick pole; the other resting on a wheel, probably denoting his having succeeded in opening some great road.

In no. 70 are seen the two victories supporting a triumphal crown, the *victoriae augusti*.

The local goddess Setlocenia, with long flowing hair, with a vessel in her hand, fills the front of one stone: and an altar inscribed to her is lodged in one of the garden walls.

No. 74 is near the goddess, a most rude figure of a cavalier on his steed.

In the same wall with her altar is no. 64, a monumental mutilated inscription, supposed in honour of Antoninus Pius.

No. 71, the next monument, notes the premature death of Julia Mamertina, at the age of twenty years and three months. A rude head expresses the lady and a setting sun, the funereal subject.

A female expressing modesty with one hand; the other lifted to her head, stands beneath an arch, as if about to bathe, and is marked in Horsely, no. 73.

In a garden house is no. 62, an altar to Jupiter, by the first cohort of the Spanish, whose tribune was Marcus Menius Agrippa.

Another, no. 66, to Mars Militaris; devoted by the first cohort of the Belgic Gauls, commanded by Julius Tutor.

And a third, no. 67, to Jupiter, by Caius Caballus Priscus, a tribune; but no mention is made of the cohort.

Since I visited this place, Mr Senhouse has favoured me with an account of other discoveries, made by the removal of the earth that covered the relics of this station: the streets and footways have been traced paved with stones from the shore, or freestone from the quarries: the last much worn by use. Many foundations of houses; the cement still very strong; and the plaster on some remains of walls, appears to have been discovered, one with freestone steps much used: fire hearths open before, enclosed with a circular wall behind: from the remains of the fuel it is evident that the Romans

---

[9] Monfaucon, *Antiq.* I, tab. civ., f. 7.

III.

ANTIQUITIES.

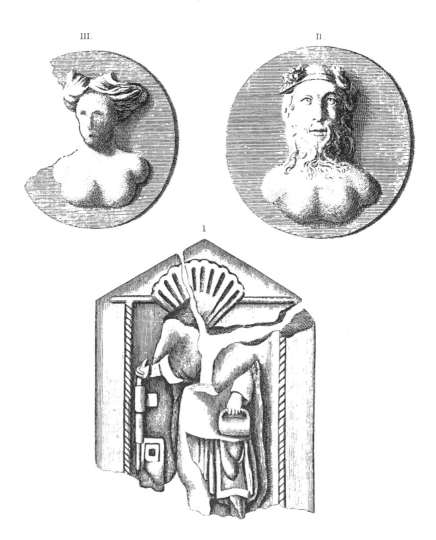

have used both wood and pit coal. Bones and teeth of various animals; and pieces of horns of stags, many of the latter sawed, have been found here: also shells of oysters, mussels, whelks and snails. Broken earthenware and the handle of a large vessel, marked *A E L*. Fragments of glass vessels and mirrors; and two pieces of a painted glass cup, which evinces the antiquity of that art.

An entire altar found in the same search, is to be added to the preceding: three of the sides are plain: the fourth has a hatchet exactly resembling those now in use, and a broad knife, or rather cleaver, with which the victims were cut up.

But the most curious discovery is a stone three feet high, the top formed like a pediment, with a neat scallop shell cut in the middle. From each side the pediment falls in straight corded molding; and between those, just beneath the scallop, is a mutilated figure, the head being destroyed; but from the body which is clothed with the sagum, and the bucket which it holds in one hand by the handle,[10] it appears to have been a Gaul, the only sculpture of the kind found in our island.

Continue my ride along the coast, enjoying a most beautiful prospect of the Solway Firth, the Ituna Aestuarium of Ptolemy, bounded by the mountains of Galloway, from the hill of Cresel, near Dumfries, to the Great and the Little Ross, not remote from Kirkcudbright.

Keep on the shore as far as the village of Allanby: then turn to the north-east, ride over a low barren woodless tract, and dismal moors, seeing on the left Cresel in Scotland, and on the right Skiddaw, both quite clear; the last now appears of an insulting height over its neighbours. Had the weather been misty it would have had its cap; and probably Cresel, according to the old proverb, would have sympathized:

> *If ever Skiddaw wears a cap,*
> *Cresel wots full well of that.*

Dine at Wigton, a small town, with some manufacturers of coarse checks. About a mile or two to the right, is old Carlile, supposed by Mr Horsley to have been the Olenacum of the Notitia.

[10] Monfaucon *Suppl.* III, 38, tab. xi.

From Wigton the country continues very flat and barren, to a small distance of Carlile. Near that city a better cultivation takes place, and the fields often appear covered with linen manufactures: cross the River Cauda, that runs through the suburbs, and enter the city at the Irish gate.

Carlile is most pleasantly situated; like Chester is surrounded with walls, but in very bad repair, and kept very dirty. The castle is ancient, but makes a good appearance at a distance. The view from it consists of an extensive tract of rich meadows, of the River Eden, here forming two branches and insulating the ground: over one is a bridge of four; over the other one of nine arches. There is besides a prospect of a rich country; and a distant view of Coldfells, Crossfells, Skiddaw, and other mountains.

The castle was founded by William Rufus, who restored the city, after it had lain two hundred years in ruins by the Danes. Richard III made some additions to it; and Henry VIII built the citadel, an oblong with three round bastions seated on the west side of the town: in the inner gate of the castle is still remaining the old portcullis; and here are shown the apartments of Mary, Queen of Scots, where she was lodged for some time after her landing at Workington; and after being for a little space entertained with flattering respect, found herself prisoner to her jealous rival.

Carlile has two other gates besides the Irish, viz. the English and the Scotch. The principal street is very spacious; in it is a guardhouse, built by Cromwell, commanding three other streets that open into this.

The cathedral, begun by Walter, deputy under William Rufus, is very incomplete, Cromwell having pulled down part in 1649 to build barracks: there remains some portion that was built in the Saxon mode, with round arches, and vast massy round pillars, whose shafts are only fourteen feet two inches high, and circumference full seventeen and a half: the rest is more modern, said to have been built by Edward III, who had an apartment to lodge in, in his frequent expeditions into Scotland. The arches in this latter building are sharp pointed, the pillars round and clustered, and the inside of the arches prettily ornamented. Above are two galleries, but with windows only in the upper; that in the east end has a magnificent simplicity, and the painted glass an uncommon neatness, notwithstanding there is not a single figure in it.

The choir was not founded till about the year 1354; the tabernacle work in it is extremely pretty; but on the aisles on each side are some strange legendary paintings of the history of St Cuthbert and St Augustine; one represents the saint visited by an unclean spirit, who tempts him in a most indecent manner, as these lines import:

> *The spyrit of Fornication to him doth aper;*
> *And thus he chasteneth hys body with thorne and with bryer.*

At the west end of the church is a large plain altar tomb called the Blue Stone: on this the tenants of the dean and chapter by certain tenures were obliged to pay their rents.

There had been only one religious house in this city; a priory of black canons founded by Henry I, replaced on the suppression, by a dean and four canons secular; but what the tyrant Henry VIII had spared, such as the cloisters and other relics of the priory, fell in after-times victims to fanatic fury; no remains are to be seen at present, except the gateway, and a handsome building called the fratry, or the lodging-room of the lay-brothers, or novices.

Before this pious foundation, St Cuthbert in 686 fixed here a convent of monks, and a nunnery, overthrown in the general desolation of the place by the Danes.

But to trace the antiquity of this city with historic regularity, the reader should learn, that after laying aside all fabulous accounts, the Britons called it Caer-Lualid, that it was named by Antonine, or the author of his itinerary Lugovallium, or 'the city of Lual on the vallum' or 'wall'.

That it was probably a place of note in the seventh century, for Egfrid presented it to St Cuthbert with fifteen miles of territory around; that the Danes entirely destroyed it in the ninth century, and that it remained in ruins for two hundred years. William Rufus in 1092, in a progress he made into these parts, was struck with the situation, founded the castle, rebuilt the town and fortified it as a bulwark against the Scots: he planted there a large colony from the south, who are said to be the first who introduced tillage in that part of the north.

Henry I, in 1122, gave a sum of money to the city, and ordered some additional fortifications. Stephen yielded it to David, King of Scotland. After the recovery into the hands of the English, it underwent a cruel siege by William the Lion in 1173; and was again besieged by Robert Bruce in 1315; and in the reign of Richard II was almost entirely destroyed by fire. The greater events from that period are unknown to me, till its rendition to the rebels in 1745, on November 16th, when its weakness made it untenable, even had it not been seized with the epidemic of the times. It was retaken by the Duke of Cumberland, on the 30th of December following, and the small self-devoted garrison made prisoners on terms that preserved them (without the shadow of impeachment of his Highness's word) for future justice.

The town at present consists of two parishes, St Cuthbert's and the cathedral, and contains about four thousand inhabitants; is handsomely built, and kept very neat. Here is a considerable manufacture of printed linens and coarse checks, which bring in near £3,000 per annum in duties to the Crown. It is noted for a great manufacture of whips, which employs numbers of children; here are also made most excellent fish-hooks; but I was told that the mounting them with flies is an art the inhabitants of Langholm are celebrated for.

Saw, at Mr Bernard Burton's, a pleasing sight of twelve little industrious girls spinning at once at a horizontal wheel, which set twelve bobbins in motion; yet so contrived that should any accident happen to one, the motion of that might be stopped without any impediment to the others.

At Mrs Cust's I was favoured with the sight of a fine head of Father Huddleston, in black, with a large band and long grey hair, with an uplifted crucifix in his hand, probably taken in the attitude in which he lulled the soul of the departing profligate Charles II.

Cross the little River Petrel, the third that bounds the city, and at about three miles east, see Warwick, or Warthwick Church, remarkable for its tribune or rounded east end, with thirteen narrow niches, ten feet eight high, and seventeen inches broad, reaching almost to the ground, and the top of each arched; in two or three is a small window. The whole church is built with good cut stone; the

IV

WARWICK CHURCH.

PLAN OF WETHEREL CELLS.

Mess. Griffiths del.   P. Maxell sculp

length is seventy feet, but it once extended above one and twenty feet farther west; there being still at that end a good rounded arch, now filled up.

This church is of great antiquity, but the date of the foundation unknown. It was granted in the time of William the Conqueror to the abbey of St Mary's, in York, and then mentioned as a chapel.[11]

Beneath it is a handsome bridge of three arches over the Eden, a beautiful river. Ride for two miles over a rich and well cultivated tract, to Corbie Castle, now a modern house, seated on an eminence above the river, which runs through a deep and finely wooded glen; that part next the house judiciously planned and laid out in walks: in one of them is the votive altar engraven in Mr Gordon's itinerary, tab. 43, with tolerable exactness, except on the top, for the hollow is triangular, not round.

The sight from this walk of the celebrated cells, and the arch of the ancient priory, were so tempting that I could not resist crossing the river to pay a visit to those curious remains. The last is the gateway of the religious house of Wetherel, with its fine elliptic arch: the house was once a cell to the abbey of St Mary, in York, given by Ranulph de Meschines, Earl of Carlile, and maintained a prior and eight monks.[12]

A little farther, in the midst of a vast precipice, environed with woods, are cut, with much labour, some deep cells in the live rock: the front and entrance (the last is on the one side) are made of fine cut stone; in the front are three windows, and a fireplace; the cells are three in number, divided by partitions of the native rock, four feet three inches thick: each is twelve feet eight inches deep, and about nine feet six wide in the lower part, where they are more extensive than in their beginning: before them, from the door to the end, is a sort of gallery twenty-three feet and a half long, bounded by the front, which hangs at an awful height above the Eden. There are marks of bolts, bars and other securities in the windows and doors; and vestiges, which show that there had been doors to the cells.

These are called Constantine's Cells, but more commonly the safeguard, being supposed to have been the retreat of the monks

---

[11] Dugdale's *Monast.* I, 397.
[12] Ibid., 389.

of the neighbouring priory, during the inroads of the Scots; no-one who sees them will doubt their security, being approachable only by a most horrible path, amidst woods that grow rather out of precipices than slopes, impending over the far subjacent river; and to increase the difficulty, the door is placed at no small height from this only access, so that probably the monks ascended by a ladder, which they might draw up to secure their retreat.

I searched without success for the inscription on the same rock, a little higher up the river. The words, as preserved in the *Archaelogia*,[13] are:

> *Maximum scripsit*
> *Le xx vv cond: casosius.*

The first line is said to be a yard distant from the other, and nearer, is a coarse figure of a deer. The meaning is too dark to be explained.

Return to Corbie; and find in the house an excellent picture of a musician playing on a bass viol; the work of a Spanish master, part of the plunder of Vigo. A large piece of the Emperor Charles V and his empress; he sitting with a stern look, as if reproving her, and alluding to a casket on a table before them. She stands, and has in her countenance a mixture of obstinacy and fear.

On the staircase is a full length of Lord William Howard, third son of the Duke of Norfolk, known in these parts by the name of 'Bald Willy'. He lived in the time of Queen Elizabeth, and was the terror of the moss-troopers, ruling with a rod of iron, but by his necessary severity, civilized the country.

There are no traces of the old castle. The manor belonging to it was granted by Henry II to Hubert De Vallibus, who consigned it to William de Odard, Lord of Corbie. In the gift of Edward I, it was held by Thomas de Richemount; from him, came to Sir Andrew de Harcla, the unfortunate Earl of Carlile, executed in the time of Edward II, and on his attainder, to Sir Richard de Salkeld: from his heirs to Lord William Howard, then of Naworth, who settled it upon his second son, in whose line it still continues.

---

[13] I, 86.

V

Moses Griffiths del.

WETHEREL CELLS.

R. Manell sculp.

Returned to Carlile, and continue there till the 30th. Cross the Eden, that flows about ten miles below into the Solway Firth. Pass over near the village of Stanwick, a mile from Carlile. The site of the Picts, or more properly Adrian's or Severus's Wall, begun by the first emperor, and completed by the last, who may with more justice be said to have built a wall of stone, near the place, where Adrian had made his of turf. For that reason the Britons styled it Gualsever, Gasever, and Mursever. But at present not a trace is to be discovered in these parts, except a few foundations, now covered with earth, to be seen in a field called Wallknow. From thence it passes behind Stanwick to Hissopholm Bank, an eminence above the river; on which are vestiges of some dikes describing a small square, the site of a fort to defend the pass; for the wall reached to the edge of the water, was continued on the opposite side, over Soceres Meadow, and extended ten or twelve miles farther, till it terminated at Bowness, on the Solway Firth. Adrian's Wall, or rather rampart, was made on the north side of the wall, and is visible in some place, but ceases at or near Brugh, the Axelodunum of the Notitia. Probably this was a station for cavalry, for near Hissop Bank is a stupendous number of horses' bones, exposed by the falling of the cliff.

Cross the Leven, and ride through the village of Arthuret. In the churchyard is a rude cross, with a pierced capital, forming the exact figure of the cross of the Knights of Malta, and it is probable, it was erected by one of that order. In the same ground was interred the remains of poor Archy Armstrong, jester, or fool to Charles I, and by accident, suitable to his profession, the day of his funeral was the first of April. Archy had long shot his bolt with great applause, till it fell unfortunately upon the prelate Laud,[14] who, with a pride and weakness beneath his rank and character, procured an order of council, the king present, for the degrading of the fool, by pulling his motley coat over his head, for discharging him of the King's service, and banishing him the court. Near the village are some high

---

[14] When the news arrived at court of the tumults in Scotland, occasioned by the attempt to introduce the liturgy (a project of Laud), Archy unluckily met with the archbishop, and had the presumption to ask his Grace, 'Who is fool now?'

and irregular sandy eminences; probably natural, notwithstanding a contrary opinion has been held, because some coins and an urn have been found in them.

Reach Netherby, the seat of the Rev Mr Graham, placed on a rising ground, washed by the Esk, and commanding an extensive view; more pleasing to Mr Graham, as he sees from it a creation of his own; lands that eighteen years ago were in a state of nature; the people idle and bad, still retaining a smack of the feudal manners: scarce a hedge to be seen: and a total ignorance prevailed of even coal and lime. His improving spirit soon wrought a great change in these parts: his example instilled into the inhabitants an inclination to industry: and they soon found the difference between sloth and its concomitants, dirt and beggary, and a plenty that a right application of the arts of husbandry brought among them. They lay in the midst of a rich country, yet starved in it; but in a small time they found, that instead of a produce that hardly supported themselves, they could raise even supplies for their neighbours: that much of their land was so kindly as to bear corn for many years successively without help of manure, and for the more ungrateful soils, that there were limestones to be had, and coal to burn them. The wild tract soon appeared in form of verdant meadows or fruitful cornfields: from the first, they were soon able to send to distant places cattle and butter: and their dairies enabled them to support a numerous herd of hogs, and carry on a considerable traffic in bacon: their arable lands, a commerce as far as Lancashire in corn.

A tract distinguished for its fertility and beauty, ran in form of a valley for some space in view of Netherby: it has been finely reclaimed from its original state, prettily divided, well planted with hedges, and well peopled: the ground originally not worth six pence an acre, was improved to the value of thirty shillings: a tract completely improved in all respects, except in houses, the ancient clay-dabbed habitations still existing. I saw it in that situation in the year 1769: at this time a melancholy extent of black turbary, the eruption of Solway moss, having in a few days covered grass and corn; levelled the boundaries of almost every farm; destroyed most of the houses, and driven the poor inhabitants to the utmost distress, till they found (which was not long) from their landlord every relief that a humane mind could suggest. Happily his fortune favoured his inclination to do good: for the instant loss of four hundred pounds a year could prove no check to his benevolence.

On visiting the place from whence this disaster had flowed, it was apparently a natural phenomenon, without anything wonderful or unprecedented. Pelling Moss, near Garstang, had made the same sort of eruption in the present country; and Chat Moss, between Manchester and Warrington, in the time of Henry VIII, as Leland expresses it, 'brast up within a mile of Morley-haul, and destroied much grounde with mosse thereabout, and destroid much fresch water fische thereabout, first corrupting the stinking water Glasebrooke, and so Glasebrooke carried stinking water and mosse into Mersey water, and Mersey corruptid carried the roulling mosse, part to the shores of Wales, part to the isle of Man, and sum into Ireland; and in the very top of Chatley more, where the mosse was hyest and brake, is now a fair plaine valley as was in tymes paste, and a rylle runnith hit, and peaces of smaul trees be found in the bottom'.

Solway Moss consists of sixteen hundred acres; lies some height above the cultivated tract, and seems to have been nothing but a collection of thin peaty mud; the surface itself was always so near the state of a quagmire, that in most places it was unsafe for anything heavier than a sportsman to venture on, even in the driest summer.

The shell or crust that kept this liquid within bounds, nearest to the valley, was at first of sufficient strength to contain it; but by the imprudence of the peat-diggers, who were continually working on that side, at length became so weakened, as not longer to be able to resist the weight pressing on it. To this may be added, the fluidity of the moss was greatly increased by three days rain of unusual violence, which preceded the eruption; and extended itself in a line as far as Newcastle: took in part of Durham, and a small portion of Yorkshire, running in a parallel line of about equal breadth; both sides of which, north and south, experienced an uncommon drought. It is singular that the fall of Newcastle Bridge and this accident happened within a night of each other.

Late in the night of the 17th of November, of the last year, a farmer, who lived nearest the moss, was alarmed with an unusual noise. The crust had at once given way, and the black deluge was rolling towards his house, when he was gone out with a lantern to see the cause of his fright: he saw the stream approach him; and first thought that it was his dunghill, that by some supernatural cause, had been set in motion; but soon discovering the danger, he gave notice to his neighbours with all expedition: but others received no other advice but what this Stygian tide gave them: some by its noise, many by its entrance into their houses, and I have been assured that some were surprised with it even in their beds: these passed a horrible night, remaining totally ignorant of their fate, and the cause of the calamity, till the morning, when their neighbours, with difficulty, got them out through the roof. About three hundred acres of moss were thus discharged, and above four hundred of land covered: the houses either overthrown or filled to their roofs; and the hedges overwhelmed; but providentially not a human life lost. Several cattle were suffocated; and those which were housed had a very small chance of escaping. The case of a cow is so singular as to deserve mention. She was the only one out of eight, in the same cow-house, that was saved, after having stood sixty hours up to the neck in mud and water; when she was relieved, she did not refuse to eat, but would not taste water: nor could even look at it without showing manifest signs of horror.

The eruption burst from the place of its discharge like a cataract of thick ink; and continued in a stream of the same appearance, intermixed with great fragments of peat, with their heathy surface; then flowed like a tide charged with pieces of wreck, filling the whole valley, running up every little opening, and on its retreat, leaving upon the shore tremendous heaps of turf, memorials of the height this dark torrent arrived. The farther it flowed, the more room it had to expand, lessening in depth, till it mixed its stream with that of the Esk.

The surface of the moss received a considerable change: what was before a plain, now sunk in the form of a vast basin, and the loss of the contents so lowered the surface as to give to Netherby a new view of land and trees unseen before.

Near this moss was the shameful rendition in 1542, of the Scotch army, under the command of Oliver Sinclair, minion of James V (to Sir Thomas Wharton, Warden of the Marches). The nobility, desperate with rage and pride, when they heard that favourite proclaimed general, preferred an immediate surrender to a handful of enemies, rather than fight for a king who treated them with such contempt. The English commander obtained a bloodless victory: the whole Scotch army was taken, or dispersed, and a few fugitives perished in this very moss: as a confirmation it is said, that a few years ago some peat-diggers discovered in it the skeletons of a trooper and his horse in complete armour.

In my return visit the ancient border-house at Kirk Andrews, opposite site to Netherby: it consists of only a square tower, with a ground floor, and two apartments above, one over the other: in the first floor it was usual to keep the cattle; in the two last was lodged the family. In those very unhappy times, every one was obliged to keep guard against perhaps his neighbour; and sometimes to shut themselves up for days together, without any opportunity of tasting the fresh air, but from the battlemented top of their castlelet. Their windows were very small; their door of iron. If the robbers attempted to break it open, they were annoyed from above by the flinging of great stones, or by deluges of scalding water.[15]

As late as the reign of our James I, watches were kept along the whole border, and at every ford by day and by night: setters, watchers, searchers of the watchers, and overseers of the watchers were appointed. Besides these cautions, the inhabitants of the marches were obliged to keep such a number of slough dogs, or what we call bloodhounds: for example, 'in these parts, beyond the Esk, by the inhabitants there were to be kept above the foot of Sark, 1 dog. Item, by the inhabitants of the insyde of Esk, to Richmond Cluch, to be kept at the Moot, 1 dog. Item, by the inhabitants of the parish of Arthuret, above Richmond Clugh, to be kept at the Barley-head, 1 dog; and so on throughout the border.' The chief officers, bailiffs and constables throughout the district being directed to see that the inhabitants kept their quota of dogs, and paid their contributions for their maintenance. Persons who were aggrieved, or had lost anything, were allowed to pursue the 'hot trode' with

---

[15] *Life of Lord Keeper Guildford*, 138.

hound and horn, with hue and cry, and all other accustomed manner of hot pursuit.[16]

The necessity of all this was very strong; for before the accession of James I to these kingdoms, the borders of both were in perpetual feuds: after that happy event, those that lived by hostile excursions, took to pillaging their neighbours; and about that period got the name of moss-troopers, from their living in the mosses of the country.

They were the terror of the limits of both kingdoms; at one time amounted to some thousands, but by the severity of the laws, and the activity of Lord William Howard, were a length extirpated. The life and manners of one of the plundering chieftains is well exemplified by the confession of Giordie Bourne, a noted thief, who suffered when Robert Cary, Earl of Monmouth, was warden of one of these marches: he fairly acknowledged, that he had 'lived long enough to do so many villainies as [he had] done; that [he had] layne with above forty mens wives, what in England, what in Scotland; that [he had] killed seven Englishmen with his owne hands, cruelly murthering them; that [he had] spent his whole time in whooring, drinking, stealing, and taking deep revenge for slight offences'.[17]

Return to Netherby. This house is placed on the site of a Roman station, the *castra exploratorum* of Antoninus, and was well situated for commanding an extensive view around. 'By' signifies a habitation; thus not very remote from one another, Netherby, Middleby, and Overby. The first, like Ellenborough, has been a rich fund of curiosities for the amusement of antiquaries: at present the ground they were discovered in is covered with a good house, and useful improvements; yet not long before Leland's time 'ther hath bene marvelus buyldings, as appere by ruinus walles, and men alyve have sene rynges and staples yn the walles at yet had bene stayes or holdes for shyppes'.[18] There is a tradition that an anchor had been

---

[16] *Nicholson's Border Laws*, 127. In the Appendix, is to be seen an order for the security of the borders.
[17] Cary's *Memoirs*, 2nd ed., 123.
[18] Leland's *Itin.* VII, 56, 3rd ed.

found not remote from Netherby, perhaps under the high land at Arthuret, i.e. 'Arthur's head', beneath which it appears as if the tide had once flowed.

Everything has been found here that denotes it to have been a fixed residence of the Romans; a fine hypocaust, or bath was discovered a few years ago, and the burial place, now a shrubbery, was pointed out to me. The various altars, inscriptions, utensils, and every other antiquity collected on the spot, are carefully preserved, and lodged in the greenhouse, with some others collected in different parts of the country, which gave me an opportunity of forming the following catalogue, illustrated with some figures for the amusement of those who are fond of this study.

I. The inscription which preserves the memory of the cohort, lieutenant and proprietor, who founded the *Basilica Equestris equitata exercitatoria* at this place. This was a sort of public riding school, for exercising the cavalry and infantry, who were to serve mixed with them. To this explication of Dr Taylor, *Ph. Trans.*, vol. I, iii may be added this shrewd remark of that gentleman, that the dedication of this edifice to the emperor Marcus Aurelius Severus Alexander, by these words, '*Devota numini majestatique ejus*', brings under suspicion the opinion of the emperor's inclination to Christianity, and aversion to those idolatrous compliments, for according to Lampridus, '*Dominum se appellari vetuit*'.

II. An altar about three feet high, inscribed:

> *Deo sancto Cocidio Paternus Maternus Tribunus*
> *Coh. 1. Nervane ex evocato Palatino. V. S. L. M.*

This seems to be devoted to the local deity, Cocidius, by some veteran, who had been discharged, and promoted. Mr Horsely, no. XVIII. Cumberland, preserves a fragment inscribed to this deity, by *Cohors prima Aelia Dacorum*.

III. The altar with the Greek inscription, found at Corbridge, in Northumberland, engraven in *Archaelogia* II. On one side is a patera; on the other, a most elegant *praefericulum*. The inscription seems no more than this, *you see me an altar* [dedicated] *to Astarte; Pulcher erected it*. The person was probably a Syrian, who serving in the Roman army, assumed a Roman name: at least such is the opinion of the gentleman I consulted.

IV. The altar found in one of the rooms in the hypocaust, at Netherby, addressed *Deae sanctae Fortunae conservatrici Marcus Aurelius Salvius Tribunus, Coh. I. ael. Nispanorum oo Eq. V.S.L.M.* It is to be observed, that this person's name is in the inscription on the basilica.

V. A small altar *Deo Veteri sancto ... ... V.S.L.M.* Mr Horsely preserves some inscriptions to Vitires, a local deity: perhaps the sculptor may have in this place inserted the two *e*'s instead of the *i. i.*

VI. The altar preserved by Mr Gordon, inscribed *Deo Moconti vitiries. Flaviae secund. V.S.L.M.*

VII. Another, fragment *Deo Belatuca* ... or to Belatucadrus, a provincial name for Mars.

VIII. The altar found near Cambeck, and transferred to Netherby, inscribed ... . *B. V. omnium gentium templum olim vetustate conlabsum Jul. Pitianus, P.P. restituit.*[19]

IX. The first sculpture that merits notice is that figured by Mr Horsley, no. 49, Cumberland, and by Mr Gordon, tab. 37: they both justly style it the best of the Roman work of this nature in Britain; and the first properly makes it a genius, and probably that of the emperor. The figure is erect, three feet three inches high, holding in one hand a patera over an altar; in the other a cornucopia; the last frequently observed both in sculpture and in medals. On his head is a mural crown: each of these particulars are to be met with in Monfaucon, tom. i. part. ii. in the figures of tab. cc. The whole length of the stone is seven feet four inches: in the lower part is a long perpendicular groove, with another short and transverse near the middle: in this, I conjecture might have been fixed an iron, forming part of the stand of a lamp, which was customarily placed burning before the statues of deities.

X. A figure in a close dress, not unlike a carter's frock, or what Monfaucon calls *sagum clausum*, reaching down to the heels:

---

[19] None of these altars or stones have any remarkable sculpture; therefore no part of them merit engraving, except the pretty vessel on no. III.

on one side is a boar, on the other a wheel, and beneath that an altar: in the left hand of the figure is part of a cornucopia. The figure is evidently Gaulish, but the history is obscure: the boar is an emblem of Caledonia: the wheel a known type of fortune. It is also a concomitant of Tuisco, a Saxon or northern deity. As the Roman armies in this kingdom were latterly composed of different Gaulish and foreign nations, their deities were introduced, and intermixed with those of the Romans, a most superstitious people, ready and accustomed to adopt those of every country. We need not be surprised at the variety of figures found in this place, where it is evident that liberty of conscience was allowed by there having been so near to a temple of every nation, a latitudinarian Pantheon.

XI is a second figure resembling the former, only that a sort of close short mantle covers the shoulders and breast. It has the wheel, altar and cornucopia; but beneath the feet appear the *crupezia*, such as are beneath those of the celebrated statue of the dancing fawn.

XII is another figure, in a close sagum or saic. By it is a vessel, standing on two long supports; the figure seems about to fling in what it holds in the right hand: the other leans on what resembles an ear of corn.

XIII is a figure sitting in a chair, clothed in garments much plainted and folded: on the lap are apples or fruits. Nehalennia, a Zeland goddess, is represented in this attitude,[20] and her lap thus filled: the habit differs; but this deity might have been adopted by another nation, who dressed her according to its own mode.

XIV is a curious group of three figures, standing with their backs to a long seat, with elbows. They are habited in a loose saic, reaching but little below the knees: that in the middle distinguished by a pointed flap, and a vessel filled whether with fruit or corn is not very evident. These may perhaps be the *Deae Matres* of the barbarous nations, and introduced here by some of the German levies, there having been found in Britain three altars dedicated to them by the Tungrian cohort. They were local deities, protectresses of certain towns or villages among the Gauls and Germans,[21] by

[20] Monfaucon II, 443.
[21] *Archaelogia* III.

VI

I.

II.

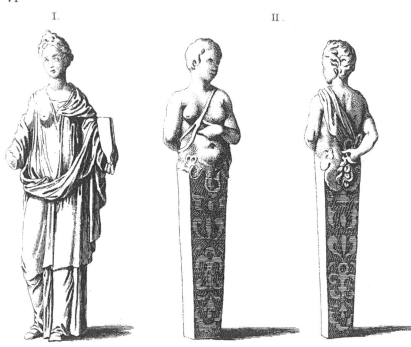

III.

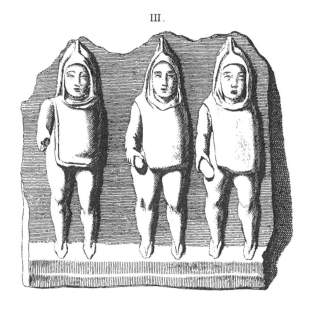

ANTIQUITIES.

whom they were transported into Britain; which it acknowledged in two inscriptions, where they are called *trans marinae*. If they were rural deities the contents of the cup is very apt. I may remark that the Ancients in general were fond of the number three; and the Gauls are known to group their deities very frequently in triplets: a number the most complete, as it regards, beginning, middle, and end.[22]

XV. Another group of three very singular figures; each with a pointed hood, a sort of breastplate hanging loosely, and their feet and legs clothed. In the right hand of each is a stone.

These seem to have been a rude species of soldiery, who fought with stones; but whether British, or foreign barbarians, auxiliary to the Romans, is not certain.

Among the antiquities of other kinds is a very beautiful small figure of a female in brass, whose dress folds with peculiar elegance. By the rudder in her hand, it seems to have been a Fortune.

A small brazen Hermes or Terminus: as it is ornamented with festoons and fruit, it probably was destined to guard the limits of orchards or gardens.

Two brasses: one with the head of a female, with a large turban-like head-dress. The other is the head of Jupiter.

A small brass case, probably designed for a thin medal: a silver brooch: a small pair of pincers, for the purpose of extirpating hairs; a practice much in use among the Romans.

A most elegant urn, found full of ashes: a strong vessel of mixed metal, seemingly a mortar: a glass bead, the *ovum anguinum* of the Romans, and *glain naidr* of the Britons: this has a wire ring through the orifice, which gives reason to suspect that they were strung together like beads.

The numbers X, XI, XIII, and XIV, are engraven in the eighteenth plate of the quarto edition of the Tour of 1769. The remainder in the IIIrd, VIth, and VIIth of this volume.

Take a ride to Liddel's Strength, or the Mote. A strong entrenchment two miles south-west of Netherby, on a steep and lofty clay cliff, above the River Liddel, commanding a vast extent of

[22] Gordon, tab. xxxvi, xxxix & lx.

VII

P·74

74

74

7¹

74

74

74

94

view: has at one end a very high mount, from whence the country might be explored to very great advantage: in the middle is the foundation of a square building, perhaps the praetorium? This place is small, rather of a circular form, strongly entrenched on the weak side; has before it a sort of half moon, with a vast fosse and dike as a security. From this place to Netherby is the vestige of a road. That this fortress had been originally Roman is probable, but since their time has been applied to the same use by other warders. 'It was', says Leland, 'the moted place of a gentilman cawled Sir Water Seleby, the which was killyd there and the place destroyed yn King Edward the thyrde when the Scottes whent to Dyrham'.[23]

It was taken by storm by David II. The governor, Sir Walter, would have compounded for his life by ransom, but the tyrant, after causing his two sons to be strangled before his face, ordered the head of the father, distracted with grief, to be struck off.[24]

[23] Leland *Itin.* VII, 55.
[24] Stow's *Chronicle*, 243.

III

DUMFRIESSHIRE

Pentonlins—Cannonsby—Carsidel—Broomholme—Langholme—
Gratna—Annan—Ruthwell—Burrens Camp—Burnswork Camps—
Hoddam Castle—Caerlaveroc Castle—Newby Abbey—Dumfries—
Lincluden Abbey—Drumlanrig—Morton Castle—Durisdeer—Tibbir
Castle

D ESCEND the hill, and crossing the Liddel, enter in Liddesdale, a
portion of the county of Dumfries: a most fertile and well-
cultivated tract of low arable and pasture land. Keep by the
riverside for three miles farther to Pentonlins, where is a most
wild but picturesque scene of the river, rapidly flowing along
rude rocks, bounded by cliffs, clothed on each side by trees. The
bottom the water rolls over assumes various forms; but the most
singular are beds of stone regularly quadrangular, and divided
by a narrow vacant space from each other, resembling immense
masses of *Ludi helmontii*, with their septa lost. Below these,
the rocks approach each other, leaving only a deep and narrow
channel, with a pretty wooden Alpine bridge over a depth of
furious water, black and terrible to the sight. The sides of the
rock are strangely perforated with great and circular hollows,
like pots; the work of the vortiginous motion of the water in
great floods.

A farmer I met with here told me, that a pebble, naturally
perforated, was an infallible cure, hung over a horse that was hag-
ridden, or troubled with nocturnal sweats.

Return and pass through the parish of Cannonsby, a small fertile plain, watered by the Esk; where some canons regular of St Augustine had pitched their priory at least before the year 1296, when William, prior of the convent, swore allegiance to Edward I.[1] The parish is very populous, containing above two thousand souls. Much coal and limestone is found here.

Most part of the houses are built with clay: the person who has building in view, prepares the materials, then summons his neighbours on a fixed day, who come furnished with victuals at their own expense, set cheerfully to work, and complete the edifice before night.

Ascend a bank on the south side of this valley, to a vast height above it: the scenery is great and enchanting: on one side is a view of the River Esk, far beneath, running through a rocky channel, and bounded by immense precipices; in various places suddenly deepening to a vast profundity; while in other parts it glides over a bottom covered with mosses, or coloured stones, that reflect through the pure water taints glaucous, green, or sappharine: these various views are in most places fully open to sight; in others suffer a partial interruption from the trees that clothe the steep bank, or shoot out from the brinks and fissures of the precipices; the trees are in general oak, but often intermixed with the waving boughs of the weeping birch.

Two precipices are particularly distinguished: one called Carsidel, the other Gilnochie's Garden: the last is said to have been the retreat of a celebrated outlaw; but originally had evidently been a small British fortress, guarded on one side by the steeps of the precipice, on the other by a deep entrenchment.

The ride was extremely diversified through thick woods, or small thickets, with sudden transitions from the shade into rich and well-husbanded fields, bounded on every side with woods; with views of other woods still rising beyond. No wonder then that the inhabitants of these parts yet believe the fairies revel in these delightful scenes.

[1] Keith's *Scotch Bishops*, 240.

Cross the Esk, through a ford with a bottom of solid rock; having on one side the water precipitating itself down a precipice forming a small cataract, which would afford a scene not the most agreeable to a timid mind. The water too was of the most crystalline, or colourless clearness, no stream I have ever seen being comparable; so that persons who ford this river are often led into distresses, by being deceived as to its depth, for the great transparency gives it an unreal shallowness.

This river is inhabited by trouts, parrs, loaches, minnows, eels and lampreys; and what is singular, the chub, which with us loves only the deep and still waters bounded by clayey banks.

On the opposite eminence see Holhouse, a defensible tower like that at Kirk Andrews, and one of the seats of the famous Johnny Armstrong, Laird of Gilnockie, the most popular and potent thief of his time, and who laid the whole English borders under contribution, but never injured any of his own countrymen. He always was attended with twenty-four gentlemen well mounted: and when James V went his progress in 1528, expressly to free the country from marauders of this kind, Gilnockie appeared before him with thirty-six persons in his train,[2] most gorgeously apparelled; and himself so richly dressed, that the king said, 'What wants that knave that a king should have?' His Majesty ordered him and his followers to immediate execution, in spite of the great offers Gilnockie made; who finding all application for favour, vain, he according to the old ballad, boldly told the king:

> To seik hot water beneath cold yce,
>   Surely it is a great folie;
> I haif asked grace at a graceless face,
>   But there is nane for my men and me.

I saw a boy, a direct descendent of this unfortunate brave, who with his whole family are said to be distinguished for their honesty and quiet disposition, happily degenerating from their great ancestor.

Continue my ride on a fine turnpike road, through beautiful woods, to Mr Maxwell's of Broomholme, environed with a most

---

[2] Lindsey, 147.

magnificent theatre of trees, clothing the lofty hills, and the whole surmounted by a barren mountain, by way of contrast.

The rent of the ground which Mr Maxwell keeps in his own hands, and that of a farm now disjoined from it, was in the unsettled times of the beginning of the last century, only five pounds Scotch, or eight shillings and four pence English. At present Mr Maxwell's share alone would take a hundred pounds sterling annual rent. This is mentioned as an illustration of the happy change of times, and the increase of revenues by the security the owners now enjoy, by the improvements in agriculture, and the cheapness of money to what they were a century and a half ago. Indeed it should be mentioned that the old rent was paid by a Maxwell to a Maxwell; and perhaps there might be some small matter of favour from the chieftain to his kinsman; but even admitting some partiality, the rise of income must be amazing.

The road continues equally beautiful, along a fertile glen, bounded by hills, and woods. Come in view of a bridge, with the pleasing motion of a mill wheel seen in perspective through the middle arch: the river was here low, and the bed appeared roughened with transverse-waved rocks, extensively spread, and sharply broken.

The town of Langholme appears in a small plain, with the entrance of three dales, and as many rivers, from which they take their names, entering into it, viz. Wachopdale, Eusdale and Eskdale; the last extends thirty or forty miles in length, and the sides as far as I could see, bounded by hills of smooth and verdant grass, the sweet food of the sheep, the great staple of the country. To give an idea of the considerable traffic carried on in these animals, the reader may be told that from twenty to thirty-six thousand lambs are sold in the several fairs that are held at Langholme in the year. To this must be added, the great profit made of the wool, sold into England for our coarser manufactures; of the sheep themselves sent into the south, and even of the cheese and butter made from the milk of the ewes.[3]

---

[3] For a fuller account of the management of the sheep of this county, vide the Appendix.

The trustees for encouraging of improvements give annual premiums to such who produce the finest wool, or breed the best tups; a wise measure in countries emerging from sloth and poverty.

The manufactures of Langholme, are stuffs, serges, black and white plaids, plains and mostly sold into England.

The castle is no more than a square tower, or border-house, once belonging to the Armstrongs. In my walk to it was shown the place where several witches had suffered in the last century: this reminds me of a very singular belief that prevailed not many years ago in these parts: nothing less than that the midwives had power of transferring part of the primeval curse bestowed on our great first mother, from the good wife to her husband. I saw the reputed offspring of such a labour; who kindly came into the world without giving her mother the least uneasiness, while the poor husband was roaring with agony in his uncouth and unnatural pains.

The magistrates of this place are very attentive to the suppression of all excessive exertions of that unruly member the tongue: the brank, an instrument of punishment, is always in readiness; and I was favoured with the sight; it is a sort of headpiece, that opens and encloses the head of the impatient, while an iron, sharp as a chisel, enters the mouth, and subdues the more dreadful weapon within. This had been used a month before, and as it cut the poor female till blood gushed from each side of her mouth, it would be well that the judges in this case would, before they exert their power again, consider not only the humanity, but the legality of this practice.

The learned Dr Plot has favoured the world with a minute description, and a figure of the instrument, and tells us, he looks on it 'as much to be preferred to the ducking stool, which not only endangers the health of the party, but also gives the tongue liberty 'twixt every dip; to neither of which this is at all liable'.[4]

Among the various customs now obsolete, the most curious was that of handfisting, in use about a century past. In the upper part of Eskdale, at the confluence of the White and the Black Esk, was held an annual fair, where multitudes of each sex repaired. The

---

[4] *Hist. Staffordshire*, 389, tab. xxxii.

unmarried looked out for mates, made their engagement by joining hands, or by handfisting, went off in pairs, cohabited till the next annual return of the fair, appeared there again, and then were at liberty to declare their approbation or dislike of each other. If each party continued constant, the handfisting was renewed for life: but if either party dissented, the engagement was void, and both were at full liberty to make a new choice; but with this proviso, that the inconstant was to take the charge of the offspring of the year of probation. This custom seemed to originate from the want of clergy in this country in the days of popery: this tract was the property of the abbey of Melross, which through economy discontinued the vicars that were used to discharge here the clerical offices: instead, they only made annual visitations for the purposes of marrying and baptising, and the person thus sent, was called 'book in bosom', probably from his carrying, by way of readiness, the book in his breast; but even this being omitted, the inhabitants became necessitated at first to take this method, which they continued from habit to practise long after the Reformation had furnished them with clergy.

Persons of rank, in times long prior to those, took the benefit of this custom; for Lindesey,[5] in his reign of James II says that 'James sixth earl of Murray begat upon Isobel Innes, a daughter of the laird of Innes, Alexander Dunbar, a man of singular wit and courage. This Isabel was but handfist with him, and deceased before the marriage; where-through this Alexander he was worthy of a greater living, than he might succeed to by the laws and practises of this realm.'[5]

Of the sports of these parts, that of curling is a favourite; and one unknown in England: it is an amusement of the winter, and played on the ice, by sliding from one mark to another, great stones of forty to seventy pounds weight, of hemispherical form, with an iron or wooden handle at top. The object of the player is to lay his stone as near to the mark as possible, to guard that of his partner, which had been well laid before, or to strike off that of his antagonist.

---

[5] p. 26, folio ed.

Return and pass the March Dike, or the Scotch border, and continue at Netherby that night.

Pass through Longtown, a place remarkable for the great trade carried on during the season of cranberries; when for four or five market, from twenty to twenty-five pounds worth, are sold each day at three pence a quart, and sent in small barrels to London.

Cross the Esk, on a bridge of five arches, a light structure, as most of the bridges of this country are. Go through the lanes which had been rendered impassable, at the time of the eruption of the Solway moss, which took its course this way to the Esk. The road was at this time quite cleared; but the fields to the right were quite covered with the black flood.

The space between the Esk and the Sark, bounded on the third side by the March Dike, which crosses from one river to the other, seems properly to belong to Scotland; but having been disputed by both crowns, was styled the debateable land. But in the reign of our James I, Sir Richard Graham obtaining from the Earl of Cumberland (to whom it was granted by Queen Elizabeth) a lease of this tract, bought it from the needy monarch, and had interest enough to get it united to the county of Cumberland, it being indifferent to James, then in possession of both kingdoms, to which of them it was annexed.

Ride by the side of the Roman road, that communicated between Netherby and the camp at Burrens. Cross a small bridge over the Sark, and again enter Scotland. On the banks of this rivulet, the English under the command of the Earl of Northumberland, and 'Magnus with a Red Main' received a great defeat from the Scots, under Douglas, Duke of Ormond, and Wallace of Craigie. Numbers of the former were drowned in their flight in Solway Firth; and Lord Piercy taken prisoner, a misfortune owing to his filial piety, in helping his father to a horse, to enable him to escape.[6]

At a little distance from the bridge, stop at the little village of Gratna, the resort of all amorous couples, whose union the

[6] *Hist. of Douglases*, 179.

prudence of parents or guardians prohibits: here the young pair may be instantly united by a fisherman, a joiner, or a blacksmith, who marry from two guineas a job, to a dram of whisky: but the price is generally adjusted by the information of the postilions from Carlile, who are in pay of one or other of the above worthies; but even the drivers, in case of necessity, have been known to undertake the sacerdotal office. If the pursuit of friends proves very hot; and there is not time for the ceremony, the frightened pair are advised to slip into bed; are shown to the pursuers, who imagining that they are irrevocably united, retire, and leave them to 'consummate their unfinished loves'. This place is distinguished from afar by a small plantation of firs, the Cyprian grove of the place; a sort of landmark for fugitive lovers. As I had a great desire to see the high priest, by stratagem I succeeded: he appeared in form of a fisherman, a stout fellow, in a blue coat, rolling round his solemn chops a quid of tobacco of no common size. One of our party was supposed to come to explore the coast: we questioned him about his price; which, after eyeing us attentively, he left to our honour. The Church of Scotland does what it can to prevent these clandestine matches; but in vain, for those infamous couplers despise the fulmin-ation of the Kirk, and excommunication is the only penalty it can inflict.

Continue my journey over a woodless flat tract, almost hedgeless, but productive of excellent oats and barley. Pass by Rig, a little hamlet, a sort of chapel of ease to Gratna, in the run-away nuptials. The performer here is an alehouse-keeper.

On the left is Solway Firth, and a view of Keswick Fells, between which and Burnswork Hill in Scotland, is a flat of forty miles, and of a great extent in length. The country grows now very uncultivated, and consists of large commons. Reach Annan, in Annandale, another division of Dumfriesshire, a town of four or five hundred inhabitants, seated on the river of the same name. Vessels of about two hundred and fifty tons can come within half a mile of the town, and of sixty as high as the bridge. This place has some trade in wine: the annual exports are between twenty and thirty thousand Winchester bushels of corn.

The castle was entirely demolished, by order of Parliament, after the accession of James VI to the crown of England, and only the ditches remain. But Annan was in a manner ruined by Wharton, Lord President of the Marches, who, in the reign of Edward VI overthrew the church, and burnt the town; the first having been fortified by the Scots,[7] under a Lyon of the House of Glames.

The Bruces were once lords of this place, as appears by a stone at present in a wall of a gentleman's garden, taken from the ruins of the castle, and thus inscribed, *Robert de Brus Counte de Carrick et senteur du val de Annand. 1300.*

After dinner make an excursion of five miles to Ruthwell, passing over the Annan on a bridge of five arches, defended by a gateway. The country resembles that I passed over in the morning, but at Newby Neck observe the ground formed into eminences, so remarkably as to occasion a belief of their being artificial, but are certainly nothing more than the freaks of nature.

The church of Ruthwell contains the ruins of a most curious monument; an obelisk once of a great height, now lying in three pieces, broken by an order of the General Assembly in 1644, under pretence of its being an object of superstition among the vulgar. When entire it was probably about twenty feet high, exclusive of pedestal and capital; making allowances in the measurement of the present pieces for fragments chipped off, when it was destroyed: it originally consisted of two pieces; the lowest, now in two, had been fifteen feet long; the upper had been placed on the other by means of a socket: the form was square and taper, but the sides of unequal breadth: the two opposite on one side at bottom were eighteen inches and a half, at top only fifteen; the narrower side sixteen at bottom, eleven at top. Two of the narrowest sides are ornamented with vine leaves, and animals intermixed with runic characters around the margin: on one of the other sides is a very rude figure of our Saviour, with each foot on the head of some beasts: above and each side him are inscribed in Saxon letters, *Jesus*

---

[7] Ayscough's *Hist. of the Wars of Scotl. and Engl.*, 321.

Christus — *judex equitatis, certo salvatoris mundi et an* — perhaps as Mr Gordon imagines, *angelorum*[8] — *Bestiae et Dracones cognoverant inde* — and lastly are the words, *fregerunt panem*.

Beneath the two animals is a compartment with two figures, one bearded, the other not, and above is inscribed, *Sanctus Paulus*.

On the adverse side is our Saviour again, with Mary Magdalene washing his feet, and the box of ointment in his hand. The inscriptions, as made out by Mr Gordon, are *Alabastrum unguenti* — *ejus Lachrymis caepit rigare pedes, ejus capills* — *capitis sui ternebat* — *et praeteriens vidi*.

The different sculptures were probably the work of different times and different nations; the first that of the Christian Saxons; the other of the Danes, who either found those sides plain; or defacing the ancient carving, replaced it with some of their own. Tradition says that the church was built over this obelisk, long after its erection; and as it was reported to have been transported here by angels, it was probably so secured for the same reason as the *santa casa* at Loretto was, lest it should take another flight.

The pedestal lies buried beneath the floor of the church: I found some fragments of the capital, with letters similar to the others; and on each opposite side an eagle, neatly cut in relief. There was also a piece of another, with Saxon letters round the lower part of a human figure, in long vestments, with his foot on a pair of small globes: this too seemed to have been the top of a cross.

Scotland has had its 'Vicar of Bray': for in this churchyard is an inscription in memory of Mr Gavin Young, and Jean Stewart his spouse. He was ordained minister in 1617, when the church was Presbyterian: soon after, James VI established a moderate sort of Episcopacy. In 1638, the famous league and covenant took place: the bishops were deposed, and their power abolished: Presbytery then flourished in the fullness of acrimony. Sectaries of all sorts invaded the church in Cromwell's time, all equally hating, persecuting, and being persecuted in their turns. In 1660, on the Restoration, Episcopacy arrived at its plenitude of power; and Presbyterianism expelled; and that sect which in their prosperity showed no mercy,

[8] Itin., 161.

now met with retributory vengeance. Mr Young maintained his post amidst all these changes, and what is much to his honour, supported his character: was respected by all parties for his moderation and learning: lived a tranquil life, and died in peace, after enjoying his cure fifty-four years.

The epitaph on him, his wife and family, merits preservation, if but to show the number of his children:

> *Far from our own, amids our own we ly:*
> *Of our dear Bairns, thirty and one us by.*

anagram

> *Gavinus junius*
> *Unius agni usui*
> *Jean Steuart*
> *a true saint*
> *a true saint I live it, so I die it.*
> *tho men saw no, my God did see it.*

This parish extends along the Solway Firth, which gains on the land continually, and much is annually washed away: the tides recede far, and leave a vast space of sands dry. The sport of salmon hunting is almost out of use, there being only one person on the coast who is expert enough to practise the diversion: the sportsman is mounted on a good horse, and furnished with a long spear: he discovers the fish in the shallow channels formed by the Esk, pursues it full speed, turns it like a greyhound, and after a long chase seldom fails to transfix it.

The salt-makers of Ruthwell merit mention, as their method seems at present quite local. As soon as the warm and dry weather of June comes on, the sun brings up and encrusts the surface of the sand with salt: at that time they gather the sand to the depth of an inch, carry it out of the reach of the tide, and lay it in round compact heaps, to prevent the salt from being washed away by the rains: they then make a pit eight feet long and three broad, and the same depth, and plaster the inside with clay, that it may hold water; at the bottom they place a layer of peat and turf, and fill the pit with the collected sand: after that they pour water on it: this filters through the sand, and carries the salt with it into a lesser pit, made at the end of the great one: this they boil in small lead pans, and procure a coarse brown salt, very fit for the purposes of salting meat or fish. James VI in a visit he made to these parts, after his accession to the crown of England, took notice of this operation, and for their industry exempted the poor salt-makers of Ruthwell from all duty on this commodity; which till the Union, was in all the Scotch acts relating to the salt duties, expected.

In this parish was lately discovered a singular road through a morass, made of wood, consisting of split oak planks, eight feet long, fastened down by long pins or stakes, driven through the boards into the earth. It was found out by digging of peat, and at that time lay six feet beneath the surface. It pointed towards the sea, and in old times was the road to it; but no tradition remains of the place it came from.

Return through Annan, and after a ride over a naked tract, reach Springkeld, the seat of Sir William Maxwell: near the house is the site of Bell Castle, where the Duke of Albany, brother to James III, and the Earl of Douglas lodged the night before their defeat at Kirkonnel, a place almost contiguous. This illustrious pair had been exiled in England, and invaded their own country on a plundering scheme, in a manner unworthy of them. Albany escaped; Douglas was taken, and finished his life in the convent of Lindores.[9]

In the burying ground of Kirkonnel is the grave of the fair Ellen Irvine, and that of her lover: she was daughter of the house of Kirkonnel; and was beloved by two gentlemen at the same time; the one vowed to sacrifice the successful rival to his resentment; and watched an opportunity while the happy pair were sitting on the banks of the Kirtle, that washes these grounds. Ellen perceived the desperate lover on the opposite side, and fondly thinking to save her favourite, interposed; and receiving the wound intended for her beloved, fell and expired in his arms. He instantly revenged her death; then fled into Spain, and served for some time against the infidels: on his return he visited the grave of his unfortunate mistress, stretched himself on it, and expiring on the spot, was interred by her side. A sword and a cross are engraven on the tombstone, with *hic jacet Adam Fleming*: the only memorial of this

---

[9] Hume's *Hist. of the Douglases*, folio 206.

unhappy gentleman, except an ancient ballad of no great merit, which records the tragical event.[10]

Excepting a glen near Springkeld, most of this country is very naked. It is said to have been cleared of the woods by Act of Parliament, in the time of James VI, in order to destroy the retreat of the moss-troopers, a pest this part of the country was infamous for: in fact the whole of the borders then was, as Lindesay expresses, no other thing but 'theft, reiff and slaughter'. They were possessed by a set of potent clans, all of Saxon descent; and, like true descendents of Ishmael, their hands were against every man, and every man's hand against them. The Johnstons of Loughwood, in Annandale; their rivals the Maxwells of Caerlaveroc, the Murrays of Cockpool, Glendonwyns of Glendonwin, Carruthers of Holmain, Irvines of Bonshaw, Jardins of Applegarth, and the Elliots of Liddesdale, may be enumerated among the great families.

But besides these were a set of clans and surnames on the whole border, and on the debateable ground, who, as my author says,[11] were not landed; many of them distinguished by *noms de guerre*, in the manner as several of our unfortunate brave are at present, such as 'Tom Trotter of the Hill', 'the Goodman Dickson of Bucktrig', 'Ralph Burn of the Coit', George Hall, called 'Pat's Geordie' there, 'the Lairds Jok', 'Wanton Sym', 'Willie of Gratna Hill', 'Richie Graham the Plump', 'John Skynbank', 'Prior John and his Bairns', 'Hector of the Harlaw', 'the Griefs and Cuts of Harlaw'; these and many more, merry men all, of Robin Hood's fraternity, superior to the little distinctions of *meum* and *tuum*.

Visit the Roman station at Burrens, in the parish of Middleby, seated on a flat, bounded on one side by the small water of Mien, and on another by a small burn. It was well defended by four ditches and five dikes; but much of both is carried away by the winter floods in the river that bounded on one side; a hypocaust had been discovered here, inscribed stones dug up, and coins found, some of

---

[10] Which happened either the latter end of the reign of James V, or the beginning of that of Mary.
[11] Taken from a fragment of a quarto book, printed in 1603, containing names of clans in every sheriffdom, etc.

them of the lower empire. Observed a place formed of square stones, which I was told contained, at the time of the discovery, a quantity of grain: I was also informed, that there had been a large vault a hundred and twenty feet long, designed for a granary; but this has long since been destroyed for sake of the materials. Mr Horsely imagines this to have been the *blatum bulgium* of Antonine, being on the north side of the wall, with a military road between it and Netherby; and that it was the place where Agricola concluded his second year's expedition. As that general was distinguished for his judicious choice of spots of encampment, so long after, his successors made use of this, as appears by a medal of Constantius Chlorus being found here, for that emperor lived about two hundred and twenty years after Agricola.

The country now begins to grow very hilly; but usefully so; the hills being verdant, and formed for excellent sheepwalks: on the sides of one called Burnswork, about two miles from Burrens, are two beautiful camps, united to each other by a rampart, that winds along the side of the hill; one camp being on the south-east, the other on the north-west: one has the praetorium yet visible; and on the north side are three round tumuli, each joined to it by a dike, projecting to some distance from the ramparts; as if to protect the gate on that quarter, for each of these mounts had its little fort: the other camp had two of these mounts on one side and one on each end; but the vestiges of these are very faint: both of these camps were surrounded with a deep ditch, and a strong rampart both on the inside and the outside of the fosse; and on the very summit of the hill is a small irregular entrenchment, intended as exploratory, for the view from thence is uninterrupted on every part. These camps are very accurately planned by Mr Gordon, tab. I, p. 16. These also were the work of Agricola, and highly probable to be, as Mr Horsely imagines, the summer camp of that at Burrens.

The view from the summit is extremely extensive: the town of Lochmaban, with its lake and ruined castle, built on a heart-shaped peninsula; Queensbury Hill, which gives title to the duke; Hartsfell, and the Loders, which dispute for height; yet a third, the Driffels, was this day patched with snow; and lastly, Ericstone, which fosters the Annan, the Clyde and the Tweed.

Descend and pass through the small town of Ecclefechan (Ecclesia Fechani) noted for the great monthly markets for cattle.

Near this place, on the estate of Mr Irvine, writer, was found an antiquity whose use is rather doubtful: the metal is gold; the length rather more than seven inches and a half; the weight 2 oz and a half and 15 gs. It is round and very slender in the middle, at each end grows thicker, and of a conoid form, terminating with a flat circular plate: on the side of one end are stamped the words *Helenus fecit*; on the other is pricked ... I I I M B. From the slenderness of the middle part, and the thickness of the ends, it might perhaps serve as a fastening of a garment, by inserting it through holes on each side, and then twisting together this pliant metal.

Keep along the plain, arrive again on the banks of the Annan, and have a very elegant view of its wooded margent, the bridge, a light structure with three arches, one of fifty-two feet, the others of twenty-five, with the turrets of Hoddam Castle a little beyond, overtopping a very pretty grove.

The castle consists of a great square tower, with three slender round turrets: the entry through a door protected by another of iron bars; near it a square hole, by way of dungeon, and a staircase of stone, suited to the place; but instead of finding a captive damsel and a fierce warder, met with a courteous laird and his beauteous spouse; and the dungeon not filled with piteous captives, but well stored with generous wines, not condemned to a long imprisonment.

This castle, or rather strong border-house, was built by John Lord Harries, nicknamed John de Reeve, a strenuous supporter of Mary Stuart, who conveyed her safe from the battle of Langside to his house of Terrigles, in Galloway, and from thence to the abbey of Dundrannan, and then accompanied her in a small vessel in her fatal flight into England. Soon after, it was surrendered to the regent Murray, who appointed the Laird of Drumlanrig Governor and Lord of the Marches.[12] Before the accession of James VI, Hoddam was one of the places of defence on the borders; for 'the house of Howdam was to be keped with ane wise stout man, and to have with him four well-horsed men, and thir to have two stark footmen

---

[12] Hollinshed's *Hist. Scotl.*, 393.

servants to keep their horses, and the principal to have ane stout footman'.[13]

In the walls about this house are preserved altars and inscriptions found in the station at Burrens: as they do not appear to have fallen under the notice of the curious, an enumeration of them perhaps will not be unacceptable; therefore shall be added in the appendix.

Near Hoddam, on an eminence, is a square building, called the Tower of Repentance. On it is carved the word 'repentance', with a serpent at one end of the word, and a dove at the other, signifying remorse and grace. It was built by a Lord Harries, as a form of atonement for putting to death some prisoners whom he had made under a promise of quarter.

Proceed over a country full of low hills, some parts under recent cultivation; others in a heathy state of nature. Reach, in a wet cultivated and woody flat, the castle and house of Comlongam; the property of Lord Stormount, and the birthplace of that ornament of our island, Lord Mansfield.

The castle consists of a great square tower, now almost in ruins, though its walls of near thirteen feet in thickness might have promised to the architect a longer duration. Many small rooms are gained out of the very thickness of the sides; and at the bottom of one, after a descent of numbers of steps, is the noisome dungeon, without light or even air-holes, except the trapdoor in the floor, contrived for the lowering in of the captives. This fortress was founded by one of the ancestors of the Murrays, earls of Annandale; a title which failed in that name about the time of the Restoration.

Ride along the shore by the end of the Lockermoss, a morass of about ten miles in length, and three in breadth, with the little water of Locker running through it. This tract, from recent survey, appears to have been overflowed by the sea, which confirms the tradition relating to such an event. This invasion of the tides was certainly but temporary, for from the numbers of trees, roots, and other vegetable marks found there, it is evident that this morass was, in some very distant period, an extensive forest. Near a place

---

[13] *Border Laws*, App., 197.

called Kilbain I met with one of the ancient canoes of the primeval inhabitants of the country, when it was probable in the same state of nature as Virginia, when first discovered by Captain Philip Amidas. The length of this little vessel was eight feet eight, of the cavity six feet seven; the breadth two feet; depth eleven inches; and at one end were the remains of three pegs for the paddle: the hollow was made with fire, in the very manner that the Indians of America formed their canoes, according to the faithful representation by Thomas Harriot, in de Bry's publication of his drawings.[14] Another of the same kind was found in 1736, with its paddle, in the same morass: the last was seven feet long, and dilated to a considerable breadth at one end; so that in early ages necessity dictated the same inventions to the most remote regions.[15] These were long prior to our *vitilia navigia*; and were in use in several ancient nations: the Greeks called them Μονοξυλα and σκαφη: some held three persons, others only one;[16] and of this kind seems to have been that now mentioned. Those used by the Germans were of a vast size, capable of holding thirty men;[17] and the Gauls on the Rhône had the same species of boats, but were indifferent about their shape, and content if they would but float, and carry a large burden.[18]

At Mr Dickson's, of Lockerwood, saw a curiosity of another nature, found in the neighbourhood: a round pot of mixed metal, not unlike a small shallow mortar, with two rings on one side, and two handles on the other.

Over Lockermoss is a road remarkable for its origin: a stranger, a great number of years ago, sold some goods to certain merchants at Dumfries upon credit: he disappeared, and neither he nor his heirs ever claimed the money: the merchants in expectation of the demand very honestly put out the sum to interest; and after a

---

[14] A servant of Sir Walter Raleigh, sent to Virginia to make drawings and observations.

[15] My ingenious friend Mr Stuart tells me, that the Greeks still make use of canoes of this kind, to cross small arms of the sea; and that they still style them Μονοξυλα, from being formed of one piece of wood.

[16] *Polyaeni Stratagem*, lib. V, ch. 23, 509. *Vellius Paterculus*, lib. II, ch. 107.

[17] Plinii, *Hist. Nat.* XVI, ch. 40.

[18] Livii, lib. XXI, ch. 26.

lapse of more than forty years, the town of Dumfries obtained a gift of it, and applied the same towards making this useful road. Another is now in execution by the military, which is also to pass over Lockermoss, and is intended to facilitate the communication between North Britain and Ireland, by way of Port Patric.

In this morning's ride, pass by a square enclosure of the size of half an acre, moated round. This was a place of refuge; for in family disputes, such was truly necessary, and here any person who came, remained in inviolable security.

See the isle of Caerlaveroc, with a border-house in the middle, built by a Maxwell. This place is far from the sea; but styled an isle because moated.

Visit Wardlaw, a small hill with a round British camp, surrounded with two fosses on the top; and on the south side the faint vestiges of a Roman camp, now much ploughed up. The prospect from this eminence is fine, of the firth, the discharge of the river Nith or Nid, the Nobius of Ptolemy; and a long extent of the hills of Galloway.

The Roman encampment on this hill might probably be the Uxelum of Ptolemy, especially if we are to derive that word from the British, *uchel*, 'high': for the site of the fortress of Caerlaveroc, is on such a flat as by no means to admit of that epithet, or to be allowed to have been the ancient Uxelum as Mr Horsely conjectures.

The castle has undergone its different sieges: the first that appears in history and the most celebrated was in the year 1300, when Edward I sat down before it in person. Enraged at the generous regard the Scots showed for their liberty, and the unremitted efforts made by their hero Wallace, to free his country from a foreign yoke, the English monarch summoned his barons, and all the nobility who held of him by military tenure to attend with their forces at Carlile, on the feast of St John the Baptist. On that occasion, as the poet of the expedition relates, there appeared, *'foissant et vint et sept banieres'*,[19] each of which, with the arms of the baron, are illuminated in a beautiful manner; and

---

[19] I am indebted to Marmaduke Tunstall, Esq., for the MS account of this siege, finely copied from the original, in the museum; which appears to have been composed in very old and bad French, soon after the event it celebrates.

VIII

Moses Griffith del.

CAERLAVEROC CASTLE.

in the catalogue are the names of the most puissant peers of this kingdom, with a little eulogy on each;[20] as a specimen, is given that on Robert Clifford, in whom it may be supported valour and beauty were combined:

> Si Je estoi une pucellette,
> Je le douroie cuer et cors,
> Tant est de lui bons li recors.

The poet then describes the castle and its situation with great exactness; and gives it the very same form and site it has at present: so that I cannot help thinking that it was never so entirely destroyed, but that some of the old towers yet remain:

> Kaerlaverok casteaus estoit
> Si fort ki siege ne doubtoit;
> Ainz ki li rois illicec venist,
> Car rendre ni le convenist.
> James mais kil fust a son droit,
> Garniz quant besogns en vendroit
> De gens de engins et de vitaille,
> Com uns escus estoit de taille,
> Car ni ot ke trois costez entour,
> Et en chescune angle une tour.
> Mes ki le une estoit jumilee,
> Tant hauti et tant longue et tant lei,
> Ke par desouz estoit la porte
> A Pont tournis, bien faite et forte,
> Et autres defenses asses, etc.

It is worth observing, that it was taken by force of engines, and the English as late as the time in question used much the same method of attack as the Greeks and Romans did: for they drove the enemy from the walls by showers of stones, flung from engines similar to the *catapultae* of the ancients; and they used also *ariettes* or battering rams:

> Entre les assaus esmaia,
> Ffrere Robert ki envoia
> Meinte piere par Robinet;
> Juq au soir des le matinet

---

[20] Appendix.

> *Le jour devant cesse ne avoit,*
> *De autre part ancore i levoit*
> *Trois autres engins moult plus grans*
> *Et il penibles et engrans,*
> *Ke le chastel du tout confondi*
> *Tant il receut mo't piere ensonde.*
> *Deschocs et kang's atteint sent*
> *A ses coups rein ne se dessent.*

On the surrender Edward behaved with more moderation than was usual to him: for his laurels were wont to be blighted with deeds unworthy of his heroism: but in this case the poor relics of the garrison experienced his clemency:

> *Lors son issirent ce est la some*
> *Ke de uns ke de autret foissant home*
> *A grant merveille resguardes*
> *Mes tenus furent et guardez*
> *Tant ke li Roys en ordena*
> *Ki vie et membre leur donna*
> *Et a chasm robe nouuele*
> *Lors fu joieuse la nouuli.*
> *A toute li ost du chastel pris*
> *Ki tant estoit de noble pris.*

It appears that the king immediately mounted his colours on the castle; and appointed three barons of the first reputation to take charge of it:

> *Puis fist de Rou porter amont*
> *Sa banniere et law seynt Eymont*
> *La saint George et la saint Edwart*
> *Et o celes par droit eswart*
> *La Segrave et le Herifort*
> *Et cele au Seigneur di Cliffort*
> *A ki le chasteans fut donnes.*

Notwithstanding the care Edward took to secure this place, it was retaken by the Scots the following year; but very soon after was repossessed by the English,[21] after a very long siege. It appears that the Scots again recovered it, for in one of the invasions of

---

[21] Maitland's *Hist. Scot.* II, 460.

the former, the gallant owner, Sir Eustace Maxwell supported a siege in it of some weeks, and obliged the enemy to retire; but considering that it might fall into the hands of the English, and become noxious to his country, generously dismantled it, and for that piece of disinterested service was properly rewarded by his prince, who remitted to him and his heirs for ever, the annual pecuniary acknowledgements they paid to the crown for the castle and lands of Caerlaveroc.[22] It was again rebuilt; but in 1355 (being then in possession of the English) was taken by Roger Kirkpatric, and levelled to the ground.[23] Notwithstanding these repeated misfortunes, it was once more restored; and once more ruined, by the Earl of Sussex in 1570.[24] From this time the lords of the place seem for some interval to have been discouraged from any attempt towards restoring a fortress so distinguished by its misfortunes; for Camden in 1607, speaks of it as only a weak house belonging to the barons of Maxwell: yet once more Robert, first Earl of Nithsdale, in 1638, ventured to re-establish the stronghold of the family: still it was ill-fated; for in the course of Cromwell's usurpation, it was surrendered on terms ill preserved; and a receipt was given for the furniture by one Finch; in which among other particulars is mention of eighty beds, a proof of the hospitality or the splendour of the place. The form of the present castle is triangular; at two of the corners had been a round tower, but one is now demolished; and on each side the gateway, which forms the third angle, are two rounders. Over the arch is the crest of the Maxwells (placed there when the castle was last repaired) with the date, and this motto, 'I bid ye fair', meaning Wardlaw, the hill where the gibbet stood; for in feudal times, it seems to have been much in use.

The castle yard is triangular: one side which seems to have been the residence of the family, is very elegantly built; has three storeys, with very handsome window cases: on the pediment of the lower

---

[22] Crawford's *Peerage of Scotland*, 370.

[23] Major, *De Gestis Scotorum*, 248 more probably rendered defenceless.

[24] Camden's annals in *Kennet* II, 429. It appears to me that the present are the ancient towers, so exactly do they answer to the old poetic description; but that the owners, till the year 1638, neglected it as a fortress, yet inhabited it as a mansion.

are coats of arms; over the second legendary tales; over the third, I think Ovidian fables, all neatly cut in stone. The opposite side is plain. In front is a handsome doorcase, leading to the great hall, which is ninety-one feet by twenty-six. The whole internal length of that side a hundred and twenty-three.

The Maxwells, lords of Caerlaveroc, are of great antiquity: but their history mixed with all the misfortune and all the disgrace so frequent in ill-governed times. They and the Johnstons had perpetual feuds: in 1593 the clans had a conflict at the Holyness of Dryse; the chieftain of the Maxwells, and many of his sons, were slain. John, a surviving son, takes his revenge: a meeting between him and Johnston, a predecessor of the Marquis of Annandale, was appointed in order to compromise all differences: both met, attended only by a single friend to each; the friends quarrel; the Laird of Lockerwood goes to part them, but is shot through the back by the other chieftain; who deservedly met his fate on the scaffold a few years after. His forfeiture was taken off, and his brother not only restored but created Earl of Nithsdale: in 1715 the title was lost by the conviction of the Earl of that day; who escaped out of the tower the night before execution, by the disguise of a female dress. The estate by virtue of entail was preserved to the heirs.

Continue my ride along the coast to the mouth of the Nith, which empties itself into the vast estuary, where the tide flows in so fast on the level sands that a man well mounted would find difficulty to escape, if surprised by it. The view of the opposite side of Cressel, and the other Galloway hills, is very beautiful, and the coast appeared well wooded. In a bottom lies Newby Abbey, founded by Devorgilla, daughter to Alan, Lord of Galloway, and wife to John Baliol, Lord of Castle Bernard, who died and was buried here: his lady embalmed his heart, and placed it in a case of ivory, bound with silver, near the high altar; on which account the abbey is oftener called 'Sweetheart' and *'Sauvi Cordium'*.

Pass by Port Kepel, the firth gradually contracting itself; and to this place vessels of two hundred tons may come. The country on both sides the river is extremely beautiful; the banks decorated with numerous groves and villas, richly cultivated and well-enclosed.

The farmers show no want of industry: they import, as far as from Whitehaven, lime for manure, to the annual amount of twenty-five hundred pounds, paying at the rate of six pence for the Winchester bushel: they are also so happy as to have great quantities of shell marl in the neighbouring morasses; and are now well rewarded for the use of it: much wheat and barley are at present the fruits of their labour, instead of a very paltry oat; and good hay instead of rushes now clothe their meadows. Reach Dumfries, a very neat and well-built town, seated on the Nith, and containing about five thousand souls. It was once possessed of a large share of the tobacco trade, but at present has scarcely any commerce. The great weekly markets for black cattle are of much advantage to the place; and vast droves from Galloway and the shire of Air pass through in the way to the fairs in Norfolk and Suffolk.

The two churches are remarkably neat, and have handsome galleries, supported by pillars. In the churchyard of St Michael are several monuments in form of pyramids, very ornamental, and on some gravestones are inscriptions in memory of the martyrs of the country, or the poor victims to the violence of the apostate Archbishop Sharp, or the bigotry of James II, before and after his accession. Powers were given to an inhuman set of miscreants to destroy upon suspicion of disaffection; or for even declining to give answers declarative of their political principles: and such who refused (before two witnesses) were instantly put to death. Many poor peasants were shot on moors, on the shores, or wheresoever their enemies met with them: perhaps enthusiasm might possess the sufferers; but an infernal spirit had possession of their persecutors. The memory of these flagitious deeds are preserved on many of the wild moors by inscribed gravestones, much to the same effect as the following in the churchyard in this city:

On John Grierson, who suffered Jan. 2, 1667.

> *Underneath this stone doth lie*
> *Dust sacrificed to tyranny:*
> *Yet precious in Immanuel's sight,*
> *Since martyr'd for his kingly right;*
> *When he condemns these hellish drudges*
> *By sufferage, Saints shall be their judges.*

Another on James Kirke, shot on the sands of Dumfries, shall conclude this dreadful subject:

> By bloody Bruce and wretched Wright
> I lost my life in great despight.
> Shot dead without due time to try
> And fit me for eternity.
> A witness of Prelatic rage
> As ever was in any age.

This place like most other considerable town in Scotland, has its Seceders' chapel: these are the rigid Presbyterians who possess their religion in all its original sourness: think their church in danger because their ministers degenerate into moderation, and wear a gown; or vindicate patronage. To avoid these horrid innovations, they separate themselves from their imaginary false brethren; renew a solemn league and covenant, and preserve to the best of their power all the rags and rents bequeathed to them by John Knox, which the more sensible preachers of this day are striving to darn and patch.

Here I first found on this side the Tweed, my good old mother church become a mere conventicler, and her chaplain supported by a few of her children, disposed to stick to her in all conditions.

Enquired for the convent of Dominicans, and the church in which Robert Bruce and his associates slew John Cummin, Lord of Badenock, and owner of great part of the lordship of Galloway. Cummin had betrayed to Edward I the generous design of Bruce to relieve his country from slavery; in resentment Bruce stabbed him; on retiring was asked by his friends, whether he was sure of his blow, but answering with some degree of uncertainty, one of them, Roger Kirkpatric replied, 'I mak sicker,' returned into the church and completed the deed. In memory, the family assumed a bloody dagger for a crest; and those words as the motto. The church thus defiled with blood was pulled down; and another built in a different place, and dedicated to St Michael, the tutelar saint of the town. Robert Bruce also built a chapel here, as soon as he got full possession of the kingdom, in which prayers were to be daily offered for the repose of the soul of Sir Christopher Seton, who was most barbously executed by Edward I for his attachment to Bruce, and for his defence of his country.

Dumfries was continually subject to the inroads of the English; and was frequently ruined by them. To prevent their invasions a great ditch and mound, called 'warders' dikes', were formed from the Nith to Lockermoss, where watch and ward were constantly kept; and when an enemy appeared the cry was 'A Loreburn, a Loreburn'. The meaning is no further known that that it was a word of alarm for the inhabitants to take to their arms: and the same word as a memento of vigilance in inscribed on a ring of silver round the ebony staff given into the hands of the provost as a badge of office on the day of annual election.

On most of the eminences of three parts, beacons were likewise established for alarming the country on any eruption of their southern neighbours: and the inhabitants able to bear arms were bound, on the firing of these signals, to repair instantly to the warden of the marches, and not to depart till the enemy was driven out of the country; and this under pain of high treason.

This regulation was established in the days of Archibald the Grim, Earl of Douglas, and afterwards renewed with much solemnity by William, Earl of Douglas, who assembled the lords, freeholders, and principal borderers at the college of Lincluden, and caused them there to swear on the holy evangelists, that they should truly observe the statutes, ordinances and usages of the marches, as they were ordained in the time of the said Archibald.

Had a beautiful view of an artificial waterfall just in front of a bridge, originally built by Devorgilla, who gave the customs arising from it to the Franciscan convent at Dumfries. It consists of nine arches, and connects this county and that of Galloway.

Cross it; pass through a small town at its foot, and walk up Gorbelly Hill, remarkable for the fine circumambient prospect of the charming windings of the Nith towards the sea, the town of Dumfries, Terregles, a house of the Maxwells, and a rich vale towards the north.

Visit the abbey of Lincluden, about half a mile distant, seated on the water of the Cluden, which is another boundary of Galloway on

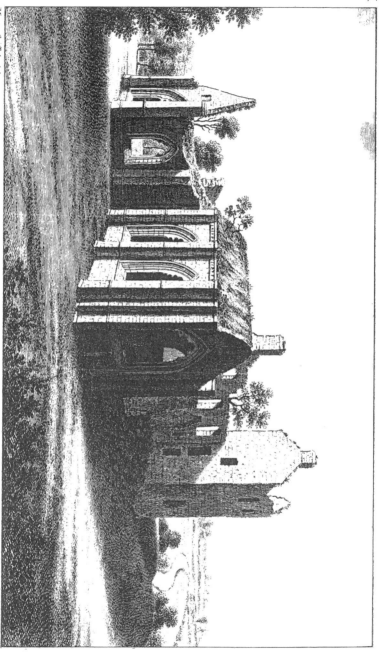

IX

Moses Griffith del.

LINCLUDEN - ABBY,

that side. This religious house is seated on a pleasant bank, and in a rich country: and was founded and filled with Benedictine nuns, in the time of Malcolm IV by Uthred, father to Roland, Lord of Galloway.[25] These were expelled by the Earl of Douglas (known by the titles of 'Archibald the Black', or 'Grim', and 'the Terrible') probably, as Major insinuates, on account of the impurity of their lives,[26] for the earl was a man in piety singular through his life, and most religious according to those times. He fixed in their places a provostry, with twelve beadsmen, and changed the name to that of the college.

Part of the house and chancel, and some of the south wall of the church are the sole remains of this ancient structure: in the chancel is the elegant tomb of Margaret, daughter of Robert III, and wife of Archibald, Earl of Douglas, first Duke of Terouan, and son of Archibald the Grim. Her effigy at full length, lay on the stone, her head resting on two cushions; but the figure is now mutilated; and her bones, till lately, were scattered about in a most indecent manner by some wretches who broke open the repository in search of treasure. The tomb is in form of an arch, with all parts most beautifully carved: on the middle of the arch is the heart, the Douglas's arms, guarded by three chalices, set crossways, with a star near each, and certain letters I could not read. On the wall is inscribed *A L'aide de Dieu*, and at some distance beneath:

> *Hic jacet D-na Margareta regis Scotiae filia quodam comitissa de Douglas Dna Gollovidiae et vallis annandiae.*

In the front of the tomb are nine shields, containing as many arms: in one are the three stars, the original coat of this great house, for the heart was not added till the good Sir James was employed in carrying that of Robert Bruce to the Holy Land: besides these, are the arms after that event; and also their arms as lords of Annandale, Galloway and Liddesdale. Near the tomb is a doorcase, richly ornamented with carving; and on top the heart and chalices, as in the former.

---

[25] Hope's *Minor Practics.*, 511. Malcolm died AD 1165.
[26] Major, *De Gest. Scot.*, 283. Archibald died AD 1400.

Countess of Galloway's Tomb.

In other parts of the remains of the church are the arms of the Douglases, or dukes of Terouan, earls of Angus, of Ormond, and of Murray: here are besides the arms of John Stewart, Earl of Athol, with the motto, 'Firth, fortune, and fil the fetters'.

Beneath one of the windows are two rows of figures; the upper of angels, the lower of a corpse and other figures, all much defaced, but seemingly designed to express the preparations for the interment of our Saviour.

Behind the house are vestiges of a flower garden, with the parterres and scrolls very visible; and near that a great artificial mount, with a spiral walk to the top, which is hollowed, and has a turf seat around to command the beautiful views; so that the provost and his beadsmen seem to have consulted the luxuries as well as necessaries of life.

Return to Dumfries, where Mr Hill, surgeon, favoured me with the sight of the head of an old lady, excellently painted, about forty years ago, by Mr John Patoun, son to a minister in this town. After painting three years in Scotland, about the year 1730 he went to London, where he read lectures on the theory of his art: at length was tempted to make a voyage to Jamaica, where he died in a few weeks, leaving behind him the character of a good man, and able artist.

Before we left the town, we were honoured with its freedom, bestowed on us in the politest manner by the magistrates.

Continue my journey due north through the beautiful Nithsdale, or Vale of Nith, the river meandering with bold curvatures along rich meadows; and the country, for some space, adorned with groves and gentlemen's seats. At a few miles distance from Dumfries, leave on the left, Bardanna and Keir, conjectured by Mr Horsely to have been the Carbantorigum of Ptolemy. Travel over small hills, either covered with corn, or with herds of cattle, flocks or black-faced sheep, attended by little pastors, wrapped in their maides,[27] and setting the seasons at defiance. The river still keeps its beauty, wandering along a verdant bottom, with banks on each side clothed with wood; and the more distant view hilly. Ride through a tract

---

[27] A sort of long cloak.

covered with broom, an indication of barrenness; and arrive in sight of Drumlanrig, a house of the Duke of Queensbury, magnificently seated on the side of a hill, an immense mass, embosomed in trees. Cross a handsome bridge of two arches, of a vast height above the Nith, which fills the bottom of a deep and wooded glen; and, after a long ascent through a fine and well-planted park, arrive at the house: a square building, extending an hundred and forty-five feet in front, with a square tower at each corner, and three small turrets on each: over the entrance is a cupola, whose top is in shape of a vast ducal coronet: within is a court, and at each angle a round tower, each containing a staircase: everywhere is a wearisome profusion of hearts carved in stone, the Douglas arms: every window, from the bottom to the third storey, is well secured with iron bars; the two principal doors have their grated guards; and the cruel dungeon was not forgot: so that the whole has the appearance of a magnificent state prison. Yet this pile rose in composed times; it was built by William, Duke of Queensbury, begun in 1679 and completed in 1689. His Grace seemed to have regretted the expense; for report says, that he denounced, in a writing on the bundle of accounts, a bitter curse on any of his posterity who offered to inspect them.

The apartments are numerous: the gallery is a hundred and eight feet long, with a fireplace at each end: it is ornamented with much of Gibbon's carvings, and some good portraits; observed among them.

The first Duchess of Somerset, half length, no cap, with a small lovelock.

William, Duke of Queensbury, distinguished in the reigns of Charles and James II, by many court favours, by his services to those monarchs, by his too grateful return in assisting in the cruel persecutions of his countrymen averse to the test, and by his honourable disgrace, the moment James found him demur to a request subversive, if complied with, of the religion and liberties of Great Britain.

John, Earl of Traquair, Lord High Treasurer of Scotland in the turbulent reign of Charles I, a prudent friend of the indiscreet Laud, and like him a zealous churchman; but unlike him, waited for a proper season for bringing his project to bear, instead of precipitating matters like the unfortunate prelate. A faithful servant to the Crown; yet, from his wife advice brought under the scandal of duplicity. Was cleared early from the suspicion by the noble historian; and soon after more indisputably by his impeachment, and by his conviction by the popular party; by his imprisonment; by his taking arms in the royal cause on his release; by his second confinement; by the sequestration of his estates: and finally by the distressful poverty he endured till death, he gave full but unfortunate testimony of untainted loyalty.

John, Earl Rothes, Chancellor of Scotland, in his gown, with the seals by him. He was in power during the cruel persecutions of the Covenanters in Charles II's time; and discharging his trust to the satisfaction of the court, was created Duke of Rothes, a title that died with him.

A head of the Duke of Perth, a bushy wig: a post-abdication duke, a converted favourite of James II and Chancellor of Scotland at the time of the Revolution, when he retired into France.

George Douglas, Earl of Dunbarton, in armour; a great wig and cravat. Instructed in the art of war in the armies of Louis XIV was general of the forces in Scotland under James II dispersed the army of the unfortunate Argyle. A gallant officer, who, when James was at Salisbury, generously offered to attack the Prince of Orange with his single regiment of the Scottish Royal, not with the hope of victory, but of giving him such a check as his sovereign might take advantage of: James, with equal generosity, would not permit the sacrifice of so many brave men. Dunbarton adhered to his king in all fortunes, and on the abdication partook of his exile.

General James Douglas, who in 1691 died at Namur.

Earl of Clarendon, son of the Chancellor, half-length, in his robes.

A good portrait of a Tripoli ambassador.

In the gardens, which are most expensively cut out of a rock, is a bird cherry, of a great size, not less than seven feet eight inches in girth; and among several fine silver firs, one thirteen feet and a half in circumference.

In my walks about the park see the white breed of wild cattle, derived from the native race of the country; and still retain the primeval savageness and ferocity of their ancestors: were more shy than any deer; ran away on the appearance of any of the human species, and even set off at full gallop on the least noise; so that I was under the necessity of going very softly under the shelter of trees or bushes to get a near view of them: during summer they keep apart from all other cattle, but in severe weather hunger will compel them to visit the outhouses in search of food. The keepers are obliged to shoot them, if any are wanted: if the beast is not killed on the spot it runs at the person who gave the wound, and who is forced, in order to save himself, to fly for safety to the intervention of some tree.

These cattle are of middle size, have very long legs, and the cows are fine-horned: the orbits of the eyes and the tips of the noses are black: but the bulls have lost the manes attributed to them by Boethius.

Ride to Morton Castle, about four miles distant, seated on a steep projection, in a lofty situation, near the Anchenlec Hills. This was originally the seat of Dunenald, predecessor of Thomas Randolph, afterwards created Earl of Murray by Robert Bruce, when the castle and that of Auchencass, near Moffat, was disposed of to Douglas of Morton, predecessor of the earls of Morton: but at the time that title was conferred, the castle and lands of Morton being settled on a son of a second marriage of that family, the Parliament, on a protestation on his part, declared, that the bestowing that title should not prejudice his right to the castle and lands, but that it was taken from a place called Morton in West Lothian.

At present remains only one front, with a number of small windows, each to be ascended on the inside by a flight of steps: at each end is also a rounded tower. I find little of its history, any farther than that it was among the castles demolished by David II[28] on his return from England, probably in compliance with a private agreement made with Edward III.

Two miles North from Morton stood the castle of Durisdeer, demolished at the same time with the former. In the church of

[28] Guthrie III, 70.

Durisdeer is the mausoleum of the family of Drumlanrig: over the door of the vault are four spiral pillars supporting a canopy, all of marble: and against the wall is a vast monument in memory of James, Duke of Queensbury: his grace lies reclined on his arm, with the collar of S. S. round his neck. The Duchess, in her robes, recumbent; four angels hold a scroll above, with this inscription:

Hic
in eodem tumulo
cum Charissmis conjugis cineribus
misci voluit suis
Jacobus Dux Queensburiae et Doverni;
Qui
ad tot et tanta honoris
Et negotiorum fastigia
Quae nullus antea subditus
attegit, evectus, Londini
fato cessit sexta die
Julii anno Christi Redemptoris
1711

And beneath is an affectionate and elegant epitaph on his duchess, who died two years before his Grace.

Visit Tibbir Castle, about a mile below Drumlanrig, placed on a small hill above the little stream, the Tibbir. Nothing remains but the foundations overgrown with shrubs. It is supposed to have been a Roman fort, but that in after-times the Scots profiting of the situation, and what had been done before, built on the place a small castle; which tradition says, was surprised by a strategem in time of William Wallace.[29]

The beauties of Drumlanrig are not confined to the highest part of the grounds; the walks, for a very considerable way, by the sides of the Nith, abound with most picturesque and various scenery: below the bridge and sides are prettily wooded, but not remarkably lofty; above, the views become wildly magnificent: the river runs through a deep and rocky channel, bounded by vast wooded cliffs, that rise suddenly from its margin; and the prospect down from the summit is of a terrific depth, increased by the rolling of the black waters

[29] Gordon's *Itin.*, 19.

beneath: two views are particularly fine; one of quick repeated, but extensive, meanders amidst broken sharp-pointed rocks, which often divide the river into several channels, interrupted by short and foaming rapids, coloured with a moory taint. The other is of a long strait, narrowed by the sides, precipitous and wooded, approaching each other equidistant, horrible from the blackness and fury of the river, and the fiery red and black colours of the rocks, that have all the appearance of having sustained a change by the rage of another element.

Cross the bridge again, and continue my journey northward for six or seven miles, on an excellent road, which I was informed was the same for above twenty miles farther, and made at the sole expense of the present Duke of Queensbury: his Grace in all respects a warm friend to his country, and by *praemia* promotes the manufactures of woollen stuffs, and a very strong sort of woollen stockings; and by these methods will preserve on his lands a useful and industrious population, that will be enabled to eat their own bread, and not oppress their brethren, or be forced into exile, as is the case in many other parts of North Britain.

The ride was, for the most part, above the Nith; that in many places appeared in singular forms: the most striking was a place called Hell's Cauldron, a sudden turn, where the water eddies in a large hole, of a vast depth and blackness, overhung, and darkened by trees. On the opposite side is the appearance of a British entrenchment; and near Durisdeer is said to be a small Roman fortress; the Roman road runs by it, and is continued from thence by the wellpath, through Crawford Moor to Elvenfoot, has been lately repaired, and is much preferable to the other through the mountains, which would never have been thought of but for the mines in the lead hills.

The river assumes a milder course; the banks bordered with fields, and those opposite well wooded. On an eminence is the house of Eliock, environed with trees, once one of the possessions of Crichton, father to the Admirable; and before, at some distance, is the town of Sanquhar, with the ruins of the castle, the ancient seat of the lords Crichton. The parish is remarkable for the manufacturer of woollen stockings, and the abundance of its coal.

IV

LANERKSHIRE, OR CLYDESDALE; RENFREWSHIRE

⊏━⊐➤●⊂⊏━⊐

Leadhills—Douglas Castle—Lanerk—Falls of the Clyde—Cartland Crags—Hamilton—Bothwell Bridge—Glasgow—Kirkpatric—Dunglass—Port Glasgow—Greenock—Cruickston Castle—Paisley—Renfrew

QUIT Nithsdale, and turn suddenly to the right; pass through the glen of Lochburn between vast mountains, one side wooded to a great height, the other naked, but finely grassed, and the bottom washed by the Menoch, a pretty stream; the glen grows very narrow, the mountains increase in height, and the ascent long and laborious. Ride by Wanlock Head in the parish of Sanquhar, the property of the Duke of Queensbury; sometimes rich in lead ore. Cross a small dike at the top of the mountain, enter Lanerkshire, or Clydesdale; and continue all night at the little village of Leadhills, in the parish of Crawford: the place consists of numbers of mean houses, inhabited by about fifteen hundred souls, supported by the mines; for five hundred are employed in the rich *sous terrains* of this tract. Nothing can equal the barren and gloomy appearance of the country round: neither tree nor shrub, nor verdure, nor picturesque rock, appear to amuse the eye: the spectator must plunge into the bowels of these mountains for entertainment; or please himself with the idea of the good that is done by the well-bestowed treasures drawn from these inexhaustible mines, that are still rich, baffling the efforts of two centuries. The space that has yielded ore is little more than a mile square, and is a flat or pass among the mountains: the veins of lead run north and south; vary, as in other places, in their depth, and are from two or four feet thick: some have been found filled with ore within two fathoms of the surface; others sink to the depth of ninety fathoms.

The ore yields in general about seventy pounds of lead from a hundred and twelve of ore; but affords very little silver: the varieties are the common plated ore, vulgarly called 'potter's': the small or steel-grained ore; and the curious white ores, lamellated and fibrous, so much searched after for the cabinets of the curious. The last yields from fifty-eight to sixty-eight pounds from the hundred, but the working of this species is much more pernicious to the health of the workmen than the common. The ores are smelted in hearths, blown by a great bellows, and fluxed with lime. The lead is sent to Leith in small carts, that carry about seven hundred weight, and exported free from duty.

The miners and smelters are subject here, as in other places, to the lead distemper, or 'mill-reek', as it is called here; which brings on palsies, and sometimes madness, terminating in death in about ten days. Yet about two years ago died, at this place, a person of primeval longevity: one John Taylor, miner, who worked at his business till he was a hundred and twelve: he did not marry till he was sixty, and had nine children; he saw to the last without spectacles; had excellent teeth till within six years before his death, having left off tobacco, to which he attributed their preservation: at length, in 1770, yielded to fate, after having completed his hundred and thirty-second year.

Native gold has been frequently found in this tract, in the gravel beneath the peat, from which it was washed by rains, and collected in the gullies by persons who at different times have employed themselves in search of this precious metal: but of late years these adventurers have scarce been able to procure a livelihood. I find in a little book, printed in 1710, called *Miscellanea Scotia*,[1] that in old times much gold was collected in different parts of Scotland. In the reign of James IV, the Scots did separate the gold from the sand by washing. In the following, the Germans found gold there, which afforded the King great sums: three hundred men were employed for several summers, and about £100,000 sterling procured. They did not dispose of it in Scotland, but carried it into Germany. The same writer says, that the Laird of Marcheston got gold in Pentland Hills; that some was found in Langham waters, fourteen miles from Leadhill House; in Meggot Waters, twelve miles; and Phinland, sixteen miles. He adds, that pieces of gold, mixed with spar and other substances, that weighed thirty ounces were found; but the largest piece I have heard of does not exceed an ounce and a half, and is in the possession of Lord Hopetoun, the owner of these mines.

Continue my journey through dreary glens or melancholy hills, yet not without seeing numbers of sheep. Near the small village of Crawford John, procured a guide over five miles of almost pathless moors, and descend into Douglasdale, watered by the river that gives the name; a valley distinguished by the residence of the family of Douglas, a race of turbulent heroes, celebrated throughout Europe for deeds of arms; the glory, yet the scourge of their country; the terror of their princes; the pride of northern annals of chivalry.

They derive their name from *Sholto du Glasse*, or 'the black and grey warrior' (as their history relates)[2] a hero in the reign of Solvathius, King of Scotland, who lived in the eighth century: with more certainty, a successor of his, of the name of William, went into Italy in quest of adventures, and from him descended the family of the Scoti of Placentia,[3] that flourished in the last age, and may to this time continue there. But the Douglases first began to rise into power in the days of the good Sir James, who died in 1330. During a century and a half their greatness knew no bounds; and their

---

[1] For a further account of gold found in Scotland, see p. 74 of the second part of this tour.
[2] Hume's *Hist. of the Houses of Douglas*, 3.
[3] Idem, 5.

arrogance was equally unlimited: that high spirit which was wont to be exerted against the enemies of their country, now degenerated into faction, sedition and treason: they emulated the royal authority; they went abroad with a train of two thousand armed men; created knights, had their counsellors, established ranks, and constituted a parliament:[4] it is certain that they might almost have formed a house of peers out of their own family; for at the same time there were not fewer than six earls of the name of Douglas.[5] They gave shelter to the most barbarous banditti, and protected them in the greatest crimes; for, as honest Lindsay expresses:

> *Oppression, ravishing of women, sacrilege, and all other kinds of mischief, were but a dalliance: so it was thought leisome to a depender on a Douglas to slay or murder, for so fearful was their name, and terrible to every innocent man, that when a mischievous limmer was apprehended, if he alleged that he murdered and slew at a Douglas's command, no man durst present him to justice.*[6]

Douglas Castle, the residence of these reguli, seems to have been prostrated almost as frequently as its masters: the ruin that is seen there at present is the remains of the last old castle, for many have been built on the same site. The present is an imperfect pile, begun by the late duke: in the front are three round towers; beneath the base of one lies the noble founder, and the tears of the country painted above. He was interred there by his own directions, through the vain fear of mingling his ashes with those of an injured dead.

The windows are Gothic: the apartments are fitting up with great elegance, which show that the storms of ambition have been laid, and that a long calm of ease and content is intended to succeed.

The inscription on the foundation stone of the present castle deserves preservation, as it gives a little of the history:

> *Hoc latus*
> *Hujus munitiffimi Praedii*
> *Familae de Douglas*

---

[4] Buchanan, *Rerum Scot.*, lib. XI., sect. 9.
[5] Camden *Br.* II, 1211.
[6] p. 26.

Ter solo aequati
Et semel atque iterum instaurati
Imperantibus
Edwardo primo Angliae
Et apud Scotos Roberto
primum sic dicto
Tandem surgere caepit
Novis munitionibus firmatum
Jussu et sumptibus
Serenissimi et potentissimi Archibaldi
Ducis de Douglas, etc., etc.
Principis familae ejus nominis
In Scota antiquissimae
Et maxime notabilis
Anno Christi
MDCCLVII.

Near the castle are several very ancient ash trees, whose branches groaned under the weight of executions when the family knew no law but its will.

In the church were deposited the remains of several of this great name. First appears the effigies of good Sir James, the most distinguished of the house, the favourite of Robert Bruce, and the knight appointed as most worthy to carry his master's heart to be interred beneath the high altar in the temple of Jerusalem. He set out, attended with a train of two hundred knights and gentlemen, having the gold box, containing the royal heart, suspended from his neck. He first put into the port of Sluys, on the coast of Flanders, where he stayed for twelve days, living on board in regal pomp (for he did not deign to land) and all his vessels were of gold.[7] Here he was informed that Alphonso, King of Spain was engaged in war with the Saracen King of Grenada: not to lose his blessed opportunity of fighting against the enemies of the cross, he and his knights sailed instantly for Valentia, was most honourably received by the Spanish monarch, luckily found him on the point of giving battle; engaged with great valour, was surrounded by the infidels, slain in the fight, and the heart of Robert Bruce, which was happily rescued, instead of visiting the Holy Land, was carried to the convent of

---

[7] Froissart, lib. I, ch. 21.

Melros, and the body of Sir James to his church; where his figure lies crosslegged, his Holiness having decreed that services against the infidels in Spain should have equal merit with those performed in Palestine.

Near him, beneath a magnificent tomb, lies Archibald, first Earl of Douglas, and second Duke of Terouan, in France; his father, slain at the battle of Verneuil, being honoured by the French king with that title. He lies in his ducal robes and coronet. This earl lived quite independent of his prince, James I, and through resentment to the minister, permitted the neighbouring thieves of Annandale to lay waste the country, when his power, perhaps equal to the regal, might have suppressed their barbarity. He died in 1438.

The Douglases and Perceys were rivals in deeds of arms; and fortune, as usual, smiled or frowned alternately on each of these potent families.

James the Fat, seventh Earl of Douglas, next appears in effigy on another tomb: a peaceable chieftain, who seems to have been in too good case to give any disturbance to the commonwealth. He died in 1443; and his lady, Beatrix de Sinclair, lies by him. Their offspring is also enumerated in the inscription.

Ride for some time in Douglasdale, a tract deficient in wood, but of great fertility: the soil fine, and of an uncommon depth; yielding fine barley and oats, most slovenly kept, and full of weeds: the country full of gentle risings. Arrive in a flat extent of ground, descend to the River Clyde, cross a bridge of three arches, ascend a steep road, and reach Lanerk: a town that gives name to the county. Here the gallant Wallace made his first effort to redeem his country from the tyranny of the English; taking the place and slaying the governor, a man of rank.[8] The castle stood on a mount on the south side of the town; and not far to the east, is a ruined church, perhaps belonging to the convent of Franciscans, founded by Robert Bruce, in 1314.

Not very far from Lanerk are the celebrated Falls of the Clyde: the most distant are about a half hour's ride, at a place called Corylin; and are seen to most advantage from a ruinous pavillion in

[8] Buchanan, lib. VIII, ch. 18.

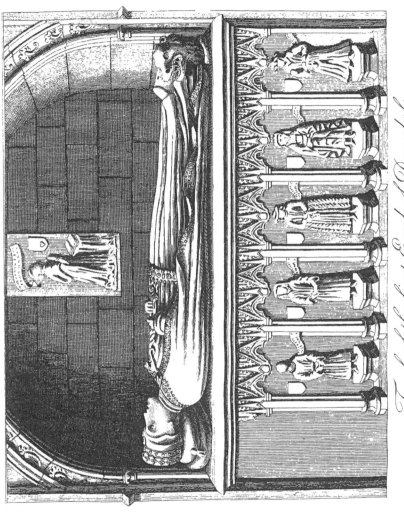

Tomb of the first Earl of Douglas.

a gentleman's garden, placed in a lofty situation. The cataract is full in view, seen over the tops of trees and bushes, precipitating itself, for an amazing way, from rock to rock, with short interruptions, forming a rude slope of furious foam. The sides are bounded by vast rocks, clothed on their tops with trees: on the summit and very verge of one is a ruined tower, and in front a wood, overtopped by a verdant hill.

A path conducts the traveller down to the beginning of the fall, into which projects a high rock, in floods insulated by the waters, and from the top is a tremendous view of the furious stream. In the cliffs of this savage retreat the brave Wallace is said to have concealed himself, meditating revenge for his injured country.

On regaining the top the walk is formed near the verge of the rocks, which on both sides are perfectly mural and equidistant, except where they overhang; the river is pent up between them at a distance far beneath; not running, but rather sliding along a stony bottom sloping the whole way. The summits of the rock are wooded; the sides smooth and naked; the strata narrow and regular, forming a stupendous natural masonry. After a walk of above half a mile on the edge of this great chasm, on a sudden appears the great and bold fall of Boniton, in a foaming sheet, far-projecting into a hollow, in which the water shows a violent agitation, and a far-extending mist arises from the surface. Above that is a second great fall; two lesser succeed: beyond them the river winds, grows more tranquil, and is seen for a considerable way, bounded on one side by wooded banks, on the other by rich and swelling fields.

Return the same way to Lanerk: much barley, oats, peas and potatoes are raised about the town, and some wheat: the manure most in use is a white marble, full of shells, found about four feet below the peat, in a stratum five feet and a half thick: it takes effect after the first year, and produces vast crops. Numbers of horses are bred here, which at two years old are sent to the marshes of Airshire, where they are kept till they are fit for use.

Again pass over the bridge of Lanerk, in order to visit the great fall of Stonebiers, about a mile from the town: this has more of the horrible in it than either of the other two, and is seen with more difficulty: it consists of two precipitous cataracts falling one above the other into a vast chasm, bounded by lofty rocks, forming an amazing theatre to the view of those who take the pains to descend to the bottom. Between this and Corylin is another fall called Dundofflin; but being satiated for this time with the noise of waters, we declined the sight of it.

Return over the bridge, and walk to Cartland Crags: a zigzag den of great extent, bounded by rocks of a very uncommon height, and almost entirely clothed with trees. It is a place of laborious access from above, so difficult is it amidst the shade of trees to find a way free from precipice. The bottom is watered by the River Mouse; and the sides, at every short turn, finely varied with the different appearance of rock, wood and precipice. Emerge into the open space; remount our horses, and ride for some miles along a rich vale, with the Clyde passing along the bottom: all parts are rich in corn, meadows, orchards and groves. Cross the Nathan. At Nathan Foot, gain the heights, which are far less fertile; and, after going over the River Avon, reach the town of Hamilton.

The original name of this place, or the lands about it, was Cadzow, or Cadyow, a barony granted to an ancestor of the noble owner on the following occasion: In the time of Edward II, lived Sir Gilbert de Hamilton, or Hampton,[9] an Englishman of rank; who, happening at court to speak in praise of Robert Bruce, received on the occasion an insult from John de Spenser, chamberlain to the king; whom he fought and slew: dreading the resentment of that potent family,[10] he fled to the Scottish monarch, who received him with open arms, and established him at the place the family now possesses: whose name in aftertimes was changed from that of Cadzow to Hamilton; and in 1445 the lands were erected into a lordship, and the owner, Sir James, sat in Parliament as Lord Hamilton.

The same nobleman founded the collegiate church at Hamilton in 1451, for a provost and several prebendaries. The endowment was ratified at Rome by the pope's Bull, which he went in person to procure.[11]

---

[9] In Leicestershire, vide Burton's hist. of that county, 126.
[10] Buchanan VIII, ch. 49.
[11] Moyses, 34.

The old castle of Hamilton, being possessed by certain of the name who had been guilty of the deaths of the Earls of Lenox and Murray, was on the 19th of May 1579 surrendered; and by the order of the king and council, entirely demolished.[12]

Hamilton House, or palace, is at the end of the town: a large disagreeable pile, with two deep wings at right angles with the centre: the gallery is of great extent, furnished (as well as some other rooms) with most excellent paints:

That of Daniel in the lions' den, by Rubens, is a great performance: the fear and devotion of the prophet finely expressed by the uplifted face and eyes, his clasped hands, his swelling muscles, and the violent extension of one foot: a lion looks fiercely at him, with open mouth, and seems only restrained by the Almighty Power from making him fall a victim to his hunger: and the deliverance of Daniel is more fully marked by the number of human bones scattered over the floor, as if to show the instant fate of others, in whose favour the deity did not interfere.

The marriage feast, by Paul Veronese, is a fine piece; and the obstinacy and resistance of the intruder, who came without the wedding garment, is strongly expressed.

The treaty of peace between England and Spain, in the reign of James I, by Juan de Pantoxa, is a good historical picture. There are six envoys on the part of the Spaniards, and five on that of the English, with the names inscribed over each: the English are the Earls of Dorset, Nottingham, Devonshire, Northampton, and Robert Cecil.

Earls of Lauderdale and Lanerk settling the covenant; both in black, with faces full of puritanical solemnity.

James, Marquis of Hamilton, and Earl of Cambridge, in black, by Vansomer. This nobleman was high in favour with James VI, Knight of the Garter, Lord High Steward of the Household, and Lord High Commissioner of the Parliament; and so much in the esteem and affection of his master as to excite the jealousy of Buckingham. He died in 1625, at the early age of thirty-three. Such symptoms attended his death, that the public attributed it to poison, and ascribed the infamy to the duke.[13]

[12] Crawford's *Peerage*, 119.
[13] Wilson, 285.

His son James, Duke of Hamilton, with a blue riband and white rod. A principal leader of the Presbyterian party in the time of Charles I, dark, uncommunicative, cunning. He managed the trust reported in him in such a manner as to make his politics suspected by each faction: and notwithstanding he was brought up in the school of Gustavus Adolphus in a military capacity, his conduct was still more contemptible: he ruined the army he faintly led into England, rather to make his royal master subservient to the design of the Scots, than to do his Majesty any real service. Was shamefully taken, and ended his days upon a scaffold.

Next to his is the portrait of his brother, and successor to the title, William, Earl of Lanerk; who behaved at the battle of Worcester with genuine heroism, was mortally wounded, and died with every sentiment of calmness and piety; regretting the enthusiasm of his younger days, and his late appearance in the royal cause.

James, Duke of Hamilton, who fell in the duel with Lord Mohun. The first a leader of the Tory party in the reign of Queen Anne; the last a strong Whig: each combatant fell; whether the duke died by the hands of an assassin second, or whether he fell by those of his antagonist, the violence of party leaves no room to determine.

Next appears a full length, the finest portrait in this kingdom: a nobleman in red silk jacket and trousers; his hair short and grey; a gun in his hand, attended by an Indian boy and with Indian scenery around: the figure seems perfectly to start from the canvas, and the action of his countenance, looking up, has matchless spirit. It is called the portrait of William, Earl of Denbigh, miscalled Governor of Barbados. His daughter married the first Duke of Hamilton, which strengthens the opinion of its being that of her father. The painter seems to have been Rubens: but from what circumstances of his Lordship's life he placed him in an Indian forest, is not known.

The old Duke of Chatelherault, in black, with the order, I think, of St Michael, pendent from his neck; which he accepted with the title, and a pension, from Francis I of France, at the time he was Earl of Arran, and regent of Scotland. He was declared next in succession to the crown, in case of failure of heirs in Mary Stuart: a rank that his feeble and unsteady conduct would have disabled him from filling with dignity.

A head of Catherine Parr, on wood; by Holbein.

Another, said to have been that of Anne Bullen: very handsome; dressed in a ruff and kerchief, edged with ermine, and in a purple gown: over her face a veil, so transparent as not to conceal 'The bloom of young desire and purple light of love'.

Maria Dei Gratia Scotorum Regina, 1586, aet. 43. A half-length: a stiff figure, in a great ruff, auburn locks, oval but pretty full face, of much larger and plainer features than that at Castle Braan; a natural alteration, from the increase of her cruel usage, and of her ill health: yet still preserves a likeness to that portrait. I was told here that she sent this picture, together with a ring, a little before her execution, to the representative of the Hamilton family, as an acknowledgement of gratitude for their sufferings in her cause.

Earl Morton, regent of Scotland: a nobleman of vast but abused abilities; rapacious, licentious, unprincipled; restrained by no consideration from gaining his point; intrepid till the last hour of his being, when he fell on the scaffold with those penitential horrors that the enormous wickedness of his past life did naturally inspire.[14]

The rough reformer, John Knox; a severe reprover of the former. The earl, at the funeral of Knox, in a few words delivered this honourable testimony of his spirit: 'There lies he who never feared the face of man.'

Alexander Henderson: a vain, insolent and busy minister during the troubles of Charles I, who was deputed by his brethren to persuade his Majesty to extirpate Episcopacy out of Scotland: but the king, an equal bigot, and better casuist, silenced his arguments; and Henderson, chagrined with his ill success, retired, and died of a broken heart.

A head of Hobbes (as a contrast to the two former) with short thin grey hair.

Lord Belhaven, author of the famous speech against the Union.

Philip II. A full-length, with a strange figure of Fame bowing at his feet, with a label, and this motto, *Pro merente adsto*.

Two half-lengths, in black, one with a fiddle in his hand, the other in a grotesque attitude, both with the same countenances,

---

[14] Spotiswood, 314. *Lives of the Douglases*, 356.

good, but swarthy; mistakenly called David Rizzio's, but I could not learn that there was any portrait of that unfortunate man.

Irresistible beauty brings up the rear, in form of Miss Mary Scott, a full-length, in white satin; a most elegant figure: and thus concludes the list with what is more powerful than all that has preceded; than the arms of the warrior, the art of the politician, the admonitions of the churchman, or the wisdom of the philosopher.

About a mile from the house, on an eminence, above a deep wooded glen, with the Avon at the bottom, is Chatelherault, so called from the estate the family once possessed in France: is an elegant banqueting-house, with a dog kennel, gardens, etc., and commands a fine view. The park is now much enclosed; but I am told there are still in it a few of the wild cattle of the same kind with those I saw at Drumlanrig.

Continue my journey: cross the Clyde at Bothwell Bridge, noted for the defeat of a small army of enthusiasts, in 1679, near the place, by the Duke of Monmouth, who distinguished himself that day more by his humanity, than his conduct; but it is probable he disliked a service against men to whose religious principles he had no aversion: he might likewise aim at future popularity in the country.

Bothwell Church was collegiate, founded by Archibald the Grim, Earl of Douglas, in 1398, for a provost and eight prebendaries. The outside is said to be encrusted with a thin coat of stone, but I confess it escaped my notice. In it are interred the founder and his lady, daughter of Andrew Murray, son to King David Bruce, with whom he got the lordship of Bothwell.

The castle, now in ruins, is beautifully seated on the banks of the Clyde: tradition and history are silent about the founder. It is said to have been a principal residence of the Douglases; and while Edward I was in possession of Scotland, was the chief station of his governor; and after the battle of Bannockbourne, was the prison of some of the English nobility taken in that fatal field. Major says that in 1337 it was taken by the partisans of David Bruce, and 'levelled to the ground'.[15] That seems a favourite phrase of the historian; for

[15] p. 232.

to me it appears to be in the same state with that of Caerlaveroc, and was only dismantled; for in both, some of the remaining towers have all the marks of the early style of building.

On the south side of the Clyde, opposite to the castle, are the remains of Blantyre, a priory of canons regular, founded before the year 1290; mention being made in that year of 'Frere William Priour de Blantyr.'[16]

The country from Bothwell Bridge is open, very fertile, composed of gentle risings, diversified with large plantations. Reach Glasgow; the best built of any second-rate city I ever saw: the houses of stone, and in general well built, and many in a good taste, plain and unaffected. The principal street runs east and west, is near a mile and a half long, but unfortunately not straight; yet the view from the cross, where the two other great streets fall into this, has an air of vast magnificence. The tolbooth is large and handsome, with this apt motto on the front:

> *Haec domus odit, amat, punit, conservat, honorat,*
> *nequitiam, pacem, crimina, jura, probos.*

Next to the exchange: within is a spacious room, with full-length portraits of all our monarchs since James I, and an excellent one, by Ramsay, of Archibald, Duke of Argyle, in his robes as Lord of Sessions. Before the exchange is a large equestrian statue of King William. This is the finest and broadest part of the street: many of the houses are built over arcades, but too narrow to be walked in with any conveniency. Numbers of other streets cross this at right angles.

The market-places are great ornaments to the city, the fronts being done in very fine taste, and the gates adorned with columns of one or other of the orders. Some of these markets are for meal, greens, fish or flesh: there are two for the last which have conduits of water out of several of the pillars, so that they are constantly kept sweet and neat. Before these buildings were constructed, most of those articles were sold in the public streets; and even after the

---

[16] Keith, 239.

market-places were built, the magistrates with great difficulty compelled the people to take advantage of such cleanly innovations.

Near the meal-market is the public granary, to be filled on any apprehension of scarcity.

The guardhouse is in the great street; where the inhabitants mount guard, and regularly do duty. An excellent police is observed here; and proper officers attend the markets to prevent abuses.

The police of Glasgow consists of three bodies; the magistrates with the town council, the merchants house, and the trades house. The lord provost, three bailies, a dean of guild, a deacon convener, a treasurer, and twenty-five council men, compose the first. It must be observed that the dean of guild is chosen annually, and can continue in office but two years. The second consists of thirty-six merchants, annually elected, with the provost and three bailies, by virtue of their office, which make the whole body forty. The dean of guild is head of this house, who, in conjunction with his council, four merchants, and four tradesmen (of which the preceding dean is to be one) holds a court every Thursday, where the parties only are admitted to plead, all lawyers being excluded. He and his council have power to judge and decree in all actions respecting trade between merchant and merchant; and those who refuse to submit to their decisions are liable to a fine of five pounds. The same officer and his council, with the master of work, can determine all disputes about boundaries, and no proceedings in building shall be stopped, except by him; but the plaintiff must lodge a sufficient sum in his hands to satisfy the defendant, in case the first should lay a groundless complaint: and, to prevent delay, the dean and his assistants are to meet on the spot within twenty-four hours; and to prevent frivolous disputes, should the plaintiff be found not to have been aggrieved, he is fined in twenty shillings, and the damage sustained by the delay: but again, should he imagine himself wronged by the decision, he has power (after lodging forty shillings in the hands of the dean) of appealing to the great council of the city; and in case they also decide against him, the sum is forfeited and applied as the dean shall think fit. The same magistrate is also to see that no encroachments are made on the public streets: he can order any old houses to be pulled down that appear dangerous and, I think, has also power in some places, of disposing of, to the best bidder, the ground of any houses which the owner suffers to lie in ruins for three years, without attempting to rebuild. Besides these affairs, he superintends the weights and measures; punishes and fines transgressors; fines all unqualified persons who usurp the privileges of freemen; admits burgesses: the fines to aliens is £100 Scotch: and finally he and his council may levy tax on the guild brethren (not exceeding the above-mentioned sum at a time) for the maintenance of the wives and children of decayed brethren: the money to be distributed at the discretion of the dean, his council and the deacon convener.

The third body is the trades house: this consists of fifty-six, of which the deacon convener is the head: there are fourteen incorporated trades, each of which has a deacon, who has a right to nominate a certain number of his trade, so as to form the house: these manage a large stock, maintain a great number of poor, and determine disputes between the trades. In this place may be mentioned that the merchants' hospital, founded by the merchants of Glasgow in 1601, has a large capital to support the poor: that the town's hospital contains four hundred indigent, and is supported by the magistrates and town council, the merchants house, the trades house, and the kirk sessions. Hutchinson's hospital, founded in 1642 by two brothers of that name, has a fund of twelve thousand pounds: the town council a revenue tax of six thousand pounds per annum.

The old bridge over the Clyde consists of eight arches, and was built by William Rea, bishop of this see, about four hundred years ago. A new one has been lately added of seven arches, with circular holes between each to carry off the superfluous waters in the great floods. This bridge deviates from the original plan, which was very elegant, and free from certain defects that disgrace the present.

The city of Glasgow, till very lately, was perfectly tantalized with its river: the water was shallow, the channel much too wide for the usual quantity of water that flowed down, and the navigation interrupted by twelve remarkable shoals. The second inconveniency continually increased by the wearing away of the banks, caused by the prevalency of the south-west winds that blow here, and often with much violence, during more than half the year: thus what is got in breadth, is lost in depth; and shoals are formed by the loss of water in the more contracted bed. Springtides do not flow above three feet, or neaptides above one, at Broomylaw Quay, close to the town; so that in dry seasons lighters are detained there for several weeks, or are prevented from arriving there, to the great detriment of the city.

To remedy this evil, the city called in several engineers: at length the plan proposed by my old friend, Mr John Golburne, of Chester, that honest and able engineer, was accepted, and he entered into contract with the magistrates of Glasgow to deepen the channel to seven feet at the quay, even at neaptides. He has made considerable progress in the work, and had given the stipulated depth to within four miles of the place. For a present relief he has deepened the intermediate shoals, and particularly he has given at least four feet of water immediately below the quay, in a shoal called the Hurst, which was above a quarter of a mile long, and had over it only eighteen inches of water. Before this improvement lighters of only thirty tons burden could reach the quay: at present vessels of seventy come there with ease.

Near the bridge is the large almshouse, a vast nailery, a stoneware manufactory, and a great porter brewery, which supplies some part of Ireland:[17] besides these are manufactures of linens, cambrics, lawns, fustians, tapes, and striped linens; sugar-houses and glasshouses, great roperies; vast manufactures of shoes, boots and saddles, and all sorts of horse furniture: also vast tanneries carried on under a company who have £60,000 capital, chiefly for the use of the colonists, whose bark is found unfit for tanning. The magazine of saddles, and other works respecting that business, is an amazing sight: all these are destined for America, no port equalling this for the conveniency of situation, and speedily supplying the market. Within sight, on the Renfrew side, are collieries, and much coal is exported into Ireland, and into America.

---

[17] Dublin is extremely capable of supplying Ireland with this liquor, but as I am credibly informed, is almost prohibited the attempt by a hard and unpolitical tax.

The great import of this city is tobacco: the following state of that trade, for the these last years, exhibits its vast extent and importance:

		1769	*1770*
From Virginia,	25,457	hogsheads	29,815
Maryland	9,641		8,242
Carolina	460		913
Total	35,558		38,970

So it appears the increase of importation from Virginia, in 1770, was 4,358 hogsheads and from Carolina, 453, and that it decreased in Maryland, 1,399. But what is remarkable, that in the same year not any part of this vast stock remained unsold; the whole being disposed of in the following proportions:

	Hogsheads		*Hogsheads*
To Ireland	3,310	Bremen	1,303
France	15,706	Spain, etc.	885
Holland	10,637	Norway	557
Dunkirk	2,907	Denmark	200
Hamburgh	2,416	America	16
Total exported			37,938

Which, with 1,032, sold inland, balances the account.

In the last year 1771, the commerce still improved, for from:

	Hogsheads
Virginia	35,493
Maryland	12,530
Carolina	993
Total	49,016

The exports also increased, but not in the same proportion with those of last year:

Ireland took	3,509 hogsheads	Bremen	1,176
France	16,098	Norway	665
Holland	14,546	Denmark	390
Dunkirk	5,309	Spain, etc.	297
Hamburg	2,788	Barbados	21

	Total	44,799
	Sold inland	1,142
		45,941
So that this year it appears that there is unsold		3,075
To balance the great sum of		49,016

But this encouraging inference may be drawn: that, notwithstanding all our squabbles with the colonies, those of the first importance improve in their commerce with their mother country: receive also an equal return in the manufactures of Great Britain, which they wisely dispense to those whom unavailing associations of prohibition bind from an open traffic with us.

The origin of foreign trade in this great city is extremely worthy of attention. A merchant, of the name of Walter Gibson, by an adventure first laid the foundation of its wealth: about the year 1668 he cured and exported in a Dutch vessel, 300 lasts of herrings, each containing six barrels, which he sent to St Martin's, in France, where he got a barrel of brandy and a crown for each: the ship returning, laden with brandy and salt, the cargo was sold for a great sum: he then launched farther into business, bought the vessel, and two large ships besides, with which he traded to different parts of Europe, and to Virginia: he also first imported iron to Glasgow, for before that time it was received from Sterling and Burrowstoness, in exchange for dyed stuffs: and even the wine used in this city was brought from Edinburgh. Yet I find no statue, no grateful inscription, to preserve the memory of Walter Gibson!

Glasgow, till long after the Reformation, was confined to the ridge that extends from the high church, or cathedral, and the houses trespassed but little on the ground of each side. This place (whose inhabitants at this time are computed to be forty thousand) was so inconsiderable, in 1357, as not to be admitted into the number of the cautionary towns assigned to Edward III for the payment of the ransom of David II.[18] But the revenue of the archbishop was, at the Reformation, little less than a thousand pounds sterling per annum, besides several emoluments in corn of different kinds. Religion was, before that period, the commerce of our chief cities; in the same manner as commerce is their religion in the present age.

Some writers attribute the foundation of this see to St Kentigern, in 560, and make him the first bishop: others will give him no other rank than that of a simple saint. It is with more certainty known, that the cathedral was founded or reformed, in 1136, by John, governor to David I, and who was the first certain bishop of the place; for it was not erected into an archbishopric till 1500, when Robert Blacader had first the title.

This fine church was devoted to destruction by the wretched ministers of 1578, who assembled, by beat of drum, a multitude to effect the demolition: but the trades of the city taking arms, declared that they would bury under the ruins the first person who attempted the sacrilege; and to this sensible zeal are we indebted for so great an ornament to the place. It is at present divided into three places for divine service; two above, one beneath, and deep under ground, where the congregation may truly say, 'Clamavi ex profundis'. The roof of this is fine, of stone, and supported by pillars, but much hurt by the crowding of the pews.

In the churchyard is an epitaph on a jolly physician, whose practice should be recommended to all such harbingers of death, who by their terrific faces scare the poor patient prematurely into the regions of eternity:

> Stay, passenger, and view this stone,
> For under it lies such a one
> Who cured many while he lived;
> So gratious he no man grieved;
> Yea when his physick's force oft' failed,
> His pleasant purpose then prevailed;
> For of his God he got the grace

---

[18] Anderson's *Dict. Commerce*, I.

> To *live in mirth, and die in peace;*
> *Heaven has his soule, his corps this stone;*
> *Sigh, passenger, and then be gone.*
>   Dr Peter Low, 1612.

Besides this church are the College Church, Ramshorn, Tron, St Andrews and Wint. The English chapel, college chapel, a Highland church, three Seceding meeting-houses, a Moravian, an Independent, a Methodist, an Anabaptist, a Barony church, and one in the suburbs of the Gorbels.

But the most beautiful is that of St Andrew's, or the New Church, whose front graced with an elegant portico, does the city great credit, if it had not been disfigured by a slender square tower, with a pepperbox top; and in general the steeples in Glasgow are in a remarkably bad taste, being in fact no favourite part of architecture with the Church of Scotland. The inside of that just mentioned is finished not only with neatness but with elegance; is supported by pillars, and very prettily stuccoed. It is one of the very few exceptions to the slovenly and indecent manner in which the houses of God, in Scotland, are kept. Reformation, in matters of religion, seldom observes mediocrity; here it was at first outrageous, for a place commonly neat was deemed to savour of popery: but to avoid the imputation of that extreme, they ran into another; for in many parts of North Britain our Lord seems still to be worshipped in a stable, and often in a very wretched one: many of the churches are thatched with heath, and in some places are in such bad repair as to be half open at top; so that the people appear to worship as the Druids did of old, in open temples. It is but common justice to say, that this is no fault of the clergy, or of the people, but entirely of the landed interest; who having, at the Reformation, shared in the plunder of the church, were burdened with the building and repairing of the houses of worship. It is too frequently the case, that the gentlemen cannot be induced to undertake the most common repairs, without being threatened with a process before the lords of sessions, or perhaps having the process actually made, which is attended with odium, trouble and expense to the poor incumbents.

Near the cathedral is the ruin of the castle, or the bishop's palace, the great tower was built by John Cameron, prelate in 1426.

Buchanan relates an absurd tale, that this bishop was summoned to the great tribunal by a loud preternatural voice; that he assembled his servants, when to their great terror the call was repeated; and the bishop died in great agonies.[19] His offence is concealed from us, for he appears to have been a good and an able man.

Archbishop Bethune surrounded the palace with a fine wall, and made a bastion over one corner, and a tower over another. This castle was besieged in 1544, by the regent Arran, in the civil disputes at that time; who took it, and hanged eighteen of the garrison, placed there by Lenox, a favourer of the Reformation.

In Glasgow were two religious houses and a hospital. One of Dominicans, founded by the bishop and chapter in 1270, and another of Observantines in 1476, by John Laing, Bishop of Glasgow, and Thomas Forsyth, rector of the college.

The university was founded in 1450, by James II, Pope Nicholas V gave the bull, but Bishop Turnbull supplied the money. It consists of one college, a large building with a handsome front to the street, resembling some of the old colleges in Oxford. Charles I subscribed £200 towards this work, but was prevented from paying it by the ensuing troubles; but Cromwell afterwards fulfilled the design of the royal donor. Here are about four hundred students who lodge in the town, but the professors have good houses in the college, where young gentlemen may be boarded, and placed more immediately under the professors' eye, than those that live in private houses. An inconveniency that calls loudly for reformation.

The library is a very handsome room, with a gallery, supported by pillars; and is well furnished with books. That beneficent nobleman, the first Duke of Chandos, when he visited the college, gave £500 towards building this apartment.

In possession of the college is a very singular version of the bible, by the Rev Zachary Boyd, a worthy, learned and pious divine of this city, who lived about a century and a half ago, and dying, bequeathed to this seminary of knowledge his fortune, and all his manuscripts, but not on condition of printing his poem as is vulgarly imagined. It is probable that he adapted his verse to the intellects

---

[19] Lib. XI, ch. 25.

of his hearers, the only excuse for the variety of gross imagery, of which part of the soliloquy of Jonas in the fish's belly, will be thought a sufficient specimen:

> *What house is this? Here's neither coal nor candle;*
> *Where I no thing but guts of fishes handle.*
> *I and my table are both here within,*
> *Where day ne'er dawn'd, where sun did never shine.*
> *The like of this on earth man never saw,*
> *A living man within a monster's maw!*
> *Burryed under mountains, which are high and steep!*
> *Plunged under waters hundred fathoms deep!*
> *Not so was Noah in his house of tree,*
> *For through a window he the light did see:*
> *He sailed above the highest waves: a wonder,*
> *I and my boat are all the waters under;*
> *He and his ark might go and also come;*
> *But I sit still in such a strait'ned room*
> *As is most uncouth; head and feet together,*
> *Among such grease as would a thousand smother;*
> *Where I intombed in melancholy sink,*
> *Choaked, suffocate with excremental stink!*

Messrs Robert and Andrew Foulis, printers and booksellers to the university, have instituted an academy for painting and engraving; and, like good citizens, zealous to promote the welfare and honour of their native place, have, at vast expense, formed a most numerous collection of paintings from abroad, in order to form the taste of their *élèves*.

The printing is a considerable branch of business, and has long been celebrated for the beauty of types, and the correctness of the editions. Here are preserved, in cases, numbers of monumental, and other stones, taken out of the wall on the Roman stations in this part of the kingdom: some are well cut and ornamented: most of them were done to perpetrate the memory of the *vexillatio*, or party, who performed such or such works; others in memory of officers who died in the country. Many of these sculptures were engraven at the expense of the university; whose principal did me the honour of presenting me with a set.

The first plate is very beautiful: a Victory, reclined on a globe, with a palm in one hand, a garland in the other; a pediment above, supported by two fluted pilasters, with Corinthian capitals: beneath is a boar, a common animal in sculptures found in Britain, probably because they were in plenty in our forests. Both these are in honour of the Emperor Antoninus Pius.

None is more instructive than that engraven in plate III, on which appears a Victory about to crown a Roman horseman, armed with a spear and shield. Beneath him are two Caledonian captives, naked, and bound, with their little daggers, like the modern dirks, by them. On another compartment of the stone is an eagle and sea-goat, to denote some victory gained in the course of their work near the sea: for it was devoted by a party of the *Legio secunda Augusta*, on building a certain portion of the wall.

The XVth is monumental: the figure is very elegant, representing one gracefully recumbent, dressed in a loose robe: beneath is a wheel, denoting, that at the time of his death he was engaged with a party on the road: and by him is an animal, resembling the musimon or Siberian goat.

In this street is the house where Henry Darnly lodged, confined by a dangerous illness, suspected to arise from poison, administered at the instigation of Bothwel. Here the unhappy prince received a visit from Mary Stuart, and took the fatal resolution of removing to Edinburgh. This sudden return of her affection, her blandishments to enveigle him from his father and friends, and his consequential murder, are circumstances unfavourable to the memory of this unfortunate princess.

Take boat at the quay; and after a passage of four miles down the Clyde, reach the little flying house of Mr Golborne, now fixed on the northern bank, commanding a most elegant view of part of the county of Renfrew, the opposite shore. After breakfast survey the machines for deepening the river, which were then at work: they are called ploughs, are large hollow cases, the back is of cast iron, the two ends of wood; the other side open. These are drawn cross the river by means of capstans, placed on long wooden frames of flats; and opposite to each other near the banks of the river. Are drawn over empty, returned with the iron side downwards, which scrapes the bottom, and brings up at every return half a ton of gravel, depositing it on the bank: and thus twelve hundred tons are cleared every day. Where the river is too wide, the shores are contracted by jetties.

Proceed down the river: on the left the water of Inchinnan opens to view; the prospect up the most elegant and the softest of any in North Britain: the expanse is wide and gentle; the one bank bare, the other adorned with a small open grove. A little isle tufted with trees divides the water; beyond the fine bridge of Inchinnan receiving the united rivers of the White and Black Cart, and the town and spire of Paisly, backed by a long and fertile range of rising land, close the scene.

On the right is a chain of low hills, Camsey Fells, running north-west and south-east, diverging north-east, and advancing to the waterside, terminating with the rock of Dunbuc, that almost reaches to the Clyde.

Pass under Kirkpatric, where the river is about a quarter of a mile broad: at this place is a considerable manufacture of all sorts of husbandry tools, began about four years ago: but it is far more celebrated for being the supposed termination of the Roman wall, or Graham's Dike, built under the auspices of Antoninus Pius. Not the least relic is to be seen here at present: but about a mile and a half to the eastward on a rising ground above the bridge of the burn of Dalmure, near the village of Duntocher, are the vestiges of a fort and watch-tower, with a very deep fosse. The houses in the village appear to have been formed out of the ruins, for many of the stones are smoothed on the side; and on one are the letters N. E. R. O., very legible. This wall was guarded with small forts from end to end, that is to say from near Kirkpatric to within two miles of Abercorn, or, as Bede calls it, the monastery of Abercurnig, on the Firth of Forth, a space of thirty-six miles eight hundred and eighty-seven paces: of these forts ten are planned by the ingenious Mr Gordon; and numbers of the inscriptions found in them, engraven. This great work was performed by the soldiery under Lollius Urbicus, lieutenant of Antoninus, in pursuance of the plan before pointed out by the great Agricola, who garrisoned the whole space between the two firths, removing, as it was, the barbarians into another island.[20]

[20] Tacitus.

Ireland will scarce forgive me if I am silent about the birthplace of its tutelar saint. He first drew breath at Kirkpatric, had derived his name from his father, a noble Roman (a patrician) who fled hither in the time of persecution. St Patric took on himself the charge of Ireland; founded there 365 churches, ordained 365 bishops, 3,000 priests, converted 12,000 persons in one district, baptized seven kings at once, established a purgatory and with his staff at once expelled every reptile that stung or croaked.

Somewhat lower, on the same side, Dunglas projects into the water, and forms a round bay. On the point is a ruined fort, perhaps on the site of a Roman; for probably the wall might have ended here, as at this very place, the water is deep, and at all times unfordable by foot or horse. The fort was blown up in 1640, as some say, by the desperate treachery of an English boy, page to the Earl of Haddington, who, with numbers of people of rank, were miserably destroyed.[21] Below this the river widens, and begins to have the appearance of an estuary: the scene varies into other beauties; the hills are rocky, but clothed at the bottom by ranges of woods, and numbers of pretty villas grace the country. Dunbuc makes now a considerable figure: the plain of Dunbarton opens; the vast and strange bicapitated rock, with the fortress, appears full in front; the town and its spire beyond; the fine River Leven on one side, and the vast mountains above Loch Lomond, and the great base and soaring top of Ben Lomond close the view.

The Roman fleet in all probability, had its station under Dunbarton: the Glota, or Clyde, has there sufficient depth of water; the place was convenient and secure; near the end of the wall; and covered by the fort at Dunglas: the Pharos on the top of the great rock is another strong proof that the Romans made it their harbour, for the water beyond is impassable for ships, or any vessels of large burden.

After a long contest with a violent adverse wind, and very turbulent water, pass under, on the south shore, Newark; a castellated house, with round towers. Visit Port Glasgow, a considerable town, with

[21] Whitelock, 35. Crawford's *Peerage*, 182.

a great pier, and numbers of large ships: dependent on Glasgow, a creation of that city, since the year 1668, when it was purchased from Sir Patrick Maxwell of Newark, houses built, a harbour formed, and the custom-house for the Clyde established.

Proceed two miles lower to Greenock, anciently called the Bay of St Lawrence; a place still more considerable for its shipping than the former; and, like the other, a port of Glasgow, twenty-two miles distant from it. The firth here expands into a fine bastion four miles wide, and is land-locked on all sides. Dine here, contract for a vessel for my intended voyage, and return to Glasgow at night.

Cross the new bridge, at whose foot on that side is Gorbel, a sort of suburbs of Glasgow. The county of Lanerk still extends three miles down the river; but after a short ride, I enter the shire of Renfrew.

Leave, on the left, the hill of Langside, noted for the battle in 1568; which decided the fortune of Mary Stuart, and precipitated her into that fatal step of deserting her country, and flinging herself into an eighteen years captivity, terminating in the loss of her head, the disgrace of the annals of her glorious rival. Ride through a fine country to Cruickston Castle, seated on the summit of a little hill; now a mere fragment, only a part of a square tower remaining of a place of much magnificence, when in its full glory. The situation is delicious, commanding a view of a well-cultivated tract, divided into a multitude of fertile little hills.

This was originally the property of the Crocs, a potent people in this county; but in the reign of Malcolm II, was conveyed, by the marriage of the heiress, daughter of Robert de Croc, into the family of Stuarts, in after-times earls and dukes of Lenox, who had great possessions in these parts. To this place Henry Darnly retired with his enamoured Queen, Cruickston being then, as Cliefden in the time of Villiers, 'The seat of wantonness and love'. Here fame says that Mary first resigned herself to the arms of her beloved, beneath a great yew, still existing: but no loves would smile on joys commenced beneath the shade of this funeral tree; the hour was unpropitious, '*Ille dies primus Lethi, primusque malorum, causa fuit*'.

It was even said that Mary, unconscious of events, struck a coin on the occasion, with the figure of the fatal tree, honoured with a crown, and distinguished by the motto, *Dat gloria vires.*[22] But I have opportunity of contradicting this opinion from an examination of the coins themselves, whose dates are 1565, 1566, and 1567.[23] The tree is evidently a palm, circumscribed, *Exurgat Deus, dissipentur inimici ejus.* Pendent from the boughs, is the motto above cited, which is part of the following lines taken from Propertius, alluding a snail climbing up the body of the tree, a modest comparison of the honour that Henry Darnly received by the union with his royal spouse:

> *Magnum ite ascendo, sed dat mibi gloria vires, Non iuvat ex facili, lata corona jugo.*
>
> Lib. iv. El. 2.

Visit Paisley, a considerable but irregularly built town; at the distance of two miles from Cruickston, six miles west of Glasgow, two miles south-west of Renfrew, and fourteen south-east of Greenock. It was erected into a burgh of barony in the year 1488, and the affairs of the community are managed by three bailies, of which the eldest is commonly in the commission of the peace, a treasurer, a town clerk, and seventeen counsellors, who are annually elected upon the first Monday after Michaelmas. It stands on both sides of the River Cart, over which it has three stone bridges, each of two arches: the river runs from south to north, and empties itself into the Clyde, about three miles below the town: at springtides vessels of forty tons burthen come up to the quay; and, as the magistrates are now clearing and deepening river, it is hoped still larger may hereafter get up. The communication by water is of great importance to the inhabitants, for sending their goods and manufacturers to Port Glasgow and Greenock, and, if they choose it, to Glasgow; and besides, was the grand canal finished, they will have an early communication with the Firth of Forth, as the canal joins the Clyde about three or four miles north of Paisley.

---

[22] Bishop Nicholson's *Scottish Library*, 323.
[23] See also Anderson's *Coins*, tab. 165.

Notwithstanding its antiquity this town was of little consequence till within these last fifty years; before that period scarce any other manufacture was carried on but coarse linen checks, and a kind of striped cloth called 'Bengals'; both which have long been given up here: while these were the only manufacture, the inhabitants seem to have had no turn for enlarging their trade, for their goods were exposed to sale in the weekly market, and chiefly brought up by dealers from Glasgow: some of them, however, who travelled into England to sell Scots manufactures, picked up a more general knowledge of trade, and having saved a little money, settled at home, and thought of establishing other branches; to which they were the more encouraged, as their acquaintance in England was like to be of great use to them.

About 50 years ago the making of white stitching threads was first introduced into the west country by a private gentlewoman, Mrs Millar of Bargarran, who, very much to her own honour, imported a twist-mill, and other necessary apparatus, from Holland, and carried on a small manufacturer in her own family: this branch, now of such general importance to Scotland, was soon after established in Paisley; where it has ever since been on the increase, and has now diffused itself over all parts of the kingdom. In other places girls are bred to it: here they may be rather said to be born to it: as almost every family makes some threads, or have made formerly. It is generally computed, that, in the town and neighbourhood, white threads are annually made to the amount of from £40 to £50,000.

The manufacture of lawns, under various denominations, is also carried on here to a considerable amount, and to as great perfection as in any part of Europe. Vast quantities of foreign yarn are annually imported from France, Germany, etc. for this branch, as only the lower priced kinds can be made of our home manufactured yarn. It is thought the lawn branch here amounts to about £70,000 annually. The silk gauze has also been established here, and brought to the utmost perfection: it is wrought to an amazing variety of patterns; for such is the ingenuity of our weavers, that nothing in their branch is too hard for them. It is commonly reckoned that this branch amounts to about £60,000 annually.

A manufacture of ribbons has, within these twelve months, been established here, and both flowered and plain are made, in every respect as good as in any place of England. In these different branches a great number of people are employed, many of them boys and girls, who must otherwise have been idle for some years. It must be extremely agreeable to every man who wishes well to his country, to see, in the summer season, both sides of the river, and a great many other fields about town, covered with cloth and threads; and to hear, at all seasons, as he passes along the streets, the industrious and agreeable noise of weavers' looms and twist-mills. The late unfortunate stagnation of trade has been felt here, as well as in most other parts of the island; but it is hoped, if things were a little more settled, trade will revive, and the industrious artificers be again all employed.

Besides these general manufactures, several others of a more local kind are carried on here: there is a very considerable one of hard soap and tallow candles, both of which are esteemed excellent of their kinds, as the gentlemen concerned spared no expense to bring their manufacture to perfection: their candles, especially their moulded ones, are reckoned the best and most elegant that have been made in Scotland, and great quantities of them are sent to England and to the West Indies. They are made after the Kensington manner, and with this view they had a man from London, at very high wages. There are also two tanning works in town, and a copperas work in the neighbourhood.

Before the year 1735 the whole people in the parish, town and country, said their prayers in one church, and the reverend and learned Mr Robert Millar discharged the whole duties of the pastoral office for many years without an assistant: but since that period the town has increased so much, that besides the old church there are now two large ones, and two Seceding meeting-houses. The church first built, called the Laigh, or Low church, is in form of a Greek cross, very well laid out, and contains a great number of people: the other, called the High church, is a very fine building, and, as it stands, on the top of a hill, its lofty stone spire is seen at a vast distance: the church is an oblong square, of eighty-two feet by sixty-two, within the walls, built of freestone, well smoothed, having rustic corners, and an elegant stone cornice at top: though the area is so large, it has no pillars; and the seats and lofts are so well laid out, that, though the church contains about three thousand people, every one of them sees the minister: in the construction of the roof, (which is a pavillion, covered with slate, having a platform covered with lead on the top) there is something very curious; it is admired by every man of taste, and, with the whole building, was planned and conducted by the late very ingenious Bailie Whyte, of this place. The town house is a very handsome building of cut stone, with a tall spire, and a clock: part of it is let for an inn, the rest is used as a prison, and courtrooms; for here the sheriff courts of the county are held. The fleshmarket has a genteel front, of cut stone, and is one of the neatest and most commodious of the kind in Britain: butcher's meat, butter, cheese, fish, wool, and several other articles, are sold here by what they call the tron-pound of 22 English ounces and a half. The poorhouse is a large building, very well laid out, and stands opposite to the quay, in a fine free air: it is supported by a small tax, imposed upon the inhabitants quarterly. There are at present in the house above sixty, of which number about thirty-six are boys and girls, who are carefully educated, and the boys put out to business at the expense of the house. Besides these, many outpensioners have weekly supplies. Most of the mechanics of artificers in town, and several others, that fall not under these denominations, have formed themselves into societies, and have established funds for the aid of their distressed members: these funds are generally well managed, and of very great benefit to individuals.

The old part of the town runs from east to west upon the south slope of a ridge of hills, from which there is a pleasant and very extensive prospect of the city of Glasgow, and the adjacent country on all sides, but to the southward, where the view terminates on a ridge of green hills, about two miles distant. Including the late buildings and suburbs, it is about an English mile long, and much about the same breadth. So late as the year 1746, by a very accurate survey, it was found to contain scarce four thousand inhabitants: but it is now thought to have no fewer than from ten to twelve thousand, all ages included. The Earl of Abercorn's burial place is by much the greatest curiosity in Paisley: it is an old Gothic chapel, without pulpit or pew, or any ornament whatever; but has the finest echo perhaps in the world: when the end-door (the only one it has) is shut, the noise is equal to a loud and not very distant clap of thunder; if you strike a single note of music, you hear the sound gradually ascending, till it dies away, as if at an immense distance, and all the while diffusing itself through the circumambient air: if a good voice sings, or a musical instrument is well played upon, the effect is inexpressibly agreeable. In this chapel is the monument of Marjory Bruce: she lies recumbent, with her hands closed, in the attitude of prayer: above was once a rich arch, with sculptures of the arms, etc. Her story is singular: she was daughter of Robert Bruce, and wife of Walter, Great Steward of Scotland, and mother of Robert II. In the year 1317, when she was big with child, she broke her neck in hunting near this place: the Caesarean operation was instantly performed, and the child taken out alive; but the operator chancing to hurt one eye with his instrument, occasioned the blemish that gave him afterwards the epithet of 'Blear-eye'; and the monument is also styled that of the 'Queen Bleary'. In the same chapel were interred Elizabeth Muir and Euphemia Ross, both consorts to the same monarch: the first died before his accession.

About half a mile south-west of Paisley lies Maxwelton: a very neat little village, erected since the year 1746, where the manufactures of silk gauze are carried on to a considerable extent.

There is scarce a vestige remaining of the monastery, founded in 1160 by Walter son of Allan, '*Dapiser Regis Scotiae pro anima quondam regis David et anima Henrici regis Angliae et anima comitis Henrici et pro salute corporis et animae regis Malcolmi et pro animabus omnium parentum meorum, et benefactorum nec non et mei ipsius salute*', etc. The monks, who were instructed with this weighty charge, were first of the order of Cluniacs, afterwards changed to Cistercians; and lastly, the first order was again restored.

The garden wall, a very noble and extensive one of cut stone, conveys some idea of the ancient grandeur of the place: by a rude inscription, still extant, on the north-west corner, it appears to have been built by George Shaw, the abbot, in the year 1484, the same gentleman who four years after procured a charter for the town of Paisley. The inscription is too singular to be omitted:

> *Thy callit the abbot George of Shaw,*
> *About my abby gart make this waw*
> *An hundred four hundredth zear*
> *Eighty-four the date but weir.*
> *Pray for his salvation*
> *That laid this noble fundation.*

As the great stewards of Scotland were their patrons and benefactors, they enjoyed ample privileges, and very considerable revenues; they were the patrons of no fewer than thirty-one parishes, in different parts of the kingdom. The monks of this abbey wrote a chronicle of Scots affairs, called *The Black Book of Paisley*, an authentic copy of which is said to have been burnt in the abbey of Holyroodhouse, during Cromwell's usurpation: another copy taken from Mr Robert Spottiswood's library, was carried to England by General Lambert. The cartulary of the monastery is said to be still extant; the account of the charters, bulls of confirmation, donations, etc. is brought down to the year 1548. John Hamilton, the last abbot, was natural brother to the Duke of Hamilton, and, upon his promotion to the see of St Andrews, in 1546, resigned the abbacy of Paisley in favour of Lord Claud Hamilton, third son of that duke; which resignation was afterwards confirmed by Pope Julius III, in the year 1553. This Lord Claud Hamilton, titular Abbot of Paisley, upon the dissolution of the monasteries obtained from King James VI, a charter, erecting the lands belonging to the abbacy into a temporal lordship: this charter is dated at Edinburgh, July 29, 1587. He was, by the same prince, created a peer, in 1591, by the title of Lord Paisley, and died in 1621. In 1604 his eldest son had been created Lord Abercorn, and in 1606 was raised to the dignity of an earl. The family is now represented by the Right Hon. James, Earl of Abercorn, Baron Hamilton of Straban, in Ireland, etc. The lordship of Paisley was disposed of to the Earl of Angus, in the year 1652, and by him to William, Lord Cochran, afterwards Earl of Dundonald, in 1653, in which family it continued till the year 1764, when the present Earl of Abercorn repurchased the paternal inheritance of his family. The abbey church, when entire, has been a grand building, in form of a cross; the great north window is a noble ruin, the arch very lofty, the middle pillar wonderfully light, and still entire: only the chancel now remains, which is divided into a middle and two side aisles; all very lofty pillars, with Gothic arches; above these is another range of pillars, much larger, being the segment of a circle, and above a row of arched niches, from end to end; over which the roof ends in a sharp point. The outside of the building is decorated with a profusion of ornaments, especially the great west and north doors, than which scarce anything lighter or richer can be imagined.

But notwithstanding popery and Episcopacy were expelled this country, yet superstition and credulity kept full possession in these parts. In 1697 twenty poor wretches were condemned for the imaginary crime of witchcraft, and five actually suffered at the stake on June 10th in the same year.[24] One young and handsome; to whom is attributed the heroic reply mentioned in my former volume.[25] So deep was the folly of excess in belief rooted here, that full credit seems to have been given to an account that one of the condemned (a wizard) was strangled in his chair by the devil, I suppose lest he should make a confession to the detriment of the service.

The vestiges of the Roman camp at Paisley, are at present almost annihilated. Of the outworks mentioned by Camden, there are no traces of any excepting one, for at a place called Castle Head, are still left a few marks, but nothing entire. There had been a military road leading to the camp, which is supposed to have been the Vanduara of Ptolemy.

Continue my journey towards Renfrew. On the road see a mount or tumulus, with a fosse round the base, and a single stone erected on the top. Near this place was defeated and slain Somerled, Thane of Argyle, who in 1159, with a great army of banditti collected from

[24] *Narrative of the Diabolical Practices of above Twenty Wizards, etc.*, printed 1697.
[25] The girl at Warbois made a reply equally great. Her persecutors had only one circumstance against her, that of concealing herself: for when the mob came to seize her mother, she hid herself in the coal-hole. On her trial the bystanders pitying her youth and innocence, advised her to plead her belly. She replied with the utmost spirit, that notwithstanding they had power to put her to death; they never should make her destroy her reputation by so infamous a plea.

Ireland and other parts, landed in the Bay of St Laurence, and led them in rebellion against Malcolm IV.[26] That this mount was raised in memory of so signal an event is not improbable, especially as we are told by a most respectable writer,[27] that his troops retired unmolested; therefore might have leisure to fling up this usual tribute to the honour of their leader.

Reach Renfrew, the county town, now an inconsiderable place. Robert II had a palace here, which stood on a piece of ground of about half an acre, still called the Castle Hill; but nothing remains but the ditch which surrounded it. This monarch first made Renfrew an independent sheriffdom, for before it was joined to that of Lanerk.

Pass by the tower of Inch, or isle so called, from its once having been, as tradition says, surrounded by the Clyde. Mr Crawford, in his history of the county, informs us it had been the property of the barons Ross of Haulkhead.

All the land in these parts excellent, but most ill and slovenly dressed. Cross the Clyde, pass by Partic, a village where the bakers of Glasgow have very considerable mills on the water of Kelvin, and a great tract of land, at present valued at ten thousand pounds; originally granted to them by the regent Murray, in reward for their services in supplying his army with bread previous to the decisive battle of Langside. Return again to Glasgow.

[26] Major, 133.
[27] Rev Dr John Macpherson.

V

LENOXSHIRE, ARGYLE, KINTYRE

Mugdoc Castle—Loch Lomond—Ben Lomond—Buchanan—Roseneath—
Ardincapel—Loch Loung—Kilmun—Dunoon Castle—Isles of Cumray—
Isle of Bute—Rothesay—Inchmarnoc—Loch Tarbat—Isle of Arran—
Brodic Castle—Tormore—Fingal's Cave—Lamlash—Crag of Ailsa—Sanda
Isle—Campbeltown—Gigha

SET out in company with Mr Golborne, for Loch Lomond. Pass
for a few miles over a pleasant country, hilly, well-cultivated, and
often prettily planted, and thickset with neat villas. Go over the site
of the Roman wall, near Bemulie, where had been a considerable
fort, whose plan is engraven by Mr Gordon. Cross the Kelvin, and
enter the shire of Lenox, or sheriffdom of Dunbarton.

See on the right Mugdoc Castle, a square tower, the ancient seat
of the Grahams: and near it is a mount, probably the work of the
Romans, for they penetrated on this side as far as the banks of
Loch Lomond, a gold coin of Nero and another of Trajan having
been found in the parish of Drummond. The country now grows
high, moory, black, and dreary. Pass over Fenwick Bridge, flung
over a dark and rocky glen, shaded with trees, impending over a
violent torrent. Leave at some distance on the right the small house
of Moss, immortalized by the birth of the great Buchanan. Cross
a handsome bridge over the water of Enneric, and breakfast at the

village of Drummin or Drummond with the Rev Mr MacFarlane, the minister of the place. The parish, which takes its name from Druim, a back, from the ridges that run along it, is in extent nine miles by seven; and some years ago contained about a thousand eight hundred souls; but the number is much reduced by the unfeeling practice of melting several lesser farms into a greater. Arrive once more within sight of the charming Loch Lomond.

Approach its shores, go through the narrow pass of Bualmacha, where the Grampian hills finish in the lake. Many of the isles run in a line with, and seem to have been a continuation of them; appearing like so many fragments rent from them by some violent convulsion. Arrive in a beautiful bay: the braes of the hills on the right are lofty: some filled with small pebbles; others have a ferruginous look. The islands are mountainous and exhibit variety of charms. Inchcalloch, or 'the isle of nuns', has on it the remains of a church, is finely wooded; and is said to have been the seat of the fair recluses. Inchmurrin, or 'the isle of St Murrinus', is two miles long, is a deer park, and has on it the ruins of a house once belonging to the family of Lenox. On this island John Colquhoun, Laird of Luss, with several of his followers, were barbarously murdered by a party of islanders who, under conduct of Lauchlan Maclean, and Murdoc Gibson, in 1439, carried fire and sword through this part of North Britain.

Various other islands grace this fine expanse: Inchlonaig of great extent is blackened with the deep green of yews. The osprey inhabits a ruined castle on Inchgalbraith: and several little low and naked isles serve to diversify the scene. From this spot the boundaries of the water are magnificent and distinct: the wooded side of the western, and the soaring head of Ben Lomond on the eastern, form a view that is almost unequalled.

The top of this great mountain is composed of a micaceous slate, mixed with quartz. The *Sibbaldia procumbens*, a plant unknown in England, grows on the upper parts. Ptarmigans inhabit its summit; and roes the woods near its base, the most southern resort of those animals in our island.

The height of Ben Lomond from the surface of the lake is three thousand two hundred and forty feet: the prospect from the summit of vast extent: the whole extent of Loch Lomond with its wooded isles appears just beneath. Loch Loung, Loch Kettering, Loch Earn and the River Clyde form the principal waters. The mountains of Arran appear very distinct, and to the north alps upon alps fill up the amazing view.

Return the same way, and visit Buchanan, the seat of the Duke of Montrose, in a low and most disadvantageous situation, within a mile of the lake, without the least view of so delicious a water. This had been the seat of the Buchanans for six or seven ages, till it was purchased by the family of Montrose, sometime in the last century. Trees grow well about the house; and the country yields a good deal of barley and oats, some potatoes, but very little wheat.

His Grace has in his possession a portrait of his heroic ancestor James, Marquis of Montrose: his six victories, great as they were, do him less honour than his magnanimity at the hour of his death: he ascended the gibbet with a dignity and fortitude that caused the ignominy of his punishment to vanish: he fell with a gallant contempt of the cruelest insults; with that intrepid piety that blunted the malice of his enemies, and left them filled with the confusion natural to little minds, disappointed in the strained contrivances of mean revenge.

It is amusing to read the weak effects of fear, envy and rancour in the reports of the times: 'The witches (said the wretched covenants) were consulted at his birth; it was predicted that the boy would trouble Scotland; and while he was a sucking child (add they) he eat a venemous toad.'[1]

Walk in the afternoon over the neighbouring environs. See the water of Enneric that discharges itself here into the lake. Salmon in their annual migration pass up the Leven, traverse the lake, and seek this river to deposit their spawn.

The surface of Loch Lomond has for several years past been observed gradually to increase and invade the adjacent shore: and there is reason to suppose that churches, houses, and other buildings have been lost in the water. Near Luss is a large heap of stones at a distance of the shore, known by the name of the old church;

---

[1] *Staggering State of Scots Statesmen*, 14.

and about a mile to the south of that, in the middle of a large bay, between Camstraddan and the isle Inchlavanack, is another heap, said to have been the ruins of a house. To confirm this, it is evident by a passage in Camden's *Atlas Britannica*, that an island, existing in his time, is now lost, for he speaks of the isle of Camstraddan, placed between the lands of the same name and Inchlavanack, in which, adds he, was a house and orchard. Besides this proof, large trees with their branches still adhering are frequently found in the mud near the shore, overwhelmed in former times by the increase of water. This is supposed to be occasioned by the vast quantities of stone and gravel that is continually brought down by the mountain rivers, and by the falls of the banks of the Leven: the first filling the bed of the lake; the last impeding its discharge through the bed of the river.

Mr Golborne, at the request of the several proprietors, has made a voyage and survey of the lake, in order to plan some relief from the encroachment of the water. He proposes to form a constant navigation down the Leven, by deepening the channel, and cutting through the neck of two great curvatures, which will not only enable the inhabitants of the environs of Loch Lomond, to convey their slate, timber, bark, etc. to the market; but also by lowering the surface of the lake, recover some thousands of acres now covered with water.

The tide flows up the Leven two miles and a quarter. From thence as far as the lake is a rapid current, the fall being nineteen feet in five miles: the water is also full of shoals, so that in dry seasons it becomes unnavigable; and even at best the vessels are drawn up by a number of horses.

I must not leave the parish of Drummond without saying, that the celebrated Napier of Merchiston, author of the logarithms, was born at Garlies, within its precincts.

Still at Glasgow: am honoured with the freedom of the city.

Set out for Greenock, pass again through Renfrew: the country very fine, the lanes for some space well planted on both sides. Ride over Inchinnan Bridge, near which Matthew, Earl of Lenox, in 1506, built a magnificent palace: get upon some high grounds and, above the seat of Lord Glencairn, have a fine view of the

Clyde, Dunbarton, and all the northern shore. Reach Greenock: after dinner take a boat and cross into the shire of Lenox, and land where the parish of Roseneath juts out, and narrows the bay to the breadth of three miles, forming in that part a sort of strait: the prospect in the middle of this passage uncommonly fine; a contrast of fertility and savage views: to the east were the rich shores of the shires of Renfrew and Lenox, the pretty seats on the banks, and the wooded peninsula of Ardmore; and to the west appears the craggy tops of the hills of Argyleshire. Visit Roseneath House; a neat seat of the Duke of Argyle, dated 1634: the grounds well planted, the trees thriving: in one part of the walks am shown a precipitous rock, to which I was informed that the hero Wallace was pursued, and obliged to leap down to avoid captivity: his horse perished; the hero escaped unhurt. This country was the seat of the MacAulays, who struggled along with the Campbells in defence of their rights, but their genius proved the weaker.

Cross over the mouth of Loch Gair, which runs to the north six or seven miles up the country, the end overhung with lofty ragged mountains. Visit Airdencapel, a new house of Lord Frederic Campbell, situate on an eminence, commanding a most beautiful view of the Renfrew shore, and the prospect of the ports of Port Glasgow and Greenock, continually animated with the movement of ships, and the busy haunt of commerce. Ardincapel was anciently possessed by a family of the same name; but in the time of James III it was changed to that of MacAulay, from the word Aulay happening to be the Christian name of the owner.

VOYAGE

Go on board the *Lady Frederic Campbell,* a cutter of ninety tons, Mr Archibald Thompson master. Sail at half an hour past two in the afternoon; pass, on the left, the village and little bay of Gourock, a place of sailors and fishermen; on the right, the point of Roseneath, in Lenox; between which, and that of Strone, in Cowal, a portion of Argyleshire, opens Loch Loung, or 'the loch of ships', which runs north many miles up the country. This is the Skipafiord of the Norwegians, having in their tongue, the same signification. To this place, in 1263, Haco, King of Norway, detached, with sixty ships, some of his officers, who landed and destroyed all the country round Loch Lomond.[2] Immediately beyond the point of Strone the land is again divided by the Holy Loch, or Loch Seant, extending westward. On its northern shore is Kilmun, once the seat of a collegiate church, founded by Sir Duncan Campbell in 1442, and since that time the burial place of the house of Argyle.

Steer south, conveyed rather by the force of the tide than wind: the channel straight, and so narrow as to make every object distinct. On the eastern shore is the square tower of Leven, and a little farther projects the point of Cloch. Almost opposite, on the western side, are the ruins of the castle of Dunoon: this fortress was possessed by the English in 1334, but was taken in behalf of David Bruce, by Sir Colin Campbell, of Lochow, who put the garrison to the sword; in reward he was made hereditary governor, and had the grant of certain lands towards its support.

The view down the firth now appears extremely great: the shire of Renfrew bounds one side; the hills of Cowal, sloping to the water edge, and varied with woods and cornlands, grace the other: in front are the greater and the lesser Cumray, the first now remarkable for its church, dedicated to St Columba,[3] and at present for the quarries of beautiful freestone; the last for the abundance of rabbits: the isle of Bute, with its fertile shore, lies oblique, and the stupendous mountains of Arran, soar at some distance far, far above.

[2] *Universas villas in circuitu Lacus Lokuofrii vastarunt.* Torfoeus, *Hist. Oracad.,* 167.

[3] Dean of the Isles, 6.

XII

Moss Griffith del.

ROTHESAY CASTLE.

E. Morell sculp.

Am carried by the point and castle of Towart, the flat southern extremity of Cowal, leaving on the east the shire of Air. Towart is the property of the Lamonds, who, during the civil wars, siding with Montrose, were besieged in it, and on the surrender, put to the sword.[4] At a distance is pointed out to me, in that county, the site of Largs, distinguished in the Scottish annals for the final defeat of the Norwegians, in 1263, which put an end to their invasions, and restored to Scotland the possession of the Hebrides.

Steer towards the coast of Bute, and in the evening land at the little point of Squolog, and walk up to Mount Stewart, the seat of the Earl of Bute; a modern house, with a handsome front and wings: the situation very fine, on an eminence in the midst of a wood, where trees grow with as much vigour as in the more southern parts, and extend far beneath on each side; and throstles, and other birds of song, fill the groves with their melody.

The isle of Bute is about twenty measured miles long; the breadth unequal, perhaps the greatest is five miles; the number of acres about twenty thousand; of inhabitants about four thousand: here are two parishes, Kingarth and Rothesay; at the last only the Erse language is used. It must be observed also, that in the last church were buried two of the bishops of the Isles,[5] but whether it was at times the residence of the prelates does not appear.

The country rises into small hills, is in no part mountainous, but is highest at the south end. The strata of stone along the shore from Rothesay Bay to Cilchattan, is a red grit, mixed with pebbles; from the first, transverse to Scalpay Bay, is a bed of slate, which seems to be a continuation of that species of stone, rising near Stonehive, on the eastern side of Scotland, and continued, with some interruptions, to this island; but is of a bad kind, both at its origin and termination. In the south end is some limestone: some spotted stone, not unlike lava, is found near the south end.

The quadrupeds of this island are hares, polecats, weasels, otters, seals, and as a compliment to the soil, moles. Among the birds, grouse and partridge are found here.

---

[4] Buchanan's *Clans* I, 152.
[5] Keith, 180.

The cultivation of an extensive tract on this eastern side is very considerable. In the article of enclosure, it has the start of the more southern counties of this part of the kingdom: the hedges are tall, thick and vigorous: the white thorns and wicken trees now in full flower; and about two thousand acres have been thus improved. The manures are coral and sea shells, seaweeds and lime. I observed in many places whole strata of corals and shells of a vast thickness, at present half a mile from the sea, such losses has that element sustained in these parts. The island is destitute of coal, but still much lime is burnt here, not only for private use, but for exportation at a cheap rate to the ports of Greenock and Port Glasgow.

The produce of the island is barely oats and potatoes. The barley yields nine from one: the oats four. Turnips and artifical grasses have been lately introduced with good success: so that the inhabitants may have fat mutton throughout the year. A great number of cattle are also reared here. The highest farm here is sixty pounds a year, excepting a single sheep farm which rents for two hundred; but the medium is about twenty-five. Arable land is set at nine or ten shillings an acre; the price of labourers is eight pence a day. Rents are at present mostly paid in money: the rentroll of the island is about four thousand pounds a year. Lord Bute possesses much of the greater share; and two or three private gentlemen own the rest.

The air is in general temperate: no mists or thick rolling fogs from the sea, called in the north a 'harle', ever infest this island. Snow is scarcely ever known to lie here; and even that of last winter, so remarkable for its depth and duration in other places, was in this island scarce two inches deep. The evils of this place are winds and rains, the last coming in deluges from the west.

When the present Earl of Bute came to his estate, the farms were possessed by a set of men, who carried on at the same time, the profession of husbandry and fishing to the manifest injury of both. His Lordhsip drew a line between these incongruent employs, and obliged each to carry on the business he preferred, distinct from the other: yet in justice to the old farmers, notice must be taken of their skill in ploughing even in their rudest days, for the ridges were straight, and the ground laid out in a manner that did them much credit. But this new arrangement, with the example given by his

Lordship of enclosing, by the encouragement of burning lime for some; and by transporting gratis to the nearest market the produce of all, has given to this island its present flourishing aspect.

This isle with that of Arran, the greater and the lesser Cumray, and the Inchmarnoc, form a county under the name of Bute. This shire and that of Cathness send a member to Parliament alternately.

Civil causes are determined here as in other counties of this part of the kingdom, by the sheriff-depute, who is always resident: he is the judge in smaller matters, and has a salary of about a hundred and fifty pounds a year. Justices of peace have the same powers here, and over the whole county, as in other places: but in North Britain no other qualification is required, after nomination, than taking out their commissions, and giving the usual oaths.

Criminals are lodged in the county jail at Rothesay, but are removed for trial to Inveraray; where the judges of the court of justiciary meet twice a year for the determining of criminal causes of a certain district.

The Earl of Bute is admiral of the county by commission from his Majesty, but no way dependent on the Lord High Admiral of Scotland; so that if any maritime case occurs within his jurisdiction (even crimes of as high a nature as murder or piracy) his Lordship, by virtue of the powers as admiral, is sufficient judge, or he may delegate his authority to any deputies.

Visit the south part of the island: ride to the hill of Cilchattan, a round eminence, from whence is a vast view of all around, insular and mainland. Observe, on the face of the hills, that the rocks dip almost perpendicularly, and form long columnar stacks, some opposing to us their sides, others their angles: are hard and cherty, but not basaltic; a term I apply to the jointed columns resembling those of the Giant's Causeway.

Descend to the ruin of old Kingarth Church. Two cemeteries belong to it, a higher and a lower: the last was allotted for the interment of females alone; because, in old times, certain women being employed to carry a quantity of holy earth, brought from Rome, lost some by the way, and so incurred this penalty for their negligence; that of being buried separated from the other sex.

Near this place is a circular enclosure called the Devil's Cauldron: it is made of stone, of excellent masonry, but without mortar, having the inside faced in the most smooth and regular manner. The walls at present are only seven feet six inches high, but are ten feet in thickness: on one side is an entrance, wide at the beginning, but grows gradually narrower as it approaches the area, which is thirty feet diameter.

Mr Gordon has engraven, in tab. iii, a building similar to this, near the course of the wall, called Cairnfual, and styles it a *castellum*. This, I presume, could never have been designed as a place of defence, as it is situated beneath a precipice, from whose summit the inmates might instantly have been oppressed by stones, or missile weapons: perhaps it was a sanctuary; for the name of the church, Kingarth implies, *kin*, 'chief' or 'head', *garth,* 'a sanctuary';[6] the common word for places of refuge, 'girth' being corrupted from it.

The south end of Bute is more hilly than the rest, and divided from the other part by a low sandy plain, called Langalchorid, on which are three great upright stones, the remains of a Druidical circle, originally composed of twelve.

Return over a coarse country, and pass by lands, lately enclosed with hedges, growing in a very prosperous manner. Pass by Loch Ascog, a small piece of water; and soon after by Loch Fad, about a mile and three quarters long, narrow, rocky on one side, prettily wooded on the other. The other lochs are Loch Quyen, and Loch Greenan; and each has its river. Reach Rothesay, the capital; a small but well-built town, of small houses, and about two hundred families; and within these few years much improved. The females spin yarn; the men support themselves by fishing. The town has a good pier, and lies at the bottom of a fine bay, whose mouth exactly opens opposite to that of Loch Streven, in Cowal: here is a fine depth of water, a secure retreat; and a ready navigation for foreign parts might most advantageously be established here.

The castle has been built at different times; the present entrance by Robert III. The rest is quite round, with round towers at the sides and is of unknown antiquity. Husbec, grandson of Somerled, was killed in the attack of a castle in Bute, perhaps of this.[7] Haco took the castle and whole island in the year 1263.[8] It was seized by Edward Baliol,

---

[6] *Garth* originally meant no more than 'yard' or 'enclosure'.
[7] Torfoeus.
[8] Buchanan.

in 1334, when possessed by the high steward of Scotland, a friend of the Bruces, and heir to the crown.[9] In the year following, the whole island, as well as that of Arran, was ravaged by the English, under the command of Lord Darcy, Lord Justice of Ireland. Soon after, the natives of Arran and Bute arose,[10] and, unarmed, made an attack with stones on Alan Lile, the English governor, put his party to flight, and recovered the fortress. It became in after-times a royal residence: Robert III lived there for a considerable time;[11] much attention was bestowed on it, for in the reign of James V we find, that one of the articles of accusation against Sir James Hamilton, was his not accounting for three thousand crowns, destined 'to reform the castle and palace of Rosay'.[12] In 1544, the Earl of Lenox, assisted by the English, made himself master of the place: and in the beginning of the last century (on what occasion I do not recollect) it was burnt by the Marquis of Argyle.

Bute is said to derive its name from *bothe*, 'a cell', St Brandan having once made it the place of his retreat; and for the same reason, the natives of this isle, and also of Arran, have been sometimes styled 'Brandani'. It was from very early times, part of the patrimony of the Stuarts: large possessions in it were granted to Sir John Stuart, natural son of Robert II by one of his mistresses, but whether by his beloved More or Moreham, or his beloved Mariota de Cardny, is what I cannot determine.[13]

Continue our ride along a hilly country, open, and under tillage: past on the right, the castle and bay of Cames, long the property of the Bannentynes: turn to the west, descend to the shore, and find our boat ready to convey us to the vessel, which lay at anchor a mile distant, under Inchmarnoc.

An island so called from St Marnoc, where appear the ruins of a chapel, and where (according to Fordun)[14] had been a cell of monks. The extent of this little isle is about a mile, has a hundred

---

[9] Boethius, 317.
[10] Major, 229.
[11] Boethius, 339.
[12] Lindesay, 165.
[13] Vide Sir James Dalrymple's *Collections*, Edinburgh 1705, xxxviii, lxxxiii.
[14] Lib. II, ch. 10.

and twenty acres of arable land, forty of brushwood, near three hundred of moor, and has vast strata of coral and shells on the west side. It is inhabited by a gentleman on half-pay, who, with his family, occupies the place under Lord Bute.

Weigh anchor at three o'clock in the morning: am teased with calms, but amused with a fine view of the circumambient land: the peninsula of Cantyre, here lofty, sloping, and rocky, divided by dingles, filled with woods, which reach the water edge, and expand on both sides of the hollows: Inchmarnoc and Bute lie to the east; the mountainous Arran to the south; Loch Fine, the Sinus Lelalonnius of Ptolemy, opened on the north, between the point of Skipnish in Cantyre, and that of Lamond in Cowal, and showed a vast example of water wildly bounded: numbers of herring-busses were now in motion, to arrive in time at Campbeltown, to receive the benefit of the bounty, and animated the scene.

Turn northward, leave the point of Skipnish to the south-west, and with difficulty get through a strait of about a hundred yards wide, with sunk rocks on both sides, into the safe and pretty harbour of the eastern Loch Tarbat, of capacity sufficient for a number of ships, and of a fine depth of water. The scenery was picturesque; rocky little islands lie across one part, so as to form a double port; at the bottom extends a small village; on the Cantyre side is a square tower, with vestiges, of other ruins, built by the family of Argyle to secure their northern dominions from the inroads of the inhabitants of the peninsula: on the northern side of the entrance of the harbour the rocks are of a most grotesque form: vast fragments piled on each other; the faces contorted and undulated in such figures as if created by fusion of matter after some intense heat; yet did not appear to me a lava, or under any suspicion of having been the recrement of a volcano.

Land at the village, where a great quantity of whisky is distilled.

Visit the narrow neck of land which joins Cantyre to South Knapdale: it is scarcely a mile wide, is partly morassy, partly intersected by strata of rocks, that are dipping continuations from the adjacent mountains of each district. There have been plans for cutting a canal through this isthmus to facilitate the navigation between the western ocean and the ports of the Clyde, and to take away the necessity of sailing through the turbulent tides of the Mull of Cantyre: it is supposed to be practicable, but at vast expense; at an expense beyond the power of North Britain to effect, except it could realise those sums which the wishes of a few of its sons had attained in idea. While I meditate on the project, and in imagination see the wealth of the Antilles sail before me, the illusion bursts, the shores are covered with wracked fortunes; real distress succeeds the ideal riches of Alnaschar, and dispels at once the beautiful vision of Aaron Hill, and the much-affected traveller.[15]

Ascend a small hill, and from the top have a view of the western Loch Tarbat, that winds along for about twelve miles, and is one continued harbour, for it has eight fathom water not very remote from this extremity, and opens to the sea on the west coast, at Aird Patric: the boundaries are hilly, varied with woods and tracts of heath; the country yields much potatoes and some corn: but the land is so interrupted with rocks that the natives, instead of the plough, are obliged to make use of the spade.

The time of the tides vary greatly at the terminations of each of the harbours: at this the flood had advanced in the east loch full three-quarters; in the other only one hour. According to some remarks Mr James Watt, of Glasgow, favoured me with the springtides in East Tarbat flow ten feet, in very extraordinary tides, two feet higher. The tides in the west loch are most irregular; sometimes neither ebb nor flow; at other times ebb and flow twice in a tide, and the quantity of the false ebb is about one foot. The mean height of the Firth of Clyde is greater than that of West Tarbat.

It is not very long since vessels of nine or ten tons were drawn by horses out of the west loch into that of the east, to avoid the dangers of the Mull of Cantyre, so dreaded and so little known was the navigation round the promontory. It is the opinion of many that these little isthmuses, so frequently styled 'Tarbat' in North Britain, took their name from the above circumstance; *tarruing*, signifying 'to draw', and *bata*, 'a boat'. This too might be called, by way of pre-eminence, 'the Tarbat', from a very singular circumstance related by Torfoeus.[16] When Magnus the Barefooted, King of Norway,

---

[15] Vide Tour of 1769, first ed., 215, second ed., 228.
[16] *Hist. Orcad.*, 73.

obtained from Donaldbane of Scotland the cession of the Western Isles, or all those places that could be surrounded in a boat, he added to them the peninsula of Cantyre by this fraud: he placed himself in the stern of a boat, held the rudder, was drawn ever over this narrow tract, and by this species of navigation wrested the country from his brother monarch.

In the afternoon attempt to turn out, but am driven back by an adverse gale.

Get out early in the morning into the same expanse as before: land on Inchbui, or 'the yellow isle'; an entire rock, covered with the *Lichen parientinus*. Sail by Inchskaite; amused by the sporting of seals. Hail a small fishing boat, in order to purchase some of its cargo: am answered by the owner, that he would not sell any, but that part was at my service; a piece of generosity of greater merit, as in this scarce season the substance of the whole family depended on the good fortune of the day. Thus in these parts hospitality is found even among the most indigent.

Most of the morning was passed in a dead calm: in the afternoon succeeded brisk gales, but from points not the most favourable, which occasioned frequent tacks in sight of port: in one broke our topsail yard. During these variations of our course, had good opportunity of observing the composition of the isle of Arran: a series of vast mountains, running in ridges across the whole; their tops broken, serrated, or spiring; the summit of Goatfield rising far above the rest, and the sides of all sloping towards the water edge: a scene, at this distance, of savage sterility.

Another calm within two miles of land: take to the boat, and approach Loch Ranza, a fine bay, at the north end of the isle of Arran, where I land in the evening. The approach was magnificent: a fine bay in front, about a mile deep, having a ruined castle near the lower end, on a low far-projecting neck of land, that forms another harbour, with a narrow passage; but within has three fathoms of water, even at the lowest ebb. Beyond is a little plain watered by a stream: and inhabited by the people of a small village. The whole is environed with a theatre of mountains and in the background the terraced crags of Crianan Athol soar above.

Visit the castle, which consists of two square parts united, built of red gritstone: in one room is a chimney-piece, and fireplace large enough to have roasted an ox: but now strewed with the shells of limpets, the hard fare of the poor people who occasionally take refuge here.

This fortress was founded by one of the Scottish monarchs, and is of some antiquity, for Fordun, who wrote about the year 1380, speaks of this and Brodic, as royal castles.

The village of Ranza and a small church lie a little farther in the plain. The last was founded and endowed by Ann, Duchess of Hamilton, in aid of the church of Kilbride; one of the two parishes this great island is divided into.

Am informed of a basking shark that had been harpooned some days before, and lay on the shore, on the opposite side of the bay. Cross over to take a view of a fish so rarely to be met with in other parts of Great Britain; and find it a monster, notwithstanding it was much inferior in size to others that are sometimes taken; for there have been instances of their being from thirty-six to forty feet in length.

This was twenty-seven feet four inches long. The tail consisted of two unequal lobes: the upper five feet long: the lower three. The circumference of the body great: the skin cinereous: and rough. The upper jaw much longer than the lower. The teeth minute, disposed in numbers along the jaws. The eyes placed at only fourteen inches distance from the tip of the nose. The apertures to the gills very long, and furnished with strainers of the substance of whalebone.

These fish are called in the Erse, *cairban*; by the Scotch, 'sailfish', from the appearance of the dorsal fins above water. They inhabit most parts of the western coasts of the northern seas: Linnaeus says within the Arctic circle: they are found lower, on the coast of Norway, about the Orkney Isles, the Hebrides; and on the coast of Ireland in the Bay of Balishannon, and on the Welsh coast about Anglesea. They appear in the firth in June in small shoals of seven or eight, continue there till the end of July and then disappear. They are most inoffensive fish; feed either on exsanguious marine animals, or on algae, nothing being ever found in their stomachs except some dissolved greenish matter.

They swim very deliberately with their two dorsal fins above water, and seem quiescent as if asleep. They are very tame or

XIII

LOCH RANZA BAY, And the manner of fishing the basking Shark.

Miss Griffith del.

R. C. Carrel sculp.

very stupid; and permit the near approach of man: will suffer a boat to follow them without accelerating their motion till it comes almost within contact, when a harpooner strikes his weapon into the fish as near the gills as possible: but they are often so insensible as not to move until the united strength of two men has forced in the harpoon deeper: as soon as they perceive themselves wounded, they fling up their tail and plunge headlong to the bottom, and frequently coil the rope round them in their agonies, attempting to disengage themselves from the weapon by rolling on the ground, for it is often found greatly bent. As soon as they discover that their efforts are in vain, they swim away with amazing rapidity, and with such violence that a vessel of 70 tons, has been towed by them against a fresh gale: they sometimes run off with 200 fathoms of line, and with two harpoons in them; and will find employ to the fishers for twelve and sometimes twenty-four hours before they are subdued. When killed they are either hauled on shore, or if at a distance, to the vessel's side. The liver (the only useful part) is taken out and melted into oil in vessels provided for that purpose: a large fish will yield eight barrels of oil, and two of sediment, and prove a profitable capture.

The commissioners of forfeited estates were at considerable expense in encouraging this species of fishery; but the person they confided in, most shamefully abused their goodness; so at present it is only attempted by private adventurers.

Return, land again and walk through a pretty wood of small trees, up the side of a hill that bounds the western side of the bay. A gigantic frog of the species called by Linnaeus, *Bombina*,[17] presented itself on the path. In the course of our ramble, fall in with the manse, or minster's habitation; pass a cheerful evening with him, and meet with hearty welcome, and the best fare the place would afford. Return to our ship, which had anchored in the bay.

---

[17] Vide *Enumeration of Animals and Plants*, 231.

Procure horses, and (accompanied by Mr Lindsay, the minister) ride up the valley, cross the little River Ranza, and leave that and a corn-mill on the right. Ascend the steeps of the barren mountains, with precipices often on the one side of our path, of which our obstinate steeds preferred the very margin. See to the west the great crags of Grianan Athol, with eagles soaring over their naked summits. Pass through woods of birch, small, weather-beaten and blasted: descend by Macfarlane's Cairn, cross the water of Sannocks, near the village of the same name: see a low monumental stone; keep along the eastern coast; hear a sermon preached beneath a tent formed of sails, on the beach; the congregation numerous, devout, and attentive, seated along the shore, forming a group picturesque and edifying.

Dine at the Corry; a small house, belonging to a gentleman of Airshire, who visits this place for the benefit of goats' whey.

Much barrenness in the morning's ride: on the mountains were great masses of moorstone; on the shore, millstone, and red gritstone.

The ride is continued along the coast, beneath low cliffs, whose summits were clothed with heath that hung from their margins, and seemed to distil showers of crystalline water from every leaf, the effect of the various springs above. Meet a flock of goats, skipping along the shore, attended by their herdsman; and observed them collecting, as they went, and chewing with great delight, the sea plants. Reach Brodic Castle, seated on an eminence amidst flourishing plantations, above a small bay, open to the east. This place has not at present much the appearance of a fortress, having been modernized; is inhabited by the Duke of Hamilton's agent, who entertained me with the utmost civility. It is a place of much antiquity, and seems to have been the fort held by the English under Sir John Hastings, in 1306, when it was surprised by the partisans of Robert Bruce, and the garrison put to the sword. It was demolished in 1456 by the Earl of Ross, in the reign of James II, is said to have been rebuilt by James V and to have been garrisoned in the time of Cromwell's usurpation. Few are the records preserved of these distant places, therefore very wide must be their historic gaps.

Arran, or properly Arrinn, or 'the island of mountains', seems not to have been noticed by the ancients, notwithstanding it must have been known to the Romans, whose navy, from the time of Agricola, had its station in the Glota Aestuarium, or the Firth of Clyde: Camden indeed makes this island the Glota of Antonine, but no such name occurs in his itinerary; it therefore was bestowed on Arran by some of his commentators.

By the immense cairns, the vast monumental stones, and many relics of Druidism, this island must have been considerable in very ancient times. Here are still traditions of the hero Fingal, or Fin MacCoul, who is supposed here to have enjoyed the pleasures of the chase; and many places retain his name: but I can discover nothing but oral history that relates to the island, till the time of Magnus the Barefooted, the Norwegian victor, who probably included Arran in his conquests of Cantyre.[18] If he did not conquer that island, it was certainly included among those that Donaldbane was to cede; for it appears that Acho, one of the successors of Magnus, in 1263, laid claim to Arran, Bute, and the Cumrays, in consequence of that promise: the two first be subdued, but the defeat he met with at Largs soon obliged him to give up his conquests.[19]

Arran was the property of the Crown: Robert Bruce retired here during his distresses, and met with protection from his faithful vassals: numbers of them followed his fortunes; and, after the battle of Bannockbourn he rewarded several, such as the MacCooks, MacKinnons, MacBrides, and MacLouis, or Fullertons, with different charters of lands in their native country. All these are now absorbed by this great family, except the Fullertons and a Stuart, descended from a son of Robert III who gave him a settlement here. In the time of the Dean of the Isles, his descendent possessed Castle Douan; and 'He and his bluid', says the Dean, 'are the best men in that countrey.'

The manner in which Robert Bruce discovered his arrival to his friends, is so descriptive of the simplicity of the times, that it merits

---

[18] Torfoeus, 71.
[19] Buchanan, lib. VII, ch. 62.

notice, in the very words of the faithful old poet, historian of that great prince:

> *The King then blew his horn in by,*
> *And gart his men that were him by,*
> *Hold them still in privitie:*
> *And syn again his horn blew he:*
> *James of Dowglas heard him blow,*
> *And well the blast soon can he know:*
> *And said surelie yon is the King,*
> *I ken him well by his blowing:*
> *The third time therewith also he blew,*
> *And then Sir Robert Boyde him knew,*
> *And said, yon is the King but dreed,*
> *Go we will forth to him good speed.*

Barbour

About the year 1334 this island appears to have formed part of the estate of Robert Stuart, Great Steward of Scotland, afterwards Robert II. At that time the inhabitants took arms to support the cause of their master, who afterwards, in reward, not only granted at their request an immunity from their annual tribute of corn, but added several new privileges, and a donative to all the inhabitants that were present.[20]

In 1456 the whole island was ravaged by Donald, Earl of Ross, and Lord of the Isles. At that period it was still the property of James II, but in the reign of his successor, James III when that monarch matched his sister to Thomas, Lord Boyd, he created him Earl of Arran, and gave him the island as a portion: soon after, on the disgrace of that family, he caused the countess to be divorced from her unfortunate husband; and bestowed both the lady and island on Sir James Hamilton, in whose family it continues to this time, a very few farms excepted.

Arran is of great extent, being twenty-three miles from Sgreadan Point north to Beinnean south; and the number of inhabitants are about seven thousand, who chiefly inhabit the coasts; the far greater part of the country being uninhabitable by reason of the vast and barren mountains. Here are only two parishes, Kilbride and Kilmore,

---

[20] Boethius, 318.

with a sort of chapel of ease to each, founded in the last century, in the golden age of this island, when it was blessed with Anne, Duchess of Hamilton, whose amiable disposition and humane attention to the welfare of Arran, render at this distant time, her memory dear to every inhabitant. Blessed preeminence! when power and inclination to diffuse happiness concur in persons of rank.

The principal mountains of Arran are, Goatfield, or Gaoilbheinn, or 'the mountain of the winds', of a height equal to most of the Scottish Alps, composed of immense piles of moorstone, in form of woolpacks, clothed only with lichens and mosses, inhabited by eagles and ptarmigans. Beinn-Bharrain, or 'the sharp-pointed'; Ceum-na-Caillich, 'the step of the carline' or 'old hag'; and Grianan Athol, 'that yields to none in ruggedness'.

The lakes are Loch Jorsa, where salmon come to spawn. Loch Tana; Loch-na-h-Jura, on the top of the high hill; Loch Mhachrai, and Loch-knoc-a-charbeil, full of large eels. The chief rivers are, Abhan-mhor, Moina-mhor, Slaodrai-machrai and Jorsa; the two last remarkable for the abundance of salmon.

The quadrupeds are very few: only otters, wild cats, shrew-mice, rabbits and bats: the stags which used to abound, are now reduced to about a dozen. The birds are eagles, hooded crows; wild pigeons, stares, black game, grouse, ptarmigans, daws, green plovers and curlews. Mrs Stuart, in ascending Goatfield, found the secondary feather of an eagle, white with a brown spot at the base, which seemed to belong to some unknown species. It may be remarked that the partridge, at present inhabits this island, a proof of the advancement of agriculture.

The climate is very severe: for besides the violence of winds, the cold is very rigorous; and snow lay here in the valley for thirteen weeks of the last winter. In summer the air is remarkably salubrious, and many invalids resort here on that account, and to drink the whey of goats' milk.

The principal disease here is the pleurisy: smallpox, measles and chin-cough visit the island once in seven or eight years. The practice of bleeding twice every year seems to have been intended as a preventative against the pleurisy: but it is now performed with the utmost regularity at spring and fall. The Duke of Hamilton keeps a surgeon in pay; who at those seasons makes a tour of the island. On notice of his approach, the inhabitants of each farm assemble in the open air; extend their arms; and are bled into a hole made in the ground, the common receptacle of the vital fluid.

In burning fevers a tea of wood sorrel is used with success, to allay the heat.

An infusion of ramsons or *Allium ursinum* in brandy is esteemed here a good remedy for the gravel.

The men are strong, tall and well-made; all speak the Erse language, but the ancient habit is entirely laid aside. Their diet is chiefly potatoes and meal; and during winter, some dried mutton or goat is added to their hard fare. A deep dejection appears in general through the countenances of all: no time can be spared for amusement of any kind; the whole being given for procuring the means of paying their rent; of laying in their fuel, or getting a scanty pittance of meat and clothing.

The leases of farms are 19 years. The succeeding tenants generally find the ground little better than a *caput mortuum*; and for this reason; should they at the expiration of the lease leave the lands in a good state, some avaricious neighbours would have the preference in the next setting, by offering a price more than the person who had expended part of his substance in enriching the farm could possibly do. This induces them to leave it in the original state.

The method of letting a farm is very singular: each is commonly possessed by a number of small tenants; thus a farm of forty pounds a year is occupied by eighteen different people, who by their leases are bound, conjunctly and severally, for the payment of the rent to the proprietor. These live in the farm in houses clustered together, so that each farm appears like a little village. The tenants annually divide the arable land by lot; each has his ridge of land, to which he puts his mark, such as he would do to any writing: and this species of farm is called *runrig*, i.e. 'ridge'. They join in ploughing; every one keeps a horse or more; and the number of those animals consume so much corn as often to occasion a scarcity; the corn and peas raised being (much of it) designed for their subsistence, and that of the cattle, during the long winter. The pasture and moorland annexed to the farm is common to all the possessors.

All the farms are open. Enclosures of any form, except in two or three places, are quite unknown: so that there must be a great loss of time in preserving their corn, etc. from trespass. The usual manure is seaplants, coral and shells.

The *runrig* farms are now discouraged; but since the tenements are let by *roup*, or auction, and advanced by an unnatural force to above double the old rent, without any allowance for enclosing; any example set in agriculture; any security of tenure, by lengthening the leases; affairs will turn retrograde, and the farms relapse into their old state of rudeness; migration will increase (for it has begun) and the rents be reduced even below their former value: the late rents were scarce twelve hundred a year; the expected rents three thousand.

The produce of the island is oats; of which about five thousand bolls, each equal to nine Winchester bushels, are sown: five hundred of beans, few peas, and above a thousand bolls of potatoes, are annually set: notwithstanding this, five hundred bolls of oatmeal are annually imported, to subsist the natives.

The livestock of the island is 3,183 milk cows; 2,000 cattle, from one to three years old; 1,058 horses; 1,500 sheep; and dried for winter provision, or sold at Greenock. The cattle are sold from forty to fifty shillings per head, which brings into the island about £1,200 per annum: I think that the sale of horses also brings in about £300. Hogs were introduced here only two years ago. The herring fishery round the island brings in £300. The sale of herring nets, £100, and that of thread about £300, for a good deal of flax is sown here. These are the exports of the island; but the money that goes out for mere necessaries is a melancholy drawback.

The women manufacture the wool for the clothing of their families; they set the potatoes, and dress and spin the flax. They make butter for exportation, and cheese for their own use.

The inhabitants in general are sober, religious and industrious: great part of the summer is employed in getting peat for fuel, the only kind in use here; or in building or repairing their houses, for the badness of the materials requires annual repairs: before and after harvest they are busied in the herring fishery; and during winter the men make their herring nets; while the women are employed in

spinning their linen and woollen yarn. The light they often use is
that of lamps. From the beginning of February to the end of May,
if the weather permits, they are engaged in labouring their ground:
in autumn they burn a great quantity of fern, to make kelp. So
that, excepting at New Year's Day, at marriages, or at the two or
three fairs in the island, they have no leisure for any amusements:
no wonder is there then at their depression of spirits.

This forms part of the county of Bute, and is subject to the same
sort of government: but besides, justice is administered at the baron's
baily court, who has power to fine as high as twenty shillings; can
decide in matters of property, not exceeding forty shillings; can
imprison for a month; and put delinquents into the stocks for three
hours, but that only during day time.

Take a ride into the country: descend into the valley at the head
of the bay; fertile in barley, oats and peas. See two great stones, in
form of columns, set erect, but quite rude: these are common to
many nations; are frequent in North Wales, where they are called
main hirion, i.e. 'tall stones', *meini gwir*, or 'men pillars', and *lleche*:
are frequent in Cornwall, and are also found in other parts of our
island: their use is of great antiquity; are mentioned in the Mosaic
writings as memorials of the dead, as monuments of friendship, as
marks to distinguish places of worship, or of solemn assemblies.[21]
The northern nations erected them to perpetuate the memory of
great actions, such as remarkable duels; of which there are proofs
both in Denmark and in Scotland; and the number of stones was
proportionable to the number of great men who fell in the fight:[22]
but they were besides erected merely as sepulchral for persons of
rank who had deserved well of their country.[23]

Not far from hence is a stone, the most singular that I ever
remember to have seen, and the only one of the kind that ever fell
within my observation: this lies on the ground, is twelve feet long,
two broad, one thick; has at one end the rude attempt to carve
a head and shoulders, and was certainly the first deviation from

[21] Joshua XXIV, 26.
[22] Wormii, *Monum Dan.*, 62, 63. Boethius, *Scot. Prisc. et Recentes Mores*, 10.
[23] *Hist. Scot.*, 20.

the former species of monument; the first essay to give to stone a resemblance to the human body. All that the natives say of this, that it was placed over a giant, and is called MacBhrolchin's Stone.

Ascend a steep hill, with vast gullies on the side; and, on descending, arrive in a plain inhabited by curlews, resorting there to breed, and which flew round our heads like lapwings. At a place called Monquil is a small circle of small stones, placed close to each other: whether a little Druidical place of worship, or of assembly; or whether a family place of sepulture, as is usual with the northern nations, is not easy to determine.[24] If an urn is found in the centre of this coronet, as is not uncommon, the doubt will cease.

Pass by the River Machrai, flowing through a rocky channel, which, in one part has worn through a rock, and left so contracted a gap at the top as to form a very easy step across. Yet not long ago a poor woman in the attempt, after getting one foot over, was struck with such horror at the tremendous torrent beneath, that she remained for some hours in that attitude, not daring to bring her other foot over, till some kind passenger luckily came by, and assisted her out of her distress.

Arrive at Torness, an extensive plain of good ground, but quite in a state of nature: seems formerly to have been cultivated, for there appear several vestiges or dikes, which might have served as boundaries. There is a tradition that in old times the shores were covered with woods; and this was the habitable part.

The want of trees in the internal part at present, and the kindly manner in which they grow about Brodic, favour this opinion.

On this plain are the remains of four circles, in a line, extending north-east by south-west; very few stones are standing to perfect the enclosure, but those are of a great size; and stand remote from each other. One is fifteen feet high and eleven in circumference. On the outside of these circles are two others: one differs from all I have seen, constituting of a double circle of stones and a mound within the lesser. Near these are the relics of a stone chest, formed

---

[24] *Olaus Magnus*, lib. I, ch. 16. Various circles of this nature are engraven in Dahlbert's *Suecia Hodierna et Antiqua*, tab. 104. Other very curious antiquities similar to these, are preserved in tab. 280, 281, 315, 322, and 323.

of five flat stones, the length of two yards in the inside: the lid or top is lost. In the middle of these repositories were placed the urn filled with the ashes of the dead to prevent its being broken; or to keep the earth from mixing with the blunt remains. In all probability there had been a cairn or heap of stones above.

By the number of the circles; and by their sequestered situation, this seems to have been sacred ground. These circles were formed for religious purposes: Boethius relates, that Mainus, son of Fergus I, a restorer and cultivator of religion after the Egyptian manner (as he calls it) instituted several new and solemn ceremonies: and caused great stones to be placed in form of a circle; the largest was situated towards the south, and served as an altar for the sacrifices to the immortal gods.[25] Boethius is right in part of his account: but the object of the worship was the sun,[26] and what confirms this, is the situation of the altar pointed towards that luminary in his meridian glory. In this place the altar and many of the stones are lost; probably carried to build houses and dikes not very remote from the place.

At a small distance farther is a cairn of a most stupendous size, formed of great pebbles: which are preserved from being scattered about by a circle of large stones, that surround the whole base: a circumstance sometimes usual in these monumental heaps.[27]

Descend through a narrow cleft of a rock to a part of the western shore called Drum-an-Dùin, or 'the ridge of the fort', from a round tower that stands above. The beach is bounded by cliffs of whitish gritstone, hollowed beneath into vast caves. The most remarkable are those of Fin MacCoul, or Fingal, the son of Cumhal, the father of Ossian, who, tradition says, resided in the island for the sake of hunting. One of these caverns is a hundred and twelve feet long, and thirty high, narrowing to the top like a Gothic arch; towards the end it branches into two: within these two recesses, which penetrate far, are on each side several small holes, opposite to each other: in these were placed transverse beams, that held the pots in which the

[25] Boethius, lib. II, 15.
[26] Doctor Macpherson, 314, and Mr Macpherson, 162.
[27] Borlase *Antiq. Cornwal*, tab. xvii, fig. 4.

heroes seethed their venison; or probably, according to the mode of the times, the bags formed of skins of animals slain in the chase,[28] which were filled with flesh, and served as kettles sufficiently strong to warm the contents; for the heroes of old devoured their meat half raw, holding, that the juices contained the best nourishment.[29]

On the front of the division between these recesses, and on one side, are various very rude figures, cut on the stone, of men, of animals, and of a claymore or two-handed sword: but whether these were the amusements of the Fingallian age, or of after-times, is not easy to be ascertained; for caves were the retreats of pirates as well as heroes. Here are several other hollows adjacent, which are shown as the stable, cellars and dog-kennel of the great MacCoul: one cave, which is not honoured with a name, is remarkably fine, of great extent, covered with a beautiful flat roof, and very well lighted by two august arches at each end: through one is a fine perspective of the promontory Carn-baan, or 'the white heap of stones', whose side exhibits a long range of columnar rocks (not basaltic) of hard grey whinstone, resting on a horizontal stratum of red stone: at the extremity one of the columns is insulated, and forms a fine obelisk.

After riding some time along the shore, ascend the promontory: on the summit is an ancient retreat, secured on the land side by a great dike of loose stones, that encloses the accessible part; within is a single stone, set erect; perhaps to mark the spot where the chieftain held his council, or from whence he delivered his orders.

From this stone is a fine view of Cantyre, the western side of Arran, being separated from it by a strait about eight miles wide.

Leave the hills, and see at Feorling another stupendous cairn, a hundred and fourteen feet over, and of a vast height; and from two of the opposite sides are two vast ridges; the whole formed of rounded stones, or pebbles, brought from the shores. These immense accumulations of stones are the sepulchral protections of the heroes among the ancient natives of our islands: the stone chests, the

---

[28] Major, lib. V, 215.
[29] Boethius, *Mores Scot.*, II.

repository of the urns and ashes, are lodged in the earth beneath; sometimes one, sometimes more, are found thus deposited; and I have one instance of as many as seventeen of these stone chests being discovered under the same cairn. The learned have assigned other causes for these heaps of stones; have supposed them to have been, in times of inauguration, the places where the chieftain-elect stood to show himself to the best advantage to the people; or the place from whence judgment was pronounced; or to have been erected on the roadside in honour of Mercury; or to have been formed in memory of some solemn compact.[30] These might have been the reasons, in some instances, where the evidences of stone chests and urns are wanting; but those generally are found to overthrow all other systems.

These piles may be justly supposed to have been proportioned in size to the rank of the person, or to his popularity: the people of a whole district assembled to show their respect to the deceased, and, by an active honouring of his memory, soon accumulated heaps equal to those that astonish us at this time. But these honours were not merely those of the day; as long as the memory of the deceased endured, not a passenger went by without adding a stone to the heap: they supposed it would be an honour to the dead, and acceptable to his manes:

> *Quanquam festinas, non est mora longa: licebit*
> *Injecto ter pulvere, curras.*

This moment there is a proverbial expression among the Highlanders allusive to the old practice: a suppliant will tell his patron, '*Curri mi cloch er do charne*', 'I will add a stone to your cairn', meaning 'when you are no more I will do all possible honour to your memory.'[31]

There was another species of honour paid to the chieftains, that I believe is still retained in this island, but the reason is quite lost; that of swearing by his name, and paying as great a respect to that

---

[30] Vide Rowland's *Mon. Ant.*, 50 and Borlase *Antiq. Cornwal*, 209.
[31] Dr Macpherson, 319.

as to the most sacred oath:[32] a familiar one in Arran is, by Nail: it is at present unintelligible, yet is suspected to have been the name of some ancient hero.

These cairns are to be found in all parts of our islands, in Cornwall, Wales, and all parts of North Britain; they were in use among the northern nations; Dahlberg, in his 323rd plate has given the figure of one. In Wales they are called *carneddau*; but the proverb taken from them, with us, is not of the complimental kind: '*Karn ar dy ben*', or 'a cairn on your head' is a token of imprecation'.

Dine at Skeddag , a small hamlet: after dinner, on the roadside, see, in Shiskin or Seasgain churchyard, a tomb called that of St Maolios, that is, 'the servant of Jesus'. The saint is represented in the habit of a priest, with a chalice in his hands, and a crozier by him: the stone was broken about half a year ago by some sacrilegious fellow, in search of treasure; but an islander, who stood by, assured me, that the attempt did not go unpunished, for soon after the audacious wretch was visited with a broken leg.

St Maolios was a companion of St Columba: the last chose Iona for the place of his residence; this saint fixed on the little island of Lamlash, and officiated by turns at Shiskin, where he died at the age of a hundred, and was there interred.

In this evening's ride pass by some farms, the only cultivated tract in the internal parts of the country: saw one of forty pounds a year, which had sixty acres of arable land annexed to it. Am informed that the general size or value of farms was eight or nine pounds a year.

Return to Brodic Castle. Take a ride to visit other parts of the island: go through the village of Brodic, at a small distance beneath the castle. Visit Glencloy, a plain, on which are five earthen tumuli, or barrows, placed in a row, with another on the outside of them: on the top of one is a depression, or hollow; on that of another is a circle of stones, whose ends just appear above the earth. These are probably the memorial of some battle: the common men were placed

---

[32] Boethius, lib. I, 4.

beneath the plain barrows; the leaders under those distinguished by the stones.

Pass by the ruins of Kirkmichel Chapel: visit Mr Fullerton, descended from the MacLouis, originally a French family, but settled in this island near seven hundred years. He is one of the lesser proprietors of this island: his farm is neat, well-cultivated, and enclosed with very thriving hedges. Robert Bruce, out of gratitude for the protection he received from this gentleman's ancestor, Fergus Fullerton, gave him a charter, dated at Arnele, Nov 26, in the second year of his reign, for the lands of Killmichel and Arywhonyne, or Straithoughlain, which are still in the family.

A mile farther is a retreat of the ancient inhabitants, called Torranschian Castle, surrounded with a great stone dike. Here Robert Bruce sheltered himself for some time, under the protection of MacLouis.

Two miles farther east, near the top of the great hill Dunfuin, on the brow, is a great stratum of most singular stone, of a dull black-green cast, smooth glossy surface, shattery in its composition, semi-transparent, in small pieces, and of a most vitreous appearance: it sometimes breaks into forms rather regular, and like those of that species called Iceland crystal; but cannot be reduced to that class, as it strikes fire with steel, and refuses to ferment with acids. Some pieces, more mature, break like glass; of which it seems an imperfect species, less pure than the Iceland agate,[33] and like that to have been the effect of a volcano.

The other fossil productions of this island, that I had an opportunity of seeing, were,

An iron ore, *Bolus martialis*, Cronsted, sect. 87,207.

A most ponderous white spar, in all probability containing lead, found near Sannox.

The stone called *Breccia quartzosa*, Cronsted, sect. 275.

Schistus ardesia of Linnaeus, p. 38, no. 5. A fine smooth black kind of slate.

Granites durus grieseus of Cronsted, sect. 270, no. 26. Like our Cornish moorstone, but the particles finer.

---

[33] *Pumex vitreus*. Lin. *Syst.* III, 182.

Very fine and large black crystals, that would be useful to seal-cutters and lapidaries.

Great variety of beautiful sardonyxes; and other beautiful stones, indiscriminately called Scotch pebbles.

A coalmine has formerly been worked near the Cock of Arran, at the north end of the island. The coal had all the qualities of that of Kilkenny, and might prove of the utmost benefit to this country, was the work pursued; not only as it might prove the means of restoring the salt-pans, which formerly flourished here, but be of the utmost benefit to agriculture, in burning the limestone which abounds in many parts.

In the course of my ride, on the other side of the hill of Dunsuin, facing the bay of Lamlash, saw, on the roadside a cairn, of a different kind to what I had seen before: it was large, of an oblong form, and composed like the others, of round stones; but along the top was a series of cells, some entire, but many fallen in; each was covered with a single flat stone of a great size, resting on others upright, that served as supports; but I could not count them by reason of the lapse of the lesser stones. Dr Borlase says that in Cornwall the number of upright stones are three; but in Wales they sometimes exceed that number.

These cells are called in Wales, *cromlech* and *cest-va en*, or 'stone chests': are spoken of largely by Mr Rowland,[34] and by Dr Borlase,[35] and by Wormius, under the name of *ara*, or 'altar';[36] the first is divided in his opinion, for he partly inclines to the notion of their having been altars, partly to their having been sepulchres: he supposes them to have been originally tombs, but that in after-times sacrifices were performed on them to the heroes deposited in them: but there can be no doubt of the former. Mr Keyser preserves an account of King Harold having been interred beneath a tomb of this kind in Denmark; and Mr Wright discovered in Ireland a skeleton deposited beneath one of these *cromlech*.[37] The great similarity

[34] 48.
[35] 213, etc.
[36] 105.
[37] Louthiana.

of the monuments throughout the north, evinces the sameness of religion to have been spread in every part, perhaps with some slight deviations. Many of these monuments are both British and Danish; for we find them where the Danes never penetrated. It must not be forgotten, that at one end of the cairn in question are several great stones, some extending beyond the cairn; and on one side is a large erect stone, perhaps an object of worship.

Return near the shore at the head of Brodic Bay, and see a vast stratum of coral and shells, the gift of the sea some ages ago, some part being covered with peat.

In the afternoon leave Brodic Castle, cross a hill, descend by the village of Kilbride, and reach the harbour of Lamlash, where our vessel lay at anchor in the safest port in the universe, a port perfectly Virgilian: a beautiful semilunar bay forms one part: while the lofty island of Lamlash extending before the mouth secures it from the east winds: leaving on each side a safe and easy entrance. The whole circumference is about nine miles; and the depth of the water is sufficient for the largest ships. This is the place of quarantine: at this time three merchantmen belonging to Glasgow lay here for that purpose, each with the guard-boat astern.

In the bottom of the bay was a fine circular basin or pier now in ruins; the work of the good Duchess of Hamilton.

Land on the island of Lamlash, a vast mountain, in great part covered with heath; but has sufficient pasture and arable land to feed a few milk cows, sheep and goats, and to raise a little corn and a few potatoes.

In the year 1558, the English fleet under the Earl of Sussex, after ravaging the coast of Cantyre, at that time in possession of James MacConnel, landed in this bay, and burned and destroyed all the neighbouring country; proceeded afterwards to Cumray, and treated it in the same manner.

Buchanan gives this the Latin name of Molas and Molassa, from its having been the retreat of St Maolios: for the same reason it is called the Holy Island, and Hellan Leneow, or that of saints, and sometimes Ardnamolas.[38] St Maolios's cave, the residence of that

---

[38] Fordun, lib. II, ch. 10.

holy man, his well of most salutary water, a place for bathing, his chair, and the ruins of his chapel are shown to strangers; but the walk is far from agreeable, as the island is greatly infested with vipers.

The Dean of the Isles says, that 'on this isle of Molass was foundit by John Lord of the Isles ane Monastry of Friars which is decayit'. But notwithstanding this, it contributed largely to support of others on the mainland. Thus Lamlash and the lands round the bay; and those from Corry to Loch Ranza, were annexed to the abbey of Kilwhinnin. And those of Shiskin, Kilmore, Torelin, and Benans to that of Sandale or Saddel in Cantyre. I imagine that I must have seen the site of it from the top of Carnbaan: therefore take the liberty of mentioning it as having been a convent of Cistercians, founded by Reginaldus, son of Somerled, Lord of the Isles: the same Somerled who was slain near Renfrew in 1164. Here was also a castle belonging to the successors of that petty prince; whose owner Angus, Lord of the Isles, gave protection during his distresses to Robert Bruce.

Weighed anchor at half an hour past one in the morning, and going through the south passage of the harbour, get into the middle of the firth. Have a magnificent view on all sides of Arran and Lamlash, and the coast of Cantyre on one side; and of the coasts of Cunningham and Carrick on the other. In front lay the hills of Galloway and the coast of Ireland; and the vast crag of Ailsa, appearing here like an inclined haycock, rose in the midst of the channel. In our course leave to the west the little and low island of Plada, opposite to, and as if rent from that of Arran, a circumstance the name from *bladhan*, 'to break', seems to import.

After a very tedious calm reach the craig of Ailsa, and anchor on the north-east within fifty yards of the side in twelve fathom water, gravelly bottom. On this side is a small beach: all the rest is a perpendicular rock for an amazing height, but from the edges of the precipice, the mountain assumes a pyramidal form: the whole circumference of the base is two miles. On the east side is a stupendous and amazing assemblage of precipitous columnar rocks of great height rising in wild series one above the other: beneath these, amidst the ruins that had fallen from time to time, are groves of elder trees, the only trees of the place; the sloping surface being almost entirely covered with fern and short grass. The quadrupeds that inhabit this rock are goats and rabbits: the birds that nestle in the precipices are numerous as swarms of bees; and not unlike them in their flight to and from the crag. On the verge of the precipice dwell the gannets and the shags. Beneath are guillemots, and the razorbills: and under them the grey gulls and kittiwakes, helped by their cry to fill the deafening chorus. The puffins made themselves burrows above: the sea-pies found a scanty place for their eggs near the base. Some land birds made this their haunt: among them ravens, hooded crows, pigeons, wheatears and rock larks; and what is wonderful, throstles exerted the same melody in this scene of horror as they do in the groves of Hertfordshire.

Three reptiles appeared here very unexpectedly: the naked black snail, the common and the striped shell-snail: not volunteer inhabitants, but probably brought in the salads of some visitants from the neighbouring shores.

This rock is the property of the Earl of Cassils, who rents it for £33 per annum to people who come here to take the young gannets for the table; and the other birds for the sake of their feathers. The last are caught when the young birds are ready for their flight. The fowler ascends the rocks with great hazard, is provided with a long rod, furnished at the end with a short hair line with a running noose. This he slings round the neck of the bird, hawls it up and repeats it till he takes ten or twelve dozen in an evening.[39]

Land on the beach; and find the ruins of a chapel, and the vestiges of places inhabited by fishermen who resort here during the season for the capture of cod, which abound here from January to April, on the great bank, which begins a little south of Arran, passes this rock, and extends three leagues beyond. The fish are taken with long lines, very little different from those described in the third volume of the *British Zoology*, p. 193; a repetition is unnecessary: the fish are dried and then salted; but there are seldom sufficient caught for foreign exportation.

---

[39] I cannot learn where these feathers are used.

XIV

CRAG OF AILSA.

Moses Griffith del.   P. Mazell sculp.

With much difficulty ascend to the castle, a square tower of three storeys, each vaulted, placed pretty high on this only accessible part of the rock. The path is narrow, over a vast slope, so ambiguous that it wants but little of a true precipice: the walk is horrible, for the depth is alarming. It would have been thought that nothing but an eagle would have fixed his habitation here; and probably it was some chieftain not less an animal of rapine. The only mark of civilization I saw in the castle was an oven; a conveniency which many parts of North Britain are yet strangers to.

In 1597, one Barclay of Ladyland undertook the romantic design of possessing himself of this rock; and of fortifying it for the service of the Spaniards. He arrived there with a few assistants, as he imagined, undiscovered; but one day walking alone on the beach, he unexpectedly encountered Mr John Knox who was sent to apprehend him: and the moment he saw the unfriendly party, in despair, rushed into the sea, and put an end to his existence.[40]

Made a hearty dinner under the shade of the castle; and even at that height procured fine water from a spring within a hundred yards of the place. The view of the bay of Girvan, in Carrick, within nine miles, and that of Campbeltown, about twenty-two, bounded each side of the firth.

The weather was so hot that we did not ascend to the summit; which is said to be broad, and to have had on it a small chapel, designed (as is frequent on the promontories of foreign shores) for the devout seaman to offer up his prayer, of supplication for a safe voyage, or, of gratitude for a safe return.

In the evening return on board, and steer towards Campbeltown, but make very little way, by reason of the stillness of the night.

In the morning find ourselves within nine miles of the town, having to the south (near the end of Cantyre) Sanda, or Avoyn, or 'island of harbours';[41] so called from its being the station of the Danish fleets, while that nation possessed the Hebrides; a high island, about two miles long, inhabited by four families. In

---

[40] Spotiswood's *Hist. of Scot.*, 446, 447.
[41] Buchanan, lib. I, 35. The Dean of the Isles calls it Avoyn, 'fra the armies of Denmark callit in their leid, Havin'.

Fordun's time here was the chapel of St Annian, and a sanctuary for the refuge of criminals.[42] Near it is Sheep Island; and a mile to the east lies Peterson's Rock, dreaded by mariners. The Mull, or extremity of Cantyre, lies at a small distance beyond this group.

Direct Mr Thompson to carry the vessel round the Mull, and to wait under the isle of Gigha. Take the boat, and make for Campbeltown: after seven miles reach the mouth of the harbour, crossed by a small and high island, with a deep but narrow passage on one side: on the other, connected to the land by a beach, dry at the ebb of the tides, and so low, that strange ships, mistaking the entrance, sometimes run on shore. The harbour widens to a very considerable extent, is two miles in length, and of a considerable depth of water, even close to the town, which lies at the bottom.

Campbeltown is now a very considerable place, having risen from a petty fishing town to its present flourishing state in less than thirty years. About the year 1744 it had only two or three small vessels belonging to the port: at present there are seventy-eight sail, from twenty to eighty tons burden, all built for, and employed in, the herring fishery; and about eight hundred sailors are employed to man them. This town in fact was created by the fisher; for it was appointed the place of rendezvous for the busses; two hundred and sixty have been seen in the harbour at once; but their number declines since the ill-payment of the bounty. I do not know the gradual increase of the inhabitants here; but it is computed that there are seven thousand in the town and parish. Two ministers officiate; besides another for the church of the Seceders, called the relief house. This is a remarkable neat building, and quite shames that of the established church: was raised by a voluntary subscription of £2,300 collected chiefly among the posterity of oppressed natives of the Lowlands, encouraged to settle here (in times of persecution) by the Argyle family. These still keep themselves distinct from the old inhabitants, retain the zeal of their ancestors, and obstinately averse to patronage, but are esteemed the most industrious people in the country.

[42] Fordun, lib. II, ch. 10.

The ancient name of this place was Cean-loch-chille-Ciarain, or 'the end of the loch of St Kerran', a saint of the neighbourhood. The country, of which it is the capital, is Cantyre, the most southern part of Argyleshire; derived from *ceann*, 'a head' and *tire*, 'of the land': was the country of the Epidii of the Romans; and the extremity, the Epidii Promontorium, now the Mull of Cantyre, noted for the violence of the adverse tides, compared to the force of a mill-race, from whence the modern name. Magnus the Barefooted made a conquest of it, and added it to the Hebrides, making an island of it by the *ratio ultima regum*. Torfoeus says, that the ancient name was Saltiria, or Satiria, perhaps Norwegian.[43]

This peninsula, from the Tarbat to the Mull, is above forty miles long, and from five to twelve miles broad: is hilly, but, comparative to other parts, cannot be called mountainous: is open, and in general naked; but near Campbeltown are some thriving plantations. The country is at present a mixture of heath and arable land: the land is good, capable of bearing wheat, but little is raised for want of mills to grind it: either the inhabitants buy their flour from England, or send the grain they have to be ground in the shire of Air. Much bere is sown here, great quantities of potatoes raised, and near £800 worth annually exported. Numbers of black cattle are reared, but chiefly killed at home, and salted for the use of the busses at Campbeltown. Much butter and cheese is made; the last large and bad. There are, besides, sheep and goats; the last killed for winter provision.

Notwithstanding the quantity of bere raised, there is often a sort of dearth; the inhabitants being mad enough to convert their bread into poison, distilling annually six thousand bolls of grain into whisky. This seems a modern liquor, for in old times the distillation was from thyme, mint, anise, and other fragrant herbs;[44] and ale was much in use with them. The former had the same name with the *usquebaugh*, or 'water of life'; but, by Boethius's account, it was taken with moderation.

---

[43] Torfoeus, 73.
[44] Boethius, *De Moribus Scot.*, II.

The Duke of Argyle, the principal proprietor of this country, takes great pains in discouraging the pernicious practice; and obliges all his tenants to enter into articles, to forfeit five pounds and the still, in case they are detected in making this *liqueur d'enfer*; but the trade is so profitable that many persist in it, to the great neglect of manufactures. Before this business got ground, the women were accustomed to spin a great deal of yarn (for much flax is raised in these parts) but at present they employ themselves in distilling, while their husbands are in the field.

Rural economy is but at a low ebb here: his Grace does all in his power to promote that most useful of arts, by giving a certain number of bolls of burnt lime to those who can show the largest and best fallow; and allowing ten per cent out of the rents to such farmers who lay out any money in solid improvements; for example, in enclosing, and the like. The duke also shows much humanity in another instance, by permitting his tenants, in the places of his estates where stags inhabit, to destroy them with impunity; resigning that part of the ancient chieftains' magnificence, rather than beasts of chase should waste the bread of the poor.

Cantyre was granted to the house of Argyle after a suppression of a rebellion of the MacDonalds of the Isles (and I suppose of this peninsula) in the beginning of the last century,[45] and the grant was afterwards ratified by Parliament.[46] The ancient inhabitants were the MacDonalds, MacEachrans, MacKays, and MacMaths.

Take a ride along the west side of the bay. See, in Kilkerran churchyard, several tombs of artificers, with the instruments of their trades engraven: amongst others appear a goose, and shears, to denote that a tailor lay beneath. A little further, on the shore, are the ruins of Kilkerran Castle, built by James V when he visited this place in order to quell a rebellion: he was obliged to fly to it for protection, and, as is said, to abandon it to the fury of the insurgents, who took the fortress, and hung his governor.

Turn to the south, and visit some caves in the rocks that face the firth: these are very magnificent, and very various; the tops are

[45] *Br. Biography* II, 1141.
[46] Crawford's *Peerage*, 19.

lofty, and resemble Gothic arches; one has on all sides a range of natural seats; another is in form of a cross, with three fine Gothic porticos, for entrances; this had been the residence of St Kerran; had formerly a wall at the entrance, a second about the middle, and a third far up, forming different apartments. On the floor is the capital of a cross, and a round basin, cut out of the rock, full of fine water, the beverage of the saint in old times, and of sailors in the present, who often land to dress their victuals beneath this shelter. An ancient pair, upwards of seventy years of age, once made this their habitation for a considerable time.

Return, view the cross, in the middle of the town: a most beautiful pillar, richly ornamented with foliage, and with this inscription on one side: *Haec: est: crux: Domini: YVARI: M: H: EACHYRNA: quondam: Rectoris: de KYRECAN: et: Domini: ANDRE: nati: ejus: Rectoris de KIL: COMAN: qui hanc cruce fieri faciebat*. Mr Gordon (by report only) mentions this as a Danish obelisk, but does not venture the description, as he had not opportunity of seeing it: his informant said, that it was brought from Iona, which concurs with the tradition of this place.

At night am admitted freeman of Campbeltown, and, according to the custom of the place, consult the Oracle of the Bottle about my future voyage, assisted by a numerous company of brother burgesses.

Leave Campbeltown with a full sense of all the civilities received there. Ride over a plain about five miles wide. See on the roadside a great wheel, designed for the raising water from the neighbouring collieries. The coal is eight feet thick, dips one yard in five, and points north-east by north-west; is sold on the bank for four shillings per ton; but sufficient is not yet raised for the use of the country.

This plain is fruitful, pretty much enclosed, and the hedges grow well; a great encouragement to further experiments: the improved land is rented here from fifteen to twenty shillings an acre.

Observe on the roadside the ruins of the chapel of Cillchaovain, or Kilchyvain: within are some old gravestones, engraven with figures of a two-handed sword, and of dogs chasing deer.

Ride three miles along the sands of Machrai'-Shanais Bay, noted for the tremendous size and roaring of its waves in stormy seasons;

and for the loss of many ships, which by reason of the lowness of the land are deceived into destruction.

Dine at a tolerable house at Bar: visit the great cave of Bealach-a'-Chaochain, near the shore. Embark in a rotten, leaky boat, and passing through six miles of rippling sea, find late at night our vessel safe at anchor, under the east side of the isle of Gigha, in the little harbour of Caolas Gioglam, protected by Gigha, and the little isle of Cara on the west and south; and by a chain of vast rocks to the east: numbers appear just peeping above water in several parts; and others that run out far from the Cantyre shore correspond with these so exactly, as to make it probable that they once formed the same bed.

Land on Gigha: an island about six miles long, and one broad; the most eastern of the Hebrides: this, with Cara, forms a parish in the county of Bute, in the presbytery of Cantyre. Has in it no high hills, and is a mixture of rock, pasture, and arable land. Produces barley, bere, oats, flax, and potatoes. Malt is made here and exported; and about a hundred and fifty bolls of bere; insomuch that sometimes the natives themselves feel the want of it, and suffer by a scarcity arising from their own avarice. They also rear more cattle than they can maintain, and annually lose numbers for want of fodder.

The island is divided into thirty marklands, each of which ought to maintain fourteen cows and four horses; besides producing a certain quantity of corn. The bere yields five, the oats three-fold. Each markland is commonly occupied by one farmer, who has several married servants under him, who live in separate cottages, and are allowed to keep a few cattle and sheep. The wages are from three to four pounds a year to the men servants; from twenty to thirty shillings to the women. The young men employ themselves in the summer in the herring fishery; but during winter give themselves up entirely to an inactive life.

This island contains about five hundred inhabitants: and the revenue is about six hundred a year; most of it belonging to Mr Macneile of Taynish. In old times the laird was styled Thane of Gigha: his family has been long owner of these little territories, this sea-girt reign; but was dispossessed of it in 1549, by the clan

Donald;[47] and recovered it again; but history omits the time of restoration. Discontent has even reached this small island; and two families have migrated to America.

Breakfast with the minister, who may truly be said to be wedded to this flock. The ocean here forbids all wandering, even if inclination excited: and the equal lot of the Scotch clergy is a still stronger check to every aspiring thought: this binds them to their people; and invigorates every duty towards those to whom they consider themselves connected for life; this equal lot may perhaps blunt the ambition after some of the more specious accomplishments; but makes more than amends by sharpening the attention to those concerns which end not with this being.

Visit the few wonders of the isle: the first is a little well of a most miraculous quality, for in old times, if ever the chieftain lay here wind-bound, he had nothing more to do than cause the well to be cleared, and instantly a favourable gale arose. But miracles are now ceased.

Examine the ruins of a church, and find some tombs with two-handed swords, the *claidh-da-laimh* of the hero deposited beneath.

A little farther, at Kilchattan, is a great rude column, sixteen feet high, four broad, and eight inches thick, and near it, a cairn. On a line with this, at Cnoc-a'-Chara, is another, and still higher in the same direction, at Cnoc-a'-Crois, is a cross and three cairns; probably the cross, after the introduction of Christianity, was formed out of a pagan monument similar to the two former.

In a bottom a little east from these, is a large artificial mount of a square form, growing less and less towards the top, which is flat, and has the vestage of a breast wall around. The mount Romelborg in Sweden, engraven by M. Dahlberg, no. 325, is somewhat similar: this probably was the work of the Danes, the neighbouring nation.

Return to the shore: observe a vast bed of most pure and fine sand, useful in the glass manufacturer: the same species but defiled with a mixture of sea-sand, appears again on the opposite coast of Cantyre.

[47] Dean of the Isles, 7.

The birds that appear here at present are the common gull, common sandpiper, and sea-pie. The great Arctic diver, of the *British Zoology*, sometimes visits these seas: and is styled in the Erse, *murbhuachaille*, or 'the herdsman of the ocean'; because, as is pretended, it never leaves that element, never flies, and hatches the young beneath its wing.

The weather extremely fine; but so calm that Mr Thompson is obliged to tow the vessel out of this little harbour, which is of unequal depths, but unfit for vessels that draw more than fourteen feet water. Pass under Cara, an isle one mile long, divided by a narrow channel, south of Gigha, is inhabited by one family, and had once a chapel. At the south end it rises into a hill exactly formed like a loaf of bread. The property of this little place is in Mr MacDonald of Largis.

Attempt to steer for the island of Islay, but in vain. Am entertained with the variety and greatness of the views that abound the channel, the great Sound of Jura; to the east the mountains of Arran overtop the far-extending shores of Cantyre; to the west lies Jura, mountainous and rugged; four hills, naked and distinct, aspire above the rest, two of them known to the seamen by the name of 'the paps', useful in navigation: far to the north, just appears a chain of small isles; and to the south, the island of Rathry, the supposed Ricnea, or Ricinia of Pliny,[48] on the coast of Ireland, which stretches beyond far to the west.

[48] lib. IV., ch. 16.

VI

A BRIEF HISTORY
OF THE HEBRIDES,
THE HEBRIDES (1)

A Brief History of the Hebrides—Jura—Isle of Fruchlan—Paps of Jura—
Ilay—Sunderland—Loch Guirm—Dounvollan—Sanegmor Cave—Loch
Finlagan—Ilay—Oronsay—Colonsay

THE leisure of a calm gave ample time for reflection on the history
and greater events of the islands now in view, and of the others,
the objects of the voyage. In justice to that able and learned writer
the Rev Dr John Macpherson, late minister of Slate in Skie, let me
acknowledge the assistance I receive from his ingenious essay on
this very subject: for his labours greatly facilitate my attempt; not
undertaken without consulting the authors he refers to; and adding
numbers of remarks overseen by him, and giving a considerable
continuation of the history. It would be an ostentatious task to
open a new quarry, when such heaps of fine materials lie ready to
my hand.

All the accounts left us by the Greek and Roman writers are
enveloped with obscurity; at all times brief, even in their descriptions
of places they had easiest access to, and might have described with
the most satisfactory precision; but in remote places their relations

furnish little more than hints, the food for conjecture to the visionary antiquary.

That Pytheas, a traveller mentioned by Strabo, had visited Great Britain, I would wish to make only apocryphal: he asserts, that he visited the remoter parts; and that he had also seen Thule, the land of romance amongst the ancients; which all might pretend to have seen; but every voyager, to swell his fame, made the island he saw last, the *ultima Thule* of his travels. If Pytheas had reached these parts he might have observed, floating in the seas, multitudes of gelatinous animals, the Medusae of Linnaeus, and out of these have formed his fable: he made his Thule a 'composition of neither earth, sea, nor air; but like a composition of them all'; then, catching his simile from what floated before him, compares it to the lungs of the sea,[1] the Aristotelian idea of these bodies; and from him adopted by naturalists, successors to that great philosopher. Strabo very justly explodes these absurd tales, yet allows him merit in describing the climate of the places he had seen. As a farther proof of his having visited the Hebrides, he mentions their unfriendly sky, that prohibits the growth of the finer fruits; and that the natives are obliged to carry their corn under shelter, to beat the grain out, least it should be spoiled by the defect of the sun, and violence of the rains.[2] This is the probable part of his narrative: but when the time that the great geographer wrote is considered; at a period that these islands had been neglected for a very long space by the Romans; and when the difficulties of getting among a fierce and unfriendly nation must be almost insuperable, doubts innumerable, respecting the veracity of this relater, must arise: all that can be admitted in favour of him is, that he was a great traveller, that he might have either visited Britain, with some of the nations commercing with our isle, or have received from them accounts, which he afterwards dressed out mixed with the ornaments of fable. A traffic must have been carried on with the very northern inhabitants of our islands in the time of Pytheas, for one of the articles of commerce, mentioned by Strabo, the ivory bits, were made either of the teeth of the walrus, or of a species of whale native of the northern seas.

[1] *Hist. Ang.*, lib. XV. Strabo, lib. II, 71.
[2] Strabo, lib. IV, 139. This is also mentioned by Diodorus Siculus.

The geographer Mela, who flourished in the reign of Claudius, is the next who takes notice of our lesser islands. He mentions the Orcades as consisting of thirty; the Aemodae of seven. The Romans had then made a conquest of the former, and might have seen the latter; but from the words of the historian, it is probable that the Shetland islands were those intended; for he informs us, that the Aemodae were carried out over against Germany: the site of the Hebrides will not admit of this description, which agrees very well with the others; for the ancients extended their Germany, and its imaginary islands, to the extreme north.

Pliny the Elder is the next that mentions these remote places. He lived later than the preceding writers, and of course his information is fuller: by means of intervening discoveries, he has added ten more to the number of the Orcades: is the first writer that mentions the Haebudes, the islands in question; and joins in the same line the Aemoda, or, as it is in the best editions more properly written, the Acmodae,[3] or extreme point of the Roman expeditions to the north; as the Shetland isles in the highest probability were. Pliny and Mela agree in the number of the Aemoda, or Acmodae; the former makes that of the Hebrides thirty; an account extremely near the truth, deducting the little isles, or rather rocks, that surrounded most of the greater and many of them so indistinct as scarcely to be remarked, except on an actual survey.

Solinus succeeds Pliny: if he, as is supposed, was contemporary with Agricola, he has made very ill use of the light he might have received from the expeditions of that great general, whose officers might have furnished the historian with better materials than those he has communicated. He has reduced the number of the Haebudes, to five: he tells us, that 'the inhabitants were unacquainted with corn; and that they lived on fish and milk; that they had one king, as the islands were only separated from each other by narrow straits; that their prince was bound by certain rules of government, to do justice: and was prevented by poverty from deviating from the true course; being supported by the public, and allowed nothing that he could call his own: not even a wife; but then he was allowed free

---

[3] Lib. IV., ch. 16.

choice, by turns one out of every district of any female that caught his affection; which deprived him of all ambition about a successor'.[4]

By the number of these islands, and by the minute attention given by the historian to the circumstance of their being separated from each other by very narrow straits, I should imagine, that which is now called the Long Island and includes Lewis, North Uist, Benbecula, South Uist, and Barra, to have been the five Haebudes of Solinus, for the other great islands, such as Skie, etc., are too remote from each other to form the preceding very characteristic description of that chain of islands. These might naturally fall under the rule of our petty prince; almost the only probable part of Solinus's narrative.

After a long interval appears Ptolemy, the Egyptian geographer: he also enumerates five Ebuda; and has given each a name; the western Ebuda, the eastern, Ricina, Maleos, Epidium. Camden conjectures them to be the modern Skie, Lewis, Rathry or Racline, Mull, and Ilay: and I will not controvert his opinion.

The Roman historians give very little light into the geography of these parts. Tacitus, from whom most might have been expected, is quite silent about the names of places; notwithstanding he informs us that a fleet by command of Agricola performed the circumnavigation of Britain. All that he takes notice of is the discovery and the conquest of the Orkneys: it should seem that with the biographers of an ambitious nation, nothing seemed worthy of notice, but what they could dignify with the glory of victory.

It is very difficult to assign a reason for the change of name from Ebudae to Hebrides; the last is modern: and seems as the annotator on Dr Macpherson supposes, to have arisen from the error of a transcriber, who changed the 'u' into 'ri'.

From all that has been collected from the ancients, it appears, that they were acquainted with little more of the Hebrides than the bare names: it is probable that the Romans, either from contempt of such barren spots, from the dangers of seas, the violence of the tides, and horrors of the narrow sounds in the inexperienced ages of navigation, never attempted their conquest, or saw more of them,

---

[4] Polyhistor, ch. 35.

than what they had in sight, during the few circumnavigations of Great Britain, which were expeditions, more of ostentation than of utility.

The inhabitants had probably for some ages their own governors: one little king to each island, or to each group as necessarily required. It is reasonable to suppose, that their government was as much divided as that of Great Britain, which it is well known, was under the direction of numbers of petty princes before it was reduced under the power of the Romans.

No account is given in history of the time these islands were annexed to the government of Scotland. If we may credit our Saxon historians, they appear to have been early under the dominion of their Picts; for Bede and Adamnanus inform us that soon after the arrival of St Columba in their country, Brudeus, a Pictish monarch made the saint a present of the celebrated island of Iona.[5]

But neither the holy men of this island, nor the natives of the rest of the Hebrides, enjoyed a permanent repose after this event.

The first invasion of the Danes does not seem to be easily ascertained: it appears that they ravaged Ireland, and the isle of Rathry, as early as the year 735. In the following century their expeditions became more frequent: Harold Harfager, or 'the Light-Haired', pursued in 875, several petty princes, whom he had expelled out of Norway; who had taken refuge in the Hebrides, and molested his dominions by perpetual descents from those islands. He seems to have made a rapid conquest: he gained as many victories as he fought battles; he put to death the chief of the pirates, and made an indiscriminate slaughter of their followers.[6] Soon after his return, the islanders repossessed their ancient seats: and in order to repress their insults, he sent Ketil the Flat-nosed, with a fleet and some forces for that purpose. He soon reduced them to terms; but made his victories subservient to his own ambition; he made alliances with the reguli he had subdued; he formed intermarriages, and confirmed to them their old dominions. This effected, he sent back the fleet to Harold; openly declared himself independent, made himself Prince

[5] Bede, lib. III, ch. 4. Adamnanus, *Vit. Columbae*, lib. II., ch. 10 and 28.
[6] Torfoeus, 10.

of the Hebrides; and caused them to acknowledge him as such, by the payment of tribute, and the badges of vassalage.[7] Ketil remained during life, master of the islands, and his subjects appear to have been a warlike set of freebooters, ready to join with any adventurers. Thus when Eric, son of Harold Harfager, after being driven out of his own country, made an invasion of England, he put with his fleet into the Hebrides, received a large reinforcement of people, fired with the hopes of prey, and then proceeded on his plan of rapine.[8] After the death of Ketil, a kingdom was in after-times composed out of them, which from the residence of the little monarch in the Isle of Man was styled that of Man.[9] The islands became tributary to that of Norway for a considerable time,[10] and princes were sent from thence to govern:[11] but at length they again shook off the yoke. Whether the little potentates ruled independent, or whether they put themselves under the protection of the Scottish monarchs, does not clearly appear: but it is reasonable to suppose the last, as Donaldbane is accused of making the Hebrides the price of the assistance given him by the Norwegians against his own subjects. Notwithstanding they might occasionally seek the protection of Scotland, yet they never were without princes of their own. From the *Chronicles of the Kings of Man* we learn, that they had a succession.[12]

In 1089 is an evident proof of the independency of the islanders on Norway; for, on the death of Lagman, one of their monarchs, they sent a deputation to O'Brian, King of Ireland, to request a regent of royal blood to govern them during the minority of their young prince. They probably might in turn compliment in some other respects their Scottish neighbours: the islanders must have given them some pretence to sovereignty, for, in 1093, Donaldbane, King of Scotland, calls in the assistance of Magnus the Barefooted, King of Norway, and bribes him with a promise of all the islands:[13]

---

[7] Torfoeus, 14.
[8] Torfoeus, 23.
[9] Torfoeus, 29.
[10] Camden, 1444.
[11] Ibid.
[12] In Camden.
[13] Buchanan, lib. VII, ch. 23.

Magnus accepts the terms, but at the same time boasts that he does come to invade the territories of others, but only to resume the ancient rights of Norway. His conquests are rapid and complete, for, besides the islands, by an ingenious fraud he adds Cantyre to his dominions.[14]

The Hebrides continued governed by a prince dependent on Norway, a species of viceroy appointed by that court; and who paid, on assuming the dignity, ten marks of gold, and never made any other pecuniary acknowledgement during life: but if another viceroy was appointed, the same sum was exacted from him.[15] These viceroys were sometimes Norwegian, sometimes natives of the isles. In 1097 we find, that Magnus deputes a nobleman, of the name of Ingemund.[16] Yet they seem at times to have shaken off their independency, and to have assumed the title of King. Thus in 1206 we find, King John gives to his brother monarch Reginald, King of the Isles, a safe conduct; and in six years after, that Reginald swears fidelity to our monarch, and becomes his liegeman. It is probable they suited their allegiance to their conveniency; acknowledging the superiority of England, Scotland, or Norway according to the necessity of the times. Thus were the Hebrides governed, from the conquest, by Magnus, till the year 1263, when Acho, or Haquin, King of Norway, by an unfortunate invasion of Scotland, terminating in his defeat at Largs, so weakened the powers of his kingdom, that his successor, Magnus IV, was content in 1266 to make a cession of the islands to Alexander II; but not without stipulating for the payment of a large sum, and of a tribute of a hundred marks for ever, which bore the name of the annual of Norway. Ample provision was also made by Magnus in the same treaty, for the security of the rights and properties of his Norwegian subjects, who chose to continue in the isles; where many of their posterity remain to this day.

Notwithstanding this revolution, Scotland seems to have received no real acquisition of strength: the islands still remained governed

---

[14] Torfoeus, 73.
[15] *Hist. Normannorum*, 1000.
[16] *Chron. Man.*

by powerful chieftains, the descendants of Somerled, Thane of Heregaidel, or Argyle, who, marrying the daughter of Olave, King of Man, left a divided dominion to his sons Dugal and Reginald: from the first were descended the MacDougals of Lorn: from the last the powerful clan of the MacDonalds. The lordship of Argyle with Mull, and the islands north of it fell to the share of the first; Ilay, Cantyre, and the southern isles were the portion of the last: a division that formed the distinction of the Sudereys and Nordereys, which will be farther noticed in the account of Iona.

These chieftains were the scourges of the kingdom; they are known in history but as the devastations of a tempest: for their paths were marked with the most barbarous desolation. Encouraged by their distance from the seat of royalty; and the turbulence of the times, which gave their monarchs full employ, they exercised a regal power, and often assumed the title; but are more generally known in history by the style of the Lord of the Isles, or the Earls of Ross; and sometimes by that of the great Macdonald.

Historians are silent about their proceedings, from the retreat of the Danes, in 1263, till that of 1335, when John, Lord of the Isles, withdrew his allegiance.[17] In the beginning of the next century his successors were so independent, that Henry IV sent two ambassadors in the years 1405, and 1408 to form an alliance with the brothers, Donald and John: this encouraged them to commit fresh hostilities against their natural prince. Donald, under pretence of a claim to the earldom of Ross,[18] invaded and made a conquest of that county; but penetrating as far as the shire of Aberdeen, after a fierce but undecisive battle with the royal party, thought proper to retire, and in a little time to swear allegiance to his monarch, James I.[19] But he was permitted to retain the county of Ross, and assume the title of Earl. His successor, Alexander, at the head of ten thousand men, attacked and burnt Inverness: at length, terrified with the preparations made against him, fell at the royal feet, and obtained pardon as to life, but was committed to strict confinement.

[17]   Rymer's *Foedera* I, 140, 159.
[17b] Buchanan, lib. IX, ch. 22.
[18]   Rymer's *Foedera* VIII, 418, 527.
[19]   Boeth., lib. XVI, 342.

His kinsman and deputy, Donald Balloch, resenting the imprisonment of his chieftain, excited another rebellion, and destroyed the country with fire and sword: but on his flight was taken and put to death by an Irish chieftain, with whom he sought protection.

These barbarous inroads were very frequent with a set of banditti, who had no other motive in war but the infamous inducement of plunder. In p. 147 we see their cruel invasion of the shire of Lenox, and the horrible massacre in consequence.

In the reign of James II in the year 1461, Donald, another petty tyrant, an Earl of Ross and Lord of the Isles, renewed the pretence of independency; surprised the castle of Inverness, forced his way as far as Athol, obliged the earl and countess, with the principal inhabitants, to seek refuge in the church of St Bridget, in hopes of finding security from his cruelty by the sanctity of the place; but the barbarian and his followers set fire to the church, put the ecclesiastics to the sword, and, with great booty, carried the earl and countess prisoners to his castle of Claig, in the island of Ilay.[20] In a second expedition, immediately following the first, he suffered the penalty of his impiety: a tempest overtook him, and overwhelmed most of his associates; and he, escaping to Inverness, perished by the hands of an Irish harper:[21] his surviving followers returned to Ilay, conveyed the Earl and Countess of Athol to the sanctuary they had violated, and expiated their crime by restoring the plunder, and making large donations to the shrine of the offended saint.

John, successor to the last Earl of Ross, entered into alliance with Edward IV,[22] sent ambassadors to the court of England, where Edward empowered the Bishop of Durham, and Earl of Worcester, the Prior of St Johns of Jerusalem, and John, Lord Wenlock, to conclude a treaty with him, another Donald Balloch, and his son and heir, John. They agreed to serve the king with all their power,

---

[20] Buchanan, lib. XII, ch. 19.
[21] Holinshead *Hist. Scot.*, 279.
[22] For the sake of making a diversion in their favour, both Edward III and Henry IV condescended to enter into alliance with these reguli.

and to become his subjects: the earl was to have a hundred marks sterling for life in time of peace, and two hundred pounds in time of war; and these island allies, in case of the conquest of Scotland, were to have confirmed to them all the possessions to the north of the Scottish sea; and in case of a truce with the Scottish monarch, they were to be included in it.[23] But about the year 1476, Edward, from a change of politics, courted the alliance of James III and dropped his new allies. James, determined to subdue this rebellious race, sent against them a powerful army, under the Earl of Athol, and took leave of him with this good wish, 'Furth, Fortune, and fil the fetters'; as much as to say, 'Go forth, be fortunate, and bring home many captives': which the family of Athol have used ever since for its motto. Ross was terrified into submission, obtained his pardon, but was deprived of his earldom, which by Act of Parliament was then declared unalienably annexed to the crown; at the same time the king restored to him Knapdale and Cantyre,[24] which the earl had resigned, and invested him anew with the lordship of the Isles, to hold them of the king by service and relief.[25]

Thus the great power of the Isles was broken; yet for a considerable time after, the petty chieftains were continually breaking out into small rebellions, or harassed each other in private wars; and tyranny seems but to have been multiplied. James V found it necessary to make the voyage to the isles in person, in 1536; seized and brought away with him several of the most considerable leaders, and obliged them to find security for their own good behaviour, and that of their vassals. The names of these chieftains were (according to Lindesay[26]) Mydyart, MacConnel, MacLoyd of the Lewis, MacNiel, MacLane, MacIntosh, John Mudyart, MacKay, MacKenzie, and many others; but by the names of some of the above, there seem to have been continental as well as insular malcontents. He examined the titles of their holdings, and finding several to have been usurped, reunited their lands to the crown. In the same voyage he had the glory of causing surveys to

[23] Rymer's *Foed.* XI, 483, 484.
[24] Beoth. *Hist. Scot.*, App. 393.
[25] Holinshead, *Chr. Scot.*, 282.
[26] p. 152.

be taken of the coasts of Scotland, and of the islands, by his pilot, Alexander Lindesay; which were published in 1583, at Paris, by Nicholas de Nicholay, geographer to the French monarch.[27]

The troubles that succeeded the death of James occasioned a neglect of these insulated parts of the Scottish dominions, and left them in a state of anarchy: in 1614, the MacDonalds made a formidable insurrection, oppugning the royal grant of Cantyre to the Earl of Argyle, and his relations.[28] The petty chieftains continued in a sort of rebellion, and the sword of the greater, as usual in weak government, was employed against them: the encouragement and protection given by them to pirates, employed the power of the Campbells during the reign of James VI and the beginning of that of Charles I.[29]

But the turbulent spirit of the old times continued even to the present age. The heads of clans were by the divisions, and a false policy that predominated in Scotland during the reign of William III flattered with an unreal importance: instead of being treated as bad subjects, they were courted as desirable allies; instead of feeling the hand of power, money was allowed to bribe them into the loyalty of the times. They would have accepted the subsidies, notwithstanding they detested the prince that offered them. They were taught to believe themselves of such consequence that in these days turned to their destruction. Two recent rebellions gave legislature a late experience of the folly of permitting the feudal system to exist in any part of its dominions. The act of 1748 once deprived the chieftains of all power of injuring the public by their commotions.[30] Many of these reguli second this effort of legislature, and neglect no opportunity of rendering themselves hateful to their unhappy vassals, the former instruments of ambition. The halcyon

[27] *Br. Topograph.*, 627.
[28] *Feuds of the Clans*, 99. *Biogr. Britan.* II, 1141.
[29] In the beginning of the last century the islanders were continually harassing Ireland with their plundering invasions; or landing there to support rebellions; at length it was made treason to receive these 'Hebridian Redshanks', as they were styled. Camden II, 1407.
[30] The act for abolishing heritable jurisdictions, etc.

days are near at hand: oppression will beget depopulation; and depopulation will give us a dear-bought tranquillity.

The remainder of the day is past in the Sound of Jura: about twelve at noon a pleasant but adverse breeze arose, which obliged us to keep on towards the north, sometimes tacking towards the coast of Lower Knapdale, black with heathy mountains, verdant near the shores with tracts of corn: advance towards Upper Knapdale, rugged and Alpine: am told of a dangerous rock in the middle of the channel. About one o'clock on June 30, receive notice of getting into the harbour of the small isles of Jura, by the vessel's touching ground in the entrance. On the appearance of daylight find ourselves at anchor in three fathom and a half water, in a most picturesque bay, bounded on the west by the isle of Jura, with the paps overshadowing us; and to the east several little islands clothed with heath, leaving narrow admissions into the port at north and south: in the maps this is called the Bay of Meil.

Land on the greater isle, which is high and rocky. A boat filled with women and children crosses over from Jura, to collect their daily wretched fare, limpets and periwinkles. Observe the black guillemots in little flocks, very wild and much in motion.

Mr Campbell, principal proprietor of the island, is so obliging as to send horses: land in Jura, at a little village, and see to the right on the shore the church, and the minister's manse. Ride westward about five miles to Ardfin, the residence of Mr Campbell, seated above the Sound of Ilay.

Jura, the most rugged of the Hebrides, is reckoned to be about thirty-four miles long, and in general ten broad, except along the Sound of Ilay: is composed chiefly of vast mountains, naked and without the possibility of cultivation. Some of the south, and a little of the western sides only are improvable: as is natural to be supposed, this island is ill-peopled, and does not contain above seven or eight hundred inhabitants; having been a little thinned by the epidemic migrations.

The very old clans are the MacIlvuys and the MacRaines: but it seems to have changed masters more than once: in 1549, Donald of Cantyre, MacGuillayne of Doward, MacGuillayne of Kinlockbuy, and MacDuffie of Colonsay were the proprietors: MacLean of Mull had also a share in 1586.[31] At present Mr Campbell by purchase from Mr Campbell of Shawfield; Mr MacNeile of Colonsay, Mr Campbell of Shawfield; and the Duke of Argyle divide this mass of weather-beaten barrenness among them.

In 1607 Jura was included in the lordship of Cantyre, by charter, dated the last of May, then granted to Archibald, Earl of Argyle.

The produce is about three of four hundred head of cattle, sold annually at £3 each, to graziers who come for them. About a hundred horses are also sold annually: here are a few sheep with fleeces of most excellent fineness, and numbers of goats. In good seasons sufficient bere and oats are raised as will maintain the inhabitants: but they sometimes want, I suppose from the conversion of their grain into whisky. But the chief food of the common people is potatoes and fish and shellfish. It is to be feared that their competence of bread is very small. Bere produces four or five-fold; oats three-fold.

Fern ashes bring in about a hundred pounds a year: about two hundred tons of kelp is burnt annually, and sold from three pounds ten to four pounds per ton.

Sloes are the only fruits of the island. An acid for punch is made of the berries of the mountain ash: and a kind of spirit is also distilled from them.

Necessity hath instructed the inhabitants in the use of native dyes. Thus the juice of the tops of heath boiled supplies them with a yellow; the roots of the white water lily with a dark brown. Those of the yellow water iris with a black: and the *Galium verum*, *rù* of the islanders with a very fine red, not inferior to that from madder.

The quadrupeds of Jura are about a hundred stags. Some wildcats, otters, stoats, rats and seals. The feathered game, black cocks, grouse, ptarmigans, and snipes. The stags must here have been once more numerous, for the original name of the island was Deiry, or 'the isle of deer', so called by the Norwegians from the abundance of those noble animals.

[31] Dean of the Isles.

The women are very prolific, and very often bear twins. The inhabitants live to a great age, and are liable to very few distempers. Men of ninety work; and there is now living a woman of eighty who can run down a sheep. The account given by Martin of Gillour MacCrain, was confirmed to me. His age exceeded that of either Jenkins or Par: for he kept a hundred and eighty Christmases in his own house, and died in the reign of Charles I. Among the modern instances of longevity I forgot to mention John Armour, of Campbeltown, aged one hundred and four, who was a coxswain in our navy, at the time of the peace of Utrecht; and within these three years was stout enough to go out a-shooting.

This parish is supposed to be the largest in Great Britain, and the duty the most troublesome and dangerous: it consists of Jura, Colonsay, Oransay, Skarba, and several little isles divided by narrow and dangerous sounds; forming a length of not less than sixty miles; supplied by only one minister and an assistant.

Some superstitions are observed here to this time. The old women, when they undertake any cure, mumble certain rhythmical incantations; and, like the ancients, endeavour *decantare dolorem*. They preserve a stick of the wicken tree, or mountain ash, as a protection against elves.

I had some obscure account here of a worm, that in a less pernicious degree, bears some resemblance to the *Furia infernalis* of Linnaeus,[32] which in the vast bogs of Kemi drops on the inhabitants, eats into the flesh and occasions a most excruciating death. The fillan, a little worm of Jura, small as a thread and not an inch in length, like the *furia*, insinuates itself under the skin, causes a redness and great pain, flies swiftly from part to part; but is curable by a poultice of cheese and honey.

After dinner walk down to the Sound of Ilay, and visit the little island of Fruchlan, near to the shore, and a mile or two from the eastern entrance. On the top is a ruined tower of a square form, with walls nine feet thick; on the west side the rock on which it stands is cut through to a vast depth, forming a fosse over which had been the drawbridge. This fortress seemed as if intended to

---

[32] *Faun. Suec.*, no. 2070.

guard the mouth of the sound; and was also the prison where the MacDonalds kept their captives, and in old times was called the castle of Claig.

Ride along the shore of the sound: take boat at the ferry, and go a mile more by water: see on the Jura side some sheelins or summer huts for goatherds, who keep here a flock of eighty for the sake of the milk and cheese. The last are made without salt, which they receive afterwards from the ashes of sea-tang, and the tang itself which the natives lap it in.

Land on a bank covered with sheelins, the habitants of some peasants who attend the herds of milk cows. These formed a grotesque group; some were oblong, many conic, and so low that entrance is forbidden, without creeping through the little opening, which has no other door than a faggot of birch twigs, placed there occasionally: they are constructed of branches of trees, covered with sods; the furniture a bed of heath, placed on a bank of sod; two blankets and a rug; some dairy vessels, and above, certain pendent shelves made of basket work, to hold the cheese, the produce of the summer. In one of the little conic huts, I spied a little infant asleep, under the protection of a faithful dog.

Cross, on foot, a large plain of ground, seemingly improvable, but covered with a deep heath, and perfectly in a state of nature. See the Arctic gull, a bird unknown in South Britain, which breeds here on the ground: it was very tame, but, if disturbed, flew about like the lapwing, but with more flagging wing. After a walk of four miles, reach the paps: left the lesser to the south-east, preferring the ascent of the greatest, for there are three; Beinn-a-Chalaois, or 'the mountain of the sound'; Beinn Sheunta, or 'the hallowed mountain'; and Beinn-an-Òir, or 'the mountain of gold'. We began to scale the last; a task of much labour and difficulty; being composed of vast stones, slightly covered with mosses near the base, but all above bare, and unconnected with each other. The whole seems a cairn, the work of the sons of Saturn; and Ovid might have caught his idea from this hill, had he seen it.

> *Affectasse serunt regnum celeste Gigantes,*
> *Atlaque congestos struxisse ad sidera montes*

XV

Sheelins in JURA and a distant View of the Paps.

A Cottage in ILAY.

Gain the top, and find our fatigues fully recompensed by the grandeur of the prospect from this sublime spot: Jura itself afforded a stupendous scene of rock, varied with little lakes innumerable. From the west side of the hill ran a narrow stripe of rock, terminating in the sea, called, the Slide of the Old Hag. To the south appeared Ilay, extended like a map beneath us; and beyond that, the north of Ireland; to the west, Gigha and Cara, Cantyre and Arran, and the Firth of Clyde, bounded by Airshire; an amazing tract of mountains to the north-east, as far as Ben Lomond; Skarba finished the northern view; and over the western ocean were scattered Colonsay and Oransay, Mull, Iona, and its neighbouring group of isles; and still further the long extents of Tirey and Col just apparent.

On the summit are several lofty cairns, not the work of devotion, but of idle herds, or curious travellers. Even this vast heap of stones was not uninhabited: a hind passed along the sides full speed, and a brace of ptarmigans often favoured us with their appearance, even near the summit.

The other paps are seen very distinctly; each inferior in height to this, but all of the same figure, perfectly mamillary. Mr Banks and his friends mounted that to the south, and found the height to be two thousand three hundred and fifty-nine feet: but Beinn-an-Òir far overtopped it; seated on the pinnacle, the depth below was tremendous on every side.

The stones of this mountain are white (a few red), quartzy and composed of small grains; but some are brecciated, or filled with crystalline kernels, of an amethystine colour. The other stones of the island that fell under my observation, were a cinereous slate, veined with red, and used here as a whetstone; a micaceous sandstone; and between the small isles and Ardefin, abundance of a quartzy micaceous rockstone.

Return by the same road, cross the sound, and not finding the vessel arrived, am most hospitably received by Mr Freebairn, of Freeport, near Port Askaig, his residence on the southern side of the water, in the island of Ilay. Walk into the interior parts: on the way see abundance of rock and pit-marl, convertible in the best of manures. Visit the mines, carried on under the directions of

Mr Freebairn, since the year 1763: the ore is of lead, much mixed with copper, which occasions expense and trouble in the separation: the veins rise to the surface, have been worked at intervals for ages, and probably in the time of the Norwegians, a nation of miners. The old adventurers worked by trenching, which is apparent everywhere: the trenches are not above six feet deep; and the veins which opened into them not above five or six inches thick; yet, by means of some instrument, unknown to us at present, they picked or scooped out the ore with good success, following it in that narrow space to the length of four feet.

The veins are of various thickness; the strings numerous, conducting to large bodies, but quickly exhausted. The lead ore is good: the copper yields thirty-three pounds per hundred; and forty ounces of silver from a ton of metal. The lead ore is smelted in an air furnace, near Freeport; and as much sold in the pig, as, since the first undertaking by this gentleman, has brought in six thousand pounds.

Not far from these mines are vast strata of that species of iron called bog ore, of the concreted kind: beneath that large quantities of vitriolic mundic.

On the top of a hill, at some distance little distance, are some rocks, with great veins of emery running in the midst, in a horizontal direction, and from one to three feet thick.

A small quantity of quicksilver has been found in the moors, which ought to encourage a farther search.

Continue the walk to the neighbouring hill of Dun Bhorairaig: on the summit is a Danish fort, of a circular form, at present about fourteen feet high, formed of excellent masonry, but without mortar: the walls are twelve feet thick; and within their very thickness is a gallery, extending all around, the cavern for the garrison, or the place where the arms were lodged secure from wet. The entrance is low, covered at top with a great flat stone, and on each side is a hollow, probably intended for guardrooms, the inside of the fort is a circular area, of fifty-two feet diameter, with a stone seat running all round the bottom of the wall, about two feet high, where might have been a general resting-place of chieftains and soldiers.

On the outside of the fort, is another work, under which is the vestige of a subterraneous passage conducting into it, a sort of sallyport. Round the whole of this ancient fortress is a deep fosse. Three of these forts are generally within sight, so that in case of any attempt made on any one, a speedy alarm might be given to the others. Each was the centre of a small district; and to them the inhabitants might repair for shelter in case of any attack by the enemy: the notice was given from the fort, at night by the light of a torch, in the day by the sound of trumpet: an instrument celebrated among the Danes, sometimes made of brass, sometimes of horn.[33] The northern bards speak hyperbolically of the effect of the blast blown by the mouth of the heroes. The great Roland caused his trumpet Olivant to be heard twenty miles, and by the sound scattered about the very brains of one of his hearers.[34]

Return, and see on the roadside the ruins of chapel dedicated to St Columba; and near it an ancient cross.

Several gentlemen of the island favour me with a visit; and offer their service to conduct me to whatever was worthy of attention. Set out, in their company, on horseback, and ride south, crossing the country; find the roads excellent, but the country quite open; and too much good land in a state of nature, covered with heath, but mixed with plenty of natural herbage. See some stunted woods of birch and hazels, giving shelter to black game. On Imiriconart, or 'the plain ridge', are the vestiges of some butts, where the great MacDonald exercised his men at archery. Reach and dine at Kilarow, a village seated on Loch-in-Daal, a vast bay, that penetrates very deeply into the island. Opposite Bomore, ships of three hundred tons may ride with safety; which renders it a very convenient retreat.

Near Kilarow is the seat of the proprietor of the island. In the churchyard, is now prostrate a curious column, perhaps the shaft of a cross, for the top is broken off; and near it is a flat stone, with a hole in the middle, the probable pedestal. The figures and inscriptions are faithfully expressed in the plate.

---

[33] Wormii, *Museum*, 378. Boat's *Nat. Hist. Ireland*, 197. Smith's *Hist. Cork* II, 404.
[34] Wormii, *Mon. Dan.*, 381.

The two most remarkable gravestones are, one of a warrior, in a close vest and sleeves, with a sort of filibeg reaching to his knees, and the covering of his head of a conic form, like the *bared* of the ancient Irish:[35] a sword in his hand, and dirk by his side. The other has on it a great sword; a beautiful running pattern of foliage round it; and a griffin, a lion, and another animal at one end: near to them is a plain tablet, whether intended to be engraven, or whether, like Peter Papin, Lord of Utrique, he was a new knight, and wanted a device, must remain undetermined.

On a little flat hill, near the village, are the remains of the gallows: this was the place of execution in the days of the lords of the Isles. From hence is a pretty view of the loch, and the church and village of Bomore.

This part of the island is in many places bounded by a sort of terrace near twenty-two feet high, entirely formed of rounded sea-worn pebbles, now some hundred of yards distant from the medium line between high and low-water mark; and above twenty-five yards above it. This is another proof of the loss sustained by the sea in the Scottish islands; which, we know, makes more than reprisals in other places.

Ride along the head of the bay; at Tralaig, on a heathy eminence that faces the sands, are three deep hollows; their insides once lined with stone: these had been the watch-towers of the natives, to attend the motions of any invaders from the sea. Observe near them a great column of rude stone.

Pass by two deep channels, at present dry: these had been the harbour of the great MacDonald; had once piers, with doors to secure his shipping; a great iron hook, one of the hinges, having lately been found there.

The vessels then in use were called *birlings*, probably corrupted from *byrdinga*,[36] a species of ship among the Norwegians: but by the size of the harbours, it is plain that the navy of this potentate was not very considerable.

Turn a little out of the road to see the site of one of his houses, called Kilchoman, and a deep glen, which is pointed out to me as

[35] Mr O'Connor's *Diss. Hist. Ireland*, 112.
[36] Torfoeus, 106.

the place where he kept his fat cattle: such a conveniency was very necessary, as most of the establishment of the great MacDonald's household was paid in kind. Mr Campbell, of Ballole, favoured me with the state of it in 1542, which was as follows:

North Cantyre	South Cantyre
In money, £125 10 B.	In money, £162 8 B. 48
Oatmeal, 388 stones three-quarters	Meal, 480 st. 2 pt.
Malt, 4 ch. 10 bolls	Malt, 25 ch. 14 B. 2 fir.
Marts, i.e. a stall-fed ox, 6	Marts, 48
Cow, 1	Mutton, 53
Muttons, 41	Cheese, 342 ft. three-quarters
Cheese, 307 st. three-quarters	

Ilay and Reinds[37]

Money, £45 1d. Meal, 2,593 st. Marts, 301 Murron, 301 Cheese, 2161, 3 pt. Geese, 301 Poultry, 301

	£	B	d
Total in money, £332 18 6	332	18	6
Meal, 3,061 st. three-quarters, 2 pt. at 2 B	366	2	10
Malt, 30 chal. 8 bolls, 2 fir. at 5 B	122	2	6
Marts, 356, at 2 marks	553	6	8
Mutton, 595, at 2 B	45	11	10
Cheese	237	2	0
Geese, 301, at 4d	6	0	4
(Poultry, 301, at 2d)			
In Scotch money	1,666	2	11

Observe, near this place, a tract quite covered with clover, sown by nature. Proceed west, and am conducted to Sunderland,[38] the seat of — Campbell, Esq. The improvements of his lands are excellent, and the grass so good, and the fields so clean, as to vie with any place. Near the house, in a well-sheltered nook, is an apple orchard,

[37] A tract of Ilay to the west between Kilarow and Sunderland.
[38] Near this place is the dangerous bay of Sallego.

which bore plentifully: these, with strawberries, are the fruits of these remote islands; the climate denies other luxuries of this nature: and even in these articles, Pomona smiles but where she finds a warm protection.

About a mile from the house, on the coast, separated from the land by a deep but dry chasm, is a large rock, with a pretty large area on the top: on it are vestiges of various habitations, the retreat of the ancient natives in times of irresistible invasion: here they were secure, for the ascent is as difficult and hazardous as most I have undertaken. The place is called Burgcoul, and by the name refers to Fingal, or Fin MacCoul.

Sat up late, which gave me opportunity of knowing the lightness of the night in the island at this season: for at half an hour past one in the morning, I could read the small print of a newspaper.

Visit Loch Guirm, about two miles distant from Sunderland; a water of four miles in circumference, shallow, but abounding with trout. It is most remarkable for a regular fort of the MacDonalds, placed in a small island, but now in ruins: the form is square, with a round bastion at each corner; and in the middle are some walls, the remains of the buildings that sheltered the garrison: beneath one side, between the two bastions, was the place where MacDonald secured his boats: they were drawn beneath the protection of the wall of the fort, and had another on their outside, built in the water, as an additional security. The Dean of the Isles says that in his time this castle was usurped by MacKillayne, of Doward.

Dine at Mr Campbell's, of Balnabbi. His land is quite *riante*; his pastures in good order; and his people busily employed in haymaking: observed one piece of good grass ground, which he assured me was very lately covered with heath, now quite destroyed by the use of shell-sand. Perhaps it may seem trifling to mention, that some excellent new potatoes were served up at dinner; but this circumstance, with the forwardness of the hay harvest, shows what may be effected by culture in this island, when the tenure is secure, for both Sunderland and Balnabbi are proprietors.

See, near the house, three upright stones, of a stupendous size, placed nearly equidistant: the largest was seventeen feet high, and three broad.

Ride two miles north-west to Dounvollan, where some high rocks project one behind the other into the sea, with narrow isthmuses between: on the ascent of each are strong dikes, placed transversely, and a path leading towards the top; and on some parts are hollows, probably the lodging of the occupiers. The last of these rocks terminate in a precipice over the sea, and was the dernier resort of the defendants: such were the fortifications of the barbarous ages: here, were the assailants successful, the garrison had no alternative but to perish by the edge of the sword, or to precipitate themselves into the ocean.

In various parts of this neighbourhood are scattered small holes, formed in the ground, large enough to hold a single man in a sitting posture: the top is covered with a broad stone, and that with earth: into these unhappy fugitives took shelter after a defeat, and drawing together sods, found a temporary concealment from enemies, who in early times knew not the giving or receiving of quarter. The incursions of barbarians were always short; so that the fugitives could easily subsist in their earths till the danger was over. Men were then almost in a state of nature: how strong was their resemblance to beasts of prey! The whole scenery of this place was unspeakably savage, and the inhabitants suitable. Falcons screamed incessantly over our heads, and we disturbed the eagles perched on the precipice.

Continue clambering among the rocks impending over the sea, and split by intervals into chasms, narrow, black and of a stupendous depth; whose bottoms appeared and disappeared according to the momentary coruscations of the furious foam of the waves, rolling from the heavy ocean. Proceed along a narrow path, surrounding the face of a promontory hanging over the water, skipping nimbly over a way that fear alone could make dangerous, laughing at a bulky companion whom the rest had distanced.

Descend a steep tract, and found part of our company (who chose a less picturesque road) in possession of the fine cave of Saneg-mor: the entrance was difficult; but after some travail found the inside of an august extent and height; the roof solid rock, which returned with the noise of thunder, the discharge of our muskets. Within this cave was another straight before us, with a fine arched entrance: several of the company had got into it, and passing with their tapers backwards and forwards, from recess to recess, appeared at our distance like the gliding spectres of Shakespeare in the pit of Acheron. We followed, and found our grotto divided into numbers of far-winding passages, sometimes opening into fine expanses, again closing, for a long space, into galleries, passable but with difficulty: a perfect subterraneous labyrinth. A bagpiper preceded: at times the whole space was filled with the sound, which died away by degrees to a mere murmur, and soon after again astonished us with the bellowing, according as the meanders conducted him to, or from our singular stations.

Take leave of the hospitable family of Sunderland: ride along a different road across the island; pass by some cairns, and some ancient fences on the heaths. Reach the head of Loch Druinard, a place celebrated for the battle of Traii-dhruinard, in 1598, between the Lord of the Isles, and Sir Lauchlan Maclean, of Mull: the last, with fifteen hundred men, invaded Ilay, with a view of usurping it from his nephew: the first had only eleven hundred, and was at first obliged to retreat till he was joined by a hundred and twenty fresh forces: this decided the engagement. Sir Lauchlan was slain, with four score of his principal kinsmen, and two hundred of his soldiers, who lay surrounding the body of their chieftain. A stone still on the spot, was erected in memory of his fall.

Sir Lauchlan consulted a witch, the Oracle of Mull, before he set out on his expedition; and received three pieces of advice: first, not to land on a Thursday: a storm forced him into disobedience. The second, not to drink of a certain spring: which he did through ignorance. The third, not to fight beside Loch Druinaird: but this the fates may be supposed to have determined.

Ride by Loch Finlagan, a narrow piece of water, celebrated for its isle, a principal residence of the great MacDonald. The ruins of this place and chapel still exist, and also the stone on which he stood when he was crowned King of the Isles. This custom seems to have been common to the northern nations. The Danes had their *kongstolen*.[39]

The ceremony, (after a new lord had collected his kindred and vassals) was truly patriarchal. After putting on his armour his

[39] *Stephanii notae* in *Sax. Gramm.*, 29.

helmet and his sword, he took an oath to rule as his ancestors had done; that is, to govern as a father would his children: his people in return swore that they would pay the same obedience to him as children would to their parent. The dominions of this potentate about the year 1586 consisted only of Islay, Jura, Knapdale and Cantyre. So reduced were they, from what they had been, before the deprivation of the great Earl of Ross in the reign of James III.

Near this is another little isle, where he assembled his council: Ilan-na-Corlle, or, 'the island of council'; where thirteen judges constantly sat to decide differences among his subjects; and received for their trouble the eleventh part of the value of the affair tried before them.[40]

In the island were buried the wives and children of the lords of the isles; but their own persons were deposited in the more sacred ground of Iona.

On the shores of the lake are some marks of the quarters of his *carnauch* and *gilliglasses*, the military of the isles: the first signifying a strong man; the last, a grim-looking fellow. The first were light-armed, and fought with darts and daggers; the last with sharp hatchets.[41] These are the troops that Shakespeare alludes to, when he speaks of a Donald, who

> From the Western Isles
> of Kernes and Gallow glasses was supplied.

Upon the shore are the remains of a pier, and on a stone is cut, *A. II.* or, Aeneas II, one of the lords of the Isles, in whose reign it was founded.[42] This proves sufficiently that MacDonald was not their general title, as some have imagined: the mistake arose from two of the name of Donald, who were most remarkable for the ravages they made in Scotland, in the reign of Edward Baliol, in 1368, and in that of James I in 1410. As the title is popular still in the isles, I choose to continue what is so much in use.

---

[40] These were the Armin or Tierna heads of the principal families; who also assessed the Lord of the Isles with their advice.

[41] Camden, 1421.

[42] Boethius, 383. Fordun says, that the Lord of the Isles had here '*duas mansioness, et Castrum Domanowalk*'.

Besides those already mentioned, the lords had a house and chapel at Laganon, on the south side of Loch-an-Daal: a strong castle on a rock in the sea, at Dunowaick, at the south-east end of the country; for they made this island their residence after their expulsion from that of Man, in 1304.

There is a tradition, that while the Isle of Man was part of the kingdom of the Isles, that the rents were for a time paid in this country: those in silver were paid on a rock, still called Creig-a-Nione, or, 'the rock of the silver rent': the other, Creg-a-nairgid, or, 'the rock of rents in kind'. These lie opposite to each other, at the mouth of a harbour on the south side of this island.

Return to Freeport, and go on board my vessel, now at anchor on the Jura side of the sound, in Whitefarlane Bay.

The isle of Ilay, Isla, or, as it is called in Erse, Ile, is of a square form, deeply indented on the south by the great bay of Loch-an-Daal, divided from Jura, on the north-east, by the sound, which is near fourteen miles long, and about one broad. The tides most violent and rapid: the channel clear, excepting at the south entrance, where there are some rocks on the Jura side.

The length of Ilay, from the point of Ruval to the Mull of Kinoth, is twenty-eight miles; is divided into the parishes of Kildalton, Kilarow, Kilchoman, and Kilmenie. The latitude of Freeport, 55° 52' 29' N.[43] The face of the island is hilly, but not high: the loftiest hills are Aird Inisdail, Diur Bheinn, and Sgarbh Bhein. The land in many parts is excellent, but much of it is covered with heath, and absolutely in a state of nature.

The produce is corn of different kinds; such as bere, which sometimes yields eleven-fold; and oats six-fold: a ruinous distillation prevails here; insomuch that it is supposed that more of the bere is drank in form of whisky than eaten in the shape of bannocks. Wheat has been raised with good success in an enclosure belonging to the proprietor; but in an open country where most of the cattle go at large, it is impossible to cultivate that grain; and the tenants are unable to enclose. Much flax is raised here, and about £2,000 worth,

[43] I am greatly indebted to Dr Lind for the true latitude; and for a beautiful map of the isle from which I take my measurements.

XVI

Inside of a WEAVERS COTTAGE in ILAY

Grignion Sc.

sold out of the island in yarn, which might better be manufactured on the spot, to give employ to the poor natives.

A set of people worn down with poverty: their habitations scenes of misery, made of loose stones; without chimneys, without doors, excepting the faggot opposed to the wind at one or other of the apertures, permitting the smoke to escape through the other, in order to prevent the pains of suffocation. The furniture perfectly corresponds: a pothook hangs from the middle of the roof, with a pot pendent over a grateless fire, filled with fare that may rather be called a permission to exist, than a support of vigorous life: the inmates, as may be expected, lean, withered, dusky and smoke-dried. But my picture is not of this island only.

Notwithstanding the excellency of the land, above a thousand pounds worth of meal is annually imported, a famine threatened at this time; but was prevented by the seasonable arrival of a mealship; and the inhabitants like the sons of Jacob of old, flocked down to buy food.

Ale is frequently made in this island of the young tops of heath, mixing two thirds of that plant with one of malt, sometimes adding hops. Boethius relates that this liquor was much used among the Picts, but when that nation was extirpated by the Scots, the secret of making it perished with them.[44]

The country blessed with fine manures: besides sea-wrack, coral, shell-sand, rock and pit-marl, it possesses a tract of thirty-six square miles of limestone. What treasures, if properly applied, to bring wealth and plenty into the island.

Numbers of cattle are bred here, and about seventeen hundred are annually exported at the price of fifty shillings each. The island is often overstocked, and numbers die in March for want of fodder. None but milk cows are housed: cattle of all other kinds, except the saddle horses, run out during winter.

The number of inhabitants is computed to be between seven and eight thousand. About seven hundred are employed in the mines and in the fishery: the rest are gentlemen farmers, subtenants or servants. The women spin. Few as yet have migrated.

---

[44] *Descr. Regni Scotorum*, 8.

The servants are paid in kind; the sixth part of the crop. They have houses gratis: the master gives them the feed for the first year, and lends them horses to plough annually the land annexed.

The air is less healthy than that of Jura: the present epidemical diseases are dropsies and cancers: the natural effects of bad food.

The quadrupeds of this island are stoats, weasels, otters and hares: the last small, dark-coloured, and bad runners. The birds are eagles, peregrine falcons, black and red game; and a very few ptarmigans. Red-breasted goosanders breed on the shore among the loose stones, wild geese in the moors. Herons in the island in Loch Guirm. The fish are plaice, smeardab, large dabs, mullets, ballan, lumpfish, black goby, greater dragonet, and that rare fish the lepadogaster of M. Gouan.

Vipers swarm in the heath: the natives retain the vulgar error of their stinging with their forked tongues; that a sword on which the poison has fallen will hiss in water like a red-hot iron; and that a poultice of human ordure is an infallible cure for the bite.

In this island several ancient diversions and superstitions are still preserved: the last indeed are almost extinct, or at most lurk only amongst the very meanest of the people.

The late wakes or funerals, like those of the Romans, were attended with sports, and dramatic entertainments, composed of many parts, and the actors often changed their dresses suitable to their characters. The subject of the drama was historical and preserved by memory.

The active sports are wrestling. Another is performed by jumping on a pole held up horizontally by two men; the performer lights on his knees, takes hold with both hands, bends and kisses it; and then springs off. He who succeeds in the feat when the pole is at the highest elevation, carries the prize.

A second game of activity is played by two or three hundred, who form a circle; and every one places his stick in the ground before him, by way of barrier. A person called the odd man stands in the middle, and delivers his bonnet to any one in the ring. This is nimbly handed round, and the owner is to recover it: and on succeeding, takes the place of the person, whom he took it from; and that person again takes the middle place.

There are two other trials of strength: firstly, throwing the sledgehammer. The other seems local. Two men sit on the ground foot to foot: each lays hold of a short stick; and the champion that can pull the other over is the winner.

The power of fascination is as strongly believed here as it was by the shepherds of Italy in times of old:

> *Nescio quis teneros oculis mihi fascinat agnos?*

But here the power of the evil eye affects more the milch cows than lambs. If the good housewife perceives the effect of the malicious on any of her kine, she takes as much milk as she can drain from the enchanted herd, for the witch commonly leaves very little. She then boils it with certain herbs, and adds to them flints and untempered steel: after that she secures the door, and invokes the three sacred persons. This puts the witch into such an agony, that she comes nilling-willing to the house, begs to be admitted, to obtain relief by touching the powerful pot: the good woman then makes her terms; the witch restores the milk to the cattle, and in return is freed from her pains.

But sometimes to save the trouble of those charms (for it may happen that the disorder may arise from other causes than an evil eye), the trial is made by immersing in milk a certain herb, and if the cows are supernaturally affected, it instantly distils blood.

The unsuccessful lover revenges himself on his happy rival by charms potent as those of the shepherd Alphesibaeus, and exactly similar:

> *Necte tribus nodis ternos Amarylli colores:*
> *Necte, Amarylli, modo.*

Donald takes three threads of different hues, and ties three knots on each, three times imprecating the most cruel disappointments on the nuptial bed: but the bridegroom to avert the harm, stands at the altar with an untied shoe, and puts a sixpence beneath his foot.

A present was made me of *clach clun ceilach*, or 'cock-knee stone', believed to be obtained out of that part of the bird; but I have unluckily forgotten its virtues. Not so with the *clach crubain*, which is to cure all pains in the joints. It is to be presumed both these amulets have been enchanted; for the first very much resembles a common pebble; the other is that species of fossil shell called *gryphites*.

I was also favoured with several of the nuts, commonly called Molucca beans, which are frequently found on the western shores of this and others of the Hebrides. They are the seeds of the *Dolichos urens*, *Guilandina Bonduc.*, *G. Bonducetta*, and *Mimosa scandens* of Linnaeus, natives of Jamaica. The fifth is a seed called by Bauhin, *Fructus exot: orbicularis fulcis nervisque quatuor*, whose place is unknown. The four first grow in quantities on the steep banks of the rivers of Jamaica, and are generally supposed to drop into the water, and to be carried into the sea: from thence by tides and currents, and the predominancy of the east wind, to be forced through the Gulf of Florida, into the North American ocean, in the same manner as the sargasso, a plant growing on the rocks in the seas of Jamaica. When arrived in that part of the Atlantic, they fall in with the westerly winds, which generally blow two-thirds of the year in that tract; which may help to convey them to the shores of the Hebrides and Orkneys.[45] I was for resolving this phenomenon into shipwrecks and supposing that they might have been flung on these coasts out of some unhappy vessels: but this solution of mine is absolutely denied, from the frequency and regularity of the appearance of these seeds. American tortoises, or turtle, have more than once been taken alive on these coasts, tempest-driven from their warm seas; and part of the mast of the Tilbury man-of-war, burnt at Jamaica, was taken up on the western coast of Scotland; facts that give probability to the first opinion.

History furnishes very few materials for the great events or revolutions of Ilay. It seems to have been long a seat of empire, probably jointly with the Isle of Man, as being most conveniently situated for the government of the rest of the Hebrides; for Crovan, the Norwegian, after his conquest of that island, in 1066, retired and finished his days in Ilay.[46] There are more Danish or Norwegian names of places in this island than any other; almost all the present

---

[45] *Phil. Trans.*, abridged, III, 540.
[46] *Chron. Man.*

farms derive their titles from them, such as Persibus, Torridale, Torribolse, and the like. On the retreat of the Danes it became the seat of their successors, the lords of the Isles, and continued after their power was broken, in the reign of James III in their descendants, the MacDonalds, who held, or ought to have held, it from the crown. It was in the possession of a Sir James MacDonald, in the year 1598, the same who won the battle of Traii-dhruinard before mentioned. His power gave umbrage to James VI, who directed the Lord of MacLeod, Cameron of Lochiel, and the MacNeiles of Barra, to support the Macleanes in another invasion. The rival parties met near the hill of Benbigger, east of Kilarow; a fierce engagement ensued, and the MacDonalds were defeated, and almost entirely cut off. Sir James escaped to Spain; but returned in 1620, was pardoned, received a pension, and died the same year at Glasgow, and in him expired the last of the great MacDonalds. But the king, irritated by the disturbances raised by private wars, waged between these and other clans, resumed the grant made by his predecessor,[47] and transferred it to Sir John Campbell, of Calder, who held it on paying an annual feu duty of five hundred pounds sterling, which is paid to this day. The island was granted to Sir John, as a reward for his undertaking the conquest; but the family considered it as a dear acquisition, by the loss of many gallant followers, and by the expenses incurred in support of it. At present it is in possession of Mr Campbell, of Shawfield, and the rents are about £2,300 per annum.

Weigh anchor at three o'clock in the morning: with the assistance of the tide get out of the sound. See, on the north-west side, the place where that gallant enemy Thurot lay, at different times, expecting the fit opportunity of his invasion, to be determined by the news he had of the success of the Brest squadron. He was told that he lay in a dangerous place; but he knew that his security constituted, in case a superior force came against him, in being able either to take to sea, or escape through the sound, according to the quarter the attack came from. His generosity and humanity is spoken of

---

[47] *Feuds of the Isles*, 99.

XVII

Moses Griffith del.

MONASTERY IN ORANSAY.

P. Mazell sculp.

in high terms by the islanders; and his distress appeared very deep when he was informed of the miscarriage of Conflans' fleet.

Leave, on the Ilay coast, near the mouth of the sound, the celebrated cave of Uamh-fhearnaig, or Uam-mhòr. Fourteen or fifteen families retire to it during the fine season, as their sheelins, or summer residence; and three families reside in it the whole year.

About eight or nine miles from the mouth of the sound lie the isles of Oransay and Colonsay. The stillness of the day made the passage tedious; which induced us to take boat: the view, midway, was very fine of Ilay and Jura, of the opening into Loch Tarbat, a bay penetrating deep into Jura, and affording anchorage for large vessels; as was experienced a very few years ago, by one of eight hundred tons, driven in during night: the master found an opening, and passed providentially between two rocks, at a small distance from each other; and finding himself in smooth water, dropped anchor, and lay secure in a fine natural wet dock. A discovery worthy the attention of mariners.[48]

Beyond Jura appears the Gulf of Corryvrekan, bounded by the isle of Skarba; the mountains of Mull succeed; and before us extend the shores of two islands, the immediate objects of our visit. Land about one o'clock on Oransay. The ship arrives soon after, and anchors within Ghudimal, which, with two or three other little rocky isles, forms a harbour.

After about a mile's walk reach the ruins of the ancient monastery, founded (as some say) by St Columba, but with more probability by one of the lords of the Isles, who fixed here a priory of canons regular of Augustine, dependent on the abbey of Holyrood, in Edinburgh. The church is fifty-nine feet by eighteen, and contains the tombs of numbers of the ancient islanders, two of warriors recumbent, seven feet long; a flattery perhaps of the sculptor, to give to future ages exalted notions of their prowess. Besides these, are

---

[48] Mariners have overlooked the account of this harbour given by Alexander Lindsay, pilot to James V, in his navigation round Scotland, in 1536, who pronounced it to have good anchorage. James in person executed the great design of taking charts of the coasts of his dominions, and sounding the most distant and dangerous rocks.

scattered over the floor lesser figures of heroes, priests and females; the last seemingly of some order: and near them is a figure, cut in stone, of full size, apparently an abbess.

In a side chapel, beneath an arch, lies an abbot, of the name of MacDufie, with two of his fingers elated, in the attitude of benediction: in the same place is a stone enriched with foliage, a stag surrounded with dogs, and a ship with full sail: round is inscribed, *hic jacet Murchardus Macdufie de Collonsa, An. Do. 1539, mense mart. ora me ille. ammen.*

This Murchardus is said to have been a great oppressor, and that he was executed, by order of the Lord of the Isles, for his tyranny. Near his tomb is a long pole, placed there in memory of the ensign staff of the family, which had been preserved miraculously for two hundred years: on it (report says) depended the fate of the MacDufian race, and probably the original perished with this Murchadus.

Adjoining to the church is the cloister: a square of forty-one feet; one of the sides of the inner wall is ruined; on two of the others are seven low arches, one seven feet high including the columns, which are nothing more than two thin stones,[49] three feet high, with a flat stone on the top of each, serving as a plinth; and on them two other thin stones, meeting at top, and forming an acute angle, by way of arch: on the foreside are five small round arches; these surround a court of twenty eight feet eight inches. This form is peculiar (in our part of Europe) to this place; but I am told that the same is observed in some of the religious houses in the islands of the archipelago.

Several other buildings join this, all in a ruinous state; but a most elegant cross is yet standing, twelve feet high, one foot seven broad, five inches thick.

St Columba, when he left Ireland, made a vow never to settle within sight of his native country: accordingly when he and his friend Oran landed here, they ascended a hill, and Ireland appeared full in view. This induced the holy men to make a sudden retreat; but Oran had the honour of giving name to the island.

---

[49] On one of these there is an inscription, which was copied, but by some accident lost.

XVIII

I. CROSS IN ORANSAY.
II. II. CROSS IN ILAY.

XIX

Cloisters in the ABBY of ORANSAY.

XX

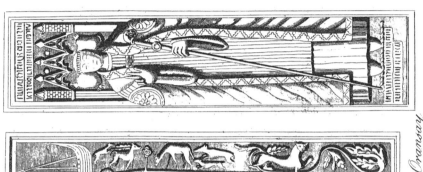

Tombs in the Monastery of Oransay.

Ascend the very hill that the saint did. Lofty and craggy, inhabited by red-billed choughs, and stares. On the top is a retreat of old inhabitants, protected by a strong stone dike and advanced works. On the plain below is a large round mount, flat at top; on which had probably been a small Danish fort, such as are frequently seen in Ireland. Nearer the shore in the east side of the island is a large conic tumulus; and on the same plain, a small cross placed where a MacDufie's corpse is said to have rested.

Take boat and visit Bird Island, and some other rocks divided by narrow passages, filled by a most rapid tide. Saw several eider ducks and some sheldrakes. The islanders neglect to gather the down of the former; which would bring in a little money.

This is the bird called by the Dean of the Isles, 'colk'. From the circumstance of its depluming its breast, he fables that 'at that time her fleiche of fedderis falleth of her hailly, and sayles to the mayne sea againe, and never comes to land quhyll the zeir end again, and then she comes with her nev fleiche of fedderis: this fleiche that she leaves zeirly upon her nest hes nae pens in the fedderis, bot utter fine downes'.

The seals are here numerous. A few are caught in nets placed between these rocks. The great species is taken on Du Hirtach, a great rock about a mile round, ten leagues to the west; reported to be the nearest of any to America.

Oransay is three miles long: the south part low and sandy, the rest high and rocky. Is divided from Colonsay by a narrow sound dry at low water. This island is a single farm, yielding bere, flax, and much potatoes; which are left in their beds the whole winter, covered with sea-wrack, to protect them from the frost. The manure is shell-sand and wrack: the last laid on grass will produce but one crop; on cornland it will produce two. Sixty milch cows are kept here: and this year eighty head of cattle were sold from the island at three pounds apiece: some butter and cheese are also exported.

This island is rented by Mr MacNeile, brother to the proprietor of both islands. The rent is not more than forty pounds a year: yet according to the custom of the isles, the farm employs a number of servants, viz. a chief labourer, who has fifty shillings a year, and a stone of meal per week: a principal herdsman, whose wages are grass for two cows, and meal sufficient for his family: a cowherd who has twenty-four shillings a year and shoes: one under him, whose wages are about sixteen shillings: and a calfherd, who is allowed ten shillings. Besides these are two other men, called from their employ *aoireannan*, who have the charge of cultivating a certain portion of land; and also overseeing the cattle it supports; these have grass for two milch cows, and six sheep; and the tenth sheaf, the produce of the ground, and as many potatoes as they choose to plant. The maidservants are a housekeeper, at three pounds a year: a principal dairy maid, twelve marks Scots, each half year: and five other women, five marks.

Cross the sound at low water, and enter the island of Colonsay. Twelve miles long, three broad, full of rocky hills, running traversely, with variety of pretty meandering vales full of grass, and most excellent for pasturage. Even the hills have plenty of herbage mixed with the rock. The valleys want enclosures and want woods, the common defect of all the Hebrides. They yield bere and potatoes, much of the first is used in distillation, to the very starving of the islanders, who are obliged to import meal for their subsistence. About two hundred and twenty head of cattle are annually exported at £3 each. In 1736 the price was only five and twenty shillings; but the rise commenced two years after the rebellion. Yet even this advance does not enrich the people of this pretty island, for their whole profit is exhausted in the purchase of bread, which their own industry ought to supply.

Oats are sown here about the middle of April, and yield three and a half. Bere produces eight fold. Forty or fifty tons of kelp are annually made in both islands. The materials are collected on the shores in the middle of April, and the kelp exported in August, at the rate of £3 10s or £4 per ton.

Their poverty prevents them from using the very means Providence has given them of raising a comfortable subsistence. They have a good soil, plenty of limestone, and sufficient quantity of peat. A sea abounding the fish, but their distressed state disables them from cultivating the one, and taking the other. These two islands contain eight thousand four hundred acres, of which about two thousand six hundred are arable. How inadequate then is the produce of cattle; and how much more so is that of corn!

The soil of this island is far superior in goodness to that of Oransay; yet how disproportionably less are the exports: Oransay owes its advantages to the good management of the tenant.

In both islands are between five and six hundred souls. The old inhabitants were the MacDufies and the MacVurechs. The first were chief, 'This isle', says the Dean, 'is brukit be ane gentle capitane callit Mac-Dufyke and pertend of auld to Clandonald of Kyntyre', and it is now 'brukit be ane gentle capitane callit Macneile', who has never raised his rents, has preserved the love of his people, and lost but a single family by migration.

This island, since the time of Dean, was the property of the Argyle family, who sold it to an ancestor of the present proprietor about sixty years ago. I conjecture that the ancient owner might have forfeited by engaging in the last rebellion of the MacDonalds; and that it was included in the large grant of islands made to the Campbells, in reward for their services.

Met with nothing very interesting in the ride. Pass by a chain of small lakes, called Loch Fad, by two great erect stones monumental, at Cilchattan; and by a ruined chapel. There are three others; but notwithstanding from this circumstance, Oransay and Colonsay might be supposed to have been isles of sanctity, yet from the Reformation till within the last six years, the sacrament had been only once administered.

Reach Ciloran, the seat of the proprietor, Mr MacNeile, who entertained us with much politeness. His house is well-sheltered, and trees grow very vigorously in its neighbourhood. There is scarcely an island, where valleys protected from winds, may not be found, in which trees might be planted to great advantage. Ash and maple would succeed particularly well: and in many places the best kinds of willows would turn to good account, and produce a manufacture of baskets and hampers, articles our commercial towns have a great demand for.

Rabbits abound here: about a hundred and twenty dozen of their skins are annually exported.

Barnacles appear in vast flocks in September, and retire the latter end of April or beginning of May. Among the domestic fowls I observed peacocks to thrive well in the farm at Oransay. So far north has this Indian bird been naturalized.

Neither frogs, toads nor vipers are found here; or any kind of serpent, except the harmless blindworm.

I met with no remarkable fossils. Black talc the *Mica lamellata martialis nigra* of Cronsted, sect. 95, is found here, both in large detached flakes, and immersed in indurated clay. Also rock-stone formed of glimmer and quartz. An imperfect granite is not unfrequent.

In the morning, walk down to the eastern coast of the island, to a creek guarded by the little rocky isle of Olamsay, where small vessels may find shelter. Find Mr Thompson plying off at a mile's distance. Go on board; and sail for Iona. The lofty mountains of Mull lay in front: the eastern views were Ilay, Jura, Scarba, and the entrance of the gulf of Corryvrekan, beyond lies Lorn, and at a distance soars the high hill of Crouachan.

Steer to the north-west; but our course greatly delayed by calms: take numbers of grey gurnards in all depths of water, and find young herrings in their stomachs.

VII

THE HEBRIDES (2)

Sound of Iona — Iona — Staffa — *Account of Staffa* by Joseph Banks

Towards evening arrive within sight of Iona, and a tremendous chain of rocks, lying to the south of it, rendered more horrible by the perpetual noise of breakers. Defer our entrance into the sound till daylight.

About eight of the clock in the morning, very narrowly escape striking on the rock Bònirevor, apparent at this time by the breaking of a wave: our master was at some distance in his boat, in search of sea-fowl, but alarmed with the danger of his vessel, was hastening to its relief; but the tide conveyed us out of reach of the rock, and saved him the trouble of landing us; for the weather was so calm as to free us from any apprehensions about our lives. After riding for three hours, anchor in the Sound of Iona, in three fathoms water, on a white sandy bottom; but the safest anchorage is on the east side, between a little isle and that of Mull: this sound is three miles long and one broad, shallow, and in some parts dry at the ebb of springtides: it is bounded on the east by the island of Mull; on the west, by that of Iona, the most celebrated of the Hebrides.

Multitudes of gannets were now fishing here: they precipitated themselves from a vast height, plunged on their prey at least two fathoms deep, and took to the air again as soon as they emerged. Their sense of seeing must be exquisite; but they are often deceived, for Mr Thompson informed me, that he had frequently taken them

232

XXI

GENERAL VIEW OF JONA.

P. C. Amet sculp

by placing a herring on a hook, and sinking it a fathom deep, which the gannet plunges for and is taken.

The view of Iona was very picturesque: the east side, or that which bounds the sound, exhibited a beautiful variety; an extent of plain, a little elevated above the water, and almost covered with the ruins of the sacred buildings, and with the remains of the old town still inhabited. Beyond these the island rises into little rocky hills, with narrow verdant hollows between (for they merit not the name of valleys) and numerous enough for every recluse to take his solitary walk, undisturbed by society.

The island belongs to the parish of Ross, in Mull; is three miles long and one broad; the east side mostly flat; the middle rises into small hills; the west side very rude and rocky: the whole is a singular mixture of rock and fertility.

The soil is a compound of sand and comminuted sea shells, mixed with black loam; is very favourable to the growth of bere, natural clover, crowsfoot and daisies. It is in perpetual tillage, and is ploughed thrice before the sowing: the crops at this time made a promising appearance, but the seed was committed to the ground at very different times; some, I think, about the beginning of May, and some not three weeks ago. Oats do not succeed here; but flax and potatoes come on very well. I am informed, that the soil in Col, Tir-I, and north and south Uist, is similar to that in Iona.

The tenants here *runrig*, and have the pasturage in common. It supports about a hundred and eight head of cattle, and about five hundred sheep. There is no heath in this island: cattle unused to that plant give bloody milk; which is the case with the cattle of Iona transported to Mull, where that vegetable abounds; but the cure is soon effected by giving them plenty of water.

Servants are paid here commonly with a fourth of the crop, grass for three or four cows, and a few sheep.

The number of inhabitants is about a hundred and fifty: the most stupid and the most lazy of all the islanders; yet many of them boast of their descent from the companions of St Columba.

A few of the more common birds frequent this island: wild geese breed here, and the young are often reared and tamed by the natives.

The beautiful sea-bugloss makes the shores gay with its glaucous leaves and purple flowers. The eryngo, or seaholly, is frequent; and the fatal belladonna is found here.

The *Granites durus rubescens*, the same with the Egyptian, is found in Nuns Isle, and on the coast of Mull: a *Breccia quartzosa*, of a beautiful kind, is common; and the rocks to the south of the Bay of Martyrs is formed of the Swedish trapp, useful to glassmakers.[1]

Iona derives its name from a Hebrew word, signifying a dove, in allusion to the name of the great saint, Columba, the founder of its fame. This holy man, instigated by his zeal, left his native country, Ireland, in the year 565, with the pious design of preaching the gospel to the Picts. It appears that he left his native soil with warm resentment, vowing never to make a settlement within sight of that hated island. He made his first trial at Oransay, and on finding that place too near to Ireland, succeeded to his wish at Hy, for that was the name of Iona, at the time of his arrival. He repeated here the experiment on several hills, erecting on each a heap of stones; and that which he last ascended is to this day called Carnan-chul-reb-Eirinn, or 'the eminence of the back turned to Ireland'.

Columba was soon distinguished by the sanctity of his manners: a miracle that he wrought so operated on the Pictish king, Bradeus, that he immediately made a present of the little isle to the saint. It seems that his Majesty refused Columba an audience; and even proceeded so far as to order the palace gates to be shut against him; but the saint, by the power of his word, instantly caused them to fly open.

As soon as he was in possession of Iona he founded a cell of monks, borrowing his institutions from a certain Oriental monastic order.[2] It is said that the first religious were canons regular, of whom the founder was the first abbot: and that his monks, till the year 716, differed from those of the church of Rome, both in the observation of Easter, and in the clerical tonsure. Columba led here an exemplary life, and was highly respected for the sanctity of

---

[1] Cronsted, no. cclxvii.
[2] Sir Roger Twisden's *Rise of Monastic States*, 36.

his manners for a considerable number of years. He is the first on record who had the faculty of second-sight, for he told the victory of Aidan over the Picts and Saxons on the very instant it happened. He had the honour of burying in his island, Convallus and Kinnatil, two kings of Scotland, and of crowning a third. At length, worn out with age, he died, in Iona, in the arms of his disciples; was interred there, but (as the Irish pretend) in after-times translated to Down; where, according to the epitaph, his remains were deposited with those of St Bridget and St Patric:

> Hic tres in Duno tumulo tumulantur in uno;
> Brigida, Particius, atque Columba pius.

But this is totally denied by the Scots; who affirm, that the contrary is shown in a life of the saint, extracted out of the pope's library, and translated out of the Latin into Erse, by Father Calohoran; which decides, in favour of Iona, the momentous dispute.[3]

After the death of St Columba, the island received the name of Y-Columb-Cill, or, 'the isle of the cell of Columba'. In process of time the island itself was personified, and by a common blunder in early times converted into a saint, and worshipped under the title of St Columbkilla.

The religious continued unmolested during two centuries: but in the year 807 were attacked by the Danes, who with their usual barbarity put part of the monks to the sword, and obliged the remainder, with their abbot Cellach, to seek safety by flying from their rage. The monastery remained depopulated for seven years; but on the retreat of the Danes received a new order, being then peopled by Cluniacs, who continued there till the Dissolution, when the revenues were united to the see of Argyle.

Took boat and landed on the spot called the Bay of Martyrs: the place where the bodies of those who were to be interred in this holy ground, were received, during the period of superstition.

Walked about a quarter of a mile to the south, in order to fix on a convenient spot for pitching a rude tent, formed of oars and sails, as our day residence, during our stay on the island.

---

[3] MS in Advoc. Libr. 1693.

Observe a little beyond, an oblong enclosure, bounded by a stone dike called Clachan Druinach, and supposed to have been the burial place of the Druids, for bones of various sizes are found there. I have no doubt but that Druidism was the original religion of this place; yet I suppose this to have been rather the common cemetery of the people of the town, which lies almost close to the Bay of Martyrs.

Having settled the business of our tent, return through the town, consisting at present of about fifty houses, mostly very mean, thatched with straw of bere pulled up by the roots, and bound tight on the roof with ropes made of heath. Some of the houses that lie a little beyond the rest seemed to have been better constructed than the others, and to have been the mansions of the inhabitants when the place was in a flourishing state, but at present are in a very ruinous condition.

Visit every place in the order that they lay from the village. The first was the ruin of a nunnery, filled with canonesses of St Augustine, and consecrated to St Oran. They were permitted to live in community for a considerable time after the Reformation, and wore a white gown; and above it a rotchet of fine linen.[4]

The church was fifty-eight feet by twenty: the roof of the east end is entire, is a pretty vault made of very thin stones, bound together by four ribs meeting in the centre. The floor is covered some feet thick with cow-dung; this place being at present the common shelter for the cattle; and the islanders are too lazy to remove this fine manure, the collection of a century, to enrich their grounds.

With much difficulty, by virtue of fair words, and a bribe, prevail on one of these listless fellow to remove a great quantity of this dunghill; and by that means once more expose to light the tomb of the last prioress. Her figure is cut on the face of the stone; an angel on each side supports her head; and above them is a little plate and a comb. The prioress occupies only one half of the surface: the other is filled with the form of the Virgin Mary, with head crowned and mitred; the child in her arms; and, to denote her Queen of

[4] Keith, 280.

Heaven, a sun and moon appear above. At her feet is this address, from the prioress: *Sancta Maria ora pro me*. And round the lady is inscribed, *Hic jacet Domina Anna Donaldi Terleti[5] filia quondam Prioriss de Jona quae obiit an~o m° d° xim° ejus animam Altissimo commendamus*.

Mr Stuart, who some time past visited this place, informed me, that at that time he observed this fragment of another inscription: *Hic jacet Mariota filia Johan: Lauchlani Domini de…* .

Besides this place of sepulchre, was another on the outside, allotted for the nuns; where, at a respectable distance from the virtuous recluses, lies in solitude, a frail sister.

This nunnery could never have been founded (as some assert) in the days of St Columba, who was no admirer of the fair sex; in fact he held them in such abhorrence, that he detested all cattle on their account, and would not permit a cow to come within sight of his sacred walls; because, *''Sfar am bi bo, bi'dh bean, 'Sfar am bi bean, bi'dh mallacha'*: 'Where there is a cow, there must be a woman; and where there is a woman, there must be mischief.'

Advance from hence along a broad paved way, which is continued in a line from the nunnery to the cathedral: another branches from it to the Bay of Martyrs: and a third narrower than the others, points towards the hills.

On this road is a large and elegant cross, called that of MacLeane, one of three hundred and sixty, that were standing in this island at the Reformation,[6] but immediately after were almost entirely demolished by order of a provincial assembly, held in the island. It seems to have been customary in Scotland for individuals to erect crosses, probably in consequence of some vow, or perhaps out of a vain hope of perpetuating their memory.

Arrive at Reilig Ourain, or 'the burying-place of Oran': a vast enclosure; the great place of interment for the number of monarchs who were deposited here; and for the potentates of every isle, and their lineage; for all were ambitious of lying in this holy spot. The place is in a manner filled with gravestones, but so overgrown with

---

[5] Or Charles.
[6] *Short Descr. of Iona*, 1693. Advoc. Libr. MS.

weeds, especially with the common butterbur, that very few are at present to be seen.

I am very desirous of viewing the tombs of the kings, described by the Dean of the Isles, and from him by Buchanan: the former says that in his time there were three, built in form of little chapels:[7] on one was inscribed, *Tumulus Regum Scotiae*. In this were deposited the remains of forty-eight Scottish monarchs, beginning with Fergus II and ending with the famous Macbeth: for his successor, Malcolm Canmore, decreed, for the future, Dumfermline to be the place of royal sepulchre.[8] Of the Scottish monarchs interred in Iona, sixteen are pretended to be of the race of Alpin, and are styled, *rigbrid Ailpeanach*.

Fergus was the founder of this mausoleum (Boethius calls it *abbatia*[9]) and not only directed, that it should be the sepulchre of his successors, but also caused an office to be composed for the funeral ceremony.

The next was inscribed *Tumulus Regum Hiberniae*, containing four Irish monarchs; and the third, *Tumulus Regum Norwegiae*, containing eight Norwegian princes, or more probably viceroys of the Hebrides, while they were subject to that crown.

That so many crowned heads, from different nations, should prefer this as the place of their interment, is said to have been owing to an ancient prophecy:

> *Seachd bliadna romb'n bhrà*
> *Thig muir thar Eirin re aon tra'*
> *Sthar Ile ghu irm ghlais*
> *Ach Snàmhaidh I cholum clairich.*

Which is to this effect: 'Seven years before the end of the world, a deluge shall drown the nations: the sea, at one tide, shall cover Ireland, and the green-headed Ilay; but Columba's isle shall swim above the flood.'

But of these celebrated tombs we could discover nothing more than certain slight remains, that were built in a ridged form, and

---

[7] p. 19.
[8] Boethius, lib. VII, 122.
[9] lib. VII, 119.

arched within; but the inscriptions were lost. These are called *Iomaire nan righ*, or, 'the ridge of the kings'. Among these stones were found two with Gaelic inscriptions, and the form of a cross carved on each: the words on one were, *Cros Domhail fat'asich*, or, 'the cross of Donald Longshanks': the other signified the cross of Urchvine o Guin. The letters were those of the most ancient Irish alphabet, exhibited in Vallancy's *Irish Grammar*.

Among the same stones is also the following: *Hic jacent quatuor Priores de HY, Johannes, Hugenius, Patricius; in decretis olim Bacularius qui obiit an. Dom. millessmo quingentessimo.*

I am indebted to Mr Stuart for these three inscriptions, which he met with in his former voyage; arriving before the growth of the all-covering weeds. Mr Frazier, son to the Dean of the Isles, informed Mr Sacheverel, governor of the Isle of Man, who visited Iona in 1688, that his father had collected there three hundred inscriptions, and presented them to the Earl of Argyle; which were afterwards lost in the troubles of the family.

The chapel of St Oran stands in this space, which legend reports to have been the first building attempted by St Columba: by the working of some evil spirit, the walls fell down as fast as they were built up.

After some consultation it was pronounced, that they never would be permanent till a human victim was buried alive. Oran, a companion of the saint, generously offered himself, and was interred accordingly: at the end of three days St Columba had the curiosity to take a farewell look at his old friend, and caused the earth to be removed. To the surprise of all beholders, Oran started up, and began to reveal the secrets of his prison-house; and particularly declared, that all that had been said of hell was a mere joke. This dangerous impiety so shocked Columba, that, with great policy, he instantly ordered the earth to be flung in again: poor Oran was overwhelmed, and an end for ever put to his prating. His grave is near the door, distinguished only by a plain red stone.

Boethius[10] gives us reason to suppose, before this period, Iona to have been the habitation of the weird sisters and cacodemons, for

[10] lib. VI, 90.

King Natholocus, like Saul of old, consulted in this island an old witch, of uncommon fame: no wonder, therefore, that the prince of darkness should be interested in the overthrow of edifices that were to put an end to his influence.

In Oran's chapel are several tombs, and near it many more: within, beneath a recess formed with three neat pointed arches, is a tombstone with a ship and several ornaments. I forget whether the sails were furled: in that case the deceased was descended from the ancient kings of Man of the Norwegian race,[11] who used those arms.

Near the south end is the tomb of the Abbot MacKinnon's father, inscribed, *Haec est crux Lauchlani Mc. Fingon et ejus filii Johannis Abbatis de Hy. facta an. Dom. m++ cccclxxxix.*

Another of MacDonald of Ilay and Cantyre, commonly called Innus, or Angus Oig, the chief of the name. He was a strong friend to Robert Bruce, and was with him at the battle of Bannockbourne. His inscription is, *Hic jacet corpus Angusii filii Domini Angusii Mc. Domhnill de Ilay.*

In another place lies the gravestone of Ailean Nan Sop, a *ceatharnarch*, or head of a party, of the name of MacLeane; from whom is descended the family of Torloisg. The stone is ornamented with carving and a ship.

A MacLeane, of Col, appears in armour, with a sword in his left hand. A MacLeane, of Duart, with armour, shield and two-handed sword. And a third, of the same name of the family of Lochbuy: his right hand grasps a pistol, his left a sword. Besides these, are numbers of other ancient heroes, whose very names have perished, and they deprived of their expected glory: their lives were, like the path of an arrow, closed up and lost as soon as past; and probably in those times of barbarism, as fatal to their fellow creatures.

About seventy feet south of the chapel is a red unpolished stone; beneath which lies a nameless king of France. But the memory of the famous old doctor of Mull has had a better fate, and is preserved in these words: *Hic jacet Johannes Betonus Maclenorum familiae,*

---

[11] Dr Macpherson.

*redicus, qui mortuus est 19 Novembris 1657. Aet. 63. Donaldus
Betonus fecit. 1674.*

> *Ecce cadit jaculo victricis mortis iniquae;*
> *Qui toties alios solverat ipse malis.*
> *Soli Deo Gloria.*

A little north-west of the door is the pedestal of a cross: on it are
certain stones, that seem to have been the supports of a tomb.
Numbers who visit this island (I suppose the elect impatient for
the consummation of all things) think it incumbent on them to
turn each of these thrice round, according to the course of the sun.
They are called *clacha-bràth*, for it is thought that the *bràth*, or
end of the world, will not arrive till the stone on which they stand
is worn through. Originally, says Mr Sacheverel, here were three
noble globes, of white marble, placed on three stone basins, and
these were turned round, but the synod ordered them, and sixty
crosses, to be thrown into the sea. The present stones are probably
substituted in place of these globes.

The precinct of these tombs was held sacred, and enjoyed
the privileges of a girth, or sanctuary.[12] These places of retreat
were by the ancient Scotch law, not to shelter indiscriminately
every offender, as was the case in more bigoted times in Catholic
countries: for here all atrocious criminals were excluded; and only
the unfortunate delinquent, or the penitent sinner shielded from the
instant stroke of rigorous justice. The laws are penned with such
humanity and good sense, that the reader cannot be displeased with
seeing them in their native simplicity:[13]

> *Gif any fleis to Halie Kirk moved with repentance confesses*
> *there that he heavily sinned, and for the love of God is come*
> *to the house of God for safetie of himself, he sall nocht tine*
> *life nor limme bot quhat he has taken frae anie man he sall*
> *restore sameikill to him, and sall satisfie the King according*
> *to the law of the countrie.*
>
> *And swa sall swere upon the Halie Evangell that there-*
> *after he sall never commit reif nor theift.*
>
> Alex., 11, ch. 6.

---

[12] Fordun, lib. II, ch. 10.
[13] From the *Regiam Majestatem.*

XXII

a. Maria Griffith del.

S. Noodie.

CATHEDRAL IN JONA.

'If ane manslayer takes himself to the immunitie of the
Kirk, he sould be admonissed and required to come forth
and present himself to the law; to know gif the slauchter
was committed be forthocht felonie or murther.

'And gif he be admonissed, and will not come furth; fra
that time furth in all time thereafter he sal be banished and
exiled as ane committer of murther and forethocht felonie;
keep and reservand to him the immunitie of the kirk to the
whilk he take himself.'

Rob., 11, ch. 9.

Particular care was also taken that they should receive no injury
during their retreat: penalties were enacted for even striking; but for
the murder of any, 'The King was to have from the slayer twentye nine
kyes and ane zoung kow; and the offender was also to assithe to the
friends of the defunct conforme to the laws of the cuntrie.' Wil., ch. 5.

The cathedral lies a little to the north of this enclosure: is in the
form of a cross. The length from east to west is a hundred and
fifteen feet. The breadth twenty-three. The length of the transept
seventy. Over the centre is a handsome tower: on each of which is
a window with stonework of different forms in every one.

On the south side of the chancel are some Gothic arches
supported by pillars, nine feet eight inches high, including the
capitals; and eight feet nine inches in circumference. The capitals
are quite peculiar; carved round with various superstitious figures,
among others is an angel weighing of souls.

The altar was of white marble veined with grey, and is vulgarly
supposed to have reached from side to side of the chancel: but Mr
Sachverel, who saw it when almost entire, assures us that the size
was six feet by four.[14]

The demolition of this stone was owing to the belief of the
superstitious; who were of opinion, that a piece of it conveyed
to the possessor success in whatever he undertook. A very small
portion is now left; and even that we contributed to diminish.

Near the altar is the tomb of the abbot MacKinnon. His figure
lies recumbent, with this inscription round the margin, *Hic jacet*
Johannes MacFingone abbas de Hy, qui obiit anno Domini:

---

[14] p. 132.

Millessimo quingentessimo, cujus animae propitietur Deus altissimus. Amen.

On the other side is the tomb and figure of Abbot Kenneth.

On the floor is the effigy of an armed knight, with a whelk by his side, as if he just had returned from the feast of shells in the hall of Fingal.

Among these funereal subjects, the interment (a few years ago) of a female remarkable for her lineage must not be omitted. She was a direct descendant, and the last of the clan An Oister, *ostiarri*, or doorkeepers to the monastery. The first of the family came over with Columba, but falling under his displeasure, it was decreed on the imprecation of this irritable saint, that never more than five of his clan should exist at one time; and in consequence when a sixth was born, one of the five was to look for death. This, report says, alway happened till the period that the race was extinguished in this woman.

It is difficult to say when the present church was built: if we may credit Boethius, it was rebuilt by Malduinus, in the seventh century, out of the ruins of the former. But the present structure is far too magnificent for that age. Most of the walls are built with red granite from the nun's isle in the sound.

From the south-east corner are two parallel walls about twelve feet high, and ten feet distant from each other. At present they are called *dorus tràgh*, or 'the door to the shore': are supposed to have been continued from the cathedral to the sea, to have been roofed, and to have formed a covered gallery the whole way.

In the churchyard is a fine cross, fourteen feet high, two feet two inches broad, and ten inches thick, made of a single piece of red granite. The pedestal is three feet high.

Near the south-east end is Mary's chapel. Besides this, we are informed, that there were several others founded by the Scottish monarchs, and the reguli of the isles.[15]

The monastery lies behind the cathedral. It is in the most ruinous state, a small remnant of a cloister is left. In a corner are some black stones, held so sacred, but for what reason I am ignorant,

---

[15] Buchanan, lib. I, ch. 37. Dean of the Isles, 19.

Inside of the CATHEDRAL of IONA.

XXIII

XXIV

I. Abbot MacKinnon's Tomb. II. The Abbess. III. The Warrior. IV. Sculpture round the Capitals of two of the Pillars.

that it was customary to swear by them: perhaps from their being neighbours to the tutelar saint, whose grave is almost adjacent.

Boethius gives this monastery an earlier antiquity than perhaps it can justly claim.[16] He says that after the defeat of the Scots, at the battle of Munda, AD 379, the survivors with all religious fled to this island, and were the original founders of this house. But the account given by the Venerable Bede is much more probable, that St Columba was the original founder, as has been before related.

This isle, says the Dean, 'hes beine richlie Dotat by the Scotch kings': and mentions several little islands that belonged to it, which he calls Soa, Naban, Moroan, Reringe, Inchkenzie, Eorsay, and Kannay. If these had been the endowments, they would never serve to lead the religious into the temptation of luxury: but they were in possession of a considerable number of churches and chapels in Galway, with large estates annexed, all which were taken from them, and granted to the canons of Holyroodhouse by William I between the years 1172 and 1180.[17]

Columba was the first abbot: he and his successors maintained a jurisdiction over all the other monasteries that branched from this; and over all the monks of this abbey that exercised the priestly or even episcopal function in other places. One of the institutes of Loyola seems here to have been very early established, for the *élèves* of this house seem not to think themselves freed from their vow of obedience to the Abbot of Iona. Bede speaks of the singular pre-eminence,[18] and says that the island always had for a governor an abbot-presbyter, whose power (by a very uncommon rule) not only every province, but even the bishops themselves, obeyed. From this account, the enemies to Episcopacy have inferred, that the rank of bishop was a novelty, introduced into the church in corrupt times; and the authority they assumed was an errant usurpation, since a simple abbot for so considerable a space was permitted to have

---

[16] Lib. VI, 108, 109.

[17] Sir James Dalrymple's Coll., 271, 272.

[18] *Habere autem solet ipsa insula rectorem semper Abbatem Presbyterum, cujus juri et omnis Provincia et ipsi etiam Episcopi ordine inusitato debeant esse subjecti.* Lib. III, ch. 4.

the superiority. In answer to this, Archbishop Usher advances that the power of the abbot of Iona was only local and extended only to the bishop who resided there:[19] for after the conquest of the Isle of Man by the English, and the division of the see after that event, the Bishop of the Isles made Iona his residence, which before was in Man. But notwithstanding this, the Venerable Bede seems to be a stronger authority, than the Ulster annals quoted by the archbishop, which pretend no more than that a bishop had always resided in Iona, without even an attempt to refute the positive assertion of the most respectable author we have (relating to church matters) in those primitive times.

North of the monastery are the remains of the bishop's house: the residence of the bishops of the Isles after the Isle of Man was separated from them. This event happened in the time of Edward I. On their arrival the abbots permitted to them the use of their church, for they never had a cathedral of their own, except that in the Isle of Man. During the time of the Norwegian reign, which lasted near two hundred years, the bishops were chosen without respect of country, for we find French, Norwegian, English, and Scotch among the prelates, and they were generally, but not always, consecrated at Drontheim. Even after the cession of the Ebudae to Scotland by Magnus, the patronage of this bishopric was by treaty reserved to the Archbishop of Drontheim.[20] This see was endowed with thirteen islands;[21] but some of them were forced from them by the tyranny of some of the little chieftains; thus for example, Rasa, as the honest Dean says, was pertaining to MacGyllychallan by the sword, and to the Bishop of the Isles by heritage.

The title of these prelates, during the conjunction of Man and Sodor, had been universally mistaken, till the explications of that most ingenious writer, Dr Macpherson: it was always supposed to have been derived from Soder, an imaginary town, either in Man or in Iona: whose derivation was taken from the Greek *soter* or 'saviour'.[22] During the time that the Norwegians were

[19] *De Brit. Eccles. Primord.*, cap. xv, 701.
[20] Sir David Dalrymple's *Annals Scotland*, 178.
[21] The Dean.
[22] p. 282, and Torfoeus, in many parts of his *History of Orkneys*.

in possession of the isles, they divided them into two parts: the northern, which comprehended all that lay to the north of the point of Ardnamurchan, and were called the Nordereys, from *norder*, 'north', and *ey* 'an island'. And the Sudereys took in those that lay to the south of that promontory. This was only a civil division, for the sake of governing these scattered dominions with more facility; for a separate viceroy was sent to each, but both were subject to the same jurisdiction civil and ecclesiastical. But as the Sudereys was the most important, that had the honour of giving name to the bishopric, and the Isle of Man retained both titles, like as England unites that of France, notwithstanding many centuries have elapsed since our rights to the now usurped titles are lost.

Proceed on our walk. To the west of the convent is the abbot's mount, overlooking the whole. Beneath seem to have been the gardens, once well cultivated, for we are told that the monks transplanted from other places, herbs both esculent and medicinal.

Beyond the mount are the ruins of a kiln, and a granary: and near it, was the mill. The lake or pool that served it lay behind; is now drained, and is the turbary, the fuel of the natives: it appears to have been once divided, for along the middle runs a raised way, pointing to the hills. They neglect at present the conveniency of a mill, and use only querns.

North from the granary extends a narrow flat, with a double dike and fosse on one side, and a single dike on the other. At the end is a square containing a cairn and surrounded with a stone dike. This is called a burial place: it must have been in very early times contemporary with other cairns, perhaps in the days of Druidism; for Bishop Pocock mentions, that he had seen two stones seven feet high, with a third laid across on their tops, an evident *cromlech*: he also adds, that the Irish name of the island was Inish Drunish; which agrees with the account I have somewhere read, that Iona had been the seat of Druids expelled by Columba, who found them there.

Before I quit this height, I must observe, that the whole of their religious buildings were covered on the north side by dikes, as a protection from the northern invaders, who paid little regard to the sanctity of their characters.

The public was greatly interested in the preservation of this place, for it was the repository of most of the ancient Scotch records.[23] The library here must also have been invaluable, if we can depend upon Boethius, who asserts, that Fergus II assisting Allaric the Goth, in the sacking of Rome, brought away as share of the plunder, a chest of books, which he presented to the monastery of Iona. Aenas Sylvius (afterwards Pope Pius II) intended, when he was in Scotland, to have visited the library in search of the lost books of Livy, but was prevented by the death of the King, James I. A small parcel of them were in 1525 brought to Aberdeen,[24] and great pains were taken to unfold them, but through age and the tenderness of the parchment, little could be read; but from what the learned were able to make out, the work appeared by the style to have rather been a fragment of Sallust than of Livy. But the register and records of the island, all written on parchment, and probably other more antique and valuable remains, were all destroyed by that worst than Gothic synod, which at the Reformation declared war against all science.[25]

At present, this once celebrated seat of learning is destitute of even a schoolmaster; and this seminary of holy men wants even a minister to assist them in the common duties of religion.

Cross the island over a most fertile elevated tract to the southwest side, to visit the landing place of St Columba; a small bay, with a pebbly beach, mixed with variety of pretty stones, such as violet-coloured quartz, nephritic stones, and fragments of porphyry, granite and Zoeblitz marble: a vast tract near this place was covered with heaps of stones, of unequal sizes: these, as is said, were the penances of monks who were to raise heaps of dimensions equal to their crimes: and to judge by some, it is no breach of charity to think there were among them enormous sinners.

[23] Vide MacKenzie, Stillingfleet, Lluyd.

[24] Boethius lib. VII, 114. Paulus Jovius, quoted by Usher, *Br. Eccl.*, 597. I am informed that numbers of the records of the Hebrides were preserved at Drontheim till they were destroyed by the great fire which happened in that city either in the last, or present century.

[25] MS, Advocates Library.

On one side is shown an oblong heap of earth, the supposed size of the vessel that transported St Columba and his twelve disciples from Ireland to this island.

On my return saw, on the right hand, on a small hill, a small circle of stones, and a little cairn in the middle, evidently Druidical, but called 'the hill of the angels', Cnoc-nar-Aimgeal; from a tradition that the holy man had there a conference with those celestial beings soon after his arrival. Bishop Pocock informed me, that the natives were accustomed to bring their horses to this circle at the feast of St Michael, and to course round it. I conjecture that this usage originated from the custom of blessing the horses in the days of superstition, when the priest and the holy water-pot were called in: but in latter times the horses are still assembled, but the reason forgotten.

The traveller must not neglect to ascend the hill of Dun-ii; from whose summit is a most picturesque view of the long chain of little islands, neighbours to this; of the long low isles of Col and Tir-I to the west; and the vast height of Rum and Skie to the north.

At eight of the clock in the morning, with the first fair wind we yet had, set sail for the sound: the view of Iona, its clustered town, the great ruins, and the fertility of the ground, were fine contrasts, in our passage to the red granite rocks of the barren Mull.

Loch Screban, in Mull, soon opens to our view. After passing a cape, placed in our maps far too projectingly, see Loch-in-a-Gaal; a deep bay, with the isles of Ulva and Gometra in its mouth.

On the west appears the beautiful group of the Treashunish Isles.[26] Nearest lies Staffa, a new Giant's Causeway, rising amidst the waves; but with columns of double the height of that in Ireland; glossy and resplendent, from the beams of the eastern sun. Their greatest height was at the southern point of the isle, of which they seemed the support. They decreased in height in proportion as they advanced along that face of Staffa opposed to us, or the eastern side; at length appeared lost in the formless strata: and the rest of the island that appeared to us was formed of slopes to the water

---

[26] These are most erroneously placed in the maps, a very considerable distance too far to the north.

XXV

Ru-entiach

Rutreanish or Ruth-en-i-sleuth

Crinberg or Cairnberg

Fiadda

bei more

Lunga

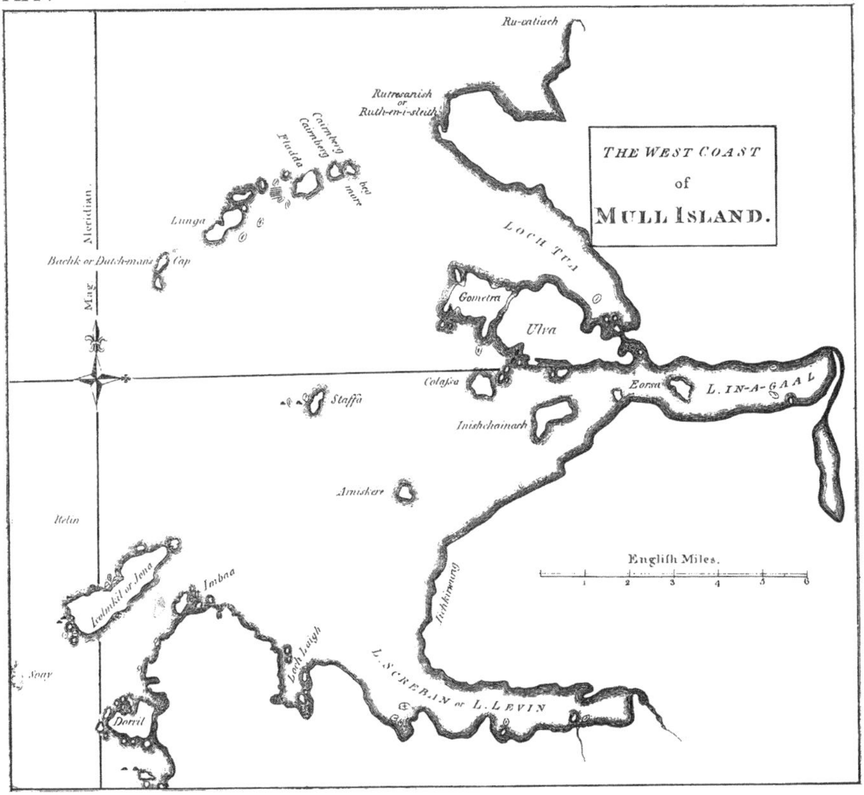

THE WEST COAST
of
MULL ISLAND.

LOCH TUA

Bachk or Dutchmans Cap

Mag. Meridian.

Gometra

Ulva

Colafsa

Earsa

L. IN-A-GAAL

Staffa

Inishchainach

Amiskere

English Miles.
1 2 3 4 5 6

Helin

Inchkil or Iona

Imbna

Loch Lough

Inchkenneg

L. SCREBAN or L. LEVIN

Soar

Dorril

edge, or of rude but not lofty precipices. Over part of the isle, on the western side, was plainly to be seen a vast precipice, seemingly columnar, like the preceding. I wished to make a nearer approach, but the prudence of Mr Thompson, who was unwilling to venture in these rocky seas, prevented my farther search of this wondrous isle: I could do no more than cause an accurate view to be taken of its eastern side, and of those of the other picturesque islands then in sight. But it is a great consolation to me, that I am able to lay before the public a most accurate account communicated to me through the friendship of Mr Banks.

ACCOUNT of STAFFA
by
JOSEPH BÁNKS, Esq.

In the Sound of Mull we came to anchor, on the Morvern side, opposite to a gentleman's house, called Drummen: the owner of it, Mr MacLeane, having found out who we were, very cordially asked us ashore: we accepted his invitation, and arrived at his house; where we met an English gentleman, Mr Leach,[27] who no sooner saw us than told us, that about nine leagues from us was an island where he believed no one even in the Highlands had been,[28] on which were pillars like those of the Giant's Causeway: this was a great object to me who had wished to have seen the causeway itself, would time have allowed: I therefore resolved to proceed directly, especially as it was just in the way to the Columbkill; accordingly having put up two days provisions, and my little tent, we put off in the boat about one o'clock for our intended voyage, having ordered the ship to wait for us in Tobirmore, a very fine harbour on the Mull side.

At nine o'clock, after a tedious passage, having had not a breath of wind, we arrived, under the direction of Mr McLeane's son, and Mr Leach. It was too dark to see any thing, so we carried our tent and baggage near the only house upon the island, and began to cook our suppers, in order to be prepared for the earliest dawn, to enjoy that which from the conversation of the gentleman we had now raised the highest expectations of.

The impatience which everybody felt to see the wonders we had heard so largely described, prevented our morning's rest; everyone was up and in motion before the break of day, and with the first light arrived at the south-west part of the island, the seat of the most

[27] I cannot but express the obligations I have to this gentleman for his very kind intentions of informing me of this matchless curiosity; for I am informed that he pursued me in a boat for two miles, to acquaint me with what he had observed: but, unfortunately for me, we out-sailed his liberal intention.

[28] When I lay in the Sound of Iona, two gentlemen, from the isle of Mull, and whose settlements were there, seemed to know nothing of this place; at least they never mentioned it as anything wonderful.

XXVI

View down the Firth of Clyde.

remarkable pillars; where we no sooner arrived than were struck with a scene of magnificence which exceeded our expectations, though formed, as we thought, upon the most sanguine foundations: the whole of that end of the island supported by ranges of natural pillars, mostly above 50 feet high, standing in natural colonnades, according as the bays or points of land formed themselves; upon a firm basis of solid unformed rock, above these, the stratum which reaches to the soil or surface of the island, varied in thickness, as the island itself formed into hills or valleys; each hill, which hung over the columns below, forming an ample pediment; some of these above 60 feet in thickness, from the base to the point, formed by the sloping of the hill on each side, almost into the shape of those used in architecture.

Compared to this what are the cathedrals or the places built by men? Mere models or playthings, imitations as diminutive as his works will always be when compared to those of nature. Where is now the boast of the architect? Regularity the only part in which he fancied himself to exceed his mistress, Nature, is here found in her possession, and here it has been for ages underscribed.[29] Is not this the school where the art was originally studied, and what has been added to this by the whole Grecian school? A capital to ornament the column of nature, of which they could execute only a model; and for that very capital they were obliged to a bush of acanthus: how amply does nature repay those who study her wonderful works!

With our minds full of such reflections we proceeded along the shore, treading upon another Giant's Causeway, every stone being regularly formed into a certain number of sides and angles, till in a short time we arrived at the mouth of a cave, the most magnificent, I suppose, that has ever been described by travellers.

The mind can hardly form an idea more magnificent than such a space, supported on each side by ranges of columns; and roofed by the bottoms of those, which have been broke off in order to

[29] Staffa is taken notice of by Buchanan, but in the slightest manner; and among the thousands who have navigated these seas, none have paid the least attention to its grand and striking characteristic, till this present year.

This island is the property of Mr Lauchlan MacQuaire, of Ulva, and is now to be disposed of.

form it; between the angles of which a yellow stalagmitic matter has exuded, which serves to define the angles precisely; and at the same time vary the colour with a great deal of elegance, and to render it still more agreeable, the whole is lighted from without; so that the farthest extremity is very plainly seen from without, and the air within being agitated by the flux and reflux of the tides, is perfectly dry and wholesome, free entirely from the damp vapours with which natural caverns in general abound.

We asked the name of it. Said our guide, 'The cave of Fhinn.' 'What is Fhinn?' said we. 'Fhinn MacCoul, whom the translator of Ossian's works has called Fingal.' How fortunate that in this cave we should meet with the remembrance of that chief, whose existence, as well as that of the whole epic poem is almost doubted in England.

Enough for the beauties of Staffa. I shall now proceed to describe it and its productions more philosophically.

The little island of Staffa lies on the west coast of Mull, about three leagues north-east from Iona, or the Columb Kill: its greatest length is about an English mile, and its breadth about half a one. On the west side of the isle is a small bay, where boats generally land: a little to the southward of which the first appearance of pillars are to be observed; they are small, and instead of being placed upright, lie down on their sides, each forming a segment of a circle: from thence you pass a small cave, above which, the pillars now grown a little larger, are inclining in all directions: in one place in particular a small mass of them very much resemble the ribs of a ship:[30] from hence having passed the cave, which if it is not low water, you must do in a boat, you come to the first ranges of pillars, which are still not above half as large as those a little beyond. Over-against this place is a small island, called in Erse, Boo-sha-la or more properly Buachaille, or 'the herdsman', separated from the main, by a channel not many fathoms wide; this whole island is composed of pillars without any stratum above them; they are still small, but by much the nearest formed of any about the place.

---

[30] The Giant's Causeway has its bending pillars; but I imagine them to be very different from these. Those I saw were erect, and ran along the face of a high cliff, bent strangely in their middle, as if unable, at their original formation, while in a soft state, to support the mass of incumbent earth that pressed on them.

View of the ERECT COLUMNS near the SHAGS CAVE, on the Island of STAFFA.
Taken from the Sea.

P.º Mazel sculp.

FINGAL'S CAVE IN STAFFA.

The first division of the island, for at high water it is divided into two, makes a kind of cone, the pillars converging together towards the centre: on the other, they are in general laid down flat, and in the front next to the main, you see how beautifully they are packed together; their ends coming out square with the bank which they form: all these have their transverse sections exact, and their surfaces smooth, which is by no means the case with the large ones, which are cracked in all directions. I much question however, if any one of this whole island of Buachaille is two feet in diameter.

The main island opposed to Boo-sha-la and farther towards the north-west is supported by ranges of pillars pretty erect, and though not tall, (as they are not uncovered to the base) of large diameters; and at their feet is an irregular pavement, made by the upper sides of such as have been broken off, which extends as far under water as the eye can reach. Here the forms of the pillars are apparent; these are three, four, five, six, and seven sides; but the numbers of five and six are by much the most prevalent. The largest I measured was of seven; it was four feet five inches in diameter. I shall give the measurement of its sides, and those of some other forms which I met with:

No. 1. 4 sides diam. 1 ft. 5 in. No. 2 5 sides diam. 2 ft. 10 in.

Side	Ft.	In.	Side	Ft.	In.
1	1	5	1	1	10
2	1	1	2	1	10
3	1	6	3	1	5
4	1	1	4	1	$7\,^1/_2$
			5	1	8

No. 3. 6 sides diam. 3 ft. 6 in. No. 4. 7 sides diam. 4 ft. 5 in.

Side	Ft.	In.	Side	Ft.	In.
1	0	10	1	2	10
2	2	2	2	2	4
3	2	2	3	1	10
4	1	11	4	2	0
5	2	2	5	1	1
6	2	9	6	1	6
			7	1	3

XXIX

VIEW OF BOOSHALA FROM THE CLIFF ABOVE IT.

XXX

Miller del.

B. Mazell Sculp.

BENDING PILLARS IN STAFFA.

Isle of Boo-sha-la & bending Pillars opposite to it.

The surfaces of these large pillars in general are rough and uneven, full of cracks in all directions; the transverse figures in the upright ones never fail to run in their true directions: the surfaces upon which we walked were often flat, having neither concavity nor convexity: the larger number however were concave, though some were very evidently convex; in some places the interstices within the perpendicular figures were filled up with a yellow spar: in one place a vein passed in among the mass of pillars, carrying here and there small threads of spar. Though they were broken and cracked through and through in all directions, yet their perpendicular figures might easily be traced: from whence it is easy to infer, that whatever the accident might have been, that caused the dislocation, it happened after the formation of the pillars.

From hence proceeding along shore, you arrive at Fingal's Cave: its dimensions though I have given, I shall here again repeat in the form of a table:

	Feet	Inches
Length of the cave from the rock without	371	6
from the pitch of the arch,	250	0
Breadth of ditto at the mouth	53	7
at the farther end	20	0
Height of arch at the mouth	117	6
at the end	70	0
Height of an outside pillar	39	6
of one at the north-west corner	54	0
Depth of water at the mouth	18	0
at the bottom	9	0

The cave runs into the rock in the direction of north-east by east by the compass.

Proceeding farther to the north-west you meet with the highest ranges of pillars, the magnificent appearance of which is past all description: here they are bare to their very basis, and the stratum below them is also visible: in a short time it rises many feet above the water, and gives an opportunity of examining its quality. Its surface rough, and has often large lumps of stone sticking in it, as if half immersed; itself, when broken, is composed of a thousand heterogeneous parts, which together have very much the appearance of a lava; and the more so as many of the lumps appear to be of the very same stone of which the pillars are formed: this whole stratum lies in an inclined position, dipping gradually towards the south-east. As hereabouts is the situation of the highest pillars, I shall mention my measurements of them and the different strata in this place, premising that the measurements were made with a line, held in the hand of a person who stood at the top of the cliff, and reaching to the bottom, to the lower end of which was tied a white mark, which was observed by one who stayed below for the purpose: when this mark was set off from the water, the person below noted it down, and made signal to him above, who made then a mark in his rope: whenever this mark passed a notable place, the same signal was made, and the name of the place noted down as before: the line being all hauled up, and the distances between the marks measured and noted down, gave, when compared with the book kept below, the distances, as for instance in the cave:

No. 1 in the book below, was called from the water to the foot of the first pillar, in the book above; No. 1 gave 36 feet 8 inches, the highest of that ascent, which was composed of broken pillars.

No. 1 Pillar at the west corner of Fingal's Cave

		Feet	Inches
1	From the water to the foot of the pillar	12	10
2	Height of the pillar	37	3
3	Stratum above the pillar	66	9

No. 2 Fingal's Cave

1	From the water to the foot of the pillar	36	8
2	Height of the pillar	39	6
3	From the top of the pillar to the top of the arch	31	4
4	Thickness of the stratum above	34	4
	By adding together the three first measurements, we got the height of the arch from the water	117	6

No. 3 Corner pillar to the westward of Fingal's Cave

Stratum below the pillar of lava-like matter	11	0
Length of pillar	54	0
Stratum above the pillar	61	6

No. 4 Another pillar to the westward

Stratum below the pillar	17	1
Height of the pillar	50	0
Stratum above	51	1

No. 5 Another pillar farther to the westward

Stratum below the pillar	19	8
Height of the pillar	55	1
Stratum above	54	7

The stratum above the pillars, which is here mentioned, is uniformly the same, consisting of numberless small pillars, bending and inclining in all directions, sometimes so irregularly, that the stones can only be said to have an inclination to assume a columnar form; in others more regular, but never breaking into, or disturbing the stratum of large pillars, whose tops every where keep an uniform and irregular line.

Proceeding now along shore round the north end of the island, you arrive at Oua-na-Scarve, or 'the cormorant's cave': here the stratum under the pillars is lifted up very high; the pillars above it are considerably less than those at the north-west end of the island, but still very considerable. Beyond is a bay, which cuts deep into the island, rendering it in that place not more than a quarter of a mile over. On the sides of this bay, especially beyond a little valley, which almost cuts the island into two, are two stages of pillars, but small; however having a stratum between them exactly the same as that above them, formed of innumerable little pillars, shaken out of their places, and leaning in all directions.

Having passed this bay, the pillars totally cease; the rock is of a dark brown stone, and no signs of regularity occur till you have passed round the south-east end of the island (a space almost as large as that occupied by the pillars) which you meet again on the west side, beginning to form themselves irregularly, as if the stratum had an inclination to that form, and soon arrive at the bending pillars where I began.

The stone of which the pillars are formed, is a coarse kind of basalt, very much resembling the Giant's Causeway in Ireland, though none of them are near so neat as the specimens of the latter, which I have seen at the British Museum; owing chiefly to the colour, which in our's is a dirty brown, in the Irish a fine black: indeed the whole production seems very much to resemble the Giant's Causeway, with which I should willingly compare it, had I any account of the former before me.[31]

[31] As this account is copied from Mr Banks' journal, I take the liberty of saying (what by this time that gentleman is well acquainted with) that Staffa is a genuine mass of basalt, or 'giant's causeway'; but in most respects superior to the Irish in grandeur. I must add that the name is Norwegian; and most properly bestowed on account of its singular structure: Staffa being derived from *staf*, 'a staff', 'prop', or, figuratively, 'a column'.

VIII

THE HEBRIDES (3)

Cairnberg—Cannay—Rum—MacKinnon's Castle—The Kyle—Beinn-na-caillich—Isle of Rasa—Skie—Talyskir—Loch Bracadale—Dunvegan—Duntuilm Castle

PROCEED with a fine breeze; see, beyond Staffa, Baca-beg, and the Dutchman's Cap, formed like a Phrygian bonnet: next succeeds Lunga varying into grotesque shapes as we recede from it:[1] the low flats of Flada next show themselves: and lastly the isles of Cairnberg More and Beg; the first noted for its ancient fortress, the outguard to the Sudereys, or southern Hebrides.

In the year 1249, John Dungadi, appointed by Acho of Norway, King of the Northern Hebrides, was entrusted with the defence of this castle; and, in return for that confidence, declined to surrender it to Alexander III of Scotland, who meditated the conquest of these islands. It was in those days called Kiarnaburgh, or Biarnaburgh.[2] The MacLeanes possessed it in 1715, and during the rebellion of that year, was taken and retaken by each party.

In our course observe at a distance, Tirey, or Tir-I, famous for its great plain, and the breed of little horses. To the north, separated from Tirey by a small sound, is the isle of Col. I must not omit

---

[1] At the bottom of the print of the rocks of Cannay, is a very singular view of Lunga, and the Dutchman's Cap, as they appeared about eight or nine miles distant, the first south-south by west the last south-west by south.

[2] Torfoeus, 164.

observing, that the first, is reported, by a very sensible writer, to be well adapted for the culture of tobacco.[3]

Pass the point Ruth-an-i-sleith, in Mull, when Egg high and rounded, Muck small, and the exalted tops of the mountainous Rum, and lofty Skie, appear in view. Leave on the east, Calgaray Bay, in Mull, with a few houses, and some signs of cultivation; the first marks of population that had shown themselves in this vast island.

The entrance of the Sound of Mull now opens, bounded to the north by cape Ardnamurchan, or, the height of the boisterous sea; and beyond, inland, soar the vast summits of Benevish, Morvern and Crouachan.

Towards afternoon the sky grows black, and the wind freshens into a gale, attended with rain, discouraging us from a chase of seals, which we proposed on the rock Heiskyr, a little to the west, where they swarm. To the west of Cannay, have a sight of the rock Humbla, formed of basaltic columns.[4]

Leave, three leagues to the west, the cairns of Col, a dangerous chain of rocks, extending from its northern extremity.

Sail under the vast mountains of Rum, and the point of Bredon, through a most turbulent sea, caused by the clashing of two adverse tides. See several small whales, called here pollacks, that when near land are often chased on shore by boats: they are usually about ten feet long, and yield four gallons of oil. At seven o'clock in the evening find ourselves at anchor in four fathom water, in the snug harbour of the isle of Cannay, formed on the north side by Cannay, on the south by the little isle of Sanda: the mouth lies opposite to Rum, and about three miles distant: the western channel into it is impervious, by reason of rocks. On that side of the entrance next to Sanda is a rock to be shunned by mariners.

As soon as we had time to cast our eyes about, each shore appeared pleasing to humanity; verdant, and covered with hundreds

---

[3] *Accompt. Current betwixt England and Scotland,* by John Spruel.
[4] This was discovered by Mr Murdock Mackenzie.

of cattle: both sides gave a full idea of plenty, for the verdure was mixed with very little rock, and scarcely any heath: but a short conversation with the natives soon dispelled this agreeable error: they were at this very time in such want, that numbers for a long time had neither bread nor meal for their poor babes: fish and milk was their whole subsistence at this time: the first was a precarious relief, for, besides the uncertainty of success, to add to their distress, their stock of fish-hooks was almost exhausted; and to ours, that it was not in our power to supply them. The ribons, and other trifles I had brought would have been insults to people in distress. I lamented that my money had been so uselessly laid out; for a few dozens of fish-hooks, or a few pecks of meal, would have made them happy. The Turks erect *caravansaras*. Christians of different opinions concur in establishing *hospitia* among the dreary Alps, for the reception of travellers. I could wish the public bounty, or private charity, would found in fit parts of the isles or mainland, magazines of meal, as preservatives against famine in these distant parts.

The crops had failed here the last year: but the little corn sown at present had a promising aspect: and the potatoes are the best I had seen: but these were not fit for use. The isles I fear annually experience a temporary famine: perhaps from improvidence, perhaps from eagerness to increase their stock of cattle, which they can easily dispose of to satisfy the demands of a landlord, or the oppressions of an agent. The people of Cannay export none, but sell them to the numerous busses, who put into this *portus salutis* on different occasions.

The cattle are of a middle size, black, long-legged, and have thin staring manes from the neck along the back, and up part of the tail. They look well, for in several parts of the islands they have good warm recesses to retreat to in winter. About sixty head are exported annually.

Each couple of milch cows yielded at an average of seven stones of butter and cheese: two thirds of the first and one of the last. The cheese sold at three and six pence a stone; the butter at eight shillings.

Here are very few sheep: but horses in abundance. The chief use of them in this little district is to form an annual cavalcade at

Michaelmas. Every man on the island mounts his horse unfurnished with saddle, and takes behind him either some young girl, or his neighbour's wife, and then rides backwards and forwards from the village to a certain cross, without being able to give any reason for the origin of this custom. After the procession is over, they alight at some public house, where, strange to say, the females treat the companions of their ride. When they retire to their houses an entertainment is prepared with primeval simplicity: the chief part consists of a great oatcake, called *struan Michaeil*, or 'St Michael's cake', composed of two pecks of meal, and formed like the quadrant of a circle: it is daubed over with milk and eggs, and then placed to harden before the fire.

Matrimony is held in such esteem here that an old maid or old bachelor is scarcely known; such firm belief have they in the doctrine of the ape-leading disgrace in the world below. So, to avoid that danger the youth marry at twenty, the lasses at seventeen. The fair sex are used here with more tenderness than common, being employed only in domestic affairs, and never forced into the labours of the field. Here are plenty of poultry and of eggs.

Abundance of cod and ling might be taken; there being a fine sandbank between this isle and the rock Heiskyr, and another between Skie and Barra; but the poverty of the inhabitants will not enable them to attempt a fishery. When at Campbeltown I enquired about the apparatus requisite, and found that a vessel of twenty tons was necessary, which would cost two hundred pounds; that the crew should be composed of eight hands, whose monthly expenses would be fourteen pounds; that six hundred fathom of long-line, five hundred hooks, and two stuoy lines (each eighty fathoms long) which are placed at each end of the long-lines, with buoys at top to mark the place when sunk, would all together cost five guineas; and the vessel must be provided with four sets: so that the whole charge of such an adventure is very considerable, and past the ability of these poor people.[5]

The length of the island is about three miles; the breadth near one: its surface hilly. This was the property of the Bishop of the Isles,

---

[5] In *Br. Zool.* III, 193, is an account of a fishery of this nature.

but at present that of Mr MacDonald of clan Ronald. His factor, a resident agent, rents most of the island, paying two guineas for each pennyland; and these he sets to the poor people at four guineas and a half each; and exacts, besides this, three days labour in the quarter from each person. Another head tenant possesses other pennylands, which he sets in the same manner, to the impoverishing and very starving of the wretched inhabitants.

The pennylands derive their name from some old valuation. The sum requisite to stock one is thirty pounds: it maintains seven cows and two horses; and the tenant can raise on it eight bolls of small black oats, the produce of two; and four of bere from half a boll of seed; one boll of potatoes yields seven. The two last are manured with sea-tang.

The arable land in every farm is divided into four parts, and lots of cast for them at Christmas: the produce, when reaped and dried, is divided among them in proportion to their rents; and for want of mills is ground in the quern. All the pasture is common, from May to the beginning of September.

It is said that the factor has in a manner banished sheep, because there is no good market for them; so that he does his best to deprive the inhabitants of clothing as well as food. At present they supply themselves with wool from Rum, at the rate of eight pence the pound.

All the clothing is manufactured at home: the women not only spin the wool, but weave the cloth: the men make their own shoes, tan the leather with the bark of willow, or the roots of the *Tormentilla erecta*, or tormentil, and in defect of wax-thread, use split thongs.

About twenty tons of kelp are made in the shores every third year.

Sickness seldom visits this place: if any disorder seizes them the patients do no more than drink whey, and lie still. The smallpox visits them about once in twenty years.

All disputes are settled by the factor, or, if of great moment, by the justices of the peace in Skie.

This islands Rum, Muck, and Egg, form one parish. Cannay is inhabited by two hundred and twenty souls; of which all, except four families, are Roman Catholics; but in the whole parish there is neither church, manse, nor school: there is indeed in this island a catechist, who has nine pounds a year from the royal bounty. The minister and the popish priest reside in Egg; but, by reason of the turbulent seas that divide these isles, are very seldom able to attend their flocks. I admire the moderation of their congregations, who attend the preaching of either indifferently as they happen to arrive. As the Scotch are economists in religion, I would recommend to them the practice of one of the little Swiss mixed cantons, who, through mere frugality, kept but one divine; a moderate honest fellow, who, steering clear of controversial points, held forth to the Calvinist flock on one part of the day, and to his Catholic on the other. He lived long among them much respected, and died lamented.

The Protestant natives of many of the isles observe Yule and Pasch, or Christmas and Easter; which among rigid Presbyterians is esteemed so horrid a superstition, that I have heard of a minister who underwent a censure for having a goose to dinner on Christmas day; as if any one day was more holy than another, or to be distinguished by any external marks of festivity.

In popish times here was probably a resident minister; for here are to be seen the ruins of a chapel, and a small cross.

Much rain and very hard gales the whole night; the weather being, as it is called in these parts, broken.

Bad weather still continues, which prevented us from seeing so much of this land as we intended, and also of visiting the rock Humbla. Go on shore at the nearest part, and visit a lofty slender rock, that juts into the sea: on one side is a little tower, at a vast height above us, accessible by a narrow and horrible path: it seems so small as scarce to be able to contain half a dozen people. Tradition says that it was built by some jealous regulus, to confine a handsome wife in.

To the north-west above this prison, is the Compass Hill, in Erse called Sgar Dhearg, or 'the red projecting rock'. On the top the needle in the mariners compass was observed to vary a whole quarter; the north point standing due west: an irregularity probably owing to the nature of the rock, highly impregnated with iron.

XXXII

Mar. Griffith, del.

I. Mazell Sculp.

VIEW IN CANNAY.

In the afternoon some coal was brought, found in the rocks Duneudain, but in such small veins as to be useless. It lies in beds of only six inches in thickness, and about a foot distant from each other, divided by strata of whinstone. Fuel is very scarce here, and often the inhabitants are obliged to fetch it from Rum.

A continuation of bad weather. At half an hour after one at noon, loose from Cannay, and after passing with a favourable gale through a rolling sea, in about two hours, anchor in the isle of Rum, in an open bay, about two miles deep, called Loch Sgriosard, bounded by high mountains, black and barren: at the bottom of the bay is the little village of Kinloch, of about a dozen houses, built in a singular manner, with walls very thick and low, with the roofs of thatch reaching a little beyond the inner edge, so that they serve as benches for the lazy inhabitants, whom we found sitting on them in great numbers, expecting our landing, with that avidity for news common to the whole country.

Entered the house with the best aspect, but found it little superior in goodness to those of Ilay; this indeed had a chimney and windows, which distinguished it from the others, and denoted the superiority of the owner: the rest knew neither windows nor chimneys. A little hole on one side gave an exit to the smoke: the fire is made on the floor beneath; above hangs a rope, with the pot-hook at the end to hold the vessel that contains their hard fare, a little fish, milk, or potatoes. Yet, beneath the roof I entered, I found an address and politeness from the owner and his wife that were astonishing: such pretty apologies for the badness of the treat, the curds and milk that were offered; which were tendered to us with as much readiness and good will, as by any of old Homer's dames, celebrated by him in his *Odyssey* for their hospitality. I doubt much whether their cottages or their fare was much better; but it must be confessed that they might be a little more cleanly than our good hostels.

Rum, or Ronin as it is called by the Dean, is the property of Mr MacLeane, of Col; a landlord mentioned by the natives with much affection. The length is about twelve miles; the breadth six: the number of souls at this time three hundred and twenty-five; of families, with their wives, were at this time all alive, except five, three widowers and two widows. They had with them a hundred and two sons and only seventy-six daughters: this disproportion prevails in Cannay, and the other little islands; in order, in the end, to preserve a balance between the two sexes; as the men are, from their way of life, so perpetually exposed to danger in these stormy seas, and to other accidents that might occasion a depopulation, was it not so providentially ordered.[6]

The island is one great mountain, divided into several points; the highest called Aisgobhall. About this bay, and towards the east side, the land slopes towards the water side; but on the south-west forms precipices of a stupendous height. The surface of Rum is in a manner covered with heath, and in a state of nature: the heights rocky. There is very little arable land, excepting about the nine little hamlets that the natives have grouped in different places; near which the corn is sown in diminutive patches, for the tenants here *runrig* as in Cannay. The greatest farmer holds five pounds twelve shillings a year, and pays his rent in money. The whole of the island is two thousand marks.[7]

The little corn and potatoes they raise is very good; but so small is the quantity of bere and oats that there is not a fourth part produced to supply their annual wants: all the subsistence the poor people have besides, is curds, milk and fish. They are a well-made and well-looking race, but carry famine in their aspect. Are often a whole summer without a grain in the island; which they regret not on their own account, but for the sake of their poor babes. In the present economy of the island, there is no prospect of any improvement. Here is an absurd custom of allotting a certain stock to the land; for example, a farmer is allowed to keep fourteen head of cattle, thirty sheep, and six mares, on a certain tract called a pennyland.[8] The person who keeps more is obliged to repair out

---

[6] In Chester, and other large towns, though the number of males exceeds the number of females born; yet when arrived to the age of puberty the females are much more numerous than males; because the latter, in every period of life, are more liable to fatal diseases.

[7] A Scotch mark is little more than thirteen pence farthing.

[8] The division into pennylands, and much of the rural economy agree in both islands.

of his superfluity any loss his neighbour may sustain in his herds or flocks.

A number of black cattle is sold, at thirty or forty shillings per head, to graziers, who come annually from Skie, and other places. The mutton here is small, but the most delicate in our dominions, if the goodness of our appetites did not pervert our judgment: the purchase of a fat sheep was four shillings and six pence: the natives kill a few, and also of cows, to salt for winter provisions. A few goats are kept here: abundance of mares, and a necessary number of stallions; for the colts are an article of commerce, but they never part with the fillies.

Every pennyland is restricted to twenty-eight 'sums' of cattle: one milk cow is reckoned a sum, or ten sheep: a horse is reckoned two sums. By this regulation every person is at liberty to make up his sums with what species of cattle he pleases; but then is at the same time prevented from injuring his neighbour (in a place where grazing is in common) by rearing too great a stock. This rule is often broken; but by the former regulation, the sufferer may repair his loss from the herds of the avaritious.

No hay is made in this island, nor any sort of provender for winter provision. The domestic animals support themselves as well as they can on spots of grass preserved for that purpose. In every farm is one man, from his office called *fear cuartaich*, whose sole business is to preserve the grass and corn: as a reward he is allowed grass for four cows, and the produce of as much arable land as one horse can till and harrow.

Very few poultry are reared here, on account of the scarcity of grain.

No wild quadrupeds are found, excepting stags: these animals once abounded here, but they are now reduced to eighty, by the eagles, who not only kill the fawns, but the old deer, seizing them between the horns, and terrifying them till they fall down some precipice, and become their prey.

The birds we observed were ring-tail eagles, ravens, hooded crows, white wagtails, wheatears, titlarks, ring-ouzels, grouse, ptarmigans, curlews, green plovers, fasceddars or Arctic gulls, and the greater terns: the Dean mentions gannets, but none appeared while we were in the island.

At the foot of Sgor-mor, opposite to Cannay, are found abundance of agates, of that species called by Cronsted, sect. lxi, 6, *Achates chalcedonisans*, improperly, white cornelians: several singular strata, such as grey quartzy stone, Cronsted sect. cclxxiv; another, a mixture of quartz and basaltes, a black stone, spotted with white, like porphyry, but with the appearance of lava: fine grit, or freestone, and the cinereous indorated bole of Cronsted, sect. lxxxvii.

Land again: walk five miles up the sides of the island, chiefly over heath and moory ground: cross two deep gullies, varied with several pretty cascades, falling from rock to rock: pass by great masses of stone, corroded as if they had lain on the shore. After a long ascent reach Loch-nan-grun, a piece of water amidst the rocks, beneath some of the highest peaks of the mountains. Abundance of terns inhabit this loch. Return excessively wet with constant rain.

Notwithstanding this island has several streams, here is not a single mill; all the molinary operations are done at home: the corn is 'graddaned', or burnt out of the ear, instead of being thrashed: this is performed two ways; first, by cutting off the ears, and drying them in a kiln, then setting fire to them on a floor, and picking out the grains, by this operation rendered as black as coal. The other method is more expeditious, for the whole sheaf is burnt, without the trouble of cutting off the ears: a most ruinous practice, as it destroys both thatch and manure, and on that account has been wisely prohibited in some of the islands. Graddaned corn was the parched corn of Holy Writ. Thus Boaz presents his beloved Ruth with parched corn; and Jesse sends David with an ephah of the same to his sons in the camp of Saul. The grinding was also performed by the same sort of machine the quern, in which two women were necessarily employed: thus it is prophesied 'two women shall be grinding at the mill, one shall be taken, the other left'. I must observe too that the island lasses are as merry as their work of grinding the graddan, the καχζος of the ancients, as those of Greece were in the days of Aristophanes,

Who warbled as they ground their parched corn.[9]

---

[9] *Nubes*, Act I, scene 2. Graddan is derived from *grad*, 'quick', as the process is so expeditious.

The quern or *bra* is made in some of the neighbouring counties, in the mainland, and costs about fourteen shillings. This method of grinding is very tedious: for it employs two pairs of hands four hours to grind only a single bushel of corn. Instead of a hair sieve to sift the meal the inhabitants here have an ingenious substitute, a sheepskin stretched round a hoop, and perforated with small holes made with a hot iron. They knead their bannock with water only, and bake or rather toast it, by laying it upright against a stone placed near the fire.

For want of lime they dress their leather with calcined shells: and use the same method of tanning it as in Cannay.

The inhabitants of Rum are people that scarcely know sickness: if they are attacked with a dysentery they make use of a decoction of the roots of the *Tormentilla erecta* in milk. The smallpox has visited them but once in thirty-four years, only two sickened, and both recovered. The measles come often.

It is not wonderful that some superstitions should reign in these sequestered parts. Second sight is firmly believed at this time. My informant said that Lauchlan MacKerran of Cannay had told a gentleman that he could not rest for the noise he heard of the hammering of nails into his coffin: accordingly the gentleman died within fifteen days.

Molly MacLeane (aged forty) has the power of foreseeing events through a well-scraped blade-bone of mutton. Some time ago she took up one and pronounced that five graves were soon to be opened; one for a grown person: the other four for children; one of which was to be of her own kin: and so it fell out. These pretenders to second sight, like the Pythian priestess, during their inspiration fall into trances, foam at the mouth, grow pale, and feign to abstain from food for a month, so overpowered are they by the visions imparted to them during their paroxysms.

I must not omit a most convenient species of second sight, possessed by a gentleman of a neighbouring isle, who foresees all visitors, so has time to prepare accordingly: but enough of these tales, founded on impudence and nurtured by folly.

Here are only the ruins of a church in this island; so the minister is obliged to preach, the few times he visits his congregation, in the open air. The attention of our popish ancestors in this article, delivers down a great reproach on the negligence of their reformed descendants: the one leaving not even the most distant and savage part of our dominions without a place of worship; the other suffering the natives to want both instructor, and temple.

The weather grows more moderate; at one o'clock at noon sail from Rum, with a favourable and brisk gale, for the isle of Skie. Soon reach the point of Slate, at the south end, a division of that great island, a mixture of grass, a little corn and much heath. Leave on the right the point of Arisaig. Pass beneath Armadale in Skie, a seat beautifully wooded, gracing most unexpectedly this almost treeless tract. A little farther to the west opens the mouth of Loch-in-Daal, a safe harbour, and opposite to it on the mainland, that of Loch Iurn, or 'the lake of hell', with black mountains of tremendous height impending above.

The channel between the shire of Inverness and Skie now contracts; and enlarges again to a fine bay opposite to Glenelg, between the mainland and Dunan Ruagh, where is good anchorage under Skie. At the north end of this expanse, the two sides suddenly contract, and at Kul-ri form a strait bounded by high lands, not a quarter of a mile broad; the flood which runs here at the spring tides at the rate of seven knots an hour, carried us through with great rapidity, into another expanse perfectly landlocked, and very picturesque. We were now arrived amidst an amphitheatre of mountains; the country of Kintail bounded us on the north and east; and Skie (which from Loch-in-Daal became more lofty) confined us with its now wooded cliffs to the south. The ruins of an ancient castle, seated on the pinnacle of a rock, and some little isles formed our western view. These of old belonged to the MacKinnons, a very ancient race, who call themselves clan Alpin, or the descendants of Alpin, a Scotch monarch in the ninth century. Some of the line have still a property in Skie.

The violent squalls of wind darting from the apertures of the hills teased us for an hour, but after various tacks at last Mr Thompson anchored safely beneath MacKinnon's Castle, amidst a fleet of busses, waiting with anxiety for the appearance of herrings, this year uncommonly late. The hard rains were no small advantage to our scenery. We lay beneath a vast hill called Glaisbhein, clothed with birch and oaks, inhabited by roes: cataracts poured down in various places amidst the woods, reminding me of the beautiful cascades between Scheideck and Meyringen, in the canton of Underwald. This part is in the district of Strath, a portion of Skie.

Land at a point called the Kyle, or passage, where about fourscore horses were collected to be transported *à la nage* to the opposite shore, about a mile distant, in the same manner as, Polybius informs us, Hannibal passed his cavalry over the rapid Rhône.[10] They were taken over by fours, by little boats, a pair on each side held with halters by two men, after being forced off a rock into the sea. We undertook the conveyance of a pair. One, a pretty grey horse, swam admirably; the other was dragged along like a log; but as soon as it arrived within scent of its companions before landed, revived, disengaged itself, and took to the shore with great alacrity. Some very gentleman-like men attended these animals, and with great politeness offered their services.

Among the crowd was a lad *erectis auribus*; his ears had never been swaddled down, and they stood out as nature ordained; and I dare say his sense of hearing was more acute by this liberty.

The horned cattle of Skie are swam over, at the narrow passage of Kul-ri, at low water. Six, eight, or twelve are passed over at a time, of the one to the tail of the preceding, and so to the next; the first is fastened to a boat, and thus are conveyed to the opposite shore. This is the great pass into the island, but is destitute even of a horseferry.

At five in the morning quit our situation, and passing through a narrow and short sound, arrive in another fine expanse, beautifully landlocked by the mainland (part of Ross-shire) the islands of Rona and Croulin; Rasa, distinguished by the high hillock, called Duncanna; Scalpa, and the low verdant isle of Pabay, in old times the seat of assassins.[11] Skie shows a verdant slope for part of its shore: beyond soar the conic naked hills of Strait, and still farther the ragged heights of Blaven.

[10] Lib. III, ch. 8.
[11] In the time of Dean, all these little isles were full of woods, at present quite naked.

XXXIII

Maria Gegfele del

Dryas octopetala

Chelonia Sileviles

Ab Novel sculp.

See, behind us, the ruins of the castle, and the entrance of the bay we had left, the openings into the great lochs Kisserne and Carron, and, as a background, a boundless chain of rugged mountains. The day was perfectly clear, and the sea smooth as a mirror, disturbed but by the blowing of two whales, who entertained us for a considerable space by the *jet d'eaux* from their orifices.

Mr MacKinnon, junior, one of the gentlemen we saw with the horses, overtakes us in a boat, and presses us to accept the entertainment of his father's house of Coire-chattachan, in the neighbouring part of Skie. After landing near the isle of Scalpa, and walking about two miles along a flat, arrive at the quarters so kindly provided; directing Mr Thompson to carry the vessel to the north part of Skie.

The country is divided by low banks of earth, and, like the other islands, has more pasturage than corn. In my walk to Kilchrist, the church of the parish of Strath, saw, on the roadside strata of limestone and stone-marl, and former grey, the last white, and in many parts dissolved into an impalpable powder, and ready to the hands of the farmer. It is esteemed a fine manure, but better for corn than grass.

Near the church are vast strata of fine white marble, and some veined with grey, which I recognized to have been the bed, from whence the altar at Iona had been formed. Observe also great quantities of white granite, spotted with black. Messrs Lightfoot and Stuart ascend the high limestone mountain of Beinn-shuardal, and find it in a manner covered with that rare plant the *Dryas octopela*.

On my return an entertained with a rehearsal, I may call it, of the *luagh*, or, 'walking of cloth', a substitute for the fulling mill: twelve or fourteen women, divided into two equal numbers, sit down on each side of a long board, ribbed lengthways, placing the cloth on it: first they begin to work it backwards and forwards with their hands, singing at the same time, as at the quern: when they have tired their hands, every female uses her feet for the same purpose, and six or seven pairs of naked feet are in the most violent agitation, working one against the other: as by this time they grow very earnest in their labours, the fury of the song rises; at length it arrives to such a pitch, that without breach of charity you would imagine a troop of female demoniacs to have been assembled.

They sing in the same manner when they are cutting down the corn, when thirty or forty join in chorus, keeping time to the sound of a bagpipe, as the Grecian lasses were wont to do to that of a lyre during vintage in the days of Homer.[12] The subject of the songs at the *luaghadh*, the quern, and on this occasion, are sometimes love, sometimes panegyric, and often a rehearsal of the deeds of the ancient heroes, but commonly all the tunes slow and melancholy.

Singing at the quern is now almost out of date since the introduction of water-mills. The laird can oblige his tenants, as in England, to make use of this more expeditious kind of grinding; and empowers his miller to search out and break any querns he can find, as machines that defraud him of the toll. Many centuries past, the legislature attempted to discourage these awkward mills, so prejudicial to the landlords, who had been at the expense of others. In 1284, in the time of Alexander III it was provided, that 'na man fall presume to grind quheit, maishloch, or rye, with hand mylne, except he be compelled by storm, or be in lack of mills quhilk sould grind the samen. And in this case gif a man grindes at hand mylnes, he sal gif the threttein measure as multer, and gif anie man contraveins this our prohibition, he sall tine his hand mylnes perpetuallie.'

Walk up Beinn-a-Caillich, or, 'the hill of the old hag'; one of those picturesque mountains that made such a figure from the sea. After ascending a small part, find its sides covered with vast loose stones, like the Paps of Jura, the shelter of ptarmigans: the top flat and naked, with an artificial cairn, of a most enormous size, reported to have been the place of sepulture of a gigantic woman in the days of Fingal. The prospect to the west was that of desolation itself; a savage series of rude mountains, discoloured, black and red, as if by the rage of fire. Nearest, joined to this hill by a ridge, is Bein-an-Ghrianan, or 'the mountain of the sun'; perhaps venerated in ancient times. Malmore, or the round mountain, appears on the north. The serrated tops of Blaven affect with astonishment; and

---

[12] *Iliad*, XVIII, line 570.

XXXIV

Moses Griffith del.

Women at the QUERN and the LUAGHAD with a view of TALYSKIR

Grignion Sc.

XXXV

Moses Griffith del.

R. Havell sculp.

VIEW FROM BEINN, NA, CAILLICH IN SKIE.

beyond them, the clustered height of Quillin, or, the mountain of Cuchullin, like its ancient hero, 'stood like a hill that catches the clouds of heaven'.[13] The deep recesses between these alps, in times of old, possessed 'the sons of the narrow vales, the hunters of deer'; and to this time are inhabited by a fine race of stags.

The view to the north-east and south-west is not less amusing: a sea sprinkled over with various isles, and the long extent of coast soaring into all the forms of Alpine wildness. I must not omit that the point of Camisketel, on the south of Skie, was showed to me at a distance, famous for the cave which gave shelter for two nights to the young adventurer, and his faithful guide, the ancient MacKinnon.

Leave Coire-chattachan, after experiencing every civility from the family; and from the Rev Mr Nicholson, the minister. Wind along the bottoms of the steep hills. Pass by the end of Loch Slappan to the south. See a stone dike or fence called Paraicnam Fiadh, or 'the enclosure of the deer', which seems once to have been continued up a neighbouring hill. In one angle is a hollow, in the days of Ossian, a pitfall covered with boughs for the destruction of the animals chased into it. Places of this name are very common, and very necessary, when the food of mankind was the beasts of the field.

Turn towards the northern coast; pass by the end of Lochsligachan, and soon after by the side of the small fresh water Loch-na-Caiplich, filled with that scarce plant *Eriocaulon decangulare*, first discovered by Mr James Robertson. Breakfast at Sconser, one of the post offices, an inn opposite to Rasa, an island nine miles long and three broad, divided from Skie by a sound a mile broad. On the shore, the house of Mr MacLeod, the owner of Rasa, makes a pretty figure. The Dean speaks of this island as having 'maney deires, pairt of profitable landes inhabit, and manurit, with twa castles, to wit, the castle of Kilmorocht, and the castle of Brolokit, with twa fair orchards at the saids twa castles with ane parish kirke, called Kilmolowocke.' In his time, he says, 'it pertaining to Macghyllichallan of Raasay

---

[13] His residence is said to have been at Dunscaich, in this island. The literal meaning of *quillin*, or *cullin*, is 'a narrow dark hollow'.

be the sword, and to the bishope of the isles be heritage.' This usurper was a vassal of MacLeod of Lewis, who probably consigned it to his chieftain, from whom the present proprietor derives his family.

Continue our journey pointing to the south-west. Meet great droves of fine cattle, on their way to change the pasture. See a small quantity of very poor flax, raised from the seed of the country, a very unprofitable management: but the greatest part of the land was covered with heath. Leave to the left the mountains of Cuchullin, Cullin, or Quillin, which reach to the sea. Come to the end of Loch Bracadale, which pierces the island on this side. Skie is so divided by branches of the sea that there is not a place five miles distant from a port; such numbers of good harbours are there in a place destitute of trade, and without a single town. Near the end of this loch the ground is more cultivated; but all the cornland is dug with the *caschrom* or 'crooked spade', instead of being ploughed: eight men are necessary to dig as much in a day as a single plough would turn up: the harrows are commonly tied to the horses' tails; but in very wet land, the men and women break the sods by dragging over them a block of wood, with five teeth and a long handle, called *raachgan*.

Descend through a narrow pass, and arrive instantly in a tract flat as any in Holland, opening to the west with a fine distant view of North and South Uist, and other parts of the long island: bounded on the other three sides by high precipices, enlivened with cataracts formed by the heavy rains. In a wood in a snug corner lies Talyskir, inhabited by Mr Macleod, Lieutenant-Colonel in the Dutch service, who with the utmost hospitality sheltered us from the inclemency of the day. This house belongs to the chief of the name; and in old times was always the portion of a second son: he enjoyed it for life, with the view of giving him the means of educating his children; who after that were left to the care of fortune; which custom filled foreign service with a gallant set of officers. Daughters of chieftains were generally portioned with cattle; and often with a set of stout men, who in feudal times were valuable acquisitions to the husband, who estimated his wealth by the power of his people, for he instantly adopted and incorporated them with his own clan.

It will not be impertinent to mention here the origin of the Scotch regiments in the Dutch service. They were formed out of some independent companies, sent over either in the reign of Elizabeth or James VI. At present the common soldiers are but nominally national, for since the scarcity of men, occasioned by the late war, Holland is no longer permitted to draw her recruits out of North Britain. But the officers are all Scotch, who are obliged to take oaths to our government, and to qualify in presence of our ambassador at the Hague.

See here a claymore, or great two-handed sword, probably of the same kind with the *ingentes gladii* of the Caledonians, mentioned by Tacitus: an unwieldly weapon, two inches broad, doubly edged: the length of the blade three feet seven inches; of the handle, fourteen inches; of a plain transverse guard, one foot; the weight six pounds and a half. These long swords were the original weapons of our country, as appears by a figure of a soldier, found among the ruins of London, after the great fire, AD 1666, and preserved at Oxford:[14] his sword is of a vast length, his hair flowing, his legs bare, his lower garment short, and fastened by a girdle round his waist; the sagum is flung carelessly over his breast and one arm, ready to be flung off, as custom was, in time of action. The great broadsword, and much the same kind of dress, were preserved in the Highlands to the last age, at the battle of Killicrankie: the upper garment was thrown off by the Highlanders, in order to enable them to use this two-handed instrument with greater effect. But the enormous length of weapon has been found useless against the firmness of determined troops, from the battle of the Mons Grampius,[15] to the recent victory of Culloden. The short swords of the forces of Agricola, and the bayonets of the British regulars, were equally superior.

Col. Macleod favours me with a weapon, common to the Roman, Scandinavians, and Britons. It is a brazen sword, whose blade is twenty-two inches long; the handle (including a round hollow pummel) five and a half; the middle of the blade swells out on both sides, and the edges very sharp; the end pointed; we

---

[14] Monfaucon, *Antiq*. IV, 16, tab. x.
[15] Taciti, *Vit. Agric.*, ch. 36.

are told that the scabbards are of brass, but this was destitute of one.[16] The weapon was found in Skie. The same kind is met with in many parts of Scotland and of Wales, which the Danes have visited; and they have been frequently discovered in tumuli, and other sepulchres, in Denmark and Holsace, deposited there with the urns in honour of the deceased.[17] Others, similar, have been found in Sweden.[18]

Walk down the east side of the vale, and see the well of Cuchullin. Take boat near the lofty insulated rock, Stach-in-Nuchidar, or that of the fuller, pyramidal and inclining: am rowed beneath a range of magnificent cliffs, at whose base were lodged plenty of white crystalized zeolite, and vast rocks of stone, of the appearance of lava, filled with rounded kernels.

Our boat's crew were islanders, who gave a specimen of marine music, called in the Erse, *iorrams*: these songs, when well-composed, are intended to regulate the strokes of the oars, and recall to mind the customs of classical days:

> *Mediae flat margine puppis*
> *Qui voce alternos nautarum temperet ictus,*
> *Et remis dectet fonitum, pariterque relatis,*
> *Ad numerum plaudat resonantia caerula tonsis.*
> Silius, lib. IV.

But in modern times they are generally sung in couplets, the whole crew joining in chorus at certain intervals: the notes are commonly long, the airs solemn and slow, rarely cheerful, it being impossible for the oars to keep a quick time: the words generally have a religious turn, consonant to that of the people.

Visit a high hill, called Briis-mhawl, about a mile south of Talyskir, having in the front a fine series of genuine basaltic columns, resembling the Giant's Causeway: the pillars were above twenty feet high, consisting of four, five and six angles, but mostly of five: the columns less frequently jointed than those of the Irish; the joints

[16] Sibbald, *Append. Hist. Fife*, 18.
[17] *Wormii Mon. Dan.*, 48. tab. 50. Worm., *Mus.*, 354. *Jacob. Mus. Reg. Havinae*, pars II, sect. iii.
[18] Dahlberg, *Suec. Ant.*, tab. 314.

being a great and unequal distances, but the majority are entire: even those that are jointed are less concave and convex on their opposite surface than the columns of the former. The stratum that rested on this colonnade was very irregular and shattery, yet seemed to make some effort at form. The ruins of the columns at the base made a grand appearance: these were the ruins of the creation: those of Rome, the work of human art, seem to them but as the ruins of yesterday.

At a small distance from these, on the slope of a hill, is a tract of some roods entirely formed on the tops of several series of columns, even and close set, forming a reticulated surface of amazing beauty and curiosity. This is the most northern basalt I am acquainted with; the last of four in the British dominions, all running from south to north, nearly in a meridian: the Giant's Causeway appears first; Staffa succeeds; the rock Humbla about twenty leagues further, and finally the column of Briis-mhawl: the depth of ocean in all probability conceals the lost links of this chain.

Take leave of Talyskir. See very near to the house the vestiges of some small buildings, and by them a heap of stones, with a basaltic column set erect in the middle. Cross a range of barren lands for four miles: reach Loch Bracadale. Exchange our horses for a boat. Pass over this beautiful land-locked harbour abounding with safe creeks. Cod fish swarm here in the herring season pursuing the shoals: a man with a single hand-line caught in three hours as many as were sold for three guineas, at the rate of two pence apiece. Land, after a traject of four miles, and find ready a new set of horses.

This seems to me the fittest place in the island for the forming of a town. The harbour is deep and unspeakably secure. It is the Milford Haven of these parts; it opens at its mouth to the best part of the sea. Skie has not in it a single town or even village. But what is a greater wonder, there is not a town from Campbelton in the Firth of Clyde to Thurso, at the end of Cathness, a tract of above two hundred miles.

Proceed: ride by, a Struan, a beautiful Danish fort on the top of a rock, formed with most excellent masonry. The figure as usual circular. The diameter from outside to outside sixty feet, of the inside forty-two. Within are the vestiges of five apartments, one in the centre, four around: the walls are eighteen feet high. The entrance six feet high, covered with great stones.

About a furlong north-west of this, is another large rock precipitous on all sides but one. On that is the ruin of a very thick wall, and the traces of a dike quite round, even on the inaccessible parts. Between which and the wall is a large area. This seems to have been built without regularity, yet probably belonged to the same nation. Each seems designed to cover an assemblage of people who lived beneath their protection in a hostile country, for under both are remains of numbers of small buildings with regular entrances. The last enclosure is supposed to have been designed for the security of the cattle, of which, these freebooters had robbed the natives; and this species is distinguished by the name of *boaghun*.

These fortresses are called universally in the Erse, *duns*. I find that they are very rare in the country from whence they took their origin; no people will give themselves the trouble of fortifying amidst the security of friends. Mr Frederic Suhm of Copenhagen, whom I had the pleasure of addressing on this subject, could point out but a single instance, of a similar tower, and that on the Suallsberg, a mountain half a Norwegian league distant from Drontheim. But we expect further elucidations from a skilful antiquary now on the tour of the country.

About two miles farther, see near the roadside, two large conoid cairns: pass near the end of Lochcaroy, a branch of the noble Loch Bracadale, and soon after reach the castle of Dunvegan, the seat of Mr Macleod, a gentleman descended from one of the Norwegian viceroys, governors of the isles while they bore a foreign yoke. But the antiquity of his descent is an accident that would convey little honour to him; had he not a much more substantial claim; for to all the milkiness of human nature usually concomitant with his early age, is added, the sense and firmness of more advanced life. He feels for the distresses of his people, and insensible of his own, with uncommon disinterestedness has relieved his tenants from their oppressive rents; has received instead of the trash of gold, the treasure of warm affections, and unfeigned prayer. He will soon experience the good effects of his generosity; gratitude, the result of the sensibility still existing among those accustomed to a feudal

XXXVI

DANISH FORT IN SKIE.

government, will show itself in more than empty words; and in time they will not fail exerting every nerve to give his virtue the due reward. Feudal governments, like that of unmixed monarchy, has its conveniences and its blessings. The last rarely occur from the imperfection of human nature: one Being only can lay claim to that: therefore it is the business of every honest man to resist the very appearance of undivided power in a prince, or the shadow of independency in a subject. The Highlanders may bless the hand that loosened their bonds: for tyranny more often than protection was the attendance on their vassalage. Yet still from long habitude, and from the gleams of kindness that darted every now and then amidst the storms of severity, was kindled a sort of filial reverence to their chieftain: this still is in a great degree retained, and may, by cherishing, return with more than wonted vigour. The noxious part of the feudal reign is abolished; the delegated rod of power is now no more. But let not the good part be lost with the bad: the tender relation that patriarchal government experiences, should still be retained: and the mutual inclination to beneficence preserved. The chieftain should not lose, with the power of doing harm, the disposition of doing good. Such are the sentiments of Mr MacLeod, which ripen into actions that, if persisted in, will bring lasting comfort into his own bosom, and the most desired of blessings amongst a numerous clan.

The castle of Dunvegan is seated on a high rock, over a loch of the same name, a branch of Loch Falart. Part is modernised, but the greatest portion is ancient: the oldest is a square tower, which with a wall round the edge of the rock, was the original strength of the place. Adjacent is a village and the post office; for from hence a packet-boat, supported by subscription, sails every fortnight for the Long Island.

Here is preserved the *braolauch shi*, or 'fairy flag of the family', bestowed on it by Titania the Ben-shi, or wife to Oberon, King of the Fairies. She blessed it at the same time with powers of the first importance, which were to be exerted on only three occasions: but on the last, after the end was obtained, an invisible being is to arrive and carry off standard and standard-bearer, never more to be seen. A family of clan y Faitter had this dangerous office, and held by it, free lands in Bracadale.

XXXVII

Miss Griffith del.

R. Roffe sculp.

DUNVEGAN CASTLE.

The flag has been produced thrice. The first time in an unequal engagement against the clan Ronald, to whose sight the MacLeods were multiplied ten-fold. The second preserved the heir of the family, being then produced to save the longings of the lady: and the third time, to save my own; but it was so tattered, that Titania did not seem to think it worth sending for.

This was a superstition derived from the Norwegian ancestry of the house: the fable was caught from the country, and might be of use to animate the clan. The Danes had their magical standard, *reafan*, or 'the raven', embroidered in an instant by the three daughters of Lodbroke, and sisters of Hinguar, Hubba, or Ivar.[19] Sigurd had an enchanted flag given him by his mother, with circumstances somewhat similar to the Dunvegan colours: whosoever bore it in the day of battle was to be killed; accordingly in one of his battles three standard-bearers were successively slain; but on the death of the last he obtained the victory.[20]

Here is preserved a great ox-horn, tipped with silver: the arm was twisted round its spires, the mouth brought over the elbow, and then drank off. The northern nations held this species of cup in high esteem, and used the capacious horns of the great aurochs.[21] They graced the hospitable halls of kings,[22] and out of them the ancient heroes quenched their thirst: Haquin,[23] weary with slaughter, calls aloud for the mighty draught:

> *Heu labor immensus, fessos quam vellicat artus!*
> *Quis mihi jam praebet cornua plena mero?*

In this castle is also preserved, a round shield, made of iron, that even in its decayed state weighs near twenty pounds; itself a load in these degenerate days: yet they were in use no longer ago than the beginning of the last century. Each chieftain had his armour-bearer, who proceeded his master in time of war, and, by

---

[19] Affer., *Vit. Alfred*, 10.

[20] Torfoeus, 27.

[21] *Urorum cornibus, Barbari septentrionales potant, urnasque binas capitis unius cornua implent.* Plinii, lib. II, ch. 37.

[22] *Saxo Grammat.*, 94.

[23] Wormii, *Mon. Dan.*, 389.

my author's account,[24] in time of peace; for they went armed even to church, in the manner the North Americans do at present in the frontier settlement, and for the same reason, the dread of savages.

In times long before those, the ancient Scotch used round targets, made of oak, covered with the hides of bulls; and long shields, narrow below and broad above, formed of pieces of oak or willow, secured with iron: I guess them to be of the same kind with the Norwegian shields figured by Wormius,[25] and probably derived from the same country. They had also a guard for their shoulders, called Scapul;[26] and for offensive weapons had the bow, sword, two-handed sword, and Lochaber axe, a weapon likewise of Norwegian origin. But the image-tombs of ancient warriors are the best lectures on this subject.

Mr MacQueen informs me, that near this place is an *anait*, or Druidical place of worship, of which there are four in Skie, much of the same situation and construction. This lies in the heart of an extensive moor, between the confluence of two waters. To the east stands one hill, to the west another: which gradually slope down toward the plain, and from which a clear prospect might be had of all that passed below. From one of these waters to the other is a strong stone wall, forming an equilateral triangle: the rocks face it towards the water, and every crevice is filled with stones regularly laid; so that it seems to have been on that spot inaccessible in former days. Near the centre of this triangle, is a small square edifice of quarried stones; and on each side of the entrance which leads to it from the wall, are the remains of two houses, both within and without. In those lodged the priests and their families: the servants most probably on the outside. A strong turf rampart protected also the wall from water to water, across a rising ground, which hath been cut through by a road leading from the Tempul-na-Anait (as the edifice is called) a great way into the moor. There is no tradition of the use of this place. My learned friend supposes it to have been designed for the worship

---

[24] Timothy Pont's MS, Advoc. Library.
[25] Vide fig. 1, tab. xx.
[26] Ibid.

of the Earth, Bendis or Diana, which, according to Hesychius, was supposed to be the same. Plutarch gives the same goddess the title of *Anait*, the name of this place of worship; and Pliny speaks of a country in Armenia, called Anaitica, from Anaitis, a goddess in great repute there, where a noble temple had been built, which was plundered of its immense riches by the soldiers of Antony in his Parthian expedition. Pausanias also speaks of the temple of Diana the Anait. These temples were erected when the purity of the Celtic religion had been debased by the extravagance of fancy, and idols introduced. Here we may suppose that this deity was worshipped in the utmost simplicity.

Proceed on our journey; pass over a black and pathless tract of moor and bog, for about fifteen miles. Dine on a soft spot of heath, with that appetite which exercise and the free air never fail to create. Arrive on the banks of Loch Grisernis, a branch of Loch Snisart: take boat; observe that the ropes for the fishing nets are made of the purple melic grass, the *pundglas* of the Highlanders, remarkable for lasting long without rotting. After a passage of a mile, land at Kingsburgh; immortalized by its mistress, the celebrated Flora Macdonald, the fair protectress of a fugitive adventurer; who, after some days' concealing himself from pursuit, in the disguise of the lady's maid, here flung off the female habit.

Mr MacDonald did me the favour of presenting me with three very curious pieces of antiquity: an urn, a *glain naidr*, or serpent-bead, and a denarius, found not remote from his house. The first is an urn of elegant workmanship, found in a stone chest, formed of six flags as before described: this urn was filled with ashes; was placed not prone, as that mentioned in the former volume, but with the mouth up, and covered with a light thin stone. This was discovered beneath an immense cairn.

The *glain naidr,* or Druidical bead, as it is vulgarly called, is an unique in its kind, being of a triangular shape; but, as usual, made of glass, marked with figures of serpents coiled up. The common people in Wales and in Scotland retain the same superstitions relating to it as the ancients, and call it by the name of serpent-stone. The Gauls, taught by their priests, believed the strangest tales of their serpents, described from the prose of Pliny, in a most spirited manner, by

the ingenious Mr Mason, who thus makes his Druid demand of a
sapient brother:

> *But tell me yet*
> *From the grot of charms and spells,*
> *Brennus, has thy holy hand*
> *Where our matron sister dwells;*
> *Safely brought the Druid wand,*
> *And the potent adder-stone,*
> *Gender'd 'fore the autumnal moon?*
> *When in undulating twine*
> *The foaming snakes prolific join;*
> *When thsy hiss, and when they bear*
> *Their wond'rous egg aloof in air;*
> *Thence, before to earth it fall,*
> *The Druid in his holy pall,*
> *Receives the prize,*
> *And instant flies,*
> *Follow'd by the envenom'd brood,*
> *Till he cross the silver flood.*

The ancients and moderns agree in their belief of its powers; that
good fortune attends the possessor wherever he goes. The stupid
Claudius, that *Ludibrium aulae Augusti*, put to death a Gaulish
knight, for no other reason than that he carried an *ovum anguinum*,
a serpent-stone, about him.[27] The vulgar of the present age attribute
to it other virtues; such as its curing the bite of the adder, and giving
ease to women in childbirth, if tied about the knee. So difficult is
it to root out follies that have the sanction of antiquity.

The last favour that I was indebted to Mr MacDonald for, is a
denarius, of the Emperor Trajan, found on a moor near the shore
of Loch Grisernis; a probable, but not a certain evidence that the
Romans had landed in this island. We have no lights from history to
enable us to say what was done during the reign of that emperor: in
the succeeding, Adrian reduced the bounds of the empire to the place
still called his wall, and lost all communication with the islands; but
in the following reign they were extended to their ancient bounds,
and the isles might be visited from the *glota estuarium,* the station
of the fleet, and the money in question lost at that time in Skie. But

---

[27] *Plinii,* lib. XXIX, ch. 3. *Equitem Romanum e Vocontiis,* a people of Dauphiny.

its being found there may be accounted for by another supposition: that of its having been the booty of an island soldier, taken from the Romans in some of the numberless skirmishes in one of the following reigns, and brought here as a mark of victory.

I observe that the great scallop-shell is made use of in the dairies of this country for the skimming of milk. In old times, it had a more honourable place, being admitted into the halls of heroes, and was the cup of their festivity. As Doctor Macpherson expresses it:

> 'The whole tribe filled the hall of the chieftain; trunks of trees covered with moss were laid in form of tables from one end to the other; whole beeves or deer were roasted and laid before them on rough boards, or hurdles of rods woven together: the pipers played while they sat at table, and silence was observed by all. After the feast was over, they had ludicrous entertainments; a practice still continued in part of the highlands: the females retired, and the old and young warriors sat in order, down from the chieftain, according to their proximity in blood to him; the harp was then touched, the song was raised, and the sligà-crechin, or the drinking-shell, went round.'

Am lodged this night in the same bed that formerly received the unfortunate Charles Stuart. Here he lay one night, after having been for some time in a female habit under the protection of Flora Macdonald. Near this place he resumed the dress of his own sex by the assistance of the master of the house, Mr Alexander Macdonald, who suffered a long imprisonment on that account; but neither the fear of punishment, nor the promises of reward, could induce him to infringe the rights of hospitality, by betraying an unhappy man who had flung himself under his protection.

Leave Kingsburgh, travel on a good horse road, pass by a cairn, with a great stone at the top, called the High Stone of Ugg. I must remark, that the Danes left behind them in many places the names of their deities, their heroes, and their bards: thus in the rock Humbla is perpetuated the name of Humblus,[28] one of their ancient kings; the isle of Gunna assumed the title of one of the *Valkyriae*, the fatal sisters;[29] Ulva takes its name from the bear-begotten hero,

---

[28] *Sax. Gram.*, 5.
[29] Torfoeus, 36.

Ulvo;[30] and the stone of Ugg seems to have been erected in memory of the poet Uggerus.[31]

Beneath is the fertile bottom of Ugg, laughing with corn: ascend a hill, and on the other side descend into the parish of Kilmore; the granary of Skie. Leave, on the left, Muggastot, the principal house of Sir Alexander MacDonald, lineally descended from the lords of the Isles: all the estates at present possessed by that gentleman were bestowed by John, the last regulus, the Earl of Ross, on his brother Hugh, and confirmed by a charter dated at Aros, in the year 1449, and afterwards by James IV at Sterling, in 1495.

Beneath the house was the lake of St Columba, now drained; once noted for a monastery of great antiquity, placed in an island. The ruins evince its age, being built with great stones, without mortar, in the manner customary in the times of Druidism. The cells and several rooms are still very distinguishable. The chapel is of a later date, and built with mortar, as are all the other chapels in Skie, and in the little islands along its shores: these chapels were served by the monks: the place they landed on, in order to discharge these religious duties, was called Pein-orah, or 'the land of prayer'; for after solemnly recommending themselves, and the object of their journey, to the Most High, they separated, and took their respective routes.

Pursue our journey. A minister, who gave us the pleasure of his company, observed to us, that a couple were in pursuit of him in order to have their nuptials celebrated: unwilling to be the cause of deferring their happiness. I begged he would not on my account delay the ceremony: we took possession of a cottage; the minister laid before them the duties of the marriage state, asked, whether they took each other willingly, joined their hands, and concluded with a prayer. I observed that the bridegroom put all the powers of magic to defiance, for he was married with both shoes tied with their latchet.

Not many years have elapsed since it was customary in some parts of the north of Scotland for the lairds to interfere in the marriages

[30] *Sax. Gram.*, 193.
[31] Ibid., 88.

of their vassals, and direct the pairing of their people. These strange tyrannies, these oppressions of inclination, seem to have occasioned the law of Alexander I, to prevent such a foundation for domestic misery: it is indeed the case of the widow only that he took into consideration, 'Na widow', says the statute, 'should be compelled to marie gif sche please to live without ane husband, but sche sould give securitie that sche sall not marie without consent of hir lord, gif sche holds of ane other than the king.'

Take a repast at the house of Sir Alexander MacDonald's piper, who, according to ancient custom, by virtue of his office, holds his lands free. His dwelling, like many others in this country, consists of several apartments; the first of his cattle during winter, the second is his hall, the third for the reception of strangers, and the fourth for the lodging of his family; all the rooms within one another.

The owner was quite master of his instrument, and treated us with several tunes. In feudal times the MacDonalds had in this island a college of pipers; and the MacLeods had the like; these had regular appointments in land, and received pupils from all the neighbouring chieftains. The MacKarters were chief pipers to the first; the MacKrumens to the last.

The bagpipe has been a favourite instrument with the Scots, and has two varieties: the one with short pipes, played on with the fingers; the other with long pipes and sounded with the mouth: this is the loudest and most ear-piercing of all music, is the genuine Highland pipe, and suited well the warlike genius of the people, roused their courage to battle, alarmed them when secure, and collected them when scattered; solaced them in their long and painful marches, and in times of peace kept up the memory of the gallantry of their ancestors, by tunes composed after signal victories; and too often kept up the spirit of revenge, by airs expressive of defeats or massacres from rival clans. One of the tunes, wild and tempestuous, is said to have been played at the bloody battle of Harlaw, when Donald, Lord of the Isles, in 1410, opposed the powers of James I under the conduct of Alexander Stuart, Earl of Mar.

Neither of these instruments were the invention of the Danes, or, as is commonly supposed, of any of the northern nations; for their ancient writers prove them to have been animated by the *clangor tubarum.* Notwithstanding they have had their sack-pipe long amongst them, as their old songs prove,[32] yet we cannot allow them the honour of inventing this melodious instrument; but must assert, that they borrowed it from the invaded Caledonians. We must still go farther, and deprive even that ancient race of the credit; and derive its origin from the mild climate of Italy, perhaps from Greece.

There is now in Rome a most beautiful bas-relief, a Grecian sculpture of the highest antiquity; of a bagpiper playing on his instrument, exactly like a modern Highlander. The Greeks had their Ασχχυλης, or instrument composed of a pipe and blown-up skin: the Romans in all probability borrowed it from them, and introduced it among their swains, who still use it under the names of *piva* and *cornu musa.*[33]

That master of music, Nero, used one;[34] and had not the empire been so suddenly deprived of that great artist, he would (as he graciously declared his intention) have treated the people with a concert; and, among other curious instruments, would have introduced the *utricularius,* or bagpipe, Nero perished, but the figure of the instrument is preserved on one of his coins, but highly improved by that great master. It has the bag and two of the vulgar pipes, but was blown with a bellows, like an organ, and had on one side a row of nine unequal pipes, resembling the syrinx of the god Pan.[35] The bagpipe, in the unimproved state, is also represented in an ancient sculpture, and appears to have had two long pipes or drones,[36] and a single short pipe for the fingers. Tradition says, that the kind played on by the mouth was introduced by the Danes. As theirs was wind music, we will admit that they might have made improvement, but more we cannot allow: they were skilled in the use of the trumpet; the Highlanders in the *piohb,* or bagpipe.

> *Non tuba in usu illis, conjecta at tibia in utrem*
> *Dat belli signum, et martem vocat horrida in arma.*[37]

[32] From Dr Solander.
[33] From Dr Burney.
[34] Suetonius, lib. VI, ch. 54.
[35] Monfaucon, *Antiq. Suppl.* iii, 188, tab. 73, f. 2.
[36] Ibid., f. 12.
[37] Melvini, *Topog. Scotiae.*

Proceed two miles farther; pass under a high hill, with a precipitous front, styled Sgor-more, or, 'the great projection'; and immediately after reach Duntuilm Castle, or, 'the castle of the round grassy eminence', placed at the verge of a high precipice over the sea; the ground adjacent formed of fine verdant turf.

Find our vessel at anchor under the little rocky Elan-tuilm, lofty, and of a picturesque form.

Take leave of several gentlemen, who, according to the worthy custom of these islands, conveyed us from place to place, and never left us till they had delivered us over to the next hospitable roof, or seen us safely embarked. Among others who did me this honour, was Dr John MacLean, whose family have been hereditary physicians, for some centuries, to that of MacDonald. They have been educated at the expense of the chieftain; and receive to this day an appointment in land, holding the farm of Shulista at the gates of the ancient residence of the MacDonalds, the castle of Duntuilm, which the doctor enjoys together with a pension from the late Sir James MacDonald.

Duntuilm Castle is a ruin, but was inhabited as late as 1715. It was the original seat of the MacDonalds, in Skie: near it, a hill, called Cnock-an-Eirick, or, 'the hill of pleas': such eminences are frequent near the houses of all the great men, for on these, by the assistance of their friends, they determined all differences between their people: the place was held sacred, and to the respect paid to the decisions delivered from the summit, may in some measure be attributed the strict obedience of a fierce and military race to their chieftain.

Near this place was pointed to me the spot where an incestuous pair (a brother and sister) had been buried alive, by order of the chieftain.

In the rocks are abundance of small compressed *ammonitae*, and on the shores saw fragments of white quartz, the hectic stone so often mentioned by Martin.

Skie is the largest of the Hebrides, being above sixty measured miles long; the breadth unequal, by reason of the numbers of lochs, that penetrate far on both sides. It is supposed by some to have been the eastern Aebudae of the ancients; by others, to have been

Moses Griffith del.

P.C. Canot sculp.

DUNTULME CASTLE.

the Dumna. The modern name is of Norwegian origin, derived from *ski*, 'a mist'; and from the clouds (that almost constantly hang on the tops of its lofty hills) was styled, *Ealand Skianach, or,* 'the cloudy island'.[38] No epithet could better suit the place; for, except in the summer season, there is scarcely a week of fair weather: the summers themselves are also generally wet, and seldom warm.

The westerly wind blows here more regularly than any other, and arriving charged with vapour from the vast Atlantic, never fails to dash the clouds it wafts on the lofty summits of the hills of Cuchullin, and their contents deluge the island in a manner unknown in other places. What is properly called the rainy season commences in August: the rains begin with moderate winds; which grow stronger and stronger till the autumnal equinox, when they rage with incredible fury.

The husbandman then sighs over the ruins of his vernal labours: sees his crops feel the injury of climate: some laid prostrate; the more ripe corn shed by the violence of the elements. The poor foresee famine, and consequential disease: the humane tacksmen agonize over distresses, that inability, not want of inclination, deprives them of the power of remedying. The nearer calls of family and children naturally first excite their attention: to maintain and to educate are all their hopes, for that of accumulating wealth is beyond their expectation: so the poor are left to Providence's care: they prowl like other animals along the shores to pick up limpets and other shellfish, the casual repasts of hundreds during part of the year in these unhappy islands. Hundreds thus annually drag through the season a wretched life: and numbers, unknown, in all parts of the western Highlands (nothing local is intended) fall beneath the pressure, some of hunger, more of the putrid fever, the epidemic of the coasts, originating from unwholesome food, the dire effects of necessity. Moral and innocent victims who exult in the change, first finding that place 'where the wicked cease from troubling, and where the weary are at rest'.

The farmer labours to remedy this distress to the best of his power, but the wetness of the land late in spring prevents him

---

[38] Dr Macpherson, 282.

from putting into the ground the early seed of future crops, bere and small oats: the last are fittest for the climate: they bear the fury of the winds better than other grain, and require less manure, a deficiency in this island. Poverty prevents him from making experiments in rural economy: the ill success of a few made by the more opulent, determines him to follow the old tract, as attended with more certainty, unwilling, like the dog in the fable, to grasp at the shadow and lose the substance, even poor as it is.

The produce of the crops very rarely are in any degree pro-portioned to the wants of the inhabitants: golden seasons have happened, when they have had superfluity; but the years of famine are as ten to one. The helps of the common years are potatoes: it is difficult to say whether the discovery of America by the Spaniards has contributed to preserve more lives by the introduction of this vegetable; or to have caused more to perish by the insatiable lust after the precious metals of the new world.

The difficulties the farmer undergoes in this bad climate are unknown in the south; there he sows his seed, and sees it flourish beneath a benign sun and secured from every invasion. Here a wet sky brings a reluctant crop:[39] the ground, enclosed only with turf mounds, accessible to every animal. A continual watch employs numbers of his people. Some again are occupied in repairing the damages sustained by their houses from storms the preceding year; others are labouring at the turbaries, to provide fuel to keep off the rigour of the severe season: or in fencing the natural (the only) grasses of the country to preserve their cattle from starving; which are the true and proper staple of these islands.

The quantity of corn raised in tolerable seasons in this island, is esteemed to be about nine thousand bolls. The number of mouths to consume them, in the presbytery of Skie,[40] near thirteen thousand: migrations, and depression of spirit, the last a common cause of

---

[39] The moment the corn is cut down, a certain number of sheaves are gathered in a heap, and thatched on the top: the first dry moment that happens, the thatch is taken off, and the sheaves now dry, are carried in; and this is repeated till the whole crop is secured.

[40] Which comprehends Rum, Cannay, Muck and Egg, besides the seven parishes in this great island.

depopulation, having since the year 1750 reduced the number from fifteen thousand to between twelve and thirteen: one thousand having crossed the Atlantic, others sunk beneath poverty, or in despair, ceased to obey the first great command, 'Increase and Multiply'.

In that year the whole rent of Skie was three thousand five hundred pounds. By an unnatural force some of the rents are now doubled and trebled. People long out of all habit of industry, and used to the convivial tables of their chieftain, were unable instantly to support so new a burden: in time not very long preceding that, they felt the return of some of their rents: they were enabled to keep hospitality; to receive their chieftain with a well-covered board; and to feed a multitude of poor. Many of the greater tacksmen were of the same blood with their chieftains; they were attached to them by the ties of consanguinity as well as affection: they felt from them the first act of oppression, as Caesar did the wound from his beloved Brutus.

The high advance of the price of cattle is a plea for the high advance of rents; but the situation of the tacksman here is particular: he is a gentleman, and boasts the same blood with his laird (of five hundred fighting men that followed Macleod in 1745 in his Majesty's army, four hundred were of his kindred): has been cherished by him for a series of years often with paternal affection: has been used to such luxuries as the place affords; and cannot instantly sink from a good board to the hard fare of the common farmer. When the chieftains riot in all the luxuries of South Britain, he thinks himself entitled to share a due degree of the good things of this life, and not to be for ever confined to the diet of brochan or the compotation of whisky. During the feudal reign their love for their chieftains induced them to bear many things, at present intolerable. They were their pride and their glory: they strained every nerve in support of them, in the same manner as the French through vanity, refuse nothing to aggrandize their *grand monarque*.

Resentment drove many to seek a retreat beyond the Atlantic: they sold their stock, and in numbers made their first essay. They found, or thought they found, while their passions were warm, a happy change of situation: they wrote in terms savouring of romance, an account of their situation: their friends caught the contagion; and numbers followed; and others were preparing to follow their example. The tacksmen from a motive of independency: the poor from attachment; and from excess of misery. Policy and humanity, as I am informed, have of late checked this spirit so detrimental to the public. The wisdom of legislature may perhaps fall on some methods to conciliate the affections of a valuable part of the community: it is unbecoming my little knowledge of the country to presume to point out the methods. It is to be hoped the head will, while time permits, recollect the use of the most distant members.

The proper products of this and all the Hebrides are men and cattle: the use of the first need not be insisted on, for England cannot have forgot its sad deficiency of recruits towards the end of the late long and destructive war: and what it owed in the course of it to North Britain. In respect to cattle, this in particular bears the pre-eminence of having the largest breed of all the Highlands. The greater tenants keep their cattle during winter in what are called winter-parks, the driest and best ground they have: here they are kept till April, except the winter proves very hard, when they are foddered with straw: in April the farmer turns them to the moor-grass (cotton-grass) which springs first, and at night drives them into the dry grounds again.

The poorer tenants, who have no winter-parks, are under the necessity of keeping the cattle under the same roof with themselves during night; and often are obliged to keep them alive with the meal designed for their families. The cows are often forced, through want of other food, to have recourse to the shores, and feed on the sea plants at low water: by instinct they will, at ebb of tide, hasten from the moors, notwithstanding they are not within sight of the sea.

One of the greater farms in Skie is thus stocked:

Fifty cows, and their followers, viz. 20 young heifers, fit for bull; 30 ditto, three years old; 35 ditto, two years old; 40 yearlings, or sterks. Of these the owner can sell only twenty cows at forty-five shillings each at an average; can make butter and cheese for his family, but none for sale, for their best cow will not yield above three English quarts of milk at a meal. Such a farm was formerly rented for sixteen pounds a year, at present is raised to fifty. The greatest rent in the island is eighty pounds, but the medium from thirty to forty.

In Skie when a tacksman has a greater farm than he can manage, he often sets off part to a bowman or *aireach*, who takes care of the stock of cattle on a certain tract; and binds himself to give to the tacksman every year four stone of cheese, and two of butter, from each couple of milch cows. If there is any arable ground, he is provided with horses and a plough; and seed sufficient to sow it; and receives part of the crop; and some additional grass ground for two or three milch cows, for his trouble.

There is certainly much ill management in the direction of the farms: a tacksman of fifty pounds a year often keeps twenty servants; the laziest of creatures, for not one will do the least thing that does not belong to his department. Most of them are married, as in Ilay. Their common food is brochan, a thick meal pudding, with milk, butter or treacle; or a thinner sort, called *easoch*, taken with their bannocks. This number of servants seemed to answer the retainers in great families before that pernicious custom was abolished by Henry VII; in feudal times they were kept here for the same bad end. The cause is now no more, but the habit cannot suddenly be shaken off; charity forbids one to wish it, till some employ is thought of for them; otherwise, like the poor cottagers before-mentioned, starving must be their portion.

Cattle is at present the only trade of the island: about four thousand are annually sold, from forty shillings to three pounds a head. The loss sustained in Skie by the severity of the last winter, and the general failure of the crops the preceding season, amounted to five thousand; perhaps in some measure owing to the farms being overstocked.

About two hundred and fifty horses are purchased from hence every year.

Here are no sheep but what are kept for home consumption, or for the wool for the clothing of the inhabitants. Hogs are not introduced here yet, for want of proper food for those animals.

Goats might turn to good advantage if introduced into the few wooded parts of the island. These animals might be procured from the neighbourhood of Loch Ness; for being naturalized to the climate, would succeed better than any imported from the southern parts of Europe, or from Barbary. As an inducement, I must inform the natives of the Hebrides that in the Alpine part of Wales a well-haired goat skin sells for seven and sixpence or half a guinea.

About three hundred tons of kelp are made here annually, but it is thought not to answer, as it robs the land of so much manure.

There are not above two or three slated houses in the island; the general thatch is fern, root and stalk, which will last above twenty years.

The roots of the *Crobus tuberosus*, the *cormeille* or 'carmel' of the Highlanders, are in high esteem in this and the other islands: they sometimes chew them, at others make a fermented liquor with them. They imagine that they promote expectoration, and that they are very efficacious in curing any disorders of the breast or lungs: they also use it as a remedy against hunger, chewing it as some of our poorest people do tobacco,[41] to put off that uneasy sensation.

Ligusticum scoticum, Scotch parsley, or the *shunis* of this island, is also much valued; in medicine, the root is reckoned a good carminative, and an infusion of the leaves is thought a good purge for calves. It is besides used as a food, either as a salad, raw, or boiled as greens.

Very few superstitions exist here at present: pretenders to second-sight are quite out of repute, except among the most ignorant, and at present are very shy of making boast of their faculties.

Poor Browny, or Robin Goodfellow, is also put to flight. This serviceable sprite was wont to clean the houses, helped to churn, thrashed the corn, and would belabour all who pretended to make a jest of him. He was represented as stout and blooming, had fine flowing hair, and went about with a wand in his hand. He was the very counterpart of Milton's lubber fiend, who

> *Tells how the drudging goblin sweat*
> *To earn his cream-bewl duly set;*
> *When in one night, ere glimpse of morn,*

---

[41] Vide Mr Spence's *Life of Mr Robert Hill*, Taylor, 102.

> His shadowy flail hath thrash'd the corn
> That ten day-lab'rers could not end;
> Then lays him down the lubber fiend,
> And stretch'd along the chimney's length,
> Basks at the fire his hairy strength.

The *Gruagach* is a deity in form representing the last; and who was worshipped in old times by libations of milk; and milkmaids still retain the custom by pouring some on certain stones that bear his name. *Gruagach* signifies 'the fair-haired', and is supposed by Mr MacQueen to have been an emblem of Apollo, or the sun; and to correspond with the epithet Χευσοχομος. A stone was dug up near Musselburgh, dedicated Apollini Granno, 'Grianich the Sunny', an epithet probably borrowed from the Caledonians. The same deity might also receive the title of Galaxius from the libation of milk still retained in those parts.[42]

A wild species of magic was practised in the district of Trotterness, that was attended with a horrible solemnity. A family who pretended to oracular knowledge practised these ceremonies. In this country is a vast cataract, whose waters falling from a high rock, jet so far as to form a dry hollow beneath, between them and the precipice. One of these impostors was sowed up in the hide of an ox, and to add terror to ceremony, was placed in this concavity: the trembling enquirer was brought to the place, where the shade and the roaring of the waters, increased the dread of the occasion. The question is put, and the person in the hide delivers his answer, and so ends this species of divination styled *taghairm*.

But all these idle tales are totally exploded, and good sense and polished manners prevail, instead of that barbarity which in 1598 induced James VI to send here a new colony to civilize the natives; who were so little disposed to receive their instructors, that his Majesty was in the end obliged to desist from his design.[43] At present the island forms part of the shire of Inverness. The sheriff of that county appoints a substitute who resides here, and takes cognizance of small disputes about property, and petty crimes; but, on account of the distance, avoids harassing the inhabitants, by

[42] See Mr MacQueen's curious account in the Appendix to the third volume.
[43] *Jonstoni Rerum Britain Hist.*, lib. VIII, 249.

requiring their attendance on the lords of Sessions and Justiciary Courts at Inverness, the jurymen being selected from among the gentry and inhabitants of the mainland.

After a most tempestuous night, loose from our harbour at two o'clock at noon. Go through a narrow channel at the north end, a rock lying in the middle. Have to the west a view of Fisher's Rock; and to the north a strange chain of rocky isles, very singular in their appearance; and varying in their forms in the process of our course. The highest is called Bordh mor MhicLeod, or 'MacLeod's great table.'[44] Another is called Flada. On the first Mr Thompson took in our absence the little petrel, which with numbers of others were lurking beneath the loose stones, and betrayed themselves by their loud twittering. These are the least of palmipeds; the dread of mariners, who draw a certain presage of a storm from their appearance; for they always collect in numbers at the approach of a tempest beneath the stern; running along the waves in the wake of the ship, with a swiftness incredible. This bird is the Camilla of the ocean: like her:

> *She swept the seas, and as she skim'd along,*
> *Her flying feet unbath'd on billows hung.*

The seamen call them 'Mother Cary's chickens': some devotees styled them petrels, from the attempt of the apostle St Peter to tread the water. They are seen in all parts of the ocean; and were not overlooked by the ancients, who named them *cypselli*, and take notice of this remarkable particular.

Mr Thompson also shot one of those enormous seals, or the great seal, *Syn. quad.* no. 266; but to my great regret it sunk as soon as killed.

Have a full view of the isle of Lewis, the Lodhus of the Norwegians: and off it a group of little isles called Siant, or Schant, and somewhat to the north of those is the fine harbour, and town of Stornoway. It was my intention to have steered for that port, but was dissuaded from it by the accounts I had from the gentlemen of Skie, that a putrid fever raged there with great violence.

---

[44] Two views of these wild rocks (2) as they appeared from Duntuilm; the other (3) as they appeared from the east in our passage, are engraved at the bottom of the view in Loch Iurn.

IX

ROSS-SHIRE, SUTHERLAND, INVERNESS-SHIRE

———◆———

Loch Broom—Assynt—Little Loch Broom—Dundonnel—Loch Maree—
Inchmaree—Gairloch—Applecross—Glenelg—Loch Iurn—Knoydart—
Moydart—Point of Ardnamurchan

DIRECT our course for Loch Broom, in the county of Ross. An easy breeze carries us off the cape Ruthanri, in the maps Rowrie. About eight o'clock in the morning of July 25, find ourselves near a considerable number of small isles, with a most dreary appearance, miscalled the Summer Islands. Within is a great bay six miles broad and eight deep, bounded by vast and barren mountains, patched with snow. The wind chops about and blows very fresh, so that after many teasing tacks, about nine o'clock in the evening drop anchor under Isle Martin, in the bottom of the bay, which is here called Loch Kinnard. To the south is a hill, which we landed on, and ascended, and saw on the other side great Loch Broom, or Braon, narrow, of a vast depth, and running many miles up the country. At its head receives a river frequented by salmon in April.

This parish is one of the largest on the mainland of Scotland, being thirty-six miles long and twenty broad. It has in it seven places of worship, three catechists,[1] and about two thousand examinable persons: but is destitute of a parochial school. None of the people except the gentry understand English. The country is inhabited by the MacKenzie, even quite from Kintail, whose chieftain is the Earl of Seaforth.

It is a land of mountains, a mixture of rock and heath, with a few flats between them producing bere and black oats, but never sufficient to supply the wants of the inhabitants.

Cattle are the great support of the country, and are sold to graziers who come for them even as far as from Craven in Yorkshire, at the rate of thirty shillings to three pounds a head. A great deal of butter and cheese is sold to the busses. Land is set here by the 'davoch' or 'half davoch'; the last consists of ninety-six Scotch acres of arable land, such as it is, with a competent quantity of mountain and grazing ground. This maintains sixty cows and their followers; and is rented for fifty-two pounds a year. To manage this the farmer keeps eight men and eight women servants; and an overseer, who are all paid partly in money and partly in kind. The common servants have thirty shillings per annum, house, garden, six bolls of meal and shoes. The dairy maids thirteen shillings and four pence and shoes: the common drudges six and eight pence and shoes.

The tender cattle are housed during winter. The common manure of the country is dung, or sea-wrack.

Still on board. The weather very bad.

Land at the bottom of the bay, in Ross-shire. Procure horses. Observe some houses built for the veteran soldiers and sailors; but as usual, all deserted. Proceed up Stathkennard, which with Coygach that bounds the north side of the bay is a forfeited estate, and unalienably annexed to the crown. The commissioners give all possible encouragement to the tenants; and have power to grant longer leases than the lairds are inclined to do, which keeps the people under the government contented, and banishes from their minds all thoughts of migration.

---

[1] A catechist is one who goes from house to house to instruct the people in the principles of religion, and in the catechisms, approved by the General Assembly; are appointed by its committee, and are supported out of his Majesty's bounty.

XXXIX

Cornus herbacca.

Eriocaulon decungulare.

Moses Griffiths del.

P. Mazell sculp.

Kindness and hospitality possess the people of these parts. We scarce passed a farm but the good woman, long before our approach, sallied out and stood on the roadside, holding out to us a bowl of milk or whey.

Ascend a very high mountain, and pass through a birch wood, over a pretty little loch: various other woods of the same kind were scattered over the bottoms; but the trees were small. Roots of pines filled all the moors, but I saw none of those trees standing. Pass under some great precipices of limestone, mixed with marble: from hence a most tremendous view of mountains of stupendous height and generally of conoid forms. I never saw a country that seemed to have been so torn and convulsed: the shock, whenever it happened, shook off all that vegetates: among these aspiring heaps of barrenness, the sugar-loaf hill of Suil-bhein made a conspicuous figure: at their feet, the blackness of the moors by no means assisted to cheer our ideas.

Enter Assynt, in Sutherland. Ride by Loch Camloch; enjoy some diversity of the scene, for it was prettily decorated with little wooded islands. Reach Ledbeg, where we obtained quarters, and rough hospitality.

This country is environed with mountains; and all the strata near their base, and in the bottoms, are composed of white marble, fine as the Parian: houses are built with it, and walls raised; burnt it is the manure of the country; but oftener nature dissolves, and presents it ready prepared to the lazy farmer.

This tract seems the residence of sloth; the people almost torpid with idleness, and most wretched: their hovels most miserable, made of poles wattled and covered with thin sods. There is not corn raised sufficient to supply half the wants of the inhabitants: climate conspires with indolence to make matters worse; yet there is much improveable land here in a state of nature: but till famine pinches they will not bestir themselves: they are content with little at present, and are thoughtless of futurity; perhaps on the motive of Turkish vassals, who are oppressed in proportion to their improvements. Dispirited and driven to despair by bad management, crowds were now passing, emaciated with hunger, to the eastern coast, on the report of a ship being there loaden with meal. Numbers of the miserables of this country were now migrating: they wandered in the state of desperation; too poor to pay, they madly sell themselves for their passage, preferring a temporary bondage in a strange land, to starving for life in their native soil.

Every country has had its prophets: Greece its Cassandra, Rome its sibyls, England its Nixon, Wales its Robin Ddu, and the Highlands their Kenneah Oaur. Kenneah long since predicted the migrations in these terms:

> *Whenever a MacCleane with long hands, a Frazier with a black spot on his face, a Macgregor with the same on his knee, and a club-footed MacCleod, of Rasa, should have existed; whenever there should have been successively three Macdonalds of the name of John, and three Mackinnons of the same Christian name; oppressors would appear in the country, and the people change their own land for a strange one.*

The predictions, say the good wives, have been fulfilled, and not a single breach in the oracular effusions of Kenneah Oaur.

In a country where ignorance and poverty prevail it is less wonderful that a tragical affair should happen, similar to that at Tring, near our polished capital. About three years ago lived in this neighbourhood, a woman of more than common strength of understanding: she was often consulted on the ordinary occurrences of life, and obtained a sort of respect which excited the envy of another female in the same district. The last gave out that her neighbour was a witch; that she herself had a good genius, and could counteract the evils dreaded from the other: at length she so worked on the weak minds of the simple vulgar, that they determined on destroying her rival, and effected their purpose by instigating a parcel of children to strangle her. The murder was inquired into, but the inciters had so artfully concealed themselves, that they escaped their reward, and no punishment was inflicted, except what was suited to the tender years of the deluded children.

Assynt parish contains between three and four thousand souls; and sends out five hundred head of cattle annually; and about two or three lasts of salmon are taken every year in the water of Innard, on the coast.

I saw here a male and female red-throated diver; which convinces me of my mistake in supposing another to have been of this species.[2]

It was our design, on leaving the ship, to have penetrated by land, as far as the extremity of the island; but we were informed that the way was impassable for horses, and that even a Highland foot-messenger must avoid part of the hills by crossing an arm of the sea. Return the same road through a variety of bog and hazardous rock, that nothing but our shoeless little steeds could have carried us over. At length we arrive safely on board the ship:

> A wond'rous token
> Of heaven's kind care, with necks unbroken.

Found in our harbour some busses, just anchored, in expectation of finding the shoals of herrings usually here at this season; but at present were disappointed: a few were taken, sufficient to convince us of their superiority in goodness over those of the south: they were not larger, but as they had not wasted themselves by being in roe, their backs and the part next to the tail were double the thickness of the others, and the meat rich beyond expression.

Mr Anderson gives to the Scotch a knowledge of great antiquity in the herring fishery:[3] he says that the Netherlanders resorted to these coasts as early as AD 836, to purchase salted fish of the natives; but imposing on the strangers, they learned the art, and took up the trade, in after-times of such immense emolument to the Dutch.

Sir Walter Raleigh's observations on that head, extracted from the same author, are extremely worth the attention of the curious, and excite reflections on the vast strength resulting from the wisdom of well-applied industry.

In 1603, remarks that great man, the Dutch sold to different nations, as many herrings as amounted to £1,759,000 sterling.

In the year 1615, they at once sent out 2,000 busses, and employed in them 37,000 fishermen.

In the year 1618, they sent out 3,000 ships, with 50,000 men, to take the herrings, and 9,000 more ships to transport and sell the fish, which by sea and land employed 150,000 men, besides those

---

[2] *Br. Zool.* II, 415.
[3] *Dict. Commerce* I, 41.

first mentioned. All this wealth was gotten on our coasts; while our attention was taken up in a distant whale fishery.

The Scottish monarchs for a long time seemed to direct all their attention to the preservation of the salmon fishery; probably because their subjects were such novices in sea affairs. At length James III endeavoured to stimulate his great men to these patriotic undertakings; for by an Act of his third Parliament, he compelled 'certain lords spiritual and temporal, and burrows, to make ships busses and boats with nets and other pertinents for fishing. That the same should be made in each burgh; in number according to the substance of each burgh and the least of them to be of twenty tunn: and that all idle men be compelled by the sheriffs in the country to go on board the same.'

But his successors, by a very false policy, rendered this wise institution of little effect; for they in a manner prevented their subjects from becoming a maritime people, by directing that no white fish should be sent out of the realm, but that strangers may come and buy them;[4] that freeports be first served; the cargoes sold to the freemen, who are to come and transport the same.[5] The Dutch at this very time having an open trade.

It is well known that there have been many attempts made to secure this treasure to ourselves, but without success: in the late reign a very strong effort was made, and bounties allowed for the encouragement of British adventurers: the first was of thirty shillings per ton to every buss of seventy tons and upwards. This bounty was afterwards raised to fifty shillings per ton, to be paid to such adventurers who were entitled to it by claiming it at the places of rendezvous. The busses are from twenty to ninety tons burden, but the best size is eighty. A vessel of eighty tons ought to take ten lasts, or a hundred and twenty barrels of herrings, to clear expenses, the price of the fish to be admitted to be a guinea a barrel: a ship of this size ought to have eighteen men and three boats: one of twenty tons should have six men; and every five tons above, require an additional hand.

---

[4] James V, *Parlem.* VII.
[5] James IV and James VI.

To every ton are two hundred and eighty yards of nets; so a vessel of eighty tons carries twenty thousand square yards: each net is twelve yards long, and ten deep; and every boat takes out from twenty to thirty nets, and puts them together so as to form a long train: they are sunk at each end of the train by a stone, which weighs it down to the full extent: the top is supported by buoys, made of sheepskin, with a hollow stick at the mouth, fastened tight; though this the skin is blown up, and then stopped with a peg, to prevent the escape of air. Sometimes these buoys are placed at the top of the nets; at other times the nets are suffered to sink deeper, by the lengthening the cords fastened to them, every cord being for that purpose ten or twelve fathoms long. But the best fishers are generally in more shallow water.

The nets are made at Greenock, in Knapdale, Bute and Arran; but the best are procured from Ireland; and, I think, from some part of Caernarvonshire.

The fishing is always performed in the night, unless by accident. The busses remain at anchor, and send out their boats a little before sunset, which continue out, in winter and summer, till daylight; often taking up and emptying their nets, which they do ten or twelve times a night in case of good success. During winter it is a most dangerous and fatiguing employ, by reason of the greatness and frequency of the gales in these seas, and in such gales are the most successful captures; but by the providence of heaven, the fishers are seldom lost; and, what is wonderful, few are visited with illness. They go out well prepared, with a warm greatcoat, boots and skin aprons, and a good provision of beef and spirits. The same good fortune attends the busses, who in the tempestuous season, and in the darkest nights, are continually shifting in these narrow seas from harbour to harbour.

Sometimes eighty barrels of herrings are taken in a night by the boats of a single vessel. It once happened in Loch Slappan, in Skie, that a buss of eighty tons might have taken two hundred barrels in one night, with ten thousand square yards of net; but the master was obliged to desist, for want of a sufficient number of hands to preserve the capture.

The herrings are preserved by salting, after the entrails are taken out; an operation performed by the country people, who get three half-pence per barrel for their trouble; and sometimes, even in the winter, can gain fifteen pence a day. This employs both women and children, but the salting is only entrusted to the crew of the busses. The fish are laid on their backs in the barrels, and layers of salt between them. The entrails are not lost, for they are boiled into an oil: eight thousand fish will yield ten gallons, valued at one shilling the gallon.

A vessel of eighty tons takes out a hundred and forty-four barrels of salt: a drawback of two shillings and eight pence is allowed for each barrel used for the foreign or Irish exportation of the fish; but there is a duty of one shilling per barrel for the home consumption, and the same for those sent to Ireland.

The barrels are made of oak staves chiefly from Virginia; the hoops from several parts of our own island, and are made either of oak, birch, hazel, or willow: the last from Holland, liable to a duty.

The barrels cost about three shillings each, they hold from five to eight hundred fish, according to the size of the fish, are made to contain thirty-two gallons. The barrels are inspected by proper officers: a cooper examines if they are statuteable and good; if faulty, he destroys them, and obliges the maker to stand to the loss.

The herrings in general are exported to the West Indies, to feed the Negroes, or to Ireland, for the Irish are not allowed to fish in these seas. By having a drawback of five pence a barrel, and by repacking the fish in new barrels of twenty-eight gallons, they are enabled to export them to our colonies at a cheaper rate than the Scots can do.

The trade declines apace; the bounty, which was well paid at first, kept up the spirit of the fishery; but for the last six years the detention of the arrears has been very injurious to several adventurers, who have sold out at thirty per cent loss, besides that of their interest.

The migration of the herrings has been very fully treated of in the third volume of the *British Zoology*: it is superfluous to load this work with a repetition; I shall therefore only mention the observations that occur to me in this voyage, as pertinent to the present place.

Loch Broom has been celebrated for three or four centuries as the resort of herrings. They generally appear here in July: those that turn into this bay are part of the brigade that detaches itself from the western column of that army that annually deserts the vast depths of the Arctic Circle, and come, heaven-directed, to the seats of population, offered as a cheap food to millions, whom wasteful luxury or iron-hearted avarice has deprived, by enhancing the price, of the wonted supports of the poor.

The migration of these fish from their northern retreat is regular: their visits to the Western Isles and coasts, certain: but their attachment to one particular loch, extremely precarious. All have their turns; that which swarmed with fish one year, is totally deserted the following; yet the next loch to it be crowded with the shoals. These changes of place give often full employ to the busses, who are continually shifting their harbour in quest of news respecting these important wanderers.

They commonly appear here in July; the latter end of August they go into deep water, and continue there for some time, without any apparent cause: in November they return to the shallows, when a new fishery commences, which continues till January; at that time the herrings become full of roe, and are useless as articles of commerce. Some doubt whether these herrings that appear in November are not part of a new migration; for they are as fat, and make the same appearance, as those that composed the first.

The signs of the arrival of the herrings are flocks of gulls, who catch up the fish while they skim on the surface; and of gannets, who plunge and bring them up from considerable depths. Both these birds are closely attended to by the fishers.

Codfish, haddocks, and dogfish follow the herrings in vast multitudes; these voracious fish keep on the outsides of the columns, and may be a concurrent reason of driving the shoals into bays and creeks. In summer they come into the bays generally with the warmest weather, and with easy gales. During winter the hard gales from the north-west are supposed to assist in forcing them into shelter. East winds are very unfavourable to the fishery.

In a fine day, when the fish appear near the surface, they exhibit an amazing brilliancy of colours; all the various coruscations that dart from the diamond, sapphire and emerald, enrich their tract: but during night, if they break, i.e. play on the surface, the sea appears on fire, luminous as the brightest phosphorus.

During a gale, that part of the ocean which is occupied by the great shoals, appear as if covered with the oil that is emitted from them.

They seem to be greatly affected by lightning: during that phenomenon they sink towards the bottom, and move regularly in parallel shoals one above the other.

The enemies that assail these fish in the winter season are varied, not diminished: of the birds, the gannets disappear; the gulls still continue their persecutions; whales, pollacks[6] and porpoises are added to their number of foes: these follow in droves; the whales deliberately, opening their vast mouths, taking them by hundreds. These monsters keep on the outside, for the body of the phalanx of herrings is so thick as to be impenetrable by these unwieldy animals.

The herring fishers never observe the remains of any kind of food in the stomachs of that fish, as long as they are in good condition: as soon as they become foul or poor, they will greedily rise to the fly, and be taken like the whiting pollack.

They do not deposit their spawn in sand, or mud, or weeds, like other fish, but leave it in the water, suspended in a gelatinous matter, of such a gravity as prevents it from floating to the surface, or sinking to the bottom. The fishermen discover this by finding the slimy matter adhering to the hay ropes sometimes in use to hold the stone that sinks the nets, the middle part being slimed over, the top and bottom clear.

Before I leave this bay it must be observed that there are here, as in most of the lochs, a few, a very few of the natives who possess a boat and nets; and fish in order to sell the capture fresh to the busses: the utmost these poor people can attain to are the boat and nets; they are too indigent to become masters of barrels, or of salt, to the great loss of the public as well as theirselves. Were magazines of salt established in these distant parts; was encouragement given to these distant Britons, so that they might be enabled, by degrees, to

---

[6] A small whale, whose species I cannot determine.

furnish themselves with the requisites for fishing, they would soon form themselves into seamen, by the course of life they must apply themselves to; the busses would be certain of finding a ready market of fish, ready cured; the natives taught industry, which would be quickened by the profits made by the commodity, which they might afford cheaper, as taken at their very doors, without the wear and tear of distant voyages, as in the present case. Half of the hands employed now in fishing and curing generally come out as raw seamen as the inhabitants of these parts: they do not return with much greater experience in the working of a ship, being employed entirely in the boats, or in salting of the herrings, and seem on board as awkward as marines in comparison of able seamen. A bounty on these home captures would stimulate the people to industry; would drive from their minds the thoughts of migrations; and would never lessen the number of seamen, as it would be an incitement for more adventurers to fit out vessels, because they would have a double chance of freight, from their own captures, and from those of the residents, who might form a stock from shoals of fish, which often escape while the former are wind-bound, or wandering from loch to loch.

Weigh anchor, and sail with a favourable breeze towards the mouth of the bay, with a design of returning south; but towards evening the wind changes, cold weather and hard adverse gales succeed, which oblige us to tack and anchor in the mouth of Little Loch Broom, an arm of the sea, about seven miles long, and not half a mile broad, bounded by high mountains, covered in many parts with birch woods. The hill Tallochessie may vie with the highest I have seen.

For two hours amuse ourselves with taking with hand-lines abundance of cod, some dogfish, and a curious ray.

The night was most tempestuous: our situation was disagreeable, as Mr Thompson thought our vessel would drive, and that he should be obliged to cut his cables, and put to sea; which, under the circumstances of a black night, a furious storm, and rocky narrows, did not contribute to the repose of freshwater seamen.

The wind grows moderate: in weighing anchor discover on the cable several very uncommon asteriae. No sooner was our anchor on board, but a furious squall arises, and blows in blasts like a hurricane, driving us before it at a vast rate, till we arrived within a mile of the bottom of the loch. Drop anchor, but without effect; are obliged to weigh again, while the furious gale engages an attention to the sails, and flings us into a double perplexity in this narrow strait, where for an hour our tacks were almost perpetual, and the vessel frequently in no small danger. The blasts from the mountains were tremendous, not only raising a vast sea, but catching up the waves in eddies, and raising them up in the air to a surprising height. At length we were relieved from our distress by a successful anchorage, under a high and finely wooded hill, in eight fathoms water, but within a small distance, of eighty.

Procure horses, by favour of Kenneth MacKenzie, Esq., of Dundonnel. Ride about a mile on the side of the hill, above the loch; arrive in a small but fertile plain, winding among the vast mountains, and adorned with a pretty river and woods of alder. Here we were rejoiced with the sight of enclosures long strangers to us: the hay was good, the bere and oats excellent; but the manner of manuring, called in these parts 'tathing', was very singular: many of the fields were covered with the boughs of alders, lately cut: these are left during the whole winter to rot; in March the ground is cleared of the undecayed parts, and then ploughed. Fern is also used for the same end.

Reach Dundonnel. Determined to go by land to visit Loch Maree, a great lake to the south: and direct Mr Thompson to sail, and wait for us at Gairloch.

We found ourselves seated in spot equalized by few in picturesque and magnificent scenery. The banks of the river that rushes by the house is fringed with trees; and the course often interrupted by cascades. At a small distance the ground begins to rise: as we mount, the eye is entertained with new objects; the river rolling beneath the dark shade of alders, an extent of plain composed of fields bounded by groves; and as the walk advances, appears a deep and tremendous hollow, shagged with trees, and winding far amidst the hills. We are alarmed with the roar of invisible cataracts, long before their place is discovered; and find them precipitating themselves down narrow chasms of stupendous depths, so narrow at the top, that

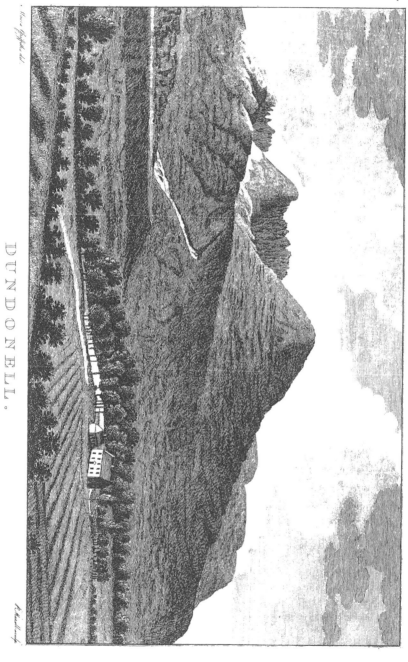

XL

DUNDONELL.

Highlanders in the eagerness of the chase will fearlessly spring over these barathra. They meander for miles amidst the mountains, and are the age-worn work of water, branch off into every glen, hid with trees of various species. Torrents roll over their bottoms often darting down precipices of a thousand forms, losing themselves beneath the undermined rocks, and appearing again white with the violence of the fall. By laying aside the boughs, and creeping to the verge, got sight of these otherwise latent cataracts; but the prospect sufficiently tired my head. Besides these darksome waters, multitudes of others precipitate themselves in full view down the steep sides of the adjacent hills; and create for several hundreds of feet a series of most magnificent falls.

Above rises a magnificent hill, which as far as the sight can reach is clothed with birch and pines, the shelter of stags, roes and black game.

To the west is a view where the awful, or rather the horrible predominates. A chain of rocky mountains, some conoid, but united by links of a height equal to most in North Britain, with sides dark, deep, and precipitous, with summits broken, sharp, serrated, and spiring into all terrific forms; with snowy glaciers lodged in the deep-shaded apertures. These crags are called *squrfein,* or 'hills of wind'; they rather merit the title of *squrshain,* or 'rocks of wind'; for here Aeolus may be said to make his residence, and be ever employed in fabricating blasts, squalls and hurricanes, which he scatters with no sparing hand over the subjacent vales and lochs.

Most agreeably detained with the good family of Dundonnel by a violent fall of rain, which rendered the waters impassable. Observe after dinner that cloudberries,[7] that grow on the adjacent mountains, were served as a dessert.

After taking a *deoch-an-doruis,* or a 'door-cup', proceed south, ascend a steep hill far above a bank wooded with various trees, among others the witch-elm grew native. To the west were the vast mountains, naked, rugged and dreary, their bases sloping furrowed with long clefts, emptying their precipitated waters into the river beneath. Descend into a vale with birch trees thinly scattered over it: and the extremity crossed by a high rock wooded and divided

[7] *Rubus Chamaemorus.*

in the middle by a vast and foaming cataract, the waters of Loch Nan-niun, or 'the lake of birds'. On the west side is an amazing mountain steeply sloping, composed of a whitish marble, so extensive, smooth, glossy and even, as to appear like an enormous sheet of ice; and is, I doubt not, as slippery. Our guide called the hill Lecach. The opposite side of the vale was precipitous; varied with trees and cascades, that fell among the branches. The whole of this scene was truly Alpine.

Ascend again. Arrive amidst strata of red and white marble, the way horrible, broken, steep and slippery; but our cautious steeds tried every step before they would venture to proceed. Black morassy heaths succeed, named Gliann-dochartai. Dine on the side of a rill at the bottom, on plentiful fare provided by our kind host, whose son, Mr MacKenzie, and another gentleman of the name, kindly undertook the charge of us to the next stage. Ride through a narrow strath called Kinlochewe, where we first saw the signs of houses and a little cultivation since morning. This terminates in a meadowy plain, closed at the end with Loch Maree: the night proved wet, and tempestuous: we therefore determined to defer the voyage till next day; and to take shelter in a whisky house the inn of the place. Mr MacKenzie complimented Mr Lightfoot and me with the bedstead, well covered with a warm litter of heath: we lay in our clothes, wrapped ourselves in plaids; and enjoyed a good repose. Our friends did not lose their sleep; but great was our surprise to see them form their bed of wet hay, or rather grass collected from the fields; they flung a plaid over it, undressed, and lay most comfortably, without injury, in what, in a little time, must have become an errant hotbed: so blest with hardy constitutions are even the gentlemen of this country!

At seven in the morning, take a six-oared boat, at the east end of Loch Maree: keep on the north shore beneath steep rocks, mostly filled with pines waving over our heads. Observe on the shore a young man of good appearance, hailing the boat in the Erse language. I demanded what he wanted: was informed, a place in the boat. As it was entirely filled, I was obliged to refuse his request. He follows us for two miles through every difficulty, and by his voice and gestures threatened revenge. At length a rower thought fit to acquaint us, that he was owner of the boat, and only wanted admission in lieu of one of them. The boat was ordered to shore, and the master taken in with proper apologies and attempts to soothe him for his hard treatment. Instead of insulting us with abuse, as a Charon of South Britain would have done, he instantly composed himself, and told us through an interpreter that he felt great pride in finding that his conduct gained any degree of approbation.

Continue our course. The lake, which at the beginning was only half a mile broad, now, nearly half its length, widens into a great bay, bending towards the south, about four miles in breadth, filled with little isles, too much clustered and indistinct.

Land on that called Inchmaree, the favoured isle of the saint, the patron of all the coast from Applecross to Loch Broom. The shores are neat and gravelly; the whole surface covered thickly with a beautiful grove of oak, ash, willow, wicken, birch, fir, hazel, and enormous hollies. In the midst is a circular dike of stones, with a regular narrow entrance: the inner part has been used for ages as a burial place, and is still in use. I suspect the dike to have been originally Druidical, and that the ancient superstition of Paganism had been taken up by the saint, as the readiest method of making a conquest over the minds of the inhabitants. A stump of a tree is shown as an altar, probably the memorial of one of stone; but the curiosity of the place is the well of the saint; of power unspeakable in cases of lunacy. The patient is brought into the sacred island, is made to kneel before the altar, where his attendants leave an offering in money: he is then brought to the well, and sips some of the holy water: a second offering is made; that done, he is thrice dipped in the lake; and the same operation is repeated every day for some weeks: and it often happens, by natural causes, the patient receives relief, of which the saint receives the credit. I must add that the visitants draw from the state of the well an omen of the disposition of St Maree: if his well is full, they suppose he will be propitious; if not, they proceed in their operations with fears and doubts: but let the event be what it will, he is held in high esteem: the common oath of the country is, by his name: if a traveller passes by any of his resting-places, they never neglect to leave an offering; but the saint is so moderate as not to put him to any expense: a stone, a stick, a bit of rag contents him.

This is the most beautiful of the isles; the others have only a few trees sprinkled over their surface.

About a mile farther the lake again contracts. Pass beneath a high rock, formed of short precipices, with shelves between, filled with multitudes of self-sown pines, making a most beautiful appearance.

The south side of the water is bounded with mountains adorned with birch woods, mixed with a few pines; a military road runs along its length. The mountains are not very high, but open in many parts to give a view of others, whose naked and broken tops shooting into sharp crags, strangely diversify the scene, and form a noble termination.

Towards the bottom of the lake is a headland, finely wooded to the very summit. Here the water suddenly narrows to the breadth of a hundred yards, and continues so for near a mile, the banks clothed with trees, and often bending into little semilunar bays to the very extremity; from whence its waters, after the course of a mile, a continual rapide, discharge into a deep and darksome hole, called Poolewe, which opens into the large bay of Loch Ewe.

The lake we had left is eighteen miles long: the waters are said to be specifically lighter than most others, and very rarely frozen: the depth is various, in some places sixty fathoms; but the bottom is very uneven: if ten feet of water were drained away, the whole would appear a chain of little lakes.

The fish are salmon, char and trout; of the last is a species weighing thirty pounds.

Land; are received by the Rev Mr Dounie, minister of Gairloch, whom we attend to church, and hear a very edifying plain comment on a portion of scripture. He takes us home with him, and by his hospitality makes us experience the difference between the lodgings of the two nights.

Take a view of the environs; visit the mouth of the river, where the salmon fishery supplies the tenant with three or four lasts of fish annually. On the bank are the remains of a very ancient iron furnace. Mr Dounie has seen the back of a grate, marked *S. G. Hay*, or Sir George Hay, who was head of a company here in the time of the Queen Regent; and is supposed to have chosen this remote place for the sake of quiet in those turbulent times.

Potatoes are raised here on the very peat moors, without any other drains than the trenches between the beds. The potatoes are kiln-dried for preservation.

It is to be hoped that a town will form itself here, as it is the station of a government packet, that sails regularly from hence to Stornoway, in Lewis, a place now growing considerable, by the encouragement of Lord Seaforth, the proprietor. This is a spot of much concourse: for here terminates the military road, which crosses from the east to the west sea, commencing at Inverness, and passing by Fairburn and Strathbraan to this place. Yet I believe the best inn on the last thirty miles is that of Mr Roderick MacDonald, our landlord the last night but one.

Ride above six miles south, and reach Gairloch; consisting of a few scattered houses, on a fine bay of the same name. Breakfast at Flowerdale; a good house, beautifully seated beneath hills finely wooded. This is the seat of Sir Hector MacKenzie, whose ancestor received a writ of fire and sword against the ancient rebellious owners: he succeeded in this commission, and received their lands for his pains.

The parish of Gairloch is very extensive, and the number of inhabitants evidently increase, owing to the simple method of life, and the conveniency they have of drawing a support from the fishery. If a young man is possessed of a herring net, a hand-line, and three or four cows, he immediately thinks himself able to support a family, and marries. The present number of souls are about two thousand eight hundred.

Herrings offer themselves in shoals from June to January: codfish abound on the great sandbank, one corner of which reaches to this bay, and is supposed to extend as far as Cape Wrath; and south, as low as Rona, off Skie; with various branches, all swarming with cod and ling. The fishery is carried on with long-lines, begins in February, and ends in April. The annual capture is uncertain, from five to twenty-seven thousand. The natives labour under some oppressions, which might be easily removed to the great advancement of this commerce. At present the fish are sold to some merchants from Campbeltown, who contract for them with the laird, a two pence halfpenny apiece, after being cured and dried in the sun. The merchants take only those that measure eighteen inches from the gills to the setting on of the tail; and oblige the people to let them have two or one of all that are beneath that length. The fish are sent to Bilbao: ling has also been carried there, but was rejected by the Spaniards. This trade is far from being pushed to its full extent; is monopolized, and the poor fishers cruelly forced to sell their fish for three halfpence apiece to those who sell it to the merchants.

The want of a town is very sensibly felt in all those parts: there is no one commodity, no one article of life, or implement of fishery but what is gotten with difficulty, and at a great price, brought from a distance by those who are to make advantage of the necessities of the people. It is much to be lamented that after the example of the Earl of Seaforth, they do not collect a number of inhabitants by feuing their lands, or granting leases for a length of years for building: but still so much of the spirit of the chieftain remains, that they dread giving an independency to their people; a false policy, as it would enrich both parties; and make the landlord more respectable, as master of a set of decent tenants, than of thousands of barefooted half-starved vassals. At present adventurers from distant parts take the employ from the natives: a town would create a market; a market would soon occasion a concourse of shipping, who would then arrive with a certainty of a cargo ready taken for them; and the mutual wants of stranger and native would be supplied at an easy rate.

By example of a gentleman or two, some few improvements in farming appear. Lime is burnt: sea-tang used as manure: and shell-sand imported by such who can afford the freight. But the best trade at present is cattle: about five hundred are annually sold out of this parish, from the price of one pound seven to two pounds five apiece. About eighty horses, at three pounds each, and a hundred and fifty sheep at three pounds per score. The cattle are blooded at spring and fall: the blood is preserved to be eaten cold.

We found our vessel safely arrived at anchor with many others, under the shelter of a little isle, on the south side of the bay. Weigh, and get under sail with a good breeze. Pass by the mouth of Loch Torridon: a few leagues farther by Applecross Bay, small, with populous and well-cultivated shores. The back ground most uncommonly mountainous.

Applecross house is inhabited by a most hospitable gentleman as fame reports: we lamented therefore our ability to pay our respects.

On the right leave the isles of Rona and Rasa and Scalpay: before us is Croulin, and beyond soar the vast hills of Skie. Sail close under Croulin inhabited by two families: producing a little corn and a few cattle. Almost opposite to its southern end is the common entrance into the two great lochs, Kisserne and Carron.

Pass the sound between Skie and Kintail; anchor about nine o'clock, and once more sleep beneath MacKinnon's Castle.

In sailing down the bay, had to the north-east a full view of Kintail in Ross-shire, the original seat of the MacKenzies, or rather MacKenneths,[8] a patronymic from their great ancestor Kenneth, son of Colin Fitzgerald, of the house of Desmond in Ireland. To him Alexander III made a grant of these lands for his good services at the battle of Largs. His posterity, a warlike race, filled all the lands; for the heroes of North Britain like polyps, multiply the more exceedingly by cuts and wounds.

Leave to the east the entrance to Loch Loung and Loch Duach; two miles from the south side of the last are the dangerous passes of Glensheil and Strachell; where, on June 10, 1719, a petty rebellion, projected by Cardinal Alberoni, and to have been supported by the Spaniards was suppressed. A tempest dispersed the hostile squadron, and only about three hundred forces arrived. The Highlanders made a poor stand at Strachell; but were quickly put to flight, when they had opportunity of destroying the king's forces by rolling down

---

[8] These were the chief gentlemen, in 1603, in the sheriffdom of Inverness, which at that time included the shire of that name, Ross, Strathnavern, Cathness, Sutherland, and the Northern Hebrides: Macloyd of Lewis, Macloyd of Harries, Donald Gormesoun, Macneil of Barray, Mulcalloun of Rosay, John Mudzart, captain of the Clanrannalts, The Laird of Glengarry, The Laird of Knoydart, Mac-kenzie, Laird of Garloche, Laird of Balnagownie, Laird of Fowles, Sherrife of Cromartie, Dumbeith, Forse, Otansceale, Mackye, Neil Hutchesoun, in Assent, Mackentosche, captain of the Clanchaniroun, Laird of Glenewes, Raynold Macraynold, of Keppache.

stones from the heights. I must not omit that among the clans that appeared in arms, was a large body lent by a neighbouring chieftain, merely for the battle of that one day; and win or lose was to return home that night.

Pass through the Kilru, buffetted severely on the way by violent squalls. Land on the east side in the parish of Glenelg, in the county of Inverness. The vessel anchors three miles distant on the opposite side of the bay, under Skie.

Walk up to the church; and observe near it a singular tree, whose boughs had bent to the grounds, and taking root formed a strange arbour. Pass by the barracks of Bernera, built in 1722, handsome and capacious, designed to hold two hundred men: at present occupied only by a corporal and six soldiers. The country should lament this neglect. They are now quite sensible of the good effects of the military, by introducing peace and security: they fear lest the evil days should return, and the ancient thefts be renewed, as soon as the banditti find this protection of the people removed.

Walk up the valley of Glenelg, or 'the vale of deer': visit Mr MacLeod, the minister, and receive all the welcome that the *Res angusta Domus* would permit. He showed us, at a small distance from his house, the remains of a mine of black lead, neglected on account of the poverty of what the adventurers found near the surface; but it is highly probable, that at a proper depth it may be found to equal that of Cumberland. A poor kind of bog iron ore is also found here.

Above the manse, on the top of a hill, is a British fortress, diked round with stone, and in the middle is the vestige of a circular enclosure, perhaps of a building, the shelter of the officers. Within sight is another of these retreats, which are called in the Erse *bàdhun*, or, 'the place of refuge'.

This valley is the property of Mr MacLeod, of Dunvegan, acquired by a marriage of an ancestor with a daughter of Lord Bisset. The parish is of vast extent, and comprehends Knodiart and North Morar. Glenelg has near seven hundred inhabitants, all Protestants; the other two districts are almost entirely of the popish persuasion. The reader who has the curiosity to know the number of Roman Catholics in these parts of North Britain, may satisfy his curiosity in the Appendix, from an abstract taken from the report made by the gentlemen appointed by the General Assembly, in 1760, to visit these remote Highlands, and the Hebrides, for the purpose of enquiring into the state of religion in those parts.

This part of Glenelg is divided into two valleys; Glenmore where the barracks are, from which is a military road of fifty-one miles extent, reaching to Fort Augustus: the other is Glenbeg. The parish sends out a considerable number of cattle: these valleys would be fertile in corn, was it not for the plague of rain, which prevents tillage to such a degree, that the poor inhabitants feel the same distress as their neighbours.

Walk back by the barracks to Glenbeg, to visit the celebrated edifices attributes to the Danes: the first is placed about two miles from the mouth of the valley. The more entire side appears of a most elegant taper form: the present height is thirty feet six inches; but in 1722, some Goth purloined from the top, seven feet and a half, under pretence of applying the materials to certain public buildings. By the appearance of some ruins that now lie at the base, and which have fallen off since that time, I believe three feet more may be added to the height, which will make the whole, about forty-one.

The whole is built with dry walls, but the courses most beautifully disposed. On one side is a breach of at least one quarter of the circumference. The diameter within is thirty-three feet and a half, part is seven feet four inches thick, but is formed thinner and thinner till it reaches the top, whose breadth I forgot to cause to be measured. This inside wall is quite perpendicular, so that the inner diameter must have been equal from top to bottom: but the exterior wall slopes, increasing in thickness till it reaches the ground.

In the thickness of the wall were two galleries; one at the lower part, about six feet two inches high, and two feet five at the bottom, narrowing to the top; flagged, and also covered over with great flat stones. This gallery ran quite round, and that horizontally, but was divided into apartments: in one place with six flags, placed equidistant from each other; and were accessible above by means of a hole from another gallery: into the lower were two entrances (before the ruin of the other side there had been two others) above each of these entrances were a row of holes, running up to the top, divided by flags appearing like shelves: near the top was a circle of projecting stones, which probably were intended to hold the beams that formed the roof: above is another hole like the former. None of these openings pass through, for there is not the least appearance of window nor opening on the outside wall. All these holes are square; are too small to admit the human body, so were probably designed to lodge arms, and different other matters, secure from wet or harm.

Over the first gallery was another, divided from it only by flags. This also went round, but was free from any separation: the height was five feet six; only twenty inches wide at bottom. This was also covered with flags at top.

At a distance above, in the broken sides of the wall, was another hole; but it seemed too small for a gallery. The ascent was not safe, so could not venture up. The height was taken by a little boy, who scrambled to the top.

The entrance was a square hole, on the west side: before it were the remains of some building, with a narrow opening that led to the door. Almost contiguous to this entrance or portico, was a small circle formed of rude stones, which was called the foundation of the Druid houses. It probably was formed for some religious purpose. I was told there were many others of this kind scattered over the valley.

At less than a quarter of a mile distant from this stands the second tower, on a little flat on the side of the hill. The form is similar, but the number of galleries differs: here are three, the lowest goes entirely round; but at the east end is an aperture now of a small depth, but once of such extent, that the goats which sheltered in it were often lost: on that account the entrance was filled with stones. This is six feet high, four feet two inches broad, and flagged above and below.

A second gallery was of the same height, but the breadth of the floor only three feet five.

The third gallery was of such difficult access that I did not attempt to get up: it was so narrow and low, that it was with difficulty that the child who climbed to it could creep through.

XLI

DANISH EDIFICES.

The present height of this tower is only twenty-four feet five inches; the diameter thirty; the thickness of the lower part of the wall twelve feet four.

I could not perceive any traces of the winding stairs mentioned by Mr Gordon: but as these buildings have suffered greatly since that gentleman saw them, I have no doubt of his accuracy.

These were in all probability places of defence; but it is difficult to say anything on the subject of their origin, or by what nation they were erected. They are called here *Caisteal Teilbah*, or 'the castles of Teilba', built by a mother for her four sons, as tradition, delivered in this translation of four Erse lines, informs:

> *My four sons a fair clan,*
> *I left in the strath of one glen:*
> *My Malcomb, my lovely Chonil,*
> *My Telve, my Troddan.*

There had been two others, totally demolished, and each named after her children. Mr Gordon mentions others of this kind; one at Glendunin, two at Easter Fearn in Ross-shire, and two or three in Lord Reay's country; one of which is called the Dune of Dornadilla, from an imaginary prince, who reigned two hundred and sixty years before the Christian era. This appears to be so well described by an anonymous writer in the Edinburgh magazine, that it will possibly be acceptable to the reader to find it copied in the note.[9]

---

[9] *In the most northern part of Scotland, called Lord Reay's country, not far from Tongue, and near the head of the river which runs into the North sea at Loch Bribal, is the remains of a stone tower, which I apprehend to be Druidic work, and to be the greatest piece of antiquity in this island. It is surprising that it is so little known even to the natives of that country: I don't remember to have ever seen it mentioned in any book whatever, nor do I recollect whether Mr Pennant has received any information concerning it. This tower is called by the neighbouring inhabitants, the Dune of Dornadilla. It is of a circular form, and now nearly resembling the frustrum of a cone: whether, when perfect, it terminated in a point, I cannot pretend to guess; but it seems to have been formerly higher, by the rubbish which lies round it. It is built of stone, without cement, and I take it to be between twenty and thirty feet high still. The entrance is by a very low and narrow door, to pass through which one is obliged to stoop much; but, perhaps, the ground may have been raised since the first erection.*

The rain, which poured in a deluge during the whole of this walk, attended with a most violent gale, prevented us from going abroad: but we found a most comfortable lodging under the hospitable roof of the good minister.

The whole morning continued wet and boisterous. In the evening cross over to Skie: see, near the shore, cut on the live rock, an inscription in rude characters. It must have been of great antiquity, as it was discovered by the accidental digging of peat at the depth of four feet.

Weigh anchor at eight o'clock in the morning, and turn out with wind and tide averse. After a struggle of three or four miles, put into Loch Iurn, or 'the lake of hell', on the Inverness coast, and anchor about two o'clock near a little isle on the south side, four miles within the mouth. Land on the north side, three miles distant from our ship, and visit Mr Macleod, of Arnisdale: I shall never forget the hospitality of the house: before I could utter a denial, three glasses

---

When one is got in, and placed in the centre, it is open over head. All round the sides of the walls are ranged stone shelves, one above another, like the shelves in a circular beaufait, reaching from near the bottom to the top. The stones which compose these shelves are supported chiefly by the stones which form the walls, and which project all round just in that place where the shelves are, and in no others: each of the shelves is separated into several divisions as in a bookcase. There is some remains of an aukward staircase. What use the shelves could be applied to I cannot conceive. It could not be of any military use from its situation at the bottom of a sloping hill, which wholly commands it. The most learned among the inhabitants, such as the gentry and clergy, who all speak the Irish language, could give no information or tradition concerning its use, or the origin and meaning of its name. But some years since I happened, at an auction of books, in London, to look into a French book, containing Gaulish antiquities, and there I saw a print of the remains of a Druidic temple in France, which greatly resembles the tower I am speaking of, having like shelves in it. And, reading a late pamphlet on the antiquity of the Irish language, I think I can partly trace the origin of the name Dornadilla. At page 24, the author says, that dorn *means 'a round stone', so that* abdorn *would mean 'the round stone of the priest';* na *is 'of' and* Di *is 'God': at page 45, he says, in the last line,* ulla *means 'a place of devotion'; so that* Dorna Diulla *will signify 'the round stone place of the worship of God'; or perhaps it might allude to some round stone preserved within as a sacred emblem of divinity. As I am not acquainted with the Irish language, if any of your correspondents can give any better account, either of the nature of such Druidic temples, or of this name in particular, it will, perhaps, be acceptable to others, as well as to your humble servant.*

of rum cordialized with jelly of bilberries, were poured into me by the irresistible hand of good Madam MacLeod. Messrs Lightfoot and Stuart sallied out in high spirits to botanise: I descended to my boat to make the voyage of the lake.

Steer south-east. After a small space the water widens into a large bay, bending to the south, which bears the name of Barrisdale: turn suddenly to the east, and pass through a very narrow strait, with several little isles on the outside; the water of a great depth, and the tide violent. For four miles before us the loch was straight, but of an oval form; then suddenly contracts a second time. Beyond that was another reach, and an instantaneous and agreeable view of a great fleet of busses, and all the busy apparatus of the herring fishery; with multitudes of little occasional hovels and tents on the shore, for the accommodation of the crews, and of the country people who resort here at this season to take and sell herrings to the strangers. An unexpected sight, at the distance of thirteen miles from the sea, amidst the wildest scene in nature.

A little farther the loch suddenly turns due south, and has a very narrow inlet to a third reach: this strait is so shallow as to be fordable at the ebb of springtides; yet has within, the depth of ten and seventeen fathoms: the length is about a mile; the breadth a quarter. About seven years ago it was so filled with herrings, that had crowded in, that the boats could not force their way, and thousands lay dead on the ebb.

The scenery that surrounds the whole of this lake has an Alpine wildness and magnificence; the hills of an enormous height, and for the most part clothed with extensive forests of oak and birch, often to the very summits. In many places are extensive tracts of open space, verdant, and only varied with a few trees scattered over them: amidst the thickest woods aspire vast grey rocks, a noble contrast! Nor are the lofty headlands a less embellishment; for through the trees that wave on their summit, is an awful sight of sky, and spiring summits of vast mountains.

On the south side, or the country of Knoydart, are vast numbers of pines, scattered among the other trees, and multitudes of young ones springing up. A conflagration had many years ago destroyed a fine forest; a loss which in a little time, it is to be hoped will be

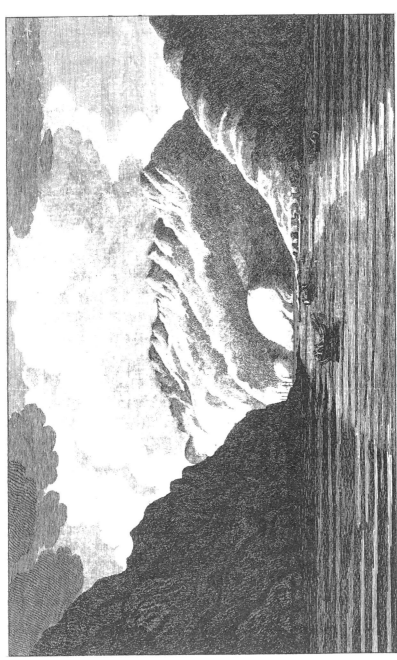

XLII

Mark Griffith del.

S. Hazell Sculp.

LOCK JURN.

repaired. Besides this, I can add some other pine forests to my former list:[10] that near Loch Maree; Abernethy and Rothmurchu; both belonging to gentlemen of the name of Grant; Glenmore, the Duke of Gordon's: and Glentaner, the property of Lord Aboyne. Our old botanists are silent about these British productions, till the time of Mr Evelyn and Mr Ray. This species of pine seems not to have been cultivated in England, till the former, as he says, received some seeds from that unhappy person, the late Marquis of Argyle: but Speed, in his chronicle, mentions the vast size of those on the banks of Loch Argicke, and their fitness for masts, as appeared by the report from commissioners sent there for that purpose, in the time of James VI.[11] Taylor, the water-poet, speaks in high terms of those in Braemar, that 'there are as many as will serve to the end of the world, for all the shippes, carracks, hoyes, galleys, boates, drumlers, barkes and water craftes, that are now in the world, or can be these forty years'.[12]

It is not wonderful, that the imagination, amidst these darksome and horrible scenes, should figure to itself ideal beings, once the terror of the superstitious inhabitants: in less enlightened times a dreadful spectre haunted these hills, sometimes in form of a great dog, a man, or a thin gigantic hag called Glaslich. The exorcist was called to drive away these evil *genii*: he formed circle within circle, used a multitude of charms, forced the demon from ring to ring, till he got it into the last entrenchment, when, if it proved very obstinate by adding new spells, he never failed of conquering the evil spirit, who, like that which haunted the daughter of Raguel, was:

> *With a vengeance sent*
> *From Media post to Egypt, there fast bound.*

In our return from the extremity of this sequestered spot, are most agreeably amused with meeting at least a hundred boats, rowing to the place we were leaving, to lay their nets; while the persons on shore were busied in lighting fires, and preparing a

[10] First, second, third edit., 183, 194, 212.
[11] Speed's *Chronicle*, IX.
[12] *Pennilesse Pilgrimage*, 136.

repast for their companions, against their return from their toilsome work.

So unexpected a prospect of the busy haunt of men and ships in this wild and romantic tract, afforded this agreeable reflection: that there is no part of our dominions so remote, so inhospitable, and so unprofitable, as to deny employ and livelihood to thousands; and that there are no parts so polished, so improved, and so fertile, but which must stoop to receive advantage from the dreary spots they so affectedly despise; and must be obliged to acknowledge the mutual dependency of part on part, howsoever remotely placed, and howsoever different in modes or manner of living. Charles Brandon's address to his royal spouse may well be applied to both extremes of our isle:

> *Cloth of gold, do not despise,*
> *Altho' thou art match'd with cloth of frize.*
> *Cloth of frize, be not too bold,*
> *Altho' thou art match'd with cloth of gold.*

Return to Arnisdale, and pass a most cheerful evening. Mr Lightfoot returned happy in having found the *Azalea procumbens*: Mr Stuart laden with fine specimens of amianthus and black talc.

Return on board at midnight: the night most excessive dark; but every stroke of our oars, every progressive motion of our boat, flung a most resplendent glory around, and left so long and luminous a train in our wake, as more than compensated the want of stars in the firmament. This appearance was occasioned by myriads of noctilucous Nereids, that inhabit the ocean, and on every agitation become at certain times apparent, and often remain sticking to the oars, and, like glow-worms, give a fine light. Mr Thompson informed us, that they were most brilliant before rain and tempest. He was not deceived in his predictions.

There is not an instance of any country having made so sudden a change in its morals as this I have just visited, and the vast tract intervening between these coasts and Loch Ness. Security and civilization possess every part; yet thirty years have not elapsed since the whole was a den of thieves, of the most extraordinary kind. They conducted their plundering excursions with the utmost policy, and reduced the whole art of theft into a regular system.

From habit it lost all the appearance of criminality: they considered it as labouring in their vocation; and when a party was formed for an expedition against their neighbour's property, they and their friends prayed as earnestly to heaven for success, as if they were engaged in the most laudable design.

The constant petition at grace of the old Highland chieftains, was delivered with great fervour, in these terms: 'Lord! Turn the world upside down, that Christians may make bread out of it.' The plain English of this pious request was, that the world might become, for their benefit, a scene of rapine and confusion.

They paid a sacred regard to their oath; but as superstition must, among a set of banditti, infallibly supersede piety; each, like the distinct casts of Indians, had his particular object of veneration: one would swear upon his dirk, and dread the penalty of perjury; yet make no scruple of forswearing himself upon the bible: a second would pay the same respect to the name of his chieftain: a third again would be most religiously bound by the sacred book: and a fourth, regard none of the three, and be credited only if he swore by his crucifix. It was always necessary to discover the inclination of the person, before you put him to the test: if the object of his veneration was mistaken, the oath was of no signification.

The greatest robbers were used to preserve hospitality to those that came to their houses, and, like the wild Arabs, observed the strictest honour towards their guests, or those that put implicit confidence in them. The Kennedys, two common thieves, took the Young Pretender under protection, and kept him with faith inviolate, notwithstanding they knew an immense reward was offered for his head. They often robbed for his support, and to supply him with linen, they once surprised the baggage horses of one of our general officers. They often went in disguise to Inverness to buy provisions for him. At length, a very considerable time after, one of these poor fellows, who had virtue to resist the temptation of thirty thousand pounds, was hanged for stealing a cow, value thirty shillings.

The greatest crime, among these felons, was that of infidelity among themselves: the criminal underwent a summary trial, and, if convicted, never missed of a capital punishment. The chieftain had his officers, and different departments of government; he had his judge, to whom he entrusted the decision of all civil disputes: but in criminal causes, the chief, assisted perhaps by some favourites, always undertook the process.

The principal men of his family, or his officers, formed his council; where everything was debated respecting their expeditions. Eloquence was held in great esteem among them, for by that they could sometimes work on their chieftain to change his opinion; for, notwithstanding he kept the form of a council, he always reserved the decisive vote in himself.

When one man had a claim on another, but wanted power to make it good, it was held lawful for him to steal from his debtor as many cattle as would satisfy his demand, provided he sent notice (as soon as he got out of reach of pursuit) that he had them, and would return them, provided satisfaction was made on a certain day agreed on.

When a *creach* or 'great expedition' had been made against distant herds, the owners, as soon as discovery was made, rose in arms, and with all their friends, made instant pursuit, tracing the cattle by their track for perhaps scores of miles. Their nicety in distinguishing that of their cattle from those that were only casually wandering, or driven, was amazingly sagacious. As soon as they arrived on an estate where the track was lost, they immediately attacked the proprietor, and would oblige him to recover the track from his land forwards, or to make good the loss they had sustained. This custom had the force of law, which gave to the Highlanders this surprising skill in the art of tracking.

It has been observed before, that to steal, rob and plunder with dexterity, was esteemed as the highest act of heroism. The feuds between the great families was one great cause. There was not a chieftain but that kept, in some remote valley in the depth of woods and rocks, whole tribes of thieves in readiness to let loose against his neighbours; when, from some public or private reason, he did not judge it expedient to resent openly any real or imaginary affront. From this motive the greater chieftain-robbers always supported the lesser, and encouraged no sort of improvement on their estates but what promoted rapine.

The greatest of the heroes in the last century, was Sir Ewin Cameron, whose life is given in the other volume. He long resisted the power of Cromwell, but at length was forced to submit. He lived in the neighbourhood of the garrison fixed by the usurper at Inverlochy. His vassals persisted in their thefts, till Cromwell sent orders to the commanding-officer, that on the next robbery he should seize on the chieftain, and execute him in twenty-four hours, in case the thief was not delivered to justice. An act of rapine soon happened: Sir Ewin received the message; who, instead of giving himself the trouble of looking out for the offender, laid hold of the first fellow he met with, sent him bound to Inverlochy, where he was instantly hanged. Cromwell, by his severity, put a stop to these excesses, till the time of the restoration, when they were renewed with double violence, till the year 1745.

Rob Roy Macgregor was another distinguished hero in the later end of the last, and the beginning of the present century. He contributed greatly towards forming his profession into a science; and establishing the police above mentioned. The Duke of Montrose unfortunately was his neighbour: Rob Roy frequently saved his Grace the trouble of collecting his rents; used to extort them from the tenants, and at the same time give them formal discharges. But it was neither in the power of the Duke or of any of the gentlemen he plundered to bring him to justice, so strongly protected was he by several great men to whom he was useful. Roy had his good qualities: he spent his revenue generously; and strange to say, was a true friend to the widow and orphan.

Every period of time gives a new improvement to the arts. A son of Sir Ewin Cameron refined on those of Rob Roy, and instead of dissipating his gains accumulated wealth. He, like Jonathan Wild the Great, never stole with his own hands, but conducted his commerce with an address, and to an extent unknown before. He employed several companies, and set the more adroit knaves at their head; and never suffered merit to go unrewarded. He never openly received their plunder; but employed agents to purchase from them their cattle. He acquired considerable property, which he was forced to leave behind, after the battle of Culloden gave the fatal blow to all their greatness.

The last of any eminence was the celebrated Barrisdale, who carried these arts to the highest pitch of perfection: besides exerting all the common practices, he improved that article of commerce called 'the black-meal' to a degree beyond what was ever known to his predecessors. This was a forced levy, so called from its being commonly paid in meal, which was raised far and wide on the estate of every nobleman and gentleman, in order that their cattle might be secured from the lesser thieves, over whom he secretly presided, and protected. He raised an income of five hundred a year by these taxes; and behaved with genuine honour in restoring, on proper consideration, the stolen cattle of his friends. In this he bore some resemblance to our Jonathan; but differed, in observing a strict fidelity towards his own gang; yet he was indefatigable in bringing to justice any rogues that interfered with his own. He was a man of a polished behaviour, fine address, and fine person. He considered himself in very high light, as a benefactor to the public, and preserver of general tranquillity; for on the silver plates, the ornaments of his Baldrick, he thus addresses his broadsword:

Hae tibi erunt artes, pacis compontere mores:
Parcere subjectis et debellare superbos.

After a most tempestuous and rainy night, sail at eight o'clock in the morning, designing to reach the Sound of Mull; but the wind proving contrary, we ran over to isle Oransay, in the isle of Skie, a safe harbour: where we continued confined by adverse winds till the next day.

At half an hour after one at noon, sail. As soon as we got out, we found a vast swell from the fury of the last night's storm; the waves mountainous, but, thanks to a gentle breeze, we made our way finely through them.

Pass on the east, Loch Nevish, or 'the lake of Heaven', a fine and picturesque inlet.

Polmorrer where small craft may lie. About a mile inland from this bay is the great freshwater lake called Loch Morrer: next is the country of Arisaig, and its celebrated point; for within this, a little to the south, in Loch-nan-Ua, or 'the bay of caves', landed the young pretender, on July 25, 1745; and from hence concluded his Phaetontic expedition, September 20th of the following year. The two frigates that lay there in May of the same summer, with arms and ammunition, had an engagement off this point with two of ours; and maintained their station. They landed part of their stores, but finding the cause desperate, returned to France with several of the fugitives from the battle of Culloden.

Sail by Loch Hallyort, and the country of Moydart, the most southerly part of the shire of Inverness. Leave to the west the point of Slate in Skie: the vast hills of Blaven and Cuchullin open to view: then succeeds the mountainous Rum; keep close under the isle of Egg, distinguished by the lofty spire of Squregg. Pass immediately under the point of Ardnamurchan, the most northern part of Argyleshire.

X

THE HEBRIDES (4)

Mull—Tobirmoire Bay—Aros—Kerrera Isle—Dunstaffage—Loch Etive—
Lismore—Scarba—Ardmaddie

Turn into the Sound of Mull, a fine opening five miles broad:
to the east of the point is Loch Sunart, penetrating deeply
into the country of Morvern. At the head, is Strontian, noted
for a lead mine. About nine o'clock at night anchor in Tobirmoire
Bay, in the isle of Mull. This bay is a most beautiful circular
basin, formed by Mull on one side, and the isle of Calve on the
other. All the banks are verdant and embellished at this time
with three cascades. It takes its name from a chapel and well,
dedicated to the Virgin Mary. Here in 1588 the *Florida*, one of
Philip's invincible Armada was blown up after the dispersion of
the fleet: some say by accident; others by the desperate resolution
of a Scotchman. Several attempts were made to recover the sunk
treasure. One in 1688, by William Sacheverel Esq., who fitted
up diving bells; and tried them with success at the depth of ten
fathoms: and report says, he got up much treasure. A piece of
the wreck was given me by an old inhabitant of the place; to be
preserved in memory of this signal providence, so beautifully
acknowledged by Queen Elizabeth in the motto of the medal struck
on the occasion:

Afflvait Deus, et dissipantur.

In this bay also the unfortunate Earl of Argyle may be said to have wrecked both life and fortune, in the year 1680: for in this place he made the first landing with a few friends, in his fatal invasion in concert with the unhappy Duke of Monmouth. The most inhuman medal I ever saw (next to that in memory of the massacre of Paris, by Charles IX) is one in my possession, struck by James II on occasion of the sad catastrophe of these two noblemen. Their heads are placed on two altars, at whose base are their bleeding corpses: the motto, *Ambitio malesuada ruit.*

A little north is Bloody Bay, so called from a sea-fight between a MacDonald of the Isles and his son. The former was supported by Hector Obbar MacLeane, the same, who died gloriously at the battle of Floddon, covering his monarch, James IV from the arrows of the English archers.

On the opposite shore of Morvern is Dun-an-Gal, a ruined castle of the MacLeanes. In this the rebels of 1719 put a small garrison; which soon surrendered to one of our men of war that attacked it.

Leave Tobirmoire at eight o'clock in the morning; and about half an hour past ten, anchor opposite to Aros Castle seated on a rock above the sea, and once a seat of MacDonald of the Isles. At the foot of the rock is the ruin of an oval pier, where he secured his boats.

Breakfast with Mr. Campbell, of Aros, and collect a few parculars of this rough island: that it is twenty-four Scotch miles long, and about the same in breadth; that it is divided into three great parishes, viz. Toracy, Ross, and Kilmore, or Kilninian, containing in all near four thousand catechisable persons; that it is in general rocky and barren, and does not yield corn enough for its inhabitants; that it sends out annually about eighteen hundred head of cattle, sold from thirty to fifty shillings apiece; that there are but few sheep; that the graziers have suffered greatly this year by the loss of cattle; but that none of the people have as yet migrated. That the usual manure is shell-sand, which the farmers procure from Tirey. That there is coal in the island nearly inaccessible by the badness of the roads, and that this most important article, which alone would bring wealth and comfort to the isles, is unaccountably neglected!

The island originally was part of the dominions of the lords of the Isles; but in after-times became the possession of the antient and valiant family of the MacLeanes, who still retain half. The other moiety is the litigated property of the Duke of Argyle; whose ancestor possessed himself of it in 1674, on account of a debt: and after the courts of law had made an adjudication in his favour, he was obliged to support their decree by force of arms.

Sail again down the sound, which in general is about four miles broad: the coast on both sides slopes and is patched with cornland. The northern coast is Morvern, the celebrated country of Fingal.

Leave on that side Loch Aylin, a safe harbour, with a most contracted entrance. A little farther is Castle Ardtornish, a ruin on a low headland jutting into the sound, where in 1461, John, Earl of Ross, and Lord of the Isles, lived in regal state.[1] His treaty with Edward IV is dated, *ex castello nostro Ard-Thornis Oct^{ris}, 19.* AD *1461.*[2]

On the Mull side is MacAllester's Bay, and below that, where the sound opens to the east is Castle Duart, once the seat of the MacLeane, lords of the island; but now garrisoned by a lieutenant and a detachment from Fort William. Morvern, near Ardtornish, begins to grow lofty and wooded; and Mull beyond this castle appears very mountainous.

Traverse the broad water of Loch Linnhè, which leads up to Lochaber. Have a fine view of the vast mountains, and the picturesque hills of Glenco. Pass the southern end of Lismore, and steer north between that isle and Middle Lorn. Sail by the isle of Kerrera noted for the death of Alexander II in 1249, while he lay there with a mighty fleet meditating the conquest of the Hebrides, then possessed by the Norwegians.

Opposite to this island, in Lorn, is the bay of Oban, where are the custom-house and post office.

On a great rock within land, precipitous on three sides, is the castle of Dunolly, once the residence of the chieftains of Lorn.

---

[1] Guthrie IV, 68.
[2] Rymer's *Foed.* XI, 487.

XLIII

Miss Griffith. del.

DUNSTAFFAGE CASTLE.

R. Magilbray. sc.

Continue our course; and passing with difficulty through a very narrow sound, formed by the Ilan Beach, and the mainland, arrive in a fine bay. Anchor under the ancient castle of Dunstaffage, or Stephen's Mount; and instantly receive, and accept, a most polite invitation from the owner, Mr Campbell.

This castle is fabled to have been founded by Ewin, a Pictish monarch, contemporary with Julius Caesar, naming it after himself Evonium. In fact, the founder is unknown; but it is certainly of great antiquity, and the first seat of the Pictish and Scottish princes. In this place was long preserved the famous stone, the palladium of North Britain; brought, says legend, out of Spain, where it was first used as a seat of justice by Gethalus, coeval with Moses. It continued here as the coronation chair till the reign of Kenneth II, who removed it to Scone, in order to secure his reign; for, according to the inscription:

> *Ni fallat fatum, Scoti, quocunque locatum*
> *Invenient lapidem, regnare tenentur ibidem.*

Mr Campbell showed to me a very pretty little ivory image, found in a ruinous part of the castle, that was certainly cut in memory of this chair, and appears to have been an inauguration sculpture. A crowned monarch is represented sitting in it, with a book in one hand, as if going to take the coronation oath.

The castle is square; the inside only eighty-seven feet; partly ruinous, partly habitable. At three of the corners are round towers; one of them projects very little. The entrance is towards the sea at present by a staircase, in old times probably by a drawbridge, which fell from a little gateway. The masonry appears very ancient: the tops battlemented. This pile is seated on a rock, whose sides have been pared to render it precipitous, and to make it conform to the shape of the castle.

In 1307, this castle was possessed by Alexander MacDougal, Lord of Argyle, a friend to the English; but was that year reduced by Robert Bruce, when MacDougal sued for peace with that prince, and was received into favour.[3]

---

[3] Barbour.

I find, about the year 1455, this to have been a residence of the lords of the Isles; for here James, last Earl of Douglas, after his defeat in Annandale,[4] fled to Donald the regulus of the time, and prevailed on him to take arms, and carry on a plundering war, against his monarch James II.

At a small distance from the castle is a ruined chapel, once an elegant building, and at one end an enclosure, a family cemetery, built in 1740. Opposite to these is a high precipice, ending abrupt, and turning suddenly toward the south-east. A person concealed in the recess of the rock, a little beyond the angle, surprises friends stationed at some distance beneath the precipice, with a very remarkable echo of any word, or even sentence he pronounces, which reaches the last distinct and unbroken. The repetition is single; but remarkably clear.

After breakfast ride along the edge of a beautiful bay, with the borders fertile in spots. The bere almost ripe. Cross a ferry at Connel or Conf Huil, or 'the raging flood', from a furious cataract of salt water, at the ebb of springtides. This place is the discharge of the waters of Loch Etive into the sea; where it suddenly contracts to a small breadth; and immediately above, certain rocks jut out, which more immediately direct the vast pent-up waters to this little strait, where they gush out with amazing violence, and form a fall of near ten feet.

Loch Etive runs far up the country, and receives the waters of Loch Aw at Bunaw. Here is at times a considerable salmon fishery; but at present very poor. See at a distance, on the northern bank, the site of Ardchattan, a priory of monks of Valliscaulium founded AD 1230, by Duncan MacCoul, ancester of the MacDougals of Lorn. Here Robert Bruce is said to have held a parliament; but more probably a council, for he remained long master of this country, before he got entire possession of Scotland.

A mile from Connel, near the shore, is Dun-mac-Sniochain, the ancient Beregonium, or Berogomum. The foundation of this city, as it is called, is attributed, by apocryphal history, to Fergus II and was called the chief in Scotland for many ages. It was at best such

---

[4] *Lives of the Douglases*, 203.

XLIV

M Griffith Pinx.^t   R. Murray Sc.

a city as Caesar found in our island at the time of his invasion; an *oppidum*, or fortified town, placed in a thick wood, surrounded with a rampart and fosse, a place of retreat from invaders.[5] Along the top of the beach is a raised mound, the defence against a sudden landing. This, from the idea of here having been a city, is styled, Straid-a-Mhargai, or Market Street: within this are two rude erect columns, about six feet high, and nine and a half in girth: behind these a peatmoss: on one side a range of low hills, at whose nearest extremity is an entrenchment called Dun-valirè. On the western side of the morass is an oblong insulated hill, on whose summit, the country-people say, there had been seven towers: I could only perceive three or four excavations, of no certain form, and a dike round them.

In most parts of the hill are dug up great quantities of different sorts of pumices, or scoria, of different kinds: of them one is the *Pumex cinerarius*; the other the *Pumex molaris* of Linnaeus; the last very much resembling some that Mr Banks favoured me with from the island of Iceland. The hill is doubtless the work of a volcano, of which this is not the only vestige in North Britain.

Ride on a fine road to Ardmuchnage, the seat of the late Sir Duncan Campbell; a very handsome house, and well finished. Sir Duncan, at the age of forty began to plant, and lived to see the extensive plantations in his garden, and on the picturesque hills round his lands, arrive to perfection. The country about rises into a lofty but narrow eminence, now finely wooded, extending in a curvature, forming one side of an enchanting bay; the other impending over the sea.

On my return observe, near the hill of the seven towers, a Druidical circle, formed of round stones placed close together. The area is twenty-six feet in diameter; and about ten feet distant from the outside is an erect pillar seven feet high. At such stones as these, my learned friend, the late Dr William Borlase remarks,[6] might have stood the officers of the high priest, to command silence among the people; or some inferior person, versed in the ceremonies, to

---

[5] *De Bello Gallico*, lib. V, ch. 21.
[6] *Antiq. Cornwal.*

observe that none were omitted, by warning the officiating priest, in case any escaped his memory.

Return, and lie on board.

Weigh anchor at six o'clock in the morning. Sail by the back of Lochnel Hill, forming a most beautiful crescent, partly cultivated, partly covered with wood to the summit. Land near the north end of the isle of Lismore, which is about nine miles long, one and a half broad, and contains about fifteen hundred inhabitants.[7] It derives its name from *lios mor*, or 'the great garden': but tradition says it was originally a great deer forest; and, as a proof, multitudes of stag horns of uncommon sizes are perpetually dug up in the mosses. At present there is scarce any wood; but the lesser vegetables grow with uncommon vigour. The chief produce of the land is bere and oats. The first is raised in great quantity, but abused by being distilled into whisky. The crops of oats are generally applied to the payment of rent; so that the inhabitants are obliged for their subsistence annually to import much meal.

The ground has in most parts the appearance of great fertility, but is extremely ill-managed, and much impoverished by excess of tillage, and neglect of manure. Pit- and rock-marl are found here. The whole isle lies on a limestone rock, which in many places peeps above ground, forming a long series of low sharp ridges. No use can be made of this as a manure for want of fuel to burn it. The peat here is very bad, being mixed with earth; it must first be trampled with the feet into a consistence; is then formed into small flat cakes, and must afterwards be exposed on the ground to dry.

About a hundred head of cattle are annually exported, which are at present remarkably small: they seem to have degenerated, for I saw, at Ardmuchnage, the skull of an ox, dug up in this island, that was of much larger dimensions than of any now living in Great Britain.

Horses are in this island very short-lived. They are used when about two or three years old: and are observed soon to lose all their

[7] Or between 900 and 1,000 examinable persons.

teeth. Both they and the cows are housed during winter, and fed on straw.

Otters are found here: but neither foxes, hares, nor rats. Mice are plentiful, and very destructive.

There are three small lakes. Two abound with fine trout: the third only with eels. Variety of the duck kind frequent these waters during winter.

Walk up to a Danish fort: at present the height is seventeen feet: within the wall is a gallery, and round the area a seat, as in that described in Ilay.

Visit the church, now a mean modern building. In the churchyard are two or three old tombs, with claymores engraven on them: here is also a remarkable tomb, constituting of nothing more than a thick log of oak. This substitute for a gravestone must have been in this country of great antiquity, there being no word in the Erse language to express the last, it not being styled *leichd lithidh*, 'a gravestone', but *darag lithidh* or, 'a gravelog'. On a live rock are cut the radii of a dial, but the index is lost. On another rock is a small excavated basin, perhaps one of the rock basins of Dr Borlase, in times of Druidism used for religious purposes.

This island had been the site of the Bishop of Argyle: the see was disjoined from that of Dunkeld about the year 1200, at the request of John the Englishman, bishop of that diocese. There are no relics of the cathedral or the bishop's house, whose residence was supposed to have been latterly in the castle of Achanduin, on the west side of the isle, opposite to Duart in Mull.

The inhabitants in general are poor, are much troubled with sore eyes; and in the spring are afflicted with a costiveness that often proves fatal. At that season all their provisions are generally consumed; and they are forced to live on sheeps' milk boiled, to which the distemper is attributed.

The isle of Lismore forms but a small part of the parish. The extent is not to be comprehended by an Englishman. From the point of Lismore to the extremity of Kinlochbeg is forty-two computed miles, besides nine in Kingerloch. It comprehends this isle, Appin Duror, Glenco, Glencreran and Kingerloch, and contains 3,000 examinable persons, under the care of one minister and two missionaries.

Get on board, and have in mid-channel, a most delightful view: the woods of Loch Nell; the house of Airds; beyond is the castle of Ellenstalker, seated in a little isle; the country of Appin; the vast mountains of Lochaber; Dunolly, Lismore, and various isles of grotesque appearance.[8] To the south appear the Slate islands, Scarba, Jura, and Ilay; and to the west, Oransay and Colonsay.

Sail between Inch and the Maire isles, leaving the noted Slate island of Eusdale to the east, and close to it Suil and Luing, chiefly the property of the Earl of Breadalbane: within these are the harbours of Eusdale, of Cuain, between Luing and Suil; Bardrise, off Luing; and below, is that of Blackmuil Bay.

Opposite to Luing, on the west, is a group of rough little isles, of which Plada and Belnabua are productive of slate. In the broad basin between these and Luing, is a most rippling tide; even in this calm forces us along with vast celerity and violence: the whole surface disordered with eddies and whirlpools, rising first with furious boilings, driving and vanishing with the current. Anchor under the east side, beneath the vast mountain of Scarba; an island of great height, about five miles long, chiefly covered with heath, but on this side are some woods, and marks of cultivation. Mr MacLeane lives on this side, and favours us with a visit, and offers his service to show us the celebrated gulf of Corryvrekan; which we did not wait till morning to see, as our expectations were raised to the highest pitch, and we thought of nothing less than that it would prove a second maelstrom. We accordingly took a most fatiguing walk up the mountain, through heath of an uncommon height, swarming with grouse. We arrived in an ill hour, for the tide did not suit, and we saw little more than a very strong current.

This morning we take boat; and after rowing two miles, land and walk along the rocks till we reach a fit place for surveying this phenomenon. The channel between this isle and Jura is about a mile broad, exposed to the weight of the Atlantic, which pours

---

[8] Among them that of Durisfuire. Vide title-page.

in its waters here with great force, their course being directed and confined by the sound between Colonsay and Mull. The tide had at this time made two hours flood, and ran with a furious current, great boilings, attended with much foam;[9] and in many places formed considerable whirlpools. On the side of Jura the current dashes, as is reasonable to suppose, against some sunk rocks. It forms there a most dreadful backtide, which in tempests catches up the vessels that the whirlpools fling into it; so that almost certain destruction attends those that are so unfortunate as to be forced in at those seasons. It was our ill-luck to see it in a very pacific state, and passable without the least hazard.

The chief whirlpool lies on the Scarba side, near the west end. Here, as that skilful pilot, Mr Murdock Mackenzie, assured me, it is of various depths, viz, 36, 47, 83, and 91 fathoms; and of some places unfathomable: the transitions sudden, from the lesser to the greater depths: the bottom all sharp rocks with vast chasms between; and a fathomless one where the greatest vortex lies, from which, to the eastern end of Scarba, close to shore, the depths are 13, 9, 12.

There is another whirlpool off a little isle, on the west end of Jura: which contributes to the horrors of the place. In great storms, the tides run at the rate of fifteen miles an hour; the height of the boilings are said to be dreadful; and the whole rage of the waters unspeakable. It is not therefore wonderful that there should have been here a chapel of the Virgin, whose assistance was often invoked, for my historian says, that she worked numbers of miracles, doubtlessly in favour of distressed mariners.[10]

Scarba contains forty inhabitants. Mr Macleane the proprietor resides here. When he favoured us with his company, he came with two of his sons and their tutor; for in North Britain, there is no gentleman of ever so small an estate, but strictly attends to the education of his children, and the sure foundation of their future fortune. A person properly qualified and easily procured at a cheap

---

[9] From its varied colours it is called Coirebhreatain; or, 'the spotted or plaided cauldron'.

[10] Fordun, lib. II, ch. 10.

rate, attends in the family; where the father sees that justice is done to them, at far less expense than if he sent them to distant schools.

Leave Scarba; pass between Nether Lorn and the isles of Luing and Suil to the east, and of Toracy and Shuna to the west, all inhabited; and the first almost covered with excellent corn. In Toracy is an ancient tower once belonging to the great MacDonald who made it his half-way hunting seat in his progress from Cantyre to his northern isles: for which reason it was called Dogcastle: and here he made it a most laudable rule to reside, till he had spent the whole of his revenue collected in the neighbourhood. According to the report, these isles, and part of the neighbouring mainland, form a parish, whose church is in Suil.[11]

Take boat; turn at the point of Suil, am carried by a rapid tide through the gut of Cuan, visit Eusdale, the noted slate island; whose length is about half a mile, and composed entirely of slate, intersected, and in some parts covered, with whinstone, to the thickness of sixteen feet: the stratum of slate is thirty-six, dipping quick south-east to north-west. In order to be raised, it is at first blasted with powder; the greater pieces are then divided, carried off in wheelbarrows, and lastly split into the merchantable sizes, from eighteen by fourteen inches, to nine by six: and put on board at the price of twenty shillings per thousand. About two millions and a half are sold annually to England, Norway, Canada, and the West Indies. In the slates are multitudes of cubic pyritae. In one place, about sixteen feet above high-water mark, just over the slates, is a thick bed of small fragments, worn smooth, as if by the action of the waves; and mixed with them are multitudes of the common sea shells: a proof of the vast retreat of the ocean in these parts.

There are many other good slate quarries in this neighbourhood, as, on the isles of Suil, Luing, Balnahua and Kerrera, and some few opposite to them on the coast of Nether Lorn.

The boat takes us the length of the western side of Suil. At the north point, turn into Clachan Firth, the narrowest strait I ever was in, dividing that island from Lorn, in parts so contracted as

---

[11] Made by the gentlemen sent, in 1760, by order of the General Assembly, to inspect the state of religion in the islands, etc. MS.

would admit the flinging an arch from shore to shore. The depth is very various: in some parts fifty fathoms; in others, so shallow as to be fordable at the ebb of springtides. On the banks of the island and mainland, the strata of stone rise in form of walls, of a great height, and not above two feet and a half thick, extending far, so as easily to be mistaken for the bounds of an enclosure.

Arrived in the beautiful bay of Ardmaddie, or 'the height of the wolves'. A house small, but elegant, stands in front, and the sides of the bay high, entirely clothed with wood. Here I find the kindest welcome from my worthy acquaintance, Captain Archibald Campbell, tenant here to the Earl of Breadalbane; who, with the utmost friendship, during the voyage charged himself with the care of my groom and my horses. Here I also took leave of Mr Archibald Thompson; whose attention to the objects of my enquiries, obliging conduct throughout, and skill in his profession, demand my warmest acknowledgements. Thus ended this voyage of amusement, successful and satisfactory in every part, unless where embittered with reflections on the sufferings of my fellow-creatures. Gratitude forbids my silence respecting the kind reception I universally met with; or the active zeal of every one to facilitate my pursuits; or their liberal communication of every species of information, useful or entertaining.

I retired to my chamber, filled with reflections on the various events of my voyage; and every scene by turns presented itself before my imagination. As soon as my eyes were closed, I discovered, that the slumber of the body was but the waking of the soul.[12] All I had seen appeared to have been dull and clouded to my apprehension, serving to evince, that 'our waking conceptions do not match the fancies of our sleep'.[13] I imagined myself again gently wafted down the Sound of Mull; bounded on each side by the former dominions, of mighty chieftains; or of heroes immortalized in the verse of Ossian. My busy fancy was worked into a species of enthusiasm, and for a time it

> Bodied forth
> *The forms of things unknown;*
> *Turned them to shape, and gave to airy nothing*
> *A local habitation and a name.*

[12] Brown's *Religio Medici.*
[13] Ibid.

A figure, dressed in the garb of an ancient warrior, floated in the air before me: his target and his claymore seemed of no common size, and spoke the former strength of the hero. A graceful vigour was apparent in his countenance, notwithstanding time had robbed him of part of his locks, and given to the remainder a venerable hoariness. As soon as he had fixed my attention, he thus seemed to address himself to me:

'Stranger, thy purpose is not unknown to me; I have attended thee (invisible) in all thy voyage; have sympathised with thee in the rising tear at the misery of my once-loved country; and sighs, such as a spirit can emit, have been faithful echoes to those of thy corporeal frame.

'Know, that in the days of my existence on earth, I possessed an ample portion of the tract thou seest to the north. I was the dread of the neighbouring chieftains; the delight of my people, their protector, their friend, their father. No injury they ever received, passed unrevenged; for no one excelled me in conferring benefits on my clan, or in repaying insults on their enemies. A thousand of my kindred followed me in arms, wheresoever I commanded. Their obedience was to me implicit, for my word was to them a law: my name, the most sacred of oaths. I was (for nothing now can be concealed) fierce, arrogant, despotic, irritable: my passions were strong, my anger tremendous: yet I had the arts of conciliating the affections of my people, and was the darling of a numerous brave. They knew the love I bore them: they saw, on a thousand occasions, the strongest proofs of my affection. In the day of battle I have covered the weak with my shield; and laid at my feet their hostile antagonists. The too grateful vassal, in return, in the next conflict, has sprung before me, and received in his own bosom the shaft that has been levelled at mine. In retreats from overpowering numbers, I was ever last in the field. I alone have kept the enemy at bay, and purchased safety for my people with a hundred wounds.

In the short intervals of peace, my hall was filled with my friends and kindred: my hospitality was equal to my deeds of arms; and hecatombs of beeves and deer covered my rude but welcome tables. My nearest relations sat next to me, and then succeeded the bravest of my clan; and below them, the emulous youth leaned forward, to hear the gallant recital of our past actions. Our bards rehearsed the valiant deeds of our great ancestors, and inflam'd our valour by the sublimity of their verse, accompanied with the inspiring sound of the ear-piercing *peebirechts*.

'The crowds of people that attended at an humble distance, partook of my bounty; their families were my care: for I beheld in their boys a future support of the greatness of my house: an hereditary race of warriors.

'My numerous kindred lived on lands the gift of my distant progenitors, who took care to plant their children near the main stock: the scions took firm root, and proved, in after-times, a grateful shelter to the parent tree, against the fury of the severest storms. These I considered, not as mercenary tenants, but as the friends of good and of adverse fortune. Their tenures were easy; their *duchas* involate.[14] I found my interest interwoven with theirs. In support of our mutual welfare, they were enabled to keep a becoming hospitality. They cherished their neighbouring dependents; and could receive my visits in turn with a well-covered board.

'Strong fidelity and warm friendship reigned among us; disturbed perhaps by the momentary gusts of my passions: the sun that warmed them might experience a short obscurity; but the cloud soon passed away, and the beams of love returned with the fulness of years and of glory; and finished my course, attended to my grave with the full *coranach* of my lamenting people.

'My progeny for a time supported the great and wild magnificence of the feudal reign. Their distance from court unfortunately prevented them from knowing that they had a superior; and their ideas of loyalty were regulated only by the respect or attention paid to their fancied independency. Their vassals were happy or miserable, according to the disposition of the little monarch of the time. Two centuries, from my days, had elapsed, before their greatness knew its final period. The shackles of the feudal

---

[14] From *dulhaich*, 'native country'. They held their farms at a small rent, from father to son, by a kind of prescribed right, which the Highlanders called *duchas*. This tenure, in the feudal times, was esteemed sacred and inviolable.

government were at length struck off; and possibly happiness was announced to the meanest vassal. The target, the dirk, and the claymore, too long abused, were wrested from our hands, and we were bid to learn the arts of peace; to spread the net, to shoot the shuttle, or to cultivate the ground.

'The mighty chieftains, the brave and disinterested heroes of old times, by a most violent and surprising transformation, at once sunk into the rapacious landlords; determined to compensate the loss of power, with the increase of revenue; to exchange the warm affections of their people for sordid trash. Their visits, to those of their forefathers, are like the surveys of a cruel land-jobber, attended by a set of quick-sighted vultures, skilled in pointing out the most exquisite methods of oppression, or to instruct them in the art of exhausting their purses of sums to be wasted in distant lands. Like the taskmasters of Egypt, they require them to make brick without straw. They leave them in their primeval poverty, uninstructed in any art for their future support; deprived of the wonted resources of the hospitality of their lord, or the plentiful boards of his numerous friends. They experience an instantaneous desertion; are flung at once into a new state of life, and demand the fostering hand as much as the most infant colony. When I hover over our vales, I see the same nakedness exist, the same misery in habitation, the same idle disposition. Would I could have seen the same spirit and vigour as in days of yore! But the powers of their souls are sunk with oppression, and those of their bodies lost with want. They look up in despair at our deserted castles; and, worn out with famine and disease, drop into an unnoticed grave.

'The ties of affection amongst relations are now no more: no distinction is at present made between proximity of blood and the most distant stranger. Interest alone creates the preference of man to man. The thousands that with joy expected the return of their chieftain, now retire with sullen grief into their cottages; or, in little groups, express their rage in curses both loud and deep. No vassal now springs to receive the weapon levelled at the breast of the Lord, but rather wishes to plant his own in the bosom of the oppressor.

'The ancient Native, full of the idea of the manly look of the warriors and friends of his youth, is lost in admiration at the degenerate progeny: feature and habit are changed; the one effeminated, the other become ridiculous by adopting the idle fashions of foreign climes: lost to the love of their country, lost to all the sweet affections of patriarchal life! What then, may I say, are the fruits of your travels? What arts have you brought home, that will serve to bring subsistence to your people? To recompense them for your drafted revenues? What to clothe the naked? To feed the hungry? To furnish them with more comfortable protection from the inclemency of the weather? They require no great matters: a small portion of a raiment; a little meal. With sad comparison they learn, that chieftains still exist, who make their people their care: and with envy they hear of the improving state of the vassals of an Argyle, an Athol, a Breadalbane, and a Bute.

'Return to your country: inform them with your presence: restore to them the laudable part of the ancient matters; eradicate the bad. Bring them instructors, and they would learn. Teach them arts adapted to their climate: they would brave the fury of our seas in fishing. Send them materials for the coarser manufactures; they would with patience sit down to the loom; they would wave the sails to waft your navies to victory; and part of them rejoice to share the glory in the most distant combats. Select a portion of them for the toils of the ocean: make your levies, enroll them; discipline them under able veterans, and send annually to our ports the smaller vessels of your tremendous navy. Trust them with swords, and a small retaining pay. If you have doubts, establish a *place d'armes*, in vacant times, the deposit of their weapons, under proper garrison. They would submit to any restrictions: and think no restraints, founded on the safety of the whole, an infringement of liberty, or an invasion of property. Legislature has given them their manumission; and they no longer consider themselves as part of the livestock of their chieftain. Draft them to distant climes, and they will sacrifice their lives in the just cause of government with as much zeal as their forefathers did under the lawless direction of my valiant ancestors. Limit only the time of their warfare; sweeten it only with the hopes of a return to their native country, and they will become willing substitutes for their southern brethren. Occupied in the soft arts of peace, those should extend your manufactures; and these would defend your commerce. Persuade their governors to experience their zeal; and let courtly favour rise and fall with their actions. Have not thousands in the late war proved their sincerity? Have not thousands expiated with their blood the folly of rebellion, and the crimes of their parents?

'If you will totally neglect them: if you will not reside among them; if you will not, by your example, instruct them in the science of rural economy, nor cause them to be taught the useful arts: if you cannot obtain leave for them to devote themselves to the service of their country, by deeds of arms; do not at least drive them to despair, by oppression: do not force them into a distant land, and necessitate them to seek tranquillity by a measure which was once deemed the punishment of the most atrocious criminals. Do not be guilty of treason against your country, by depriving it of multitudes of useful members, whose defence it may too soon want, against our natural enemies. Do not create a new species of disaffection; and let it not receive a more exalted venom, in a continent replete with the most dangerous kind. Extremes of change are always the worst. How dreadful will be the once-existent folly of Jacotibism, transformed into the accused spirit of political libertinism!

'Leave them (if you will do no more) but the bare power of existence in their native country, and they will not envy you your new luxuries. Waste your hours in the lap of dissipation: resign yourself up to the fascinations of Acrasia; and sport in the bower of bliss. Cover your tables with delicacies, at the expense of your famished clans. Think not of the wretches, at those seasons, lest your appetite for the hors d'ouvres be palled, and you feel a momentary remorse for deaths occasioned by ye, ye thoughtless deserters of your people! With all my failings, I exult in innocence of such crimes; and felicitate myself on my aerial state, capable of withdrawing from the sight of miseries I cannot alleviate, and of oppressions I cannot prevent.'

A
TOUR
in
SCOTLAND
and
VOYAGE TO THE HEBRIDES
1772

Part 2

ADVERTISEMENT

———⟫●⟪———

THIS volume brings my journey of 1769 and 1772 to a conclusion. I beg leave to return thanks to the several gentlemen who gave themselves the trouble of supplying me with materials, and with variety of remarks and strictures, that have served to correct the many mistakes I may have committed. I hold myself peculiarly indebted to

— Fraser, Esq., of Inverness;
The Rev Mr Macintyre, of Glenurchie;
The Rev Dr Ferguson, of Mouline;
The Rev Mr Bisset, of Logierait;
John Mackenzie, Esq., of Delvin;
Mr Thomas Marshall, of Perth;
Dr Drummond;
The Rev Mr Duff, of Tibbirmoor;
The Rev Mr Scott, of Meigle;
John Haliburton, Esq., of Dundee;
The Rev Mr Bell, of Aberbrothic;
Patrick Scott, Esq., of Rossie;
Mr Alexander Christie, late Provost of Montrose;
Robert Barclay, Esq., of Urie;
Professor Watson, of St Andrews;
George Skene, Esq., of Careston;
Mr James Gillies, of Brechin;
George Chalmers, Esq., of Dumferline;
and superlatively to

Mr George Allan, of Darlington.

I must apologize to the public for so hastily passing over two places of which ampler accounts might have been expected. I have lived so long in Chester that a more minute history of it ought to have been given; but after all, it would have seemed trivial, on the appearance of the labours of the Rev Dr Foot Gower, which the public has very long expected. I shall rejoice on a future occasion to have opportunity of drawing from so rich a magazine, a variety of materials for a farther elucidation of the respectable capital of so respectable a county.

I wish I could assign as good a reason for my worse than neglect of the venerable Lincoln. When I passed through it in 1769, I must have been planet-struck, not to have observed the amazing beauties of the external as well as internal architecture of the cathedral. I could not stifle my remorse. Last year I hastened thither; and with all signs of contrition, made the *amende honorable* before the great door. I trust that my penitence was accepted by the whole chapter. A recantation of the little respect I paid to its external elegance will be a subject of a future volume, a tour through the eastern parts of the Mercian Kingdom.

Downing,
March 1, 1776

THOMAS PENNANT.

XI

ARGYLE,
PERTHSHIRE (1)

Ardmaddie—Parish of Suil—Inverarey—Glenurchie—Inchhail—Fraoch
Elan—Kilchurn Castle—Tynedrum—Strathfillan—Glendochart—Killin—
Loch Tay—Fortingal—Isle of Loch Tay—Taymouth

PASS this day at Ardmaddie. The house commands a beautiful
view of the bay, and of the isle of Suil, where the parish church
and the manse of the minister of the parish are placed, accessible at
all times, by reason of the narrowness of the channel of Clachan.
This tract is hilly, finely wooded near the house, and on the adjacent
part of the shore: contains about eleven hundred examinable
persons, and abounds with cattle. A quarry of white marble, veined
with dull red, is found on the west side of the bay.

This parish lies in Nether Lorn, a district of the vast country of
Argyle. These divisions (for there are three Lorns) were, in the time
of Robert Bruce, possessed by the MacDougals, opponents of that
prince; passed from them to the Stuarts; but in the fifteenth century
were transferred into the family of the Campbells,[1] by the marriages
of three coheiresses, daughters of the last Stuart, Lord of Lorn. Sir
Colin, of Glenurchie, surnamed the black, took to his share Isabel
the eldest: disposed of the second to his half-brother Archibald;

---

[1] MS Hist. of the Campbells.

377

and reserved for his nephew (Colin, first Earl of Argyle, then under his guardianship) the youngest Marrate-na-Nhaghn, or Margaret the Rhymer.

This county was part of the ancient Ergadia, or Iar-ghael, or land of the western Caledonians, which extended as far as Gairloch, in the shire of Ross. It formed part of the dominions of the old Scots, whose kingdom reached from the Firth of Clyde, along the whole coast, even as far as Dungsby Head, in Caithness.[2]

Leave Ardmaddie. Ride along a fine road, for some time by the side of an arm of the sea, called, from the plenty of shells, Loch Fuchan. Go by a heap of stones, called Cairnalpin, because from hence the bodies of the Alpiniades, or successors of that monarch, were embarked for interment in the sacred ground of Iona. After quitting this loch, arrive in a barren tract of black heathy land, enlivened now and then with some pretty lakes. Reach the banks of Loch Aw, where the fine water is contracted to the breadth of about three quarters of a mile. Am wafted over in a horse-boat; land on a spot styled Port Sonnachan, and after about ten miles riding, pass between hills, finely planted with several sorts of trees, such as Weymouth pines, etc. and reach the town and castle of Inveraray,[3] seated on a small but beautiful plain, on the side of Loch Fine. This had long been the seat of the Campbells. It was inhabited about the latter end of the fourteenth century by Colin, surnamed Iongallach, or 'the Wonderful', on account of his marvellous exploits; and, I may add, his odd whims: among which, and not the least, may be reckoned the burning of his house at Inveraray on receiving a visit from the O'Neiles of Ireland, that he might have pretence to entertain his illustrious guests in his magnificent field equipage. The great tower, which was standing till very lately, was built by the black Sir Colin, for his nephew, the first Earl of Argyle, at that time a minor.[4] I do not discover any date to ascertain the time of its foundation, any further than that it was prior to the year 1480, the

---

[2] Dr Macpherson, 334.

[3] In Gaelic, *Inner Aora*.

[4] In the quarto edition of the *Tour*, 1769, is a print, supposed to be that of the old castle, copied from one inscribed with its name; but the Gordons claim it as a view of Castle Gordon, the seat of their chieftains.

I

Maria Griffiths del.   W. C. Cartwright.

INVERARAY CASTLE.

time of Sir Colin's death. The power of the family, and the difficult approach to the place, preserved it from the insult of enemies, excepting in two instances: in December, 1644, amidst the snows of this severe climate, the enterprising Montrose poured down his troops on Inveraray, through ways its chieftain thought impervious. The Marquis of Argyle made his escape in a little fishing boat, and left his people to the merciless weapons of the invaders, who for a twelvemonth carried fire and sword through the whole Campbell race, retaliating, as is pleaded, the similar barbarities of its leader.[5]

After the unfortunate expedition of his son, in 1685, this place and people experienced a fresh calamity: another clan, deputed by the Government to carry destruction throughout the name, was let slip, armed with the dreadful writ of fire and sword, to act at discretion among an unhappy people; seventeen gentlemen of the name were instantly executed. On the spot is erected a column, with an inscription, commemorating, with a moderation that does honour to the writer, the justice of the cause in which his relation fell.

In 1715, Archibald, Duke of Argyle, then Earl of Ilay, collected a few troops in this place, in order to prevent the rebels from becoming masters of so important a pass, through which they might have led their forces to Glasgow, and from thence into the north of England. General Gordon approached within a small distance, reconnoitred it, and actually cut fascines to make the attack; but was deterred from it by the determined appearance of the garrison.

The figure of the magnificent bridge over the Aray is given in the frontispiece. That fine structure, built at the expense of government, was destroyed by the violent autumnal flood of this year.

The portraits in the castle are few; of them two only merit notice. The first is a head of the Marquis of Argyle, his hair short, his dress black, with a plain white turnover. A distinguished person during the reign of Charles I, and the consequent usurpation. A man, as his own father styled him, of craft and subtlety. In his heart no friend to the royal cause, temporising according to the complexion

[5] Montrose's *Wars*, 43.

of the times; yielding an hearty but secret concurrence with the disaffected powers, and extending a feigned and timid aid to the shackled royalty of Charles II, when he entrusted himself to his northern subjects, in 1650. At all times providing pleas of merit with both parties, apparently sincere with the usurpers only: with them he took an active part during their plenitude of power,[6] yet at first claimed only protection, freedom, and payment of his debts due from the English Parliament.[7] His interest seems to have been constantly in view: while Charles was in his hands he received from that penetrating prince a promissory note for great honours and great emoluments.[8] He is charged with encouraging his people in various acts of murder and cruelty;[9] but the provocations he had received, by the horrible ravages of Montrose, may perhaps extenuate retaliation on such of his neighbours, who, for any thing that appears, partook of the excesses. He is charged also with possessing himself of the estates of those who were put to death by his authority: a charge not repelled in his fine defence on his trial. His generosity in declining to take an open part in the prosecution of his arch enemy, Montrose, would have done him great honour, had he not meanly placed himself in a window, to see the fallen hero pass in a cart to receive judgment.[10] On the Restoration he fell a victim to his *manes*. It was intended that he should undergo the same ignominious death, which was afterwards changed to that of beheading. 'I could,' says he, 'die like a Roman, but I choose rather to die like a Christian.' He fell with heroism: in his last moments with truth exculpating himself from having any concern in the murder of his royal master; calming his conscience with the opinion, that his criminal compliances were but the epidemic disease and fault of the times. His guilt of treason was indisputable; but the act of grace in 1641, and the other in 1651, ought to have been his securities from a capital punishment.

---

[6] Whitelock, 563, 567.
[7] The same, 529.
[8] *Br. Biogr.* II, 1150.
[9] *State Trials* V, 376, 377.
[10] Carte IV, 529.

Here is also a head of his son, the Earl of Argyle, a steady, virtuous, but unfortunate character. Firm to his trust through all the misfortunes of his royal master, Charles II. Was appointed colonel of his guards in 1650, but scorned to receive his commission from the tyrannical states of his country, and insisted on receiving it from his Majesty alone. Neither the defeats at Dunbar, or at Worcester, abated his zeal for the desperate cause; he betook himself to the Highlands, and for a long time resisted the usurping powers: notwithstanding he was cast off, and his adherents declared traitors, by the zealous marquis, his father.[11] Suffered, after his submission to the irresistible tyranny of the times, a long imprisonment. His release, at the Restoration, subjected him but to fresh troubles: ingratitude seems to have been the first return to his services. A bare recital of his success with the king, in repelling certain injuries done him, was entitled 'leasing-making', or creating dissensions between his majesty and his subjects. For this, by the Scottish law, he was condemned to lose his head: a sentence too unjust to be permitted to be put into execution. After a long imprisonment, was restored to favour, to his fortune, and to the title of earl. In all his actions he preserved a patriotic, yet loyal moderation: but in 1681, delivering in an explanation of an oath he was to take, as a test not to attempt any alteration in church or state,[12] he was again disgraced, tried, and a second time condemned; and the infamous sentence would have been executed, had he not escaped from the power of his enemies. In 1685, in concert with the Duke of Monmouth, he made a fatal attempt to restore the liberties of his country, then invaded by James II. He failed in the design, and was put to death on his former sentence.

On the day of execution, he eat his dinner, and took his afternoon's nap with his usual composure, falling with a calmness and constancy suitable to the goodness of his life.

A little before his death he composed his epitaph, I think still to be seen in the Greyfriars churchyard, Edinburgh. The verses are rather to be admired, as they showed the serenity of his mind, at that awful period, than for the smoothness of the numbers: but

[11] Whitelock, 563.
[12] *State Trials* II, 851.

the translation, by the Rev Mr Jamison, of Glasgow, cannot but
be acceptable to every reader of taste:

> *Audi, Hospes, quicunque venis, tumulumque revisis,*
> *Et rogitas quali crimine tinctus eram.*
> *Non me crimen habet, non me malus abstulit error,*
> *Et vitium nullum, me pepulit patria.*
> *Solus amor patriae, verique immensa cupido*
> *Dissuetas iussit sumere tela manus.*
> *Opprimor, en! Rediens, vi sola et fraude meqrum,*
> *Hostibus et saevis victima terna cado.*
> *Sit licet hic noster labor irritus, haud Deus aequus*
> *Despiciet populum saecula cuncta suum.*
> *Namque alius veniet fatis melioribus ortus*
> *Qui toties ruptum sine beabit opus.*
> *Sat mihi credo datum (quamvis caput ense secetur)*
> *Hinc petor aetheri Lucida templa poli.*

> *Thou, Passenger, who shalt have so much time,*
> *As view my grave, and ask what was my crime:*
> *No stain of error, no black vices' brand,*
> *Did me compel to leave my native land.*
> *Love to my country, truth condemn'd to die,*
> *Did force my hands forgotten arms to try.*
> *More from friends' fraud my fall proceeded hath,*
> *Than foes, tho' thrice they did attempt my death.*
> *On my design tho' Providence did frown,*
> *Yet God at last will surely raise his own.*
> *Another hand, with more successful speed,*
> *Shall raise the remnant, bruise the serpent's head.*

The fine woods and cascades at Esachossen must not pass
unnoticed; nor the fertile tract of cornland between it and the
sea; nor the deer-park called Beauchamp, with its romantic glen;
nor the lake Duloch, near the foot of Glenshiera, a fresh water,
communicating with Loch Fine, which receives into it salmon, sea-
trout, flounders, and even herrings, so that the family, during the
seasons, find it a never-failing reservoir of fish.

The tunny frequents this and several other branches of the sea,
on the western coast during the season of herrings, which they
pursue:[13] the Scotch call it the 'mackerel-sture', or 'stor', from its

---

[13] *Br. Zool.* III, 223. IV, tab. 43.

enormous size, it being the largest of the genus. One, that was taken off Inveraray, when I was there in 1769, weighed between four and five hundred pounds. These fish are taken by a hook, baited with a herring; and notwithstanding their vast bulk, soon lose their spirit, and tamely submit to their fate. Their capture is not attended to as much as it merits; for they would prove a cheap and wholesome food to the poor. The few that are caught are cut in pieces, and either sold fresh, or salted in casks. Tunnies are the great support of the convents in the countries that bound the Mediterranean Sea, where they swarm at stated seasons, particularly beneath the great promontories of Sicily, the Thunnoscopia of the ancients,[14] because watchmen were placed on them to observe the motions of the tunnies, and give signals of their approach to the fishermen. In Scotland they arrive only in small herds of five or six, are discovered by their playing near the surface, and by their agility and frequent leaps out of the water.

In the midst of the duke's estate, not far from the castle, is a tract of about a hundred a year value, the property of the Earl of Breadalbane; a gift of a chieftain of this house to an ancestor of his lordship, in order to maintain the vast train of followers that attended on the great in feudal days: so that, whenever the owner of Taymouth payed his respects to his lord in Inveraray, the suite might be properly accommodated; the difficulty of supplying so vast an addition to the family with forage might be obviated; and quarrels prevented between two such little armies of retainers.

Return north; and reach Cladich, a village on the banks of Loch Aw, so named from Evah, heiress of the country about the year 1066, when the name was first changed from that of Loch Cruachan. I have here the pleasure of meeting Mr MacIntyre, minister of Clachan-disart, in the beautiful vale of Glenurchie. He conducts me to a cairn, in which had been found the ashes perhaps of some ancient hunter, and the head of a deer, probably buried with them, from the opinion that the departed spirit might still be delighted with its favourite employ during the union with the body:

Eadem sequitur tellure repostos.

---

[14] Strabo, lib. V. Oppian., *Halieut.*, lib. III, 638.

The custom of burning the dead was common to the Caledonians as well as the Gauls.[15] Both were attentive to the security of these poor remains; thought a neglect, impiety; and the violation of them the greatest act of enmity. The Highlanders to this day retain a saying, derived from this very remote custom. If they would express the malice of an enemy, they would tell him, that was it in his power, he would wish to see their ashes floating on the water: '*Dhurige tu mo luath le Uisge.*'

Take boat, and visit Inchhail, a little isle, on which had been a cell of Cistercians, dependent on Dunkeld. Amidst the ruins of the church are some tombs of rude sculpture; among others, one of a Campbell of Inveraw, of uncommon workmanship indeed!

Pass under Fraoch Elan, a small but lofty island tufted with trees, with the ruins of a fortress appearing above.

A little higher to the north opens the discharge of the lake; a narrow strait, shagged on each side with woods. From hence, after a turbulent course of three miles, a series of cataracts, the water drops into Loch Etive, an arm of the sea.

On the side of this strait is a military road leading from Dalmalie to Bunaw; and near it is the cave of MacPhaidan, a chieftain, who, taking part against his country with Edward I, was pursued and slain in this retreat by the hero Wallace.

Visit Kilchurn Castle, a magnificent pile, now in ruins, seated on a low isle, near the southern border of the lake, whose original name was Elan-keil guhirn. The fortress was built by Sir Colin Campbell, Lord of Lochow, who died, aged 80, in 1480; others say, by his lady, during the time of his absence, on an expedition against the infidels, to which he might have been obliged by his profession, being a knight of Rhodes. His successors added greatly to it. Within are some remains of apartments, elegant, and of no great antiquity. The view from it of the rich vale, bounded by vast mountains, is fine; among which Crouachan soars pre-eminently lofty.

This island was probably the original seat of the O'Duimhms, lords of Lochow, the ancestors of the Campbells, who in the reign

[15] *Cum mortuis cremant atque defodiunt apta viventibus olim.* Mela., lib. III, ch. 2.

of Malcolm Canmore, assumed their present name, on account of the marriage of a Malcolm MacDuimhm (who had gone into France in quest of adventures) with the heiress of Bellus Campus, or Beauchamp in Normandy. From those lands Giallaespig, or Archibald, his son took the name of Campbell, came into England with the Conqueror, and visiting the country of his ancestors, married Evah, sole daughter of the chieftain; and thus became possessor of the estate of Lochow. This barony, and the land of Ardscordyrche, were confirmed, by Robert I, to Colin, son of Nigel Campbell, by the tenure of providing for the King's service, whenever it was demanded, a ship of forty oars, completely furnished and manned, and the attendance customary with the other barons of Argyleshire.[16]

I must not leave this parish without mentioning a deep circular hollow, in form and of the size of a large cauldron, in a morass near Hamilton's Pass, on the south side of the lake. There is a tradition that this was one of the vats frequent in the Highland turbaries, from which the old natives drew an unctuous substance, used by them to dye their cloth black, before the introduction of copperas, etc. The ingredient was collected from the sides of the hole, and surface of the water; the cloth or yarn was boiled in it, and received a lasting colour.

Continue my journey for some time through the vale of Glenurchie, possessed by the Campbells since the time of Sir Colin before mentioned,[17] ancestor of the Breadalbane line, the famous knight of Rhodes, surnamed from his complexion and from his travels Duibh-na-Roimh, or 'black Colin of Rome'.[18] This tract is of great fertility, embellished with little groves, and watered by a fine stream. The view bounded on one side by the great hill of Crouachan, and on the other by that of Benlaoighe. The valley now contracts into a glen, abounding with cattle, yet destitute both of arable land and meadow; but the beasts gather a good sustenance from the grass that springs among the heath. See frequently on the

[16] Anderson's *Diplomata*, XLVII.
[17] Buchanan's *Clans*, 139.
[18] MS Hist. of the Campbels.

roadsides small verdant hillocks, styled by the common people, *shi-an*, or 'the fairy-haunt', because here, say they, the fairies, who love not the glare of day, make their retreat, after the celebration of their nocturnal revels.

Pass by a little lake, whose waters run into the western sea. On the roadside a lead-mine is worked to some advantage, by means of a level. The veins are richest near the surface, but dwindle away towards the soles. At this place enter the district of Breadalbane, in Perthshire, and breakfast at Tynedrum, or 'the house of the height', being the most elevated habitation in North Britain. Breadalbane also signifying the loftiest tract of Albin, or Scotland. These hills are a part of that lofty range commencing at Loch Lomond, traversing the country to the firth of Dornoch, and called by some writers, Drumalbin. In my passage, in 1769, from the King's House to this place, I rode near the mountains of Bendoran. One of them is celebrated for the hollow sound it sends forth about twenty-four hours before any heavy rain. 'The spirit of the mountain shrieks',[19] warns the peasants to shelter their flocks; and utters the same awful prognostics, that Virgil attributes to those of Italy:

> *Continuo ventis surgentibus, aut freta ponti*
> *Incipiunt agitata tumescere: et aridus altis*
> *Montibus audiri fragor.*

> *When winds approach, the vex'd sea heaves around:*
> *From the bleak mountain comes a hollow sound.*

Warton

Immediately below the village of Tynedrum rises the River Tay, which takes its course into the eastern sea; such opposite currents have two streams, not half a mile distant from each other. Ride over the small plain of Dalrie, perhaps the seat of the Dalreudini mentioned by Bede,[20] or the ancient government of Dalrieta, noticed by Camden.[21] On this spot was the conflict between Robert Bruce, and the forces of Argyleshire, under MacDougal, Chieftain of Lorn,

[19] Ossian.
[20] lib. I, ch. 1.
[21] p. 1241.

II

BROTCHE.

M. Griffiths del.   P. Mazell sculp.

when the former was defeated. A servant of Lorn had seized on Bruce, but the prince escaped by killing the fellow with a blow of his battle-axe; but at the same time lost his mantle and brooch, which the assailant tore away in his dying agonies. The brooch was long preserved in the family; at length destroyed by a fire, that consumed the house of Dunolly, the residence of the representative. In default of that, the annexed plate exhibits one probably not inferior in magnificence. It had been the property of MacLeane, of Lochbuy, in the isle of Mull, and is said to be made of silver found on the estate. The workmanship is elegant, and seems to be of the time of Queen Elizabeth.[22] It is about five inches diameter at bottom. Round the upper margin is a low upright rim; within that are ten obeliscs, about an inch and a quarter high, prettily studded, and the top of each ornamented with a river pearl. These surround a second rim; from that rises a neat case, whose sides project into ten demi-rounders, all neatly studded. In the centre is a round crystalline ball, a magical gem, such as described in the tour of 1769.[23] This case may be taken off; has a considerable hollow, in which might have been kept amulets or relics, which, with the assistance of the powerful stone, must needs prove an infallible preservative against all harms.

Enter Strathfillan, or the vale of St Fillan, an abbot, who lived in the year 1703, and retired here the latter end of his days. He is pleased to take under his protection the disordered in mind; and works wonderful cures, say his votaries, even to this day. The unhappy lunatics are brought here by their friends, who first perform the ceremony of the 'deasil', thrice round a neighbouring cairn; afterwards offer on it their rags, or a little bunch of heath tied with worsted; then thrice immerge the patient in a holy pool of the river, a second Bethesda; and, to conclude, leave him fast bound the whole night in the neighbouring chapel. If in the morning he is found loose, the saint is supposed to be propitious; for if he continues in bonds, his cure remains doubtful: but it often happens

[22] This fine ornament is in the possession of the Rev Mr Lort, late Greek Professor at Cambridge, who favoured me with the loan of it.
[23] 2nd and 3rd edition.

that death proves the angel that releases the afflicted, before the morrow, from all the troubles of this life.

The deasil,[24] or turning from east to west, according to the course of the sun, is a custom of high antiquity in religious ceremonies. The Romans practised the motion in the manner now performed in Scotland.[25] The Gaulish Druids made their circumvolution in a manner directly reverse: but the Druids of Gaul and Britain had probably the same reason for these circumambulations; for as they held the omnipresence of their God, it might be to instruct their disciples, that wheresoever they turned their face, they were sure to meet the aspect of the deity.[26] The number of turns was also religiously observed in very ancient days: thus the arch enchantress, Medea, in all her charms attends to the sacred three:

> Ter se convertit, ter sumtis flumine crinem
> Irrovait aquis; ternis ululatibus ora
> Solvit, et in dura submisso poplite terra,
> Nox, ait, etc.

> She turn'd her thrice around, and thrice she threw
> On her long tresses and nocturnal dew;
> Then yelling thrice a most terrific sound,
> Her bare knee bended on the flinty ground.

The saint, the object of the veneration in question, was of most singular service to Robert Bruce, inspiring his soldiery with uncommon courage at the battle of Bannockbourne,[27] by a miracle wrought the day before in his favour. His Majesty's chaplain was directed to bring with him into the field, the arm of the saint, lodged in a silver shrine. The good man, fearing, in case of a defeat, that the English might become masters of the precious limb, brought only the empty cover: but, while the king was invoking the aid of St Fillan, the lid of the shrine, placed before him on the altar, opened and shut of its own accord: on inspection, to the wonder

---

[24] From *deas* or *des*, 'the right-hand', and *syl*, 'the sun'.
[25] *Hist. Nat.*, lib. XXXVIII, ch. 2.
[26] Borlase's *Antiq. Cornwal.*, 126.
[27] Boethius, 302.

of the whole army, the arm was found restored to its place; the soldiers accepted the omen, and, assured of victory, fought with an enthusiasm that ensured success. In gratitude for the assistance he received that day from the saint, he founded here, in 1314, a priory of canons regular, and consecrated it to him. At the Dissolution, this house, with all the revenues and superiorities, were granted to an ancestor of the present possessor the Earl of Breadalbane.[28]

This part of the country is in the parish of Killin, very remote from the church. As the chapel here is destitute of a resident minister, Lady Glenurchy, with distinguished piety, has just established a fund for the support of one; has built a good house for his accommodation, and Lord Breadalbane has added to the glebe.

This tract is at present almost entirely stocked with south-country sheep, which have in a manner expelled the breed of black cattle. Sheep are found to turn more to the advantage of the proprietors; but whether to the benefit of the community, is a doubt. The live stock of cattle of this kingdom decreases: from whence will our navy be victualled? or how will those, who may be able to purchase animal food, be supplied, if the mere private interest of the farmer is suffered universally to take place? Millions at this time look up to legislature for restrictions, that will once more restore plenty to these kingdoms.

Pass near the seat of Rob Roy, the celebrated freebooter mentioned in the former volume.

Enter Glendochart, and go by the sides of Loch Dochart, beautifully ornamented with trees. In a lofty island embosomed in wood, is the ruin of a castle, one of the nine under the rule of the great knight of Lochow. It was once taken by the Macgregors, in a manner that did credit to the invention of a rude age. The place was not accessible during summer; the assailants therefore took advantage of a frost, formed vast fascines of straw and boughs of trees, rolled these before them on the ice, to protect them against the arrows of the garrison, till they could get near enough to make their attack, by scaling at once the walls of the fortress. The Veltae of the northern nations were of this kind:[29] the ancient Swedes and

---

[28] Keith, 241.
[29] Olaus Magnus de Gent., lib. VII, ch. 8, 9.

Goths practised an attack of the same nature; but did, what perhaps the Macgregors might also have done, wait for a high wind in their favour, roll the Veltae as near as possible to the fort, set them on fire, and under favour of the flame, distressing the besieged, never failed of a successful event.

I must observe that the Macgregors were of old a most potent people. They possessed Glenurchie; were owners of Glen Lion, and are even said to have been the original founders of Balloch or Taymouth, or, at least, to have had their residence there before they were succeeded by the Campbells.[30]

Somewhat farther, opposite to the farm of Achessan, is a small lake, noted for a floating island, fifty-one feet long, and twenty-nine broad, that shifts its quarters with the wind. It has (like the islands of the Vadimonian lake, so elegantly described by the younger Pliny[31]) strength sufficient to carry an involuntary voyage, the cattle that might be surprised feeding on this *mobile solum*, deceived with the appearance of its being farm land. It cannot indeed boast of carrying on its surface the darksome groves of those of the Cutilian waters; but, like the Lydian Calamina,[32] may be launched from the sides of the lake with poles, and can show plenty of coarse grass, some small willows, and a little birch tree.[33]

Proceed by the sides of the Tay, since its passage through Loch Dochart, assuming the name of the lake. The pearl fishery in this part of the river, some years ago, was carried on with great success, and the pearls were esteemed the fairest and largest of any.

The military road through this country is planned with a distinguished want of judgment; a series of undulations, quite unnecessary, distress the traveller for a considerable part of the way. Near Achline the eye begins to be relieved by the sight of the enclosures; and some plantations begin to hide the nakedness of

[30] Buchanan's *Clans*, 138, 139.
[31] Epist. lib. VIII, cp. 20.
[32] Plinii, *Hist. Nat.*, lib. II, ch. 95.
[33] The thickness of this isle is twenty-five inches. Perhaps, as Mr Gahn affirms to be the case of other floating islands, this might have originated from the twisted roots of the *Sebaenus mariscus*, and *Scriptus caespitosus*, converted into a more firm mass by the addition of the *Carex Caespitosus*. Vide *Amaen. Acad.* VII, 166.

the country. On approaching the village of Killin, every road and every path was filled with groups of people, of both sexes, in neat dresses, and lively plaids, returning from the sacrament. A sober and decent countenance distinguished every party, and evinced the deep sense they had of so solemn a commemoration. Breadalbane in general is exempt from the charge of impropriety of conduct of these occasions, which happens sometimes; and by the undiscerning, the local fault is indiscriminately attributed to the whole.

Cross two bridges. The river here forms two islands, beautifully planted with firs: Inishbuy, the most easterly, is remarkably picturesque, the water rolling with tremendous force on each side for a long tract over a series of broken rocks, and short but quick-repeated cataracts, in a channel of unspeakable rudeness.

Reach Killin, or Cill-Fhin, from the tradition of its having been the burial-place of Fingal. Here is an excellent inn, built by Lord Breadalbane, who, to the unspeakable comfort of the traveller, established others at Dalmalie, Tynedrum, and Kenmore, where they are as acceptable as *caravanseras* in the East.

Mount Strone Clachan, a hill above Mr Stuart's, the minister's, house; and am overpayed for the labour of the ascent by a most enchanting view. A most delicious plain spreads itself beneath, divided into verdant meadows, or glowing with ripened corn; embellished with woods, and watered with rivers uncommonly contrasted. On one side, pours down its rocky channel the furious Tay: on the other, glides between its wooded banks the gentle Lochy, forming a vast bend of still water, till it joins the first; both terminating in the great expanse of Loch Tay. The northern and southern boundaries suit the magnificence of the lake: but the northern rise with superior majesty in the rugged heights of Finlarig, and the wild summits of the still loftier Laurs, often patched with snow throughout the year. Extensive woods clothe both sides, the creation of the noble proprietor.

At the foot of the first, amidst woods of various trees, lie the ruins of the castle of the same name, the old seat of the Campbells, the knights of Glenurchie, and built by Sir Colin between the years 1513 and 1523.[34] The venerable oaks, the vast chestnuts, the ash trees,

[34] Black, *Book of Taymouth.*

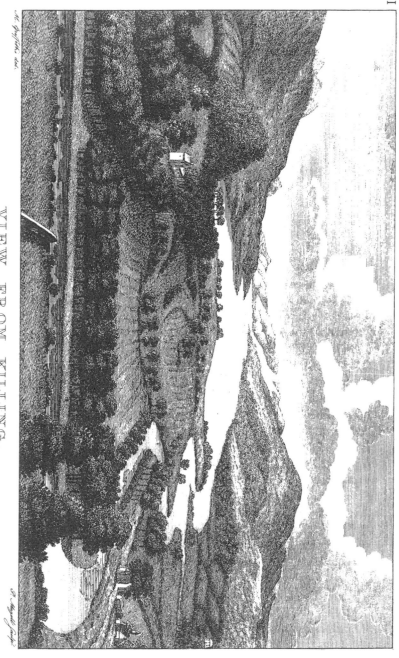

III

VIEW FROM KILLING.

M. Griffith, del.

and others of ancient growth give a fine solemnity to the scene, and compliment the memory of progenitors, so studious of the benefit of posterity. Tradition is loud in reports of the hospitality of the place, and blends with it tales of gallantry; one of festivity, terminating in blood and slaughter. Amidst the mirth of a christening, in the great hall of Finlarig, inhabited, I think, at that time by Sir Robert, son of the chieftain; news arrived that the MacDonalds of Keppoch, had made a *creach* into the lands of some of their friends, had acquired a great booty, and were at that time passing in triumph over the hill of Stroneclachan. The Campbells, who were then assembled in numbers to honour the occasion, took fire at the insult, and, warm with the convivial cheer, started from the table to take sudden revenge. They ascended the hill with thoughtless bravery to begin the attack, were overpowered, and twenty cadets of the family left dead on the spot. News of the disaster was immediately sent to Taymouth, the residence of the chieftain, who dispatched a reinforcement to those who had escaped. They overtook the MacDonalds at the braes of Glenurchie, defeated them, slew the brother of the chieftain, rescued the booty, and returned back triumphing in the completion of their revenge.

Cross a large arch over the Lochy, winding to the north-west, through a small but elegant glen, whose fertile bottom is finely bounded by woods on both sides. Turn short to the east, and continue my journey on a fine road, at a considerable height above Loch Tay. The land slopes to the water edge, and both above and below the highway, forms a continued tract of cultivated ground, rich in corn, and varied with groves and plantations. The abundance of inhabitants on this side surpasses that of any place in Scotland of equal extent; for from Finlarig to the forks of the Lion, about fifteen miles, there are not fewer than seventeen hundred and eighty souls, happy under a humane chieftain. Their habitations are prettily grouped along the sides of the hill; are small and mean, often without windows or doors; and are the only disgrace to the magnificence of the scenery.

The opposite part of the lake is less populous, and less fertile; yet, from the vast patches of cornland, and the frequent woods, exhibits a most beautiful view.

In going through Laurs observe a Druidical circle; less complete indeed than one, that should have been mentioned before, at Kinnel, a little south-west of Killin; which consists of six vast stones, placed equidistant from each other.

The windings of the lake in the course of the ride become very conspicuous, appearing to form three great bendings, the whole showing the shape of a capital 'S'. Its length is about fifteen miles, the breadth one: the depth in many places a hundred fathoms; and, even within as many yards of the shore, is fifty fathoms deep. It abounds with fish, such as pike, perch, salmon, char, trout, samlets, minnows, lampreys, and eels. A species of trout is found here, that weighs thirty pounds.

All this country abounds with game, such as grouse, ptarmigans, stags, roes, etc.

Roes are in a manner confined to Glen Lion, where they are protected by the principal proprietor. Foxes are numerous and destructive. Martins are rare, but the yellow-breasted was lately taken in the birch woods of Rannoch. The otter is common. The vulgar have an opinion, that this animal has its king or leader: they describe it as being of a larger size, and varied with white. They believe that it is never killed, without the sudden death of a man, or some other animal, at the same instant: that its skin is endued with great virtues, is an antidote against all infection, and preservative to the warrior from wounds, and ensures the mariner from all disasters on the watery element.

The cock of the wood, or capercaillie, or 'capercalze', a bird of this genus, once frequent in all parts of the Highlands, is now confined to the pine forests north of Loch Ness. From the size it is called 'the horse of the woods'; the male sometimes weighing fifteen pounds. The colour of the breast is green, resembling that of the peacock: above each eye is a rich scarlet skin, common to the grouse genus: the feet of this and the black cock are naked, and the edges of the toes serrated; for these birds, sitting upon trees, do not want the thick feathery covering with which nature hath clothed those of the red game and ptarmigan, who, during winter, are obliged to reside bedded in the snows. Bishop describes three of the species found in Scotland:[35] the capercaillie, which he truly says

[35] *Hist. Scotiae.*, 24. The female of the capercaillie is of the colour of the common grouse.

feeds on the extreme shoots of the pine: the common grouse, with its feathered feet; and the black cock. He omits the ptarmigan. It has been my fortune to meet with every kind: the three last frequently; the capercaillie only at Inverness.

Woodcocks appear in Breadalbane, in the beginning or middle of November; but do not reach Ardmaddie, or, I may say, any part of the western coast of the Highlands till the latter end of December or beginning of January. They continue there in plenty till the middle or latter end of March, according to the mildness or rigour of the season; and then disappear at once. In the first season they continue arriving in succession for a month; and in every county in Scotland (where they are found) fly regularly from east to west. Their first landing-places are in the eastern counties, such as Angus, Merns, etc., usually about the end of October; but their stay in those parts is very short, as woods are so scarce. Woodcocks are very rarely seen in Caithness; and there are still fewer in the Orkneys, or in the more remote Hebrides: one or two appear there, as if by accident driven thither by tempests, not voluntary migrants. There is no account of these birds having ever bred in Scotland, any more than of the fieldfare and redwing; yet all three make their summer residence in Norway; from whence, in all probability, many of them visit our islands.

Sea eagles breed in ruined towers, but quit the country in winter; the black eagles continue there the whole year. They were so numerous a few years ago in Rannoch, that the commissioners of the forfeited estates gave a reward of five shillings for every one that was destroyed. In a little time such numbers were brought in, that the honourable board thought fit to reduce the reward to three shillings and six pence: but a small advance, in proportion as the birds grew scarcer, in all probability would have effected their extirpation. But to resume the journey.

The whole road on the side of the lake is excellent, often crossed by gullies, the effects of the great rains, or torrents from the melted snow. The public are indebted to Lord Breadalbane, not only for the goodness of the way, but for above thirty bridges, all made at his expense, to facilitate the passage. Cross the opening into the little plain of Fortingal, mentioned in my former tour, noted for its camp, the most northern work of the Romans that I could get any intelligence of. It seems to have been the *castellum* of some advanced party in the time of Antonine, or Commodus, or perhaps a temporary station in that of Severus, in whose reign the Romans abandoned these parts. A copper vessel, with a beak, handle, and three feet, was found in it. I did not hear of any coins met with on the spot: but, in digging the foundation of a tower near Taymouth, fourteen silver denarii were discovered; but none of a later date than Marcus Aurelius.

I must also commemorate again the wonderful yew tree in the churchyard of Fortingal, whose ruins measure fifty-six feet in circumference. The middle part is now decayed to the ground; but, within memory, was united to the height of three feet; Captain Campbell, of Glen-Lion, having assured me that, when a boy, he has often climbed over, or rode on, the then connecting part. Our ancestors seem to have had a classical reason, for planting these dismal trees among the repositories of the dead; and a political one, for placing them about their houses: in the first instance, they were the substitutes of the *invisa cupressus*; in the other, they were the designed provision of materials for the sturdy bows of our warlike ancestors

> *Who drew,*
> *And almost joined, the horns of the tough Yew.*

In the days of archery so great was the consumption of this species of wood, that the bowyers were obliged to import staves of yew for making the best sort of bows.[36] This tree is not universally dispersed through England, in its native state; or, at least, is now in most parts eradicated, on account of its noxious qualities: yet is still to be found in quantities on the lofty hills that bound the water of the Winander, those near Rydal in Westmoreland, and on the face of many precipices in different parts of this kingdom.

Not far from the church is the house of Col. Campbell, of Glen Lion, a beautiful vale, that runs several miles up the country, watered by a river of the same name.

---

[36] Statute 33. Henry VIII, ch. IX, sect. 6.

I must add to my account of the crystal gem in possession of that gentleman, that there was a remarkable one in possession of Sir Edward Harley, of Brampton Brian, set in a silver ring, resembling the meridian of a globe, with a cross on the top, and on the rim the virtuous names of Uriel, Raphael, Michael, and Gabriel. This predicted death, dictated receipts for the cure of all curables;[37] and another, of much the same kind, even condescended to recover lost goods.[38] It was customary in early times to deposit these balls in urns or sepulchres. Thus twenty were found at Rome in an alabastrine urn, cased with two great stones, and lodged in a hollow made in each to receive it. The contents were (besides the balls), a ring with a stone set in it; a needle, a comb, and some bits of gold, mixed with the ashes: the needle showed these remains to have been those of a lady.

In the tomb of Childeric, King of France, was found another of these balls. Some Merlin might have bestowed it on him; which must have been an invaluable gift, if it had the same powers with that given by our magician to the British prince:

> *Such as the glassy globe that Merlin made,*
> *And gave unto King Ryence for his gard,*
> *That never foes his kingdom might invade,*
> *But he it knew at home before he hard*
> *Tydings thereof, and so them still debar'd.*
> *It was a famous present for a prince,*
> *And worthy worke of infinite rewarde,*
> *That treasons cou'd betray, and foes convince:*
> *Happy this realme had it remayned ever since!*[39]

Approach near Taymouth, keeping still on the side of the lake. Leave on the right, not far from the shore, the pretty isle of Loch Tay, tufted with trees, shading the ruins of the priory. From the ancient inhabitants of this holy island, the present noble owner has liberty of fishing in the lake at all times of the year; which is denied to the other landowners in the neighbourhood. But it was necessary for the monks to be indulged with that privilege, as their

---

[37] Aubrey's *Miscellanies*, 129.
[38] Aubrey's *Miscellanies*, 131.
[39] Spenser's *Fairy Queen*, Book III, ch. II, stanza 21.

IV

VIEW FROM TAYMOUTH.

very existence depended on it. To this island the Campbells retreated at the approach of the Marquis of Montrose, where they defended themselves for some time against that hero. A shot narrowly missed him, which enraged him to that degree as to cause him instantly to carry fire and sword through the whole country. It was taken and garrisoned; but in 1654 was surrendered to General Monk.[40]

On the right is a plantation, the orchard of the monastery. In it is a black cherry tree that measures, four feet from the ground, ten feet three inches in circumference. These trees are called in Scotland, 'Guines', from a notion of their being brought originally from thence.

Cross the Tay on a temporary bridge, just below its discharge from the lake. A most elegant bridge is now constructing in this place, under the direction of captain Archibald Campbell, at the expense of Lord Breadalbane, consisting of three large arches; and a smaller on each side, in case of floods. Reach Taymouth, his lordship's principal house; originally called Balloch Castle, or 'the castle at the discharge of the lake'; was built by Sir Colin Campbell, sixth knight of Lochow, who died in the year 1583. The place has been much modernised since the days of the founder; has the addition of two wings, and lost its castellated form, as well as the old name. We are informed that this Sir Collin was 'ane great justiciar all his tyme throchtht quhille he fuftenit that dadlie feid of the Clangregour ane lang space. And besydis that he caused execust to the death many notable lymmeris. He behaddit the Laird McCregr himself at Candmoir in presence of the Erle of Atholl, the justice clerk, and sundrie other noblemen.'[41]

By a poem I met with in the library at Taymouth, it appears, that this unfortunate chieftain, surnamed Duncan Laider, or the strong, made a very good end; and delivered, in penitential rhymes, in Spenser's manner, an account of his past life, his sorrow for his sins, and his pathetical farewell to the various scenes of his plundering

---

[40] Whitelock's *Mem.*, 592.
[41] *Black Book.*

exploits. Like Spenser, he personifies the vices: The two first stanzas
will suffice for a specimen of his manner:

> *Quhn passit wes the tyme of tendir age,*
> *And youth with insolence maid acquentance,*
> *And wickitness enforced evill courage,*
> *Quhill might with Crueltie maid alliance;*
> *Then Falshead tuke on him the governance,*
> *And me betaucht ane houshald for to gyde*
> *Callit evill companie, baith to gang and ryde.*

> *My maister-houshald wes heich Oppressioun,*
> *Reif my steward that cairit of na wrang;*
> *Murbure, Slauchtir, ay of ane professioun,*
> *My cubicularis, bene thir yearis lang:*
> *Recept, that oft tuik money ane fang,*
> *Wes porter to the yeltis, to oppin wyde,*
> *And Covatice was chamberlane at all tyde.*

The most remarkable part of the furniture of Taymouth is the
portraits: here being a most considerable collection of the works
of Jameson, the Scotch Van Dyck, an *élève* of this family.

In the same room with the famous genealogical picture are about
twenty heads of persons of the same family. Among them is the last Sir
Duncan Campbell, a favourite of James VI; and not less so of Anne of
Denmark; who, after the accession, often by letter solicited his presence
at her new court; and sent him, as a mark of innocent esteem, a ring
set with diamonds, and ornamented with a pair of doves.

The other pictures of Jameson's performance are in a small
parlour; but unfortunately much injured by an attempt to repair
them. There are the heads of:

William Graham, Earl of Airth, 1637. He was originally Earl
of Menteith, a title derived from a long train of ancestors. He
was much favoured by Charles I, who indulged his pride by
conferring on him, at his request, the earldom of Strathearn, which
he pretended to, as being descended from David Stuart, nephew
to David II. Unfortunately his vanity induced him to hint some
pretensions to the crown. Charles punished his folly by depriving
him of both earldoms; but, relenting soon after, created him Earl
of Airth, with precedence due to the creation of Malise, earl of
Menteith by James I.

John, Lord Lesly, 1636, afterwards Duke of Rothes.[42] He died in 1681; and had, according to the extravagant folly of the times, a funeral of uncommon magnificence.[43]

James, Marquis of Hamilton, 1636, afterwards Duke of Hamilton.

Anne, Marchioness of Hamilton, 1636, daughter to the former, and, on the death of his brother, heiress to the title and fortune. The lady who is distinguished for her works of piety and charity, in the isle of Arran, by the glorious title of 'the Good'.

Archibald, Lord Napier, 1636, grandson of the celebrated John Napier, author of the logarithms.

William, Earl Marshal, 1637, a remarkable sufferer in the causes of Charles I and II: rewarded, on the Restoration, with the privy seal of Scotland.

The Lord of Loudon, 1637, afterwards Chancellor of Scotland.

Thomas Hamilton, Lord Binning, son of the first Earl of Haddington, and successor to the title. In 1640, being commandant of the garrison of Dunglas, then held for the Covenanters, was blown up, with several other persons of quality, as Crawfurd asserts, by the desperate treachery of his page, an English boy, who set fire to the powder magazine.

John, Earl of Mar, 1636, made Knight of the Bath at the creation of Henry, Prince of Wales.

Sir Robert Campbell, of Glenurchie, 1641.

Sir John Campbell, of Glenurchie, 1642.

In the drawing room are two portraits, by Van Dyck, of two noble brothers, distinguished characters in the unhappy times of Charles I. The first may be styled one of the most capital of that great painter's performances. Sir Robert Walpole, the best judge of paintings in his time, was of that opinion, and would have given any price for it. There is particular reason for the exquisite finishing of this picture: Van Dyck was patronized by his Lordship, lived with him at Holland house, and had all opportunity to complete it at full leisure. The beautiful, the courteous, the gallant Henry Rich, Earl of Holland, is represented at

[42] Vide vol. I, p. 93.
[43] Represented in four large plates, published by Thomas Sommers.

full length, dressed with the elegance he might have appeared in to win the affections of the queen of his unfortunate master. He appears in a white and gold doublet; a scarlet mantle, laced with gold, flows gracefully from him; his white boots are ornamented with point; his armour lies by him. Charles was struck with jealousy at the partiality shown to this favourite by Henrietta. He directed his Lordship to confine himself to his house; nor was the restraint taken off, till the Queen refused, on that account, to cohabit with her royal spouse. But neither loyalty to his master, nor tenderness to his fair mistress, could prevent him from joining the popular party, after receiving every favour from the court, his earldom, the garter, command of the guard, and groom of the stole. With unsettled principles, he again deserted his new friends, shifting from side to side. At length, immediately before the murder of his sovereign, roused by the dangers of one he was so much indebted to, he made a single effort in his favour; but, on the first appearance of danger (as he had done more than once) fled the attack, was taken, and ended his days on the scaffold, falling timidly, inglorious, unpitied.

In the same room is the portrait of his elder brother Robert, Earl of Warwick, High Admiral of England, in the service of the Parliament. The ships in the back ground denote his profession. His person, like the Earl of Holland's, elegant; his mind more firm, and his political conduct more coherent. He left a court he had no obligation to: adhered to the Parliament as long as it existed, and supported himself by the power of Cromwell, as soon as the tyrant had destroyed that instrument of his ambition. He was of great popularity with the puritanical party, kept open house for the divines of the times, was a constant attendant at their sermons 'made merry with them and at them, which they dispensed with. He became the head of their party, and got the style of a Godly Man. Yet of such a license in his words and in his actions, that a man of less virtue could not be found out.'[44] What a picture of fanatical priesthood, which could endure, for its own end, the vices of the great; yet, at the same time, be outrageous against the innocent pleasures of the multitude!

[44] Clarendon.

In the dining room are portraits of a later time. John, the first Earl of Breadalbane, a half-length, in his robes. His lady, daughter to the unfortunate Holland, is in another frame, near him. His Lordship was unhappily a distinguished character in the reign of King William. He had formed a humane plan for conciliating the affections of the clans by bribing them into loyalty, till reflection and cooler times would give them opportunity of seeing the benefits that would result from change of government. The chieftains at once attended to his proposals; and, at the same time, gave assurance to their old master, that they would preserve terms no longer than was consistent with his interest. Enraged at their perfidy, and perhaps actuated by feudal resentment, he formed the common scheme in North Britain, of extirpation by fire and sword. The most pernicious indeed of the clans was singled out for execution; but the manner and the season were attended with circumstances of such a nature, that caused the indifferent to shudder; the clans to resent with a long and fatal revenge.

In the library is a history of Thebes, in verse.

History of the world in folio, with wooden plates, by Michael Wolgemut, and William Pleydenwurff, prior to Albert Durer: the first was master to that great artist.

The will of Duncan Laider, before quoted; a long poem in manuscript.

His Lordship's policy[45] surrounds the house, which stands in a park, one of the few in North Britain where fallow deer are seen.

The ground is in remarkably fine order, owing to his Lordship's assiduity in clearing it from the stones with which it was once covered. A blaster was kept in constant employ, to blast with gunpowder the great stones; for, by reason of their size, there was no other method of removing them.

The *berceau* walk is very magnificent, composed of great lime trees, forming a fine Gothic roof, four hundred and fifty yards long: probably that species of architecture might owe its origin to such arched shades. The south terrace on the banks of the Tay is

---

[45] This word signifies here, improvements, or demesne: when used by a merchant or tradesman, means warehouses, shops, and the like.

eighteen hundred yards long; that on the north, two thousand two hundred, and is to extend as far as the junction of the Tay and the Lion, about eighteen hundred more: each are fifty feet wide, and kept with the neatness of the walks of a London villa. The river runs with great rapidity, is clear but not colourless; for its pellucidness is like that of brown crystal, as is the case with most of the rivers in Scotland. The Tay has here a wooden bridge, two hundred feet long, leading to a white seat on the side of the hill, commanding a fine view up and down Strathtay. The rich meadows beneath, the winding of the river, the beginning of Loch Tay, the discharge of the river out of it, the pretty village and church of Kinmore, form a most pleasing and magnificent prospect.

The view from the temple of Venus, is that of the lake, with a nearer sight of the church and village: the two sides of the fine water are seen to vast advantage.

Much flax is cultivated in these parts. A few years ago, when *praemia* were given for the greatest crops, from seventy to a hundred and twenty hogsheads of linseed were annually sown; and each peck yielded two stones of dressed flax; and when the yarn sold highest, two thousand pounds worth has been sold out of the country. The present low price affects the trade of the country, yet still more flax is imported than the land produces.

Oats, bere, and potatoes are the other crops.[46] Oats yield from four to six-fold at the most, oftener less; bere, from eight to ten, at an average, six. The corn raised seldom suffices the number of inhabitants; for they are often obliged to have recourse to importation.

Every person has his potato garden; and they often change the sort: the London Lady has been found to succeed best, which in some farms yields from seven to ten-fold. Some people have distilled from this root a very strong spirit, which has been found to be cheaper than what is distilled from any grain. Starch is also made of it; and, in some families, bread.

---

[46] A variety of barley with square heads, and four rows of grain, called by Old Gerard, 'beare barley', or 'barley big', and *Hordeum polystichum vernum*, to distinguish it from the common kind, which he styles *Hordeum dystichon*. It suits barren lands, and ripens early, which recommends the use in this rainy climate.

Corcar, or the *Lichen omphaloides*, is an article of commerce; great quantities have been scraped from the rocks, and exported for the use of the dyers, at the price of a shilling or sixteen pence a stone.

A good many sheep are now reared here. The best fat wethers sell for eleven shillings each. Those of the old small kind for only six. Much wool is sent out of the country.

The best black cattle have been sold for five guineas per head; but the usual price of the four year old is about five and forty shillings. While on this subject, I cannot help mentioning the distressful state of this country, previous to the rebellion; for, till the year 1745, Lord Breadalbane was obliged to keep a constant guard for the protection of his vassals' cattle, or to retain spies among the thievish clans, having too much spirit to submit to pay the infamous tax of 'blackmeal' to the plundering chieftains.

Few horses are reared here. Such which feed on the tops of the higher hills are often affected with a distemper that commonly proves fatal, if a remedy is not applied within twenty-four hours. It attacks them in the months of July and August, usually after a fall of rain, or before the dew rises in the morning. A universal swelling spreads over the body: the remedy is exercise, chasing, or any method that promotes urine and perspiration. The vulgar attribute this evil to a certain animal that scatters its venom over the grass; but more probably it arises from some noxious vegetable hitherto unobserved.

Cross the Lion at a ford near its union with the Tay. To the north soars the rocky hill of Shi-hallin, or 'the Paps'; and to the left lies the road to Rannoch, noted for its lake and pine forest.

Visit Castle Menzies, the seat of Sir Robert Menzies, placed romantically at the foot of the northern side of Strathtay. The woods that rise boldly above, and the grey rocks that peep between, are no small embellishment to the vale. Far up the hill are the remains of a hermitage, formed by two sides of native rock, and two of wall, some centuries past, the retreat of the chief of the family, who, disgusted with the world, retired here, and resigned his fortune to a younger brother.

Cross Tay Bridge, and visit on the opposite side, Moness, a place Mr Fleming is so happy as to call himself owner of. A neat walk conducts you along the sides of a deep and well-wooded glen, enriched with a profusion and variety of cascades, that strike with astonishment. The first, which lies on the left, runs down a rude staircase with numbers of landing-places, and patters down the steps with great beauty. Advancing along the bottom, on the right, is a deep and darksome chasm, water-worn for ages; the end filled with a great cataract, consisting of several breaks. The rocks more properly arch than impend over it, and trees imbrown and shade the whole.

Ascend a zigzag walk, and, after a long labour, cross the first cascade. The path is continued among the woods to the top of the hill. Emerge into a cornfield, re-enter the wood, and discover, from the verge of an immense precipice, another cataract, forming one vast sheet, tumbling into the deep hollow, from whence it gushes furiously, and is instantly lost in a wood beneath.

No stranger must omit visiting Moness, it being an epitome of every thing that can be admired in the curiosity of waterfalls.

Leave Taymouth. Soon reach the eastern extremity of Lord Breadalbane's estate; which, I may now say from experience, reaches near a hundred miles; having seen the other end among the slate islands in the western sea.

Ride along the banks of the Tay. The river flows in frequent reaches of considerable length, which are finely bordered with cornfields, intermixed with small groves; both which spread on both sides, far up the hills. Cross Taybridge, and continue the same sort of pleasing ride, with one variation only, and that for a small space where the banks heighten, and are clothed with hanging woods; and near them are a few risings covered with broom.

XII

PERTHSHIRE (2)

Athol—Logierait—Dalshian—Mouline—Killicrankie—Dunkeld—
Inchstuthel—Loncarty

A LITTLE below Taybridge enter that division of Perthshire
called Athol, infamous, says Camden, for its witches; with
more truth, at present, to be admired for its high improvements,
natural and moral.

Enter the parish of Logierait, containing about 2,200 inhabitants.
Go through the little town of Logierait, in feudal days the seat of the
regality court, where the family of Athol had an extensive civil and
criminal jurisdiction. By power delegated from the crown, the great
men had formerly courts, with 'sock, sack, pitt and gallous,[1] toill
and hame, infangthief and outfangthief, bad power to hald courts
for slauchter; and to doe justice upon ane man taken with theift,
that is seised thairwith in hand have-and, or on back bearand'.
Justice was administered with great expedition, and too often with
vindictive severity: originally the time of trial and execution was
to be within three suns: about the latter end of the last century, the
execution was extended to nine days after sentence: but, on a rapid
and unjust execution in a petty Scotch town, in the year 1720, the
time was to be deferred for forty days, on the south, and sixty on

---

[1] Women are usually punished by drowning.

the north, of the Tay, that the case might reach the royal ear, and majesty have opportunity of exerting its brightest prerogative.

Above the town is the poor remnant of the castle, defended on the accessible side by a deep ditch: the other is of great steepness. It is said to have been a hunting-seat of Alexander III, who in 1285 was killed by a fall, in pursuit of his favourite amusement. The prospect from hence is fine; for three beautiful vales, and two great rivers, the Tay and the Tumel, unite beneath. This was selected as the place of execution, that the criminal might appear a striking example of justice to so great an extent of country. I must add, that *L'Executeur de la haute justice* had his house free, and two pecks of meal, and a certain fee, for every discharge of his office.

Descend, and am ferried over the Tumel: reach the great road to Blair, and turning to the left, reach Dalshian; where, on the summit of a little hill, in an area of a hundred and sixty feet diameter, is the ruin of St Catherine's Chapel: on the accessible side of the hill is a ditch of great depth. This place seems to have been an ancient British post; and that in after-times the founder of this chapel might prefer the situation on account of the security it might afford to the devotees, in a barbarous age. There are in other parts of this parish remains of chapels, and other religious foundations, as at Killichassie, Tillipurie, Chapeltown, and Pilgir; and at Killichange, may be seen a ruin, surrounded with woods, with the rolling waters of the Tumel adding solemnity to the situation.

Enter the parish of Mouline, Ma-oline, or 'the little lake', from the wet situation of that part: that called the Hollow of Mouline is the most fertile. Their manufactures, and those of Logieriat, are the same: in both great quantities of flax being spun into yarn; and much flax imported from Holland and the Baltic for that purpose, besides what is raised in the country. Notwithstanding the apparent fertility of these vales, the produce of oats, bere, and potatoes, is not equal to the consumption; but quantities of meal are imported. Barley bread is much used in these parts, and esteemed to be very wholesome.

To the honour of the landlords of all the tracts I passed over since my landing, none of the tenants have migrated. They are encouraged in manufactures and rural economy. The ladies promote the article of cleanliness among the lower orders of females by little *praemia*: for example, the Duchess of Athol rewards with smart hats the lasses who appear neatest in those parts, where her Grace's influence extends.

In this parish are considerable natural woods of oak: they are cut down once in twenty years for the sake of the bark, which is here an important article of commerce. The timber sells at little or no price, being too small for use.

The common diseases of this country (I may say of the Highlands in general) are fevers and colds. The putrid fever makes great ravages. Among the *nova cohors febrium* which have visited the earth, the ague was till of late a stranger here. The *glacach*, or as it is sometimes called, 'the MacDonalds disorder', is not uncommon. The afflicted finds a tightness and fulness in his chest, as is frequent in the beginning of consumptions. A family of the name of MacDonald, an hereditary race of MacHaons, pretend to the cure by *glacach*, or handling of the part affected, in the same manner as the Irish Mr Greatrack, in the last century, cured by stroking. The MacDonalds touch the part, and mutter certain charms; but, to their credit, never accept a fee on any entreaty.

Common colds are cured by 'brochan', or water gruel, sweetened with honey; or by a dose of butter and honey melted in spirits, and administered as hot as possible.

As I am on this subject, I shall in this place continue the list of natural remedies, which were found efficacious before they began to

> Fee the doctor
> For his nauseous drought.

Adult persons freed themselves from colds, in the dead of winter, by plunging into the river; immediately going to bed under a load of clothes, and sweating away their complaint.

Warm cow's milk in the morning, or two parts milk and one of water, a little treacle and vinegar made into whey, and drank warm, freed the Highlander from an inveterate cough.

The chincough was cured by a decoction of apples, and of the mountain ash, sweetened with brown sugar.

Consumptions, and all disorders of the liver, found a simple remedy in drinking of buttermilk.

Stale urine and bran made very hot, and applied to the part, freed the rheumatic from his excruciating pains.

Fluxes were cured by the use of meadow sweet, or jelly of bilberry, or a poultice of flour and suet; or new churned butter; or strong cream and fresh suet boiled, and drank plentifully morning and evening.

Formerly the wild carrot boiled, at present the garden carrot, proved a relief in cancerous, or ulcerous cases. Even the faculty admit the salutary effect of the carrot poultice in sweetening the intolerable foetor of the cancer, a property till lately neglected or unknown. How reasonable would it be therefore, to make trial of these other remedies, founded, in all probability, on rational observation and judicious attention to nature!

Persons affected with the scrofula imagined they found benefit by exposing the part every day to a stream of cold water.

Flower of daisies, and narrow and broad leaved plantane, were thought to be remedies for the *ophthalmia*.

Scabious root, or the bark of ash tree burnt, was administered for the toothache.

The water *ranunculus* is used instead of *cantharides* to raise blisters.

But among the useful plants, the *corr* or *cormeille*[2] must not be omitted, whose roots dried are the support of the Highlanders in long journeys, amidst the barren hills destitute of the supports of life; and a small quantity, like the alimentary powders, will for a long time repel the attacks of hunger. Infused in liquor it is an agreeable beverage, and, like the *nepenthe* of the Greeks, exhilarates the mind. From the similitude of sound in the name, it seems to be the same with *chara*, the root discovered by the soldiers of Caesar at the siege of Dyrrachium,[3] which steeped in milk was such a relief to the famished army. Or we may reasonably believe it to have been the Caledonian food described by Dio,[4] of which the quantity of

[2] *Orobus tuberosus*, wood pease. Huds. *Fl. Ang.*, 274.
[3] Caesar, *De Bel. Civili*, lib. III.
[4] *In Vita Severi*.

V

Azalea procumbens

Sibbaldia procumbens

Moses Griffiths del   P. Mazell sculp

a bean would prevent both hunger and thirst: and this, says the historian, they have ready for all occasions.

Among the plants of mere rarity, must be reckoned the trailing thyme leaved azalea, and the reclining *sibbaldia*. The first is found on Crouachan, the last on Benmore.

Mr John Stuart informed me, that he had discovered, in some part of Breadalbane, the *Betula nana*, or dwarf birch. This plant grows in plenty in some boggy ground in the canton of Schweitz, where the natives believe it to be the species with which our Saviour was scourged; and from that period it was cursed with a stunted growth.

For burns, they boil cream till it becomes oil, and with it anoint the part.

The itch declines in proportion as cleanliness gains ground. It may happen that that disorder may be sought in the purlieus of St Giles's, and the other seats of filth, poverty, and debauchery, in our great towns.

During the unhappy civil wars of this kingdom in the last century, a loathsome and horrible distemper, originating from the vices of mankind, made its appearance in the Highlands, and was supposed to have been communicated first by the Parliament's garrison at Inverlochy. It has since diffused itself over most parts of the Highlands, and even crept into the Lowlands, seeming to have accomplished the divine menace, in visiting the sins of the father upon the children to the third and fourth generation. The recital is disagreeable, but too curious to be suppressed; and, therefore, not to betray the delicate mind into a disgusting narrative, I throw it into the Appendix, and leave the perusal to the choice of the reader.

I shall now proceed from the disorders of the body to those of the soul; for what else are the superstitions that infect mankind? A few unnoticed before are still preserved, or have till within a small space been found in the places I have visited, and which may merit mention, as their existence in a little time may happily be lost.

After marriage, the bride immediately walks round the church, unattended by the bridegroom. The precaution of loosening every knot about the new-joined pair is strictly observed, for fear of the penalty denounced in the former volumes. It must be remarked that the custom is observed even in France, *'Nouer l'aiguillette'* being a common phrase for disappointments of this nature.

Matrimony is avoided in the month of January, which is called in the Erse 'the cold month'; but, what is more singular, the ceremony is avoided even in the enlivening month of May. Perhaps they might have caught this superstition from the Romans, who had the same dread of entering into the nuptial state at that season; for the amorous Ovid informs us:

> *Nec viduae taedis eadem, nec virginis apta*
> *Tempora, quae nupsit non diuturna fuit.*
> *Hac quoque de causa, si te proverbia tangunt,*
> *Mense malas Maio nubere vulgus ait.*
> Fasti V, 485.

> *No tapers then shall burn; for never bride,*
> *Wed in ill season, long her bliss enjoy'd.*
> *If you are fond of proverbs, always say,*
> *No lass proves thrifty, who is wed in May.*

After baptism, the first meat that the company tastes, is 'crowdie', a mixture of meal and water, or meal and ale thoroughly mixed. Of this every person takes three spoonfulls.

The mother never sets about any work till she has been 'kirked'. In the Church of Scotland there is no ceremony on the occasion: but the woman, attended by some of her neighbours, goes into the church, sometimes in service time, but oftener when it is empty; goes out again, surrounds it, refreshes herself at some public house, and then returns home. Before this ceremony she is looked on as unclean, never is permitted to eat with the family; nor will any one eat of the victuals she has dressed.

It has happened that, after baptism, the father has placed a basket, filled with bread and cheese, on the pot-hook that impended over the fire in the middle of the room, which the company sit around; and the child is thrice handed across the fire, with the design to frustrate all attempts of evil spirits, or evil eyes. This originally seems to have been designed as a purification, and of idolatrous origin, as the Israelites made their children pass through the fire to Moloch. The word used for charms in general is *colas* or 'knowledge', a proof of the high repute they were once held in. Other charms were styled *paiders*, a word taken from the *Pater Noster*. A necklace is called *padreuchain*, because on turning every bead they used one of these *paiders*. Other charms again are called *toisgeuls*, from the use of particular verses of the Gospel.

The superstition of making pilgrimages to certain wells or chapels is still preserved. That to St Fillan's is much in vogue: and others again to different places. The object is relief from the disorders mankind labour under. In some places the pilgrims only drink of the water: in others, they undergo immersion.

A Highlander, in order to protect himself from any harms apprehended from the fairy tribe, will draw round himself a circle with a sapling of the oak. This may be a relic of Druidism; and only a continuation of the respect paid to the tree held in such veneration by the priesthood of our ancestors.

They pay great attention to their lucky and unlucky days. The Romans could not be more attentive on similar occasions: and surely the Highlander may be excused the superstition, since Augustus could say, that he never went abroad on the day following the *nundinae*, nor began any serious undertaking on the *nonae*, and that, merely to avoid the unlucky omen.[5] The Scottish mountaineers esteem the May 14th unfortunate, and the day of the week that it has happened to fall on. Thus Thursday is a black day for the present year.

They are also very classical in observing what they first meet on the commencement of a journey. They consider the looks, garb and character of the first person they see. If he has a good countenance, is decently clad, and has a fair reputation, they rejoice in the omen. If the contrary, they proceed with fears, or return home, and begin their journey as second time.

The *Beltein*, or the rural sacrifice, on the first of May, O.S., has been mentioned before. Hallow Eve is also kept sacred: as soon as it is dark, a person sets fire to a bush of broom fastened round a pole: and, attended with a crowd, runs round the village. He then flings it down, keeps great quantity of combustible matters in it, and makes a great bonfire. A whole tract is thus illuminated at the

---

[5] Suetonius, *Vit. Aug.*, ch. 92.

same time, and makes a fine appearance. The carrying of the fiery pole appears to be a relic of Druidism; for, says Doctor Borlase,[6] *faces preferre*, was esteemed a species of paganism, forbidden by the Gallic councils, and the *accensores factularum* were condemned to capital punishment, as if they sacrificed to the devil.

The Highlanders form a sort of almanac or presage of the weather of the ensuing year in the following manner. They make observation on twelve days, beginning at the last of December, and hold as an infallible rule, that whatsoever weather happens on each of those days, the same will prove to agree in the correspondent months. Thus, January is to answer to the weather of December 31st. February to that of January 1st; and so with the rest. Old people still pay great attention to this augury.

To these superstitions may be added certain customs now worn out, which were peculiar to this country.

In old times the great Highland families sent their heir, as soon as he was weaned, to some wealthy tenant, who educated him in the hardy manner of the country, at his own expense. When the foster-father restored the child to his parents, he always sent with him a number of cows, proportioned to his abilities, as a mark of the sense he had of the honour done him. A strong attachment ever after subsisted between the two families: the whole family of the foster-father was received under the protection of the chieftain, and held in the highest esteem.

To this day the greater chieftains are named by their clans from some of their ancestors, eminent for strength, wisdom, or valour. Thus the Duke of Argyle is styled Mac-chailean-mhoir, 'the son of the great Colin'. Lord Breadalbane, Mac-chailean-mhic-dhonachi, 'the son of Colin, son of Duncan'. The head of the family of Dunstaffnage, Mac-Innais an Duin, or 'the son of Angus of the hill'.

Most of the old names of the Highlanders were derived from some personal property. Thus Donald or Donshuil signifies 'brown eye'; Finlay, 'white head'; Duncan, 'brown head'; Colin or Coaluin, 'beautiful'; and Gormla, 'a blue eye'.

[6] *Antiq. Cornwall*, 131.

The old Highlanders were so remarkable for their hospitality that their doors were always left open, as if it were to invite the hungry travellers to walk in, and partake of their meals. But if two crossed sticks were seen at the door, it was a sign that the family was at dinner, and did not desire more guests. In this case the churl was held in the highest contempt; nor would the most pressing necessity induce the passenger to turn in. Great hospitality is still preserved through all parts of the country to the stranger, whose character or recommendations claim the most distant pretensions. But this virtue must cease, or, at best, lessen, in proportion as the inundation of travellers increases: a quick succession of new guests will be found to be a trouble and an expense unsupportable: but they will have this consolation, that good inns will be the consequence even of a partial subversion of the hospitable system.

Strict fidelity is another distinguishing character of the Highlanders. Two instances, taken from distant periods, will be sufficient proofs of the high degree in which they possess this shining virtue. In the reign of James V when the clan Chattan had raised a dangerous insurrection, attended with all the barbarities usual in those days, the Earl of Murray raised his people, suppressed the insurgents, and ordered two hundred of the principal prisoners to execution. As they were led one by one to the gallows, the Earl offered them a pardon in case they would discover the lurking-place of their chieftain; but they unanimously told him, that, were they acquainted with it, no sort of punishment should ever induce them to be guilty of breach of trust to their leader.[7]

The other example is taken from more recent and mercenary days. In the year 1746, when the Young Pretender preferred the preservation of an unhappy life by an inglorious flight to the honour of falling heroically with his faithful followers in the field of Culloden, he for five months led the life of a fugitive, amidst a numerous and various set of mountaineers. He trusted his person often to the lowest and most dissolute of the people; to men pinched with poverty, or accustomed to rapine: yet neither the fear of punishment for assisting the wretched wanderer, nor the dazzling allurement of the reward of

[7] Lessey, *De Origine, Moribus, et Rebus Festis Scotorum*, 405.

thirty thousand pounds, could ever prevail on any one to violate the laws of hospitality, or be guilty of a breach of trust. They extricated him out of every difficulty; they completed his deliverance, preserving his life for mortifications more afflicting than the dreadful hardships he sustained during his long flight.

Soon after entering the parish of Mouline, leave, on the right, Edradour. At this place, on the top of a steep den, are the remains of a circular building, called the Black Castle, about sixty feet diameter within side, and the walls about eight feet thick. There is another about a mile west from the village of Mouline, near Balyou'an, and a third on an eminence south of the former. One of these answers to another similar at Killichange, in the parish of Logierait. Some conjecture these round buildings to have been intended for making signals with fires in case of invasions: others think them to have been *tighfasky*, or a storehouse for the concealment of valuable effects in case of sudden inroads. The first is a very probable opinion, as I can trace, approaching towards the west sea, a chain of these edifices, one within sight of the next, for a very considerable way. It is not unlikely, if search was made, but that they may even extend to the east sea, so as to form a series of beacons cross this part of the kingdom.

My worthy fellow-voyager, Mr Stuart, has, from remarks on several in the neighbourhood of Killin, enabled me to trace them for several miles. To begin with the most eastern, next to those I have mentioned, there is one on the hill of Drummin, opposite to Taymouth, on the side of the vale: another lies within view, above the church of Fortingal: on the hill Druim-an-Timhoir, is a third, opposite to Alt-mhuic, east of Miggerny; one under the house of Cashly, called Castal-mhic-nèil; and another, about half a mile west, of the name of Castal-a-chon-bhaican, a crooked stone, called Con-bhacan, being erected about two hundred feet east from it, and so named, from a tradition that the Nimrods of old times tied their dogs to it with a leathern thong, when they returned from the chase. The figure of this building differs from the others, being oval:[8]

---

[8] The *saghs na ain eighe*, or 'the work of one night', engraved. Book III; tab. viii, of Mr Wright's *Louthiana*, is similar to this.

the greatest length within the wall is seventy-one feet; the breadth forty; the thickness at the sides twelve feet, at the ends only eight. The door at the east end low and narrow, covered with a flag.

But the most entire is that styled Castal-an-Dui, lying at the foot of the hill Grianan, on the farm of Cashly, three miles west from Miggerny. On the north-west side is a stone twenty-nine feet long, and nine thick, which supplies part of the building on the outside. The form of this building is a circle: the thickness from eleven to twelve feet; and within the place where the great stone stands, is an additional strength of wall, about eight feet thick. The most complete place is nine feet and a half high: the diameter within the wall is forty-five feet. The greatest part of the stones used in this edifice are from three to six feet long, and from one and a half to three feet thick.

About three hundred yards west from this is another, called Castal-an-Deirg. A mile farther west is another, of the name of Fiam-nam-Bònean; and lastly, within sight of this, five miles distant, on the side of a hill called Ben-chastal, is one more, the most westerly of any we have yet had intelligence of. Most, if not all of these, lie in Glen Lion. The tradition of the inhabitants respecting them is included in these lines:

> Dà chaisteal-deug aig Feann
> Ann an crom-ghleann nar clach.

That is, 'Fingal, the king of heroes, had twelve towers in the winding valley of the grey-headed stones.'

I must mention two others, that are out of the line of these, yet might be subservient to their use. One lies on the north side of Loch Tay, about five miles east of Killin, above the public road. The other, called Caisteal Baraora, on the south side, about a quarter of a mile from the lake, and a measured mile east of Achmore, the seat of Mr Campbell, of Achalader.

On the top of a great eminence, a furlong from this, are the remains of a vast enclosure, a stronghold, of the same nature with that I saw in Glenelg;[9] to which the inhabitants might drive their

---

[9] *Voyage to the Hebrides*, 336.

cattle in time of invasion, on the signals given from the round towers. The form tends to an oval; the greatest length is three hundred and sixty feet; the breadth one hundred and twenty. No part of the wall is entire, but the stones that formed it lie in ruins on the ground to the breadth of fifteen feet. Within, near the east end, is the foundation of a rectangular building, thirty-eight feet long, ten broad. This post commands a vast view of the west end of Breadalbane, almost to the head of the vallies of Glen Dochart, and Glen Lochy; and at a very small distance from it is seen the hill of Drummin, from whose round tower the signal might easily be received.

The round edifices of this internal part of Scotland, and those of the coast and of the islands, seem to have been erected for the same purpose, but probably by different architects. The former are the labours of much less skilful workmen; the stones more rude, the facings less exact and elegant, but not inferior to the manner now in use in the common dry walled houses of the country.

I cannot but think that all these buildings were originally constructed by the natives; and that those so frequent in the islands, and of such superior workmanship, might have been rebuilt by the Danes and Norwegians, on the same model, but more artificially than those they found on the spot. From all the enquiries I have made among the natives of Scandinavia, I do not learn that any such buildings are known there, a single instance excepted on the Sualesberg,[10] a mountain half a Norwegian league distant from Drontheim. If no more are discovered, it is probable that the invaders did not bring this mode of building with them. But they might have considered the use and conveniency of these structures, and adopted the plan, making such improvements as appeared to them necessary. Thus in some they formed walls, with galleries within; and in others, erected small buildings in the areas,[11] to

---

[10] The building alluded to was the work of King Suerre, who died in 1202, about a hundred and four years after these isles were made subject to Norway by Magnus the Barefooted. Suerre might therefore have taken the model of this single tower from the Hebrides.

[11] Vide the *Voyage to the Hebrides*, 219, 292, 358.

protect them from the inclemency of the weather; for being in an enemy's country, the Danes were obliged to use them as little garrisons: on the contrary, the natives never might consider them in any other light than as short and temporary retreats from an invading enemy. It is also pretty certain, that the Danes either never reached some of the places where we now see these buildings, or, at least, never made any more than a short inroad. On the other hand, they possessed the islands, and some of the coasts for a long series of years; and had ample time to form any improvements that were agreeable to them.

A few other antiquities are also found in this parish. On a plain below Dirnanean in Strathardle, is a circular mount, composed of small stones, mixed with earth, coated with turf, on whose summit is an erect four-sided stone, of a considerable size. This seems a sepulchral memorial of some person of rank, whose urn is probably beneath. Another stone of the same kind is also to be seen at some distance from it, at the edge of the river.

At the east end of the same plain is the appearance of a grave, sixteen feet long, with a large stone at each end. In the language of the country, this is styled 'the grave of high blood', from a tradition, that a Danish prince was slain and interred here. It is suspected that a skirmish might have been fought here, and the slain in general buried in this place.

Of castles of a more modern date, this parish boasts only one, in the hollow of Mouline, of a square form, built with bad whinstone, cemented with hot lime, so strong as scarcely to be broken. Two round towers yet remain, and a transverse wall. The vestige of the ditch is still to be traced. The inhabitants ascribe the building to one of the Cummins; but Sir James Balfour,[12] with more certainty, gives it to Thomas of Galloway, Earl of Athol, and acquaints us, that it was the residence of the ancient earls.

Proceed on my way; and, after a short ride through a barren and dreary tract, am again enraptured with the charms of Faskally, which appears like fairy ground, amidst the wild environs of craggy mountains, skirted with woods; is seated in a beautiful meadow,

[12] MS.

on one side bordered with woods, on the other bounded by the Tumel, rival in size to the Tay, which at a small distance appears again gushing from between the wooded rocks, and tumbling down a precipice of great height, to water these delicious scenes.

Salmons annually force their passage even up this furious cataract; and are taken here in a most artless manner: a hamper, fastened to a wicker rope, pinned into a cleft of the rock by a stick, is flung into the stream: now and then a fish, in the fall from its effort to get up, drops into this little ware. It is not to be supposed that the owner can enrich himself by the capture: in fact, the chance of his good fortune is hired out at the annual rent of one pound fourteen shillings.

At other times the fisher flings into the stream below, a crowfoot, or caltrop, fastened to a long rope. On this instrument the salmon often transfix themselves, and are drawn up to land. Another method, of much risk to the adventurer, is at times practised. A person seats himself on the brink of the precipice, above the cataracts, and fixes one foot in the noose of a wicker-cord: here he expects the leap of a salmon, armed with a spear: the moment the fish rises, he darts his weapon at the hazard of falling into the water by his own effort, or the struggle of his prey.

A little to the east of this fall the Garrie unites itself with the Tumel; a river that rises from a lake thirteen computed miles above Blair. The noted pass of Killicrankie is formed by the hills that impend over it on each side; the waters of the Garrie rushing beneath in a deep, darksome, and horrible channel; in the last century a pass of much danger and difficulty, a path hanging over a tremendous precipice, threatening destruction to the least false step of the traveller; at present a fine road, formed by the soldiery lent by Government, and encouraged by six pence per day added to the pay, gives an easy access to the remoter Highlands. A fine arch over the Garrie joins the once impervious sides.

Near the north end of this pass, in its unimproved and arduous state, on an open space, was fought the celebrated battle of Killicrankie; when the gallant Viscount Dundee fell in the moment of victory, and with him all the hopes of the abdicating monarch. The enemies of this illustrious hero made his eulogy: Mackay, the defeated general, in the course of his flight, pronouncing the death of his antagonist; 'Was Dundee alive,' says he, 'my retreat would not have been thus uninterrupted.' His body was interred in the church of Blair. His glory required no inscription to perpetuate it: yet the elegance of his epitaph, composed by Dr Archibald Pitcairn, merits repetition, doing equal honour to the hero and poet:

> *Ultime Scotorum, potuit quo sospite solo*
>   *Libertas patriae salva fuisse tuae.*
> *Te moriente novos accepit Scotia cives:*
>   *Acceptique novos te moriente Deos.*
> *Illa tibi superesse negat, tu non potes illi,*
>   *Ergo Caledoniae nomen inane vale.*
> *Tuque vale gentis priscae fortissime Ductor,*
>   *Optime Scotorum atque ultime, Grame, vale.*

> *O last and best of Scots! who didst maintain*
> *Thy country's freedom from a foreign reign;*
> *New people fill the land, now they are gone;*
> *New Gods the temples, and new kings the throne:*
> *Scotland and thou did each in other live,*
> *Thou coud'st not her, nor cou'd she thee survive;*
> *Farewel, thou, living, that didst support the State,*
> *And cou'dst not fall, but by thy country's fate.*
> Dryden

Continue my ride to Athol House, in the Blair of Athol, seated on an eminence above a plain, watered by the Garrie; a most outrageous stream, whose ravages have greatly deformed the valley by the vast beds of gravel it has left behind.

The house, or castle is of uncertain antiquity: the oldest part is called Cummin's Tower, being supposed to have been built by John, commonly called de Strathbogy, who enjoyed the title of Athol, in right of his wife. It became the principal seat of his successors. In 1644 the Marquis of Montrose possessed himself of it, and was joined by a large body of the Athol Highlanders, to whose bravery he was indebted for the victory at Tibbirmoor. In the troubles of 1653, the place was taken by storm by Colonel Daniel,[13] an officer of Cromwell, who, unable to remove a magazine of provision

---

[13] Whitelock, 582.

lodged there, destroyed it by powder. In 1689, it occasioned one of the greatest events of the time, being the cause that brought on the celebrated battle of Killicrankie. An officer belonging to Viscount Dundee flung himself into it, and refusing to deliver it to Lord Murray, son to the Marquis of Athol, was by him threatened with a siege. His Lordship, to effect the reduction, assembled a body of forces, and marched towards the place. Dundee knew the importance of preserving this pass, and the communications with the Highland clans, in whom he had the greatest confidence.[14] With his usual expedition, he joined the garrison; and in a few days after concluded his glorious life with the well-known defeat of the royal forces under Mackay.

The last siege it experienced was in 1746, when it was gallantly defended by Sir Andrew Agnew against the rebels, who retired from before it a few weeks preceding the battle of Culloden. As soon as peace was established, a considerable part of that fortress was reduced in height, and the inside most magnificently furnished.

The views in front of the house are planted with so much form, as to be far from pleasing; but the picturesque walks amidst the rocks on the other side, cannot fail to attract the admiration of every traveller of taste. The late noble owner, with great judgment, but with not less difficulty, cut, or rather blasted out, walks along the vast rocks and precipices, that bound the rivers Banovy and Tilt. The waters are violent, and form in various places cascades of great beauty. Pines and trees of several species wave solemnly over the head, and darken the romantic scene. The place appeared to great advantage: for the Highland, as well as other beauties, have their good and their bad days. The glen, that in 1769 I thought deficient in water, now, by reason of the rains, looked to great advantage, and finished finely the rich scenery of rock and wood.

The Yorke Cascade, a mile from the house, merits a visit. It first appears tumbling amidst the trees, at the head of a small glen. The waters are soon joined by those of another that dart from the side. These united waters fall into a deep chasm, appear again, and, after forming four more cataracts, are lost in the Tilt; which likewise

[14] Balcarras's *Memoirs*, 99.

disappears, having for a considerable space excavated the rock we stood on; running invisible, with a roaring torrent, before it emerges today.

It is but of late that the North Britons became sensible of the beauties of their country; but their search is at present amply rewarded. Very lately a cataract of uncommon height was discovered, covered on the Bruer, a large stream about two miles north from this place. It is divided into five falls, visible at once, and in a line with each other: the four uppermost form together a fall of a hundred feet: the fifth alone is nearly the same height; so that when the whole appear in front, in high floods, they seem one sheet of near two hundred feet: a sight scarcely to be paralleled in Europe.

Trees of all kinds prosper here greatly: larches of twenty years growth yield plank of the breadth of fifteen inches. The late duke annually lessened the nakedness of the hills, and extended his plantations far and wide. His attention to the culture of rhubarb must not pass unnoticed: for his benevolent design of rendering common and cheap this useful medicine, is blessed with the utmost success. The roots which he had cultivated in the light soils, familiar to those of the Tartarian deserts, the native place, increase to a vast size: some when fresh having been found to weigh fifty pounds, and to equal in smell, taste, and effect to those we import at an enormous expense to our country. On being dried they shrink to one quarter of their original weight. There is reason to suppose that the Scotch rhubarb may be superior in virtue to the foreign, the last being gathered in all seasons, as the Mongol hunters chance to pass by. They draw up the roots indiscriminately, pierce them at one end, and sling them on their belts; and then leave them to dry on their tents without further care.

Leave Athol House. Return by Faskally along the great road to the junction of the Tumel with the Tay. Nature hath formed, on each side of the vale, multitudes of terraces, some with grassy sides, others wooded. Art hath contributed to give this road an uncommon magnificence: such parts, which want clothing, are planted not only with the usual trees, but with flowering shrubs: and the sides of the way are sodded in the neatest manner. In a little time the whole way

VI

Drawn fecit.

R. Wayct sculp.

D U N K E L D.

from Dalnacardoch to Perth, near forty-five miles, will appear like a garden: if our sister Peg goes on at this rate, I wish, that, from a confessed slattern, she does not become downright finical.

On approaching Dunkeld, the vale becomes very narrow: at last leaves only space for the road and the river, which runs between hills covered with hanging woods. The town of Dunkeld is seated on the north side of the Tay; is supposed to take its name from the words *dun*, 'a mount', and Gael, the old inhabitants, or Caledonians, and to have been the Castrum Caledoniae, and the Oppidum Caledoniorum of the old writers.[15] At present I could not hear of any vestiges of Roman antiquity. The town is small, has a share of the linen manufacture, and is much frequented in summer by invalids, who resort here for the benefit of drinking goats' milk and whey.

This place in very early days became the seat of religion. Constantine III, King of the Picts, at the instance of Adamnanus is said to have founded here a monastery of Culdees, in honour of St Columba, about the year 729. These religious had wives according to the custom of the eastern church, only they were prohibited from cohabiting *dum vicissim administrarunt*. About 1127 that pious prince David I converted it into a cathedral, displaced the Culdees, and made Gregory their abbot, the first bishop, who obtained from pope Alexander III ample protection and confirmation.[16] The revenue, at the Reformation, was £1,505 10s 4d Scots, besides a large contribution of different sorts of grain.[17]

The present church was built by Robert Arden, the nineteenth bishop, who was interred in it, about the year 1436.[18] Except the choir, which serves as the parish church, the rest exhibits a fine ruin, amidst the solemn scene of rocks and woods. The extent within is 120 feet by 60. The body is supported by two rows of round pillars, with squared capitals. The arches Gothic.

In the vestry room is a large monument of the Marquis of Athol, who died in 1703. It is hung with the arms of all the numerous connections of this illustrious house, which, by its great ancestor

[15] Boethius, lib. IX, 167. Buchanan, lib. II, ch. 22.
[16] Keith, 46.
[17] Maitland, *Hist. Scot.* I, 244.
[18] Monteith's *Epitaphs*, 229.

Sir James Stuart, called the Black Knight of Lorn, and first Earl of Athol of the present family, may boast of being related to every crowned head in Europe, excepting the Grand Segnior.

In the body of the church is a tomb with the recumbent effigies in armour, of Alexander Stuart, Earl of Buchan, third son of Robert II by Elizabeth More: a person of most uncommon impiety;[19] and for his cruelty justly styled the Wolf of Badenoch. Yet his epitaph, when entire, ran thus:

> *Hic jacet bonae memoriae, Alexander Senescallus comes de Buchan et dominus de Badenoch, qui obiit 24. Novemb. 1394.*

The cathedral was demolished in 1559: the monuments were destroyed in 1689, by the garrison that was placed there at that time. I looked in vain for the tomb of Marjory Scot, who died at Dunkeld, January 16th, 1728. Her epitaph was composed by Alexander Pennicuik, and is said to have been inscribed in memory of her longevity. It thus addresses the reader:

> *Stop Passenger, until my Life you read,*
> *The Living may get knowledge from the Dead.*
> *Five Times five Years I liv'd a virgin Life;*
> *Five Times five Years I liv'd a happy Wife;*
> *Ten Times five Years I liv'd a Widow chaste,*
> *Now wearied of this mortal Life I rest,*
> *Betwixt my Cradle and my Grave were seen*
> *Eight mighty Kings of Scotland, and a Queen,*
> *Four Times five Years a Commonwealth I saw,*
> *Ten Times the Subjects rise against the Law;*
> *Thrice did I see old Prelacy pull'd down,*
> *And thrice the Cloak was humbled by the Gown.*
> *An End of Stuart's Race I saw, nay more,*
> *I saw my Country sold for English Ore.*
> *Such Desolations in my Time have been;*
> *I have an End of all Perfection seen.*

The great ornament of this place is the Duke of Athol's extensive improvements, and magnificent plantations, bounded by crags with summits of a tremendous height. The gardens extend along

---

[19] 3rd ed. *Tour Scot.*, 279 or Appendix, octavo, 67.

the side of the river, and command from different parts the most beautiful and picturesque views of wild and gloomy nature that can be conceived.

Ascend the hill; and from a southern brow have a view of a chain of small lakes, on whose banks is Leagh Wood, an estate granted by James III to John Stuart, Earl of Athol, as a reward for his victory over the great Macdonald of the Isles.

Return towards the north, along an extensive flat, bounded on the right by vast and precipitous crags. On this plain is planted abundance of rhubarb, by way of trial whether it will succeed as well in these wild tracts as in the manured soils. Walk through a narrow pass, bounded by great rocks. One retains the name of the King's Seat,[20] having been the place where the Scottish monarchs placed themselves, in order to direct their shafts with advantage at the flying deer driven that way for their amusement. A chase of this kind had very nearly prevented the future miseries of the unhappy Mary Stuart. The story is well told by William Barclay, in his treatise *Contra Monarchomachos*: it gives a lively picture of the ancient manner of hunting; and, on that account, will perhaps be acceptable to the reader in an English dress:

> *I once had a sight of a very extraordinary sort, which convinced me of what I have said. In the year 1563, the Earl of Athol, a prince of the blood royal, had, with much trouble and vast expense, a hunting-match for the entertainment of our most illustrious and most gracious Queen. Our people call this a Royal Hunting. I was then a young man, and was present on the occasion: two thousand Highlanders, or wild Scottish, as you call them here, were employed to drive to the hunting ground all the deer from the woods and hills of Atholl, Badenoch, Marr, Murray, and the countries about. As these Highlanders use a light dress, and are very swift of foot, they went up and down so nimbly, that in less than two months time they brought together two thousand red deer, besides roes and fallow deer. The Queen, the great men, and a number of others, were in a glen when all these deer were brought before them; believe me, the whole body moved forward in something like battle*

---

[20] By mistake the view of this place, in the first and second editions of the Tour, is called the King's Seat, near Blair.

order. This sight still strikes me, and ever will strike me: for they had a leader whom they followed close wherever he moved.

This leader was a very fine stag with a very high head: this sight delighted the Queen very much, but she soon had cause for fear; upon the Earl's (who had been from his early days accustomed to such sights) addressing her thus, 'Do you observe that stag who is foremost of the herd, there is danger from that stag, for if either fear or rage should force him from the ridge of that hill, let every one look to himself, for none of us will be out of the way of harm; for the rest will follow this one, and having thrown us under foot, they will open a passage to this hill behind us.' What happen'd a moment after confirmed this opinion: for the Queen ordered one of the best dogs to be let loose on one of the deer; this the dog pursues, the leading stag was frightened, he flies by the same way he had come there, the rest rush after him and break out where the thickest body of the Highlanders was; they had nothing for it but to throw themselves flat on the heath, and to allow the deer to pass over them. It was told the Queen that several of the Highlanders had been wounded, and that two or three had been killed outright; and the whole body had got off, had not the Highlanders, by their skill in hunting, fallen upon a strategem to cut off the rear from the main body. It was of those that had been separated that the Queen's dogs and those of the nobility made slaughter. There were killed that day 360 deer, with five wolves, and some roes.

From the summit of the King's Seat is a beautiful prospect to the north of Strathtay; and to the south, a still finer one of the winding of the river, through a tract enriched with cornfields, and varied with frequent woods; and, at a distance, the celebrated wood of Birnam, and hill of Dunsinane.

On descending into the gardens, visit the house, or rather villa, belonging to the Duke of Athol; small, but furnished with peculiar elegance: the windows are finely painted by Mr Singleton, an *élève* of the house, whose performances do him much credit.

Cross the Tay, to visit the improvements on the banks of the great torrent, Bran, which rushes most impetuously over its rugged bottom. All this part is a mixture of cultivation, with vast rocks springing out of the ground, among which are conducted variety of walks, bordered with flowers and flowering shrubs, and adorned with numbers of little buildings, in the style of the Oriental gardens.

Continue my ride on the west side of the Tay, and soon quit this august entrance into the Scottish Alps. The mountains gradually sink, the plain expands, and agriculture increases. Arrive in the plain of Stormont, a part of Strathmore, or the great plain, being the most extensive of any in North Britain, bounded on the north by the Grampian Hills, on the south by those of Ochil, and of Seidlaw, and on the east by the sea; stretching at one extremity within a small distance of Sterling, at the other to Stonehive in the Merns, but distinguished in different places by different names.

Pass by a neat settlement of weavers, called, from the inhabitants, Spittlefields. This country is very populous, full of spinners, and of weavers of buckrams and coarse cloths or stentings; of which twelve millions of yards are annually exported from Perth. Much flax is raised here, and the country is full of corn, but not sufficient to supply the numerous inhabitants. Late at night reach Inchstuthel, the modern Delvin, the seat of John Mackenzie, Esq.,[21] where I found a continuation of Highland hospitality.

The situation of this house is of strange singularity; on a flat of a hundred and fifty-four Scotch acres,[22] regularly steep on every side, and in every part of equal height; that is to say, about sixty feet above the great plain of Stormont, which it stands on. The figure is also remarkable, and much better to be expressed by the engraving than by any description of mine.

---

[21] Mr Mackenzie's father, who was a good antiquary, held this to have been part of the land granted by Kenneth to the gallant Hay, the hero of the battle of Loncarty, whose descendents possessed it four or five centuries.

[22] The difference between the measures of land in Scotland, and those used in England, is in proportion to the Scots fall of six Scots ells length, and the English perch, which by statute is in length five yards and a half, whereby the acres stand thus: one Scots acre is one acre, one rood, and one perch English; 100 Scots acres is 125 acres, two roods, 33 perches: so that the proportion is nearly as four is to five. It is to be observed, that there is no statute for the Scots chain, as there is for the English; only a very old custom, which seems to have been brought from the Paris Royal arpent, which is nearly the same with that used at present in Scotland, and called the Scots acre.

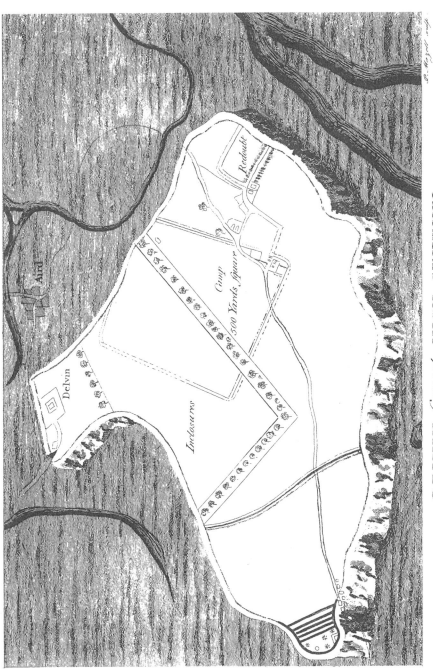

VII

Aird

Delvin

Inclosures

Camp
500 Yards Square

Redoubt

DELVIN formerly INCH-STUTHIEL.

Two nations took advantage of this natural strength, and situated themselves on it. The Picts, the long possessors of these eastern parts of the kingdom, in all probability had here an *oppidum*, or town, such as uncivilized people inhabited in early times; often in the midst of woods, and fortified all round with a dike. Here we find the vestiges of such a defence; a mound of stones and earth running along the margin of the steep, in many places entire: in others, time or accident hath rendered it less visible, or hath totally destroyed it. The stones were not found on the spot; but were brought from a place two miles distant, where quarries of the same kind are still in use.

Another dike crosses the ground, from margin to margin, in the place it begins to grow narrow. This seems intended as the first defence against an enemy, should the inhabitants fail in defending their outworks, and be obliged to quit their station and retire to a stronger part. Near the extremity is what I should name their citadel; for a small portion of the end is cut off from the rest by five great dikes, and as many deep fosses; and within that is the stronghold, impregnable against the neighbouring nations.

This place had also another security which time hath diverted from them: the River Tay once entirely environed the place, and formed it into an island, as the name in the ancient language, which it still retains, imports; that of Inchstuthel, or 'the isle of Tuthel'. The river at present runs on one side only: but there are plain marks on the north in particular, not only of a channel, but of some pieces of water, oblong, narrow, and pointing in the direction the Tay had taken, before it had ceased to insulate this piece of ground. I cannot ascertain the period when its waters confined themselves to one bed; but am informed that a grant still exists from one of the James's of a right of fishing in the river, at Caput-mac-Athol, east of the place.

It is not to be imagined that there can be any traces of the habitations of a people who dwelt in the most perishable hovels: but as the most barbarous nations paid more attention to the remains of the dead, than to the conveniency of the living, they formed, either for the protection of their relics of their chieftains from insults of man, or savage beast, or for sepulchral memorials, mounts of different sizes. Ancient Greece and ancient Latium concurred in the same practice with the natives of this island. Patroclus among the Greeks, and Hector among the Trojans, received but the same funeral honours with our Caledonian heroes, and the ashes of Dercennus the Laurentine monarch had the same simple protection.[23] The urn and pall of the Trojan warrior might perhaps be more superb than those of a British leader: the rising monument of each had the common materials from our mother earth:

> *The snowy Bones his Friends and Brothers place,*
> *With tears collected, in a golden vase.*
> *The golden vase in purple palls they rolled*
> *Of softest texture and inwrought with gold.*
> *Last o'er the urn the sacred earth they spread,*
> *And rais'd a tomb, memorial of the dead.*[24]

Or, as it is more strongly expressed by the same elegant translator, in the account of the funeral of Patroclus:

> *High in the midst they heap the swelling bed*
> *Of rising earth, memorial of the dead.*[25]

Monuments of this kind are very frequent over the face of this plain: the tumuli are round, not greatly elevated, and at their basis surrounded with a fosse. Many bones have been found in some of the barrows, neither lodged in stone chests nor deposited in urns.

The Romans, in their course along this part of Britain, did not neglect so fine a situation for a station. Notwithstanding the great change made by enclosures, by plantation, and by agriculture, there are still vestiges of one station five hundred yards square. The side next to Delvin House is barely to be traced: and part of another borders on the margin of the bank. There is likewise a small square redoubt, near the edge, facing the East Inch in the Tay; which covered the station on that side.

The first was once enclosed with a wall fourteen feet thick, whose foundations are remembered by two farmers of the name

---

[23] *Aeneid.*, lib. XI, lin. 849.
[24] Pope's *Homer's Iliad*, book XXIV, line 1003.
[25] The same, book XXIII, line 319.

of Stertan, aged about seventy; who had received from their father and grandfather frequent accounts of ashes, cinders, brick, iron, utensils, weapons, and large pieces of lead, having been frequently found on the spot, in the course of ploughing:[26] and to the west of this station, about thirty years ago, were discovered the vestiges of a large building, the whole ground being filled with fragments of brick and mortar. A rectangular hollow made of brick is still entire: it is about ten or twelve feet long, three or four feet wide, and five or six feet deep. Boethius calls this place the Tulina of the Picts; and adds, that in their time, it was a most populous city; but was deserted and burnt by them on the approach of the Romans under Agricola. He also informs us that it bore the name of Inchstuthel in his days.[27] The materials from which this historian took the early part of his work are unknown to us, any further than what we learn from himself, that they were records sent to him in 1525 from Iona; but by whom compiled, remains undiscovered. I do not doubt this assertion; nor do I doubt but that some truths collected from traditions may be scattered amidst the innumerable legendary tales, so abundant in his first books. This I would wish to place among the former, as the actual vestiges of two nations are still to be traced on the spot. I would also call it the Orrea of the Romans, which the learned Stukeley supposes to have been Perth, notwithstanding he places it in his map north-east of the Tay, and on the very spot where the present Delvin stands.[28]

Leave Delvin. Cross the Tay, at the ferry of Caputh. Pass over a short tract of barren country. On the banks of a small rill are vestiges of an encampment, as is supposed, of the Danes, and to have been called from those invaders Gally Burn, or 'the burn of the strangers'. A little farther, in a very fertile improved country, is Loncarty, celebrated for the signal victory obtained by the Scots, under Kenneth III,[29] over the Danes, by means of the gallant peasant Hay, and his two sons, who, with no other weapons than yokes which they snatched from their oxen then at plough, first put a

---

[26] By letter from the Rev Mr Bisset, minister of Caputh.
[27] *Hist. Scotiae.*, lib. IV, 64.
[28] In his account of Richard of Cirencester.
[29] Who began his reign in 976.

stop to the flight of their countrymen, and afterwards led them on to conquest. These spirited lines are a perfect picture of the action:

Quo ruitis, Cives? Heia! Hosti obvertite vultus!
  Non pudet infami vertere terga fuga?
Hostis ego vobis; aut ferrum vertite in hostem.
  Dixit, et armatus dux praeit ipse jugo.
Qua, qua ibat vastum condensa per agmina Danum
  Dat stragem. Hinc omnis consequiturque fuga.
Servavit cives. Victorem reppulit hostem.
  Unus cum natis agminis instar erat.
Hic Decios agnosce tuos magnae aemula Roma,
  Aut prior hac; aut te his Scotiae major adhuc.[30]

The noble families of Hay derive their descent from this rustic hero, and, in memory of the action, bear for their arms the instrument of their victory, with the allusive motto of '*Sub Jugo*'. Tradition relates, that the monarch gave this deliverer of his country, in reward, as much land as a greyhound would run over in a certain time, or a falcon would surround in its flight: and the story says that he chose the last.

Over this tract are scattered numbers of tumuli, in which are frequently found bones and entire skeletons, sometimes lodged in rude coffins, formed of stones, disposed in that form; at other times deposited only in the earth of the barrow. In one place is an upright stone, supposed to have been laid over the place of sepulture of the Danish leader. The present names of two places on this plain certainly allude to the action and to the vanquished enemy. Turn-again Hillock points out the place where the Scots rallied, and a spot near eight tumuli, called Danemerk, may design the place of greatest slaughter.

---

[30] Joh. Johnstoni, *Heroes Scoti*.

XIII

PERTHSHIRE (3),
FIFE (1)

———————◆———————

Perth—Strathearn—Innerpeffrey—Loch Monival—Loch Earn—Comerie—
Castle Drummond—Kemp's Castle—Ardoch—Tullibardine—Dupplin—
Ruthven House—Perth Bridge—Scone—Gowrie—Errol—Lindores
Abbey—Balmerino Abbey

CONTINUE my ride through a fine plain, rich in corn; the crops
of wheat excellent. The noble Tay winds boldly on the left;
the eastern borders are decorated with the woods of Scone. The
fine bridge now completed, the city of Perth, and the hills and
rising woods beyond, form a most beautiful finishing of the
prospect.

Perth, till about the year 1437,[1] the capital of Scotland, and
residence of its princes, the seat of its parliaments and its courts of
justice, is placed in the middle of a verdant plain, which it divides
into two parts, one called the North, and the other the South Inch.
Boethius asserts that it is not of any great antiquity, and that it was
founded by William the Lion, after the destruction of Bertha, AD
1210, a place about two miles to the north. He adds that William
gave his new foundation the name of St John's Town, in honour
of the saint; but other writers pretend that it first had the name of

---

[1] Gall's *Gabions*, 24.

Perth from the owner of the land on which it was built: but it is more probable that the derivation is from the ancient Bertha.

But leaving the uncertainty of etymology; it is clear that Perth is much more ancient than Boethius seems to admit. That it was a place of commerce in the year 1128, is evident from the charter of David I to the abbey of Holyroodhouse, in which he gives the monks a hundred shillings out of his small tithes there, or out of the duties arising from the first merchant ships which might arrive in that port:[2] and that it was a town of strength in 1160, is equally apparent from the siege of Malcolm IV, which it sustained that year against Feretach, Earl of Strathearn, who was obliged to retire from before the place.[3] It is undeniably true that Perth suffered a great misfortune from an inundation at the time Boethius has mentioned, which destroyed several houses, carried away the bridge, and obliged the king and royal family to save themselves in a little boat.[4] The town stood then on, or nearly on, the same ground it does at present; therefore William can only be styled the restorer, not the founder, of this fine city.

It soon became considerable, not only on account of its being a royal residence, but likewise by reason of the vast commerce which its situation on one of the first rivers in North Britain would naturally convey. Its importance soon gave it walls and fortifications. Major calls it the only walled city in Scotland.[5] The castle stood near the Skinnergate Street. The importance of the place made it frequently experience the calamities of war. Edward I, when he overran Scotland, possessed himself of this city. In 1307 Robert Bruce, after a siege of six weeks, by a feigned retreat and sudden return made himself master of it, when defended for the English by John, Earl Warren, and Earl of Strathearn.[6] The English soon repossessed themselves of it; and Edward II made Perth for some time his residence. In 1312 Bruce again made himself master of it by a scalade, putting to the sword his traitorous countrymen, but

---

[2] Maitland's *Hist. Edinburgh*, 145.
[3] Roger de Hovenden, *Inter Scrip. post Bedam*, 492.
[4] Major, 138.
[5] p. 20
[6] *Hist. Scot.*, 20.

permitting the English garrison to return in safety to their own country: he then levelled the walls to the ground, and filled all the ditches. After the fatal battle of Dupplin in 1332, Baliol, with small opposition, entered the place, and left it in possession of the enemies of his country. Edward III, who knew its importance, repaired the walls, and restored the fortifications at the expense of the rich abbeys of Arbroth, Cowper, Lindores, Balmerinoch, Dumferline, and St Andrew's; and placed there, as governor, Sir Thomas Orchard. It remained under a foreign yoke but a small time; for in 1340 Robert Stuart, guardian of Scotland, with a strong army, and the assistance of a French fleet, restored it once again to its natural masters.

I do not recollect that it underwent any siege from that period till the religious wars of 1559; when the queen regent, provoked by the insult of the inhabitants on all she held venerable and holy, placed there a garrison of French.[7] The zeal however of the congregation soon collected a potent army to its relief under Argyle, who, after a short siege, obliged the garrison to capitulate and retire.

Perth from that time remained in peace above a century. In 1644 the Marquis of Montrose seized the place, after the battle of Tibbirmoor; and Cromwell, in July 1651, after a weak defence from a weak garrison, made himself master of this important city: and, to secure the possession, the English commissioners ordered a citadel to be built on the South Inch, capable of containing five hundred men,[8] the remains of which still retain the name of Oliver's Mount.

The Earl of Mar's army, in the rebellion of 1715, lay a considerable time in this place, and spent here considerable sums of money. This circumstance contributed as much to enrich the city, as the settlement of numbers of Oliver's forces, after the establishment of peace, assisted in introducing that spirit of industry, which, to this moment, distinguishes the inhabitants.

Perth is large, well built, and populous, and contains about eleven thousand inhabitants, nine thousand of whom are of the established church of Scotland; the rest of a variety of persuasions, such as

---

[7] The reformers committed several excesses; such as interrupting the priests in their sermons, nailing a pair of ram's horns on the head of St Francis, and a cow's tail to his rump, etc.

[8] Whitelock, 528.

Episcopalians, Nonjurors, Glassites, Seceders; the second chiefly consists of a congregation of venerable females. The town has but one parish, supplied with three churches, besides the chapels for such who dissent from the established church.

The two principal streets are remarkably fine: in some of the lesser ones are still to be seen a few wooden houses in the old style; but as they decay, the magistrates prohibit the rebuilding them in the same manner. The great improvement of the town is to be dated from the year 1745, it being supposed to have increased one third since that turbulent period: for the government of this part of Great Britain had never been properly settled till a little after that time.

The Tay washes the east side of the town, and is deep enough to bring vessels of one hundred and twenty tons burden as far as the quays: and, if Dutch-built, or flat-bottomed, even of two hundred tons burden. This enables the inhabitants of Perth to carry on a most considerable trade. The exports are as follow: of white and brown linens, about seventy-five thousands pounds worth are annually sent to London, besides a very great quantity that is disposed of to Edinburgh and Glasgow: and London, Manchester and Glasgow take about ten thousand pounds worth of linen yarn.

Linseed oil forms a considerable article of commerce. Seven water-mills belonging to this place are in full employ, and make, on a medium, near three hundred tons of oil, which is chiefly sent to London, and brings in from eight to nine thousand pounds. The first mill for this purpose was erected, about the beginning of this century, by John Duke of Athol. At the first a glass of whisky, mixed with half as much of the oil, was a fashionable dram; but this soon grew out of use, as well as the custom of throwing away the lintseed cakes; which are now sold at a good price, and used with the utmost success in feeding cattle. The gentleman is now living, who first introduced stall-fed beef into the market of Perth. Before that time the greatest part of Scotland lived on salt meat throughout the winter, as the natives of the Hebrides do at present, and as the English did in the feudal times.[9] So far behind

---

[9] We admire the stock of provisions in the larder of the elder Spencer about the year 1327, when, as late as May, the carcasses of 80 salted beeves, 500 bacons, and 600 muttons were found, mere relics of his winter provisions. But in those days, there was no hay, no harvested food for domestic animals.

has North Britain been in the conveniences of life, and such rapid progress has it of late made towards attaining them.

The exports of wheat and barley are from twenty-four to thirty thousand bolls.

Considerable quantities of tallow, beeswax, dressed sheepskins, dressed and raw calfskins, and raw goatskins are shipped from this place.

The export of salmon to London and the Mediterranean brings in from twelve to fourteen thousand pounds. That fish is taken here in great abundance. Three thousand have been caught in one morning, weighing, one with another, sixteen pounds apiece; the whole capture being forty-eight thousand pounds. The fishery begins at St Andrew's Day, and ends August 26th, old style. The rents of the fisheries amount to three thousand pounds a year.

It is to no purpose to search for any remains of the monastic antiquities of this place; fanatic fury having in a few hours prostrated the magnificent works of mistaken piety. 'Pull down the nests, and the rooks will fly away', was the maxim of the rough apostle Knox, and his disciples took effectual care to put in execution the opinion of their master.

The Dominicans first felt the effect of their rage. After the conclusion of one of his sermons, inciting the demolition of images and church ornaments, an indiscreet priest began the celebration of mass. A boy in his zeal flung a stone and injured a picture: the populace took that as a signal to begin the demolition, and in a very short time plundered the monastery, and laid all in ruin. This house was founded in 1231 by Alexander II. In 1437 its walls were polluted by the execrable murder of James I, the best and most accomplished prince of the name. He had retired to this convent on the rumour of a conspiracy. The attack was made: the heroism of Catherine Douglas, an attendant on the Queen, must not be passed in silence. She ran and shut the door on the first alarm; but, missing the bar which should have secured it, substituted her tender arm in the place, which was instantly crushed to pieces by the efforts of the assassins.

The Observantines, a branch of the Franciscans, had here a monastery, founded by Lord Oliphant, in 1460. It underwent the same fate with the other. In it, say the writers on the Reformation, were found eight puncheons of salt beef, wine, beer, and plenty of other provisions, besides most excellent furniture, consisting of sheets, blankets, and beds; and yet there were only eight persons in the convent: from whence they drew an inference how ill the monks observed their vows of poverty and abstinence; never considering that the religious houses were the support of the poor, and the inns of the rich; and that their regular acts of charity and hospitality obliged them to keep these large stocks of provisions, without affording the means of applying them to the purposes of selfish luxury.

The rigid order of Carthusians founded a place here. James I, on his return from his English captivity, established a convent of them in 1429, as these monkish lines express:

> *Annus millenus vicenus sicque novenus*
> *Quadringentenus Scotis fert munera plenus:*
> *Semina florum, germina morum, mystica mella*
> *Cum tibi, Scotia, sit Carthusia, sponsa novella.*

The vicar of the *grand chartreuse* in Dauphiné was the first superior. On the Dissolution, James VI created George Hay, of Nethercliff, commendator of this priory, with the title of Lord, but finding the revenue too small to support the dignity, wisely resigned it into his Majesty's hands.

Leave Perth, and pass over the South Inch, a green beautifully planted. Keep ascending a hill for a considerable space, and enjoy a rich view of the Carse of Gowrie, and of the Firth of Tay, bounded by that fine tract on one side, and the county of Fife on the other. On passing the heights of this ascent, have a full view of Strathearn: Continue my way, for some time, on the fine terrace that runs along the northern side; and finish this day's journey at Dupplin, the seat of my noble friend the Earl of Kinnoull.

In the house are several very fine pictures: among others:

The adoration of the shepherds; the worshipping of the wise men in the east; and Diogenes remarking the boy drinking out of his hand; three capital pieces, by Paulo Panini. The figures uncommonly fine.

Two monks praying: heads. By Quintin Metsis.

A fine half length of St Jerome, half naked: a figure of intense devotion. His eyes lifted up, his mouth opening. By Lamanse.

A fine head of an old woman, looking over her shoulder, keen and meagre. By Honthurst.

Heads of Polembergh, the painter, and his wife. By Honthurst.

The head of Boon, a comic painter, playing on a lute. By himself.[10]

Head of Spenser, the poetic ornament of the reign of Elizabeth; the sweet, the melancholy, romantic bard of a romantic queen; the moral, romantic client of the moral romantic patron, Sir Philip Sydney; fated to pass his days in dependence, or in struggling against adverse fortune, in a country insensible to his merit: either at court

> To loose good days, that might be better spent,
> To waste long nights in pensive discontent;
> To speed to day, to be put back tomorrow,
> To feed with hope, to pine with fear and sorrow;
> To have his prince's grace, yet want her peers;
> To have his asking, yet wait many years;
> To fret his soul with crosses and with cares,
> To cut his heart with comfortless despair;
> To fawn, to crouch, to wait, to ride, to run;
> To spend, to give, to want, to be undone.[11]

Or in Ireland to be tantalized with the appearance of good fortune; to be seated amidst scenery indulgent to his fanciful muse; yet, at length, to be expelled by the barbarous Tyrone; to have his house burnt, and his innocent infant perish in the flames; to return home; to die in deep poverty; lamenting

> That gentler wits should breed
> Where thick-skin chuffes laugh at a scholler's need.[12]

May it not be imagined, that, in the anguish of his soul, he composed his *Cave of Despair*,[13] as fine a descriptive poem as any in our language? Might not his distress furnish him with too

---

[10] For an account of these three painters consult Mr Walpole's *Anecdotes*, Vol. II, 103, 110. Vol. III, 26.

[11] *Mother Hubbard's Tale*.

[12] Quoted in the *British Biography*.

[13] Book I, canto ix.

powerful arguments for suicide, had not his Una, or his innate religion, snatched him from the danger?

Another poet, equally neglected, but of too merry a turn to sink under any pressure, is the droll Butler, whose head, beautifully painted by Sir Peter Lely, is here also. This poet, instead of whining out his complaints to insensible majesty, rallies his monarch with the same pleasantry that he exposed the ridiculous characters in his immortal poem:

> *This prince, whose ready wit and parts*
> *Conquer'd both men and women's hearts,*
> *Was so o'ercome with knight and Ralph,*
> *That he cou'd never claw it off;*
> *He never eat, nor drank, nor slept,*
> *But Hudibras still near him kept;*
> *Nor wou'd he go to church, or so,*
> *But Hudibras must with him go;*
> *Nor yet to visit concubine,*
> *Or at a city feast to dine,*
> *But Hudibras must still be there,*
> *Or all the fat was in the fire.*
> *Now, after all, was it not hard*
> *That he should meet with no reward,*
> *That fitted out this knight and 'squire*
> *This monarch so much did admire?*
> *That he shou'd never reimburse*
> *The man for equipage and horse,*
> *Is sure a strange ungrateful thing*
> *In any body but a king.*
> *But this good king, it seems, was told*
> *By some that were with him too bold,*
> *'If e'er you hope to gain your ends,*
> *Caress your foes, and trust your friends.'*
> *Such were the doctrines that were taught,*
> *'Till this unthinking king was brought*
> *To leave his friends to starve or die;*
> *A poor reward for loyalty!*[14]

Mrs Tofts, in the character of St Catherine: a beautiful picture. Mrs Tofts lived at the very introduction of the opera into this kingdom, and sung in company with Nicolini; but, being ignorant of

---

[14] Butler's remains.

Italian, chanted her recitativo in English, in answer to his Italian: but the charms of their voices overcame this absurdity. Her character may be collected from the following epigram:

> So bright is thy beauty, so charming thy song
> As had drawn both the beasts and their Orpheus along;
> But such is thy av'rice, and such is thy pride,
> That the beasts must have starv'd, and the poet have dy'd.[15]

A head of Prince Rupert, by Lely, covered with a vast wig; the unfortunate mode for that great artist, stiff and ungraceful. Rupert, after a thousand actions, distinguished as much by their temerity as valour; after several battles won and lost by his excess of courage, at once disgraced himself by a panic. Accustomed to face an enemy in the field, and to act the part of the assailant; he seems to have lost all spirit when coped up within walls. He knew so little of himself that he promised his ill-fated uncle a four months defence of the important town of Bristol; but as soon as the attack was made, he sunk beneath it, and made an almost instant surrender. After he was commanded by Charles to quit the kingdom, he still attempted some naval services; but neither acquired fame or success. After the Restoration he recovered his former reputation; and in the naval engagement with the Dutch, to which all later battles have been but play, his temerity seemed to have been lost; but his courage and conduct shone with equal lustre. His active spirit never suffered him to rest even in the intervals of peace. Love and the arts were his relaxations. Miss Hughes, an actress, was the object of the first. Among the last, we owe to him the art of *mezzotinto* scraping. He invented a metal for great guns, and a method for boring them. He also taught the first Kirkby the art of giving the fine temper to fish-hooks.

Robert Harley, Earl of Oxford, in a gown and velvet cap. By Richardson.

A beautiful miniature of Sir John Earnly, Chancellor of the Exchequer in the reign of Charles II, and one of the commissioners of the treasury in that of James II on the displacing of Hyde, Earl of Rochester. By Cooper.

---

[15] She retired from England, and died at Venice, about twelve years ago.

A head of Sir Thomas Nicholson, Attorney General. By Jameson.

George Hay, first Earl of Kinnoull, and Chancellor of Scotland in 1622, who died in 1634. His dress a black robe furred; a ruff; a laced linen cap: the seals by him. A fine full length, painted in the year 1663. Aged 63. By Mytens.

His son, the second Earl, Captain of the Guards to Charles I, a tall upright figure, with great roses in his shoes; an active but unfortunate Royalist, continued in arms as late as the year 1654, when he was totally defeated, and made prisoner, by the usurping powers in Scotland.

Sir George Hay of Meginnis; full length, in armour. Done at Rome, 1649. By L. Ferdinand.

Below stairs, in one of the bedchambers, is a half-length portrait of the celebrated James Hay, Viscount Doncaster, and Earl of Carlisle, one of the most singular characters of the age. His engaging manner recommended him to the favour of James I, who first bestowed on him the title of Lord Hay, with rank next to our barons, but without privilege of sitting in the English Parliament. Soon after, without any patent, or external ceremony, but by his mere royal fiat, before witnesses in the privy chamber, at Greenwich, he conferred on him the honour of an English peerage; and this the lawyers held to be equally valid with any formal vestiture.[16]

His Majesty then procured him the sole daughter and heiress of Lord Denny, the greatest match of that time: and never ceased heaping on him honour, favours and riches, which he seems not to have coveted for any other end than to indulge his violent passion for dress, luxury and magnificence. He was a man of the greatest expense, and introduced more excess in clothes and diet than any other that ever lived;[17] and was the inventor of all those expensive fashions from which others did but transcribe their copies. His dress in the portrait at Dupplin is an exception; being black-slashed, and puffed with white; his hair short and curled; his beard peaked: but when he made his public entry into Paris as ambassador, his cloak and hose were of white beaver, richly embroidered with gold and

---

[16] Camden's *Annals*, 1615.
[17] Clarendon I, 62.

VIII

Aliamet Sculp.

James Hay Earl of Carlisle

silver. His cloak had no other lining than embroidery, the doublet cloth of gold richly worked, and his white beaver hat brimful of embroidery. His horse was shod with silver shoes, slightly tacked on, so that every curvet flung off one to be scrambled for by the populace; and that was instantly replaced by a farrier, who attended for the purpose.[18]

Sumptuous as his apparel was on this occasion, it fell short of the dress in which he and the Earl of Holland appeared when they espoused, by proxy, Henrietta Maria; for they received her, clad in beaten silver. They certainly did not consult the Graces in this stiffness of splendour.

In his embassy into Germany the same pomp followed him. At The Hague he met with his contrast in the frugal Maurice, Prince of Orange; who being told he ought to give an entertainment to the great English ambassador, 'Let him come,' says his Highness; and looking over his simple bill of fare, seeing only one pig, ordered a couple,[19] by way of making the treat more sumptuous, nor could he be prevailed on to alter it. What a feast was this to him, who seemed to have realized the entertainments of Sir Epicure Mammon, who used to have the board covered, at the entrance of his guests, with dishes as high as a tall man could reach, filled with the greatest delicacies; and, after they had feasted their eyes, would cause them to be removed for a fresh service; who once permitted one person to carry off in his cloak-bag forty pounds worth of sweetmeats; another to eat a pie composed of ambergris, musk and magisterial of pearl.[20] It is not surprising that with all these extravagancies he wasted above four hundred thousand pounds; nor that his generosity, attended with uncommon affability and gracefulness of manners, and with a great and universal understanding, should rivet him in the affection and esteem of the whole English nation. But that with the luxury of an Apicus, he could mingle the honest sentiments of a Clarendon in his advice to his prince;[21] and that

[18] Wilson, 92, 93.
[19] Wilson, 154.
[20] Lloyd II, 62.
[21] *Cabbala*, as quoted in Drake's *Parliamentary History* V, 530.

he dared to deliver to his opiniative master disagreeable truths, and unpalatable counsels, are facts more astonishing than any of his wasteful fooleries. To conclude, he finished his life in 1636; and quitted the stage *conviva satur*,[22] dying, as the noble historian observes, with as much tranquillity of mind to all appearance, as used to attend a man of the most severe exercise of virtue; and with as little apprehension of death, which he expected many days.

In this apartment is a half-length of his son and successor to the title; but in the dining-room is a full-length of the same, a most beautiful portrait, by Cornelius Jansen. It is difficult to say which is most elegant, the person or the dress of this young nobleman, for it is drawn at an early period of life: all his father's fancy seems exerted in the habit, beset with loops and buttons: a lovelock graces one side of his neck: one hand is on his staff of office, the other on his side. His history is but brief. He married Margaret, daughter of Francis, fourth Earl of Bedford; was appointed Captain of the Yeomen of Guard to Charles I, and for taking an active part in putting the commission of array in execution, in the county of Essex, was by the Parliament sent to the Tower. In 1643 he appears among the nobility, who signed the letter at Oxford to the popular general; but soon after deserted the royal cause, and took the oath appointed by Parliament for those who flung themselves under its protection.[23] At length, distressed in his circumstances, he retired to Barbados,[24] an island granted to his father; and died in 1660.

But the most remarkable head is that of the celebrated Catherine, Countess of Desmond. She lived to the age of some years above a hundred and forty, and died in the reign of James I. Sir Walter Raleigh speaks of her marriage as a fact well known to all the noblemen and gentlemen of Munster.[25] He gives us room to think

---

[22] Old Osborn, vol. I, 157, makes him die like a blasphemous lunatic; for when his own weakness had passed a judgment, that he could not live many days, he did not forbear his entertainments, but made divers brave cloaths, as he said, 'to outface naked and despicable death withal', saying that 'Nature wanted wisdom, love or power, in making man mortal and subject to deseases'.

[23] Whitelock, 83, 145.

[24] *Staggering State,* etc., 151.

[25] *Hist. of the World,* Book I. ch. V, sect. v, 66.

that she died before the publication of his history, which was in the year 1614. Supposing then her Ladyship's age to have been a hundred and fifty at the time of her death, she might have danced in the court of King Edward, at the age of nineteen, a blooming widow; that prince not dying till 1483.

This lady was a most popular subject with the painters: besides this at Dupplin, there are not fewer than four others in Great Britain, in the same dress, and without any difference of feature. The most ancient is on board, in a bedchamber at Devonshire House, with her name and age (140) inscribed. The Hon. John Yorke has another, at his seat near Cheltenham. There is a fourth in possession of Mr Scott, printer, in Chancery Lane. And the fifth is in the standard closet in Windsor Castle. The last was a present from Sir Robert Car, Earl of Roxburgh, as is signified on the back; above that is written, with a pen, Rembrandt, which must be a mistake, for Rembrandt was not fourteen years of age in 1614, at which time it is certain that the countess was not living.[26] The picture at Dupplin, which is much in the manner of that celebrated painter, is probably a copy done by him after some original he might have met with in his own country, for it does not appear he ever visited England.

Take the earliest opportunity of paying my respects to Mr Oliphant, post-master general, at his seat of Rossie, a few miles from Dupplin. I am in a particular manner indebted to this gentleman for the liberal concern he took in my journey, by directing, that all my correspondences relating to it should be freed, and forwarded to me. A true instance of national politeness; and a peculiar honour done to myself.

In my road cross the Earn, and pass by the church of Fort Teviot, once the site of a Pictish palace, where Kenneth II departed this life,[27] and where Malcolm Canmore is said to have resided. Near this place, a little to the west, are the vestiges of a camp, occupied by Edward Baliol, immediately before the battle of Dupplin, in August 1332. Donald, Earl of Marr, regent in the minority of David II lay encamped on the hill, at no great distance from Dupplin House. By an unhappy

[26] Grainger's *Biogr.*, Vol. III, 164.
[27] Guthrie I, 156.

but common disagreement in feudal times, the other part of his forces were separated under the Earl of Dunbar, at Auchterauder, a few miles distant. This had determined Marr to stand on the defensive till he could be joined by the former: but Baliol crossing the river in the night, and beginning his attack, he was induced partly by that, partly by the reproach of timidity from the Earl of Carrick, to suffer his prudence to give way to rashness, and to renew the fight with Baliol, supported by the English archers, the best troops then in Europe. A horrible carnage ensued: three thousand Scots fell on the spot, among whom were the flower of nobility; with no farther loss to the enemy than two knights, and thirty-three squires, without that of one common man. The day was particularly fatal to the Hays. Historians relate, that the name would have been extinct, had not several of the warriors left their wives pregnant. We may be permitted to qualify this, by supposing, as seems to have been the case, that the line of the chieftain would have failed but for such an accident, a posthumous child preserving the race.

Determine on a little journey up Strathearn, and to the head of the river, at the loch of the same name. At a small distance from Dupplin, at the top of the hill, first meet with the Roman road, twenty-four feet broad, formed with great stones, and visible in many places. It continues one way by Tibbirmoor to Bertha, and from thence over the Tay, near Perth; and to the west passes a little to the north of the castle of Innerpeffery, and is continued on the other side of the river, where it falls into the camp at Strageth, and from thence to that at Ardoch. Mr Maitland seems to have traced the Roman roads and camps of North Britain with great industry, and to have discovered many that were never before observed. It was my ill fortune not to meet with his book till I had in a manner quitted the classical ground, therefore must refer the reader to his first volume of the History of Scotland for an account of these curious remains.

Proceed west. Pass by the great plantations at Gask Hall: in these woods is a small circular entrenchment; and about half a mile farther, on Gask Moor, is another, whose ditch is eleven feet wide; the area within the bank, fifty-six in diameter; and between this and Innerpeffery are two others, similar, placed so near, that everything that stirred beneath, or at a certain distance around, could be seen; having probably been the site of little observatory forts, subservient to the stations established by Agricola, on his conquest of this country.

Reach the village of Innerpeffery. At this place is a good room, with a library, for the use of the neighbourhood, founded by David, Lord Madderty, which still receives new supplies of books. Just beneath, cross the Earn, in a ferryboat, and turning to the left, visit the Roman camp at Strageth: much of it is now defaced with the plough; but many of the vast fosses and ramparts are to be seen in several parts; also the rows of fosses and ramparts facing the exterior south-west side. According to Mr Gordon, who caused it to be surveyed and engraved, the length is ninety-five paces, the breadth near eighty.

Breakfast at Mr Keir's, agent to the forfeited estate of the Duke of Perth. The ground here is fertile, and about this place (Muthel) is well cultivated; the land is manured with grey marl, filled with river shells, though lodged eight feet beneath the surface; and turnips and cabbages are raised to feed the cattle; an example, if followed, of the first importance to the country.

Proceed along the military road towards Crief. See, on the road side, a row of neat small houses, intended for quiet retreats for disbanded soldiery; but, as usual, deserted by the colonists. This seems to have been the only Utopian project of the commissioners appointed by his Majesty for the management of the forfeited estates unalienably annexed to the crown, by the act of the twenty-fifth of George II. But, as these gentlemen, with rare patriotism discharge their trust without salary, they ought not to be liable to censure, like hireling placemen, on every trifling failure.

The service that this board has been of to North Britain is so considerable, that it merits a little farther attention than I have hitherto paid it. First, I must premise that the gross rent of these estates amounts to about eight thousand pounds; but after paying certain annuities to the widows of attainted persons, ministers stipends, and other public demands, the salaries of agents, and other necessary officers, the clear residue, which comes into the hands of the receiver-general, amounts to little more than £5,000.

The application of this money has proved a great benefit to the country: out of it is paid annually two hundred pounds to schoolmasters stationed in many remote parts of the Highlands. The like sum annually for the purpose of bringing up the sons of the poorer tenants to useful trades, such as blacksmiths, cartwrights, coopers, weavers, flax-dressers, etc. who, besides the expense of their education, are furnished with a set of tools, and a reasonable aid towards enabling them to pursue their respective trades, when they return to settle in their own country.

The commissioners often send the sons of some of the better sort of tenants, into the Lowlands, and some into England, to be taught the best sort of farming. They encourage artificers to settle on the annexed estates, by affording them proper accommodation, and bestowing on them seasonable aids. They have from time to time expended large sums for the purpose of introducing and establishing the linen and the woollen manufactures, and for promoting fisheries in the Highlands; for making highways, and erecting bridges within the annexed estates, and countries adjacent. In particular, they bestowed, under sanction of his Majesty's permission, an aid of eleven thousand pounds, towards building a bridge over the Tay at Perth; a noble work, and of great national utility.

They have caused large tracts of barren and uncultivated grounds on different parts of the estates to be enclosed, and planted with oaks, firs, and other trees, now in a very prosperous condition; and which will in time be of considerable value. They allow certain sums to tenants, for enclosing their farms, free of interest for three years, after which they are to pay five per cent advance in their rent. They employ skilful persons to make trials for discovery of mines and minerals, of medical and other useful indigenous plants. They lend their aid to every undertaking of public utility, that comes within the intent of the act, and constantly keep in view and hope to accomplish the great objects of it; 'the civilizing of the inhabitants of the annexed estates, the promoting among them the protestant religion, good government, industry, manufactures, and the principles of loyalty to the present royal line'.

Soon after leaving these houses, the unfortunate proofs of their good intentions, observe, on the right and left, two great rocks, called Concraig, running east and west for a vast way; their fronts steep, and perfectly smooth and even, so as to be easily mistaken for a wall. Go over the bridge of Crief, and pass through the town. It is pleasantly seated on the side of a hill, and tolerably well-built. It possesses a small share of the coarse linen manufacture.

Turn to the north-west, and have in front a fine view of the serpentine Earn, and numbers of little hills tufted with trees, and backed by immense rugged mountains.

Pass by Auchtertyre, the seat of Sir William Murray, situated on a hill, sprinkled over with good oaks, and commanding a most elegant view. The pretty Loch Monivard lies beneath, whose bottom yields a quantity of excellent marl, which is dragged up for a manure. The church of the same name lies at a small distance from it. About the year 1511, this place was a horrid scene of feudal revenge. Walter Murray, Abbot of Inchaffray, having a claim on the tythes of this parish, then the property of the Drummonds, rode the boundaries in a manner that was interpreted by them insulting and tumultuous. They were determined to repel the abbot and his party, and at the instant were accidentally joined by an ally, the captain of Dunstaffage, who was likewise on an errand of revenging the murders of some Drummonds by certain of the name of Murray. The abbot fearing to be overpowered, took sanctuary in the church: when a shot from one of his party slew a follower of Dunstaffage, who took instant and cruel vengeance, by burning the place and all that had retired into it.

Pass by Lars, a seat of Colonel Campbell, agreeably placed amidst woods. Go through the village of Comerie, near which are four great stones, erect, and placed so as to form a square. They appear to me the portal of a Druidical temple, or place of worship, now destroyed, and that it was meant to dignify the entrance, and inspire the votaries with greater reverence, as if it was the place of peculiar sanctity. The curious, by consulting p. 187, and tab. xv. of the learned Borlase's *Antiquities*, may find a complete history of what these stones form only a part.

The valley begins now to grow very narrow, being continually intersected by small but beautiful hills, mostly clothed with woods, which occasion every half mile or less an agreeable change of scene; new valleys succeed, or little plains beyond plains, watered by the Earn, here limpid and rapid; frequently to be crossed on genuine Alpine bridges, supported by rude bodies of trees; over them others covered with boughs, well gravelled over. The higher we advanced the more picturesque the scenes grew: the little hills that before intersected the vales, now changed into great insulated rocks, some naked, others clothed with trees. We wound about their bases frequently through groves of small oaks, or by the side of the river, with continued views of the vast rugged Grampians on each hand, soaring far above this romantic scenery. Some little corn and grass filled the small plains where there was space free from trees. The last was now in harvest; but so short, that the peasants were obliged to kneel to cut it with a sickle. Their industry went so far as to induce them to cut it even among the bushes, and carry it into open places for the benefit of drying it in the free air.

At once arrive in sight of Loch Earn, a fine extent of water, about eight miles long and one broad; filling the whole vale. A pretty isle tufted with trees divides the lake at this end. The boundaries are the vast and rugged mountains, whose wooded bases bound the margin, and very rarely give any opportunity of cultivation. A fine road through woods impends over one side, and is a ride of uncommon beauty. The great rocks that lay above us guarding the lands of Glen Karken, are most wild and picturesque; for a while bend inwards, then soar precipitous, presenting a wooded front, overtopped with naked rocks, opening in parts to give a view of cornfields and farm houses, at a dreadful height above us.

This lake is the termination of Strathearn towards the north-west; and gives name to the river which gives name to the valley. The word is originally derived from the Celtic, *eryn*, or *heryn*, 'the west', as the river runs from that quarter. The Romans adopted it; and Claudian in particular speaks of this country, when celebrating the victories of the elder Theodosius:

> *maduerunt Saxone fuso*
> *Orcades: incaluit Pictorum sanguine Thule:*
> *Scotorum cumulos flevit glacialis Ierne.*[28]

> *The Orkneys first he dyed with Saxon gore,*
> *Then Thule with the Pictish blood grew hot:*
> *Icy Strathern bemoan'd huge heaps of Scots.*

---

[28] *De IV Cons. Honorii.*, lin. 31.

Return and dine at Comerie. Near this place, on a plain of some extent, is the famous camp which Mr Gordon contends to have been occupied by Agricola, immediately before the battle of Mons Grampius; and to which, in order to support his argument, he gives the name of Galgachan, as if derived from Galgacus, leader of the Caledonians, at that fatal engagement. This camp lies between the river of Earn and the little stream called the Ruchel: and on a plain too contracted for such a number of combatants, as Tacitus says there was, to form and to act in, or for their charioteers or cavalry to scour the field. There are indeed small hills at the foot of the greater, where the British forces might have ranged themselves before the battle; but the distance from the sea is an insuperable argument against this being the spot, as we are expressly informed that Agricola sent his fleet before, in order to distract and divide the attention of the enemy, and that he himself marched with his army till he arrived at the Grampian mountain, where he found Galgacus encamped. From the whole account given by Tacitus, it should be supposed, that action was fought in an open country, at the foot of certain hills, not in a little plain amidst defiles, as the valleys about Comerie consist of. A conjecture may be made hereafter concerning the spot where the Grampian victory was obtained. The battle which was fought here, might have been that occasioned by the attack of the Caledonians, on the ninth legion. Classical authority informs us, that, in the general insurrection of that gallant people in the sixth year of Agricola's command, he divided his army into three parts; one might be at Ardoch; the other at Strageth; the third or the ninth legion might be sent to push up the defiles of Comerie, in order to prevent the enemy from surrounding him, or taking advantage of their knowledge of the country, or his inferiority of numbers.[29] His three divisions lay so near, as to enable them to assist each other in case of an attack.

The Caledonian naturally directed their force against the weakest of the three armies, the ninth legion, which probably had not fully recovered the loss it sustained in the bloody attack by Boadicia.[30]

---

[29] *Ne superante numero et peritia locorum circumiretur, diviso, et ipse in tres partes exercitu incessit. Vita Agricolæ.*

[30] *Taciti Annalia,* lib. XIV, ch. 32.

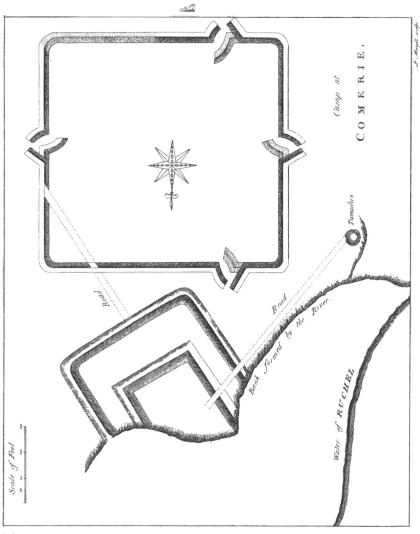

Scale of Feet

Road

Road

Bank formed by the River.

Water of RUCHEL

Tumulus

Camp at
COMERIE.

IX

J. Royde sculp.

The camp also was weak, being no more than a common one, such as the Romans flung up on their march. It has no appearance of ever having been stative; and it is probable that as soon as Agricola had, by an expeditious march, relieved this part of his army out of a difficulty they were fairly involved in, he deserted the place; and never hazarded his troops again amidst the narrows of this hostile country. Weapons, and other instruments, have been discovered on the spot, in the course of the forming the roads through this pass. A brazen spur, iron bands, a sort of iron hammer, and a most curious small iron battleaxe, or rather pickaxe, have been met with: which are evidences of a conflict on this spot.

The camp, notwithstanding it could not boast of any great strength, is beautifully designed. The four entrances are entire, guarded by curtains within and without; but there are no vestiges of the praetorium, which confirms my suspicion that the attack was begun before all the usual works were completed. On the north side of this is another square entrenchment, joined to this by a regular communication. One side had been bounded by the Ruchel; but at present that little stream has removed itself to some distance. Within this entrenchment, is another: I cannot help thinking that these works were intended as a stationary fort; it having the situation that the Romans consulted, that of a river on one side; but that it was left unfinished for the same reason that the camp was. The size of the camp is about nine hundred and seventy-five feet, by nine hundred. There are some particularities about this place worthy to be mentioned; such as the multitude of oblong hollows that lie parallel, and divided from one another by banks three feet wide, which are to be seen just on the outside of the northern agger of the camp. These seem to have been places for dressing the provisions for the soldiery, not places of interment, as was suspected; for Mr MacNab, schoolmaster of Comerie, at my request, was so obliging as to cause several of these holes to be dug through, and informed me that nothing but large quantities of wood-charcoal was to be found, the culinary fuel; and not the least trace of urn or human bones were met with to countenance the other opinion. Besides these are two remains of antiquities, both monumental. The one British, a vast upright stone, near the edge of the camp: perhaps erected, after the retreat of the Romans, by the Caledonians, over some chieftain slain in the fight. The other a vast tumulus, which probably covered the slain. This was a Roman tribute to the memory of their unfortunate countrymen. Germanicus performed such exequies over the remains of the legions of Varus in Germany, and carried the first sod to the heap. '*Primum exstruendo tumulo cespitem Caesar posuit, grasissimo munere in defunctos, et praesentibus doloris fociis.*'[31]

Visit Castle Drummond, seated boldly on a side of a hill, amidst a fine extent of woods, commanding a great view down Strathearn. The house is very unequal to the situation, being both mean and small; nor is it of any great antiquity. On the back part are some remains of the old castle, built by Sir John Drummond, hereditary steward of Strathearn, in 1493, after removing from the ancient seat of the family at Stobhall. The family derive themselves from Mauritz, an Hungarian of royal blood, who having the conduct of the mother and sisters of Edgar Atheling, in their flight from the Norman usurper, was (with his royal charge) driven by a storm into the Firth of Forth. The reigning monarch Malcolm Canmore fell in love with, and married the Princess Margaret, one of the sisters; and, in reward to Mauritz, for his skilful pilotage, made him a considerable grant of lands, and caused him to assume the name of Drymen, or 'the high ridge'; but, figuratively, the great wave of the sea, in memory of the perils from which he had delivered the fair queen.

The castle was besieged immediately after the cruel burning of the church of Monivard; the chieftain and his followers having retired thither to screen themselves from their merited punishment. It soon surrendered to the King, James IV, on condition that their lives should be preserved; but as soon as that Prince got them in his power, he carried them to Sterling, where they suffered death for their impious barbarity. It was afterwards besieged, taken and garrisoned by Cromwell's forces: and finally, at the revolution, totally demolished. The ruin of the family was completed in 1745, when the Duke of Perth, by an unfortunate attachment, forfeited

---

[31] *Taciti Ann.*, lib. I, ch. 62.

the ancient estate, to the amount of four thousand a year; and lost his life, worn out with the fatigues of the winter's campaign.

Continue my ride southerly. See, on the top of a moor about four miles from Castle Drummond, a small but strong exploratory fort, called Kemp, or, more properly, Camp Castle. The area is seventy-six feet by sixty-four, and is defended by three deep ditches. This seems to have been a place of observation subservient to that of Ardoch, two miles distant. The Roman way, which is continued from the camp at Strageth, passes by this fort, and leads me to the next. On each side are to be observed multitudes of holes, mostly of a round form, whose use I cannot conjecture. Pass through a small glen, or rather a deep hollow, which crosses the road, and see a deep and oblong trench, perhaps made as a lodgement for a small party to defend this part. A little farther, on a line with this, is a small round area, like those on Gaskmoor, but considerably stronger, being surrounded by not fewer than three fosses. Not remote from this, on the front of a deep dell, is a regular lunette, with a very strong fosse; and near that, again, another round fort, defended by two ditches.

From this lunette is a great fosse, which passes half a mile wide of Ardoch, and, as I was informed, fell into the water of Kneck, at two miles distance from its origin.

I am now in the midst of classical ground; the busy scene of action in the third year of Agricola's expeditions. Through this valley he led his troops, when he carried the terror of his arms as far as the Tay; when he passed unmolested through new-discovered nations, with the elements warring against him.[32] Here, after all the difficulties he met with in conducting his forces through the forests, and wading through estuaries first tried by himself;[33] he found an ample space for erecting of fortresses, and establishing of stations.[34] Of these, Ardoch forms the first and chief, seated at the head of two vales, and commanding a view into each: into the

[32] *Tertius expeditionum annus novas gentes aperuit, vastatis usque ad Taum (ae'stuario nomen est) nationibus, qua formidine territi hostes, quanquam conflictatum sae'vis tempestatibus, exercitum lacessere non ausi.*

[33] *Æstuaria ac sylvas ipse prae'tentare.*

[34] *Ponendisque insuper castellis spatium fuit.*

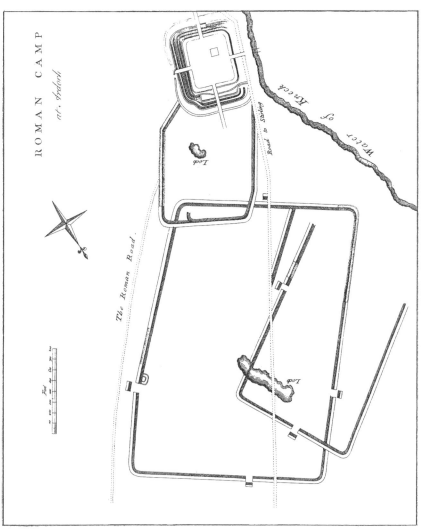

ROMAN CAMP

at Ardoch

The Roman Road.

Road to Stirling

Loch

Loch

Water of Knaick

X

fertile Strathallan, which leads to Sterling, the probable route of Agricola; and into the Glacialis Ierne, the present Strathearn, an open tract, which, under the common name of Strathmore, gave full space for the operations of this celebrated leader.

As this stationary camp was the most important, so it was secured with greater strength and artifice than any of the rest. No general ever equalled him in the judicious choice of situation: no camp he made was ever taken by storm, or obliged to surrender, or to be deserted.[35] This he fixed on an elevated situation, with one side on the steep bank of the little river of Kneck, and being fortified on that part by nature, he thought fit to give it there the security of only a single fosse. The other three have five, if not six, fosses, of a vast depth, with ramparts of correspondent heights between. The works on the south side are much injured by the plough; the others, in fine preservation. In the area is the praetorium, or the quarter of the general, in a tolerable perfect state. The area is four hundred and fifty feet, by four hundred. The four *portae*, or entrances, are plainly to be distinguished; and the road from the praetorian port to the praetorium, very visible. This station was of force sufficient to baffle any siege from a barbarian enemy: this was one of those that he made a winter garrison during the remaining time of his command in the country; and by laying in a year's magazines of provisions, freed the soldiers from all apprehensions of a blockade,[36] and enabled them to make frequent sallies.

To the north of this fortress are the outlines of three enclosures, surrounded, if I recollect right, by only single ramparts. They are the works of different periods; or perhaps might have been the summer camps to this station; or they might have been the *procestria* to the place, a sort of freetowns, built and enclosed with slight entrenchments, under the cover of the fort, which might be styled their citadel. The first is contiguous to it, and receives into the west side the Roman road. The measurements of the area are a thousand and eighty feet by eight hundred and forty. The *portae* are quite filled up.

---

[35] *Adnotabant periti, non alium ducem opportunitates locorum sapientius legisse; nullum ab Agricola positum castellum aut vi hostium expugnatum, aut pactione aut fuga desertum.*

[36] *Crebrae eruptiones; nam adversus moras obsidionis, annuis copiis firmabantur.*

Another very large one lies north of this, and part of the south, and even trespasses on, and takes in, a small portion of it. The four entrances are very visible, and each has, by way of defence, opposite to it, on the outside, a short rampart. The dimensions of this are two thousand six hundred feet, by sixteen hundred and seventy. The present road to Sterling run through the midst of this.

A third, which seems never to have been completed, breaks in on one side of the greater; it points towards the Kneck, and either never reached that water, or has been on that side totally defaced.

Many antiquities have been found about this station, such as bits of bridles, spear-heads, and armour, which are deposited at Ardoch House, the seat of Sir William Stirling, where they remained till the year 1715, when they were carried away by the soldiers. Since that time a very curious sepulchral monument has been discovered there, and presented to the college at Glasgow. It is inscribed thus:

DIS MANIBUS AMMONIUS. DAMIONIS COH. I.
HISPANORUM STIPENDIORUM XXVII. HEREDES F.C.

This is engraven in the XVth plate of the College Antiquities, and mentioned by Mr Horsley among the Scottish monuments. Sir William Stirling did me the honour of informing me, that several coins have been found there, but now dispersed; and that there is in his possession an urn, filled with ashes, a fragment of the unburnt skull, and a piece of money. The last had, in all probability, been put into the mouth of the deceased as the fare of Charon, for wafting him over Styx.

I must not omit, that opposite to Ardoch, on the other side of the Kneck, is a place called the Keir. Here, says Mr Gordon (for I did not visit it) are a great many circumvallations and ramparts of stone and earth; and regular terraces descending on the side of the hill. In Wales we have many British posts that bear the general name of *caer*; and had I time to have examined it, I should doubtless have found it to have been one.

Nor must I leave this place without observing, that from its ramparts is to be seen the plain of Sheriffmoor, where the ill-disputed battle of Dunblain was fought in 1715. The Earl of Mar lay with his army the evening before at Ardoch.

On leaving this fine relic of antiquity, proceed down Strathearn. Pass by a stupendous cairn. Cross an extensive black moor, and soon after reach Tullibardine,[37] a great old house, the original seat of the Murrays, and which gave the title of marquis to the heir of Athol. In 1715 it was made a garrison by the rebels; and for some time impeded the advance of the king's army towards Perth. Before the house, according to honest Lindsay, was shown the length and breadth of the great ship, the *Great Michael*, built by James IV, and described by his historian with most scrupulous minuteness.[38] The dimensions, says he, were expressed here by the shipwrights, by a plantation of hawthorns, which I looked for, but in vain.

Near the house is the very neat case of a small church; but the inside is quite ruinous.

Draw near the Ochil Hills, verdant and smooth; see at a small distance, at their foot, Kincardine, an ancient seat of the Montrose family. To the left is the small town of Auchterardire, which, with Muthel, Blackford, Dinin, and several other villages, were burnt

[37] From *tulloch*, 'a hillock', and *bardin*, 'bards'; this place being supposed to have been appropriated to the support of a bard. In old times districts were allotted be the great men for their support, which often became hereditary in their families. Dr Macpherson, 218.

[38] *In this same year the king of Scotland bigged a great ship, called the Great Michael, which was the greatest ship, and of most strength, that ever sailed in England or France; for this ship was of so great stature, and took so much timber, that, except Falkland, she wasted all the woods in Fife, which was oak wood, by all timber that was gotten out of Norroway: for she was so strong, and of so great length and breadth (all the wrights of Scotland, yea and many other strangers, were at her device, by the king's commandment, who wrought very busily in her, but it was year and day ere she was complete). To wit. She was twelve score foot of length, and thirty-six foot within the sides; she was ten foot thick in the wall, and boards on every side, so stack and so thick that no cannon could go through her. This great ship cumbered Scotland to get her to the sea. From that time that she was afloat, and her masts and sails complete, with tows and anchors offering thereto, she was counted to the king to be thirty thousand pounds of expences, by her artillery which was very great and costly to the king by all the rest of her orders. To wit. She bare many canons, six on every side, with three great bassils, two behind in her dock, and one before, with three hundred shot of small artillery, that is to say, myand and battered falcon, and quarter-falcon, slings, pestilent serpents, and double-dogs, with hagtor and culvering, corsbows and hand-bows. She had three hundred mariners to sail her; she had six score of gunners to use her artillery; and had a thousand men of war by her captains, shippers, and quarter-masters.*

by an order of the Pretender, dated from his court at Scone, the 17th of January, and the fifteenth year of his reign, 1715–1716. This cruel command was executed in a most uncommonly severe season; and the poor inhabitants of every age and sex left exposed to the rigour of the cold. To palliate these proceedings, the necessity of obstructing the march of the king's forces towards Perth, was pleaded: and that the Pretender, on his flight from that city, left in the hands of General Gordon, for the use of the sufferers, a large sum of money, with a letter to the Duke of Argyle, requesting a proper distribution.

Go through Dinin, and reach Dupplin at night.

Ride to see the ruins of a great cairn on the roadside, about a mile north of Dupplin, which had been lately demolished. On removing the stones, were discovered at the bottom a great number of chests, whose dimensions were two feet eight by two feet two, every one consisting of five flags; forming four sides and a lid. In all excepting one were bones, and mixed with them in some of the chests were round perforated bodies, which I suspect to have been Druidical beads; there were besides numbers of rings, heart-shaped trinkets, and others of a flat and oblong form, all made of a coarse glass.

At a small distance from this place is the plain of Tibbirmoor, where the Marquis of Montrose gained a signal victory over the Covenanters, with an inferior army of half-armed Highlanders and Irish. 'If ever God spake word of truth out of my mouth,' says one of the enthusiastic divines to his friends, 'I promise you in his name assured victory this day': but he was possessed with a lying spirit; for two thousand of their flock fell in the field, and two thousand more were taken prisoners. Tradition records a barbarous superstition of the Irish troops, who that morning put to death an innocent herdsman, they happened to meet, from the notion that victory would declare itself for the party which first drew blood.

Reach the church of Tibbirmoor, which takes its name from a holy well, dedicated to the Virgin Mary. This parish was sometime the residence of the Bishop of Dunkeld. Bishop Galfred died here in 1249; and Bishop Sinclair in 1337.[39] The last rebuilt and restored

---

[39] Mills's *Lives of the Bishops of Dunkeld*, MS.

the church of St Serf, on the north side of the water of Almond, once the chief of this parish; but, as report goes, was afterwards deserted on account of a child of Lord Ruthven's being drowned in the river, in returning from being baptised.

Below the minister's house is a rhomboid entrenchment, called the Ward: but there is not the least tradition about the design of it. A little farther is a high copped tumulus or mount, styled the Round Law, or Court Hill, such places being in these parts generally supposed to have been the seats of justice.

At a small distance from hence arrive at the high banks above the River Almond, which here waters the plain that extends to Perth, and falls into the Tay, about a mile above that city. Near this place was seated the ancient Bertha, which Boethius asserts had been the residence of the Scottish kings. Here, says he, Kenneth exercised severe justice on the great banditti.[40] This place, says Buchanan,[41] was besieged by the Danes before the battle of Loncarty; and this place, says Boethius,[42] was totally destroyed by a flood in 1210, and the city rebuilt on the spot where the present Perth stands. Notwithstanding we must deny that fact;[43] yet there are not wanting evidences of Bertha having once been of considerable note. The tide of the Tay, in former times, reached this place, an anchor has been found here; and, as I have been told, that on digging, are to be found almost everywhere old walls, vaults and causeways, far beneath the present surface of the ground. The Romans had a station on its banks, which their road pointed to: and still the falls of the cliffs produce many proofs of the truth of the assertion. About eight years ago, by the lapse of a great piece of land, was discovered great quantities of excellent iron, in short thick bars, from one to two feet in length, as if it had been cut for the conveniency of retailing.

Other falls have produced discoveries still more singular, and have layed open a species of interment, as far as I know, hitherto unnoticed. Some years ago, in the face of a broken bank, were

[40] Lib. XI, 227.
[41] Lib. VI, ch. 31.
[42] Lib. XIII, 278.
[43] See p. 43.

discovered, six pillars in a line, ten feet distance from one another, and eighteen feet high from the top of the ground to the bed of the Almond, showing out of the bank a semicircular face. These proved to have been the contents of certain cylindrical pits, sunk in the earth as places of sepulture. The urns were placed in them, and the hollows filled with earth of a different kind from the banks, and so strongly rammed in, as to remain coherent, after the former had in part been washed away. The Rev Mr Duff has described these hollows in a manner somewhat different, comparing them to the segments of a cone, with the broader part downwards; and to have been filled with bones, ashes, and fragments of urns. These funebrious vessels have been found here of different sizes; one of very uncommon dimensions as well as materials; being of fine clay only half an inch thick; and entirely plated in the inside with brass. It was capable of containing ten gallons; and was filled with ashes. Other urns of a small size have been met with in these pits; one held some wood ashes, and part of a *lacrymatory*; an evidence of the nation they belonged to. So that if we may rely on the map of Richard of Cirencester, this place might have been the Orrea of the Romans.

A mile farther, on the plain, is the ancient house of Ruthven; once the seat of the unfortunate Gowries. It consists of two square towers, built at different times; and distinct from each other; but now joined by buildings of later date. The top of one of the towers is called the Maiden's Leap, receiving its name on the following occasion: a daughter of the first Earl of Gowrie was addressed by a young gentleman of inferior rank in the neighbourhood, a frequent visitor of the family, who never would give the least countenance to his passion. His lodging was in the tower, separate from that of his mistress:

Sed vetuere patres quod non potuere vetare.

The lady, before the doors were shut, conveyed herself into her lover's apartment; but some prying Duenna acquainted the Countess with it; who cutting off, as she thought, all possibility of retreat, hastened to surprise them. The young lady's ears were quick; she heard the footsteps of the old Countess, ran to the top of the leads, and took the desperate leap of nine feet four inches over a chasm of sixty feet, and luckily lighting on the battlements of the other tower, crept into her own bed, where her astonished mother found her, and of course apologised for the unjust suspicion. The fair daughter did not choose to repeat the leap; but the next night eloped, and was married.

But this place was the scene of more serious transactions, which laid the foundation of a resentment that proved fatal to its noble master. Here was executed the generous design of freeing James VI from his worthless favourites, who were poisoning his youth with exalted notions of royal prerogative; and instilling into him those principles which, in after times, proved so destructive to his progeny. Gowrie, with numbers of other peers, inveigled James into this castle, in the year 1582, on his return from a hunting match in Athol. When he was about to depart, he was stopped by the nobles in a body, who presented him with a memorial against the ill conduct of his principal favourites. He endeavoured to free himself from restraint, but was prevented; and upon his bursting into tears, was told by the guardian of Glames, that it was 'better children weep than bearded men'. This was called 'the Raid of Ruthven'. The conspirators carried him off; but on his escape he again resigned himself to Arran, a favourite void of every species of virtue, and even after an act of oblivion, declared them guilty of high treason, and actually put Gowrie to death at Sterling, after a trial injurious to his Majesty's honour.

After the doubtful conspiracy of the two sons of this unfortunate nobleman at Perth, and after their deaths, and posthumous conviction, the very name was abolished by Act of Parliament; the house indeed was preserved; but to obliterate all memory of so detested a family, even the name of that was changed to Huntingtower.

Near this house is the stone building called the Lowswork, so styled from Low, the first contriver. This serves to divert part of the water of Almond into an aqueduct, leading to Perth, which is of the greatest service to the various mills at this present time, and anciently assisted to make the place almost impregnable, by filling the ditch that surrounded the walls. On one side of this aqueduct is the Boult of Balhousie, a stone work, perforated with an orifice, thirty-two inches round, guarded with a circle of iron at each end. This hole is permitted, by very ancient usage, to convey a portion of water to the mill of that name. A contract is still extant between the magistrates of Perth and Eviot, then owner of Balhousie, in 1464, about the repair of this boult; and very lately the same has been renewed by the Earl of Kinnoull, the present noble possessor of those lands.[44]

Mr Duff from this spot pointed to me the site of Tillilum, near Perth, once a convent of Carmelites, in the east end of the parish of Tibbirmoor. The founder is not mentioned: we only learn from Keith, that Richard Inverkeithing, Bishop of Dunkeld, built here a fine chapel and a house, in 1262, and that the synods of the diocese were wont to be kept here for fear of the 'cattaranes', or Highland robbers, till the year 1460, when Thomas Lauder, Bishop of Dunkeld, removed them to his own cathedral.[45]

In my return to Dupplin had a distant view of Methven, a place lying between Tibbirmoor and the Almond, noted for the defeat Robert Bruce received here from the English, in 1306, under Aymer de Valence, Earl of Pembroke.

The banks of this river, about two miles higher than Bertha, afforded an untimely grave to the fair friends, Bessie Bell, and Mary Gray, two neighbouring beauties, celebrated in an elegant Scotch ballad, composed by a lover deeply stricken with the charms of both. One was the daughter of the Laird of Kinvaid, the other of the Laird of Lednoch. A pestilence that raged in 1666, determined them to retire from the danger. They selected a romantic and sequestered spot, on the side of Brauchie Burn, where

> They bigged a bower on yon Burn brae,
> And thick'd it o'er with rashes.

[44] As it is my wish to preserve the memory of every benefactor to the human species, I must not omit mention of Alexander Christie, an Irish-Scot, who about fifty years ago, in this parish, at a place called Tulloch, set up the first bleaching ground; and was the first person who introduced the right culture of potatoes into this country.

[45] MS *Lives of the Bishops*.

Here they lived for some time, and as should seem, without jealousy, for they received the visits of their lover, till catching the infection, they both died, and were both interred in the lands of Lednoch, at Dronach Haugh.[46]

Leave Dupplin, and revisit Perth. Am honoured by the magistrates with the freedom of the city.

Pass over part of North Inch. On this plain, in 1396, a private war between the clan Chattan, and the clan Kay was decided in a manner parallel to the combat between the Horatii and Curiatii. A cruel feud raged between these warlike tribes, which the king, Robert III, in vain endeavoured to reconcile: at length the Earls of Crawford and Dunbar proposed, that the difference should be determined by the sword, by thirty champions on each side. The warriors were chosen, the day of combat fixed, the field appointed, the king and his nobility assembled as spectators. On reviewing the combatants, one of the clan Chattan (seized with a panic) was missing; when it was proposed, in order to form a parity of numbers, that one of the clan Kay should withdraw; but such was the spirit of that brave people, that not one could be prevailed on to resign the honour and danger of the day. At length one Henry Wind, a saddler, who happened accidentally to be present, offered to supply the place of the lost Macintosh, for the small sum of a French crown of gold. He was accepted; the combat began, and Henry fairly earned his pay, for by his prowess, victory declared itself in favour of his party. Of that of clan Chattan only ten and the volunteer were left alive, and every one of them dangerously wounded. Of the clan Kay only one survived, who declining so unequal a combat, flung himself into the Tay, and swam over unwounded to the opposite shore.[47]

Ride over the bridge of Perth, the most beautiful structure of the kind in North Britain, designed and executed by Mr Smeton. Its length is nine hundred feet; the breadth (the only blemish) twenty-two within the parapets. The piers are founded ten feet beneath the bed of the river, upon oaken and beechen piles, and the stones

[46] Gabions, *Of Perth*, 19.
[47] Buchanan, lib. X. ch. 2, 3.

XI

M. Griffiths del.

PERTH BRIDGE.

laid in *puzzalane*, and cramped with iron. The number of arches nine; of which the centre is seventy-five feet in diameter. This noble work opens a communication with all the different great roads of the kingdom, and was completed at the expense of twenty-six thousand pounds: of this the commissioners of forfeited estates, by his Majesty's permission, gave eleven thousand; Perth, two; private subscribers, four thousand seven hundred and fifty-six; the royal boroughs, five hundred. But still this great work would have met with a check for want of money, had not the Earl of Kinnoull, with his characteristic public spirit, advanced the remaining sum, and taken the security of the tolls, with the hazard only to himself.

Several preceding bridges have been washed away by the violent floods, that at times pour down from the Highlands. The first misfortune on record is that which befell it in 1210, in the time of William the Lion, before recited in p. 438. I am uncertain whether it suffered a second time before the year 1329; or whether the order given that year by Robert I, for liberty of getting stones out of the quarries of Kynkarachi and Balcormoc,[48] for the building of that, the bridge of Earn, and the church of Perth, was not for rebuilding the former, which might have lain in ruins since the days of William. After this, it met with a succession of misfortunes, in the years 1573, 1582, and 1589; and, finally, in the year 1621, when it had been just rebuilt and completed in the most magnificent manner, a fatal flood overthrew the whole: a judgment, said the people, on the iniquity of the place, for in 1606 here was held that Parliament, 'at which bishops were erected, and the lords rode first in their scarlet gowns'.[49] From that period it lay neglected, till the late successful attempt restored it at least to its former splendour.

On reaching the eastern banks of the Tay, make a digression about a mile and a half to the left, to see the celebrated abbey of Scone,[50] seated amidst beautiful woods, and, at a small distance from the river. Long before the foundation of the abbey, Scone had been a

---

[48] On opening this quarry, for the materials of the present bridge, number of the ancient tools were discovered.

[49] Gabions, 82.

[50] Or Scyon, as it is called in charter of Alexander II. Vide Anderson's *Diplomata*, no. XXX.

place of note. It is called by some the ancient capital of the Picts: but it certainly was the seat of the princes of Scotland as early as the time of Kenneth. On a tumulus, still in being, they kept their courts of justice: on this they sat to determine the pleas between their barons, whence it was called the Mons Placiti de Scona, the Mote hill of Scone. *Mote*, in the Gaelic tongue, signifies 'a court'; for in very early times it was customary for the great people to deliver their laws from eminences of this kind. Our Druids had their Gorsedd, where they 'sate aloft', and delivered their decrees, their sentences, and their orations to the people.

Legend relates, that the hill in question was called Omnis Terra,[51] being composed of earth brought here by gentlemen out of every country they had travelled in. But with more truth it may be said, that Malcolm MacKenneth, or Malcolm II, seated in the famous chair, placed on this mount, 'gave and distributed all his lands of the realm of Scotland amongst his men, and reserved nathing in propertie to himself, bot the royall dignitie, and the Mutehill in the towne of Scone'.[52] So that it should seem the very existence of his royal dignity depended on the possession of this hill of authority. But I must remark with Mr Guthrie, that this distribution ought to be taken in a more limited sense; it being incredible that any prince should thus totally divest himself of all the royal demesnes. It is most probable that he only renewed to his barons the grants of their lands, and in reward for their faithful services made their tenures sure and hereditary, which before they held precariously, and on the will of the Crown.[53]

The abbey was founded by Alexander I, in 1114, and was dedicated to the Holy Trinity and St Michael the Archangel, and filled with canons regular of St Augustine. It is said to have been originally a seat of the Culdees, which is not improbable, as it is not to be supposed that so noted a place could be destitute of some religious order. The revenues at the Reformation were considerable: amounting to £1,140 6s 6d Scots; besides sixteen chaldrons and

---

[51] Irwin's *Nomencl. Hist. Scot.*, 212.
[52] *Regiam Majest.*, I, and Boethius, lib. XI, 245.
[53] *Hist. Scotland* I, 226.

two firlots of wheat; seventy-three chaldrons thirteen bolls, two firlots and two pecks of bere; sixty-two chaldrons of meal; eighteen chaldrons and three bolls of oats; and one last of salmon.

In the church of this abbey was preserved the famous chair, whose bottom was the fatal stone, the palladium of the Scottish monarchy; the stone, which had first served Jacob for his pillow, was afterwards transported into Spain, where it was used as a seat of justice by Gethalus, contemporary with Moses. It afterwards found its way to Dunstaffage in Argyleshire, continued there as the coronation chair till the reign of Kenneth II, who to secure his empire removed it to Scone. Here it remained, and in it every Scottish monarch was inaugurated till the year 1296, when Edward I, to the mortification of North Britain, translated it to Westminster Abbey; and with it, according to ancient prophecy, the empire of Scotland.

The ceremony of placing the new monarch in the coronation chair was hereditary in the ancient earls of Fife. Edward in the midst of his usurpation, paid a strict attention to that point: the office was in Duncan, the eleventh Earl; but as he was under age, and with the king, I find in Rymer's *Foedera* a writ, dated Nov. 21, 1292, at Norham, directing one John of Perth, instead of the young Earl, to perform the ceremony of putting his creature John Baliol into the regal chair at Scone.[54]

This abbey, with the church, in the year 1559, underwent the common fate of religious houses, in the furious and ungovernable season of Reformation. This was demolished by the zealots of Dundee, in resentment of one of their company being killed by a shot from the house. The nobility who were present strove to divert their rage, being more interested in the preservation, from the prospect of sharing in the plunder of the church.

In the church is the monument of Sir David Murray, ancestor of Lord Stormont, the present owner of the place. Sir David's figure is placed in an attitude of devotion, with a long inscription, relating his lineage, offices and virtues. Charles II was crowned in this church before he set out on the expedition that terminated in the fatal battle of Worcester. The crown was placed on his head by

[54] Vol. II, 600.

the Marquis of Argyle, the wily peer being for once cheated by the young prince, who flattered him with the hope of seeing one of his daughters mother of a line of kings.[55]

In the year 1715 the old chevalier resided here for some time, and issued out six proclamations, among which was one for his coronation on the 23rd of January 1716; but before that time his resolution failed, and he fled from a crown he was unworthy to wear. His son, in 1745, made the place a short visit.

Return the same road; pass near the end of the bridge of Perth, and after a short space, ride beneath the vast rocks of Kinnoull, which threaten destruction to the traveller, from the frequent falls from this black and ragged precipice. Many awful ruins are scattered far beyond the road; one of which a few years ago overwhelmed a small cottage, and the poor inhabitants. Beautiful agates are frequently found in this hill. In examining the fragments that lay beneath, I discovered a considerable quantity of lava, a proof of its having been an ancient volcano.

In the church of Kinnoull is the magnificent monument of Chancellor Hay.[56] His Lordship is represented standing under a rich entablature, supported by three pillars: two elegantly carved, the third plain, surrounded by a coronet. His dress is a long gown, great ruff, and small close cap. The seals, and a skull are placed on a table before him. Beneath is a space designed for the epitaph, but left uninscribed. The following is part of one, destined for that purpose, composed by Dr Johnson:

> Gone is the wise Lycurgus of our time,
> The great and grave dictator of our clime;
> To whose desert the sacred sisters owe,
> As much as e'er of old they did bestow,
> Of their Pirean treasure to give fame
> To painful Curius, or grave Cato's name.
> Had thou, brave judge, liv'd in such golden days,
> Thy head had long e'er now been crown'd with bays:
> But wisdom now is richly priz'd by none,
> Nor virtue, guardian finds, till she be gone.
> Six hundred years ago how happy I,

---

[55] Clarendon VI, 395.
[56] Sir George Hay, first Earl of Kinnoull.

That day, when thy brave ancestor did dye
His face with Danic blood, he did bequeath
Life to his country at the doors of death.
Yet this brave act was clos'd with one fair day:
But thou didst still for many years display
The ensigns of thy virtue; and fierce jarrs,
Intestine broils worse than the worst of wars
Did quell combustions. Safe did keep from harm
Chaste piety; and raging wrath disarm, etc.

Soon reach the noted Carse of Gowrie, a fine tract that extends in length fourteen miles, and in breadth four, bounded on the north by a range of hills called the Braes of Gowrie; and by the River Tay on the south. Too much cannot be said of its fertility. It is covered with corn of every species; peas and clover all in great perfection; varied with orchards, plantations, and gentlemen's seats. The roads are planted on each side with trees, which, with the vast richness of the country, reminded me of Flanders; and the extensive cornlands, with the mud houses, dabbed on the outside with cowdung, for fuel, immediately brought before me the idea of Northamptonshire. It agrees with the last also, in finding during summer a great deficiency of water for common uses, and a great lack of fuel all winter; so that the following is become a proverbial saying (false, I trust, in the last instance). That the Carse of Gowrie wants water all summer, fire all winter, and the grace of God all the year through.

The view of the Tay, and the opposite shore, add great charms to the view. On the southern bank stands Elcho, a poor convent of Cistercian nuns, founded by David Lindsay of Glanerk and his mother, on a piece of ground belonging to Dumferline; endowed afterwards by Madoch,[57] Earl of Strathearn, with the lands of Kinnaird in Fife. But the recluses were never very opulent, as their whole revenue at the Reformation amounted but to sixty-four pounds, six shillings and eight pence.

A little further the Tay beings to spread considerably, and to assume the form of an estuary. At a hamlet called Hawkstone, see

---

[57] Probably Malaise or Maurice, for I see no Madoch among the earls.

on the roadside a very large stone, said to be that on which the hawk of the peasant Hay alighted, after it had performed its flight round the land which was given to the gallant rustic, in reward of his services. On it is inscribed in modern letters, I know not why, the word 'Caledonia'.

Reach Errol, a small town, remarkable for the beautiful views, particularly those from the gardens of Mr Crawford, seated on a knowl, with a rich view of land or water from every part. Here I remarked the *arbor vitae* of a very uncommon size, being five feet six inches in circumference. The seeds ripen here very well.

Observe, about a mile to the left, Castle Lion, a seat of the Lions, earls of Strathmore.

The Carse of Gowrie terminates a few miles farther, when the land grows higher; but still continues fertile and improved.

The southern boundary of the Tay is the shire of Fife, a beautiful extent of country, rising gently from the water edge. Newburgh, a port of Perth, where vessels of three hundred tons may lie, is to be seen on that shore, a little east of Abernethy. Farther on are many places of note that lie on that coast; and were seen in the course of this day's ride. The first is Lindores, a little east of Newburgh, a rich abbey, founded by David, Earl of Huntingdon, brother to William I, on his return from the Holy Land, about the year 1178. The pious inhabitants were Tyronensian monks, drawn from the abbey of Kelso, whom Boethius pronounces to have been famous for the innocency of their manners. Their revenue in money was two thousand two hundred and forty pounds, fourteen shillings and four pence Scots; and they had besides twenty-two parish churches dependent on them. The Duke of Rothesay, eldest son to Robert II, who was starved to death at Falkland by his uncle, was, according to report, buried in the church of this abbey.

A few miles more to the east, on the same shore, are the ruins of Balmerino or Balmerinach, a most beautiful abbey of Cistercians (transplanted from Melross) begun by Alexander II, and his mother Emergarda, in 1229, on lands purchased by her for a thousand marks from Richard de Ruele, who resigned this and the lands of Cultreach and Ballindean to her in 1215, for this pious use. Various other donations were bestowed on it; among which may be reckoned Corbie and Birkill, and its parks, bequeathed by Laurence of Abernethy, because the royal foundress had left him in her will a legacy of two hundred marks sterling. The preceptory of Gadvan in Fife also belonged to this abbey; and two or three of the monks always resided on it. The revenues of the place were not large, not exceeding seven hundred and four pounds two shillings and ten pence halfpenny in Scots money. At the Reformation, Balmerino was erected into a barony, in favour of Sir James Elphinston, whose descendant fell an honest victim to mistaken principles in 1746.

XIV

ANGUS (1); MERNS, OR KINCARDINESHIRE

Dundee—Broughtay Crag—Panmure—Aberbrothic—Redcastle—Lunan—
Montrose—Dunnoter—Urie—Fettercairn—Grannachie Bridge

NEAR the village of Invergowrie, quit the shire of Perth, and
enter that of Angus, and after a ride of three or four miles
arrive at its capital, the city of Dundee, a well-built town, seated
on the estuary of the Tay, about eight miles from the mouth, in
lat. 56–24.30 long, from London 3–5. 3. west, and is the third in
rank of the royal boroughs. The number of inhabitants in the town
and suburbs amount nearly to fourteen thousand. Here are three
established churches, with three ministers and two assistants, for
the discharge of the duty of the parish, which includes a certain
district near the town; besides there are two Episcopal chapels, a
meeting-house for the Glassites,[1] and three for the burgher and
antiburgher Seceders.

The town is seated on the side of a hill, and is rather irregularly
laid out. Above it is Law of Dundee, a mark to seamen. The
harbour is artificially protected by piers, and furnished with a

---

[1] Or the followers of Mr John Glass, founder of the sect of Independents in
North Britain.

quay, on which are three very handsome public warehouses, built in 1756. The largest is composed of a centre a hundred feet long, with two handsome wings, all built of freestone, and their corners adorned with rustic work. The harbour is very commodious, and very accessible by people that are acquainted with it. There are on the north shore, near the entry of the estuary, two lighthouses, very completely finished, and well attended, being the property of the fraternity of seamen at Dundee; but the want of a new survey is much to be regretted, as the sands have of late years shifted: the public therefore look up to the Admiralty expecting its attention in this important article. The port will contain about two hundred sail, has at spring tides fourteen feet water, and admits vessels of upwards of three hundred tons burden. There are at present about seventy ships belonging to the place, and one of two hundred and sixty-four tons, that is employed in the Greenland whale fishery. An attempt is now making to revive the coasting cod fishery.

The manufacturers of Dundee are linen, especially of osnaburghs, sailcloth, cordage, threads, thread-stockings, buckrams (a new work in Scotland), tanned leather, and shoes, for the London market; hats, which has set aside their importation from England for the supply of these parts; and lastly, as an article of trade may be mentioned a sugar-house, erected about seven years ago, which does considerable business. Here was, in memory of man, a manufacture of coarse woollen cloth, called plaiden, which was exported undressed, undyed, to Sweden, Germany, and the United Provinces, for clothing the troops of those countries; but this was superseded by that of osnaburghs, which commenced in the year 1747, and is now the staple of the county of Angus. In 1773, 4,488,460 yards were stamped; the price from four pence to six pence a yard. These are shipped for London, Newcastle, Leith, Burrowstoness, and Glasgow, from whence they are sent to the West Indies and America, for the clothing of the slaves. To the same places are also exported threads, soap, shoes, leather, and saddlery goods. To Sweden and Norway are sent potatoes, and dressings of flax; and in times of plenty, when exportation is allowed, corn, meal and flour. The salmon taken near Broughtay Castle is sent, salted, to Holland.

XII

THE TOWER AT DUNDEE

In respect to imports, it receives from North America, Russia, Memel and Dantzick, Sweden, Norway, Spain, Portugal, the usual exports of those countries; and from Holland, flax, for the manufacture of threads and fine linens, pot-ashes, linseed, clover-seed, old iron, and madder, for the use of dyers. Such is its present state.

The public buildings, ancient and modern, are these: the magnificent Gothic tower of the old church, a venerable and superb building, now standing by itself, giving reason to every spectator to regret the loss of the body, whose only remains are the choir, called the Old Kirk, whose west end is crossed by another building, divided into two places of worship, evidently of a later construction, and probably built out of the ruins of the old: the last, when entire, was in form of a cross, and, according to Boethius, founded by David, Earl of Huntingdon, brother to William I, of Scotland, and dedicated to the Blessed Virgin. This happened on his return from his third crusade, in which he had accompanied Richard I, in 1189, and carried with him five hundred of his countrymen. After undergoing various calamities incident to these pious warriors, on his return to his native country he was nearly perishing by shipwreck in sight of this place; when vowing to erect a temple to the Virgin, he was instantly relieved, and showed his gratitude in this superb pile.[2] It must be confessed that he called in the aid of other well-disposed people; for he obtained a mandate from the Pope, still to be seen in the Vatican,[3] recommending, to assist in the expense, a collection throughout Christendom.

The time that part of the body of the church was destroyed is not certainly known; it was probably at the time of the Reformation, when the zealots of this place made excursions far and wide to destroy the churches of other cities.

This place had several religious houses; one of Mathurines, founded by James Lindsay, whose charter was confirmed at Perth, in 1392, by Robert III. Another of Dominicans, by Andrew Abercrombie, a burgess of the town. A third, of Franciscans, by

[2] Boethius, lib. XIII, 275, 276.
[3] It was shown to Dr William Raitt, in 1740, by the Pope's librarian.

Devorgilla, daughter to Allan, Lord of Galloway; but that was supported only by alms. Lady Beatrix, dowager of William, Earl of Errol, gave them a hundred pound Scots, on condition that the monks prayed (with a low voice) for her soul, and that of her husband. In 1482 they consisted of a warden and fourteen brethren. The fort was a nunnery, whose name is barely mentioned.[4]

The town house is a most elegant structure, begun in the year 1730, and finished in 1734. It was carried on under the directions of the father of the gentlemen to whom we owe the Adelphi. It contains the post office, the court room, with vaulted repositories for the records, the guildhall, and the council-chamber.

Here is a new church, built in a style that does credit to the place, and which shows an enlargement of mind in the Presbyterians, who now begin to think, that the Lord may be praised in beauty of holiness.

There is not a relic left of the ancient castle; but its site may be found where the Lion Inn now stands.

Two or three miles east of Dundee, on the river, are the ruins of the fort called Broughtay Crag. This place was taken by the English fleet, in 1547, on the invasion of Scotland, by the Duke of Somerset. The English remained in possession of it till 1550, when it was surrendered to the French under M. Desse, who by its capture freed the Scots from a most troublesome neighbour.

This place derives its name from *dun*, 'a hill', and Tay, the river on which it stands. Boethius says, that its ancient name was Alectum, but I cannot learn on what foundation. The Roman fleet entered this estuary, and might have had a station in some part; but from diligent enquiry I cannot learn that there have been either camp or road, or coins, or any other traces of that nation discovered in the neighbourhood.

The first notice I find of it in history is on the occasion before mentioned, when the Earl of Huntingdon founded its church; and changed, as Boethius asserts, its name from Alectum to Dei Donum. It was a considerable place in the time of Edward I, who in his northern progress, in 1291, reduced it, and other places

[4] Keith, 243, 272, 274, 283.

XIII

J. Bell inv.   Moffat del.

THE NEW CHURCH AT DUNDEE.

that lay in his way. About the year 1311 it was in possession of his son, who placed there, as governor, William de Montfichet.[5] In 1423 it entered into an obligation with Edinburgh, Perth, and Aberdeen, to raise eleven thousand pounds towards paying the ransom of James I, then prisoner in England.[6] This is a proof of its wealth at that time; and an evidence of its commerce in 1458 may be collected from the royal privilege granted to it by James II, of the following tolls towards the repair of the harbour, which were thus imposed: on every ship, ten shillings; on every crayer, buss, barge, or ballinger, five shillings; on every fercost, twelve pence; on every great boat, six pence.[7]

But Dundee received a dreadful check by the siege it underwent by the English, under General Monk, in September, 1651. The governor, Major General Lumsden, was summoned; but returning a very insulting answer, Monk determined to storm the place. By means of a Scotch boy he discovered the situation of the garrison, that it was secure, and generally by noon in a state of intoxication. He made a feint, as if he intended to raise the siege; but returned instantly with his forces supplied with sheaves of wheat, cut out of the neighbouring fields; with them they filled the ditch, succeeded in their attack, and put about six hundred of the garrison to the sword. The governor perished, as Sir Philip Warwick says,[8] by the hands of a fanatic officer, after quarter was given, to the great concern of the humane Monk. The booty was immense, for besides the wealth found in the town, there were sixty sail of ships in the harbour.[9]

I must not quit Dundee without saying, that Dudhope, the seat of the gallant Viscount Dundee, lies a little north of the place. It had been the ancient residence of the Scrymseours, and was rebuilt in 1600, by Sir John Scrymseour, a family ruined in the civil wars. It fell at length to the crown, and was granted by James VII to the

[5] Ayloff's *Ancient Calendars*, 123, 306.
[6] Ibid.
[7] Anderson's *Dict. of Commerce* I, 277.
[8] *Memoirs*, 361.
[9] Vide Gumble's *Life of Gen. Monk*, 42. Whitelocke, 508, 509.

Viscount, then only Graham, of Claverhouse; on his heroic death it was given to the Marquis of Douglas, and still remains in that house.

In the morning continue my journey; and turn from Dundee northward. The country grows a little more hilly; is still much cultivated; the soil is good, but the fields of wheat grow scarcer. Leave on the left Balumbi, a ruined castle with two round towers. On the right is Claypots, one of the seats of the famous Cardinal Beaton.

Leave, knowingly, to the west, a curious monumental stone, set up in memory of the defeat of Camus, a Danish commander, slain on the spot, about the year 994. According to Mr Graham,[10] it is in form of a cross. On one side is a most rude figure of our Saviour crucified: beneath, a strange centaur-like monster with six legs. On the upper part of the other side is a man, his head surrounded with a glory, and an angel kneeling to him. Beneath are two forms like Egyptian mummies: and in the third compartment, two men with bonnets on their heads and books in their hands. The battle was fought near the village of Barray; where numbers of tumuli mark the place of slaughter. But Camus, flying, was slain here. Commissary Maul mentions a camp at Kaerboddo, fortified with rampart and fosse, to this day styled Norway Dikes.

Reach Panmure, a large and excellent house, surrounded by vast plantations. It was built about a hundred years ago, on the site of the seat of the ancient family of the Maules, in the barony of Panmure, conveyed into that house by the marriage of the heiress of the place, daughter of Sir William de Valoniis, Lord Chamberlain of Scotland in the reign of Alexander II. This barony and that of Banevin had been granted to his father Philip de Valoniis, and confirmed to himself by William to be held by the service providing half a soldier whensoever demanded.[11]

In the house are some excellent portraits of distinguished personages: among them, a half-length of the Earl of Loudon, chancellor of Scotland, during the civil wars of the last century:

[10] Itin. 154, tab. liii, fig. 1.
[11] Anderson's *Diplomata*, no. xxviii.

esteemed the most eloquent man of his time, and the most active leader of the covenanting party. We may learn from his history, that the regard pretended by the faction for the interests of religion, was mere hypocrisy. The proof may be collected from the imprisonment of this nobleman in the Tower, in the year 1639, for the highest act of treason; for joining in an offer to put his country under the protection of the French king, provided he would assist the party in their designs; for offering to unite with powers the most arbitrary in Europe, and the most cruel and inveterate persecutors of their Calvinistical brethren: but the violence of party would have induced them to have heard a mass which they pretended to abhor, provided they could reject the innocent liturgy, and tyrannize over sinking monarchy. After the quarrel of the Scots with the English Parliament, he united in the endeavours of his countrymen to restore Charles II, yet passed sentence, as chancellor, on the gallant Montrose, with all the sourness of his old friends, and with all the insolence of a Jefferies. On the defeat of the king at Worcester, his new attachments obliged him to avoid the rage of the ruling powers: he fled to the Highlands, at length made his peace, and lived in obscurity till his death in 1663.

A half-length of the first Earl of Panmure, in his robes. He was Lord of the Bedchamber to Charles I and a faithful servant to his Majesty in all fortunes. After the king's death he retired into Scotland; where, in 1654, he was fined, by an ordinance of the Protector's council, in the sum of £10,000, for no other reason than that his sons were engaged in the royal cause.

James, Earl of Panmure, in a long wig, and armour, disgraced by James II for non-compliance with that prince's designs in favour of popery; yet, at the convention of the estates at the Revolution, was a strenuous advocate in defence of his old master. In 1715 carried his attachment so far as to join the insurgents in favour of the son; behaved with gallantry at the battle of Sheriffmoor; and forfeited his estate and honours in the cause. His nephew, by his merit, recovered the title, being created, on that score, Earl of Panmure in the kingdom of Ireland; and fortune, in this instance, a judicious goddess, supplied him with the means of purchasing the large family estate.

A fine head of Prince Rupert, looking over one shoulder.

A fine portrait of the Duke of Monmouth, sitting. His hair long and beautiful; his dress, a brown satin mantle, and a laced cravat.

A head of the Duke of Hamilton, killed by Lord Mohun.

Charles XII of Sweden, with his usual savage look.

The Duc d'Aumont, the French ambassador in the reign of Queen Anne, who came over on the occasion of the peace. He is said to have paid this fine compliment to the troops that had helped to reduce the dangerous power of his master, by observing, emphatically, at a review near london, that he was very glad to see them in that place.[12]

Mr Coleshill of Chigwell, Yorkshire, a half-length, in a black cap, furred gown, with a gold chain.

His daughter, grotesquely dressed in black; her arms perfectly *hérissée* with points. She was the lady of Sir Edward Stanhope, president of the north, whose picture, in small, is by her.

Proceed eastward through an open country, and in two hours reach Aberbrothic or Arbroath, seated on the discharge of the little River Brothic into the sea, as the name imports, 'aber' in the British implying such a situation. It is a small but flourishing place, well built, and still increasing: the town has been in an improving state for the thirty last years, and the number of inhabitants greatly augmented. This is owing to the introduction of manufactures; the number, at this time, is said to be about three thousand five hundred: these principally consist of weavers of coarse brown linens, and some sailcloth; others are employed in making white and coloured threads: the remainder are either engaged in the shipping of the place, or in the necessary and common mechanic trades.

The brown linens, or osnaburghs, were manufactured here before any encouragement was given by government, or the linen company erected at Edinburgh. The merchant, who first introduced the manufacture, is still alive, and has the happiness of seeing it overspread the country. It appears from the books of the stamp-office in this town, that seven or eight hundred thousand yards are

---

[12] Communicated by the Rev Mr Granger, to whose liberal disposition I find myself often indebted.

XIV

ABBY AT ABERBROTHIE.

annually made in the place, and a small district round. Beside this export, and that of thread, much barley, and some wheat is sent abroad; but so populous is the country, that more than an equivalent of meal is imported.

The foreign imports are flax, flax-seed, and timber, from the Baltic. The coasting trade consists of coals from Barrowstoness, and lime from Lord Elgin's kilns in Fife. The first forms a considerable article of commerce, this being the last port to the north, into which that commodity may be brought, free from the heavy duty commencing after it has passed the promontory, the Red Head. The coast from the Buttoness, or northern cape of the Firth of Tay, is entirely destitute of a port, as far as the harbour of Montrose. In fact this eastern side of the kingdom is as unfavourable to the seaman as it is to the planter. Whosoever will give themselves the trouble of casting their eye on the map, will perceive that from the Humber's mouth to John a Groat's house, there is an uncommon scarcity of retreats for the distressed navigator: they occur seldom, and have often near their entrances the obstructions of sand to render the access difficult. On the western side of the kingdom nature hath dealt out the harbours with a perfect profusion; not a headland can be doubled, but what offers a safe anchorage to the distressed vessel.

Aberbrothic would have wanted a harbour, had not the aid of art been called in: for in default of a natural, a tolerable artificial one of piers has been formed, where, at springtides, which rise here fifteen feet, ships of two hundred tons can come, and of eighty at neaptides; but they must lie dry at low water. This port is of great antiquity: there is an agreement yet extant between the abbot and the burghers of Aberbrothic, in the year 1194, concerning the making of the harbour. Both parties were bound to contribute their proportions; but the largest fell to the share of the former, for which he was to receive an annual tax, payable out of every rood of land lying within the borough. This is a royal borough, and, with Montrose, Brechin, Inverbervie, and Aberdeen, returns one member to Parliament.

The glory of this place was the abbey, whose very ruins give some idea of its former magnificence: it lies on a rising above the town, and presents an extensive and venerable front; is most deliciously situated, commands a view of the sea to the east, of a fertile country to the west, bounded by the Grampian hills; and, to the south, of the openings into the firths of Tay and Forth.

The abbey was once enclosed with a strong and lofty wall, which surrounded a very considerable tract: on the south-west corner is a tower, at present the steeple of the parish church: at the south-east corner was another tower, with a gate beneath, called the Darngate, which, from the word *darn*, or 'private', appears to have been the retired way to the abbey. The magnificent church stands on the north side of the square, and was built in form of a cross: on the side are three rows of false arches, one above the other, which have a fine effect, and above them are very high windows, with a circular one above. In April last a part adjoining to the west end fell suddenly down, and destroyed much of the beauty of the place. The length of the whole church is about two hundred and seventy-five feet, the breadth of the body and side-isles, from wall to wall, sixty-seven: the length of the transept, a hundred and sixty-five feet; the breadth twenty-seven.

It seems as if there had been three towers; one in the centre, and two others on each side of the west end; part of which still remains. On the south side, adjoining to the church, are the ruins of the chapter house; the lower part is vaulted, is a spacious room, well lighted with Gothic windows. Above is another good apartment.

The great gate to the abbey fronts the north: above the arch had been a large gallery, with a window at each end. At the north-west corner of the monastery stand the walls of the regality prison, of great strength and thickness: within are two vaults, and over them some light apartments. The prison did belong to the convent, which resigned this part of its jurisdiction to a layman, whom the religious elected to judge in criminal affairs. The family of Airly had this office before the Reformation, and continued possessed of it till the year 1747, when it was sold and vested in the crown with the other heritable jurisdictions.

In the year 1445, the election of this officer proved fatal to the chieftains of two noble families. The convent had that year chosen Alexander Lindesay, eldest son of the Earl of Crawford, to be the judge or bailey of their regality: but he proved so expensive by his number of followers, and high way of living, that they were obliged to remove him, and appoint in his place Alexander, nephew to John Ogilvie of Airly, who had an hereditary claim to the place: this occasioned a cruel feud between the families: each assembled their vassals, and terminated the dispute near the town. The Lindesays were victorious, but both the principals fell in the battle, with about five hundred of their followers.

Very few other buildings remain. In the area within the great gate is to be seen part of the abbot's lodgings, built on strong vaults, three storeys high, consisting of some large and handsome rooms.

This abbey was founded by William the Lion, in 1178, and dedicated to our celebrated primate, Thomas à Becket. The founder was buried here, but there are no remains of his tomb, or of any other, excepting that of a monk, of the name of Alexander Nicol. The monks were of the Tyronensian order, and were first brought from Kelso, whose abbot declared those of this place on the first institution to be free from his jurisdiction. The last abbot was the famous Cardinal Beaton, at the same time Archbishop of St Andrews, and, before his death, as great and absolute here, as Wolsey was in England. On the Reformation, John Hamilton was commandatory abbot. In 1608 it was erected into a barony, in favour of his son James; then was conveyed to the Earl of Dysart; and finally bought by Patrick Maule, of Panmure, with the patronage of thirty-four pounds.

The revenues were very great: in the year 1562, they were reckoned two thousand five hundred and fifty-three pounds Scots, besides the vast contributions of corn from the tenants, who paid their rents in kind. The ordinance for the yearly provision of the house, in 1530, will serve to give some idea of the great charity and hospitality of the place. There was an order for buying:

800 wethers	82 chalders of malt
180 oxen	30 of wheat
11 barrels of salmon	40 of meal
1,200 dried cod fish	

All which appears additional to the produce of their lands, or what their tenants brought in. This profusion of stores would seem very extraordinary, when the number of monks did not exceed twenty-five: but the ordinance acquaints us, that the appointments of that year exceeded those of 1528, notwithstanding, in the last, the king had been there twice, and the archbishop thrice. It is evident that the house was open to all; that the great as well as the poor partook of the hospitality of it, and that this virtue increased rather than declined.

King John, the English monarch, granted this monastery most uncommon privileges; for by charter, under his great seal, he exempted it *a teloniis et consuetudine* in every part of England, except London.

In this monastery Robert Bruce convened the nobility of this kingdom, who here framed the spirited letter and remonstrance to Pope John, dated April 6, 1320; in which they trace the origin of the Scots, from the Greater Scythia, through the Tyrrhenian Sea, and the Pillars of Hercules into Spain; they inform him that they expelled the ancient Britons, destroyed the Picts, and maintained this kingdom free, through a race of 113 kings of uninterrupted lineal descent. They strongly assert their independency of the English, and disclaim the right that Edward II pretended to the kingdom. They entreat his Holiness to admonish Edward to desist from his hostilities; and heroically acquaint the pope, that even should Bruce desert their cause, they would choose another leader (so little notion had they even then of hereditary right) and never submit even to extremity to the unjust pretensions of the English monarch:

> *Cui (Roberto) tanquam illi per quem salus in populo facta est, pro nostra libertate tuenda tam jure quam meritis tenemur et volumus in omnibus adhaerere; quem si ab inceptis desisteret Regi Anglorum aut Anglicis nos aut regnum nostrum volens subjicere, tanquam inimicum nostrum, et sui nostrisque juris subversorem, statim expellere niteremur, et alium regem nostrum, qui ad defensionem nostrum sufficeret, faceremus. Quia quamdiu centum vivi remanserint, nunqum Anglorum domino aliquatenus volumus subjugari; non enim propter gloriam, divitias aut honores pugnamus, sed propter libertatem solummodo, qui nemo bonus nisi simul cum vita amittit.*

There is no immediate answer from the pope extant; but there is reason to suppose that this very important remonstrance had great weight; for in August of the same year, he sent a bull to Edward,[13] to exhort him to make peace with the Scots, in order that the operations against the infields in the Holy Land might be pursued without interruption. There is also a letter from his Holiness to the same prince,[14] to acquaint him, that at the earnest request of Robert, he had suspended the sentence of excommunication, perhaps through fear of losing the whole Scottish nation by too rigorous a procedure.

After dinner continue my journey towards Montrose. I am informed, that near the road stands the church of St Vigian, a Gothic building, supported by pillars, with aisles on each side, and standing on a pretty green mount, in the midst of a valley. This church returns a fine echo, repeating distinctly an hexameter verse.

Pass through an open country, and observe, that the plantations are vastly mossed, being exposed to the cankering blasts of the eastern winds, which bring with them frequent rains, and great volumes of black fog. Ride by extensive fields of peas and potatoes; the last a novelty till within the last twenty years.

The open country continues as far as Lunan, where the enclosures commence. To the right is the promontory, called the Red Head, forming one horn of Lunan Bay, open to the east wind. The shore in this part is high, bold, and rocky, and often excavated with vast hollows, extremely worthy the attention of the traveller: no place exhibits a greater variety; some open to the sea, with a narrow mouth; and, internally, instantly rise into lofty and spacious vaults, and so extensively meandering, that no one has, as yet, had the hardiness to explore the end.

Others of these caves show a magnificent entrance, divided in the middle by a vast column, forming two arches of a height and grandeur that shames the work of art in the noblest of the Gothic cathedrals. The voyager may amuse himself by entering in a boat on one side of the pillar, surrounding it, and returning to the sea on the other. But the most astonishing of all is the cavern, called the Geylit Pot, that almost realises in romantic form a fable in the Persian

---

[13] Rymer's *Foedera* II, 846.
[14] Idem, 848.

tales. The traveller may make a considerable subterraneous voyage, with a picturesque scenery of lofty rock above, and on every side: he may be rowed in this solemn scene till he finds himself suddenly restored to the sight of the heavens; he finds himself in a circular chasm, open to the day, with a narrow bottom, and extensive top, widening at the margin to two hundred feet in diameter: on gaining the summit a most unexpected prospect appears: he finds himself at a distance from the sea, amidst cornfields, enjoys a fine view of the country, and a gentleman's seat at a small distance from the place out of which he emerged. Such may be the amusement of the curious in the calms of the summer season: but when the storm is directed from the east, the view from the edge of this hollow is tremendous; for from the height of above three hundred feet, they may look down on the furious waves, whitened with foam, and swelling in their long confinement.

The cliffs of this shore are not without their singularities: peninsulated rocks of stupendous height, jut frequently from their front, precipitous on all sides, and washed by a great depth of water: the isthmus that joins them to the land is extremely narrow, impassable for any more than two or three persons abreast; but the tops of the rocks spread into verdant areas, containing vestiges of rude fortifications, in ancient and barbarous times the retreat of the neighbouring inhabitants from the too powerful invader.

On the south side of Lunan Water is Redcastle, once a residence of William the Lion. After crossing that water, the country becomes enclosed, and divided into fields of about eight or ten Scotch acres in size, fenced with walls or banks, planted with French furze, or with white-thorn. A great spirit of husbandry appears in these parts, especially in the parish of Craig, which I now enter. The improvements were originally begun by two brothers, Messrs. Scotts, of Rossie and Duninald, who about forty years ago made their experiment on an estate of £800 or £900 a year value; and at present they or their heirs find the reward of industry by receiving from it three thousand pounds per annum. The principal manure is lime; but every species of good husbandry is practised here, and the produce is correspondent: all kinds of grain yield six from one; the grass land is set from twenty-five to thirty shillings an acre.

The improvements made on a farm of five hundred a year, held by Mr Patrick Scott, must not be forgotten; as he has the merit of making land not worth five shillings per acre, at present worth twenty. There need no stronger proof of the improvements in husbandry, and the fertility of the land in this neighbourhood, than to mention the annual exports of bere, meal, and malt, from the port of Montrose, which in favourable seasons amount to twenty thousand bolls.

On the south side of this parish (which is a promontory between Lunan Bay and the South Esk) is a great body of bluish limestone, I may say, at present tantalizing the honest farmer, who by reason of the dearness of coal is forbidden the use of it; a fatal duty of three shillings and three pence a ton on all coal, commencing at the Red Head, to the infinite prejudice and discouragement of rural economy in three parts. The thoughtless imposition of a tax, before the use of lime was scarcely known in these parts, is now severely felt, and obliges the farmers to neglect the cheap manure Providence intended for them; and at great expense to import their lime from the Earl of Elgin's works on the Firth of Forth, which costs them about seventeen pence per boll. Nature hath denied them coal, peat, and wood; so that at present they cannot burn their lime with the imported fuel at less than twenty pence the boll.

Reach the village of Ferryden, opposite to Montrose, and crossing over the strait or entrance to the harbour, arrive there late at night.

Montrose, or more properly Mon-ross, derives its name either from Moinross, 'the fenny promontory',[15] or from Mant- er-Osc, 'the mouth of the stream';[16] is seated partly on an isthmus, partly on a peninsula, bounded on one side by the German ocean, on the other by a large bay, called the Basin or Black Sands. This peninsula is evidently a large beach, formed in old times by the sea, as appears by digging to any depth.[17] The end of this forms one

[15] Irvine's *Nomencl. Scot.*, 158.

[16] Baxter, *Gloss. Ant. Brit.*, 170.

[17] Mr Maitland, vol. I, 205, supposes that the gravel, thus discovered, to have been the materials of a Roman way, which was continued farther north: and asserts, that there are vestiges of a camp on the neighbouring links or sandy plain; but I received not the least account of any such antiquities.

side of the entrance to the harbour: a rocky point, called by Adair Scurdiness, at this time Montroseness, lies on the south side, and certain sands, called the Annot, on the northern. On the first is a square tower, a sort of lighthouse, to direct the course of vessels in dark nights. The Annot sands, after violent storms from the east, approach nearer to the ness; but are again removed to their old limits by the floods of the Esk, a circumstance to be attended to by mariners. The tide rushes up this entrance with a great head and vast fury; but the depth of water is considerable, being six fathoms in the middle, about three days before springtide. The breadth is scarcely a quarter of a mile, but the basin instantly expands into a beautiful circle of considerable diameter; but unfortunately most of it is dry at low water, except where the South Esk forms its channel, in which vessels of sixty tons will float even at the lowest ebb. Inchbroik lies on the south side of the entrance, and opposite to that is the pier, which ships of any size may reach, that can bear the ground at low water.

Montrose is built on the east side of the basin, and consists chiefly of one large street, of a considerable breadth, terminated at one end by the town house or tollboth; a handsome pile, with elegant and convenient apartments for the assemblies of the magistrates. The houses are of stone, and, like those in Flanders, often with their gable ends towards the streets. The house in which the Marquis of Montrose was born is still to be seen. The town contains about six thousand inhabitants, of which fifteen hundred are Episcopalians; the rest are of the established church, with the usual schisms of Seceders, Glassites, Nonjurors, etc. Numbers of genteel families, independent of any trade, reside here as a place of agreeable retreat, and numbers keep their carriages: these are principally of the Church of England. Their chapel, which was founded in 1722, is very neat, has a painted altarpiece, and a small organ. It is occasionally frequented by the Presbyterians, who show here a most laudable moderation. It is chiefly in the south that religious bigotry reigns, and that usually among the common people. Our bishops, who have visited Scotland, have never failed meeting with a treatment the most polite and respectful; but the introduction of the order is impracticable in a country where the natural, as well as religious objections, are so strong; for the finances of North Britain can never bear the pomp of religion, even should the people be induced to admit the ceremonial part.

In the times of popery, the Dominicans had a convent here, founded by Sir Allan Durward, in the year 1230. The friars were afterwards transported to an hospital near this city, rebuilt by Patrick Panter, but in 1524 were permitted to return to their old seat.[18] Maitland says, that their house was called the abbey of Celurca: I suppose from the ancient name of the town which Boethius bestows on it.

The town has increased one-third since the year 1745; at that time there was not a single manufacture: the inhabitants lived either by one another, or by the hiring out of ships, or by the salmon trade. At present the manufactures have risen to a great pitch: for example, that of sailcloth, or 'sailduck', as it is here called, is very considerable; in one house, eighty-two thousand five hundred and sixty-six pieces have been made since 1755. Each piece is thirty-eight yards long, and numbered from eight to one. No. eight weighs twenty-four pounds, and every piece, down to no. one, gains three pounds in the piece. The thread for this cloth is spun here, not by common wheel, but the hands. Women are employed, who have the flax placed round their waists, twist a thread with each hand as they recede from a wheel, turned by a boy at the end of a great room.

Coarse cloth for shirts for the soldiery is also made here; besides this, coarse linens, which are sent to London or Manchester to be printed; and cottons, for the same purpose, are printed at Perth. Great quantities of fine linen, lawns and cambricks are manufactured in this town, the last from two shillings and sixpence to five shillings a yard. Diapers and osnaburghs make up the sum of the weavers employ; which are exported to London, and from thence to the West Indies.

Much thread is spun here, from two shillings and six pence to five shillings a pound. It is spun both in the town and country, and brought here by the rural spinsters to be cleaned and made into parcels; and much of it is coloured here.

[18] Keith, 270.

The bleachery is very considerable, and is the property of the town: it is not only used by the manufacturers, but by private families, for the drying of their linen; all paying a certain fee to the person who rents it from the magistrates. The men pride themselves on the beauty of their linen, both wearing and household; and with greater reason, as it is the effect of the skill and industry of their spouses, who fully emulate the character of the good wife, so admirably described by the wisest of men.

The salmon fishery of these parts is very considerable; from six hundred to a thousand barrels are annually exported, valued at three pounds each; and about fifteen hundred pounds worth of kitted or pickled fish. Much of the fresh fish is sold into the country, from three halfpence to two pence halfpenny a pound. The fishery commences the second of February, and ends at Michaelmas. Its importance has been considered in very early times, and the legislature consulted its preservation by most severe penalties.[19]

Quantities of white fish, such as the cod kind, turbots, etc. might be taken on the great sand banks off this coast. The Long Fortys extend parallel to it; and beyond that lie Montrose Pits,[20] a great bank with six pits in it of uncommon depths, and singular in their situation. They are from forty to a hundred fathoms deep, reckoning from the surface of the water, and possibly may be submarine swallows. These banks swarm with fish, but are shamefully neglected, or left perhaps to foreigners. In the last century about five hundred barks and boats, which during winter were employed in the herring fishery on these coasts, during spring and part of summer, turned their thoughts to the capture of cod and ling,[21] and after curing, carried their cargoes to Holland, Hamburg, into the Baltic, to England and to France. By some mischance this fishery was lost; and the Hollanders and Hamburgers fairly beat the natives out of their trade. In the time of Henry VIII, England was supplied with salt fish from this market: the Habberdyn (Aberdeen) fish was an article in every great larder.[22]

---

[19] Vide *Tour*, 1769.
[20] Hammond's chart of the North Sea.
[21] *Accompt. Current Between England and Scotland*, 26.
[22] *Northumberland Household Book*.

Incredible numbers of lobsters are taken on this coast, from the village of Usan. Sixty or seventy thousand are sent annually to London, and sold at the rate of two pence halfpenny apiece, provided they are five inches round in the body; and if less, two are allowed for one. The attention of the natives to this species of fishery is one reason of the neglect of that of white fish, to the great loss of the whole country, which by this inattention is deprived of a cheap and comfortable diet. Agates of very beautiful kinds are gathered in great quantities beneath the cliffs, and sent to the lapidaries in London.

I cannot discover any vestiges of antiquity about this place, except a large mount called the Forthill, on the east side of the town. No marks are left of its ever having been fortified; but the materials might have been applied to other purposes: and there is a tradition that it was in full repair when Edward III was in Scotland. Boethius relates that it was a fortified place at the landing of the Danes, a little before the battle of Loncarty:[23] that those barbarians put the inhabitants to the sword, levelled the walls, and destroyed the castle. This is the only remarkable event which I can discover to have happened to the town. In this century it was distinguished by the flight of the Pretender, who, on the 4th of February, 1716, escaped on board of a frigate which lay in the road, and conveyed him safe to France.

This day we were honoured with the freedom of the town; and handsomely entertained by the magistrates. I observed that the seal of the diploma was impressed with roses allusive to its present name, which seems a poetical fiction:

> *Aureolis urbs picta rosis: mons molliter urbi*
> *Imminet, hinc urbi nomina facta canunt.*
> *At veteres perhibent quondam dixisse Celurcam,*
> *Nomine sie prisco et nobilitat novo est.*
> *Et prisca atque nova insignis virtute, virumque*
> *Ingeniis, Patriae qui peperere decus.*[24]

Leave Montrose, and after five miles riding, cross the North Esk, at North Bridge. This river and that of South Esk rise in the extreme

---

[23] Lib. XI, 228.
[24] Johnston.

northern borders of the county, among the Benchichin hills: this, flowing along Glenesk, retains the same name from the source to the sea; the other is called the White Water for a considerable way from its fountain. Near this bridge is English Maddie, the seat of the Falconers, barons of Halkerton, whose family took its name from the office of an ancestor, falconer to William the Lion. After passing the river, enter the county of Merns; or the shire of Kincardine.

Some derive the first from Merns, a valiant nobleman, who subduing the country, received it in reward from his prince Kenneth II. Camden with much probability supposes it to retain part of the name of the old inhabitants, the Vernicones of Ptolemy, it being common for the Britons in discourse to change the 'V' into 'M'. The other name is taken from its ancient capital, Kincardine, now an inconsiderable village.

Lie this night at the village of Laurencekirk. The cultivation of the land in the afternoon's ride appeared less strong than on the south side of the South Esk; but great efforts are making towards the improvement of the country. Streams of corn seem darting from the hills towards the centre of the valley, and others again radiate from the coasts: I doubt not but in a few years the obscure or heathy parts will entirely vanish, and this whole tract become one glory of cultivation.

Proceed through a fine rich bottom, called the Hollow of the Merns, bounded on one side by the Grampian hills, on the other by a rising ground, that runs almost parallel to them. The Grampians here present a low heathy front; the hollows and the eastern boundary fertile in corn. Pass near the two seats of Mess. Carnegie, and Lord Garnston. Cross the Water of Bervie, which falls into the sea a few miles to the east. Near its mouth lies the small town of Inner-bervie, made a royal burgh by David Bruce, who landed there after his long retreat into France. The rock he debarked on is to this day called Craig Davy.

Near the village of Drum-lethie the country grows hilly and heathy. Pass near Glen-bervie, the seat of Sir James Nicholson. Incline now towards the shore, and find an improvement in the country, which continues till I reach Stone-Hive or Stone-Haven, a small town built in the reign of Charles II. It is placed at the foot

DUNNOTER CASTLE.

R. Griffiths, del.

of some high cliffs in a small bay, with a most rocky bottom, in one part opening a little, so that vessels may find admittance, but that must be at high water. A pier laps over this harbour from the north side, to give them security after their entrance. The town consists of about eight hundred inhabitants. The manufactures are sailcloths and osnaburghs, which began about seven years ago; and contributed much to make the place more populous. Here is also a considerable one of knit worsted and thread stocking. Women gain four pence a day by knitting, and six pence by spinning; the men, a shilling by weaving.

The manufacturers of the Merns may be divided thus: the stocking trade employs the natives from the banks of the Dee to this place. From hence to the North Esk they are wholly occupied in weaving.

Visit the celebrated castle of Dunnoter, built on a lofty and peninsulated rock, jutting into the sea, and divided by a vast chasm, a natural fosse, from the mainland. The composition of the rock is what is commonly called 'plum-pudding stone', from the pebbles lodged in the hard cement. Kittiwakes and some other gulls breed on the sides.

The entrance is high, through an arched way. Beyond that is another, with four round holes in front, for the annoying any enemy who might have gained the first gate. The area on the top of this rock is an English acre and quarter in extent. The buildings on it are numerous, many of them vaulted, but few appeared to have been above a century and a half old, excepting a square tower of a considerable height, and the buildings that defend the approach. The sides of the rocks are precipitous, and even that part which impends over the isthmus had been cut, in order to render this fortress still more secure. The cistern is almost filled up; but had been of a great size, not less than twenty-nine feet in diameter.

The view of the cliffs to the south is very picturesque. They project far into the sea, in form of narrow but lofty capes. Their bases are often perforated with great arches, pervious to boats.

This castle was the property of the Keiths, earls marshals of Scotland, a potent and heroic family: but in the year 1715, by one fatal step, the fortune and title became forfeited; and our country lost the services of two most distinguished personages, the late earl, and his brother the general, the ablest officer of the age. According to the Scotch peerage,[25] the property of the Keiths in this country came to them, in the reign of David Bruce, by the marriage of Sir William to Margaret, daughter of Sir John Fraser: but I have been informed that this fortress had been the property of an earl of Crawford, who exchanged it for an estate in Fife, with an earl marshal, on condition that he and his dependents should, in case of necessity, be permitted to take refuge there.

About the year 1296 this castle was taken by Sir William Wallace, who, according to his historian, burnt four thousand Englishmen in it. His tale is told with wondrous simplicity; for speaking of Wallace, he says:

> *The Englishmen that durst them not abide,*
> *Before the host full fear'dly forth they flie*
> *To Dunnotar, a swake within the sea.*
> *No further they might win out of the land,*
> *They sembled there while they were four thousand,*
> *Ran to the kirk, ween'd girth to have tane,*
> *The lave remain'd upon the rock of stane.*
> *The bishop then began treaty to ma,*
> *Their lives to get out of the land to ga,*
> *But they were rude, and durst not well affy:*
> *Wallace in fire gart fet all hastily,*
> *Burnt up the kirk, and all that was therein,*
> *Attour the rock the lave ran with great din,*
> *Some hung on crags right dolefully to die,*
> *Some lap, some fell, some fluttered in the sea.*
> *No Southeron in life was left in that hold,*
> *And them within they burnt to powder cold.*
> *When this was done, feil fell on their knees down,*
> *At the bishop ask'd absolution.*
> *When Wallace leugh, said, 'I forgive you all,*
> *Are ye war-men, repent you for so small?'*
> *They rued not us into the town of Air,*
> *Out true barons when they hanged there.*

In 1336 it was re-fortified by Edward II, in his progress through Scotland; but as soon as the conqueror quitted that kingdom, the

[25] Crawford, 319.

guardian, Sir Andrew Murray, instantly retook it. History leaves us in the dark after this for a very long period. I do not recollect any mention of it till the civil wars of the last century, when it was besieged, and the church again burnt. The tradition is, that it was defended by the Earl Marshal, against the Marquis of Montrose, by the persuasion of Andrew Cant. The marquis, according to the barbarous custom of the time, set fire to the country around; which, when Andrew saw, he told the noble owner, that the flames of his houses were a 'sweet-smelling savour in the nostrils of the Lord'; supposing that his Lordship suffered for righteousness sake. This castle was inhabited till the beginning of the present century. The annotator on Camden mentions the stately rooms in the new buildings, and the library. He also speaks of St Padie's Church here, famous for being the burial place of St Palladius, who in 431 was sent by Pope Celestine to preach the gospel to the Scots.

Wait on Robert Barclay, Esq., at his seat at Urie, about a mile distant from Stonehive. This gentleman, by the example he sets his neighbours in the fine management of his land, is a most useful and worthy character in his country. He has been long a peripatetic observer of the different modes of agriculture in all parts of Great Britain: his journeys being on foot, followed by a servant with his baggage, on horseback. He has more than once walked to London, and by way of experiment has gone eighty miles in a day. He has reduced his remarks to practice, much to his honour and emolument. The barren heaths that once surrounded him, are now converted into rich fields of wheat, bere, or oats; and his clover was at this time under a second harvest.

He is likewise a great planter: he fills all his dingles with trees, but avoids planting the eminences, for he says they will not thrive on his eastern coast, except in sheltered bottoms. The few plantations on the upper grounds are stunted, cankered and moss-grown.

Mr Barclay favoured me with the following account of the progress of his improvements. He first set about them with spirit in the year 1768; since which he has reclaimed about four hundred acres, and continues to finish about a hundred annually, by draining, levelling, clearing away the stones, and liming. These, with the ploughing, feed, etc. amount to the expense of ten pounds an acre.

The first crop is commonly oats, and brings in six pounds an acre: the second, white peas, worth sometimes as much, but generally only four pounds: turnips are the third crops, and usually worth six pounds: the fourth is barley, of the same value: clover succeeds, worth about four pounds: and lastly wheat, which brings in about seven pounds ten shillings an acre, but oftener more.

As soon as the land is once thoroughly improved, it is thrown into this course: turnips, barley, clover and wheat; sometimes turnips, barley, clover and ryegrass. He sometimes breaks up the last for white peas, and afterwards for wheat: and sometimes fallows from the grass, and manures it for wheat, by folding his sheep.

The land thus improved was originally heath, and even that which was arable, produced most miserable crops of a poor degenerate oat, and was upon the whole not worth two shillings an acre; but in its present improved state is worth twenty, and the tenants would live twice as well as before the improvement.

Some of the fields have been fallowed from heath, and sown with wheat, and produced large crops. One field of thirty-four acres, which had been mostly heath, was the first year fallowed, drained, cleared of the stones, limed, etc. and sown with wheat, which produced in the London market two hundred and seventy pounds, clear of all expenses. Mr Barclay has lately erected a mill for fine flour, the only one in the county, which fully answers; and has served to encourage many of his neighbours to sow wheat where it was never known to be raised before. At present near eight hundred bolls are annually produced within ten miles of the place.

The first turnips for feeding of cattle were raised by this gentleman: and the markets are now plentifully supplied with fresh beef. For that of Aberdeen, there are frequently fifty fat beefs slaughtered in one day, from Christmas to the first of July, generally weighing forty stones Scotch apiece. Before that period fresh meat was hardly known in these parts, during the winter and spring months. Every person killed his cattle for winter provisions at Michaelmas; and this was called 'laying-in time'.

The great-grandfather of Mr Barclay was not less eminent for his improvements in affairs spiritual. The celebrated Robert Barclay made Urie his residence, and here composed that Apology for the

Quakers, which will ever remain an evidence of his abilities and his piety. His moderate disposition and cool head gave credit to the sect; for it was the peculiar happiness of George Fox to have united himself with this worthy brother, since George's tenets, as Mosheim expresses, delivered by him in a rude, confused, and ambiguous manner, were presented in a different form by the masterly hand of Barclay, who dressed them with such sagacity and art, that they assumed the aspect of a regular system. To him then is owing the purification of the opinions of the professors of it at this time. He was the great reformer of Quakerism, and his followers may exult in him as in one who would do honour to any religion.

Leave Urie, and return by the same road as far as Red Mears, where we turn to the north-west, and travel near the foot of the Grampian hills, through a fine open country. Go near the house of Captain Falconer, with excellent improvements around; and soon after by Fasque, the seat of Sir Alexander Ramsay, a gentleman distinguished for his fine method of agriculture. Stop at Fettercairn, a small village, for the sake of refreshing ourselves and horses.

In this morning's ride, observe a particular neatness in the cottages of the country. They are made either of red clay, or of sods, placed on a stone foundation; the roofs are prettily thatched, and bound by a neat network of twisted straw rope, which keeps them extremely tight.

Near Fettercairn was the residence of Finella, the daughter of a nobleman of large possessions in this country, infamous for her assassination of Kenneth III, in 994. She artfully insinuated herself into his favour, and inveigling him into her palace (under pretence of revealing some conspiracies, she was really privy to) there caused him to be murdered. The place was beset by his friends, but Finella escaping out of a window, joined the confederates in her wickedness. Such is the relation given by Boethius and Buchanan,[26] but the relations of those early times are often doubtful and often fabulous.

About two miles from this place, on the roadside, is a cairn, of a stupendous size, and uncommon form, which probably might give name to the parish. The shape is oblong, and the height at least

---

[26] Boethius, lib. XI, 233. Buchanan, lib. VI, ch. 41. Major, 94, calls the lady 'Comitissa Angusiae'.

thirty feet. At some distance from the ground the sides are formed into a broad terrace: the cairn rises again considerably above that, and consists of great loose stones, mixed with much semi-vitrified or lava-like matter. On one side is a large long stone, probably once erect. Along the top is an oval hollow, about six feet deep: its length, within, a hundred and fifty-two; the breadth, in the middle, sixty-six; the length from the outside of the surrounding dike, a hundred and sixty-seven; the breadth, eighty-three. This may be presumed to have been monumental; the northern nations thought no labour too great in paying these funeral honours to their deceased heroes. The tumulus of Haco was the size of a hill:[27] whole years, as well as whole armies, were employed in amassing these stupendous testimonies of respect. Three years were consumed in forming one, the common labour of two uterine brethren, Norwegian chieftains.[28]

Travel over an ill-cultivated flat; cross the North Esk, at the bridge of Gannachie, a vast arch, cast from rock to rock, built by subscription, by one Miller. Beneath is a vast chasm, near fifty feet deep from the top of the battlements; through this the water runs with great force. A rocky channel, with lofty and precipitous tides, fringed with wood, forms most picturesque views for above a quarter of a mile above and below the bridge.

[27] *Socii Haconis fastuosi funerandi Ducis gratia, collem spectate magnitudinis exstruunt.* Worm., *Mon. Dan.*, 33.
[28] Idem, 39.

XV

ANGUS (2),
PERTHSHIRE (4)

Edzel Castle—Catterthun—Brechin—Finehaven Hill—Aberlemni—
Forfar—Restennot Priory—Glames Castle—Denoon Castle—Meigle—
Dunsinane—Abernethy

RE-ENTER the shire of Angus; on whose borders lies the castellated house of Edzel, once the seat of the most ancient branch of the Lindsays, of the castle of Invermark, who acquired it about three hundred years ago by the marriage of an ancestor with the heiress of a Sterling, who built the house, and was Lord of Glenesk, which by this match was conveyed to them. They were remarkable for being chief over a numerous set of small tenants. Not sixty years are past since the laird kept up the parade of being attended to church by a band of armed men, who served without pay or maintenance, such duties being formerly esteemed honourable. This castle was deserted by the then owner, on account of a murder he had committed on his kinsman, Lord Spynie, in 1607. This affair involved him in difficulties, and he retired on that account, to the house of Auchmull, about two miles higher on the North Esk as the inscription on the house shows. A little after the Laird of Edzel thought proper to bestow on one Durie, a barren knowl near the house, and by charter constituted him and his family hereditary beadles of the parish, and annexed the perquisite of two bannocks for ringing the bell at the funeral of every farmer, and one for that of every cottager; which remained in the family till very lately, when it was purchased by the Earl of Panmure, the present owner of the estate. This is mentioned to show the affectation of royalty in these reguli, who made their grants and conferred places with all the dignity of majesty.

After riding two miles on black and heathy hills, ascend one divided into two summits, the higher named the white, the lower the black Catterthun, from their different colours. Both are Caledonian posts, and the first of most uncommon strength. It is of an oval form, made of a stupendous dike of loose white stones, whose convexity from the base within to that without, is a hundred and twenty-two feet. On the outside, a hollow, made by the disposition of the stones, surrounds the whole. Round the base is a deep ditch, and below that about a hundred yards, are the vestiges of another, that went round the hill. The area within the stony mound is flat; the axis or length of the oval is four hundred and thirty-six feet; the transverse diameter, two hundred. Near the east side is the foundation of a rectangular building; and on most parts are the foundations of others, small and circular: all which had once their superstructures, the shelter of the possessors of the post. There is also a hollow, now almost filled with stones, the well of the place.

The other is called brown, from the colour of the ramparts, which are composed only of earth. It is of a circular form, and consists of various concentric dikes. On one side of this rises a small rill, which running down the hill, has formed a deep gully. From the side of the fortress is another rampart, which extends parallel to the rill, and then reverts, forming an additional post or retreat.

It is to be observed, that these posts were chosen by the Caledonians with great judgment: they fixed on the summits of a hill, commanding a great view, and perfectly detached, having to the north the Grampian hills, but on that side separated from them by the lofty and rugged banks of the Westwater, which gives them additional security. Posts of this kind are, as I am informed, very common at the foot of the Grampian hills; intended as places

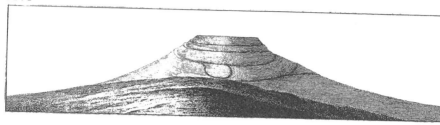

XVI

THE WHITE CATTER=THUN.

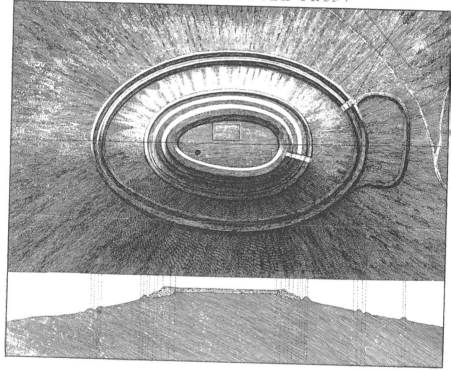

of retreat for the inhabitants on the invasion of an enemy. There is one above Phesdo, in the Merns; another called Barmkine Hill, eight miles west of Aberdeen. I have seen a long chain of similar posts in my own country; they are generally situated on high hills, overlooking the lower, or on lesser hills overlooking plains; and seem designed as asyla for the people of the low and defenceless countries.

The literal translation of Catterthun is 'camp town'. These posts are of the same kind with that made by Caractacus, on the borders of North Wales. '*Tunc montibus arduis, et si qua clementer acced; poterant, in modum valli saxa praestruit.*'[1] It is very probable that the Caledonians occupied these hills before the battle of Mons Grampius, which might have been fought in the plains below, where there was ample room for large armies to act in, and for the armed chariots to perform their careers. In these rude fastnesses the Caledonians might leave their wives and children, as was the custom of the other Britons; and then descend into the bottoms, to repel the invaders of their liberties. It is difficult to fix the spot; but there are not fewer than three Roman camps not remote from this range of hills, which Agricola might have occupied; and before one of them, drawn out his forces to have received the enemy. Of these one is at Kiethic, near Brechin; a second near Caerboddo, between Forfar and Panmure; and a third near Kennymoor called Battledikes.[2] In the neighbourhood of one of these seems to have been the celebrated action; after which he led his army to the confines of the Horesti,[3] received hostages, and ordering his fleet (then in all likelihood lying in the Tay) to perform the voyage round Britain, retired by slow marches into winter quarters.

Descend, and after travelling three miles, reach Brechin; a town consisting of one large and handsome street, and two smaller, seated on the top and side of a hill, washed by the river North Esk. At the

---

[1] Taciti *Annales*, lib. XII, ch. 33.

[2] These notices of the camps, from Maitland.

[3] Translators, misled by the sound, imagine these to have been mountaineers; but the word is probably Celtic, and should be rendered, as the ingenious Mr Aikin has done, the people of Fifeshire.

foot of the town is a long row of houses, independent of it, built on ground held in feu from the family of North Esk. It is a royal burgh, and with four others sends a member to Parliament. In respect to trade, it has only a small share in the coarser linen manufacture. It lies at no great distance from the harbour of Montrose; and the tide flows within two miles of the town, to which a canal might be made, which perhaps might create a trade, but would be of certain service in conveying down the corn of the country for exportation.

Brechin was a rich and ancient bishopric, founded by David I, about the year 1150: at the Reformation its revenues, in money and in kind, amounted to seven hundred a year; but after that event were reduced to a hundred and fifty, chiefly by the alienation of the lands and tythes by Alexander Campbell, the first Protestant bishop, to his chieftain the Earl of Argyle; being recommended to the see by his patron, probably for that very end.

The Culdees had a convent here: their abbot Leod was witness to the grant made by King David to his new abbey of Dumfermline. In after-times they gave way to the Mathurines, or Red Friars. The ruins of their house, according to Maitland, are still to be seen in the College Wynde.

Here was likewise a hospital, called Maison de Dieu, founded in 1256, by William de Brechin, for the repose of the souls of the Kings William and Alexander; of John, Earl of Chester, and Huntingdon, his brother; of Henry his father; and Juliana his mother. Albinus, Bishop of Brechin, in the reign of Alexander III, was witness to the grant. By the walls, which are yet standing, behind the west end of the chief street, it appears to have been an elegant little building.

The cathedral is a Gothic pile, supported by twelve pillars; is in length a hundred and sixty-six feet, in breadth sixty-one; part is ruinous, and part serves as the parish church. The west end of one of the aisles is entire; its door is Gothic, and the arch consists of many mouldings: the window of neat tracery: the steeple is a handsome tower, a hundred and twenty feet high; the four lower windows in form of long and narrow openings; the belfry windows adorned with that species of opening called the quatrefoil: the top battlemented, out of which rises an hexangular spire.

XVII

CHURCH & round TOWER at BRECHIN.

At a small distance from the aisle stands one of those singular round towers, whose use has so long baffled the conjectures of antiquaries.

These towers, as far as my reading or enquiries have extended, appear to have been peculiar to North Britain and Ireland: in the last frequent; in the former only two at this time exist. That at Brechin stood originally, as all I have seen do, detached from other buildings. It is at present joined near the bottom by a low additional aisle to the church, which takes in about a sixth of its circumference. From this aisle there is an entrance into it of modern date, approachable by a few steps, for the use of the ringers; the parishioners having, in time past, thought proper to hang their bells in it instead of the steeple. Two handsome bells are placed there, which are got at by means of six ladders, placed on wooden semicircular floors, each resting on the circular abutments within side of the tower.

The height from the ground to the roof is eighty feet: the inner diameter, within a few feet of the bottom, is eight feet; the thickness of the wall at that part, seven feet two inches; so that the whole diameter is fifteen feet two; the circumference very near forty-eight feet; the inner diameter at the top is seven feet eight; the thickness of the walls four feet six; the circumference thirty-eight feet eight inches; which proportion gives the building an inexpressible elegance: the top is roofed with an octagonal spire, twenty-three feet high, which makes the whole one hundred and three. In this spire are four windows, placed alternate on the sides, resting on the top of the tower; near the top of the tower are four others, facing the four cardinal points; near the bottom are two arches, one within another, in relief; on the top of the outmost is a crucifixion; between the moldings of the outmost and inner are two figures; one of the Virgin Mary, the other of St John, the cup and lamb; on each corner of the bottom of this arch is a figure of certain beasts; one, for ought I know, may be the Caledonian bear, and the other, and with a long snout, the boar; the stonework within the inner arch has a small slit, or peephole, but without the appearance of there having been a door within any modern period: yet I imagine there might have been one originally, for the filling up consists of larger stones than the rest of this curious rotund. The whole is built with most elegant masonry, which Mr Gough observed to be composed of sixty courses.[4] I am informed by Mr Gillies, of Brechin, that he has often seen it vibrate in a high wind.

The learned among the antiquaries are greatly divided concerning the use of these buildings, as well as the founders. Some think them Pictish, probably because there is one at Abernethy, the ancient seat of that nation; and others call them Danish, because it was the custom of the Danes to give an alarm, in time of danger, from high places.[5] But the manner and simplicity of building, in early times, of both those nations, was such, as to supersede that notion; besides, there are so many specimens left of their architecture, as tend at once to disprove any conjecture of that kind: the Hebrides, Cathness, and Ross-shire, exhibit relics of their buildings totally different. They could not be designed as belfries, as they are placed near the steeples of churches, infinitely more commodious for that end; nor places of alarm, as they are often erected in situations unfit for that purpose. I must therefore fall into the opinion of the late worthy Peter Collinson, that they were '*inclusoria; et arcti inclusorii ergastula*,'[6] the prisons of narrow enclosures: that they were used for the confinement of penitents; some perhaps constrained, others voluntary, Dunchad o' Braoin being said to have retired to such prison, where he died AD 987. The penitents were placed in the upper storey; after undergoing their term of probation, they were suffered to descend to the next; (in all I have seen there are inner abutments for such floors) after that, they took a second step; till at length the time of purification being fulfilled, they were released and received again into the bosom of the church.

Mr Collinson says that they were built in the tenth or eleventh century. The religious were, in those early times, the best architects;[7] and religious architecture the best kind. The pious builders either improved themselves in the art by their pilgrimages, or were foreign monks brought over for the purpose. Ireland being the land of

---

[4] *Archaeologia* II, 83.
[5] *Louthiana* III, 18.
[6] *Archaeologia* I, 307
[7] Mr Walpole's *Anecd. Painting* I, 110. Mr Bentham's *Ely*, 26.

sanctity, *patria sanctorum*, the people of that country might be the original inventors of these towers of mortification. They abound there, and in all probability might be brought into Scotland by some of those holy men who dispersed themselves to all parts of Christendom to reform mankind.

The castle of Brechin was built on an eminence, a little south of the town; but not a relic is left. It underwent a long siege in the year 1303, was gallantly defended against the English, under Edward III and, notwithstanding all the efforts of that potent prince, the brave governor Sir Thomas Maule, ancestor of the present Earl of Panmure, held out this small fortress for twenty days, till he was slain by a stone cast from an engine on August 20th, when the place was instantly surrendered.[8] James, Earl of Panmure built, in 1711, an excellent house on this spot: but in 1715 engaging in the rebellion, had but a short enjoyment of it.

I must not forget to mention the battle of Brechin, fought in consequence of the rebellion raised in 1452 on account of the murder of the Earl of Douglas in Sterling Castle. The victory fell to the Royalists, under the Earl of Huntly. The malcontents were headed by the Earl of Crawford, who retiring to his castle of Finehaven, in the frenzy of disgrace declared, he would willingly pass seven years in hell to obtain the glory which fell to the share of the rival general.[9]

This morning we were honoured with the freedom of the town: after which we continued our journey five miles to Careston, the seat of Mr Skene, where we passed the day and evening in a most agreeable manner.

After a short ride, ford the South Esk, leaving on the right the ruined castle of Finehaven, once the seat of the Lindesays, earls of Crawford. A Spanish chestnut of vast size was till of late years an ornament to the place. It was of the spreading kind; the circumference near the ground was forty-two feet eight; of the top, thirty-five, nine inches; of one of the largest branches, twenty-three feet.

Above the castle, is the hill called the castle hill of Finehaven, a great eminence or ridge, with a vast and long hollow in the top.

---

[8] Crawford's *Peerage*, 389. Camden's *Remains*, 301.
[9] Guthrie IV, 15.

Along the edges are vast masses of stone, strongly cemented by a semi-vitrified substance, or lava. These masses seem of a ton weight; they were procured out of the hill, and placed as a defence to the place, it having been a British post. The form of the hill (which ends abrupt at one end, at the other is joined by an isthmus to the neighbouring land) together with the cavity in the middle, renders it extremely fit for the purpose. The isthmus is secured by a deep ditch cut transversely.

This hill is certainly the effect of a volcano; at the one end of the hollow are two great holes of a funnel shape, the craters of the place through which the matter had been ejected. One is sixty feet in diameter, and above thirty deep; and have been much deeper, but was from time to time made more shallow by the flinging of stones, as cattle were sometimes lost in it.

On both sides of the hill are found in digging great quantities of burnt earth, that serves all the purposes of tarras or the famous *Pulvis puteolanus* or *puzzolana*, so frequent in countries that abound with volcanoes, and so useful for all works that are to lie under water.

On descending from the hill, find ourselves at Aberlemni. In the churchyard, and on the roadside are to be seen some of the curious carved stones, supposed to have been erected in memory of victories over Danes; and other great events that happened in those parts. These, like the round towers, are local monuments; but still more confined, being, as far as I can learn, unknown in Ireland; and indeed limited to the eastern side of North Britain, for I hear of none beyond the Firth of Murray, or that of Forth. The greatest is that near Forres, taken notice of in the Tour of 1769; and is also the farthest north of any. Mr Gordon describes another in the county of Mar, near the hill Benachie: the next are these under consideration. The first described by that ingenious writer,[10] is that figure which stands in the churchyard. On one side is the form of a cross, as is common to most; and proves them at least to have been the work of a Christian people. Mr Gordon very justly imagines that this was erected in memory of the victory of Loncarty; for in the upper

[10] *Itin. Septentr.*, 151.

XVIII

I. AT ABERLEMNI. *p. 170.*

II. AT GLAMES *p. 176.*

III. AT MEIGLE. *p. 180.*

part are horsemen, seemingly flying from an enemy; and beneath is another, stopped by three men on foot, armed with rude weapons, probably the peasant Hay and his two sons, putting a stop to the panic of the Scottish army, and animating his countrymen to renew the fight.

The next which I saw is on the road, with both sides full of sculpture. On one a neat cross included in a circle; and beneath two exceedingly rude figures of angels, which some have mistaken for characters. On the other side are the figures of certain instruments, to me quite unintelligible; beneath are two men sounding a trumpet, four horsemen, a footman, and several animals, seemingly wild horses pursued by dogs; under them is a centaur, and behind him a man holding some unknown animal. This is the stone mentioned by Boethius to have been put up in memory of a defeat of a party of Danes, belonging to the army of Camus, on this spot:

> *Quo loco ingens lapis est erectus. Huic animantium effigies, nonnullis cum characteribus artificiose, ut tum febat, quae rem gestam posteritati annunciarent, sunt insculptae.*[11]

On a tumulus on the roadside is a third, with various sculptures past my comprehension; but with the last are engraven, in order to exercise the conjectures of my antiquarian readers.

Near this is a fourth pillar quite plain; which was probably erected over the grave of some person, who was deemed, perhaps, unworthy the trouble of sculpture. This is as artless as any of the old British monuments, which I apprehend these carved stones succeeded. These were, from their excessive rudeness, the first efforts of the sculptor, imitative of the animal creation; and his success is such as might be expected: but in the ornaments about the crosses, and the running patterns along the sides of some, is a fancy and elegance that does credit to the artists of those early days. Boethius is willing that these engraven pillars should be supposed to have been copied from the Egyptians, and that the figures were hieroglyphic, as expressive of meaning as those found on the cases of mummies, or the sculptured obelisks of Egypt.[12]

[11] Boethius, lib. XI, 243.
[12] Boethius, lib. II, 20.

The historian's vanity in supposing his countrymen to have been derived from that ancient nation, is destitute of all authority; but his conjecture that the figures we so frequently see on the columns of this country, had their signification, and were the records of an unlettered age, is so reasonable as to be readily admitted. It was a method equally common to the most civilized and to the most barbarous nations: common to the inhabitants of the banks of the Nile, and the natives of Mexico.[13] In the northern hemisphere, monuments of this nature seem confined to the tract above-mentioned: they cannot be compared, as the learned Bishop Nicholson does, to the runic stones in Denmark and Sweden: for they will be found always attended with runic inscriptions, by any one who will give himself the trouble of consulting the antiquities of those nations.[14]

I must take notice of a new-discovered stone of this class, found in the ruins of a chapel in the den of Auldbar, near Careston, by Mr Skene, who was so obliging as to favour me with a drawing of it. On one side was a cross; in the upper compartment of the other side were two figures of men, in a sort of cloak, sitting on a chair; perhaps religious persons; beneath them is another, tearing asunder the jaws of a certain beast; near him, a spear and a harp; below, is a person on horseback; a beast like the musimon, which is supposed to have once inhabited Scotland; and lastly, a pair of animals like bullocks, or the hornless cattle of the country, going side by side. This stone was about seven feet long, and had been fixed in a pedestal found with it.

Proceed towards Forfar. About a mile on this side of the town is a moor, noted for a battle between the Picts and the Scots, in the year 831. The Scots, under Alpin, had rather the advantage: by them therefore might the great cairn near the spot be composed, which to this day is called Picts Cairnley. The base was once surrounded with a coronet of great upright columns; but only one remains, which is eleven feet high, seven broad, and eighteen feet in girth.

---

[13] *Conquest of Mexico*, 73. Purchas's *Pilgrims* III, 1068.
[14] *Wormii Mon. Danic.*, 474, 485.

Forfar, the capital of the county, contains about two thousand souls; but, since the great era of the prosperity of North Britain, has increased above half. The manufactures of linens in this neighbourhood, from four pence to seven pence a yard, are very considerable, and bring in, as is said, near twenty thousand a year.

The castle stood on a small hill near the town, but at present not a fragment is left.

The lake lies, or rather did lie, at a small distance from the castle, and, according to tradition, once surrounded the town; there being in several parts, even to this day, marks of the deserted channel: of late years it has been very considerably reduced by draining; to which the vast quantity of the fine marl at the bottom was the temptation. This fine manure is found there in strata from three to ten feet thick, and very often is met with beneath the peat in the moors. The land improved with it yields four crops successively; after which it is laid down with barley and clover. The county of Angus is supposed to be benefited, within the six last years, by this practice, by an advance of four thousand a year in the rents. Much of this is owing to an old fisherman, of this country, Mr Strachan, of Balgayloch, who invented the method of dragging up the marl from the bottom of the waters, in the same manner as the ballast is for ships.

About a mile north of Forfar, lay the cell or priory of Restennot, dependent on the abbey of Jedburgh. This house was placed in a lake, and accessible only by a drawbridge: here, therefore, the monks of Jedburgh deposited their papers, and all their valuable effects.[15]

Five miles further is the castle of Glames, a place much celebrated in our history; first for the murder of Malcolm II, who fell here by the hands of assassins, in a passage still shown to strangers. It might at the time be part of the possessions of the family of the famous Macbeth, who tells us, through the mouth of Shakespeare:

> *By Sinel's death I know I am Thane of Glames.*

This Sinel being, as Boethius informs us, father to that tyrant. Probably after his death it became forfeited, and added to the

---

[15] Keith, 140.

XIX

GLAMES CASTLE.

property of the crown; for, on the accession of Robert II, it was bestowed (then a royal palace) on his favourite, Sir John Lyon, '*propter laudabili et fideli servitio et continuis laboribus*'. The ancient buildings were of great extent, as appears by a drawing from an old print, which the Earl of Strathmore did me the honour to present to me. The whole consisted of two long courts, divided by buildings: in each was a square tower, and gateway beneath; and in the third, another tower, which constitutes the present house, the rest being totally destroyed. This has received many alterations, by the additions of little round turrets, with grotesque roofs; and by a great round tower in one angle, which was built in 1686, by the restorer of the castle, Patrick, Lord Glames, in order to contain the curious staircase, which is spiral; one end of the steps resting on a light hollow pillar, continued to the upper storey. Besides the spot of assassination, is shown the seat of poetry and music, and ancient festivity; where the bards took their place, and sung the heroism of their patron and his ancestors. In early times a chieftain was followed to court by his poets, and his ablest musicians: hence it was, that in the hall of a Celtic prince, a hundred bards have struck up at once in chorus.[16] And even about a century ago every chieftain kept two bards, each of whom had his disciples, inseparable attendants.

The most spacious rooms are, as usual in old castles, placed in the upper stories, and furnished with all the tawdry and clumsy magnificence of the middle of the last century. The habitable part is below stairs. In one of the apartments is a good portrait of the first Duke of Ormond, in armour, by Sir Peter Lely; the greatest and most virtuous character of his age.

His daughter, Countess of Chesterfield, a celebrated beauty, and the greatest coquet of the gay court of Charles II, beloved by the Duke of York, and not less by the Count Hamilton. Neglected at first by her husband, who, roused by the attentions of others to his fair spouse, became too late enamoured with her charms. At length a mutual jealousy seized the lady, and her lover Hamilton: he, in the frenzy of revenge, persuades the earl to carry her from the scene

---

[16] Dr Macpherson, 219.

of gallantry, to pass her Christmas at his seat in Derbyshire.[17] She discovers the treachery of her lover, but contrives to inveigle him to visit her in her retreat, through all the real inconveniences of bad roads, dreadful weather, and dark nights, with the additional terrors of imaginary precipices and bogs, which she had painted in her billet, to add to the misery of his journey. A bad cottage is provided for his concealment; a false confidante brings him at midnight into a cold passage, under promise of an interview: he remains there till day approaches; the night began with rain and ended with frost: he was cased with ice, perhaps complaining:

> Me tuo longos percunte noctes,
> Lydia, dormis.

He quits his station in despair, retires to his cabin, is terrified with the news of Lord Chesterfield being at home, is alarmed with the sound of the hounds, and the Earl enjoying the pleasures of the chase, peeps out, and finds the country beautiful, and neither bog nor precipice: in a word, returns to London the next night, the ridicule of the gay monarch and his merry court.[18]

I must not forget another portrait, that more immediately relates to the house of Patrick, Lord Glames; who, I am informed, wrote his own memoirs, and relates that he married the daughter of the Earl of Middleton, Lord Commissioner in the time of Charles II; and such was the simplicity of manners at that time, he brought his lady home mounted behind him, without any other train than a man on foot by the side of his horse.

In the churchyard of Glames is a stone similar to those at Aberlemini. This is supposed to have been erected in memory of the assassination of King Malcolm, and is called his gravestone. On one front is a cross; on the upper part is some wild beasts, and opposite to it a centaur: beneath, in one compartment, is the head of a wolf; these animals denoting the barbarity of the conspirators: in another compartment are two persons shaking hands; in their other hand is a battleaxe: perhaps these are represented in the act of confederacy. On the opposite front of the stone are represented an

---

[17] Breadby Hall, near Burton upon Trent.
[18] Memoires du Grammont.

eel and another fish. This alludes to the fate of the murderers, who, as soon as they had committed the horrid act, fled. The roads were at that time covered with snow; they lost the path, and went on to the lake of Forfar, which happened at the time to be frozen over, but not sufficiently strong to bear their weight: the ice broke, and they all perished miserably. This fact is confirmed by the weapons lately found in draining the lake, particularly a battleaxe, of a form like those represented in the sculpture. Several brass pots and pans were found there at the same time, perhaps part of the plunder the assassins carried off with them.

Near Glames are two other stones, one with the cross on one front, an angel on the one side, and two men with the heads of hogs on the other; probably satyrically alluding to the name of Sueno, or the swine, a Danish monarch. Beneath are four animals resembling lions: on the opposite front is a single eel. This is in the park of Glames.[19]

The other is at the village of Cossens, a mile west of the castle, and is called St Orland's stone. The cross takes up one front; on the upper part of the other are certain unknown instruments: beneath are horsemen and dogs; under them a sculpture, which in my drawing represents a boat: beneath that a cow, and another animal.[20]

I missed seeing Denoon Castle, which I am informed lies two miles to the south-west of Glames. According to Mr Gordon, it is seated on an eminence, environed with steep rocks, and almost inaccessible. On the north are two or three rows of terraces. It is of a semicircular form, and encompassed with a stupendous wall of stone and earth, twenty seven feet high, and thirty thick. The circuit three hundred and thirty-five yards. The entrances are on the south-east, and north-west. Within the area are vestiges of buildings, and there is a tradition that there was a spring in the middle. This appears to me to be the same kind of fastness as that of Catterthun.

Proceed to Belmont, the seat of the honourable Stuart Mackenzie, Lord Privy Seal of Scotland, where I found the most obliging

[19] Vide Gordon's *Itin.*, 163.
[20] Ibid. I had not an opportunity of seeing either of these. Mr Skene, of Careston, favoured me with a drawing of the last.

reception. It is seated in the parish of Meigle, where I again enter the county of Perth.

The ground of this parish is very fertile, and much improved of late by the manure of shell-marl. It yields barley, oats, some wheat, and a little rye; and, in general, more grain than the inhabitants, who amount to about twelve hundred, can consume. Much flax is raised, many potatoes planted, and of late artificial grasses begin to find a place here. Improvements in agriculture, and in making good roads, go on most prosperously under the auspices of the Lord Privy Seal. The only manufacture in the parish is that of coarse brown linens, which employs about a hundred weavers. But since a great proprietor has thought proper to debar the inhabitants from the use of a large peatmoss, it is feared that the manufacturers must remove (as many have already done) for want of that essential article, fuel.

Belmont stands entirely on classical ground; for on its environs lay the last scene of the tragedy of Macbeth. In one place is shown his tumulus, called Belly Duff, or, I should rather call it, the memorial of his fall; for to tyrants no such respect was paid; and their remains were treated with the utmost indignity among the northern nations. Thus Amlethus, after destroying the cruel Fengo, denies every honour to his body.[21] And Starcather beautifully describes the obsequies of the wicked:

> Caesorum corpora curru
> Excipiant famuli, promptusque cadavera lictor,
> Efferat, officiis merito caritura supremis,
> Et bustis indigna tegi. Non funeris illis
> Pompa rogusve pium tumuli component honorem:
> Putida spargantur campis, aviumque terenda
> Morsibus, infesto maculent rus undique tabo.[22]

By the final syllable, I should choose to style it in a monument to perpetuate the memory of the gallant Macduff. It is a verdant mount, surrounded by two terraces, with a cop at top, now shaded

[21] *Saxo Gram.*, lib. IV, 55.
[22] Idem, lib. VI, 119. *Aviumque terenda morsibus.* Shakespeare puts an idea similar to this in the mouth of Macbeth: 'Our monuments/Shall be the maws of kites.'

by broad-leaved laburnums, of great antiquity. The battle, which began beneath the castle of Dunsinane, might have spread as far as this place. Here the great stand might have been made; here Macduff might have summoned the usurper to yield; and here I imagine him uttering his last defiance:

> *I will not yield*
> *To kiss the ground before young Malcolm's feet;*
> *And to be baited with the rabble's curse.*
> *Though Birnam wood be come to Dunsinane,*
> *And thou, oppos'd, be of no woman born,*
> *Yet I will try the last. Before my body*
> *I throw my warlike shield. Lay on, Macduff!*
> *And damn'd be he that first cries, 'Hold! Enough!'*

In a field on the other side of the house is another monument to a hero of that day, to the memory of the brave young Seward, who fell, slain on the spot by Macbeth. A stupendous stone marks the place; twelve feet high above ground, and eighteen feet and a half in girth in the thickest place. The quantity below the surface of the earth only two feet eight inches; the weight, on accurate computation, amounts to twenty tons; yet I have been assured that no stone of this species is to be found within twenty miles. But the pains that were bestowed on these grateful remembrances of departed merit, may be learned from the filial piety of Harald, the son of Gormon, who employed his whole army, and a vast number of oxen, to draw a stone of prodigious size from the shore of Jutland, to honour the grave of his mother.[23]

Near the great stone is a small tumulus, called Duff's Know; where some other commander is supposed to have fallen. But Meigle is rich in antiquities: the churchyard is replete with others of a more ornamented kind, abounding with hieroglyphic columns. Mr Gordon has engraved all I saw, one excepted; however I venture to cause them to be engraved again from the drawings of my servant; for notwithstanding I allow Mr Gordon to possess great merit as a writer, yet his sketches are less accurate than I could wish.

The most curious is that marked III in the plate. In the upper part of one front are dogs and horsemen; below are represented

---

[23] Wormii, *Mon. Dan.*, 39.

four wild beasts, resembling lions, devouring a human figure. The country people call all of them Queen Vanora's gravestones; and relate that she was the wife of King Arthur; I suppose the same lady that we Welsh call Guinever, and Guenhumara to whose chastity neither historians nor bards do much credit.[24] The traditions of these parts are not more favourable to her memory. The peasants assert, that after the defeat of her lover, she was imprisoned in a fort on the hill of Barra, opposite to this place, and that there she died, and was interred in the parish of Meigle. Others again say that she was torn to pieces by wild beasts, to which this sculpture alludes; if, as Mr Gordon justly observes, the carvings might not sometimes prove the foundation of the tale.

It is reported that her grave was surrounded by three stones, in form of a triangle, mortised into one another. Some of them have holes and grooves for that purpose, but are now disjointed, and removed to different places.

The stone marked V is very curious: on it is engraved a chariot, with the driver and two persons in it; behind is a monster, resembling a hippopotamus devouring a prostrated human figure. On another stone is the representation of an elephant, or at least an animal with a long proboscis. Whence could the artists of a barbarous age acquire their ideas of centaurs, or of animals proper to the torrid zone?

Leave Belmont. Pass beneath the famous hill of Dunsinane, on the south side of Strathmore, on whose summit stood the castle, the residence of Macbeth, full in view of Birnam Wood, on the opposite side of the plain. No place could be better adapted for the seat of a jealous tyrant; the sides are steep, and of the most difficult ascent; the summit commanding a view to a great distance in front and rear. At present there are not any remains of this celebrated fortress: its place is now a verdant area, of an oval form, fifty-four yards by thirty, and surrounded by two deep ditches. On the north is a hollow road, cut through the rock, leading up to the entry, which lies on the north east, facing a deep narrow chasm, between this and the next hill. The hill has been dug into; but nothing was

[24] Jeffrey of Monmouth, 351. Percy's *Reliques* III, 4.

discovered, excepting some very black corn, which probably had undergone the operation of 'graddan', or burning. This place was fortified with great labour, for Macbeth depended on its strength and natural steepness as a secure retreat against every enemy. He summoned the thanes from all parts of the kingdom, to assist in the work. All came, excepting Macduff, which so enraged the tyrant, that he threatened to put the yoke that was on the oxen then labouring up the steep side of the hill, on the neck of the disobedient thane.[25]

A little to the eastward is a hill called the King's Seat, where tradition says, Macbeth sat, as on a watch-tower, for it commands a more comprehensive view than Dunsinane. Here his scout might be placed who brought him the fatal news of the march of Birnam Wood:

> *As I did stand my watch upon the hill,*
> *I look'd toward Birnam, and anon, methought*
> *The wood began to move!*

On the plain beneath these hills are several other monuments of antiquity, such as a great stone lying on the ground, ten feet long, called the Long Man's Grave. Here are also several tumuli composed of earth and stones of a pyramidical form, called here 'laws'. One of a considerable size, near a gentleman's seat, called Lawtown, is supposed to have been that from which Macbeth administered justice to his people. No prince ruled with more equity than he did in the beginning of his reign. He was the first of the Scottish monarchs that formed a code of laws, which were duly observed during his government; but afterwards were neglected or forgotten, as Buchanan says, much to the loss of the kingdom in general.

Continue our ride westward. Pass through Perth. Reach Dupplin, where we continue till next morning.

Cross the River Earn, at Earnbridge, near the house of Moncrief; keep on the south side of Strathearn, and breakfast in its eastern extremity, at the village of Abernethy, seated near the junction of the Earn and the Tay, and once the capital of the Pictish kingdom. The origin of these people has been greatly litigated: some suppose

---

[25] Buchanan, lib. VII, ch. 11.

them to have been foreigners imported from Scandinavia,[26] or out of Saxony; but apparently without any foundation. There is no reason to imagine them to have had any other origin than from the Caledonians, the ancient inhabitants of the country. They were the unconquered part, who on the death of Severus, recovered from his sons the conquests of the father, who harassed the Romans and southern Britons with frequent excursions, and who, with their kindred Scots, on the retreat of the Romans, forced their confinement, now called Graham's Dike, and with irresistible fury extended their dominions as far as the banks of the Humber.

Two kingdoms had been erected: the one styled that of the Picts, the other that of the Scots. Each of them were new names: the first that mentions the Picts is Eumenius the Panegyrist, who wrote in 309, and the first who speaks of the Scots is *Ammianus Marcellinus*.

The words are of Celtic origin: Pict is derived from *picteich*,[27] or *pictich*, 'a plunderer' or 'thief': it was bestowed on them by their southern neighbours, who probably experienced the cruelty of their excursions. The Caledonian offspring accepted the title, as it conveyed, in their idea, an addition of honour instead of infamy; for the northern nations, from the earliest antiquity, held robbery to have been honourable, nor does that opinion seem to be worn out to this day with some of the northern princes.

The kingdom of the Picts was on the eastern parts of North Britain: that of the Scots on the western. The last derived their name from *scottan*, 'a small flock',[28] or from *scuite*, 'wanderers'.[29] The first perhaps from their making inroads in small parties, the last from their acknowledged way of life, running about seeking whom they might devour. As soon as these two nations had established a power, wars, attended with various success, arose between them: at length the Scots proved victorious; they totally subdued their Pictish neighbours, cut off multitudes, forced numbers to fly abroad for security, overturned their kingdom, incorporated the few which were left, and made their very name to cease.

---

[26] Stillingfleet, quoted by Mr Macpherson, 79.
[27] Henry's *Hist. Britain* I, 193.
[28] Dr Macpherson, 108.
[29] Henry's *Hist. Britain* I, 193.

That the Romans might also give the name of *Picti* to the British nations from the custom of painting their bodies with woad and other dyes is incontestible, notwithstanding it is denied by many of the Scottish authors. They argue from the inconsistency of the Roman writers, some of whom assert that the Britons went naked, others that they were clothed in skins, others with garments called *brachae*. That any were so wretched as to be destitute of clothing in this severe climate is very improbable: no northern nations yet discovered were ever found in such a state of nature. But, say the former, as the Britons were clothed, why should they give themselves the trouble of adorning their bodies with paintings, since they could neither show them through vanity to their friends, or as objects of terror to their enemies? It is difficult to trace the cause of customs in such distant periods: but we know at present, from recent authority, that there are two nations, who to this day retain the custom of painting their bodies, and some of them the most concealed parts, which they are as averse to exposing as any European. Both of these people are clothed: those of Otaheite have one kind of dress; the New Zealanders another. In distant ages they may leave off the custom of tattooing their skins; and the authority of our modern voyages become as disputable as those of Caesar, Dion Cassius, or Herodian, are with some later writers. But that the painted bodies of our ancestors might be capable of striking terror into their enemies is very certain; for in action they freed themselves from the encumbrances of the looser garments, and part at least of their bodies painted with wild fancy, were left exposed to the view of the astonished foe.[30]

I could not hear that there were the least remains of antiquity at Abernethy that could be attributed to its ancient possessors. The Picts have left memorials of their seat at Inchstuthel, and marks of their retreats in time of danger on the summit of many a hill. Above the house of Moncrief, on Mordun Hill, is a fastness, formed by a bulwark of rude stones, surrounding about two acres of ground, which might have been the citadel of Abernethy, the refuge of its

[30] Mr James Macpherson, 215.

inhabitants in time of war, at least of its women, its children,[31] and its cattle; while the warriors kept the field to repel the enemy.

Here is indeed a round tower like that of Brechin; but I am more willing to give these edifices to the Irish than the Picts. The Scots have sufficient remains of antiquity to forgive this concession: the tower at Abernethy is uncovered; the height within is seventy-two feet; the inner diameter eight feet two; the thickness of the wall at top two feet seven; at bottom three feet four; the circumference near the ground forty-seven. Within is, at present, a bell, platforms, and ladders, like that in the capital of Angus.

St Brigid, a virgin of Cathness, here first dedicated herself to the services of heaven, not with vows frail as human nature, but with a resolute perseverance in the duties of the monastic life: and with her nine others adopted the same course.[32] At this place she died in 513, and left such a reputation for piety, that 'the most extravagant honors were paid to her memory. The Hebrides paid her divine honors: to her the greatest number of their churches were dedicated: from her they had oracular responses; By the divinity of St Brigid, was one of their most solemn oaths: to her they devoted the first day of February, and in the evening of that festival performed many strange ceremonies of a Druidical and most superstitious kind.'[33]

Here were preserved her relics; here, in honour of her, was founded a collegiate church; and this place was a bishopric, the metropolitan of all Scotland, till it was in 840 translated to St Andrew's by Kenneth III, after his victory over the Picts.[34] Before which it was a populous city, given by Nectanus, King of the Picts, to God and St Brigid, till the day of judgment.[35]

---

[31] *Conjuges ac liberos in loca tuta transferrent.* Tacitus, *Vit. Agricolae*, ch. 27.
[32] Spotswood's *Hist. Ch. Scotland*, 11, 12. Boethius, lib. X, 181.
[33] Dr Macpherson, 239.
[34] Keith's *Bishops*, 2.
[35] Camden, 1238.

XVI

FIFE (2)

───────➤➤❮❮⟵───────

Mugdrum Cross—Falkland—Melvil House—Dairsie—St Andrew's—Isle of May—Lundie—Levin—Kirkaldie—Inchkeith—Aberdour—Inchcolm—Dunibrissel—Inverkeithing—Dumfermline—Limekilns—Blackness

Ascend the Ochil hills, and in less than two miles cross a rivulet, and enter the shire of Fife; the nearest or most southerly part of the Roman Caledonia, the Otholinia and the Ross of the Picts.[1] The Forthever or 'over' of the Saxons, and the Fife of the present time; the last from Fifus Duffus, a warrior of the country.

Near the junction of Fife and Strathearn, not far from the spot I passed, is Mugdrum Cross, an upright pillar, with sculptures on each side, much defaced; but still may be traced figures of horsemen, and beneath them certain animals. Near this place stood the cross of the famous Macduff, Thane of Fife, of which nothing but the pedestal has been left for above a century past. On it were inscribed certain Macaronic verses, a strange jargon, preserved both by Sibbald[2] and Gordon.[3] Mr Cunningham, who wrote an essay on the cross, translates the lines into a grant of Malcolm Canmore, to the Earl of Fife, of several emoluments and privileges; among others, he allows

---

[1] Boethius, lib. IV, 61. Sibblad, *Fife*, 1.
[2] Sibbald, *Fife*, 92, 93.
[3] Gordon, 164.

XX

FALKLAND CASTLE.

it to be a sanctuary to any of Macduff's kindred, within the ninth degree, who shall be acquitted of any manslaughter, on flying to this cross, and paying nine cows and a heifer.[4]

Descend the Ochil Hills, and arrive in a pretty valley, called the Strath of Eden, bounded on the south by the Lawmond Hills, and watered by the River Eden. Go through a small town, and after crossing the vale, reach Falkland; another small town, made a royal burgh by James II in 1458. On the attainder of Murdo Stuart, seventeenth Earl, it became forfeited to the Crown in 1424. James V, who grew very fond of the place, enlarged and improved it. The remains evince its former magnificence and elegance, and the fine taste of the princely architect. The gateway is placed between two fine round towers; on the right hand joins the chapel, whose roof is of wood, handsomely gilt and painted, but in a most ruinous condition. Beneath are several apartments. The front next to the court was beautifully adorned with statues, heads in bas-relief, and elegant columns, not reducible to any order, but of fine proportion, with capitals approaching the Ionic scroll. Beneath some of these pillars was inscribed *I.R.M.G. 1537*, or Jacobus Rex, Maria de Guise.

This place was also a favourite residence of James VI, on account of the fine park, and plenty of deer. The east side was accidentally burnt in the time of Charles II, and the park ruined during Cromwell's usurpation, when the fine oaks were cut down in order to build the fort at Perth.

In the old castle was cruelly starved to death, by the villainy of his uncle the Duke of Albany, David, Duke of Rothesay, son to Robert III. For a time his life was prolonged by the charity of two women; the one supplying him with oaten cakes, conveyed to him through the prison grates: the other, a wet nurse, with milk, conveyed by means of a pipe. Both were detected, and both most barbarously put to death.[5]

Near the present place are several houses, marks of the munificence of James VI, who built and bestowed them on his

[4] Camden, 1236.
[5] Buchanan, lib. X, ch. 10.

attendants, who acknowledge his bounty by grateful inscriptions on the walls, mostly in this style:

> Al praise to God and thankis to the most excellent monarche of Great Britaine of whose princelie liberalitie this is my portioune. Nicol Moncrief. 1610.

Continue our journey along the plain, which is partly arable, partly a heath of uncommon flatness, darkened with prodigious plantations of Scotch pines. In the midst is Melvil, the seat of the Earl of Levin and Melvil; a fine house, with nine windows in front, designed by Mr James Smith, and built in 1692.

The noble owner is descended, by the female line, from Alexander Lesly, first of the title; a gallant and most trusted officer, under the great Gustavus Adolphus. To him he gave the defence of Stralsund, when besieged by the imperialists, whose commander, the impious or the frantic Walstein, swore he would take the place, though it hung in the air from heaven by a chain of adamant:[6] but Lesly disappointed his rodomontade. On his return to Scotland he headed the convenanting army, during part of the civil wars, and contributed greatly to the victory of Marston Moor, in 1644. After the death of Charles I, he favoured the loyal party, was imprisoned, and suffered sequestration; so little did the Parliament respect his former services. A neat miniature of him is preserved here, and a fine medal given him by Gustavus, for his brave defence of Stralsund.

Gustavus himself, at full length, in a short buff coat. This portrait is an original, brought out of Germany by the General.

George, Earl of Melvil, Lord High Commissioner in 1690, a post he received as a reward for his sufferings in 1683, when he had the honour of being accused of corresponding with the virtuous Lord Russel; was obliged to fly into Holland, and, on refusing to appear on being cited, suffered, till the Revolution, the forfeiture of his estate.

David, Earl of Leven, commander of the forces in North Britain, from 1706 to 1710, a fine half-length, in armour, looking over his shoulder. By Sir John de Medina.

---

[6] Hart's *Life of Gustavus* I, 99.

In the garden is a square tower, one of the summer retreats of Cardinal Beaton; and near it is Cardan's Well, named from the celebrated physician, who was sent for from Milan, to Hamilton, Archbishop of St Andrew's, who was here ill of an asthma, in 1552. Cardan effected his cure but to preserve him for a most ignominious fate, which the physician, by casting the nativity of his patient, foretold. The prelate was afterwards hanged on a live tree at Sterling, and the following cruel sarcasm composed on the occasion:

> *Vive diu, felix arbor, semperque vireto*
> *Frondibus, ut nobis talia poma feras.*

I leave Melvil. The country is well improved, enclosed, and fenced with quickset hedges. Pass by Dairsie Church, and castellated house. The church is ancient, but of elegant architecture; the tower polygonal, terminating in a spire. It is built at the edge of an eminence, over the River Eden, which washes a beautiful bottom. The view from it of the bridge, the church, and house, are uncommonly pleasing. The estate of Dairsie was once the property of the see of St Andrew, but in 1550 was feued out to Lamont of Dairsie, to be held by duty paid to this day. It was afterwards sold to Archbishop Spotswood.

After passing over a barren moor, have a most extensive view. Beneath, on the north, is the Eden, discharging itself into a small bay under Gairbridge, consisting of six arches, built by Henry Wardlaw, Bishop of St Andrew's, who died in 1440: beyond is the estuary of the Tay, great part of the county of Angus, terminating with the Red Head, which, with Fifeness in this county, forms the great bay of St Andrew's. Full in front, at the bottom of a long descent, appears the city, placed at the extremity of a plain at the water's edge. Its numerous towers and spires give it an air of vast magnificence, and serve to raise the expectation of strangers to the highest pitch. On entering the West Port, a well-built street, straight, and of a vast length and breadth, appears; but so grass-grown, and such a dreary solitude lay before us, that it formed the perfect idea of having been laid waste by the pestilence.

On a farther advance, the towers and spires, which at a distance afforded such an appearance of grandeur, on the near view showed

XXI

M. Griffith. del.

ST. ANDREWS.

themselves to be the awful remains of the magnificent, the pious works of past generations. A foreigner, ignorant of the history of this country, would naturally enquire, what calamity has this city undergone? Has it suffered a bombardment from some barbarous enemy? Or has it not, like Lisbon, felt the more inevitable fury of a convulsive earthquake? But how great is the horror on reflecting, that this destruction was owing to the more barbarous zeal of a minister, who, by his discourses, first inflamed, and then permitted a furious crowd to overthrow edifices, dedicated to that very being he pretended to honour by their ruin. The cathedral was the labour of a hundred and sixty years, a building that did honour to the country: yet in June 1559, John Knox effected its demolition in a single day.

If we may credit legend, St Andrew's owes its origin to a singular accident. St Regulus, or St Rule, as he is often called, a Greek of Achaia, was warned by a vision to leave his native country, and visit Albion, an isle placed in the remotest part of the world; and to take with him the arm-bone, three fingers, and three toes of St Andrew. He obeyed, and setting sail with his companions, after being grievously tempest-tossed, was in 370 at length shipwrecked on the coasts of Otholania, in the territory of Hergustus, King of the Picts. His Majesty no sooner heard of the arrival of pious strangers, and their precious relics, than he gave orders for their reception, presented the saint with his own palace, and built near it the church, which to this day bears the name of Regulus.

The place was then styled Mucross; or, the 'land of boars': all round was forest, and the lands bestowed on the saint were called Byrehid. The boars equalled in size the Erymanthian; as a proof, two tusks were chained to the altar of St Andrew, each sixteen inches long, and four thick. But Regulus changed the name to that of Kilrymont: here he established the first Christian priests of this country, the Culdees; a word which some derive from *cultores Dei*, or 'worshippers of God'; others, with more justice, from *keledei*, or 'dwellers in cells'. These had the power of choosing their own bishop, or overseer, professed for a long time a monastic life, and a pure and uncorrupt religion, and withstood the power of the popes. But David I, siding with his holiness in a dispute between

XXII

CATHEDRAL & CHAPEL OF S.T REGULUS AT S.T ANDREWS.

the Culdees and the prior and canons of St Andrew's, about the right of choosing a bishop, would have engaged the former to admit the last to partake of the powers of election; but on their refusal entirely divested them of their right. From that time their authority ceased, and probably their order, notwithstanding they are mentioned again in 1298, as opposing the election of Lamberton, and even appealing to the pope; a sign that the original doctrine of the Culdees was lost, and that these were only secular priests, who founded their pretensions to vote on the ancient usage of their predecessors. The Prior and canons, after this, retained the right of election.

This church was supreme in the kingdom of the Picts; Ungus having granted to God and St Andrew, that it should be the head and mother of all the churches in his dominions.[7] This was the prince who first directed that the cross of St Andrew should become the badge of the country. In 518, after the conquest of the Picts, he removed the episcopal see to St Andrew's, and the bishop was styled, *Maximus Scotorum Episcopus*. In 1441 it was erected into an archbishopric, by Sextus IV, at the intercession of James III. In 1606 the priory was suppressed, and the power of election, in 1617, transferred to eight bishops, the principal of St Leonard's College, the archdeacon, the vicars of St Andrew's, Leuchars, and Coupar.

The cathedral was founded, in 1161, by Bishop Arnold, but many years elapsed till it attained its full magnificence, it not being completed before 1318. Its length, from east to west, was three hundred and seventy feet; of the transept three hundred and twenty-two. Of this superb pile nothing remains but part of the east and west ends, and of the south side. With such success and expedition did sacrilege effect its ruin.

Near the east end is the chapel of St Regulus, a singular edifice. The tower is a lofty equilateral quadrangle, of twenty feet each side, and a hundred and three high. The body of the chapel remains, but the two side-chapels are ruined. The arches of the windows and doors are round, some even form more than semi-circles; a proof of the antiquity: but I cannot admit Hergustus, to whom it is attributed, to have been the founder.

---

[7] Camden, 1233.

The priory was founded by Alexander I in 1122, and the monks (canons regular of St Augustine) were brought from Scone, in 1140, by Robert, bishop of this see. By Act of Parliament, in the time of James I, the prior had precedence of all abbots and priors, and on the days of festival wore a mitre, and all episcopal ornaments.[8] Dependent on this priory were those of Loch Leven, Portmoak, Monimusk, the isle of May, and Pittenween, each originally a seat of the Culdees.

The revenues of the house were vast, viz. in money, £2,237 2s 10 1/2d; 38 chaldrons, 1 boll, 3 firlots of wheat; 132 ch. 7 bolls of bere; 114 ch. 3 bolls, 1 peck of meal; 151 ch. 10 bolls, 1 firlot, 1 peck and a half of oats; 3 ch. 7 bolls of peas and beans: 480 acres of land also belonged to it.

Nothing remains of the priory except the walls of the precinct, which show its vast extent. In one part is a most artless gateway, formed only of seven stones. This enclosure begins near the cathedral, and extends to the shore.

The other religious houses were, one of Dominicans, founded, in 1274, by Bishop Wishart; another of Observantines, founded by Bishop Kennedy, and finished by his successor, Patrick Graham, in 1478; and, according to some, the Carmelites had a fourth.

Immediately above the harbour stood the collegiate church of Kirkheugh, originally founded by Constantine III, who, retiring from the world, became here a Culdee. From its having been first built on a rock, it was styled, '*Praepositura sanctae Mariae de rupe*'.

On the east side of the city are the poor remains of the castle, on a rock overlooking the sea. This fortress was founded, in 1401, by Bishop Trail, who was buried near the high altar of the cathedral, with this singular epitaph:

> *Hic fuit ecclesiae directa columna, fenestra*
> *Lucida, Thuribulum redolens, campana sonora.*

The entrance of the castle is still to be seen; and the window is shown out of which it is pretended that Cardinal Beaton leaned to glut his eyes with the cruel martyrdom of George Wishart, who

---

[8] Keith, 237.

was burnt on a spot beneath. This is one of those relations, whose verity we should doubt, and heartily wish there was no truth in it;[9] and, on enquiry, we may console ourselves that this is founded on puritanical bigotry, and invented out of hatred to a persecutor sufficiently detestable on other accounts. Beaton was the director of the persecution, and the cause of the death of that pious man; and in this castle, in May, 1546, he met with the reward of his cruelty. The patience of a fierce age, as the able Dr Robertson observes, was worn out by his nefarious deed. Private revenge, inflamed and sanctified by a false zeal for religion, quickly found a fit instrument in Norman Lesly, eldest son of the Earl of Rothes. The attempt was as bold as it was successful. The cardinal at that time, perhaps instigated by his fears, was adding new strength to the castle, and, in the opinion of the age, rendering it impregnable. Sixteen persons undertook to surprise it. They entered the gates, which were left open by the workmen, early in the morning, turned out his retinue without confusion, and forced open the door of the cardinal's apartment, which he had barricaded on the first alarm. The conspirators found him seated in the chair; they transfixed him with their swords, and he expired, crying, 'I am a priest! Fie! Fie! All is gone!' He merited his death, but the manner was indefensible; as is candidly admitted by his enemy, the historian and poet, Sir David Lindsay:

> As for this cardinal, I grant,
> He was a man we might well want;
> God will forgive it soon.
> But of a truth the sooth to say,
> Altho' the loon be well away,
> The fact was foully done.

The conspirators were instantly besieged in the castle by the regent, Earl of Arran; and, notwithstanding they had acquired no greater strength than a hundred and fifty men, resisted all his efforts for five months: at length they surrendered, on the regent engaging to procure for them an absolution from the pope, and a pardon from the Scottish parliament.

[9] Brown's *Vulgar Errors*.

I shall step (rather out of course) to the church of St Nicholas, remarkable for the monument of a prelate, whose life and death bears, in some respects, a great similitude to that of the cruel Beaton. Archbishop Sharp was originally bred a rigid Presbyterian: had the full confidence of the party, and was entrusted with their interests at the time of the Restoration. Tempted by the splendour of the preferments of our church, he apostatised from his own, received in reward the archbishopric of St Andrew's, and, as is commonly the case with converts, became a violent persecutor of his deserted brethren. His career was stopped in 1675. Nine enthusiasts, some of them men of fortune, instigated by no private revenge, bound themselves by vow to sacrifice him to the sufferings of their sect. On the third of May, they met him in his coach on Magusmoor, four miles from the city, accompanied by his daughter. As soon as he saw himself pursued, he gave up all hopes of life, was taken out of his carriage, and, amidst the cries and entreaties of the lady, most cruelly and butcherly murdered. He died with the intrepidity of a hero, and the piety of a chieftain; praying for the assassins with his latest breath!

The monument is very magnificent: in the lower part is represented the manner of his death; in the middle the prelate is placed kneeling, the mitre and crozier falling from him; an angel is substituting, instead of the first, a crown of glory, with the allusive words, *pro mitra*; and above, is the bas-relief of a falling church, supported by the figure of the archbishop. This piece of flattery is attended with as flattering an epitaph: the disputable parts of his life are fully related; his undoubted charity and deeds of alms omitted.

In the church of St Salvator is a most beautiful tomb of Bishop Kennedy, who died, an honour to his family, in 1466. The Gothic work is uncommonly elegant. Within the tomb were discovered six magnificent maces, which had been concealed here in troublesome times. Once was given to each of the other three Scotch universities, and three were preserved here. In the top is represented our Saviour; around are angels, with the instruments of the passion.

With these are shown some silver arrows, with large silver plates affixed to them, on which are inscribed the arms and names of the noble youth, victors in the annual competitions in the generous art of archery, which were dropped but a few years ago; and golf is now the reigning game. That sport, and football, were formerly prohibited, as useless and unprofitable to the public; and at all 'weapon schawings', or reviews of the people, it was ordered, that 'fute-bal and golfe be utterly cryed down, and that bow-markes be maid at ilk parish kirk, a pair of buttes and schutting be used. And that ilk men schutte sex schottes at least, under the paine to be raiped upon them that cummis not, at least twa pennyes to be given to them that cummis to the bow-markes ta drinke'.[10]

The town of St Andrew's was erected into a royal borough, by David I in the year 1140, and their privileges were afterwards confirmed. The charter of Malcolm II is preserved in the tolbooth, and appears written on a bit of parchment; but the contents equally valid with what at this time would require whole skins. In this place is to be seen the monstrous axe, that, in 1646, took off the heads of Sir Robert Spotswood, and other distinguished loyalists, for the wretched preachers had declared that God required their blood. Here are kept the silver keys of the city, which, for form's sake, are delivered to the King, should he visit the place, or to a victorious enemy, in token of submission. It underwent a siege in 1337, at which time it was possessed by the English, and other partisans of Baliol; but the loyalists, under the Earls of March and Fife, made themselves masters of it in three weeks, by the help of their battering machines. It surrendered on terms of security to the inhabitants as to life, limbs and fortune.

The city is greatly reduced in the number of inhabitants; at present it scarcely exceeds two thousand. There is no certainty of the sum, when it was the seat of the primate, and in the fullness of its glory. All we know is, that during the period of its splendour, there were between sixty and seventy bakers; but at this time nine or ten are sufficient for the place. The circuit of this city is a mile, and contains three principal streets. The trade of St Andrew's was also once very considerable. I am informed, that, during the time of Cromwell's usurpation, sixty or seventy vessels belonged to

---

[10] Skene's *Scottish Acts of Parl, James II*, ch. 65.

the port; at present only one of any size. The harbour is artificial, guarded by piers, with a narrow entrance to give shelter to vessels from the violence of a most heavy sea. The manufactures, this city might in former times possess, are now reduced to one, that of golf balls; which, trifling as it may seem, maintains several people. The trade is commonly fatal to the artists, for the balls are made by stuffing a great quantity of feathers into a leathern case, by help of an iron rod, with a wooden handle, pressed against the breast, which seldom fails to bring on a consumption.

The celebrated university of this city was founded in 1411, by Bishop Wardlaw, and the next year he obtained from Benedict III the bull of confirmation. It consisted once of three colleges: St Salvator's, founded in 1458, by Bishop Kennedy. This is a handsome building, with a court or quadrangle within; on one side is the church, on another the library; the third contains apartments for students: the fourth is unfinished.

St Leonard's College was founded by Prior Hepburn, in 1512. This is now united with the last, and the buildings sold, and converted into private houses.

The new, or St Mary's College, was established by Archbishop Hamilton, in 1553; but the house was built by James, and David Bethune, or Beaton, who did not live to complete it. This is said to have been the site of a *schola illustris* long before the establishment even of the university; where several eminent clergymen taught, gratis, the sciences and languages. But it was called the new college, because of its late erection into a divinity college by the archbishop.

The university is governed by a chancellor, an office originally designed to be perpetually vested in the archbishops of St Andrew's; but since the Reformation, he is elected by the two principals, and the professors of both the colleges.

The present chancellor is the Earl of Kinnoull, who, with his characteristic zeal for promoting all good works, has established here premiums, to be distributed among the students, who make the best figure in the annual exercise. The effect is already very apparent, in exciting the ambition of a generous youth to receive these marks of distinction, that will honour their latest days.

The rector is the next great officer, to whose care is committed the privileges, discipline, and statutes of the university. The colleges have their rectors, and professors of different sciences, who are indefatigable in their attention to the instruction of the students, and to that essential article, their morals. This place possesses several very great advantages respecting the education of youth. The air is pure and salubrious; the place for exercise, dry and extensive; the exercises themselves healthy and innocent. The university is fixed in peninsulated country, remote from all commerce with the world, the haunt of dissipation. From the smallness of the society every student's character is perfectly known. No little irregularity can be committed, but it is instantly discovered and checked: vice cannot attain a head in the place, for the incorrigible are never permitted to remain the corruptors of the rest.

The students may be boarded in the colleges, or in private houses, or in those of the professors. The price at the colleges is only eight pounds for the sessions, which lasts seven months. The diet is very good, and a master always presides at the table.

The price at the professors', or at private houses, is from ten to twenty-five pounds a quarter. I observed at one of the professor's, young gentlemen from Bath, from Bourdeaux, and from Bern; a proof of the extensive reputation of the university, notwithstanding the students are far from numerous: there are at present little more than a hundred, who during sessions wear red gowns, without sleeves.

Leave St Andrew's; ascend a hill, and find the country on the heights very uncultivated, and full of moors. Here first meet with collieries on this side of North Britain. Descend into a tract, rich in corn, and enjoy a most extensive and beautiful view of the Firth of Forth, the Bodotria of Tacitus. The Bass island, with the shores of Lothian, extending beyond Edinburgh, bound the southern prospect. To the left, a few miles from the coast of Fife, appears the isle of May, about a mile in length, inaccessible on the western side. On the eastern side is safe riding for ships, in westerly storms. This isle in old times was the property of the monks of Reading, in Yorkshire; and in it David I founded a cell, dedicated to all the saints; who were afterwards superseded by Adrian, a holy man, murdered by the Danes, in Fife, and buried here. By his intercession the barren had the curse of sterility removed from them; and great was the resort hither of female pilgrims.

It was afterwards annexed to the priory of St Andrew's, having been purchased by Bishop Lamberton for that purpose, from the religious of Reading, in defiance of all the remonstrances of that tremendous monarch, the conqueror of Scotland. In later times a lighthouse has been erected on it.

Reach the shore of the fine bay of Largo; pass by the lands of the same name, bestowed in 1482 by James III on that gallant seaman, his faithful servant, Sir Andrew Wood, in order to keep his ship in trim. With two ships he attacked and took five English men-of-war, that infested the firth; and soon after had equal success against another squadron, sent out by Henry VII to revenge the disgrace.[11] The Scots, during the reigns of James III and IV, were strong rivals to England in maritime affairs.

Continue my ride along the curvature of this beautiful bay, and meet with the cheerful and frequent succession of towns, chateaux, and of well-managed farms. The country is populous; the trade is coal and salt: the last made from the seawater. The coal is exported chiefly to Middleburgh, and generally oats are brought back in return.

Go through the village of Lundie. In a field not far distant are three vast upright stones; the largest is sixteen feet high, and its solid contents two hundred and seventy. There are fragments, or vestiges, of three others; but their situation is such as baffles any attempt to guess at the form of their original disposition when the whole was entire. Near this place the Danes met with a considerable defeat from the Scots, under the conduct of Macbeth and Banquo. It is therefore probable that there stones are monuments of the victory. Mr Dougal, of Kirkaldie, who was so obliging as to favour me with their measurements, gave himself the trouble of causing the earth about them to be examined, and found, on digging about four feet deep, fragments of human bones.

Breakfast at the town of Leven, on the water of the same name, running from Loch Leven, near Kinross. The mouth forms a

[11] *Staggering State*, etc., 147.

harbour, where, at high water, vessels of a hundred tons may enter. Somewhat farther are the piers of Methel, built in the last century by David, Earl of Wemys. Go through the villages of Buckhaven, Wemys, and Easter Wemys; all in the beginning of the last century carrying on a considerable fishery. On an eminence impending over the sea is the house of Wemys, the seat of the ancient family of that name, descended from the old earls of Fife. The place derives its title from the various caverns in the cliffs beneath. On the shore is plenty of the *Ligusticum Scoticum*, the *shunish* of the Hebrides; a plant much in use in the western parts as a food.

Pass through a tract of collieries, and observe multitudes of circular holes, surrounded with a mound, and filled with water. These are called 'coal-heughs', and were once the spiracles or vent-holes to the pits, in inexperienced days of mining. The strata of coal are of great thickness, some at least nine yards. Many of the beds have been on fire for above two centuries; and there have been formerly instances of eruptions of smoke apparent in the day, of fire in the night. The violence of the conflagration has ceased, but it still continues in a certain degree, as is evident in time of snow, which melts in streams on the surface wherever there are fissures. George Agricola, the great metallurgist, takes notice of the phenomenon at this place.[12]

Buchanan, from this circumstance, fixed on the neighbourhood of Dysart for the scene of exorcism in his *Franciscanus*, and gives an admirable descriptive view of it under the horror of an eruption:

> *Campus erat late inculutus, non floribus horti*
> *Arrident, non messe agri, non frondibus arbos:*
> *Vix sterilis siccis vestitur arena myricis:*
> *Et pecorum rara in solis vestigia terris:*
> *Vicini Deserta vocant. Ibi saxea subter*
> *Antra tegunt nigras vulcania semina cautes:*
> *Sulphureis passim concepta incendia venis.*
> *Fumiseram volvunt nebulam, piceoque vapore*
> *Semper anhelat humus: caecisque inclusa cavernis*
> *Flamma furens, dum lactando penetrare sub auras*
> *Conatur, totis passim spiracula campis*

---

[12] *De Natura Fossilium*, 597. Agricola died in 1555.

Findit, et ingenti tellurem pandit hiatu:
Teter odor, tristisque habitus faciesque locorum.

A little beyond this once tremendous place is the town of Dysart, a royal burgh, large, and full of people. Leave, on the left, the castle of Ravensheugh, seated on a cliff, granted by James III to William Sinclair, on his resignation of the earldom of Orkney. Pass by Perthhead, a place of check-weavers and nailers: a modern creation, for within these sixty years, from being scarcely inhabited about four hundred families have been collected, by the encouragement of feuing. Adjoining is Kirkaldie, a long town, containing sixteen hundred inhabitants: this is another royal burgh, where I experienced the hospitality and care of Mr Oswald, its representative, during a short illness that overtook me here.

This, like most other maritime towns of Fife, depends on the coal and salt trade. The country is very populous, but far less than it was before the middle of the last century, when the fisheries were at their height. During winter it possessed a vast herring fishery; in spring a most profitable one of whitefish. One fatal check to population was the victories of Montrose. The natives of this coast were violently seized with the religious furore of the times, and took up the cause of the covenant with most distinguished zeal. Instigated by their preachers, they crowded under the banners of the godly, and five thousand fell victims to enthusiastic delusion, at the battle of Kilsyth.

Of late years many of the inhabitants have removed to the south-western parts of this kingdom; yet still such numbers remain that more provisions are consumed than even this fertile country can supply. There is one class of men on this coast, and I believe in most of the coal countries of North Britain, from whom all power of migrating is taken, be their inclinations for it ever so strong. In this very island is, to this day, to be found a remnant of slavery paralleled only in Poland and Russia: thousands of our fellow-subjects are at this time the property of their landlords, appurtenants to their estates, and transferrable with them to any purchasers. Multitudes of colliers and salters are in this situation, who are bound to the spot for their lives; and even strangers who come to settle there are bound by the same cruel custom, unless they previously stipulate to the contrary. Should the poor people remove to another place on a temporary cessation of the works, they are liable to be recalled at will, and constrained to return on severe penalties.[13] This, originally founded on vassalage, might have been continued to check the wandering spirit of the nation, and to preserve a body of people together, of whose loss the whole public might otherwise feel the most fatal effects.

During my stay at Kirkaldie I sent my servant, Moses Griffith, to Doctan, about four miles distant, where he drew the column most erroneously figured by Sir Robert Sibbald.[14] It is at present much defaced by time, but still are to be discerned two rude figures of men on horseback; and on the other sides may be traced a running pattern of ornament. The stone is between six and seven feet high, and mortised at the bottom into another. This is said to have been erected in memory of a victory, near the Leven, over the Danes in 874, under their leaders Hungar and Hubba, by the Scots, commanded by their prince, Constantine II.

Continue my journey. After proceeding about a mile, pass by the Grange, once the seat of the hero Kirkaldie, a strenuous partisan of Mary Stuart, after her storm of misfortune commenced: before, an honest opposer of her indiscretions. After an intrepid defence of Edinburgh Castle, he fell into the hands of the regent Morton, who, fearing his unconquerable spirit, basely suffered him to undergo the most ignominious death.

Leave, on the left, the ruins of Seafield Castle; a square tower, placed near the shore, in former times the seat of the Moutrays. A little farther is Kinghorn, a small town and borough. The castle was one of the seats of the kings of Scotland, till the time of Robert II, who, giving his daughter in marriage to Sir John Lyon, added this town in part of portion. At this place is the ferry between the county of Fife and the port of Leith, a traject of seven miles. Below this town, on the rocks, grows the *Ligusticum Scoticum*, or 'Scotch parsley', the *shunis* of the Hebrides; where it is often eaten raw as

[13] This disgrace, I believe, is now under consideration of Parliament, and will, I hope, be removed.
[14] *Hist. of Fife*, 34.

XXIII

PILLAR NEAR DOCTAN.

P. Mazell sculp

XXIV

Ligusticum   Scoticum

Moore Griffiths del.   P. Mazell sculp.

a salad, or boiled instead of greens. The root is esteemed a good carminative; and an infusion of the leaves in whey is used there as a purge for calves.

Opposite to Kinghorn, nearly in the middle of the firth, lies Inchkeith, an island of about a mile in length. It is said to derive its name from the gallant Keith, who so greatly signalised himself by his valour in 1010, in the battle of Barry, in Angus, against the Danes; after which he received in reward the barony of Keith, in Lothian, and this little isle. This seems to be the place that Bede calls Caerguidi, there being no other that will suit the situation he gives it in the middle of the forth.[15] His translator renders *caer* by the word 'city'; but it should be rendered a fort or post, which will give probability to Bede's account.

In 1549 the English fleet, sent by Edward VI to assist the lords of the congregation against the queen dowager, landed, and began to fortify this island,[16] of the importance of which they grew sensible after their neglect of securing the port of Leith, so lately in their power. They left here five companies to cover the workmen under the command of Cotterel; but their operations were soon interrupted by M. Desse, general of the French auxiliaries, who took the place, after a gallant defence on the part of the English. The Scots kept possession for some years; but at last the fortifications were destroyed by Act of Parliament, to prevent it from being of any use to the former.[17] The French gave it the name of *L'isle des Chevaux,* from its property of soon fattening horses.

In 1497, by order of council,[18] all venereal patients in the neighbourhood of the capital were transported there, *ne quid detrimenti Respublica caperet.* It is remarkable that this disorder, which was thought to have made its appearance in Europe only four years before, should make so quick a progress. The horror of a disease, for which there was at that period no cure known, must have occasioned this attention to stop the contagion; for even half

[15] *Hist. Eccl.,* lib. I, ch. 12.
[16] Lesly, 479.
[17] Maitland II, 1008.
[18] Vide Appendix.

a century after, one of the first monarchs in Europe, Francis I, fell a victim to it.

About a mile from Kinghorn is the precipice fatal to Alexander III, who, in 1285, was killed by a fall from it, his horse rushing down with him, when he was enjoying the pleasures of the chase. A mile beyond this is the town of Burntisland; the best harbour on the coast, formed by a rocky isle, eked out with piers, for there are none on this side the county entirely natural. This is dry at low water. The church is square, with a steeple rising in the centre. The old castle built by the Duries commanded both town and harbour. The place has a natural strength, which, with the conveniency of a port opposite to the capital, made it, during the troubles of 1560, a most desirable port. The French, allies of the Queen regent, fortified it strongly. In 1715 it was surprised, and possessed by the rebels, who here formed the bold design of passing over a body of troops to the opposite shore; which was in part executed under the conduct of Brigadier Macintosh, notwithstanding all the efforts of our men of war.

A little farther is Aberdour, another small town. The Earl of Morton has a pleasant seat here. In old times it belonged to the Viponts;[19] in 1126 was transferred to the Mortimers, by marriage, and afterwards to the Douglases. William, Lord of Liddesdale, surnamed 'the Flower of Chivalry', in the reign of David II by charter, conveyed it to James Douglas, ancestor of the present noble owner. The monks of Inchcolm had a grant for a burial place here, from Allan de Mortimer, in the reign of Alexander III. The nuns, usually styled the poor Clares, had a convent at this place.

I had the pleasure of seeing, near Aberdour, a most select collection of pictures, made by Captain Stuart, who, with great politeness, obliged me with the sight of them. It is in vain to attempt the description of this elegant cabinet, as I may say, one part or other used to be always on the march. This gentleman indulges his elegant and laudable passion so far as to form out of them *un cabinet portatif*, which is his amusement, on the road, in quarters; in short, the companions of all his motions. His house is very small:

[19] Sibbald's *Fife*, 122.

to get at his library I ascended a ladder, which reminded me of the habitation of Mynhier Biscop, at Rotterdam, the richest repository in Europe, under the poorest roof. But the comparison fails in this: Biscop was a brute; our countryman the reverse.

Two or three miles to the west lies Inchcolm; a small island, at a little distance from the shore, celebrated for the monastery founded about 1123, by Alexander I on this singular occasion. In passing the Firth of Forth he was overtaken with a violent storm, which drove him to this island, where he met with the most hospitable reception from a poor hermit, then residing here in the chapel of St Columba, who, for the three days that the King continued there tempest-bound, entertained him with the milk of his cow, and a few shellfish. His Majesty, from the sense of the danger he had escaped, and in gratitude to the saint, to whom he attributed his safety, vowed, some token of respect; and accordingly founded here a monastery of Augustines, and dedicated it to St Columba.[20] Allan de Mortimer, Lord of Aberdour, who attended Edward III in his Scotch expedition, bestowed half of those lands on the monks of this island, for the privilege of a family burial place in their church.

The buildings made in consequence of the piety of Alexander were very considerable. There are still to be seen a large square tower belonging to the church, the ruins of the church, and of several other buildings. The wealth of this place in the time of Edward III proved so strong a temptation to his fleet, then lying in the Forth, as to suppress all the horror of sacrilege, and respect to the sanctity of the inhabitants. The English landed, and spared not even the furniture more immediately consecrated to divine worship. But due vengeance overtook them; for in a storm which instantly followed, many of them perished; those who escaped, struck with the justice of the judgment, vowed to make ample recompense to the injured saint. The tempest ceased; and they made the promised atonement.[21]

The Danish monument, figured by Sir Robert Sibbald, lies on the south-east side of the building, on a rising ground. It is of a rigid

[20] Boethius, lib. XII, 263.
[21] Boethius, lib. XV, 319.

XXV

J. Falconer delin.

ABBY OF INCH-COLM.

form, and the surface ornamented with scale-like figures. At each end is the representation of a human head.

Boethius gives this island the name of Emonia, from *Y Mona*, or 'the isle of Mona'.

After leaving this place, see, on the left, Dunibrissel; the seat of the Earl of Murray. In 1592 this was the scene of the cruel murder of the 'bonny', or the handsome earl, whose charms were supposed to have engaged the heart of Anne of Denmark, and to have excited the jealousy of her royal spouse. The former at least was the popular notion of the time:

> *He was a braw gallant*
> *And he play'd at the gluve:*
> *And the bonny Earl of Murray*
> *Oh! He was the Queenes love.*

Political reasons were given for his arrest; but more than an arrest seems to have been intended, for the commission was entrusted to his inveterate enemy Huntly, who, with a number of armed men, surrounding the house in a dark night, set it on fire, on Murray's refusal to surrender: he escaped the flames, but was unfortunately discovered by a spark that fell on his helmet, and was slain, in telling Gordon of Buckie, who had wounded him in the face, 'You have spilt a better face than your awin.'

Ride through Inverkeithing, a royal burgh; and, during the time of David I, a royal residence. It was much favoured by William, who in their first charter extended its liberties from the water of Dovan to that of Levin. The Mowbrays had large possessions here, forfeited in the reign of Robert II. The Franciscans had a convent in this town; and, according to Sir Robert Sibbald, the Dominicans had another.

Separated from the bay of Inverkeithing, by a small headland, is that of St Margaret; the place where that illustrious princess, afterwards queen of Malcolm III, landed with her brother Edgar in 1068, after their flight from England, to avoid the consequences of the jealousy of the conqueror, on account of the title of the former to the crown. This passage is also called the Queen's Ferry, being afterwards her familiar passage to Dumfermline, her usual residence.

The village on this side is called the North Ferry. At this place stood a chapel, served by the monks of Dumfermline, and endowed by Robert I. Near it are the great granite quarries, which help to supply our capital with paving stones, and employ a number of vessels for the conveyance. The granite lies in perpendicular stacks, and above is a reddish earth, filled with micaceous friable nodules.

From Kinghorn to this place the firth contracts itself gradually; but here, by the jutting out of the northern shore, almost instantly forms a strait of two miles in breadth; and beyond as suddenly opens in a large and long expense. About midway of this strait lies Inchgarvie, with the ruins of a fort. This was a fine station to review the shores I had travelled, and to feast the eye with the whole circumambient view. The prospect on every part is beautiful: a rich country, diversified with the quickest succession of towns, villages, castles, and seats; a vast view up and down the firth from its extremity, not remote from Sterling, to its mouth near May island, an extent of sixty miles. To particularise the objects of this rich scene must be enumerated, the coasts of Lothian and of Fife, the isles of Garvie and Inchcolm, the town of Dumfermline; the south and north ferries, and Burrowstoness, smoking at a distance, from its numerous salt-pans and fire engines: on the south side are Hopetoun House, Dundas Castle, and many other gentlemen's seats; with Blackness Castle, once an important fortress: on the north side are Rosyth Castle, once the seat of the Stuarts; Dunibrissel, and, in the distant view, the castle and town of Burntisland; Leith, with its road often filled with ships, and a magnificent view of Edinburgh Castle on the south, assist to complete this various picture.

As I am nearly arrived at the extremity, permit me to take a review of the peninsula of Fife, a county so populous, that, excepting the environs of London, scarce one in South Britain can vie with it; fertile in soil, abundant in cattle, happy in collieries, in iron, stone, lime, and freestone, blest in manufactures, the property remarkably well divided, none insultingly powerful, to distress and often to depopulate a country, most of the fortunes of a useful mediocrity. The number of towns is perhaps unparalleled in an equal tract of coast, for the whole shore from Crail to Culross, about forty English miles, is one continued chain of towns and villages. With justice, therefore, does Johnston celebrate the advantages of the country in these lines:

> Oppida sic toto sunt sparsa in littore, ut unum
> Dixeris; inque uno plurima juncta eadem.
> Littore quot curvo Forthae volvuntur arenae
> quotoque undis refluo tunditur ora salo;
> Pene tot hic cernas instratum puppibus aequor,
> Uribus et crebris pene tot ora hominum.
> Cuncta operis intenta domus saeda otia nescit;
> Sedula cura domi, sedula cura foris.
> Quae Maria et quas non terras animosa juventus
> Ah! Fragli sidens audet adire trabe.
> Auxit opes virtus, virtuti dira pericla
> Juncta, etiam lucro damna fuere suo,
> Quae secere viris animos, cultumque dedere
> Magnanimis prosunt damna, pericla, labor.

After having passed by the Queen's Ferry, turn almost due north. See, on the road side, a great stone, called Queen Margaret's, for tradition says, she reposed herself on it in her way to Dumfermline. In a little time have a fine view of that flourishing town, and the ruins of its cathedral and palace full in front.

Dumfermline lies at the distance of four miles from the firth; is prettily situated on a rising ground, and the country round is beautifully divided by low and well-cultivated hills; and grounds are enclosed, and planted with hedgerow trees. The town wants the advantage of a river, but has a small stream for economic uses, which is conducted through the streets in a flagged channel. At its discharge it joins another rivulet, then arriving at a fall into a wooded dell of a hundred feet in depth, becomes again useful in turning five mills, placed one below the other, with room for as many more. Three of the mills are for corn; the fourth for flax; the fifth for beating iron. This dell winds about the western side of the town, is clothed with trees, and in one part contributes a most picturesque scenery to the walks laid out by Mr Chalmers, whose seat is on the opposite banks.

This place is very populous. The number of inhabitants are between six and seven thousand: and such have been the improvements in manufactures as to have increased near double its ancient number within the last twelve years. The manufactures are damasks, diapers, checks and ticking, to the amount of forty thousand pounds a year: these employ in town and neighbourhood about a thousand looms. I was informed that the number might be doubled if it was not prevented by the low duty on foreign linens, which encourages a foreign importation. But probably some other branch of British trade might receive its injury in a greater degree, was that importation to be checked.

That the iron business does not flourish more in this place is matter of surprise. Ironstone abounds. Here are collieries in all parts, even to the very entrance of the town; and the coals of such variety, that in different parts are found, besides the Scotch, those which have the qualities of the Newcastle, and of the Kilkenny. I am informed that on the Pittencrief estate are seven seams of coal in the depth of thirty fathoms, from the thickness of two to that of eight feet, all of which may be worked with a level without the assistance of any machinery. The price of coal here is from twenty pence to half a crown a ton.

The most remarkable modern building here is the tolbooth, with a slender square tower, very lofty, and topped with a conic roof. Mr Chalmers has also made a work of vast expense over the glen on the west end of the town, in order to form a communication with his estate, and to encourage buildings and improvements on that side. To effect which, he formed an arch three hundred feet in length, twelve feet wide, and ten high; covering the whole with earth, seventy-five feet thick.

This place had been at times, from very distant periods, the residence of the Scottish monarchs. Malcolm Canmor lived here, in a castle on the top of an insulated hill, in the midst of the glen; but only some poor fragments remain. A palace was afterwards built on the side next to the town, which falling to decay, was rebuilt by Anne of Denmark, as appears by the following inscription:

Propylaeum et superstructas aedes vetustate et injuriis temporum collapsas dirutasque; a fundamentis in hanc ampliorem formam, restituit et instauravit Anna Regina Frederici Danorum Regis augustissimi, Filia: Anno salutis 1600.

XXVI

M. Griffith, del.

R. Scott sculpt.

ABBY & PALACE AT DUNFERLINE.

The ruins are magnificent, and do credit to the restorer. In this palace she brought forth her unfortunate son Charles I. A gateway intervenes between the royal residence, and the magnificent abbey, begun by Malcolm Canmor, and finished by Alexander I. It was probably first intended for the pious and more useful purpose of a religious infirmary, being styled in some old manuscripts *Monasterium ab monte infirmorum'*.[22] David I changed it into an abbey, and brought into it thirteen monks from Canterbury; but at the dissolution it supported twenty-six.[23] Its endowments were very considerable. At the Reformation the revenue, in money alone, was two thousand five hundred and thirteen pounds Scots. Some of the grants were singular: that of David I gives it 'the tyth of all the gold found in Fife and Fotherif', a proof of the precious metal being then discovered in streams flowing from the hills. Another, from the same monarch, invests it with part of the seals taken near Kinghorn; and a third by Malcolm IV gives them the heads (except the tongues) of certain small whales, called 'crespies', which might be taken in such part of 'Scotchwatir' (the Firth of Forth) where the church stood: and the oil extracted from them was to be applied to its use.

The remains of the abbey are considerable, and evince its former splendour. The window of the room, near the gateway, called Frater Ball, is very beautiful. The abbot's house is adjacent. In 1303, Edward I burnt down the whole abbey, excepting the church and cells, pleading in excuse of his sacrilege, that it gave a retreat to his enemies.

Part of the church is at present in use. It is supported by three rows of massy pillars, scarcely seventeen feet high, and thirteen and a half in circumference. Two are ribbed spirally, and two marked with zigzag lines, like those of Durham, which they resemble. The arches are also Saxon or round. As the church was built by Malcolm Canmor, at the instance of Turgot, Bishop of St Andrews, (once Prior of Durham) that might be the reason it was constructed in a

[22] Keith, 246.
[23] Keith's Appendix.

XXVII

A WINDOW IN DUMFERLIN ABBEY.

similar style.[24] From this time the celebrated Iona lost the honour of being the cemetery of the Scottish monarchs. Malcolm, and his queen, and six other kings,[25] lie here; the two first apart, the others under as many flat stones, each nine feet long.

In the church is the tomb of Robert Pitcairn, abbot, or rather commendator, of Dumfermline, Secretary of State in the beginning of the reign of James VI in the regency of Lenox. He was of Morton's faction, and was sent to the court of Elizabeth, to solicit the delivery of Mary Stuart into the hands of the King's party.[26] He attended James in his confinement, after the Raid of Ruthven, and artfully endeavoured to make friends with each side; but, failing, was imprisoned in Loch Leven Castle, and died in 1584. His epitaph sets his virtues in a very high light:

> *Hic situs est Heros modica Robertus in urna*
> *Pitcarnus, patriae spes columenque suae:*
> *Quem virtus, Gravitas generoso pectore digna*
>   *Ornabant vera et cum pietate fides.*
> *Post varios vitae fluctus jam mole relicta*
>   *Corporis, Elysium pergit in umbra nemus.*

Leave Dumfermline. At a distance is pointed out to me a tumulus, planted with trees, called the Penitent Mount, from a vulgar notion, that it was formed by sacks full of land, brought there from distant places by the frail, by way of penance for their sins. At Clune am struck with the magnificence of the prospect, extending west to Ben Lomond, and east to Old Cambus; a view of the whole Forth, and the castles of Edinburgh and Stirling, two most capital objects.

Descend towards the shore; and near it, reach the limekilns, belonging to the Earl of Elgin, the greatest perhaps in the universe; placed amidst inexhaustible beds of limestones, and near immense seams of coal. The kilns are placed in a row; their openings are beneath a covered way, formed, by arches and pillars in front, into a magnificent colonnade. They lie beneath the strata of limestone, which, when broken, is conveyed into them by variety of rail roads;

[24] Boethius, lib. XII, 260.
[25] Edgar, Alexander I, David I, Malcolm IV, Alexander II and Robert Bruce.
[26] Melvil's *Memoirs*, 212.

and for shipping the lime, either burnt or crude, is a convenient pier. A hundred and twenty men are constantly employed, and a little town built for them. Above twelve thousand pounds has been expended on this useful project, which promises to turn out as much to the emolument of the noble family, which so generously engaged in it, as to the whole eastern coast of North Britian, which either wants this great fertilizer, or fuel to burn the stone they uselessly possess.

By the following account it is pleasing to observe the improving state of agriculture, and of building, in these parts of the kingdom; for the last also occasions a considerable consumption:

Sold, from Martinmas, 1770, to ditto, 1771

	£	s	d
57,515 bolls of lime shells, or unslaked lime	2,035	8	$6^{1}/_{2}$
2,852 $^{1}/_{2}$ chalders of lime,	974	11	9
37,814 carts of limestone,	864	13	$8^{1}/_{2}$
	3,874	14	0

From Martinmas, 1771, to ditto, 1772

	£	s	d
65,321 bolls of lime -shells,	3,380	7	$4^{1}/_{2}$
2,271 chalders of lime,			
52,000 carts of limestone	1,250	3	$11^{1}/_{2}$
	4,630	11	4

Opposite to Limekilns, on a rock projecting into the Forth, is Blackness Castle, once a place of great importance in preserving a communication between Edinburgh and Sterling; now a shelter to a few invalids. This fortress is a large pile, defended by towers, both square and round. Irvine says,[27] that in his time it was a state prison: he adds, that it was of old one of the Roman forts, and that it stood on the beginning of the wall. But Mr Gordon seems,

[27] *Nomenclatura*, 23.

with more truth, to place its commencement at Carin, or Caribden, west of this place. Blackness was once the port of Linlithgow, had a town near it, and a custom-house; both which were lost by the new commerce of salt and coals that rose at Burrowstoness.

XVII

PERTHSHIRE (5), CLACKMANNANSHIRE, LINLITHGOWSHIRE, LOTHIAN

Culross—Alloa—Cambuskenneth—Sterling—Bannockbourne—
Camelon—Falkirk—Carron Wharf—Linlithgow—Edinburgh—Leith—
Hawthorden—Roslin—Dalkeith—Crichton Castle—Borthwick Castle

A FTER a ride of four miles enter a portion of Perthshire, which
just touches on the Firth, at Culross; a small town, remarkable
for a magnificent house with thirteen windows in front, built about
the year 1590, by Edward, Lord Kinloss, better known in England
by the name of Lord Bruce, slain in the noted duel between him
and Sir Edward Sackville.

Some poor remains of the Cistercian abbey are still to be seen
here, founded by Malcolm, Earl of Fife, in 1217. The church was
jointly dedicated to the virgin, and St Serf, confessor. The revenue,
at the Dissolution, was seven hundred and sixty-eight pounds Scots,
besides the rents paid in kind. The number of monks, exclusive of
the abbot, were nine.

Continue my ride, in sight of vast plantations; and, in a short space enter the little shire of Clackmannan, which, with that of Kinross, alternately elect a member, their mutual representative. The small town of Clackmannan is pleasantly seated on a hill, long the seat of the chief of the Bruces, sloping on every side; and on the summit is the castle, commanding a noble view. The large square tower is called after the name of Robert Bruce; whose great sword and casque is still preserved here. The hill is prettily wooded, and, with the tower, forms a picturesque object. On the western side, cross the little River Devan, and, after a mile's ride, reach the town of Alloa, remarkable for its coal trade. Scotland exports annually, above a hundred and eighteen thousand tons of coal, out of which, I was informed, Alloa alone sends forty thousand. The town and parish is very populous, containing five thousand souls. I found here the most polite reception from Mr Erskine, representative of the family of Mar, who lives in the castle, now modernised, on one side of the town. The gardens, planted in the old style, are very extensive. In the house are some good portraits, particularly one of the celebrated Lucy, Countess of Bedford,[1] a full length, in black, with a ruff, and a coronet on her head. She sits with a pensive countenance, her face reclined on one hand and is, without beauty, an elegant figure. She was sister to John, Lord Harrington, and wife to Edward, Earl of Bedford, and became, on the death of her brother, possessed of great part of his large fortune. She affected the patronage of wits and poets; and probably possessed part of the qualities they attributed to her, or the philosophic Sir William Temple would never have condescended to celebrate her fine taste in gardening.[2] She might purchase every perfection from the former; for Donne informs us, 'She rained upon him her sweet showers of gold':[3] on Ben Johnson, haunches of venison;[4] and they, in gratitude, bestowed on her as many beauties and as many virtues as ought to have put

[1] Painted by Cornelius Jansen, in 1620, in the 38th year of her age.
[2] *Gardens of Epicurus.*
[3] As quoted by Mr Granger.
[4] Epigram 85.

vanity herself out of countenance. She makes the rough Donne declare:

> Leaving that busie praise and all appeale,
> To higher courts, senses decree is true
> The mine, the magazine, the commonweale,
> The story of beauty, in Twickham is, and you.
>   Who hath seen one, would both, as who had bin
>   In Paradise, would seek the Cherubim.[5]

In a word, her ideas became too sublime for domestic affairs; she spent her own and part of her husband's great fortunes, and, having established her character for taste, departed this life in the year 1628.

Catherine, daughter and heiress of Francis, Earl of Rutland, wife of George Villars, Duke of Buckingham. By Van Dyck. She is painted sitting with her three children, and the head of the duke in an oval above her. She afterwards married the Earl of Antrim. 'She was a lady', says the noble historian, 'of great wit and spirit; who, by her influence over Charles I forced him, under pretence of his majesty's service, to gratify her vanity, by creating her husband a marquis.'[6]

A remarkable half-length of Mary Stuart, on copper, in a gauze cloak, crown on her head, and passion-flower in her hand; sickly and pale.

A head of Anne of Denmark. A princess of so spotless a life, that malice could not find a blemish in her; therefore well might Wilson say, 'on her monument a character of virtue may be engraven'.[7] When Heaven claims her, a living queen cannot escape the same epitaph.

The Ochil Hills begin beyond Alloa to approach very near to the Forth, between which is a narrow arable tract, well-cultivated and adorned with woods. In these hills was found, in the beginning of this century, a large body of native silver, beautifully ramified; and of late years, some cobalt ore. The view of Sterling, and the

---

[5] *Poems*, 82.
[6] *Hist. of Rebellion* II, 617.
[7] *Life of James I*, 129.

windings of the Forth, now a river, are extremely elegant. Am now again in a portion of Perthshire. Turn half a mile out of the road, to visit the ancient abbey of Cambuskenneth, or rather its remains, nothing being left by the rude hand of Reformation, excepting a vast square tower, and an arched doorway, between which is a fine view of Sterling, on its sloping rock. This house was founded by David I in 1147, for canons regular of St Augustine, brought from Aroise near Arras; but the superiors were often called abbots of Sterling. Keith says, that it now belongs to St Cowan's hospital, in that city. James III and his queen were buried in this place.

After a short ride, reach the bridge of Sterling, now of stone; in the days of Sir William Wallace, of wood. On this side, the hero obtained the glorious victory over the English, commanded by the Earl of Surry, and impeded their retreat by sawing, before the fight, the posts of the bridge, which fell by the weight of fugitives.

Enter Sterling, a town says Boethius, which gave name to sterling money, because Osbert, a Saxon prince, after the overthrow of the Scots, established here a mint.[8] It was also anciently called Striveling; as is said, from the frequency of strifes or conflicts in the neighbourhood: and from this old name the present seems to have been formed.

The town contains about four thousand inhabitants; has a manufacture of tartans and shalloons, and employs about thirty looms in that of carpets. The great street is very broad; in it is the tolbooth, where is kept the standard for the wet measures of Scotland. The other streets narrow and irregular; the west side had been defended by a wall.

I cannot trace the foundation of the castle: if we may credit Boethius, it was a place of strength in the middle of the ninth century. The Romans had a camp and a military way on the west side: it might be their Alauna, but clouds and darkness rest on this part of our history.

Sterling is a miniature resemblance of Edinburgh, built on a rock of the same form with that on which the capital of North Britain is placed, with a strong fortress on the summit.

---

[8] Lib. X, 206. Sterling money is derived from the merchants of the Easterlings.

XXVIII

CAMBUSKENETH & A VIEW OF STIRLING.

The castle is of great strength, impending over a steep precipice. Within side stands the palace, built by James V, a prince that had a strong turn to the arts, as appears by his buildings here and at Falkland. This pile is large, of a square form, ornamented on three sides with pillars, resting on grotesque figures, jutting from the wall. On the top of each pillar, a fanciful statue.

Two rooms, called the Queen's and the nursery, are large; the roofs of wood, divided into squares and other forms, well carved.

A closet is shown, noted for the murder of William, Earl of Douglas, in 1452, trepanned here by a safe conduct from James II. This nobleman, too potent for legal execution, had entered into associations injurious to his prince; who commanded him to rescind the offensive alliance; and, on refusal, stabbed the earl with his own hand. In revenge, the friends of Douglas instantly burnt the town.

The parliament house is a vast room, a hundred and twenty feet long, with a timbered roof. This town, during the reigns of Mary and James VI was much frequented by the court and the nobility. In September, 1571, a bloody attempt was made here, by the Queen's party, on the regent Lenox; who was surprised, at midnight, surrounded by his friends, and in full security. Except the Earl of Morton, none of the numerous nobility made the least resistance, but surrendered themselves quietly to the enemy. Morton defended his house till it was all in flames. This gave the townsmen time to recollect their courage: they in turn attacked the assassins, who, struck with a panic, gave themselves up to their own prisoners. But the unfortunate Lenox fell a victim to the *manes* of the Archbishop of St Andrew's. Sir David Spence, to whom he had surrendered, perished in the attempt to save him, being shot by the bullet that slew his noble captive.

From the top of the castle is by far the finest view in Scotland: to the east is a vast plain, rich in corn, adorned with woods, and watered with the River Forth, whose meanders are, before it reaches the sea, so frequent and so large, as to form a multitude of most beautiful peninsulas; for in many parts the windings approximate so close as to leave only a little isthmus of a few yards. In this plain is an old abbey, a view of Alloa, Clackmannan, Falkirk, the Firth of

Forth, and the country as far as Edinburgh; on the north, the Ochil Hills, and the moor where the battle of Dumblain was fought; to the west, the strath of Menteith, as fertile as the eastern plain, and terminated by the Highland mountains; among which the summit of Ben Lomond is very conspicuous.

Among the houses of the nobility, the most superb was that of the Earl of Mar, built by the regent; the front ornamented with the arms of the family, and much sculpture. It is said to have been built from the ruins of Cambuskenneth, and that being reproached with the sacrilege, directed these words, yet extant, to be put over the gate:

> *ESSPY. SPEIK. FURTH. I CAIR. NOTHT.*
> *CONSIDIR. WEIL. I. CAIR. NOTHT.*

Near the castle are Edmonston's Walks, cut through a little wood, on the vast steeps. Nature hath strangely buttressed it up with stones of immense size, wedged between each other with more of the same kind piled on their tops. Beneath, on the flat, are to be seen the vestiges of the gardens belonging to the palace, called the King's Knot; where, according to the taste of the times, the flowers had been disposed in beds and curious knots, at this time very easily to be traced in the fantastic form of the turf.

Above these walks is the Ladies Hill; for here sat the fair to see their faithful knights exert their vigour and address in the tilts and tournaments, performed in a hollow between this spot and the castle.

The church or royal chapel was collegiate, founded by Pope Alexander IV at the request of James IV, for a dean, subdean, sacristan, chanter, treasurer, chancellor, archdean, sixteen chaplains, and six singing-boys, which, with the chaplains and a music master, were appointed by the king. The queen's confessor was the dean, who had episcopal jurisdiction. The whole most richly endowed.

The Carmelites had a house here, founded by James IV in 1494. Remorse for his father's death, seems to have instigated him to attempt these pious atonements. To this place he was wont to retire from all worldly affairs, and to perform the duties of religion with all the austerities of the devoted inhabitants.

Beneath the walls was another, of Dominicans, established in 1233, by Alexander II. In this church was interred, an imposter, who, at the instigation of the Countess of Oxford, assumed the character of Richard II. After his retreat, he found here an honourable support to the day of his death.[9]

The hospital for decayed merchants, founded by John Cowan, a merchant of this town, is very richly endowed. Here is another, founded by Robert Spittal, tailor to James IV, for the relief not only of merchants but decayed tradesmen.

This place has experienced its sieges, and other calamities of war. In 1175 it was delivered, by William, to the English, as a security, with several other places, for his acknowledgement, that he held the crown of Scotland from the kings of England. An inglorious cession, extorted by his unfortunate captivity. But Richard I, the succeeding monarch, restored them.[10]

During the wars between the English and Brucean Scots, it often changed masters. In 1299 it was in possession of Edward I, whose affairs in Scotland were at that time so bad, that he was obliged to send his governor an order to surrender. But the year following, he retook it, after a most gallant defence by William Oliphant, who gave it up on terms ill observed by the conqueror.

In 1303, it was again taken by the Scots, under Lord John Sowles: Oliphant resumed the command; and in the next year sustained a second siege. It was battered most furiously by the artillery of the age, which cast stones of two hundred weight against the walls, and made vast breaches. At length, when the garrison was reduced to a very few, the brave governor submitted and was received into mercy.

In the reign of Edward II, it was besieged by Sir Edward Bruce. The governor, Sir Philip Mowbray, made a valiant defence; but, in consequence of the battle of Bannockourne, was reduced to yield to the victorious army. During the wars of Edward III, it was reciprocally taken and retaken; the last time in 1341. The other great events of this place have slipped my memory. I must make a

---

[9] Keith, 271.
[10] Major, lib. IV, ch. 5, 135, 136.

long stride to its memorable siege in the winter of 1746, when the gallant old officer, General Blakeney, baffled all the efforts of the rebels to reduce this important place.

In the evening, pass through the small town of St Ninian, and the village of Bannockbourne.

Ascend a hill, and pass by the relics of Torwood, noted for having given shelter to Wallace, after the fatal battle of Falkirk. Some remains of an oak, beneath which the hero is said to have reposed, is still pointed out with great veneration. Over this place passes the Roman military road, which I traced before to the north of Dupplin. At some distance from this, leave, in a valley on the left, the two mounts, called Dunipace, placed on the north bank of the Carron, Caravon, or 'the winding river'. Night closed on me before I reached this place, so I must speak by quotation from an ingenious essay on the antiquities of Sterlingshire, published in the *Edinburgh Magazine*. The one, says the author, is perfectly round, and about fifty feet high. The other, which he seems unwilling to admit to be the work of art, is of an irregular form, and composed of gravel. Mr Gordon conjectures them to have been exploratory mounts: the writer of the essay, that they were sepulchral. The last seems best founded, for, if I recollect, the tops of exploratory hills are truncated or flat.

To the east of these, on the same side of the river, stood the celebrated antiquity, called Arthur's Oven, which Mr Gordon supposes to have been a *sacellum*, or little chapel, a repository for the Roman insignia, or standards.

This building was circular, upright on the sides, and rounded towards the top, in which was an opening eleven feet six inches in diameter. Beneath this was, on one side, a square aperture, like a window; under that, a door, whose top formed a Roman arch. The height to the round opening at the top, was twenty-two feet; the inner diameter of the building, at the bottom, nineteen feet six inches; round the inside, Boethius informs, were stone seats; and on the south side, an altar. He also acquaints us, that the floor was tessellated, as appeared by the fragments that might be picked up in his time.[11] He adds, that there were, on some of the stones, the

---

[11] Lib. III, 34.

sculpture of eagles, nearly defaced by age; and that there had been an inscription on a polished stone, signifying that the building was erected by Vespasian, in honour of the emperor Claudius, and the goddess Victory. This he speaks by tradition; for our Edward, conqueror of Scotland, is charged with carrying it away with him. All the old historians that take notice of this edifice, agree, that it was the work of the Romans, from the British Nennius to the Scotch Buchanan. How far that may be allowed, will be a future consideration: at present I shall only, in opposition to Mr Maitland, assert, what it was not, a mausoleum resembling the sepulchre of Metella,[12] which is a round tower, totally open at top. A more apt comparison might be found in the *calidarium* of the baths of Dioclesian,[13] whose vaulted roof, rounded, and, with a central aperture, agrees with that of the deplored Scottish antiquity.

Leave at a small distance on the left, Camelon, the site of a Roman town; whose streets and walls might be traced in the midst of the ruins in the time of Buchanan;[14] but, as I was informed, not a relic is to be seen at present worthy of a visit. The sea once flowed up to this town, if the report be true, that fragments of anchors have been found near it; and beds of oyster shells in various places, at this time remote from the Forth, which is kept embanked from overflowing the flat tract in many parts between this place and Burrowstoness. Buchanan supposes this town to have been the Caer Guidi of the venerable Bede;[15] but as that writer expressly says, that it lay in the middle of the Forth, it was probably a fortress on Inchkeith, as his Alcluith is another on the Firth of Clyde.

Lie at Falkirk, a large ill-built town, supported by the great fairs for black cattle from the Highlands, it being computed that 24,000 head are annually sold here.

Carron Wharf lies upon the river, which falls a few miles below into the Forth, and is not only useful to the great iron works erected near it, but of great service even to Glasgow, considerable

---

[12] *Antichita di Roma dell' abate Venuti*, tom. ii, 9. tab. 97.
[13] Idem. tom. i, 93, tab. 32.
[14] Lib. I, ch. 21. IV, ch. 36.
[15] *Hist. Eccles.*, lib. I, ch. 12.

quantities of goods destined for that city being landed here. The canal, which is to form a communication between this firth and that of Clyde, begins on the south side of the mouth of the Carron. Its course will be above thirty miles, assisted by thirty-nine locks. Its western termination is to be at Dalmuirburnfoot, eight miles below Glasgow; but, for the conveniency of that city, it is proposed to form another branch from the great trunk, at a place called the Stocking Bleachfield, between two and three miles distant from the city.

Near Callendar House, at a small distance east from Falkirk, are some large remains of Antoninus's Wall, or, as it is called here, Graham's Dike, from the notion that one Graham, or Grimus,[16] first made a breach in it, soon after the retreat of the Romans out of Britain. This vast work was effected by Lollius Urbicus, governor of Britain during the reign of Antoninus Pius, as appears by inscriptions found on stones discovered among the ruins of the chain of forts that defended it. Most of them are in honour of the emperor; one only mentions the lieutenant.[17] The wall itself was of turf, which in this place was forty feet broad, and the ditch thirteen feet deep. Lollius, after defeating the Britons, and recovering the country, which was, as Tacitus expresses it, 'lost as soon as won',[18] restored to the empire the boundary left by Agricola, and removed the barbarians to a greater distance.[19] It is probable, that Lollius might either place his forts on the same site with those built by Agricola, or make use of the same in case they were not destroyed; but the first is most probable, as fifty-five years had elapsed, from the time that Agricola left the island, to the re-conquest of these parts by the legate of Antonine. This wall begins near Kirkpatric, on the Firth of Clyde, and ends at Caeridden, two miles west of Abercorn, on the Firth of Forth, being, according to Mr Gordon, in length, thirty-six miles, eight hundred and eighty-seven paces;

[16] Boethius.
[17] Horsley, *Scotland*, tab. viii. See also my first volume, p. 138, where some of the inscriptions are mentioned.
[18] *Hist.*, lib. I, ch. 2.
[19] Capitolinus.

and defended, I think, by twelve, if not thirteen forts. It is probable that the Romans did not keep possession even of this wall for any length of time; for there are no inscriptions but in honour of that single emperor.

Continue our journey over a naked and barren country. Leave, on the right, the nunnery of Manwel, founded by Malcolm IV in 1156. The recluses were of the Cistercian order. Cross the water of Avon, and enter the shire of Linlithgow, and soon after have a beautiful view of the town, the castle, and the lake. This is supposed to be the Lindum of Ptolemy, and to take its name from its situation on a lake, or *lin*, or *llyn*, which the word *'lin'*, or *'llyn'*, signifies.

The town contains between three and four thousand souls, and carries on a considerable trade in dressing of white leather, which is sent abroad to be manufactured. It also employs many hands in dressing of flax, and in wool-combing: for the last, the wool is brought from the borders. Its port was formerly Blackness, but since the decline of that place, Burrowstoness, about two miles distant from Linlithgow.

The castle was founded by Edward I, who resided in it for a whole winter. But in 1307 we find that it was taken, and demolished by one Binny, a Scotsman. In the reign of Edward III, the English possessed it again; for there is extant, an order for the custody of the hospital to John Swanland.[20]

I cannot discover by whom it was rebuilt. It is at present a magnificent edifice, of a square form, finely seated above the lake. James V and VI ornamented it greatly. The inside is much embellished with sculpture: over an inner gate are niches, in former times holding the statues of a pope and cardinal; erected, as tradition says, by James V, in compliment to his holiness for a present of a consecrated sword and helmet.[21] On an outward gate, detached from the building, are the four orders of knighthood, which his Majesty bore, the garter, thistle, holy ghost, and golden fleece.

[20] *Calendar of Charters*, by Sir Jos. Aylosse, 162.
[21] Lesly, *Hist. Scot.*, 353.

XXIX

M. Griffiths del.

M. O'Donel sculp.

THE PALACE AT LINLITHGOW.

Within the palace is a handsome square: one side is more modern than the others, having been guilt by James VI, and kept in good repair, till 1746, when it was accidentally burnt by the king's forces. The pediments over the windows are neatly carved, and dated 1619.

The other sides are more ancient: in one is a room ninety-five feet long, thirty feet six inches wide, and thirty-three high. At one end is a gallery, with three arches, perhaps for music. Narrow galleries run quite round the old part, to preserve communications with the rooms; in one of which the unfortunate Mary Stuart first saw light. Her father, James V, then dying, foretold the miseries that impended over her and the kingdom. 'It came', said he, 'with a lass, and will be lost with one.'

The chapel was built by James V, and takes up one side of the square. The kitchen for the use of the kings and queens is below ground. I heard here of a letter from James VI to borrow some silver spoons for a feast; and of another to borrow from the Earl of Mar a pair of silk stockings, to appear in before the English ambassador. Though I cannot authenticate these relations of the simplicity of the times; yet I have a curious letter from the same monarch, to borrow a thousand marks, or £54 3s 4d in the year 1589, being that of his wedding, telling the lender (John Boswell, of Balmonto), 'Ye will rather hurt your self veiry far, than see the dishounour of your prince and native country with the povertie of baith set downe before the face of strangers'.

The church would be a handsome building, if not disgraced with a most ruinous floor. I was shown the place remarkable for a personated apparition that appeared to James IV while he was meditating the fatal expedition into England; and which, as honest Lindsay relates, as soon as it had delivered its message, 'vanished like a blink of sun, or a whip of a whirlwind'. The tale is told with wonderful simplicity, and would be spoiled in the abridgement: 'The King', (says the historian[22]), 'came to Lithgow where he happened to be at the time for the council, very sad and dolorous, making his devotion to God to send him good chance and fortune in his voyage. In this mean time, there came a man clad in a blue gawn

[22] p. 111.

in at the Kirk door, and belted about him in a roll of linen-cloth; a pair of botrikins on his feet, to the great of his legs, with all other hose and close conform thereto; but he had no thing on his head, but syde red yellow hair behind, and on his haffits, which wan down to his shoulders; but his forehead was bald and bare. He seemed to be a man of two and fifty years, with a great pyke-staff in his hand, and came first forward among the lords, crying and speiring for the King, saying, he desired to speak with him. While, at the last, he came where the king was sitting in the desk at his prayers: but when he saw the king, he made him little reverence or salutation, but leaned down groslings on the desk before him, and said to him in this manner, as after follows. "Sir King, my mother hath sent me to you, desiring you not to pass, at this time, where thou art purposed; for, if thou does, thou wilt not fare well in thy journey, nor none that passeth with thee. Further, she bade thee mell with no woman, nor use their counsel, nor let them touch thy body, nor thou theirs; for, if thou do it, thou wilt be confounded and brought to shame."'

In one of the streets is shown the gallery from whence Hamilton, of Bothwelhaugh, in 1570, with a blameless revenge shot the regent Murray. Hamilton had embraced the party of his royal mistress, Mary Stuart. The regent bestowed part of his estate on one of his favourites, who, in a winter's night, seized on his house, and turned his wife naked into the open fields;[23] where, before morning, she became furiously mad. Love and party rage co-operated so strongly, that he never rested till he executed his purpose. He followed the regent from place to place, till the opportunity of a slow march through a crowded street rendered his intent successful. He fled to France, and being there solicited to destroy the Admiral Coligni, he replied, with a generous resentment, that notwithstanding his injured affection compelled him to commit one murder, nothing should induce him to prostitute his sword in a base assassination.

Proceed along Strathbrock, watered by the Almond. To the right are Bathgate hills, once noted for mines of lead ore, so rich as to

---

[23] Robertson I, 511.

be deemed silver mines. Dine at Kirkliston Bridge; and, about a mile farther, cross the Almond, and enter the shire of Edinburgh. This river runs into the Forth, about four miles from this place. On the eastern bank of its influx, is the village of Cramond, once a Roman station and port. Many medals, inscriptions, and other antiquities,[24] have been discovered here. Mr Gordon says, there is one, and Mr Maitland, that there are three Roman roads leading to it; but my time would not permit me to visit the place.

On the right hand, at a small distance from our road, are some rude stones. On one, called the Catstean, a compound of Celtic and Saxon, signifying the stone of battle, is this inscription: *In hoc tumulo Jacet veta F. victi.*, supposed in memory of a person slain here.

Visit, on the roadside, Corstorphine, a collegiate church; in which are two monuments of the Foresters, ancient owners of the place, each recumbent. One preserves the memory of Sir John Forester, who made the church collegiate in 1429, and fixed here a provost, five prebendaries, and two singing boys. Here is also an inscription to the first provost, Nicholas Bannachtyne, dated 1470, concluding with request to the reader, to pray for the pope and him. Cross the water of Leith, at Coltsbridge, and soon arrive at Edinburgh.

I shall here take notice of those remarkable places which escaped my notice in my former tour; or at least merited a little further attention than I at that time paid them. I shall begin with the castle that crowns the precipitous summit of this singular city.

That fortress is of great antiquity. The ancient British name was Castell Mynydd Agned. Our long-lost Arthur, if Nennius is to be credited,[25] obtained one of his victories in its neighbourhood. His name is still retained in the great rock impending over the city, literally translated from the British, *cader*, 'the seat of Arthur'. Maitland, who gives the most probable account of the derivation of the name, attributes it to Edwin, King of Northumberland, who, from the conquests of his predecessors, was in possession of all the tract from the Humber to the Firth of Forth. Accordingly we find

---

[24] Gordon's *Itin.*, 116, 117. Horsley, 204.
[25] Ch. 62.

in very old writers, that the place was called Edwinsburch, and Edwinsburg.[26] It continued in the hands of Saxons, or English, from the invasion of Octa and Ebusa, in the year 452, till the defeat of Egfrid, King of Northumberland, in 685, by the Picts, who then repossessed themselves of it. The Saxon kings of Northumberland re-conquered it in the ninth century, and their successors retained it till it was given up to Indulfus, King of Scotland, about the year 956. All the names in this tract are of Saxon origin, and the language now spoken is full of old English words and phrases.

The castle is of great strength: and, as it was for a long time supposed to be impregnable, was called the Maiden Castle. Edward I, in 1296, made himself master of it in a few days: but, in the reign of his successor, it was, in 1313, surprised and taken by Thomas Randolph, Earl of Murray. It fell again into the hands of the English, who, in 1341, lost it by a strategem contrived by Sir William Douglas. He entered the harbour of Leith, with a vessel laden with provisions, and manned with about two hundred Highlanders. He disguised twelve in the dress of peasants, and placed the rest in ambush amidst the ruins of an abbey. He led the first up to the castle, accompanying twelve horses, laden with oats and fuel: he offered these to sale to the porter, who telling him, that the garrison stood in a great want of them, let Sir William into the gateway. They slew the porter, blockaded the gate, by killing their horses in the midst of it, and assembling their other party by sound of horn, made themselves masters of the place.

The hero Kirkcaldie, distinguished the year 1573 by a gallant defence of this castle, which he kept, in hopes of mending the fortunes of his unhappy mistress, then imprisoned in England. For three and thirty days he resisted all the efforts of the Scots and the English, excited by courage and emulation. At length, when the walls were battered down, the wells destroyed, and the whole rendered a heap of rubbish, he proposed to perish gloriously in the last entrenchment; but the garrison, which wanted his heroism, or had not the same reason for despair, mutinied, and forced him to surrender.[27]

---

[26] Vide Maitland, *Hist. Edinburgh*, 6.
[27] Robertson II, 48.

In 1650 it sustained a siege of above two months, against the Parliament army, commanded by Cromwell, and surrendered at length on very honourable terms.[28]

At the revolution, it was held for some time by the Duke of Gordon, for the abdicating prince. When his grace surrendered his charge, he made terms for every one under his command; but, with uncommon spirit and generosity, submitted his own life and interests to the mercy of the conqueror.[29] After the city was possessed by the rebels, in 1745, it underwent a short and impotent siege. The royalists, under the generals Guest and Preston kept quiet possession of it, after a few weak and unavailing hostilities.

Beneath the floor of one of the passages, were interred, the remains of William, Earl of Douglas, and his brother. These noble youths (too powerful for subjects) were inveigled here, on the faith of the royal word, and, while they were sitting at table with their prince, were seized, and hurried to the block. History mentions an uncommon circumstance. A bull's head was served up, a signal, in those days, of approaching death. The Douglases grew pale at the sight, accepting the omen.[30]

In a small room in this fortress, Mary Stuart brought into the world James VI, an event of which some uncouth rhymes on the wall inform the stranger.

The regalia of Scotland are said to be preserved here, and a room in which they are kept is pointed out, but made up, and inaccessible. According to Maitland, they were acknowledged to have been here in 1707, as appears by a formal instrument preserved by that historian.

The great cannon called Mounts Meg, made of iron bars, bound together by iron hoops, was a curiosity preserved in this fortress, till it was transported some years ago to London. It is said to have been brought here from Roxburgh, and that one of the same kind proved fatal to James II, by bursting near the royal person.

The city is of far later date than the castle. Walsingham, who wrote about the year 1440, speaks of it as a mean place, and the

---

28 Whitelock, 485.
29 *Hist. Gordons* II, 606.
30 *Hist. of the Douglases*, 154.

houses covered only with thatch: yet Froissart, who lived prior to the former, says, it was '*la principal siege du royaume, et aussi par usage le Roy d'Ecoce s'y tenoit (car il y a bon chastel, et bonne grosse ville, et beau haure)*'.[31] But it seems not to have been in any very flourishing condition, till the reign of James I, in whose last year (1436) a parliament was first held here. After those meetings were continued, its prosperity increased, and the importance of Perth, before considerable, began to lessen. Till that period, the princes and parliaments of Scotland thought the Firth of Forth a proper security against the inroads of the English, who often carried their depredations as far as this city, and often sacked it.

I should mention, that, besides the castle, it was also guarded by walls and gates. The first began near the southern base of the castle; and, protecting the town on the south and east, terminated near the north loch, then filled with water, and a sufficient security on that side.

The gates are numerous, but none that are now standing are in any degree remarkable. The Netherbow Port, which stood at the head of the Cannongate street, was a fine structure, built in the reign of James VI, but now demolished. A figure of it is preserved in Maitland's history of Edinburgh; and a still finer, but scarce, etching of it is sometimes met with, the work of Mr Alexander Runciman.

To pursue the description of Edinburgh, I shall begin with the great street, which, under several names, is continued almost in a line from the castle to Holyroodhouse, being in length a mile and a half, and in some places eighty feet wide, and in the part called the High Street, finely built.

In the street called the Castlehill, is the great reservoir for supplying the city with water. Below this is the lawn market, where every Wednesday are sold linen, checks, etc.

The weighing-house, which brings in a large revenue to the city, stands at the Bowhead, at the upper end of the lawn market.

Near that is the Luckenbooth, with the tolbooth, or city prison. The guardhouse is a little lower. I think the guard consists in all of

---

[31] Froissart, lib. II, 145.

XXX

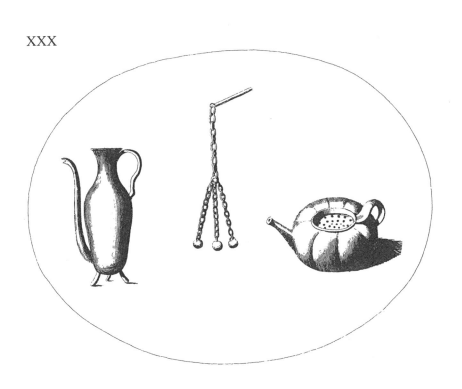

seventy-five men commanded by the provost, and three lieutenants, who are styled captains. The men are well clothed and armed. Instead of the halbert, they still retain the ancient weapon, the Lochaber axe.

In the Parliament Close, a small square, is the parliament house, where the courts of justice are held. Beneath are the advocates' library, and the register office. In my former tour, I mentioned certain curiosities preserved in the library; but neglected the notice of others in a small but select private cabinet.

Among others in the cabinet of Mr John MacGouan, discovered near this city, is an elegant brass image of a beautiful Naiad, with a little satyr in one arm. On her head is a wine-vat, or some such vessel, to denote her an attendant on Bacchus; and beneath one foot, a subverted vase, expressive of her character as a nymph of the fountains. The satyr is given her, not only to shew her relation to the jovial God, but from the opinion that the Naiads were mothers of that sylvan race.[32]

A vessel resembling a teapot, with a handle and spout. It wants a lid, but the orifice is covered with a fixed plate, full of perforations, like those of a watering-pot. Count Caylus has given a figure of a pot of this kind; but is as ignorant as myself of its use.

Some spearheads, and a brazen celt finely gilt. This embellishment of the last intimates that the instruments of that sort were not for mechanic uses; but probably the heads of javelins or ensign staffs.[33]

In the same collection is an iron whip, a most cruel instrument of punishment among the Romans. The handle is short; the lash, a chain dividing into three parts, with a bullet at the end of each. These bullets were sometimes of lead, sometimes of copper.[34] Whips of this kind are often seen in paintings of martyrdoms. It is singular, that the Europeans found among the natives of Bengal this classical scourge, or one nearly resembling it: the bullets in the Indian 'chawbuck', or whip, being affixed to thongs instead of chains.

---

[32] Monfaucon, from the authority of Nonnus. *Antiq. Expl.* I, part ii, 261.
[33] Borlasse, *Antiq. Cornwal.*
[34] Monfaucon V, part ii, 245.

The great church, divided into four places of worship; and St Giles's, with its tower terminated by a crown of stone, built by a Milne, ancestor of a celebrated race of architects, grace part of the street below the Parliament Close.

The Trone Church is remarkable for its fine Ionic front.

Here are four chapels for the use of the Protestants of the Church of England. The new one, when completed, will be a most elegant building; and the front adorned with a beautiful portico, supported by six Doric pillars, with suitable finishing. Over the altar is an Ascension by Mr Runciman; and here are besides four other paintings by the same gentleman. These, with a fine organ, are comfortable proofs of the moderation, that at present reigns in the Church of Scotland, which a few years ago would have looked with horror on these innocent decorations; and never have permitted to others what they did not approve. Perhaps the disapprobation still continues: then how far more meritorious is this toleration!

At the bottom of Cannongate stands the magnificent palace of Holyroodhouse, once an abbey of canons regular of St Augustine, founded by David I in 1128, and dedicated to the Holy Cross. This was the richest of the religious houses in North Britain, the annual revenue, at the Reformation amounting to two thousand nine hundred and twenty-six pounds Scots,[35] besides numbers of rents in kind. In 1547, it was almost ruined by the regent Duke of Somerset, who totally uncovered it, and took away with him the lead and bells.

That beautiful piece of Gothic architecture, the chapel, is now a ruin, the roof having fallen in. It was fitted up in a most elegant manner, by James VII. At the end was a throne for the sovereign, and on the sides, twelve stalls for the knights companions of the thistle; but, in 1688, the whole was demolished by the fury of the mob.

In the apartments belonging to the Duke of Hamilton, who is hereditary housekeeper, are several curious portraits. Among them, a full length of a tall youth, with his hat on a table. It is called that

---

[35] A Scotch pound is twenty pence; a Scotch mark thirteen pence.

XXXI

CARDINAL BEATON.

of Henry Darnly, but, by the countenance, I should rather imagine it to be that of Henry, Prince of Wales.[36]

A head of James IV in black, with ermine; the hair lank and short. From the great resemblance to Henry VII, I am tempted to think it the portrait of James V, who was descended from the daughter of Henry.

Mary Stuart, aged about fifteen; a half length, straight and slender; large brocade sleeves, small ruff, auburn hair.

A head of Cardinal Beaton, black hair, smooth face, a red callot. An ambitious, cruel, and licentious priest; so superior to decency that he publicly married one of his six natural six children to the master of Crawford, owned her for his daughter, and gave with her (in those days) the vast fortune of four thousand marks, Scots.

A stern half-length of John Knox, writing.

Lord John Belasys, in a red doublet and slashed sleeves; young and handsome; son of Lord Fauconberg. A person, says the noble historian, of exemplary industry and courage, who raised six regiments for the King's service, and behaved with great spirit in several engagements: at length being made commander in chief of the forces in Yorkshire, at the battle of Selby, sunk beneath the superior fortune of Sir Thomas Fairfax, and was by him taken prisoner. He received great honours at the Restoration, and lived till the year 1689.

A fine old portrait, a half-length in rich armour.

Twenty small heads, in black lead, of the family of Hamilton, and its allies. Very neat.

The life of Hercules, in ten small pieces, highly finished, but with a stiff outline, like the manner of Albert Durer. In the background are views of Flemish houses; so probably these were the work of a Flemish artist.

Edward, Earl of Jersey; a nobleman in great trust with King William; ambassador to France, and Secretary of State: in the next reign, Lord Chamberlain, and appointed Lord Privy Seal on the day of his death, August 11, 1711.

---

[36] Vide Mr Granger's *Biography* I, 213.

At Lord Dunmore's lodgings is a very fine picture, by Mytens, of Charles I and his queen going to ride, with the sky showering roses on them. The queen is painted with a lovelock, and with browner hair and complexion, and younger than any of her portraits I have seen. A black stands by them holding a grey horse; and the celebrated dwarf, Jeffrey Hudson, attends, holding a spaniel in a string. Several other dogs are sporting around. The little hero in this piece underwent a life of vast variety. He was born the son of a labourer, at Oakenham, in 1619; at the age of seven he was not eighteen inches high; at which time he was taken into the family of the Duke of Buckingham, at Burleigh-on-the-Hill, and had there the honour of being served up to table in a cold pie, to surprise the court then on a progress. On the marriage of Charles I, he was promoted to the service of Henrietta; and was even so far trusted as to be sent to France, to bring over her Majesty's midwife. In his passage he was taken by a pirate; and carried into Dunkirk. His captivity gave rise to *The Jeoffreidos*, a poem by Sir William Davenant, on his duel in that port with a turkeycock. His diminutive size did not prevent his acting in a military capacity, for during the civil wars he served as captain of horse. In following the fortunes of his mistress into France, he unluckily engaged in a quarrel with Mr Crofts, who came into the field armed only with a squirt: a second meeting was appointed, on horseback, when Jeffrey killed his antagonist at the first shot. For this he was expelled the court, which sent him to sea, when he was again captive to a Turkish rover, and sold into Barbary. On his release he was made a captain in the royal navy; and on the final retreat of Henrietta, attended her to France, and remained there till the Restoration. In 1682, this little creature was made of that importance as to be supposed to be concerned in the Popish plot, and was committed to the gatehouse; where he ended his life, at the age of sixty-three, passed with all the consequential activity of a Lilliputian hero.[37]

The precincts of this abbey, including the park (next to be mentioned) and a space as far as Duddingston, is still a place of

---

[37] Vide Fuller, Wright's *Rutlandshire*, 105, and the more entertaining account in Mr Walpole's *Anecdotes of Painting* II, 10.

refuge to the unfortunate debtor; and has its bailey, who keeps courts, and punishes offenders within his jurisdiction.

The college, founded by the citizens of Edinburgh, in 1582, in consequence of a legacy left in 1558, for that useful end, by Robert Reid, Bishop of Orkney, is a very mean building. It is built on the site of the collegiate church of Kirk-of-Field, formerly dedicated to St Mary, and in popish times supplied with a provost and ten prebends.

The museum is at present totally empty, for such has been the negligence of past times, that scarce a specimen of the noble collection deposited in it by Sir Andrew Balfour, is to be met with; any more than the great additions made to it by Sir Robert Sibbald.

The session, as they term it, of the University of Edinburgh, begins on November 1, and continues six months. Soon after the commencement a general day is appointed for matriculation, if a form can be so called, which is annually repeated by each student, as long as he stays. It was begun in the year 1764, and was looked upon as an innovation, intended both to gain a footing for some authority over the students, and to raise a fund for the public library. The manner was this: a solemn obligation (in Latin) to behave well, to respect the authority and interests of the university, and obey its laws (of which they were allowed to be entirely ignorant) was written in a book, and the students subscribed their names underneath in alphabetical order. A sum, not less than half a crown, was at the same time demanded, for the use of the library; in return for which a ticket was given, entitling the bearer to the use of books, upon depositing their value in money by way of security. I never heard of the least cognizance taken of the morals and conduct of any student; though I believe there are a few instances of expulsion, for very flagitious crimes. Degrees in physic used to be conferred like those in divinity and law, at the pleasure of the heads, without any necessity of having studied either there, or at any other university; but, on the last instance of this kind, in the year 1763, or 64, several students, piqued at a proceeding which put on a footing with themselves persons whom they thought not entitled to academical honours, mutually engaged, not to take a degree at Edinburgh. The professors, alarmed at this resolution, gave an assurance, that for the future no degree in physic should be conferred without at least two years studying at the place, and attendance upon all the medical classes. This has been, I believe, rigorously adhered to; and moreover, the examinations previous to conferring the degree, are said to be very strict. By a regulation of a later date, degrees are only granted in the summer, twice a year, during the recess from business. The number of medical students are now annually reckoned at about 300; a majority of whom, being only designed for the lower branches of the profession, stay but one session. Every one is at liberty to attend what lectures he chooses, and in what order; except that those who mean to graduate, must, during their stay, attend all the truly medical ones. They who have leisure, and means properly to complete their medical education, seldom stay less than three sessions, and frequently more. Lectures in botany, and attendance on the infirmary, go forward in the summer; and a good many of the students, especially those who come from a distance, continue at Edinburgh during that season.

This university began to be celebrated for the study of medicine about the year 1720; when a number of gentlemen, natives of this country, and pupils of the illustrious Boerhaave, settled here, and filled the professors' chairs with such abilities, as served to establish Edinburgh for the seat of instruction in the healing art. It was its peculiar good fortune to have a succession of professors of most distinguished parts, which has preserved its fame with undiminished lustre to the very present time.

Near the college is the tradesmaiden hospital, a plain, neat building, with eleven windows in front, founded, in 1707, by the mechanics of the city, for the maintenance of the daughters of their decayed brethren. Mrs Mary Erskine (of whom more will be mentioned hereafter) contributed largely towards this design, and had the honour of being entitled joint foundress. It maintains at present, fifty-two girls.

Somewhat farther, are two churches, under one roof, called the Greyfriars. The convent belonging to it was founded by James I, for the purpose of instructing his people in divinity and philosophy, and was said to have been so magnificent, that the superior, who was sent for from Zuriczee to preside, at first declined accepting it. In this church I had the satisfaction of hearing divine service performed by the celebrated Dr Robertson. It began with a hymn; the minister then repeated a prayer to a standing congregation, who do not distract their attention by bows and compliments to each other, like the good people in England. He then gave an excellent comment on a portion of scripture, which is called the lecture. After this succeeded another hymn, and prayer, the sermon, a third hymn, and the benediction.

Near this church is a pleasing group of charitable foundations, the genuine fruits of religion. Immediately behind it is the great workhouse, the receptacle of the poor of the city. When completed, it is to consist of a centre and two wings, but the last are not yet finished. It maintains about six or seven hundred persons, of all ages; each of whom contribute by their labour to their support. Besides these are about two hundred out-pensioners, who have sixpence or a shilling a week. Near it are three other buildings dependent on it; one for the reception of lunatics; the second for the sick; the third, a sort of weaving school.

The orphan hospital was begun in 1733, under the auspices of Mr Andrew Gairdiner, and other charitable persons. At present it maintains seventy poor children, who weave their own clothes, and assist in the whole economy of the house. The building is very handsome, and has nine windows in front.

To the west of this is Herriot's hospital, a magnificent pile of Gothic Grecian architecture, founded by George Herriot, goldsmith and jeweller to Anne of Denmark, who left the vast sum of near forty-four thousand pounds sterling for the building and endowment. It is destined for the support of boys, and maintains at present a hundred and three. Within is a handsome square, with the statue of the founder. In the council-room is his portrait, a half-length, by Scougal: in his hand are some jewels; for to that branch of this business he owed his fortune, particularly by the profusion bought for the wedding of the princess of Bohemia. He was member of the English Parliament; and died, aged 63, in the year 1623.

In the same room is a head of William Aytonne, mason, and builder of the hospital.

Behind this is another fine foundation, called Watson's hospital, a building with twenty-one windows in front. The founder owing his rise to the charity of a relation, established this house, for the support of about sixty boys, sons and grandsons of decayed merchants of Edinburgh. They are educated here, and apprenticed out; and after having served their times with credit, and remained after three years unmarried, receive fifty pounds to set up with.

The merchants maiden hospital lies north east of Watson's. It owes its institution to the merchants of Edinburgh, and the same Mrs Mary Erskine before mentioned, for the maintenance of the girls of distressed burgesses. It supports about sixty, who appear on Sundays in a dress truly *simplex munditiis*, in dark brown gowns, black silk handkerchiefs, and black silk bonnets.

The private acts of charity are also very considerable. Every Sunday a collection is made for the sick and necessitous. Such a religious respect do the common people pay to this fund, that nothing but extreme distress will induce them to apply for relief. It seems to them a sort of sacrilege to partake unnecessarily of a bounty destined for the miserable; and children will undergo any labour to prevent their parents from becoming burdensome to this parochial stock.

The New Town is connected to the city by a very beautiful bridge, whose highest arch is ninety-five-feet high. This bridge is flung over a deep glen, once filled with water, and called the North Loch, but at present drained. To the east and to the north of this bridge, is a motley assemblage of churches, Methodist meeting, hospitals, and Playhouse. The old Trinity collegiate church, founded by Mary of Gueldres, mother to James III is a Gothic pile. Near it is a hospital, founded on the dissolution of the former: it maintains, in a most comfortable manner, numbers of aged persons of each sex; for besides good diet, they have the luxury of a garden and library.

Leith, the port of Edinburgh, is seated about two miles to the east, is now a considerable town, divided into two parishes, called North and South Leith, separated by a river of the same name. The original name was Inverleith, and is first mentioned in 1329, in a grant of it to the citizens of Edinburgh, under whose jurisdiction it lies. They appoint out of the old magistrates a baron bailiff, who with the assistance of other officers directs the affairs of the place. It was for some time the residence of Mary of Lorrain, Queen Regent, who, followed by her court, gave rise to several handsome buildings still existing. The same princess, when she called in the assistance of the French, fixed their forces here, and caused it to be fortified, on account of the convenient harbour and its vicinity to the capital. Here Mary Stuart landed on her return from France, in 1561, and in two years after destroyed the independency of the place, by mortgaging, for a great sum of money, the superiority of it to the city of Edinburgh.[38] When Henry VIII proposed the match between his son Edward and Mary, he followed his demand in a manner worthy so boisterous a prince. In this 'rough courtship', as it was humourously styled, he sent the Earl of Hertford with a numerous army to second his demand, who burnt both this place and Edinburgh.

After that it was fortified by French, and underwent a long siege; the French behaved with spirit, and for a great length of time baffled all the attempts of the English, who supported the lords of the congregation. At length it was yielded on composition, and the fortification razed. In 1571, it was refortified by the Earl of Morton; and in little less than a century afterwards, a citadel was added by General Monk, demolished on the Restoration.

The harbour is but indifferent; yet by means of a fine pier large vessels lie here with security. The southern shore of the Forth is shallow and sandy: no part between Leith and Inchkeith is above ten fathoms deep. The northern is of a great depth, and has a rocky or foul bottom. Opposite to Kinghorn is a ledge of rocks called the Blae, which at a low ebb are only four fathom from the surface. Yet the water deepens to fifty fathoms within a ship's length. The pier is a beautiful and much frequented walk: and the annual races are on the sands, near low-water mark: It has happened often when the heats have been long, that the horses run belly deep in the flowing tide.

The disproportion of rain between this and the western side of the kingdom has been strongly exemplified here, Leith lies in a

---

[38] Robertson I, 342.

line sixty miles distant from Greenock. Some years ago, when the rope-walks of both places were uncovered, it was observed that the workmen at the last were prevented by the wet from working eighty days more at Greenock, than at Leith, and only forty days more at Glasgow; so sudden is the abatement of rain, and so quick is the change of climate, on receding from west to east.

In my return to Edinburgh, passed by Restalrig, the ancient residence of the Logans. The last possessor was accused (five years after his death) of being concerned in the Gowrie conspiracy; and was cited to appear, but proving contumacious, his estate was forfeited, his bones burnt, and his heirs declared infamous.

On the 21st of this month I visited Hawthorden, the seat of the celebrated historian and poet, Drummond, about seven miles south of Edinburgh. The house and ruined castlelet are placed on the brink of a vast precipice of freestone, with the North Esk running in a deep den beneath. In the house are preserved the portraits of the poet and his father.

In the front of the rock, just beneath the house, is cut a flight of twenty-seven steps. In the way, a gap, passable by a bridge of boards, interrupts the descent. These steps lead to the entrance of the noted caves, which have been cut with vast labour out of the rock. The descent into the great chambers is by eight steps; but, on first entrance, on right and left, are two rooms; that on the right consists of a gallery, fifteen feet long, with a space at the end (twelve feet by seven) whose sides are cut into rows of square holes, each nine inches deep, and seems to have been the pigeon-house of the place, there being an entrance cut through the rock. On the left hand is another gallery, and through the front of this is a hole, facing the bridge, which seems intended as the means to draw in the boards, and secure the retreat of the inhabitants. In this gallery is a little basin cut in the rock; perhaps a *benitoire*.

The grand apartment faces the door, and is ninety-one feet long; the beginning is twelve feet wide, the rest only five feet eight; the height six. In a recess of the broader part is a well, some fathoms deep. Above is cut a funnel, which pierces the roof to the day. Near the end of this apartment is a short turning, that leads to another gallery, twenty-three feet by five.

These curious hollows have been supposed by some to have been the works of the Picts; but to me they seem to have been designed as an asylum in troublesome times for some neighbouring inhabitants, in the same manner as Wetherell cells were for the monks of the abbey. It appears by Major, that the brave Alexander Ramsay, in 1341, made these caves his residence for a considerable time.[39] To him resorted all the gallant youth of Scotland; and to him parents sent their sons to be initiated in the art of war. From hence he made his excursions to the English borders with his pupils; each inroad was to them a lecture for valour and stratagem.

These alone attract the attention of strangers; but the solemn and picturesque walks cut along the summits, sides, and bottoms of this beautiful den, are much more deserving admiration. The vast mural fence, formed by the red precipices, the mixture of trees, the grotesque figure of many of the rocks, and the smooth sides of the Pentland hills, appearing above this wild scenery, are more striking objects to the contemplative mind.

After crossing the river, and clambering up a steep hill, discover, on the summit, a work of art, not less admirable than those of nature which we had so lately quitted, I mean, the chapel of Roslyn, Roskelyn,[40] or 'the hill in the glen'; a curious piece of Gothic architecture, founded, in 1446, by William St Clare, Prince of Orkney, for a provost, six prebendaries, and two singing boys. The outside is ornamented with a multitude of pinnacles, and variety of ludicrous sculpture. The inside is sixty-nine feet long, the breadth thirty-four, supported by two rows of clustered pillars, between seven and eight feet high, with an isle on each side. The arches are obtusely Gothic. These arches are continued across the side, but the centre of the church is one continued arch, elegantly divided into compartments, and finely sculptured. The capitals of the pillars are enriched with foliage, and variety of figures: and amidst a heavenly concert, appears a cherubin blowing the ancient Highland bagpipe. In short, in all parts is a profusion so exquisite, as seem even to have

---

[39] *De Gestis Scotorum*, lib. V, ch. 16, 236.
[40] A minute account of this chapel, its carvings, etc. are in a little book, printed by Mr William Auld, 1774.

XXXII

ROSLIN CASTLE.

affected with respect the barbarism of Knox's manual reformers, so as to induce them to spare this beautiful and venerable pile.

In a deep den far beneath, amidst wooded eminences, are the ruins of the castle, fixed on a peninsulated rock, accessible by a bridge of stupendous height. This had been the seat of the great name of Sinclair. Of this house was Oliver, favourite of James V, and the innocent cause of the loss of the battle of Solway Moss, by the hatred of the nobility to his preferred command. He lived in poverty to give a fine lesson of the uncertainty of prosperity to the pride of the worthless Arran, minion to James VI, appearing before the insolent favourite, in the garb of adversity, repeating only these words, 'I am Oliver Sinclair.'

Near this place, the English, under John de Segrave, Regent of Scotland, in 1302, received three defeats in one day from the Scots, under John Cummin and Simon Frazer.

In my return, visit St Catherine's Well, noted for the petroleum swimming on the surface. A little farther, to the left, is a noted camp of an oval form.

On returning into the city, I called at Mr Braidwood's academy of dumb and deaf. This extraordinary professor had under his care a number of young persons, who had received the Promethian heat, and divine *infaltus*; but from the unhappy construction of their organs, were (till they had received his instructions) denied the power of utterance. Every idea was locked up, or appeared but in their eyes, or at their fingers ends, till their master instructed them in arts unknown to us, who have the faculty of hearing. Apprehension reaches us by the grosser sense. They see our words, and our uttered thoughts become to them visible. Our ideas expressed in speech strike their ears in vain: their eyes receive them as they part from our lips. They conceive by intuition, and speak by imitation. Mr Braidwood first teaches them the letters and their powers; and the ideas of words written, beginning with the most simple. The art of speaking is taken from the motion of his lips; his words being uttered slowly and distinctly. Their answers are slow, and somewhat harsh.

When I entered the room, and found myself surrounded with numbers of human forms so oddly circumstanced, I felt a sort of anxiety, such as I might be supposed to feel had I been environed by another order of beings. I was soon relieved, by being introduced to a most angelic young creature, of about the age of thirteen. She honoured me with her new-acquired conversation; but I may truly say, that I could scarcely bear the power of her piercing eyes: she looked me through and through. She soon satisfied me that she was an apt scholar. She readily apprehended all I said, and returned me answers with the utmost facility. She read; she wrote well. Her reading was not by rote. She could clothe the same thoughts in a new set of words, and never vary from the original sense. I have forgot the book she took up, or the sentences she made a new version of; but the effect was as follows:

Original passage	*Version*
Lord Bacon has divided the whole of human knowledge into history, poetry and philosophy, which are referred to the three powers of the mind, memory, imagination, and reason.[41]	A nobleman has parted the total or all of man's study, or understanding, into an account of the life, manners, religion and customs of any people or country, verse or metre, moral or natural knowledge, which are pointed to the three faculties of the soul or spirit; the faculty of remembering what is past, thought or conception, and right judgement.

I left Mr Braidwood and his pupils with the satisfaction which must result from a reflection on the utility of his art, and the merit of his labours: who, after receiving under his care a being that seemed to be merely endowed with a human form, could produce the *divina particula aurae*, latent, and, but for his skill, condemned to be ever latent in it; and who could restore a child to its glad parents with a capacity of exerting its rational powers, by expressive sounds of duty, love and affection.

Before I quit Edinburgh, I must mention, that it is the first royal burgh in Scotland; is governed by a provost, who has the addition of lord, four bailies, and a dean of guild: who did me the

---

[41] This was read since, by another young lady; but that which I heard was not less difficult, nor less faithfully translated.

distinguished honour of conferring on me its freedom, after an elegant entertainment at the house of the Right Honourable John Dalrymple, Lord Provost.

I refer the reader to the Appendix for a list of the manufactures in and about this great city. If the mention of several may be thought too minute, it must be considered, how many even of the necessaries of life were wanting in North Britain, till the rising industry of the age determined that this country should supply its own deficiencies. In the time of James VI, how deplorable was its trade, for, as old Hackluyt sings, it even imported its wheelbarrows and cartwheels:

> *And the Scots bene charged knowen at the eye,*
> *Out of Flanders with little mercerie,*
> *And great plentie of haberdashers ware*
> *And half her shippes with cart-wheeles bare,*
> *And with barrowes are laden as with substance:*
> *Thus most rude ware are in her chevisance.*[42]

But notwithstanding the present progress that Scotland has made in the useful arts, it must stop at a certain point, proportionate to its wealth and population, which stand thus in respect to England: When the land tax is at 2s in the pound, Scotland pays £23,977 0s 7d and England £994,972 14s 0d that is, less than the proportion of 1 to 41. The landed property of the former is £1,000,000 per annum; of the latter £16,000,000. But if the wealth in moveables is added, the difference will be as 1 to 20. In respect to numbers of people, England has 8,000,000; Scotland only 2,000,000.

Leave Edinburgh. Ride through Dalkeith, and have the pleasure of passing the day with Sir John Dalrymple, at Cranston Castle. The country good, full of corn, and decked with numbers of small woods. Dispose of the morning by visiting the castles of Crichton and Borthwick. The first is seated on the edge of a bank, above a grassy glen. Was once the habitation of the chancellor Crichton, joint guardian, with the Earl of Callendar, of James II, a powerful and spirited statesman in that turbulent age; and the adviser of the bold but bloody deeds against the too potent Douglases; facts

[42] *Coll. Voyages* I, 187.

XXXIII

CRICHTON CASTLE.

excusable only by the plea of the necessity of state. During the life of Crichton, it was besieged, taken, and levelled to the ground, by William, Earl of Douglas, after a siege of nine months.[43]

It was rebuilt; and one part, which appears more modern than the rest, with much elegance. The front of one side of the court is very handsome, ornamented with diamond-shaped facets; and the soffits of the staircase beautifully carved; the cases of some of the windows adorned with rosettes, and twisted cordage. The dungeon, called 'the masmore', is a deep hole with a narrow mouth. Tradition says, that a person of some rank in the country was lowered into it for irreverently passing this castle, without paying his respects to the great owner.

The parish church had been collegiate; founded in 1449, by the chancellor, with the consent of his son, for a provost, nine prebendaries, and two singing boys, out of the rents of Crichton and Locherwort.

About a mile farther is Borthwick Castle, seated on a knowl in the midst of a pretty vale, bounded by hills covered with corn and woods; a most picturesque scene. It consists of a vast square tower, ninety feet high, with square and round bastions at equal distances from its base. The staterooms are on the first storey, once accessible by a drawbridge. Some of the apartments were very large; the hall forty feet long, and had its music gallery; the roof lofty, and once adorned with paintings. This castle was built by a Lord Borthwick, once a potent family. In the vault lies one of the name, in armour, and a little bonnet, with his lady by him. On the side are numbers of little elegant human figures. The place was once the property of the Earl of Bothwel, who a little before the battle of Carberry Hill, took refuge here with his fair consort.[44]

Lodge at a good inn at Blackshields; a village, as I was informed, lying in a portion of Haddingtonshire, surrounded by Lothian.

---

[43] *Lives of the Douglases*, 169.
[44] *Critical Enquiry*, etc. 3rd ed., 289.

XXXIV

BORTHWICK CASTLE

XVIII

BERWICKSHIRE, ROXBURGHSHIRE, SELKIRKSHIRE

Lauder—Thirlestane Castle—Bridgend—Melros—Old Melros—
Dryburgh—Little Den—Roxburgh Castle—Kelso

AFTER crossing a rivulet, enter the shire of Berwick. Ascend
Soutry Hill, from whence is a fine view of the Firth of Forth,
the county of Fife, the Bass Isle, and the rich county of East Lothian
immediately beneath us. This advantageous situation made it a
noted beacon, which caused it to be particularly noticed in the
old Scotch law on that account.[1] Cross a tedious dreary moor, and
descend into Lauderdale; a long narrow bottom, unenclosed, and
destitute of wood; but abundant in corn. Reach Lauder, a small
town noted for an insolent act of justice done by the nobility on the
upstart favourites of James III. Cochran, a mason, created Earl of
Mar, Hommil, a taylor, Leonard, a smith, Rogers, a musician, and
Torsisan, a fencing-master, directing all his councils. The nobility
assembled here with their vassals, in obedience to his Majesty's

---

[1] Skene's *Actes*, 38, 12th Parl., James II.

summons, in order to repel a foreign invasion; but took this opportunity to free themselves from those wretched ministers. They met in the church to consult the necessary measures; and while they were in debate, Cochran, deputed by the king, knocked at the door, to demand the cause of their assembly. His attendance, and his dress, as described by Lindesay, are most descriptive of the fellow's arrogance, 'who was well accompanied with a band of men of war, to the number of three hundred light axes, all clad in white livery, and black bends thereon, that might be known for Cochran the Earl of Mar's men. Himself was clad in a riding-pie of black velvet, with a great chain of gold about his neck, to the value of five hundred crowns; and four blowing horns, with both the ends of gold and silk, set with precious stones. His horn was tipped with fine gold at every end, and a precious stone, called a berryl, hanging in the midst. This Cochran had his beaumont born before him overgilt with gold, and so were all the rest of his horns; and all his pallions were of fine canvas of silk, and the cords thereof of fine twined silk; and the chains upon his pallions were double overgilt with gold.'[2] He was seized, thus equipped, his chain and his horns torn from him, and, with his comrades, hanged over a bridge (now demolished) in sight of the king and the whole army.

Near the town is Thirlestane Castle, a singular old house of the Earl of Lauderdale. The front small, bounded on each side with a great round tower, capped with slated cones. The inside had been heavily stuccoed by the Duke of Lauderdale, one of the noted cabal in the time of Charles II. His portrait, by Lely, is to be seen here; a much more advantageous one than that by the noble historian, who paints him 'insolent, imperious, flattering, dissembling, had courage enough not to fail, where it was absolutely necessary, and no impediment of honour to restrain him from doing anything that might gratify any of his passions'.[3]

[2] p. 78, folio ed.
[3] III, 124.

After riding two miles through a long tract of coarse sheepwalks, turn out of the great road, and enter the shire of Roxburgh. Pass by Threepwood, infamous in former days for moss-troopers; descend into a little vale, and see some ruined towers at Colmslie and Hilslap; ascend again, and soon after fall into a pretty valley well wooded and watered by the Gala; and at a house of the same name receive every civility from its owner John Scott, Esq. We have now crossed the water, and are in the county of Selkirk, or the forest of Ettrick, which was formerly reserved by the Scottish princes for the pleasure of the chase, and where they had small houses for the reception of their train. One in Galashields, the adjoining village still keeps the name of Hunter's Hall.

This country is supported chiefly by the breed of sheep, which sell from eight to twelve pounds a score. They are generally sold into the south; but sometimes into the Highlands, about the month of March, where they are kept during summer; and after being improved by the mountain grass, are returned into the Lowlands the beginning of winter. The usual weight of a wether is from thirteen to eighteen pounds of twenty-two ounces per quarter. The fleece has been of late much improved by the use of oil and butter, instead of tar; and the wool, which once was sold at five shillings and six pence, now sells for ten shillings per stone of twenty-four pounds.

The sheep inhabit the hills; but the ground is so indifferent that an acre will maintain but one. A sheep farm of fifteen hundred acres is set for eighty pounds. Numbers of cattle are reared here; and much cheese and butter made, but the last very bad in general, and chiefly used for greasing the sheep. The Dorsetshire breed has been introduced here, but in this northern climate, in two or three years, they lose their prolific nature.

I am uncertain whether a custom that prevails a little north of Coldstream, does not extend also to these parts. About Duns, the fair spinsters give much of their leisure time to the spinning of blankets for their wedding portion. On the nuptial night, the whole stock of virgin industry is placed on the bed. A friend of mine has, on such an occasion, counted not fewer than ten, thick and heavy.

Was the Penelope, who owned them, forsaken by her Ulysses, she never could complain, like the Grecian spouse, '*Non ego deserto jacuissem frigida lecto!*'

About a mile west of Galashields are very evident vestiges of the great ditch called the Catrail, which is twenty-five feet wide, bounded on each side by a great rampart. It has been traced 22 miles; passes four miles west of Hawick, up Docluch Hill, by Fairnyside hill, and Skelse Hill, across Ellen Water, ascends Carriage Hill, and goes by the Maiden Paps, reaches Pear Fell on the Dead Water, on the borders of Northumberland, and from thence may be traced beyond Langholme, pointing towards Cannonsby, on the River Esk. On several parts of its course are strong round forts, well fortified with ditches and ramparts, some even exceeding in strength those of the Romans. Whether it ever reached farther north than Gala, has not been discovered; but the tradition is, that it extended from sea to sea. Mr Gordon, the only antiquary that has explored it, traces it no farther; but has observed the chain of forts towards East Lothian. It is probable, that it was cast up by the inhabitants of the country north-west of it, as a protection against the inroads of invaders; but who they were, or what was the date of the work, are difficulties not to be determined from historical authority.

Continue my journey for a time along a fertile bottom, and, near the junction (the last in this place) of the Gala and the Tweed, a fine river, again enter the shire of Roxburgh. All the country is open, and much of it full of corn. Here the farmers injudiciously cut up the sides of the hills, and spoil their fine sheepwalks to get a little late and bad corn.

At a place called Bridgend stood, till within these few years, a large pier,[4] the remaining one of four, which formed here a bridge over the Tweed. In it was a gateway, large enough for a carriage to

---

[4] Communicated to me by a gentleman who remembers the pier, now demolished. Mr Gordon has engraved what remained in his time, in his 64th plate.

pass through, and over that a room, twenty-seven feet by fifteen, the residence of the person who took the tolls. This bridge was not formed with arches, but with great planks laid from pier to pier. It is said that it was built by David I in order to afford a passage to his abbey of Melros, which he had newly translated from its ancient site; and also to facilitate the journeys of the devout to the four great pilgrimages of Scotland, viz. Scone, Dundee, Paisley, and Melros.

Cross the new bridge; pass by Darnwick, and soon after by Skinner or Skirmish Hill, noted, in 1526, for a fray between the Earl of Angus, and the family of the Scotts, under their laird, Scott of Buccleugh. Angus had possession of the person of James V, then in his minority; and used his power with so little moderation, as to make the young prince desirous of being released. The power of the Douglases was often an overmatch for the regal. Such was the case at present; James therefore was obliged to apply to Buccleugh, a potent borderer, to attempt his deliverance. That lord, in order to bring his Majesty within the limits of his estate, encouraged all kinds of excesses among his people. This brought the king, attended by Angus, to suppress their depredations. Buccleugh appeared with his powers: a skirmish begun, the Scotts were defeated, and James was for a time obliged to submit to the tyranny of his keeper.

At a small distance lie the elegant remains of the abbey of Melros, founded in 1136, by David I, as these jingling lines import:

> *Anno milleno centeno, ter quoque deno,*
> *Ex sexto Christi, Melrose, fundata fuisti.*

David peopled it with Cistertians, brought from Rivale Abbey, in Yorkshire, and dedicated it to the Virgin Mary. At the Reformation, James Douglas was appointed commendator, who took down much of the building in order to use the materials in building a large house for himself, which is still standing, and dated 1590. Nothing is left of the abbey, excepting a part of the cloister walls, elegantly carved; but the ruins of the church are of most uncommon beauty; part is at present used for divine service, the rest uncovered; but every part does great honour to the architect, whose memory is preserved on the walls in these uncouth lines:

> *John Murdo sum tym callit was I,*
> *And born in Parysse certainly;*
> *And had in kepying all mason werk,*
> *Of Santandroys, the hye kirk*
> *Of Glasgu, Melros, and Paislay,*
> *Of Nyddysdayl, and of Galway.*
> *Pray to God and Mary baith,*
> *And sweet St John keep this haly kirk from Skaith.*

The south side and the east window are elegant past description; the windows lofty, the tracery light, yet strong. The church had been in form of a cross, and of considerable dimensions; the pillars clustered; their capitals enriched with most beautiful foliage of vine leaves and grapes. A window at the north end of the transept represents the crown of thorns. The rich work of the outside is done with uncommon delicacy and cunning. The spires of pinnacles that grace the roof; the brackets and niches, that, till 1649, were adorned with statues, are matchless performances. But what the fury of the disciples of Knox had spared, the stupid zeal of covenanting bigots destroyed. In times long prior to these it had felt the rage of impious invaders. In 1322, the baffled Edward II vented his rage on the abbeys of Melros and Dryburgh. Richard II was not more merciful to it; and in the reign of Henry VIII in 1544, two of his captains, violating the remains of the Douglases, felt the speedy resentment of their descendant, Archibald, Earl of Angus, in the battle of Ancrum Moor.

The side of the west end of the church, which remains standing, is divided into five side chapels, once probably belonging to private families; for (besides Alexander II, who lay below the great altar) it was the place of interment of the Douglases, and other potent families. James, Earl of Douglas, slain at the battle of Otterbourn, was deposited here with all the pomp that either the military or the religious profession could bestow. Here too lies the Lord of Liddesdale, the flower of chivalry, who fell an assassinated victim to the jealousy of William I, Earl of Douglas. His eulogy styles him 'terrible and fearefull in arms; meek, milde, and gentle in peace; the

MELROS.

XXXV

scourge of England, and sure buckler and wall of Scotland, whom neither hard successe could make slack nor prosperous sloathfull'.[5]

The situation of this religious house is remarkably pleasant, seated near the Tweed, and shaded with woods, above whose summits soar the venerable ruins, and the tricapitated top of Eldon Hill. On one of the heads is a Roman camp. I have since been informed of others, with military ways, to be traced in various places.

Pass by Newstead, and Redabbeystead, a house belonging once to the Knights Templars.[6] Proceed to old Melros, now reduced to a single house, on a lofty promontory, peninsulated by the Tweed: a most beautiful scene; the banks lofty, and wooded, varied with perpendicular rocks, jutting like buttresses from top to bottom. This was the site of the ancient abbey of Culdees, mentioned by Bede to have existed in 664, in the reign of the Saxon Oswy. This place was as celebrated for austerities of Dricthelmus, as ever Finchal was for those of St Godric. The first was restored to life after being dead for an entire night. During that space, he passed through purgatory and hell, had the beatific vision, and got very near to the confines of heaven. His angelic guide gave him an useful lesson on the efficacy of prayer, alms, fasting, and particularly, masses of holy men; infallible means to relieve the souls of friends and relations from the place of torment.[7]

The descriptions which Bede has given of the seats of misery and bliss are very poetical. He paints purgatory as a valley of a stupendous length, breadth, and depth; one side filled by furious storms of hail and snow; and other with lambent, inextinguishable flames. In these souls of the deceased alternately experienced the extremes of heat and cold. Both Shakespeare and Milton make use of the same idea: the first in his beautiful description of the state of the dead in *Measure for Measure*:

> *Ay, but to die and go we know not where;*
> *To lie in cold obstruction, and to rot;*
> *This sensible warm motion to become*

---

[5] *Life of the Douglases*, 78.
[6] Mentioned in the *Description of the Parish of Melros*, 7, unnoticed by Keith.
[7] Bede, lib. V, ch. 12, 196.

XXXVI

M. Griffiths del.

P. Mazell sculp.

DRYBURGH ABBY.

> *A kneaded clod; and the delighted spirit*
> *To bathe in fiery floods, or to reside*
> *In thrilling regions of thick-ribbed ice;*
> *To be imprison'd in the viewless winds,*
> *And blown with restless violence about*
> *The pendent world!*

Milton's thought is dressed only in different words:

> *At certain revolutions all the damn'd*
> *Are brought; and feel by turns the bitter change*
> *Of fierce extremes, extremes by change more fierce;*
> *From beds of raging fire to starve in ice*
> *Their soft ethereal heat.*

Cross the Tweed at Dryburgh boat, and re-enter the shire of Berwick. On the northern side, in the deep gloom of wood, are the remains of the abbey of Dryburgh, founded by Hugh Morville, constable of Scotland, in the time of David I and Beatrix de Campo Bello, his wife. There are scarce any relics of the church, but much of the convent, the refectory, supported by two pillars, several vaults, and other offices; part of the cloister walls, and a fine radiated window of stonework. These remains are not inelegant, but are unadorned. This was inhabited by Premonstratensian monks, who styled the Irish abbeys of Druin la Croix and Woodburn, their daughters.[8] At the Reformation, James VI bestowed Dryburgh on Henry Erskine, second son of the Earl of Mar, whose house as commendator is still inhabited.

Continue the ride through a fine country full of gentle risings, covered with corn, and resembling Picardy. Keep still in sight of the Tweed, whose banks, adorned with hanging woods, and variety of beautiful borders, well merit the apostrophe of the old song:

> *How sweet are the banks of the Tweed!*

Pass opposite to a round tower, called Little Den, placed on a cliff above the river, once a border-house of the Kers. Cross the river at another ferry. Pass by Rutherford, where Robert III founded an hospital, dedicated to Mary Magdalene, and bestowed it on the

---

[8] *Monasticon Hibernicum*, 140, 141.

XXXVII

LITTLE-DEN.

abbey of Jedburgh, which was to maintain here a priest to pray for his soul, and those of his ancestors, kings of Scotland.[9]

Again enter the county of Roxburgh; and soon after see, on a high cliff above the water, a small Roman camp, with two deep fosses on the land side; and not far distant, an exploratory mount. The view grows more picturesque; the river, bounded by lofty cliffs, clothed with trees; and on a rising a little beyond appear the great woods of Fleurus, and the house in front, the seat of the Duke of Roxburgh.

Pass beneath the site of the once potent castle of Roxburgh, seated on a vast and lofty knowl, of an oblong form, suddenly rising out of the plain, near the junction of the Tweed and the Tiviot. On the north and west it had been defended by a great fosse. The south impends over the Tiviot; some of whose waters were diverted in former times into the castle ditch, by a dam obliquely crossing the stream, and whose remains are still visible. A few fragments of walls are all that exist of this mighty strength; the whole area being filled with trees of considerable age. At the foot was once seated a town of the same name, destroyed by James II, when he undertook the siege of the castle, and probably never rebuilt.

The ancient name of the castle was Marchidun, or 'the hill on the marches'.[10] The name of the founder eludes my enquiry. The first mention I find of it is in 1132,[11] when a treaty was concluded here on the part of King Stephen, by Thurstan, Archbishop of York, between him and David I. In 1174, after William the Lion was taken prisoner near the castle of Alnwick, Roxburgh, and four others of the strongest in Scotland were delivered to Henry II as securities for doing homage (on his release) for the crown of Scotland.[12] They were restored to the Scots by his successor. In 1296, it was taken by Edward I. In 1342, the year in which David Bruce returned from France, this fortress was restored to his crown by the valour of

---

[9] Keith, 292.
[10] Camden.
[11] Holinshead, *Hist. Scot.*, 183.
[12] Lord Lyttleton's *Henry II*, 8vo, V, 220. Major, 135.

Alexander Ramsay, who was appointed governor;[13] an honour he enjoyed but a short time, being surprised by the envious Douglas, and starved to death in the castle of Hermitage.[14] The Scots lost this fortress in the reign of Edward III, who twice celebrated his birthday in it.[15] It was put into the hands of Lord Henry Percy, after the defeat and captivity of David, at the battle of Nevil's Cross.[16] But the most distinguished siege was that in 1560, fatal to James II, a wise and gallant prince, who was slain by the bursting of one of his own cannons. A large holly, enclosed with a wall, marks the spot. His queen, Mary of Gueldres, carried on the attack with vigour, took, and totally demolished it.

We have seen before the misfortunes that attended the first of this ill-fated name. James I fell by the hands of assassins at Perth: his successor met, at this place, in the height of prosperity, with a violent death. James III was murdered by his rebellious subjects, after a battle near Bannockbourne. James IV lost his life in Flodden field. James V died of a broken heart, on the defeat at Solway: and the fate of his unhappy daughter, Mary Stuart, is unknown to none. In her son, James VI, adversity remitted for a time the persecution of the race; but resumed it with double fury against his successor Charles. His son experienced a long series of misfortunes; and the bigotted James suffered the punishment of his infatuation, and transmitted to his offspring, exile, and seclusion from the throne of their ancestors.

Pass by an enclosure called the Friary, the site of a house of Franciscans, belonging to Roxburgh. Ford the Tivot, which gives the name of Tiviotdale to all the fine country from Melros to this place, notwithstanding it is washed by the Tweed; so that the old song, with propriety, calls its inhabitants:

> *All men of pleasant Tiviotdale,*
> *Fast by the River Tweed.*

Have here a most charming view of Kelso, its ancient church, Mr Dickson's pretty house, and the elegant bridge of six arches over the

---

[13] Walsingham.
[14] Major, 243.
[15] Walsingham, 134, 146.
[16] Major, 244.

KELSO.

M. Griffith, del.

R. Wallis, sculp.

XXXVIII

Tweed, near its junction with the Tiviot. On crossing it enter that neat place built much after the manner of a Flemish town, with a square and a town house. It contains about twenty-seven hundred souls, has a very considerable market, and great quantities of corn are sold here weekly, by sample. The parish church is darksome and inconvenient, being part of that belonging to the abbey; but a new one is building, in an octagonal form, eighty-two feet in diameter, supported by a circle of pillars.

The abbey of Tyronensians was a vast pile, and to judge by the remains, of venerable magnificence. The walls are ornamented with false round arches, intersecting each other. Such intersections form a true Gothic arch, and may as probably have given rise to that mode, as the arched shades of avenues.[17] The steeple of the church, is a vast tower. This house was founded by David I when Earl of Cumberland. He first placed it at Selkirk, then removed it here in 1128. Its revenues were, in money, above two thousand a year, Scots. The abbot was allowed to wear a mitre and pontifical robes; to be exempt from episcopal jurisdiction, and permitted to be present at all general councils.

The environs of Kelso are very fine: the lands consist of gentle risings, enclosed with hedges, and extremely fertile. They have much reason to boast of their prospects. From the Chalkheugh is a fine view of the forks of the rivers, Roxburgh Hill, Sir John Douglas's neat seat, and, at a distance, Fleurus; and from Pinnacle Hill is seen a vast extent of country, highly cultivated, watered with long reaches of the Tweed, well wooded on each margin. These borders ventured on cultivation much earlier than those on the west or east, and have made great progress in every species of rural economy. Turnips and cabbages, for the use of cattle, cover many large tracts; and potatoes appear in vast fields. Much wheat is raised in the neighbourhood, part of which is sent up the Firth of Forth, and part into England.

The fleeces here are very fine, and sell from twelve to fourteen shillings the stone, of twenty four pounds; and the picked kind from eighteen to twenty. The wool is sent into Yorkshire, to Linlithgow,

---

[17] Vide, p. 37.

or into Aberdeenshire, for the stocking manufacture; and some is woven here into cloth, called plains, and sold into England to be dressed. Here is also a considerable manufacture of white leather, chiefly to supply the capital of Scotland.

From what I can collect, the country is greatly depopulated. In the reign of James VI or a little before the Union, it is said that this country could send out fifteen thousand fighting men: at present it could not raise three thousand. But plundering in those times was the trade of the borderers, which might occasion the multitude of inhabitants.

I cannot leave Kelso, without regretting my not arriving there in time to see the races, which had been the preceding week. These are founded, not on the sordid principles of gaming, or dissipation, or fraud, but on the beautiful basis of benevolence, and with the amiable view of conciliating the affections of two nations, where the good and the bad, common to every place, are only divided by a rill scarcely to be distinguished: but prejudice for a time could find no merit but within its own narrow bourne. Some enlarged minds, however, determined to break the fascination of erroneous opinion, to mix with their fellow subjects, and to instruct both the great vulgar and the small, that the northern and southern borders of the Tweed created in their inhabitants but a mere difference, without a distinction, and that virtue and good sense were equally common to both. At these races the stewards are selected from each nation: a Percy and a Douglas may now be seen hand in hand; the example of charity spreads, and may it spread, with all its sweet influences, to the remotest corner of our island!

What pleasing times to those that may be brought in contrast! when every house was made defensible, and each owner garrisoned against his neighbour; when revenge at one time dictated an inroad, and necessity at another; when the mistress of a castle has presented her sons with their spurs to remind them that her larder was empty; and that by a foray they must supply it at the expense of the borderers; when every evening the sheep were taken from the hills, and the cattle from their pasture, to be secured in the lower floor from robbers prowling like wolves for prey; and the disappointed

thief found all in safety, from the fears of the cautious owner. The
following simple lines give a true picture of the times:

> *Then Johnie Armstrong to Willie 'gan say,*
> *Billie, a riding then will we:*
> *England and us have been long at feud,*
> *Perhaps we may hit on some bootie.*

> *Then they're come on to Hutton-ha,*
> *They rade that proper place about;*
> *But the Laird he was the wiser man,*
> *For he had left na geir without.*

These were the exploits of petty robbers: but when princes
dictated an inroad, the consequences bore a proportion to their
rank. An Armstrong might drive away a few sheep; but when an
Henry directs invasion, 192 towns, towers, steads, barnekyns,
churches, and bastel-houses, are burnt; 403 Scots slain, 816 taken
prisoners; 10,316 cattle, 12,492 sheep, 1,296 nags and geldings,
200 goats, 200 bolls of corn, and 'insight geare' without measure,
carried off. Such were successes during four months of the year
1544.[18]

Cross the river, turn almost due east, and, after a ride of three
or four miles, find myself at the extremity of the kingdom. I look
back to the north, and with a grateful mind acknowledge every
benefit I received from the remotest of the Hebrides to the present
spot: whether I think of the hospitality of the rich, or the efforts of
unblameable poverty, straining every nerve to accommodate me,
amidst dreary hills, and ungenial skies. The little accidents of diet, or
of lodgings, affect not me: I look farther than the mere differences of
living, or of customs; to the good heart, and extensive benevolence,
which softens every hardship, and turns into delicacies the grossest
fare. My constitution never yet was disposed to apathy; for which I
can claim no merit, but am thankful to the author of my frame, since
'I feel not in myself those common antipathies that I can discover
in others: those national repugnancies do not touch me, nor do
I behold with prejudice the French, Italian, Spaniard, or Dutch,
much more my fellow subjects, howsoever remotely placed from

---

[18] Hayne's *State Papers*, 43 to 51.

me. But where I find their actions in balance with my countrymens, I honour, love, and embrace them in some degree. I was born in the right climate, but seem to be framed and constellated unto all: all places, all airs, make unto me one country; I am in England every where, and under every meridian.'[19]

[19] *Religio Medici*, 33.

XIX

NORTHUMBERLAND

Wark Castle—Coldstream—Flodden Field—Wooler—Chillingham Castle—Percy's Cross—Rothbury—Camhoe—Roman walls—Hermitage—Hexham—Corbridge—Bywell—Ovingham—Prudhow Castle—Newburn—Newcastle

CROSS an insignificant rill, called Riding-burn, and enter Northumberland. Pass through Carham, a village, on the southern banks of the Tweed. Here was a house of black canons, a cell to that of Kirkham, in Yorkshire. It was burnt in 1296, by the Scots, under Wallace, who gives name to this day to an adjacent field. See a fragment of Wark Castle, once the property of the Ross's, originally granted by Henry III to Robert, son of the Baron of Helmsly.[1] It passed afterwards into the family of the Greys, who took their title from the place. After the union of the two kingdoms, by the accession of James I, Lord Grey's estate rose from a thousand to seven or eight thousand pounds a year.[2] So instantly did these parts experience the benefit.

It was often attacked by the Scots, and in 1296 was taken and burnt by them. The love of a Robert de Ross for a fair Scot, occasioned this misfortune. He betrayed it to his northern neighbours, and then joined the famous Wallace.[3] In 1383, it was

[1] Dugdale's *Baron.* I, 554.
[2] *Life of Lord Keeper Guildford*, 139.
[3] Dugdale's *Baron.* I, 554.

again burnt by the Scots;[4] but after the battle of Floddon, the garrison revenged its former disgrace by cutting off numbers of the fugitives.

Leave behind us, on the northern side of the Tweed, Coldstream, the headquarters of General Monk; from whence he marched to restore monarchy to his distressed country. On the southern side is Cornhill, noted for its fine Roman camp, which we passed unwittingly on the left.[5] This town lies in a large detached part of Durham, surrounded by Northumberland.

All this country is open, destitute of trees, and almost even of hedges; for hedges are in their infancy in these parts, as it is not above seven or eight years since they have been introduced. The land is fertile, swells into gentle risings, and is rich in corn. It is miserably depopulated; a few great farmhouses, and hamlets, appear rarely scattered over the vast tracts. There are few farms of less value than a hundred and fifty pounds a year; they are generally three, four, or five hundred; and I heard of one, possessed by a single family, that even reached twenty-five hundred: in this was a single field of three thousand acres, and which took six hundred bolls of seed-wheat, of six Winchester bushels each. A humour fatal to the commonwealth prevails over many parts of the north, of flinging numbers of small tenements into a large one, in order to save the expense of building; or perhaps to avoid the multiplicity of receipts, lay a whole country into a sheepwalk. These devour poor men's houses, and expel the ancient inhabitants from their firesides, to seek their bread in a strange land. I have heard of a character (I have forgot the spot it curses) that is too barbarous and infamous to be overlooked; which has so little feeling as to depopulate a village of two hundred souls, and to level their houses to the ground; to destroy eight or ten farmhouses on an estate of a thousand a year; for the sake of turning almost the whole into a sheepwalk. There he lives, and there may he long live his own tormentor, detesting, detested by, all mankind! Wark and Learmouth, once considerable places, are now scarcely inhabited. The last, formerly

[4] Holinshead, 444.
[5] Wallis's *Northumberland* II, 461.

a great market-town, is now reduced to a single farmhouse. The inhabitants have long since been dispersed, forced to exchange the wholesome, the vigorous, the innocent lives of the rural economists, for the sickly short-lived employs of manufacturers in Birmingham, and other great towns, where disease, and often corrupted morals, cause double the consumption of people as would happen, were they permitted to enjoy their ancient seats. The want of labourers begins to be sensibly felt. As a proof, they are retained by the year; and policy dictates to their employers, the affording them good wages: each has his cottage, a piece of land, gratis, and a shilling a day in summer, and ten pence in winter. I call this good pay in a country which ought to be very cheap; if not, what are the fine effects of the great improvements? *The Spectator* speaks much of the deserts of the man that raises two ears of corn where one grew before. But who will point out the man who has the soul to make his poor brethren feel the happy effect of this art? I believe, that at present there are numbers who have raised ten for one that were known a few years ago. It would be natural to suppose, that plenty would introduce cheapness; but till the providential plenty of the present year, corn was exactly double the value of what it was fourteen years past. Yet the plenty of money has not been found doubled by the poor manufacturer or labourer. The landowner in the north has taken full care of himself. A farm of £75 per annum, twenty years ago, has been lately set for £365, another of £230 will be soon set for £1,000 per annum. An estate was bought in 1759, for £6,800; it consisted of 1,560 acres, of which 750 have been sold for £8,400. And all these improvements result from the unprincipled and iniquitous notion of making the buyer of the produce pay not only to satisfy the demand of the landlord, but to enable the farmer to make a princely fortune, and to live with a luxury the shame of the times. They have lost the respectable character of the old English yeomanry, by too close an imitation of the extravagant follies of their betters.

The oxen of these parts are very fine; a pair has been sold for sixty-five pounds. The weight of one was a hundred and sixty-eight stones. The mountain sheep are sold for half a guinea apiece; the Lowland ewes for a guinea; the wethers for a guinea and a half: the best wool from sixteen to eighteen shillings the stone, of twenty-three pounds and a half – But to pursue our journey:

Observe on the right several very regular terraces cut on the face of a hill. They are most exactly formed, a little raised in the middle, like a fine walk, and about twenty feet broad, and of a very considerable length. In some places were three, in others five flights, placed one above the other, terminating exactly in a line at each end, and most precisely finished. I am told, that such tiers of terraces are not uncommon in these parts, where they are called 'baulks'. Mr Wallis conjectures them to be places for the militia to arrange themselves on in time of war, that they might show themselves to advantage thus placed rank above rank.[6] Mr Gordon describes several which he saw in Scotland, which he conjectures to have been Roman, and formed for itinerary encampments;[7] in my opinion a less satisfactory account. It appears more reasonable, that they were designed for what Mr Wallis imagines, as nothing could more highly gratify the pride of a chieftain's heart, and in this warlike country, than to review, at one glance, his vassals placed so advantageously for that purpose.

Reach the village of Palinsburne, and, finding either provision for man or horse, have recourse to the hospitality of John Askew, Esq., of Palinsburne Hall, where all our wants were relieved in the amplest manner. From his house we visited Floddon Hill, celebrated in history for the greatest loss the Scots ever sustained. Here, in 1513, encamped James IV in his ill-advised invasion of England. According to the custom of the time, every chieftain had his separate camp, whose vestiges are apparent to this day. Infatuated with the love of Lady Heron, of Ford, a neighbouring castle,[8] he wasted his days in inactivity, and suffered the fair Delilah to visit the Earl of Surry, the general of his enemy, under pretence of receiving from her, intelligence of his motions. She betrayed her credulous lover, whose army dwindled by delay, of which clans were always impatient. The enemy unexpectedly appeared before him; he would

---

[6] *Hist. Northumberland* II, 70.
[7] *Itinerary*, 114, 115.
[8] Lindesay, 113. Drummond, 145.

neither permit a retreat, nor suffer his gallant master of artillery to annoy them in their passage over the Till.[9] Surry cut off his passage into Scotland, and brought on the engagement, that the devoted prince so much wished for: it raged chiefly near Brankston. The Scots formed a ring round their monarch, and he fell with many wounds, surrounded by the dead bodies of his faithful nobility. Not a great house in Scotland but lamented the loss of its chieftain or near relation. The body of the king was carried to London, and (after the excommunication was taken off, on representation that he had given signs of repentance in his last moments) was interred at Shene.[10] The Scots pretend that his body was never found, and that which was taken for it by the English, was that of one of his nobility; for many on that fatal day dressed themselves in the same habit. They allege, that the body found was not surrounded with the penitential chain;[11] but it is possible, as Mr Guthrie imagines, that sign of remorse for his parricide was only worn on certain days. His sword and dagger are now in the herald's office, presented by the victorious earl.[12]

Pass near Ford Castle, now the seat of Sir John Deleval, possessed in the reign of Henry III by Odonel de Ford; and by the marriage of his daughter to William Heron, passed into that family:[13] from them to the Carrs; from the Carrs to the present owner.

Cross Millefield Plain, a flat of five miles extent; observe on one part a circular camp, with a single fosse and dike; and opposite to it, a small square entrenchment. At the village of Millefield is said to have been the residence of the kings of Bernicia after Edwin.[14] On the right is Copeland Castle; a square tower, formerly the seat of the Wallaces, but in our time transferred to the Ogles, by purchase. Cross the Glen, a small river, but honoured with baptising in its waters a multitude of Northumbrians, who were converted by Paulinus, after King Edwin had embraced the faith:

---

[9]　Lindesay, 116.
[10]　Rymer's *Foedera* XIII, 385.
[11]　Lindesay, 96, 117, 118.
[12]　Lambe's *Hist. Floddon*, frontispiece.
[13]　Dugdale, Baron I, 730.
[14]　Camden II, 1097. Wallis II.

the residence of him and his queen being at that time at Adigefrin, the neighbouring Yevering.[15]

Pass by Humbledon Hill, where in 1401, the Scots under Archibald, Earl of Douglas, received a signal defeat by the English, commanded by Henry Percy, surnamed Hotspur, in which Douglas was taken prisoner. On the hill are some marks of entrenchments, which the Scots flung up before the battle. The face of this hill is also divided by multitudes of terraces, resembling those above described.

Ride through Wooler, a small town. Observe several of the people wear the bonnet, the last remains of the English dress in the reigns of Edward VI and Mary. The hills on the right approach very near us, and the country rises on both sides, and forms a mixture of cornland and sheepwalk. On the west appear the Cheviot Hills, smooth and verdant. Among them is laid the scene of the battle of Chevychace, in the celebrated ballad of that name. Notwithstanding there is nothing but ballad authority for it, yet it is highly probable that such an action might have happened between two rival chieftains, jealous of the invasion of their hunting-grounds. The limits of the kingdoms were then unsettled; and even at this time, there are debatable lands amidst these very hills. The poet has used a licence in his description of the fight, and mixed in it some events of the battle of Otterbourne, for neither a Percy nor a Douglas fell in this woeful hunting.

Turn three miles to the south-east to visit Chillingham Castle, the ancient property of the Greys, afterwards lords of Werk, now of the Earl of Tankerville. The present building is large, and of no greater antiquity than the time of James I. Here are numbers of portraits, almost entirely misnamed. In the hall is the picture of a toad, said to have been found in the centre of the stone it is painted on; and beneath are these verses:

Heus Stagyrita,
Tuo si velis quid mirabilius Euripo,
Huc venito.
Fluant, refluantque maria, et sit Lunaticus

[15] Bede, lib. II, ch. 13, 95.

Qui suo triviam spoliat honore:
En tibi novi quid, quod non portat Africa,
Nec fabulosis Nilus arenis,
Ignem, flammamque puram,
Aura tamen vitali cassam!
Coeco e recessu scissi, quod vides, saxi,
Obstetrices lucem Lithotomi dedere Manus
Vivo Busoni.

In the park are between thirty and forty wild cattle, of the same kind with those described at Drumlanrig.

Pass over a dreary country, chiefly a sheepwalk, open, and without trees; cross the Till, a small river, and on Hegely Moor see the octagonal shaft of Percy's Cross, on whose broader sides are carved the arms of the family, crescents, and pikes. This was erected in memory of Sir Ralph Percy, who was slain here, in 1463, in battle between the partisans of the house of Lancaster, and Lord Montacute. Lord Hungerford, and the other leaders, fled at the first onset; he, with the spirit of a Percy, kept his ground, and died, consoling himself, that he had 'saved the bird in his breast'; meaning, that he had preserved his allegiance to Henry, never reflecting, as the unglozing historians of old times remark, that he had abandoned that unhappy prince in his greatest necessity, and submitted to his rival, Edward.[16]

Near this cross get on an ancient military road, miscalled the Wattling Street, which runs north into Scotland, and south to Corbridge. The northern part is better known by the name of the Devil's Dike: but as there is not a single station on it, from the place it unites with the genuine Roman way, near Beuclay, it may be supposed to have been the work of the Saxons, there being variety of little rude fortresses near its course.

After a few miles riding, fall into the vale of Whittingham, enclosed with hedges of ancient standing. Leave, on the right, the conic hill of Glanton Pike, a noted beacon. Again cross the Till, at this place called the Bremish. Ride through Whittingham, a little town, on the Aln, (here a little stream) and, after passing over part of the black and dismal Rimside Moor, lie at a neat inn, called the Halfway House.

[16] Hall, in his *Reign of Edw. IV*, 3. Holinshead, 666.

Descend into a cultivated narrow vale: reach the small town of Rothbury, seated on the Coquet, which, below the town, runs through a large extent of flat freestone rock, in a slit about forty feet long and five wide, through which the stream rushes with great violence, and has worn multitudes of those circular basins called the Giant's Pots. This manor belonged to the Claverings; a name taken from a place in Essex, but their first settlement was in this county. In the reign of King John, one of them, distinguished by the name of FitzRoger, obtained a grant of this manor, with the woods belonging; but his majesty reserved to himself the liberty of hunting in them. But the last of the family resigning it to the crown, it was re-granted to the Percys, by Edward III.[17]

Cross the Coquet, on a bridge of four arches; ascend a steep hill, and arrive in a woodless, hedgeless, and uncultivated country, which continues for some miles; the enclosures either banks or stone walls. Reach Camboe, a row of neat houses on an eminence, where the country mends, and trees and hedges appear. Mr Wallis says it signifies the fort on the hill, and that in the reign of Henry III, it belonged to Sir Robert de Camboe, high-sheriff of the county.[18]

Below it is Wallington; a good house, belonging to Sir Walter Blacket, whose ancestor purchased it from the unfortunate Sir John Fenwick, beheaded in 1696, in whose family it had been from the reign of Henry IV. After a few miles pass by Swinburne Castle, crossing a little north of it, the true Wattling Street way, which runs into the shire of Roxburgh. At Chollerton, we cross the Erring, a small stream, falling just below into the North Tyne, a beautiful river, with sloping banks, finely cultivated. At a small distance south of Chollerton, cross the site of Adrian's Dike, and Severus's Wall, opposite to Walwick, the ancient Cilurnum; a station on the west bank of the Tyne. Here was stationed the body of horse, or *ala secunda astorum*, as appears by a sepulchral stone, figured by Horsely.[19] Several other monumental inscriptions have been found there, preserved by the same author. This wall,

[17] Dugdale's *Baronage* I, 106, 109.
[18] II, 526.
[19] Northumberland XXIV.

which is commonly known by the name of the Picts Wall, crosses the island from sea to sea, beginning at Boulness:[20] on the Solway Firth, and ending in a fort at Cousin's House, near the village of Wallsend, the old Segedunum, near the mouth of the Tyne, a few miles east of Pons Aelii, or Newcastle. The whole length of this vast work was sixty-eight miles and three furlongs;[21] the height, in the time of Bede,[22] twelve feet, exclusive perhaps of parapet. The thickness, from seven to nine feet. It was guarded by a multitude of towers, generally within less than a mile distant from each other; all of them sixty-six feet square. Between every two of these towers were four exploratory turrets, only four yards square: as these were within call, sentinels were placed in them to give an alarm. Besides these, were seventeen stations, at about four miles distance from each other. These are known by names such as Cilurnum, Procolitia, and the like. A military way was made by Severus, at the same time with his wall, and ran from turret to turret, and was regularly paved.[23]

More to assist my own memory, than to inform the reader, I may be permitted to name, in order of time, the number of walls or defences, formed by the Romans, or repaired by them, in order to keep our northern fellow-subjects within bounds. The first was the chain of forts, made by Agricola, from the Firth of Forth to that of Clyde, in the year 81, to protect his conquests from the incursions of the Caledonians; and, as Tacitus expresses it, to remove them, as it were, into another island.

The second was the vallum, or dike, flung up by Adrian, in the year 121. Spartian bears witness to this;[24] who informs us that Adrian visited Britain, reformed many things, and made a wall eighty miles long, to separate the barbarians from the Romans. This was made of earth and stones. It terminated on the western side of the kingdom, at Axelodunum, or Brugh, on the Solway sands, and was supposed to have reached no farther than Pons Aelii,

[20] Vide *Voyage to the Hebrides*, 62.
[21] Horsely, 121.
[22] Part is yet tolerably entire near Lanercost Abbey, in Cumberland.
[23] Horsely, 118.
[24] *Vit. Adriani*, ch. XI.

or Newcastle, on the eastern. But by an account, I very recently received from Mr Robert Harrison of that town,[25] I find, it extended on this side as far as the wall of Severus. A broken stone has lately been discovered at Wallsend, with this inscription:

HADR
MUR: COND
HOC. MARM.
POS: COSS. D.

The third was also of earth, made in the year 138, by Lollius Urbicus, lieutenant to Antoninus, who recovering the country, once conquered by Agricola, built another turf wall on the boundary left by that great general, and removed the Caledonians farther from the Roman province.[26] This is proved not only by Capitolinus, but by the inscriptions from the stations in the course of it.

The fourth in the year 210, by Severus, as above described. Notwithstanding his historian vaunts, that this emperor penetrated to the remotest parts of the island, he seemed to judge it prudent to reduce its limits to the vallum of Adrian.

If we may credit Nennius, Carausius, in 290, repaired the wall of Severus, and fortified it with seven towers. A work seemingly needless, as it was before so well supplied with forts. It seems as if Nennius confounded the wall of Antonine with that of Severus, for immediately after mentioning the last, he speaks of Pengual, and the River Cluth. The first, being Kinniel, near the end of Antonine's Wall, on the Firth of Forth; and the Cluth, the Clyde, where it terminates on the western coast.[27]

Theodosius, in 367, after driving the crowds of Scotti, Attacotti, and other barbarous invaders, out of the Roman province, repaired the boundary, built new forts, and called the parts he had recovered, Valentia, in honour of the Emperor Valens.[28]

The provincial Britons, after they were relieved from their distresses, by the assistance of a Roman legion, in 426, once more

---

[25] August 1775.
[26] Capitolinus, *Vit. Anton. Pil.*, ch. V.
[27] *Hist. Br.*, ch. XIX. I am indebted to Mr Harrison of Newcastle for the stricture on Nennius.
[28] *Ammianus Marcelinus*, lib. XXVI, ch. 4, lib. XXVIII, ch. 3.

repaired the wall of Antonine, with turf,[29] being too ignorant to effect it in any other manner. And, finally, by the advice of Gallio, and the help of a legion under his command, the wall of Severus was restored:[30] a poor security to the degenerate Britons, after the retreat of the Romans.

Proceed by the village of Wall, and from a rising ground have a fine view of the river, now enlarged by the waters of the South Tyne. Pass by Hermitage, the house of the late Dr Jurin, the celebrated natural philosopher. In ancient times St John, of Beverley, made the adjacent woods his retreat from the world; which gave name to the place. Ford the river; the beautiful bridge, lately finished, having been swept away by the floods. Enter Hexham; the Hagustald of Bede, and Hextoldesham of the Saxons. Till the 33rd of Henry VIII, it was called a 'county palatine', but at that period was stripped of its power. In ancient times it was a manor belonging to the see of York, whose prelates had here a regality and great powers. Their liberties were affirmed to them by the King's council in Parliament, in the 21st of Edward I, and by a clause in the 13th of Edward III, had *jura regalia*, and the right of levying tenths and fifteenths. The parish was also called Hexhamshire, having, till the 14th of Queen Elizabeth, been a distinct shire; but in that year was united with the county of Northumberland.

The town is ancient, finely seated on the southern banks, consisting of about five thousand inhabitants, whose chief manufacture is that of shoes and gloves; and it also carries on a considerable trade in tanning. But Hexham, like many other places, must vaunt of the glory of past times: in that of the Romans, it was probably a station, if one may judge from the half-defaced inscriptions on certain stones that antiquaries have discovered worked up in the walls of the vaults of the church;[31] the most curious of which is that inscribed with the name of emperor Lucius Septimius Severus. Antiquaries for a time universally agreed, that this place was the Axelodunum of the Notitia; but Mr Horsely, with much reason removes it to

[29] Gildas, ch. 12. Bede, lib. I, ch. 12.
[30] Gildas, ch. 14. Bede, lib. I, ch. 12.
[31] Horsely, 247. Gordon, 183, 185.

Burgh; and conjectures, that Hexham might have been the Epiacum of Ptolemy.[32]

Very early in the Saxon times it grew distinguished by its ecclesiastical splendour. Hexham and the adjacent country were part of the crown lands of the kings of Northumberland, and settled by King Egfrid, as dower on his queen, Ethelreda. Wilfrid, Bishop of York, obtained from the king a grant of it;[33] and here prevailed on him to found a bishopric, which saw but seven prelates, being overthrown in the Danish wars, about the year 821. But the magnificence of the church and monastery, founded here in 674, by Wilfrid, is spoken of in the highest terms by ancient writers. They celebrate the variety of the buildings, the columns, the ornamental carvings, the oratories, and the crypts; they also relate the pains he was at to obtain artists of the greatest skills from different parts both at home and abroad. They mention the richness of covers for the altars, the gilding of the walls with gold and silver, and the noble library, collected with amazing industry: in few words, say they, there was not such a church to be found on this side of the Alps. As this place suffered greatly by barbarity of the Danes, there is no vestige of the ancient church. The present building, which, when entire, was large and beautiful, is probably the work of Thomas, the second Archbishop of York, to which see it had been given by Henry I. The prelate, struck with the desolation of the place, established here, in 1113, a convent of canons regular of Augustines. The architecture is mixed; has much Gothic, and a little Saxon; and in one part, the narrow sharp-arched windows; all which began to be in use about that reign. The tower is large, and in the centre; the church having been in form of a Greek cross; but the west end was quite demolished by the Scots, in 1296. The town was also plundered by David II in 1346, but saved from the flames, as he intended it as a magazine for provisions.

The inside is supported by clustered pillars, with Gothic arches: the gallery above opens with Saxon arches, including in each two of

---

[32] Horsely, 109, 369.

[33] *Eddii Vita S. Wilfridi*, in Gale's Collection III, 62. See more in that magnificent and accurate work, the *History of Ely*, 21, 22, by the Rev Mr Bentham, to whom we are first indebted for this notice from Richard of Hexham's account of it.

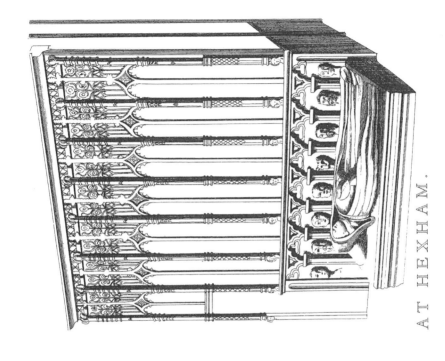

XXXIX

AT HEXHAM.

the pointed kind. On the wooden screen before the choir is painted the dance of death; in each piece the meagre monster is seizing a character of every rank. Many other paintings, now much injured by time, adorned this part. Beneath the dance on a moulding are twelve square pieces of wood; (originally there were fourteen) on each is elegantly cut in relief and gilt, a certain capital letter, and in every one a pretty cypher of other letters, which may be thus read: *ORATE PRO ANIMA DOMINI THOM: S. PRIOR HUJUS ecclesiae QUI FECIT HOC OPUS*. The letters in lower case are to supply the parts; and are conjectural to supply the sense.

The tomb of Alfwald I, King of Northumberland, assassinated in 788, by Sigga one of his nobles, is shown beneath an arch, at the south end of the north-east aisle.

An Umfravil lies recumbent, cross-legged, the privilege of crusaders. On his shield are the arms of the family, who were great benefactors to this abbey. Here is also another knight, with the same mark of holy zeal, miscalled the Duke of Somerset, beheaded here in 1463. But the arms on the shield, three gerbes, show that the deceased was not a Beaufort, who quartered the arms of England and France.

In the choir is a beautiful oratory; of stone below, and wood above, most exquisitely carved, now converted into a pew. Near that is the tomb of a religious, probably a prior. Above, in a shield, are, in Saxon characters, the letters *R.I.* These being in many parts of the building, are probably the initials of some of the pious benefactors. In a square hole in a corner of the oratory is an uncouth head of Jupiter, and in the inside a hare, the emblem of watchfulness; and on the outside is the upper part of some singular figure with a cap pendent on one side of his head; and a hare, or some animal, in his bosom. Against a pillar is a ridiculous figure of a barefooted man, with great club; perhaps a pilgrim.

Here is preserved the famous *fridstol*, or 'stool of peace'; for whosoever took possession of it was sure of remission.[34] This place had the privilege of a sanctuary, which was not merely confined

---

[34] In the minster at Beverley is a stool of this kind, called by the same name, and destined for the same use.

to the church, but extended a mile four ways,[35] and the limits each way marked by a cross. Heavy penalties were levied on those who dared to violate this sanctuary, by seizing on any criminal within the prescribed bounds; but if they presumed to take him out of the stool,[36] the offence was not redeemable by any sum; it was esteemed 'botoloss', beyond the power of pecuniary amends; and the offenders were left to the utmost severity of the church, and suffered excommunication, in old times the most terrible of punishments.

Part of the monastery still remains habitable. It was granted, on the Dissolution, to Sir Reginald Carnaby; afterwards passed to the Fenwicks, and lastly to the Blackets. The convent gate is entire, and consists of a fine round arch. This is evidently of a much older date than any of the present remains of the convent. It is of Saxon architecture; and perhaps part of the labours of the great Wilfrid.

The town house is built over an ancient gate; beyond that is an old square tower, of three floors. The lowest has beneath it two dreadful dungeons, which in this thievish neighbourhood, before the accession, were seldom untenanted.

The little rivulet, Hexold, which runs by the town, would not merit mention, if it did not give name to the place.

Proceed eastward. About three miles from Hexham, cross the Divil, on a bridge of two arches. On an eminence is a square tower, peeping picturesquely above the trees. This was part of the estate of the unfortunate Earl of Derwentwater, now vested in Greenwich hospital. On the banks of this river was fought, in 1463, the bloody battle of Hexham, between the Lancastrians and Yorkists, in which the first were defeated. The meek Henry fled with so great precipitation as to lose his abacock, or cap set with jewels, which was carried to his rival at York. His faithful consort, Margaret, betook herself, with the infant prince, to a neighbouring forest, where she was surrounded with robbers, and spoiled of her jewels and rings. The darkness of the night, and a dispute that arose among the banditti about the division of the booty, gave her opportunity of making a second escape: but while she wandered, oppressed

---

35 Steeven's *Contin.* Dugdale II, 135.
36 Richard of Hexham, as quoted by Stavely, *Hist. Ch.*, 173.

with hunger and fatigue, another robber approached with a drawn sword: her spirit now proved her safety. She advanced towards the man, and presenting to him the young prince, called out to him, 'Here friend, I commit to you the protection of the son of your king.' The man, perhaps a Lancastrian, reduced by necessity to this course of life, was affected with her gallant confidence, devoted himself to her service, and concealed his royal charge till he found opportunity of conveying them beyond the reach of their enemies.

Cross at this place the Wattling Street, which runs directly to Ebchester, the ancient Vindomona: pass the Tyne, on a bridge of seven arches, near whose northern end is Corbridge, a small town, but formerly considerable; for Leland says that in his time were the names of diverse streets, and great tokens of old foundations. Near Corbridge is Colchester, a station on the line of the wall, the old Corstopitum; the Roman way passes through it, and was continued on the other shore by the bridge, whose ruins Leland was informed of by the vicar of the parish. Mr Horsley acquaints us, that even in his time some vestiges were to be seen.[37] A little above is the small stream of Corve.[38] Leland, p. 212, of the second volume of his *Collectanea*, relates that King John, when he was at Hexham, caused great search to be made after a treasure, he had heard was hidden here, but to his disappointments found nothing but stones, old brass wire, iron and lead. Abundance of antiquary treasures have been found here since: among others, an inscription to Marcus Aurelius Antoninus; another commemorating a cohort, that made part of the wall; here is also a figure of Victory, holding in her hand, I think, a flag. But the most curious antiquities are the two Greek inscriptions, and the silver plate found in the adjacent grounds. The inscriptions are on two altars. The first is mentioned, p. 72, of the former volume; and was erected by Pulcher to the goddess Astarte. The other, in the possession of the Duke of Northumberland, is adorned on one side with a wreath; on the other, with an ox's head, and a knife; and erected, as the inscription imports, by the chief priestess Diodora, to the Tyrian Hercules.[39]

[37] *Itin.* V., 112.
[38] Ibid.
[39] Horsely, *Northumberland*, 246. *Archaeologia*. Vol. II, 92, 98. Vol. III, 324.

The other antiquity, which is also in his Grace's cabinet, is of matchless beauty and rarity: it is a piece of plate, of the weight of a hundred and forty-eight ounces, of an oblong form, twenty inches by fifteen,[40] with a margin enriched with a running foliage of vine leaves and grapes. The hollow is about an inch beneath. In this is a fine assemblage of deities. Apollo appears first, standing at the door of a temple, with wreathed pillars, with capitals of the leaves of Acanthus. In one hand is his bow; in the other a laurel branch. His feet stand on a sceptre, and near that his lyre rests against one of the columns. Beneath him is a sunflower, the emblem of Phoebus; and a griffin, that poets couple to his chariot:

> *Ac si Phoebus adest, et frenis Grypha jugalem*
> *Ripbaeo tripodas repetens destorsit ab axe*
> *Tunc sylvae,* etc.
> Claudian, VI. *Cons. Honorii.*

Vesta sits next to him, veiled and clothed with a long robe; her back leans against a round pillar, with a globe on the top, and under her the altar, flaming with eternal fire.

Ceres stands next, with her hair turned up, and tied behind: over her forehead a leaf, an emblem of vegetation; and in one hand a blunted spear. Her robe and attitude are elegant. The other hand points to her neck, and passes through a pendent fillet, hanging below her breast. Beneath her feet, and that of the succeeding figure, are two ears, perhaps of corn, but so ill executed as to leave the matter in doubt.

Minerva is placed with her back to Ceres. Her figure is by no means equivocal: her helmet, spear, shield, and the head of Medusa on her breast, sufficiently mark the goddess. Her right hand is lifted up, as if pointing to another figure, that of Diana, dressed and armed for the chase. Her lower garment is short, not reaching to her knee; over that flows a mantle, falling to the middle of her legs, and hanging gracefully over one arm. Her legs dressed in buskins:

> *Talia succincta pinguntur crura Dianae*
> *Cum sequitur fortes, fortior ipsa feras.*

---

[40] This description is borrowed from the learned Mr Roger Gale's account, and the print by Mr William Shafto.

One hand extends her bow towards Minerva; the other holds an arrow: between them is a tree branching over both of them, with several birds perched on it: among them that of Jove, immediately over the head of Minerva, perhaps to mark her as the daughter of that deity. On the side next to Diana is an altar, with a small globular body on it; probably, as my learned antiquary imagines, 'libamina ex farre, melle et oleo'.

One leg of that goddess is placed over a rock, on whose side is an urn, with a copious stream flowing from it. The rock and tree recall into Mr Gale's mind, the address of Horace, to the same deity:

> *Montium custos nemorumque virgo.*

Between the rock and the altar of eternal fire is a greyhound, looking up to her, and a dead deer; both belonging to this goddess of the chase.

Mr Gale imagines it to have been one of the lances, or sacrificing plates, so often mentioned by Virgil, on which were placed the lesser victims:

> *Dona ferunt, cumulantque oneratis lancibus aras.*

Continue our ride by the side of the Tyne. Reach Bywell, a small village, seated in a manor of the same name, which Guy de Baliol was invested with by William Rufus,[41] and which Hugh de Baliol held afterwards by the service of five knights' fees, and finding, thirty soldiers for the defence of Newcastle-upon-Tyne, as his ancestors had done from their first possession.[42]

Near the village is a handsome modern house, the seat of Mr Fenwick. A little farther is a square tower, built by the Nevils, successors to the Baliols, in the reign of Queen Elizabeth. At that time it was noted for a manufacture of bits, stirrups, and buckles, for the use of the borderers. At the same time, such was the unhappy situation of the place, that the inhabitants, through fear of the thieves of Tynedale, were obliged nightly, in summer as well as

---

[41] Dugdale's *Baron* I, 523.
[42] Blunt's *Ancient Tenures*, 14.

winter, to bring their cattle and sheep into the street, and to keep watch at the end; and when the enemy approached, to make hue-and-cry to rouse the people to save their property.[43] As this was a dangerous county to travel through, the tenants of every manor were bound to guard the judge through the precincts, but no farther. Lord Chief Justice North describes his attendants with long beards, short cloaks, long basket-hilted broad swords, hanging from broad belts, and mounted on little horses, so that their legs and swords touched the ground at every turning. His Lordship also informs us, that the sheriff presented his train with arms, i.e. a dagger, knife, penknife, and fork, all together.[44]

A little beyond Bywell are the piers of an old bridge. I have been informed, that workmen have remarked, that these piers never had any spring of arches, the superstructure therefore must have been of wood. Two or three miles farther is the village of Ovingham, in which was a cell of three black canons,[45] belonging to the monastery of Hexham, founded by Umfranvil, Baron of Prudhow, the ruins of whose castle make a fine object on the opposite bank of the river. This family came into England with the Conqueror, who bestowed on Robert with the Beard the lordship of Riddesdale, to be held for ever by the service of defending the country against thieves and wolves with the same sword with which William entered Northumberland,[46] and the barony of Prudhow, by the service of two knights' fees and a half. Odonel de Umfranvil in 1174, supported in this castle a siege against William I of Scotland, who was obliged to retire from before the place: but probably not without damaging the castle; for, we find this same Odonel, accused of oppressing and plundering his neighbours in order to repair the roof. It continued in the family till the reign of Henry VI, when on the death of the last, it fell by entail to the Tailboys, a short-lived race;[47] for on the execution of Sir William, after the battle of Hexham, it became forfeited to the crown. The

[43] Wallis II, 148.
[44] *Life of Lord Keeper Guildford*, 139, 140.
[45] Tanner's *Monast.*, 394.
[46] Dugdale's *Baron* I, 504.
[47] Idem, 508.

Duke of Northumberland is the present owner, his right is derived from the Percys, who possessed it for some ages (admitting a few interruptions from attainders, to which the name was subject) but from which they had the merit of emerging with singular honour.

Ride for some miles along the railroads, in which the coal is conveyed over to the river; and pass by numbers of coal pits. The whole road from Corbridge is the most beautiful imaginable, on the banks of the river, which runs through a narrow vale, enclosed and highly cultivated. In some parts, the borders are composed of meadows or cornfields, flanked by slopes, covered with wood. In others, the banks rise suddenly above the water, clothed with hanging groves. The country is very populous, and several pretty seats embellish the prospects: the back view to the south soon alters to barren and black moors, which extend far into Durham, and are, as I am informed, almost pathless.

Reach Newburn, a place of note preceding the conquest. In these parts presided Copsi, created, by William, Earl of Northumberland, after expelling Osulf, a governor, substituted by Morkar, the preceding earl. Osulf, being defeated, and forced into woods and deserts, gathered new forces, obliged Copsi to take refuge in the church, which he set on fire; seized him as he shunned the flames, and cut off his head.[48]

In the last century, this village was infamous for the defeat of the English, in 1640, by the Scots, who passed through the deep river in the face of our army, drawn on the opposite bank ready to receive them. A panic seized our forces and their commander; with this difference: the troops were ashamed of their flight, and wished to repair their disgrace, and to revenge it on a foe, that hardly credited its own success; but the timid general, uninfluenced by the same sense of honour, never afterwards turned his face to the enemy.[49]

At this place quit the river, and after ascending a bank, reach the fine road that extends from Carlisle to Newcastle, almost following the course of the wall.

[48] Dugdale's *Baron* I, 54.
[49] Clarendon I, 144. Whitelock, 35.

At a mile's distance from Newcastle, pass over the site of Condercum, the modern Benwel, where several inscriptions have been found, preserved in Horsley. The most remarkable is the altar, dedicated to Jupiter Dolichenus, who, with the last addition, is supposed by antiquaries to preside over iron-mines;[50] but in my opinion their arguments are an errant waste of paper. Opposite to this place the Derwent discharges itself into the Tyne.

Reach Newcastle; a vast town, seated on the steep banks of the coaly Tyne, the Vedra of Ptolemy, joined by the bridge to Gateshead, in Durham, and appears as part of it. The lower streets and 'chares', or alleys, are extremely narrow, dirty, and in general ill-built; consisting often of brewhouses, malt-houses, granaries, warehouses, and cellars. The keelmen chiefly inhabit the suburb of Sandgate and the north shore, a mutinous race, for which reason the town is always garrisoned. In the upper part, are several handsome streets.

The origin of this place is evidently Roman, like that of many of our great towns and cities. This was the Pons Aelii, a station on the line of the wall, where the Romans had a bridge to the opposite shore. No altars or inscriptions are extant to prove the name: a great and populous town has covered the ancient site, and destroyed, or absorbed into it every vestige of antiquity. Some part of the wall, which passed through the space now occupied by the present buildings must be excepted; for workmen have in the course of digging the foundations of new houses, struck on parts of it. There is also shown at Pandon Gate, the remains of one of the ancient mural towers; and at the Carpenter's tower was another. 'As old as Pandon Gate', is a common proverb in these parts, which shows its reputed antiquity. The wall had passed from the west, through the vicarage gardens, the groat market, the north part of St Nicholas's Church, and from thence to Pandon Gate.

After the Romans had deserted this island, it is not probable that this station should be entirely desolated; but we know nothing relating to it from that period, for some centuries from that great

---

[50] Horsely, 209.

event, besides a bare name, Monkchester; which shows that it was possessed by the Saxons, and noted for being the habitation of religious men. These proved the victims to the impious barbarity of some unknown enemy, who extirpated throughout these parts every house of devotion. In all Northumberland there was not a monastery; so that in 1074, when Aldwin, Alsvin, and Remfrid.[51] made their holy visitation to this place, they scarcely discovered even a church standing, and not a trace of the congenial pietists they expected to find. Their destruction must have been early; for the Venerable Bede, who died in 735, takes no notice of the place, though he mentions Jarrow, a convent, on the southern side of the Tyne, not remote from it.[52] The ruin therefore of the place cannot be attributed to the Danes, whose first invasion did not take place till after the death of that historian.

It continued an inhabited place in the year 1080, when Robert Courthose, son to William the Conqueror, returning from his expedition against Scotland, halted here with his army, and then built the present tower, that goes by his name; and changed at the same time that of Monkchester into Newcastle, whether from the novelty of the building, or in opposition to some ancient fortress, the work of the Romans or Saxons, is not certain. From this time may be dated the importance of the place; for the advantage of living in this border country, under the security of a fortress, soon caused a resort of people. If it is true, that David I (who was possessed of it as Earl of Northumberland) founded here two monasteries and a nunnery,[53] it was a place of note before the year 1153, the time of that prince's death.

The walls of Newcastle are pretty entire, with ramparts of earth within, and a fosse without. Leland informs us that they were begun in the reign of Edward I and completed in that of Edward III.[54] He ascribes their origin to the misfortune of a rich citizen, who was taken prisoner by the Scots out of the middle of the town. On his

[51] Hollinshed II, 11.
[52] *Hist. Eccl.*, lib. V, ch. 21, 210. *Vita Cudbercti*, ch. 35, 254.
[53] Tanner, 391. Keith.
[54] Leland's *Itinerary* V, 115.

redemption, he endeavoured to prevent for the future a similar disaster; for he immediately began to secure his native place by a wall; and, by his example, the rest of the merchants promoted the work: and it appears, that in the 19th of Edward I they obtained the royal licence for so salutary an end.[55] The circuit of the walls are rather more than two miles; but at present there are very considerable buildings on their outsides. All the principal towers are round: there are generally two machicollated towers between every two, which project a little over the wall.

Robert's tower was of great strength; square, and surrounded with two walls; the height of eighty-two feet; the square on the outside, sixty-two by fifty-four; the walls thirteen feet thick, with galleries gained out of them. Within was a chapel. Not long after the building, it was besieged on the rebellion of Robert Mowbray against William Rufus,[56] and taken. The town was taken by treachery by the Scots, in 1135, or the first year of King Stephen, nor was it restored to the English before 1156, when, at Chester, Malcolm IV ceded to Henry II the three northern counties. From that time, neither castle nor town underwent any siege, till the memorable one, in 1644, when, after a leaguer of two months, it was taken by storm, by the Scots, under the Earls of Callendar and Leven.

There were seven gates to the city. That of Pandon, or Pampedon, is most remarkable, leading to the old town of that name, united to Newcastle in 1299. It is said that the kings of Northumberland had a palace here, and that the house was called Pandon Hall.[57]

This town was frequently the rendezvous of the English barons, when summoned on any expedition against Scotland: and this was also the place of interview between the monarchs of each kingdom, for the adjusting of treaties. The kings of England resided at the side, an appendage to the castle, since called Lumley Place, being afterwards the habitation of the lords Lumleys. The kings and nobility of Scotland resided at the Scotch inn: the earls

---

[55] Gardner's *English Grievances*, ch. IV.
[56] Bourne, 110.
[57] Bourne, 134, 138.

of Northumberland at the great house of the same name; and the Nevils had another, styled Westmoreland Place.

The religious houses were numerous: the most ancient was a nunnery, a contemporary with the conquest,[58] to which Agas, mother to Margaret, Queen of Scotland, and Christian her sister, retired after the death of Malcolm, at Alnwick.[59] Near the Dissolution, here were ten nuns of the Benedictine order, whose revenues amounted but to thirty-six pounds per annum.

Poor as these sisters were, they were more opulent than the Carmelites, or White Friars, founded here by Edward I, whose income amounted but to nine pounds eleven and four pence, to support a prior, seven friars, and two novices, found there at the Reformation.[60]

In the close of this house was a fraternity, styled the Brethren of the Penance of Jesus Christ, or 'the brethren of the sack', to whom Henry III gave the place called the Calgarth.

The Domicans had a house founded by Sir Peter Scot, first mayor of Newcastle, and his son, about the middle of the 13th century. At the Dissolution, here were a prior and twelve friars. The remains of this house are engraven by Mr Grose.

The Franciscans, or Grey Friars, had an establishment here, founded by the family of the Carliols, in the time of Henry III. In this place Charles I was confined after he had put himself into the hands of his Scotch subjects. Part is still remaining, and with some additional building, the residence of Sir Walter Blacket. The famous Duns Scotus, the *'Doctor Subtilis'*, was of this house. He died of an apoplexy, was too suddenly buried, and coming to life in his tomb, dashed out his brains in the last struggle.

The monastery of Augustines was founded here by a Lord Ross of Werk, in the reign of Edward I.

When the grievous distemper of the leprosy raged in these kingdoms, the piety of our ancestors erected *asyla* for those poor wretches who were driven from the society of mankind. Henry I founded a hospital here for their reception; and fixed a master,

[58] Tanner, 391.
[59] Leland's *Collect.* II, 531.
[60] Bourne, 38.

brethren, and sisters; but when this disease abated, the house was appointed for the poor visited with the pestilence: a scourge that heaven in its favour has freed us from. Here were besides four other hospitals, founded for the pious purposes of redeeming the captive, for the reception of pilgrims or travellers, for the relief of distressed clergy, or the interring of the poor. Each of these in general the establishment of individuals: our present foundations the united charity of the mites of multitudes. How unequal are the merits!

But the more modern charities in this town are very considerable: firstly, the general infirmary for the sick of the counties of Durham, Northumberland and Newcastle, which, from its institution to 1771, has discharged, cured, about thirteen thousand patients. The second, is the lying-in hospital, for married women; and another charity for the support of those who lie-in at their own houses. Thirdly, a public hospital, for the reception of lunatics. Fourthly, the keelmen's hospital, a square building, with cloisters, founded, in 1702, by the poor keelmen, who allowed a penny per tide for that purpose. Besides these, are numbers of charity schools, and hospitals for the reception of the aged of both sexes.

The tower of St Nicholas's church is very justly the boast of the inhabitants. Its height is a hundred and ninety-four feet; round the top are several most elegant pinnacles, from whose base spring several very neat arches, that support the lanthorn, an open edifice, ornamented with other pinnacles of uncommon lightness. The church was originally founded in the reign of Henry I. The tower, built in the time of Henry VI by Robert Rhodes; and on the bottom of the belfry is an entreaty to pray for the soul of the founder.

The exchange contains variety of apartments, and also the courts of justice for the town. The front towards the river is enriched with two series of columns, and is of the architecture of the period of James I. The builder, Robert Trollop, is buried opposite to it in the churchyard of Gateshead. His statue pointing towards the exchange stood formerly over his grave, with these lines under his feet:

> *Here lies Robert Trollop,*
> *Who made yon stones roll-up.*
> *When death took his soul-up,*
> *His body fill'd this hole-up.*

Newcastle is divided into four parishes, with two chapels,[61] and about a dozen meeting-houses; and is a county containing a small district of ten miles circuit, a privilege bestowed on it by Henry IV rendering it independent of Northumberland. It first sent members to Parliament in the reign of Edward I and was also honoured with a sword of state.[62] It is a corporation, governed by a mayor, sheriff, and twelve aldermen. Their revenues are considerable. An annual allowance is made to the mayor of a thousand pounds, besides a coach, furnished mansion-house, and servants: he has also extra allowances for entertaining the judges on their circuit, who lodge at the mayor's house. The sheriff has also a handsome allowance for a public table. The receipts of the corporation in October, 1774, were £20,360 9s 8d, and disbursements £19,445. It is reckoned, that between this town and Gateshead, there are thirty thousand inhabitants, exclusive of those who live on each side of the river, adjacent to both places.[63] The exports are very considerable, consisting of coals, lead, glass, salt, bacon, salmon, and grinding stones. Here are not fewer than sixteen glass-houses, three sugar-houses, great manufactures of steel and iron, besides those of wrought iron at Swalwell, three miles up the river: also another of broad and narrow woollen cloth, which is carried on with great success, and not fewer than thirty thousand firkins of butter are annually sent abroad; and of tallow, forty thousand hundreds.

The great export of this place is coal, for which it has been noted for some centuries. It is not exactly known at what time that species of fuel was first dug. It is probable that it was not very early in general use. That the Romans sometimes made use of it appears in our former volume;[64] but since wood was the fuel of their own country, and Britain was overrun with forests, it was not likely that they would pierce into the bowels of the earth for a less grateful kind. But it was exported to foreign parts long before it was in use in London; for London likewise had its neighbouring forests. We find that in 1234, Henry III confirms to the good people of

---

[61] If Gateshead is included, five parishes and four chapels.
[62] Willis III, 95.
[63] Hutton's map, 1772.
[64] p. 55.

Newcastle the charter of his father, King John, granting them the privilege of digging coals in the Castlemoor, and converting them to their own profit, in aid of their fee-farm rent of a hundred a year;[65] which moor was afterwards granted to them in property by Edward III. The time of the first exportation of coals to London does not appear. In 1307, the 35th year of Edward I, they were considered in the capital as a nuisance; for on the repeated complaints of prelates, nobles, commons of Parliament, and inhabitants of London, against the stench and smoke of coals used by brewers, dyers, and other artificers, the king issued out his proclamation against the use of them: which being disregarded, a commission of oyer and terminer was issued to punish the disobedient with fines for the first offence, and for the second, by the destruction of their furnaces.[66] In 1379, we find that their use was not only tolerated, but their consumption made beneficial to the state; for, in that year, a duty of six pence per ton each quarter of a year was imposed on ships coming from Newcastle.[67] In 1421, the trade became so important as to engage the regulations of government, and orders were given about the lengths of the keels, so that the quantity of coal might be ascertained. From that period the commerce advanced continually. The present state may be collected from the following view of the shipping:[68]

Ships	*Tons*	*Chaldr. coals*	*Cwt. lead*	
3,585	689,090	330,200	123,370	coast trade
363	49,124	21,690	30,064	foreign parts
Tot.3,948	738,214	351,890	153,434	

There are about twenty-four considerable collieries, which lie at different distances, from five to eighteen miles from the river. The coal is brought down in wagons along rail roads, and discharged from certain covered places called 'staiths', built at the edge of the

---

[65] Anderson's *Dict*. I, 111, 188. Henry III, among other privileges, granted by charter to the merchants of Newcastle and their heirs, that no Jew should stay or dwell in their town. Madox, *Hist. Exch.* edition 1759, 259.

[66] Stow's *Chron.*, 209. Prynne on Coke's *Institute*, 182.

[67] *Foedera* VII, 220.

[68] Hutton's map, 1772.

water, into the keels or boats, which have the advantage of the tide flowing five or six miles above the town.

These boats are strong, clumsy, and oval, and carry twenty tons apiece. About four hundred and fifty are constantly employed: they are sometimes navigated with a square sail, but generally by two very large oars, one on the side, plied with a man and a boy; the other at the stern, by a single man, serving both as oar and rudder. Most of these keels go down to Shields, a port near the mouth of the river, about ten miles from Newcastle, where the large ships lie; for none exceeding between three and four hundred tons can come as high as the town. I must not omit that the imports of this place are very considerable. It appears that, in 1771,

810 ships, carrying	77,880,	tons from foreign parts
140	18,650	coasting trade
950	96,530	

were entered at this port; and that the customs for coal, amount to £41,000 per annum, besides the £15,000 payed to the Duke of Richmond, at one shilling per chaldron on all sent coastways.

Leave Newcastle, and cross the Tyne, in the ferryboat. Midway, have a full view of the ruins of the bridge, and of the destruction made by the dreadful flood of November, 1771, which bore down four arches, and twenty-two houses, with six of the inhabitants: one of the houses remained for a time suspended over the water; the shrieks of the devoted inmates were for a long space heard, without the possibility of affording them relief.

This bridge was of stone, and had stood above five hundred years. It consisted first of twelve arches, but by the contraction of the river by the quays on the northern side, was reduced to nine. The houses on the bridge were, generally, built at distances from each other. About the middle, was a handsome tower with an iron gate, used by the corporation for a temporary prison. At the south end, was (formerly) another tower, and a drawbridge.

By the ancient name of the station on the northern bank, Pons Aelii, it is evident, that there had been a bridge here in the time of the Romans; and I am informed that there are still vestiges of a road pointing directly to it from Chester le Street. I cannot help thinking, that part of the Roman bridge remained there till very lately; for, from the observation of workmen upon the old piers, those, as well as the piers of the bridge at Bywell, seem, originally, to have been formed without any springs for arches. This was a manner of building used by the Romans; witness the bridge built over the Danube by Trajan,[69] at Severin, twenty Hungarian miles from Belgrade, whose piers, I believe, still exist.[70] Adrian was probably the founder of the bridge at Newcastle, which was called after this family name Pons Aelii, in the same manner as Jerusalem was styled Aelia Capitolina, and the games he instituted at Pincum, in Maesia, Aeliana Pincensia. The coins discovered on pulling down some of the piers, in 1774, confirm my opinion. Several were discovered, but only three or four rescued from the hands of the workmen. All of them are coins, posterior to the time of Adrian, probably deposited there in some later repairs. One is a beautiful Faustina the elder, after her deification. Her forehead is bound with

[69] Brown's *Travels*, 3. Monfaucon, *Antiq.* IV, I, 185, tab. cxv. Brown, by mistake, attributes it to Adrian.

[70] Severin is a ruined place, a few miles above the remains of Trajan's bridge, which are still existing, about five English miles below *Demirkapi*, or 'the iron gate'. This is a narrow passage in the Danube. A quarter of an hour's walk from these remains, is an old ruined castle on the northern shore; and the next place below it is called Tchernigrad, or Maurocastro. Count Marsigli, *Topogr. Danub.*, tom. II, 22. t. x mentions, that the river, at the place, is not quite 1,000 yards wide, and that the piers can be seen at low water only; the distance of the two first of them is of 17 1/2 fathoms, and supposing all the others to be equidistant, there must have been twenty-three in all. The masonry seems to consist of a strong cement and a number of pebbles, faced with bricks; and he observed several ranges of square holes, which probably were practised in the piers for the insertion of oak timbers to form the bridge upon, which had not the least springs for arches. Captain de Schad, in the Austrian service, who, in the year 1740, navigated down the Danube, in the retinue of the ambassador to the Porte, and Count Uhlefeld, saw these low piers of Trajan's bridge, near Tchernetz, probably the same place with the abovementioned Tchernigrad, and thought them to be of freestone. Topwitch, *Enquiries on the Sea*, 203 and 241. Nicholas Ernst Kleeman, a merchant, found these piers still existing in the year 1768; but thinks the work looked more like rocks washed out by the stream than like piers: though he confesses to have seen some masonry upon the northern shore, consisting of brick and freestone, joined by a mortar as hard as the stones themselves. N. E. Kleeman's *Journey through Krim-Tartary and Turkey, 1768–1770.*

a small tiara; her hair full, twisted, and dressed *à la moderne*; round is inscribed DIVA FAUSTINA. On the reverse is Ceres, with a torch in one hand, and ears of corn in the other; the inscription *AUGUSTA. S.C.*

The next has the laureated head of Antoninus Pius. On the reverse, Apollo, with a patera in one hand; a plectrum in the other; the legend so much defaced as to be illegible.

The third of Lucius Verus (like that of Faustina, after consecration). On the reverse is a magnificent funeral pile, and the word, *CONSECRATIO, S.C.*

The original superstructure of this bridge was probably of wood, like that over the Danube: and continued, made with the same material, for several centuries. Notice is taken of it in the reign of Richard I, when Philip Poictiers, Bishop of Durham, gave licence to the burgesses of Gateshead, to give wood to whomsoever they pleased, to be spent about the River Tyne; which is supposed to mean in the repairs of the bridge and quay on the part belonging to Durham: for one third belongs to the bishop, and two to the town. So that, after it was destroyed in 1248 by a furious fire, the bishop and the town united in the expense of building the stone bridge, of which this calamity was the origin. The prelate (Walter Kirkham) had the advantage in this: for, armed with spiritual powers, he issued out indulgencies from all penances to every one that would assist either with money or labour. The town also applied to other bishops for their assistance in promoting so good a work; and they, in consequence, granted their indulgencies: but then the clergy of the north were directed by their archdeacon, to prefer the indulgencies of their own prelate to any other. In the end, both parties succeeded, and the money raised, was given to Laurentius, master of the bridge.

The boundaries of the bridge were strictly preserved. Edward III by writ, 1334, forbids the mayor and sheriffs of Newcastle to suffer their ships to lie on the southern side. And several other proofs may be brought of the strict observance of these rights of the bishop. By the calamity of November 17th, 1771, this part of the bridge was greatly damaged. An act was therefore passed this year to enable the present bishop, and his successors, to raise a sum of money by annuities equal to the purpose.

XX

THE BISHOPRIC OF DURHAM

Gateshead—Chester le Street—Lumley Castle—Coken—Priory of
Finchale—Durham—Bishops Auckland—Binchester

CROSS the water, and land in the bishopric of Durham. Enter
Gateshead; a considerable place, built on the steep banks of the
southern side of the river, containing about five hundred and fifty
houses. Camden supposes it to have been the ancient Gabrosentum,
and that it retained part of the name in its present Goatshead, as if
derived from the British *gafr*, 'a goat'. Mr Horsley justly imagines
this place to have been too near to Pons Aelii for the Romans to
have another station here, therefore removes it to Drumburgh. It
appears to me to have been very little altered from the old Saxon
name, Geats-hevod; or, 'the head of the road': and that it was so
styled from being the head of the Roman military way those new
invaders found there.

It was a place eminent for ecclesiastical antiquity. Bede mentions,
under the year 653, Uttan, brother of Adda, who had been abbot
of a monastery here;[1] but no relics of it now exist. Here are the
ruins of a beautiful chapel[2] belonging to a hospital dedicated to

[1] Lib. III, ch. 21.
[2] Engraven by Mr Grosse.

St Edmund, where four chaplains were appointed. The founder was Nicholas Farnham, Bishop of Durham, about the year 1247. In the reign of Henry VI, it was granted to the nuns of St Bartholomew, in Newcastle, and in that of Edward VI to the mayor and burgess of Newcastle. Here was besides another hospital, dedicated to the Holy Trinity, in the beginning of the reign of Henry III to which Henry de Ferlinton gave a farm, to find a chaplain, and maintain three poor men. This was refounded by James I in 1610.

Hugh Pudsey granted to the burgesses of Gateshead liberty of forestage, on paying a small acknowledgement. Edward VI annexed this place to Newcastle; but his successor Mary restored it again to the church of Durham.

Pass over a barren common, full of coalpits; then, through a rich country, enclosed and mixed with wood. Descend into a rich hollow; reach the small town of Chester le Street, the Cuneacestre of the Saxons: a small town, with good church and spire. Within are ranged, in nice order, a complete series of monuments of the Lumley family, from the founder Liulphus, down to John, Lord Lumley, who collected them from old monasteries, or caused them to be made anew, and obtained, in 1594, a licence from Tobias Matthews, Bishop of Durham, for placing them there. Over each is an inscription, with their names or history. The most remarkable is that of Liulphus, an Anglo-Saxon of distinction, who, during the distractions that reigned on the conquest, retired to these parts, and became so great a favourite with Walcher, Bishop of Durham, as to raise the envy of his chaplain Leofwin, who villainously caused Liulphus to be murdered, by one Gilbert, in his house near Durham. The bishop lay under suspicion of conniving at the horrid deed. The friends of Liulphus rose to demand justice: they obtained an interview with the bishop at Gateshead; but the prelate, instead of giving the desired satisfaction, took refuge in the church with the two offenders. On which the enraged populace, first sacrificing Gilbert and the bishop, set the church on fire, and gave the deserved punishment to the original contriver of the mischief.

In the Saxon times Chester le Street was greatly respected, on account of the relics of St Cuthbert, deposited here by Bishop Eardulf, for fear of the Danes, who at that time (about 884), ravaged the country. His shrine became afterwards an object of great devotion. King Athelstan, on his expedition to Scotland, paid it a visit, to obtain, by intercession of the saint, success on his arms; bestowed a multitude of gifts on the church, and directed, in case he died in his enterprise, that his body should be interred there. I must not omit, that at the same time that this place was honoured with the remains of St Cuthbert, the bishopric of Lindisfarn was removed here, and endowed with all the lands between the Tyne and the Were, the present county of Durham. It was styled 'St Cuthbert's patrimony'. The inhabitants had great privileges, and always thought themselves exempt from all military duty, except that of defending the body of their saint. The people of the north claimed this exemption, on account of their being under a continual necessity of defending the marches, and opposing the incursions of the Scots. The same excuse was pleaded by the town of Newcastle for not sending members to Parliament. Rymer[3] produces a discharge from Henry III to Robert, Bishop of Durham, Peter de Brus, and others, of having performed the military service they owed the king, for forty days, along with his son Edward. They, with the rest of this northern tract, asserted that they were 'hali-werke folks', that they were enrolled for holy work; that they held their hands to defend the body of the saint; and those in particular in his neighbourhood, were not bound to march beyond the confines of their country. In fact, Chester le Street was parent of the see of Durham; for when the relics were removed there, the see, in 995, followed them. Tanner says that probably a chapter of monks, or rather secular canons, attended the body at this place from its first arrival: but Bishop Beke, in 1286, in honour of the saint, made the church collegiate, and established here a dean, and suitable ecclesiastics; and, among other privileges, gives the dean a right of fishing on the Were, and the tythe of fish.[4]

At a small distance from the town, stands Lumley Castle, the ancient seat of the name. It is a square pile, with a court in the middle, and a square tower at each corner; is modernized into an

---

[3] *Foedera* I, 835.
[4] Dugdale, *Mon.* II, part 11, 5.

excellent house, and one of the seats of the Earl of Scarborough. It is said to have been built in the time of Edward I by Sir Robert de Lumley, and enlarged by his son Sir Marmaduke. Prior to that, the family residence was at Lumley (from whence it took the name), a village a mile south of the castle, where are remains of a very old hall house, that boasts a greater antiquity. The former was not properly castellated, till the year 1392, when Sir Ralph (the first Lord Lumley) obtained from Richard II 'Licentiam castrum suum de Lomley de novo aedificandum, muro de petra et calce batellare et kernellare et castrum illud sic batellatum, et kernellatum tenere', etc. This Sir Ralph was a faithful adherent to his unfortunate sovereign, and lost his life in his cause, in the insurrection, in the year 1400, against the usurping Henry. There are no dates, except one on a square tower; I. L. 1570, when, I presume, it was rebuilt by John, Lord Lumley.

The house is a noble repository of portraits, of persons eminent in the sixteenth century.

The brave, impetuous, presuming, Robert, Earl of Essex, appears in full length, dressed in black, covered with white embroidery. A romantic nobleman, of parts without discretion; who fell a sacrifice to his own passions, and a vain dependence for safety on those of an aged queen, doting with unseasonable love; and a criminal credulity in the insinuation of his foes.

Sir Thomas More; a half-length, dressed in that plainness of apparel which he used, when the dignity of office was laid aside; in a furred robe, with a coarse capuchin cap. He was the most virtuous, and the greatest character of his time; who, by a circumstance that might humiliate human nature, fell a victim for a religious adherence to his own opinion; after being a violent persecutor of others, for firmness to the dictates of their own confidence. To such inconsistencies are the best of mankind liable!

The gallant, accomplished, poetical Earl of Surry; in black, with a sword and dagger, the date 1545. The ornament (says Mr Walpole) of a boisterous, yet not unpolished court; a victim to a jealous tyrant, and to family discord. The articles alleged against him, and his conviction, are the shame of the times.

A portrait of a lady in a singular dress of black and gold, with a red and gold petticoat, dated 1560. This is called Elizabeth, third wife of Edward, Earl of Lincoln, the fair Geraldine, celebrated so highly by the Earl of Surry; but so ill-favoured in this picture, that I must give it to his first wife, Elizabeth Blount. Geraldine was the young wife of his old age. Her portrait at Woburn represents her an object worthy the pen of the amorous Surry.

Ambrose Dudley, Earl of Warwick, son of the great Dudley, Duke of Northumberland. His dress a bonnet, furred cloak, small ruff, and pendant George. This peer followed the fortunes of his father, but was received into mercy, and restored in blood; was created Earl of Warwick by Queen Elizabeth, and proved a gallant and faithful subject. He died in 1589, and lies under an elegant brass tomb in the chapel at Warwick.

Sir William Peter, or Petre, native of Devonshire, fellow of All Souls College, and afterwards secretary of state to four princes; Henry VIII, Edward VI, Mary, and Elizabeth. His prudence, in maintaining his post in reigns of such different tempers, is evident; but in that of Mary he attended only to politics; of Elizabeth, to religion.[5]

The first Earl of Bedford, engraven among the illustrious heads.

A half-length of the famous eccentric physician and chemist of the fifteenth century, *Philip Theophrastus* Paracelsus *Bombast de Hohenheim*: on the picture is added also the title of Aureolus. The cures he wrought were so very surprising in that age, that he was supposed to have recourse to supernatural aid; and probably, to give greater authority to his practice, he might insinuate that he joined the arts medical and magical. He is represented as a very handsome man, bald, in a close black gown, with both hands on a great sword, on whose hilt is inscribed the word 'AZOT'. This was the name of his familiar spirit, that he kept imprisoned in the pummel, to consult on emergent occasions. Butler humorously describes this circumstance:

> *Bombastus kept a devil's bird*
> *Shut in the pummel of his sword;*
> *That taught him all the cunning pranks*
> *Of past or future mountebanks.*[6]

[5] Dugdale's *Baron* II, 388. Prince's *Worthies of Devonshire*, 498.
[6] *Hudibras* II, ch. iii.

A head of Sir Anthony Brown, a favourite of Henry VIII, with a bushy beard, bonnet, and order of the garter. He was Master of the Horse to that prince, and appointed by him one of the executors of his will; and of the council to his young successor.

Two full-lengths of John, Lord Lumley: one in rich armour; a grey beard; dated 1588, aet. 54. The other in his robes, with a glove and handkerchief in one hand; a little black skullcap, white beard; dated 1591. This, I believe, was the performance of Richard Stevens, an able statuary, painter, and medallist, mentioned by Mr Walpole.[7]

This illustrious nobleman, restored the monuments that are in the neighbouring church, was a patron of learning, and a great collector of books, assisted by his brother-in-law, Humphrey Lhuyd, the famous antiquary. The books were afterwards purchased by James I and proved the foundation of the royal library. Mr Granger says, that they are a very valuable part of the British Museum.

His first wife, Jane Fitzallan, daughter of the Earl of Arundel; in black robes, with gloves in her hand. She was a lady of uncommon learning, having translated, from the Greek into Latin, some of the orations of Isocrates, and the Iphigenia of Euripides into English. She compliments her father highly in a dedication to him, prefixed to one of the orations, which begins, 'Cicero, Pater honoratissime, illustris'. She died before him, and was buried at Cheame in Surry.[8]

The earl himself, the last of that name; a three-quarters piece. His valour distinguished him in the reign of Henry VIII when he ran with his squadron close under the walls of Boulogne, and soon reduced it. In the following reign, he opposed the misused powers of the unhappy protector, Somerset; and yet declined connection with the great Northumberland. He supported the just rights of Queen Mary; was imprisoned by the former, but on the revolution was employed to arrest the abject fallen duke. He was closely attached to his royal mistress by similitude of religion. In his declining years, he aimed at being husband to Queen Elizabeth.[9] Had her Majesty

[7] *Anecd. Painting* I, 161.
[8] She was dead before December 30th, 1579, as appears by her father's will. Vide Ballard's *British Ladies*, 86.
[9] Camden's *Annals, Kennet*, 383.

deigned to put herself under the power of man, she never would have given the preference to age. On his disappointment, he went abroad; and, on his return, first introduced into England the use of coaches.[10]

A half length of that artful statesman, Robert, Earl of Salusbury, minister of the last years of Elizabeth, and the first of James I.

Thomas Ratcliff, Earl of Sussex, a full-length; young and handsome: his body armed, the rest of his dress white; a staff in his right hand, his left resting on a sword; on a table a hat, with a vast plume. This motto, *Amando et fidendo troppo, son ruinato.* This nobleman was a considerable character in the reigns of Mary and Elizabeth; frequently employed in embassies; in both reigns deputy of Ireland; and in the first, an active persecutor of the Protestants. He conformed outwardly to the religion of his new mistress; was appointed by her president of the north, and commanded against, and suppressed, the rebellion of the earls of Northumberland and Westmoreland, notwithstanding he secretly approved the opinions they armed in favour of. He was the spirited rival of Leicester; but the death of Sussex left the event of their dispute undetermined.

Leicester, his antagonist, is here represented, in a three-quarter piece, dated 1587; with the collar of the garter, and a staff in his hand.

A fine full-length of the Duke of Monmouth, with long hair, in armour.

A half-length of Sir Nicholas Carew, master of the horse to Henry VIII. There is vast spirit in his countenance. In his hat is a white feather; his head is bound round with a gold stuff handkerchief. He was beheaded in 1539, as Lord Herbert says for being of council with the Marquis of Exeter, a favourer of the dreaded Cardinal Pole, then in exile.[11] During the time of his confinement in the tower he imbibed the sentiments of the reformers, and died avowing their faith.[12]

[10] Idem.
[11] *Hist. Henry VIII*, 503.
[12] Hollinshead, 946.

Killegrew, gentleman of the bedchamber to Charles II, in a red sash, with his dog. A man of wit and humour; and on that account extremely in favour with the king.

A good half-length of Mr Thomas Windham, drowned on the coast of Guinea, aged 42. M. D. L. a robust figure, in green, with a red sash, and gun in his hand.

A three-quarter length, unknown, dated 1596, aged 43, dressed in a striped jacket, blue and white; black cloak and breeches, white ruff, gloves on, collar of the garter.

Here are also some illustrious foreigners. A half-length, inscribed Fernandes de Toledo, Duke of Alva, in rich armour, with his baton; short black hair, and beard. A great officer, and fortunate till his reign of cruelty. He boasted, that he had caused, during his command in the Low Countries, eighteen thousand people to perish by the executioner. He visited England in the train of his congenial master, Philip II. I imagine that this portrait was painted when the duke was young; for I have seen one (sent into England by the late Mr Benjamin Keen) now in possession of the Bishop of Ely, which represents him with a vast flowing white beard.

A three-quarter length of Andrew Doria, the great Genoese admiral, and patriot. He is dressed in black, in a cap, a collar, with the fleece pendant; a truncheon in his hand, and a dagger in his girdle. View of ships through a window.

Garcia Sarmienta Cuna; a full-length, in armour; a ruff, red stockings, white shoes, a cross on his breast, a spear in his hand. He was captain of the guard to Philip II.

A three-quarter length of a man in a scarlet robe; and over his left shoulder a white mantle; a scarlet cap tied in the middle, and open behind; a narrow white ruff; and a collar of the fleece. The scarlet robe is furred with white: on it are several times repeated these words, '*Ah! Amprins au ra jay!*' – 'Oh! Had I undertaken it!'

In the hall is a tablet, with the whole history of Liulphus, and his progeny, inscribed on a tablet, surrounded with the family arms; and round the room seventeen pictures of his descendants, down to John, Lord Lumley, who seemed to have a true veneration for his ancestors. Liulphus appears again in the kitchen, mounted on a horse of full size, and with a battleaxe in his hand. When James I, in one of his progresses, was entertained in this castle, William James, Bishop of Durham, a relation of the house, in order to give his majesty an idea of the importance of the family, wearied him with a long detail of their ancestry, to a period even beyond belief. 'O mon,' says the king, 'gang na farther, let me digest the knowledge I ha gained; for, by my saul I did na ken that Adam's name was Lumley.'

A little to the left, midway between Chester le Street and Durham, lies Coken, the seat of Mr Carr, a most romantic situation, laid out with great judgment; in former times the scene of the savage austerities of St Godric. Before his arrival, there had been an ancient hermitage, given before the year 1128, by Ralph Flambard, Bishop of Durham,[13] to the monks of Durham, who permitted that holy man to make it his residence; which he did, first with his sister,[14] and after her death entirely in solitude.

Attracted by the fame of the deceased, who died in 1170, some monks of Durham retired here. Hugh Pudsey, Bishop of Durham, made them an allowance, and granted them by charter many privileges;[15] some call him the founder of Finchale, the religious house, whose ruins are still considerable; but Tanner[16] gives that honour to his son Henry, who, about the year 1196, settled here a prior and monks of the Benedictine order, subordinate to Durham. It maintained, at the Dissolution, a prior and eight monks; when it was regranted to the dean and chapter, its value, according to Dugdale, was £122 15s 3d.

Proceed towards Durham. Near the city, on the right, stood Nevils Cross, erected in memory of the signal victory over David Bruce, of Scotland, in 1346. The army of the English was commanded by the two archbishops and three suffragans, in a conjunction with some noble lay-officers. The action was attended with great loss to the Scots; whose king, after showing the utmost valour, was taken prisoner by an Englishman, of the name of Copland.

---

[13] Dugdale's *Monast.* I, 512, where is Flambard's charter. He died in 1128.
[14] *Gulielm. Neubrigiensis* II, ch. 20.
[15] Dugdale I, 513.
[16] 114.

After admiring the beautiful situation of the city, from an adjacent hill, enter Durham; a place of Saxon foundation: the original name was Dunholme, from *dun*, 'a hill', and *holme*, 'an isle', formed by a river.[17] But it is only a lofty narrow peninsula, washed on each side by the Were, the Viurus of the Venerable Bede.[18] The city is disposed on the side of the hill, and along part of the neighbouring flat; and the buildings in general are very ancient. The approaches to it are extremely picturesque, especially that from the south, through a deep hollow, finely clothed with trees. The banks of the river are covered with woods, through which are cut numbers of walks, contrived with judgment, and happy in the most beautiful and solemn scenery. They impend over the water, and receive a most venerable improvement, from the castle and ancient cathedral, which tower far above.

This hill, till about the year 995, was an errant desert, overrun with wood, and uninhabitable. At that period, the religious of Cuneacestre, having, through fear of the Danish pirates, removed the body of St Cuthbert to Rippon, on their return back, when the danger was over, met with an admonition that determined them to deposit it in this place.[19] The corpse and the carriage became suddenly immoveable; no force could draw it a step farther. It was revealed to St Eadmer, that it should be brought to Durham; and, on that resolution, a slight strength removed it to the destined spot. With the assistance of the Earl of Northumberland, the wood was soon cleared away: a church arose, in honour of the saint, composed indeed of no better materials than rods. But this seems to have been only a temporary temple, for the whole country flocking in, assisted in building one of stone, which cost three years labour. A provost and secular canons were established here: these continued till about the year 1083, when William de Carilepho removed them,[20] placing in their room a prior and monks of the Benedictine order.

---

[17] Camden II, 946.
[18] *Eccl. Hist.*, lib. IV, ch. 18.
[19] *Hist. of the Cathedral of Durham*, annexed to Dugdale's *St Paul*, 6.
[20] Steven's *Contin.* Dugdale I, 350.

XL

CATHEDRAL CHURCH AND BRIDGE OF DURHAM.

The Saxons of these parts, unwilling to submit to the Norman yoke, retired to this as a place of strength, and built a fortress, for a time a great annoyance to the Conqueror. This they called Dunholme. The *dun*, or artificial hill, on which the great tower is built, was of their work. On the approach of William, the Saxons quitted their post. He possessed himself of so advantageous a situation, and founded the castle. This afterwards became the residence of the prelates, and, by ancient custom, the keys were, during a vacancy of the see, hung over the tomb of the tutelar St Cuthbert. The ambitious prelate, Hugh Pudsey, nephew to King Stephen, repaired and rebuilt several parts, which, during his time, had suffered by fire.[21] Hatfield, a munificent prelate in the reign of Edward III, restored such parts as he found in ruins, rebuilt the great hall, and that belonging to the constable; and added a great tower, for the farther security of the place.[22] To the mild and amiable Tunstall is owing the magnificent gate, the chapel, and some adjacent buildings;[23] and to Bishop Cosins, the first prelate of the see after the Restoration, the present beauty and magnificence of the place, after the cruel havoc made here by the brutal Haselrig.

The city, or rather the precincts of the abbey and castle, were surrounded with a wall, by Ralph Flambard,[24] in the beginning of the reign of Henry I. The admission was through three gateways: Framwell gate, at the head of a bridge of the same name; Claypath gate, near the market-place; and the Watergate, beneath the end of the Prebendaries walk. I do not find, that at any time the strength of the place was ever tried by a siege.

The cathedral stands below the castle. It was begun in 1093, by William de Carilepho, bishop of the diocese, who pulled down the old church, built by Aldwin. In this work he was assisted by Malcolm I of Scotland, and Turgot, the second prior, and his monks; who, at their own expense, and at the same time, made their own cells, and other conveniencies for the monastery.

[21] Mr Allan.
[22] *Hist. Cath. Durham*, Dugdale, 79.
[23] Goodwin, 139.
[24] Goodwin, 112.

Ralph Flambard, successor to Carilepho, had the honour of completing this superb structure, with exception of certain additions, such as the Galilee,[25] which was built by Bishop Pudsey; the stone roof, which was done by Bishop Farnham, in the time of Henry III. Bishop Skirlaw, in the reign of Richard II, built the cloisters; prior Fossor, beautified it with several fine windows, and enriched both the church and convent with variety of new works; and prior Walworth finished whatsoever his pious predecessor was prevented by death from bringing to a conclusion.[26]

The revenues of this house at the dissolution are estimated by Dugdale, at £1,366 10s 5d; by Speed, at £1,615 14s 10d. The value of the bishopric, at that time, £2,821 1s 5d clear.[27] The reader is referred to Willis's *History of Cathedrals*, I, 222, for the establishment and its revenue after that period.

This magnificent pile is 411 feet long; the breadth 80; the cross isle, 170; over its centre rises a lofty tower, reckoned 223 feet high, ornamented on the outside with Gothic work: at the west end are two low towers, once topped with two spires, covered with lead. In the inside is preserved much of the clumsy yet venerable magnificence of the early Norman style. The pillars are vast cylinders, twenty-three feet in circumference; some adorned with zigzag furrows, others with lozenge-shaped; with narrow ribs, or with spiral: the arches round, carved with zigzag; above are two rows of galleries, each with round arches or openings.

A row of small pilasters run round the sides of the church, with rounded arches, intersecting each other. The windows are obtusely pointed.

Between two of the pillars are the mutilated tombs and figures of Ralph and John, Lord Nevil. Excepting Richard de Bernardcastre, who, in 1370, erected a shrine in honour of Bede, these seem to have been the only laity admitted into this holy ground in the earlier times.

Ralph died in the year 1347, and was the first secular that was buried in this cathedral: his body was conveyed in a chariot

---

[25] Goodwin, 114.
[26] Stevens I, 152.
[27] Tanner, III.

drawn by seven horses as far as the churchyard, then carried on the shoulders of knights into the middle of the church; where the abbot of St Mary's at York, in absence of the bishop, or illness of the prior, performed the funeral office; at which were offered eight horses, four for war, with four men armed, and four for peace; and three cloths of gold, interwoven with flowers. His son, John de Nevil, redeemed four of the horses, at the price of a hundred marks. But this favour was not done gratis by the holy men of the place. Ralph had presented them with a vestment of red velvet, richly embroidered with gold, silk, great pearls and images of saints; dedicated to St Cuthbert. His widow also sent to the sacrist 120 pounds of silver, for the repairs of the cathedral; and several rich vestments for the performance of the sacred offices.[28] This was the nobleman who was so instrumental in gaining the victory of Nevils Cross.

His son John had also his merits with the pietists of this church; for by the magnificent offerings he made at the funeral of his first wife, and by some elegant and expensive work beneath the shrine of St Cuthbert, in 1389, he obtained admission for his remains in a spot not remote from his father.[29] Both their monuments are greatly mutilated; having been defaced by the Scotch prisoners, confined here after the battle of Dunbar.

In the choir is the bishop's throne, elevated to an uncommon height, erected in times of the triumph of superstition; a painful ascent to the present prelate, whose wish is directed more to distinguish himself by benevolence and sincerity, than any exterior trappings, or badges of dignity.

On the sides of the pulpit are the evangelists, finely inlaid.

The chancel and alterpiece is of stone, beautifully cut into open work,[30] and on each side are two stalls, in stone, originally designed for the resting-places of sick votaries.

On one side of the choir, is the tomb of Bishop Hatfield, who died in 1381, ornamented with as many coats of arms as would

---

[28] Dugdale's *Baron* I, 295.
[29] Idem, 297.
[30] Designed in Smith's edition of Bede, 264.

serve any German prince. Multitudes of other prelates and priors rested in this church, covered with beautiful tombs and brasses, swept away by the hand of sacrilege in the time of Henry VIII, or of undistinguishing reformation in succeeding reigns; or of fantacism, in the unhappy times of the last century.

Behind the altar stood the shrine of St Cuthbert, once the richest in Great Britain: the marks of pilgrims' feet in the worn floor, still evince the multitude of votaries: at the dissolution, his body was taken out of the tomb and interred beneath.

Beyond this, at the extreme east end, stood nine altars, dedicated to as many saints; above each is a most elegant window, extremely narrow, lofty, and sharply arched: above these, is a round window, very large and finely radiated with stonework, called St Catharine's, from its being in the form of the wheel used at her martyrdom. In this part of the church is another fine window, divided into circular portions. All the windows in this isle terminate sharply; and, were the work of a later age than that of the body of the church; probably the time of Prior Fossor.

The Galilee, or Lady's chapel, lies at the west end of the cathedral. Within are three rows of pillars, each consisting of round united columns; the arches round, sculptured on the mouldings with zigzag work.[31] This place was allotted to the female part of the votaries, who were never permitted to pass a certain line to the east of it, drawn just before the font. Here they might stand to hear divine service; but were confined to this limit on pain of excommunication. Legend assigns as the cause of this aversion in St Cuthbert to the fair sex, a charge of seduction brought against him by a certain princess, who was instantly punished by being swallowed up by the earth, which, on the intercession of the pacified saint, restored her to the king, her father. From that time, not a woman was permitted to enter any church dedicated to this holy man. Mr Grosse relates,[32] that in the fifteenth century two females, instigated by invincible curiosity, dressing themselves in man's apparel, ventured beyond

---

[31] See the view of it in Smith's edition of Bede, 805.
[32] In his account of Durham Cathedral, in his third volume.

the prohibitory line, were detected, and suffered certain penances as atonement for their crime.

In the Galilee is the tomb of the Venerable Bede. His remains were first deposited at Jarrow, then placed in a golden coffin on the right side of the body of St Cuthbert; and finally, in 1370, translated by Richard of Barnard Castle to this place.

The tomb of Bishop Langley is near that of Bede. This prelate was chancellor of England in the reign of Henry IV, but resigned that high post, on being consecrated Bishop of Durham. He obtained the cardinal's hat in 1411; and after doing many acts of munificence, died in 1437.

In the vestry room is preserved the rich plate belonging to the cathedral; and here are shown five most superb vestments for the sacred service: four are of great antiquity: the fifth was given by Charles I.

The cloisters, adjacent to the church, are 147 feet square, and very neat. The chapter house opens into them: is a plain building, in form of a theatre; on the sides are pilasters, the arches intersecting each other. At the upper end is a stone chair, in old times the seat of the bishop.

The old fratry was converted into a noble library by Dean Sudbury, who not living to complete his design, by will dated 1683, bound his heir Sir John Sudbury, to fulfil his intention. This is likewise the repository of the altars, and other Roman antiquities discovered in the bishopric. The dormitory, the loft, the kitchen, and other parts of the ancient abbey, are still existing, and still of use to the present possessors.

The prebendal houses are very pleasantly situated, and have backwards a most beautiful view. After the subversion of monarchy, Cromwell, in 1657, on the petition of the inhabitants of the county, converted the houses belonging to the dean and chapter, into a university, and assigned certain lands and revenues in the neighbourhood of the city for its support.[33] This short-lived seminary consisted of a provost, two preachers, four professors, four tutors, four schoolmasters (fellows) twenty-four scholars,

---

[33] Mr Allan.

twelve exhibitioners, and eighteen free-school scholars. They had liberty of purchasing lands as far as six thousand pounds a year; had a common seal, and many other privileges. On the accession of Richard, these new academics were not wanting in gratitude to the memory of their maker; for in their address to the successor, they compared Cromwell to Augustus, and gave him the prowess of our fifth Henry, the prudence of our seventh Henry, and the piety of our sixth Edward; and recommended to the 'vital beams of the piteous aspect of his son, his new erection, an orphan scarce bound up in its swaddling cloaths'. This orphan thrived apace; it endeavoured to confer degrees, and mimic its grown-up sisters of Oxford and Cambridge, who checked its presumptions by petitions to the new protector. But in less than two years, the ill-patched machine of government fell to pieces, and with it, this new seminary for knowledge.

There are two handsome bridges to the walks over the Were: from one the prospect is particularly fine, towards the cathedral and castle; and another bounded on each side by wood, with the steeple of Elvet, a place adjoining to Durham, soaring above. There is also a third bridge, which joins the two parts of the town, and is covered with houses.

I had heard on my road many complaints of the ecclesiastical government this county is subject to; but from the general face of the country, it seems to thrive wonderfully well under it. Notwithstanding the bishops have still great powers and privileges, yet they were stripped of still greater by statute of the 27th of Henry VIII. In the time of the Conqueror, it was a maxim, '*quicquid Rex babet extra comitatum Dunelmensem, episcopus habet intra, nisi aliqua sit concessio, aut prescriptio in contrarium.*' They had power to levy taxes, make truces with the Scots, to raise defensible men within the bishopric, from sixteen to sixty years of age. They could call a parliament, and create barons to sit and vote in it. He could sit in his purple robes to pronounce sentence of death, whence the saying, '*solum Dunelmense judicat stola et ense.*' He could coin money, hold courts in his own name, and all writs went in his own name. He claimed and seized for his own use, all goods, chattels and lands of persons convicted of treasons or felonies; could appoint the great officers under him, and do variety of acts emulating the royal authority.[34] He was Lord Paramount in the county, and the great people held most of their lands from the church. Thus the potent Nevils paid four pounds and a stag annually for Raby, and eight other manors. Two of the tenures are singular. I beg leave to present them to the reader in the form I had the honour of receiving them from the present worthy prelate:

> The valuable manor of Sockburn, the seat of the ancient family of the Conyers, in the county palatine of Durham, is held by the Blackett family, of the bishop of Durham, by the easy service of presenting a falchion to every bishop upon his first entrance into his diocese, as an emblem of his temporal power. When the present bishop made his first entrance, in the month of Sept. 1771, he was met upon the middle of Croft bridge, (where the counties of York and Durham divide), by Mr Blackett, as substitute for his brother, Sir Edward, who presented his lordship with the falchion, addressing him in the ancient form of words:
> 'Sir Edward Blackett, Bart. now represents the person of Sir John Conyers,[35] who, in the fields of Sockburn, with this falchion,[36] slew a monstrous creature, a Dragon, a Worm, or a Flying-Serpent,[37] that devoured men, women,

---

[34] These and many more are preserved in *Magna Britannia* I, 615. See also Spearman's *Enquiry*.

[35] Legend gives some other particulars of this valiant knight; which Mr Allan extracted from the Catalogue of the Harleian MSS no. 2118, 39:

> Sir Jno. Conyers de Sockburn, Knt. who slew the monstrous venom'd and poison'd Wiverne, Ask, or Worme, wch overthrew and devour'd many people in seight, for the scent of the poyson was so strong that noe person was able to abide it, yet he by the Providence of God overthrew it, and lies bured at Sockburn before the Conquest. But before he did enterprise (having but one childe) he went to the church in complete armour, and offered up his sonne to the Holy Ghost, wch monument is yet to see, and the place where the serpent lay is called Graystone.

[36] On the pommel are three lions of England, guardant. These were first borne by King John, so that this falchion was not made before that time, nor did the owner kill the dragon. The black eagle, in a field, gold, was the arms of Morkar, Earl of Northumberland. This too might be the falchion with which the earls were invested, being girt with the sword of the earldom.

[37] The Scots seem to have been intended by these dreadful animals; and the falchion bestowed with an estate, as a reward for some useful service performed by a Conyers against those invaders.

and children. The then owner of Sockburn, as a reward for his bravery, gave him the manor, with its appurtenances, to hold for ever, on condition, that he meets the Lord Bishop of Durham, with this falchion, on his first entrance into his diocese after his election to that see.

At Croft bridge the bishop was also met by the high-sheriff of the county palatine, who is an officer of his own by patent during pleasure, by the members for the county and city of Durham; and by all the principal gentlemen in the county and neighbourhood, to welcome his lordship into his palatinate, who conducted him to Darlington, where they all dined with him, after which they proceeded to Durham. Before they reached the city, they were met by the dean and chapter, with their congratulatory address; the bishop and the whole company alighted from their carriages to receive them: when the ceremony of the address, and his lordship's answer was finished, the procession moved on to the city; here they were met by the corporation, the different companies, with their banners, and a great concourse of people; they proceeded immediately to the cathedral, where the bishop was habited upon the tomb of the venerable Bede, in the Galilee, at the west end of the church; from whence he went in procession to the great altar, preceded by the whole choir, singing Te Deum: after prayers the bishop took the oaths at the altar, and was then inthroned in the usual forms, and attended to the castle by the high-sheriff and other gentlemen of the county. Pollard's lands, in this country, are holden of the bishop by the same kind of service as the manor of Sockburn. At his Lordship's first coming to Auckland, Mr Johnson met the present bishop at his first arrival there, and, presenting the falchion upon his knee, addressed him in the old form of words, saying, 'My lord, in behalf of myself, as well as of the several other tenants of Pollard's lands, I do humbly present your lordship with this falchion, at your first coming here, wherewith, as the tradition goeth, Pollard slew of old, a great and venemous serpent, which did much harm to man and beast; and by performance of this service these lands are holden.'

Leave Durham, and journey through a beautiful country, having, near the city, views of land, broken into most delightful and cultivated knowls; and, on the left, of fine hanging woods: the land much enclosed, and the hedges planted. On the right, lies

XLI

AUKLAND CASTLE.

Brancespeth Castle, originally the seat of the Bulmers, afterwards that of the Nevils, earls of Westmoreland, forfeited by the rebellion of the last in the time of Queen Elizabeth. The great steeple of Merrington is seen on the left. Turn out of the high road, and pass through the bishop's grounds, and park, and enjoy a fine view of the Were, running along a deep bottom, bounded by wooded, and well-cultivated banks. On the south side stands Bishops Aukland, a good town, with a large and square market-place. On one side is a handsome gateway, with a tower over it. This is a modern edifice, designed by Sir Thomas Robinson; that built by Bishop Skirlaw having been long since destroyed.[38] Through this gateway lies Aukland Castle, long since the residence of the bishops of Durham. It has lost its castellated form, and now resembles some of the magnificent foreign abbeys. It is an irregular pile, built at different times; but no part is left that can boast of any great antiquity. Over a bow-window are the arms of Bishop Tunstal, who died in the beginning of the reign of Elizabeth. This was originally a manor-house belonging to the see, and was first encastallated by Bishop Beke;[39] who also built a great hall, and adorned it with marble pillars; he founded a fair chapel, and collegiate church, with a dean and prebends; which church is that of St Andrews, at a small distance from the town. Excepting the church there are no relics of the labours of this prelate; the place having been bestowed by the Parliament on their furious partisan, Sir Arthur Haselrigg, who taking fancy to the place, determined to make it his chief residence. He demolished almost all the buildings he found there, and out of their ruins, erected a most magnificent house.[40]

On the Restoration, the former bishop, the munificent Cosins, was restored to his diocese. He had a palace ready for his reception, but by an excess of piety declined making use of it, from the consideration that the stones of the ancient chapel had been sacrilegiously applied towards the building of this late habitation of fanaticism. The bishop pulled it down,[41] and restoring the

---

[38] Leland, *Itin.* I, 73.
[39] Ibid.
[40] *Hist. Ch. Durham*, Dugdale, 82.
[41] Ibid.

materials to their ancient use, built the present elegant chapel. The roof is wood, supported by two rows of pillars, each consisting of four round columns, freestone and marble alternate. The shafts of some of the marble are sixteen feet high; the length of the chapel is eighty-four feet, and breadth forty-eight; the outside ornamented with pinnacles. On the floor, a plain stone, with a modest epitaph, informs us, that the pious refounder lies beneath, dying in the year 1671.

The principal apartments are, an old hall, seventy-five feet by thirty-two, the height thirty-five; and a very handsome dining parlour, ornamented with portraits of Jacob and the twelve patriarchs. Jacob bows under the weight of years. His sons, with each his scriptural attribute. The figures are animated; the colouring good. I think the painter's name is Xubero, one I do not discover in any list of artists. The pictures were bought at an auction, and presented to the place by Bishop Trevor. The same generous prelate built a suite of additional apartments; but dying before they were completed they are now furnished, in a most magnificent manner, by the present bishop.

On the old wainscot of a room below stairs, are painted the arms of a strange assemblage of potentates, from Queen Elizabeth, with all the European Princes, to the emperors of Abyssinia, Bildelgerid, Cathaye, and Tartaria; sixteen peers of the same reign, Knights of the Garter, and above them, the arms of every bishopric in England.

The castle is seated in a beautiful park, watered by the little River Gaunless, which falls, after a short course, into the Were. The park is well planted, and has abundance of vast alders, that by age have lost the habit of that tree, and assume the appearance of ancient oaks. Nothing can equal the approach through this ground to the castle, which is varied with verdant slopes, rising grounds, woods, and deep precipices, impending over the river. The great deer-house, built by Bishop Trevor, is an elegant square building, and no small embellishment to the place. Leland tells us, that in his time there was a fair park, having fallow deer, wild bulls, and kin.

On an eminence on the opposite side of the Were, is Binchester, the ancient Vinovia; where several Roman coins, altars and inscriptions have been found. Several of the latter are worked up in the walls of a gentleman's house on the station, but now scarcely legible. An account of them may be seen in Mr Horsley, p. 295. Urns full of ashes and bones, and figuline lacrymatories have been also found in the park, where the station probably extended. A military way may be traced from this place as far as Brancespethpark one way, and the other by Aukland to Peircebridge, into Yorkshire.

Proceed for a little way from Aukland, on the Roman way: leave on the left, at a mile and a half distance from the town, the church of St Andrews, Aukland, once collegiate, and well-endowed by Antony, Bishop of Durham. At the Dissolution, here were found a dean and eleven prebends.[42] A house called the deanery still remains. The chief tomb in this church is that of a Pollard; a cross-legged knight, armed in mail to his finger's ends, with a skirt, formed of stripes, reaching to his knees; a short sword, and conic helm.

Pass through St Helens Aukland and West Aukland; and after a short digression fall in with the old Roman road, which continues to Pierce or Priestbridge, where was once a chapel, founded by John Baliol, King of Scotland, and dedicated to the Virgin.[43] The gateway is still standing, in what is called the chapel garth. Till Leland's time the bridge consisted of five arches, but he says that of late it was rebuilt with three. The Tees flows beneath in a picturesque channel finely shaded on each side with trees. Near this bridge, in the field called the Tofts, had been a considerable Roman station. Urns and coins in abundance have been discovered there. A stone coffin, with a skeleton, is mentioned by Bishop Gibson; but that I apprehend to be of more modern date. The foundations of houses have been observed; and Mr Horsley imagines he could trace an aqueduct. He supposes this place to have been the Magae of the Notitia. I must observe that the Roman road is continued in a direct line between the roads to Barnard Castle and Darlington, and is continued over a small brook, and through the enclosure parallel to the Tofts, when it crosses the river about two hundred and sixty paces east of the bridge, and then falls into the turnpike-road to

---

[42] Tanner, 116.
[43] Leland, *Itin.* I, 88.

Cattarickbridge. The whole breadth of the road is still to be traced; and the stones it is formed of appear to be strongly cemented with run lime. The Romans had here a wooden bridge: the materials, such as the bodies of oaks, and several stoops, were to be seen till washed away by the great floods of 1771.

XXI

YORKSHIRE, LANCASHIRE

⟫⟫◆⟪⟪

Aldbrough—Richmond—Middleham Castle—Winsley—Bolton House—
Bolton Castle—Aysgarth—Skipton—Kighley—Halifax—Rochdale

O N crossing the Tees, enter Yorkshire. After a ride of a few
miles pass through Aldbrough, now a little village, but once a
place of eminence, as its ruins, observed by Camden, evince. In the
time of Henry I, Stephen, Earl of Albermarle and Holderness, had
a manor and castle here; the tythes of which he bestowed on the
abbey of Albemarle, in Normandy;[1] and that abbey in the reign of
Richard II granted them to the abbey of Kirkstall.[2] Henry III again
bestowed the place on Hubert de Burgh, Earl of Kent. By failure
of issue, it fell to the crown in the time of Henry IV, who gave it
to his third son, John, Duke of Bedford.[3]

Pass over a large common, called Gatherley Moor, and by
the sides of the double dike, or Roman hedge, a vast fosse, with
banks on each side, extending from the Tees to the Swale. On the
right is Diderston Hill, whether a tumulus, or exploratory, was
too distant for me to determine. After descending a hill, pass by

[1] Dugdale, *Monast.* I, 588.
[2] Idem, 589.
[3] *Britannia Magna* VI, 608.

Gilling, where Alan Fergaunt, Earl of Bretagne and Richmond, had a capital mansion-house.[4] This place was infamous for the murder of Oswyn, King of Deira, by his successor Oswy; but his Queen Aeanfled obtained permission from her husband to found here a monastery, in order to expiate so horrible a crime. At this time the place was called Ingetling, and was destroyed in the Danish wars.[5]

Near that is Ask, the seat of Sir Lawrence Dundas; in former times, if I mistake not, the property of the Asks, and forfeited in the reign of Henry VIII by Robert Ask, leader of the rebellion, styled the pilgrimage of grace, excited by the religious on the suppression of monasteries. Reach Richmond, a good town, seated (in a shire of the same name) partly on a flat, and partly on the side of a hill: on the last is the market-place, a handsome opening, in which is the chapel of the Trinity, and in the middle a large column instead of the old cross. The trade of this place is that of knit woollen stockings, in which men, women, and children are employed; the neighbourhood supplying the wool. The stockings are chiefly exported into Holland. Much wheat is sold here, and sent into the mountainous parts of the country.

There were several religious houses in this place and its neighbourhood. In the town, on the plain on the north side, was a house of Grey Friars,[6] founded in 1258, by Ralph Fitzrandal, Lord of Middleham; and had, at the Dissolution, fourteen monks. Nothing remains, excepting the beautiful tower of its church. Near this was also a nunnery.[7] About a mile east of Richmond, are the fine ruins of St Agatha, seated at the end of some beautiful meadows, upon the River Swale. It was founded in 1151, by Roaldus, constable of Richmond Castle; and at the time of the Reformation maintained seventeen white canons, or Premonstratensian monks. The abbot and religious, in 1253, agreed with Henry Fitzranulph, that he should hold of them in pure and perpetual alms, their possessions of Kerperby, on condition he paid them annually one

---

[4] Dugdale, *Baron.* I, 46.
[5] Bede, lib. II, ch. 14, 24.
[6] Tanner, 685.
[7] Idem, 672.

pound of cumin seed, a drug in no small esteem in old times.[8]
Richard Scroope, chancellor of England, was a great benefactor
to this place; for, besides his manor of Brumpton-upon-Swale,
he granted a hundred and fifty pounds a year for the support of
ten additional canons, two secular canons, and twenty-two poor
men, who were to pray for the repose of his soul, and those of his
heirs.[9] The ruins are very venerable, and the magnificent archwork
in the inside are fine proofs of the skill of the times in that species
of architecture. The arch of the gateway is extremely obtuse; that
of the windows greatly pointed.

Near this place was a hospital, dedicated to St Nicholas. I cannot
learn the founder's name, but find it was repaired in the time of
Henry VI, who gave the patronage to William Ayscough, one of
his judges; who restored the hospital at great expense, and added
another chauntry priest to the former.[10]

Nearer to Richmond, on an eminence above the river, are
the poor relics of St Martin's, a cell of nine or ten Benedictines,
dependent on the abbey of St Mary, at York. It was founded in
1100, by Wymar, chief steward to the Earl of Richmond.[11] Besides
these, were various other pious foundations on the Swale, whose
waters were sacred with the baptism of ten thousand Saxons, near
Cattarick, in 627, by Paulinus, Bishop of York.[12]

It remains now to speak of the fortifications of this ancient town:
part had been defended by walls, which took in little more than
the market-place, and had three gates. The castle stands on the
south-west part of the hill, in a lofty and bold situation, above the
Swale, and half environed by it. The remains are the walls of the
precinct, some small square towers, and one very large, all built in the
Norman style. This fortress was founded by Alan, Earl of Bretagne,[13]
newphew to the Conqueror, who commanded the rear of his army

---

[8] Dugdale, *Mon.* II, 650. And for the virtues of cumin seed consult *Old Gerard's Herbal,* 1055.
[9] Dugdale, *Mon.* II, 650.
[10] Dugdale, *Mon.* II, 479.
[11] Idem I, 401 to 404.
[12] Bede, lib. II, ch. 14.
[13] Dugdale's *Baron.* I, 46.

at the battle of Hastings, was created by him Earl of Richmond, and received from him the shire of the same name, and a hundred and sixty-six manors in the county of York alone. This country had been before the property of the brave Edwin, Earl of Mercia. The great tower was built by Conan, grandson of the former; the vault of which is supported by a fine octagonal pillar. The view from the castle is picturesque; beneath is the seat of Mr York, and beyond, a prospect up the Swale into the mountainous part of the country, rich in mineral; and on the banks of the river lived Sir John Swale, of Swale Hall, in Swaledale, fast upon the River Swale.

Cross the river, and after passing over a dreary moor, descend into a valley not more than pleasant, being totally enclosed with stone fences. Go through the small towns of Billersly and Leybourne: and soon after find an agreeable change of country, at the entrance of Wensleydale, a beautiful and fertile vale, narrow, bounded by high hills, enclosed with hedges, and cultivated far up, in many parts clothed with woods, surmounted by long ranges of scars, white rocks, smooth and precipitous in front, and perfectly even at their tops. The rapid crystal Ure divides the whole, fertilizing the rich meadows with its stream.

See, on the left, Middleham Castle. The manor was bestowed by Alan, Earl of Richmond, on his younger brother, Rinebald. His grandson, styled Robert Fitzralph, receiving from Conan, Earl of Richmond, all Wensleydale, founded this castle, about the year 1190. By the marriage of his daughter and coheir to Robert de Nevil,[14] it passed into that family, in the year 1269. In this place Edward IV suffered a short imprisonment, after being surprised by Richard Nevill, the great Earl of Warwick, and committed to the custody of his brother, the Archbishop of York, who, proving too indulgent a keeper, soon lost his royal prisoner, by permitting him the pleasure of the chase unguarded. The ruin of his house ensued. On its forfeiture, Richard, Duke of York, became possessed of it, and here lost his only son Edward. He who also made so many childless, felt in this misfortune the stroke of heaven. It is a vast building; its towers steep, and turrets square. Part was the work

---

[14] Dugdale, *Baron.* I, 291.

of Fitzralph; part of the Lord Nevill, called Darabi.[15] The hall, kitchen, and chapel were built by Beaumont, Bishop of Durham.[16] It was inhabited as late as the year 1609, by Sir Henry Lindley, knight.[17]

Visit the church of Winsley. On the floor are several carved figures on the stones, probably in memory of certain Scroopes interred there.[18] Also a figure of Oswald Dykes, in his priestly vestments, with a chalice in his hand. The inscription says that he had been rector of the parish, and died in 1607. I presume by his habit he was only nominal rector. Lord Chancellor Scroope designed to make this church collegiate, and obtained licence for that purpose from Richard II, but it does not appear that the intent was ever executed.

At a little distance beyond the church is a neat bridge of considerable antiquity, which Leland speaks of as 'the fayre bridge of three or four arches, that is on Ure, at Wencelaw, a mile or more above Midleham, made two hundred yer ago and more, by one caullyd Alwine, parson of Wincelaw'.

Visit Bolton House, a seat of the Duke of Bolton, finished about the year 1678, by Charles, Marquis of Winchester. Here are a few portraits of the Scroopes, the ancient owners.

A head of Henry, Lord Scoope, one of the lords who subscribed the famous letter to the pope, threatening his Holiness, that if he did not permit the divorce between Henry VIII and Catherine, that they would reject his supremacy.

Helen Clifford, his wife, daughter to the Earl of Cumberland. Here is another head of a daughter of Lord Dacres; third wife, according to Dugdale, of the same Lord Scroope.[19]

Another Henry, warden of the west marches in the reign of Elizabeth; in whose custody Mary Stuart remained for some time after her flight to her faithless rival.

His wife Margaret, daughter to Henry, Earl of Surrey. After the disgrace of the Earl of Essex, this lady alone stood firm to him;

---

[15] Leland.
[16] Willis's *Cathedrals* I, 240.
[17] Mr Grasse.
[18] Leland, *Itin*. VIII, 13.
[19] Dugdale's *Baron*. I, 657.

'For', says Rowland White, 'she endures much at her Majesty's hands, because she doth daily doe all the kynd offices of love to the Queen in his behalf. She weares all black, she mournes, and is pensive; and joies in nothing but in a solitary being alone; and it is thought she saies much that few wold venter to say but herself.'[20]

A head of the same lord, inscribed *Lord Harrie Scroope, Baron of Bolton*, one of the tilters before Queen Elizabeth, at the *first triumphe at the crownacion, aet. 22, 1558*.[21] To these may be added the head of his son, Thomas, Lord Scroope; and his son again, Lord Emanuel, created by Charles I, Earl of Sunderland, who died the last of this line.

Cross the Ure, on a bridge of two arches, and have from it a fine view of the river above and below, each bank regularly bounded by trees like an avenue. On the right is Bolton Castle, built, says Leland, by Richard Scroope, Chancellor of England under Richard II, after eighteen years labour, and at the expense of a thousand marks a year. Most of the timber employed was brought from Engleby Forest, in Cumberland, drawn by draughts of oxen, successively changed. He also founded here a chantry for six priests.[22] The integrity of the chancellor soon lost him the favour of his master; for on his refusal to put the seals to the exorbitant grants made to some of the worthless favourites, the king demanded them from him; at first he declined obedience, declaring he received them from the Parliament, not his Majesty.[23]

This castle is noted for having been the first place of confinement of Mary Stuart, who was removed from Carlisle to this fortress, under the care of the noble owner. Several of her letters are dated from hence. In the civil wars it underwent a siege by the Parliament forces; and was, on Nov. 5th, 1645, on conditions, surrendered, with great quantities of stores and ammunition.[24]

---

[20] Sidney's *State Papers* II, 132. The letter is dated Oct. 11th, 1599.
[21] He was one of the knights-challengers on the occasion.
[22] Leland, *Itin.* VIII, 18, 19.
[23] Rapin I, 459.
[24] Whitelock, 179.

The building is square, with a vast square tower at each corner, in which were the principal apartments. Leland observes the singular manner in which the smoke was conveyed from the chimneys of the great hall; by tunnels made in the walls, conveying it within the great piers between the windows. This castle, and the great possessions belonging to it in these parts, are the property of the Duke of Bolton, derived by the marriage of his ancestor, Charles, Marquis of Bolton, with Mary, natural daughter of Emanuel Scroope, Earl of Sunderland, last male heir of this ancient house.

Reach Aysgarth, or Aysgarth Force,[25] remarkable for the fine arch over the Ure, built in 1539. The scenery above and below is most uncommonly picturesque. The banks on both sides are lofty, rocky, and darkened with trees. Above the bridge two regular precipices cross the river, down which the water falls in two beautiful cascades, which are seen to great advantage from below. The gloom of the pendent trees, the towering steeple of the church above, and the rage of the waters beneath the ivy-bound arch, form all together a most romantic view.

A little lower down are other falls; but the finest is at about half a mile distance, where the river is crossed by a great scar, which opens in the middle, and forms a magnificent flight of steps, which grow wider and wider from top to bottom, the rock on each side forming a regular wall. The river falls from step to step, and at the lowest drops into a rocky channel, filled with circular basins, and interrupted for some space with lesser falls. The eye is finely directed to this beautiful cataract by the scars that bound the river, being lofty, precipitous, and quite a smooth front, and their summits fringed with hollies and other trees.

Near Aygsarth, or, as the cataracts are called, Aysgarth Force, was founded the convent of white monks, brought from Savigny, in France, by Akaries Fitzbardolf, in 1145. They were subject to Byland, and received from thence, in 1150, an abbot and twelve monks, who were afterwards removed to the neighbouring abbey of Jervaux.[26] This was called, from the cataracts, Fors, also Wandesleydale, and de Charitate.

---

[25] I think the old name was Attscarre.
[26] Tanner, 658.

XLII

M. Griffith, del.   D. Havell, sculp.

AYSGARTH FORCE.

Cross the ridge that divides Wensleydale from another charming valley, called Bishopsdale. All the little enclosures are nearly of the same size and form, and the meadows are laid out with the utmost regularity. It appeared as if in this spot, the plan of the Spartan legislator had taken place: it resembled the possessions of brethren, who had just been dividing their inheritance among them.

Before I quit these delicious tracts, I must remark that from Leybourne to their extremity there is scarcely a mile but what is terminated by a little town; and every spot, even far up the hills, embellished with small neat houses. Industry and competence seem to reign among the happy regions, and, highland as they are, seem distinguished by those circumstances from the slothful but honest natives of some of the Scottish Alps. Mittens and knit stockings are their manufactures. The hills produce lead; the valleys cattle, horses, sheep, wool, butter, and cheese.

Ascend a steep a mile in length, and at the top arrive on a large plain, a pass between the hills. After two miles descend into a mere glen, watered by the Wharf; ride through Buckden, and Starbottom, two villages, and lie at Kettlewel, a small mine town. There are many lead-mines about the place, and some coal; but peat is the general fuel, and oatcakes, or bannocks, the usual bread.

Continue our journey along a pleasant vale. Ride beneath Kilnseyscar, a stupendous rock, ninety-three yards high, more than perpendicular, for it overhangs at top in a manner dreadful to the traveller. The road bad, made of broken limestones uncovered. This vale ends in a vast theatre of wood, and gave me the idea of an American scene. Ascend, and get into a hilly and less pleasing country. Overtake many droves of cattle and horses, which had been at grass the whole summer in the remotest part of Craven, where they were kept from nine shillings to forty per head, according to their size. Reach Skipton, a good town, seated in a fertile expanded vale. It consists principally of one broad street, the church and castle terminating the upper end. The castle is said to have been originally built by Robert de Romely, Lord of the Honour of Skipton. By failure of male issue, it fell to William Fitzduncan, Earl of Murray, who married the daughter of Romely. William le Gros, Earl of Albemarle, by marriage with her daughter, received as portion her grandfather's estate. It fell afterwards by females to other families, such as William de Mandevil, Earl of Essex, to William de Fortibus, and Baldwin de Betun. In the time of Richard I, Avelin, daughter to a second William de Fortibus, a minor, succeeded. She became ward of King Henry III, who, on her coming of age, in 1269, bestowed her and her fortunes on his son Edmund, Earl of Lancaster;[27] but on the forfeiture of his son for treason against Edward II, the honour and castle were granted, in 1309, to Robert de Clifford, a Herefordshire baron, in whose line it continued till the last century. I know of no remarkable event that befell this castle, excepting that it was dismantled by ordinance of Parliament, in 1648, because it had received a loyal garrison during the civil wars.

It was restored, and repaired, in 1657–1658, by the famous Anne Clifford, who made it, with five other castles, her alternate residence. It is seated on the edge of a deep dingle, prettily wooded, and watered by a canal, that serves to convey limestone to the main trunk of the navigation, which passes near the town. At present the castle seems more calculated for habitation than defence. A gateway, with a round tower at each side, stands at a small distance from it. The towers in the castle are generally round, some polygonal. Over the entrance is an inscription, purporting the time of repair. The hall is worthy the hospitality of the family; has two fireplaces, a hatch to the kitchen, and another to the cellar.

The great family picture is a curious performance; and still more valuable on account of the distinguished persons represented. It is tripartite, in form of a screen. In the centre is the celebrated George Clifford, Earl of Cumberland, the hero of the reign of Elizabeth, and his lady, Margaret Russel, daughter of Francis, second Earl of Bedford. He is dressed in armour, spotted with stars of gold; but much of it is concealed by a vest and skirts reaching to his knees; his helmet and gauntlet, lying on the floor, are studded in like manner. He was born in the year 1558, and by the death of his father fell under the guardianship of his royal mistress, who

---

[27] Dugdale, *Baron.* I, 65.

XLIII

SKIPTON CASTLE.

placed him under the tuition of Dr Whitgift, afterwards Archbishop of Canterbury. He applied himself to mathematics; but soon after leaving college he felt the spirit of his warlike ancestors rise within him, and for the rest of his life distinguished himself by deeds of arms honourable to himself,[28] and of use to his country, in not fewer than twenty-two voyages against the Geryon of the time, Philip II, who felt the effects of his prowess, and the more distant ones in America. He was always successful against the enemy, but often suffered great hardships by storms, by diseases, and by famine. The wealth which he acquired was devoted to the service of the state, for he spent not only the acquisitions of his voyages, but much of his paternal fortune in building ships; and much also he dissipated by his love of horse races, tournaments, and every expensive diversion. Queen Elizabeth appointed him her champion in all her tilting matches,[29] from the thirty-third year of her reign; and in all those exercises of tiltings, turnings, and courses of the field, he excelled all the nobility of his time. His magnificent armour worn on those occasions (adorned with roses and fleurs-de-lis[30]) is actually preserved at Appleby Castle, where is, besides, a copy of this picture. In the course of the life of soldier, sailor, and courtier, he fell into the licentiousness sometimes incident to the professions: but, as the inscription on the picture imports, the effects of his early education were then felt, for he died penitently, willingly and Christianly.

His lady stands by him in a purple gown, and white petticoat, embroidered with gold. She pathetically extends one hand to two

---

[28] At an audience the earl had after one of his expeditions, the queen, perhaps designedly, dropped one of her gloves. His Lordship took it up, and presented it to her: she graciously desired him to keep it as a mark of her esteem. Thus gratifying his ambition with a reward that suited her Majesty's avarice. He adorned it with diamonds, and wore it in the front of his high-crowned hat on days of tournaments. This is expressed in the fine print of him, by Robert White.

[29] Mr Walpole, in his miscellaneous Antiquities, has favoured us with a very entertaining account of his investiture. He succeeded the gallant old knight Sir Henry Lea, in 1590, who with much ceremony resigned the office.

[30] I have seen in the collection of her Grace the Duchess Dowager of Portland, a book of drawings of all the knights-tilters of his time, dressed in their rich armour. Among others in the Earl of Cumberland, in the very armour I mention.

beautiful boys, as if in the action of dissuading her lord from such dangerous voyages, when more interesting and tender claims urged the pretence of a parent. How must he have been affected by his refusal, when he found that he had lost both on his return from two of his expeditions, if the heart of a hero does not too often divest itself of the tender sensations!

The letters of this lady are extant in manuscript, and also her diary; she unfortunately marries without liking, and meets with the same return. She mentions several minutiae that I omit, being only proofs of her great attention to accuracy. She complains greatly of the coolness of her lord, and his neglect of his daughter, Anne Clifford; and endured great poverty, of which she writes in a most moving strain to James I to several great persons, and to the earl himself. All her letters are humble, suppliant, and pathetic, yet the Earl was said to have parted with her on account of her high spirit.[31]

Above the two principal figures are painted the heads of two sisters of the earl, Anne, Countess of Warwick, and Elizabeth, Countess of Bath; and two, the sisters of the Countess; Frances, married to Philip, Lord Wharton; and Margaret, Countess of Derby. Beneath each is a long inscription. The several inscriptions were composed by Anne Clifford, with the assistance of Judge Hales, who perused and methodized for her the necessary papers and evidences.[32]

The two side leaves show the portraits of her celebrated daughter, Anne Clifford, afterwards Countess of Dorset, Pembroke, and Montgomery; the most eminent person of her age for intellectual accomplishments, for spirit, magnificence, and deeds of benevolence. Both these paintings are full-lengths: the one represents her at the age of thirteen, standing in her study, dressed in white, embroidered with flowers, her head adorned with great pearls. One hand is on a music book; her lute lies by her. The books inform us of the fashionable course of reading among people of rank in her days. I perceived among them, Eusebius, St Augustine, Sir Philip Sidney's

[31] These, and several other anecdotes of the family, I found in certain MSS, letters and diaries of the countess and her daughter.

[32] *Life of Lord Keeper North.*

Arcadia, Godfrey of Boulogne, the French Academy, Camden, Ortelius, Agrippa on the vanity of occult sciences, etc. Above are the heads of Mr Samuel Daniel, her tutor, and Mrs Anne Taylor, her governess; the last appearing, as the inscription says she was, a religious and good woman. This memorial of the instructors of her youth is a most grateful acknowledgement of the benefits she received from them. She was certainly a most happy subject to work on; for, according to her own account, old Mr John Denham, a great astronomer, in her father's house, used to say, that 'the sweet influence of the Pleiades, and the bands of Orion, were powerful both at her conception and birth'; and when she grew up, Dr Donne is reported to have said of her that 'she knew well how to discourse of all things, from predestination to slea-silk.'[33]

In the other leaf she appears in her middle age, in the state of widowhood, dressed in a black gown, and black veil, and white sleeves, and round her waist is a chain of great pearls; her hair long and brown; her wedding ring on the thumb of her right hand, which is placed on the Bible, and Charron's *Book of Wisdom*. The rest of the books are of piety, excepting one of distillations, and excellent medicines. Such is the figure of the heroic daughter of a hero father, whose spirit dictated this animated answer to the insolent minister of an ungrateful court, who would force into one of her boroughs, a person disagreeable to her:

> *I have been bullied by an usurper; I have been neglected by a court; but I will not be dictated to by a subject. Your man shan't stand.*
> *Anne Dorset, Pembroke, and Montgomery.*

Above her are the heads of her two husbands, Richard, Earl of Dorset, who died in 1624; an amiable nobleman, a patron of men and letters, and bounteous to distressed worth. The other is of that brutal simpleton, Philip, Earl of Pembroke, the just subject of Butler's ridicule, whom she married six years after the death of

---

[33] Bishop Rainbow's discourse at her funeral, in 1657.

XLIV

ANNE CLIFFORD COUNTESS OF

PEMBROKE, &c.

Æt. 81.

her first lord, yet she speaks favourably of each, notwithstanding their mental qualifications were so different: 'These two lords,' says she, 'to whom I was by the divine providence married, were in their several kindes worthy noblemen as any in the kingdom; yet it was my misfortune to have crosses and contradictions with them both. Nor did there want malicious ill-willers to blow and foment the coals of dissension between us, so as in both their lifetimes, the marble pillars of Knowle, in Kent, and Wilton, in Wiltshire, were to me but the gay arbours of anguish, insomuch as a wise man, who knew the inside of my fortune, would often say, that I lived in both these my Lords great families as the river of Roan, or Rodanus, runs thro' the lake of Geneva, without mingling any part of its streams with that of the lake.'

But she was released from her second marriage by the death of her husband, in 1650. After which the greatness of her mind burst out in full and uninterrupted lustre. She rebuilt, or repaired six of her ancient castles; she restored seven churches, or chapels; founded one hospital, and repaired another. She lived in vast hospitality at all her castles by turns, on the beautiful motive of dispensing her charity in rotation, among the poor of her vast estates. She travelled in a horse-litter; and often took new and bad roads from castle to castle, in order to find out cause of laying out money among the indigent, by employing them in the repairs. The opulent also felt the effect of her generosity, for she never suffered any visitors to go away without a present, ingeniously contrived according to their quality.[34] She often sat in person as sheriffess of the county of Westmoreland; at length died, at the age of eighty-six, in the year 1676, and was interred at Appleby. Her great possessions devolved to John, Earl of Thanet, who married Margaret, her eldest daughter, by the Earl of Dorset.

Here are four heads of this illustrious countess, in the states of childhood, youth, middle, and old age.[35] My print is taken from

[34] *Life of Lord Keeper North*, 141.
[35] She says in her diary, that in 1619, her picture was drawn by Larking. She mentions also some of the amusements of the time, such as 'glecko', at which she lost £151 and 'barley-break', at which she played on the bowling-green at Buckhurst.

one resembling the last in the gallery at Strawberry Hill, which the Hon. Horace Walpole was so obliging as to permit to be copied.[36]

In one of the rooms is a fictitious picture of the fair Rosamund, daughter of Walter de Clifford, and mistress to Henry II. She is dressed in the mode of the reign of Elizabeth; but at her ear is a red rose, an allusion of the painter to her name.

A picture of a young person, with a crown by her. Another of a man, inscribed *vultus index animi*; and a third portrait, half length, of the great Earl of Cumberland, in a white hat, are the most remarkable unnoticed.

I must mention two good octagonal rooms, in one of which is some singular tapestry, expressing the punishment of the vices. Cruauté is represented with head, hands, and feet in the stocks; and Mal Bouche and Vil Parler undergoing the cutting off of their tongues.

On the steeple of the church is an inscription, importing, that it was repaired after it had been ruined in the civil wars, by Lady Clifford, Countess of Pembroke, in 1655. Within the church are inscriptions, on plain stones, in memory of the three first earls of Cumberland. Those on the two first relate little more than their lineage; but the noble historian of the family informs us, that the first earl was brought up with Henry VIII and beloved by him. That he was one of the most eminent lords of his time, for nobleness, gallantry, and courtship, but wasted much of his estate. That the second earl at the beginning was also a great waster of his estate, till he retired into the country, when he grew rich. He was much addicted to the study and practice of alchemy and chemistry, and a great distiller of waters for medicines; was studious in all manner of learning, and had an excellent library both of handwritten books, and printed.[37]

Continue my journey through a pleasant vale, watered by the Are, or 'the gentle river', as the Celtic *ara* signifies, expressive of

[36] Mr Walpole showed me a medal, with the head of the Countess, exactly resembling the picture. On the reverse is Religion, represented by a female figure, crowned, and standing. In one hand the Bible; the left arm embraces a cross taller than herself.

[37] *Life of Lady Anne Clifford*, etc. by herself, MS.

its smooth course.[38] Along its side winds the canal, which, when finished, is to convey the manufactures of Leeds to Liverpool. Ride beneath a great aqueduct, at Kildwick, and have soon after a view of the rich valley that runs towards Leeds. Reach Kighly, at the bottom of another rich vale, that joins the former. This place has a considerable manufacture of figured everlastings, in imitation of French silks, and of shaloons and callimancoes; and numbers of people get their livelihood by spinning of wool for the stocking-weavers. The ancient family of Kighly take their name from this town. One of them, Henry Kighly, 'obtained from Edward I for this his manour, the privileges of a market and fair, and a free-warren, so that none might enter into those grounds to chace there, or with design to catch any thing pertaining to the said warren, without the permission and leave of the said Henry and his successors'.[39]

After crossing some very dismal moors, varied with several tedious ascents and descents, reach, at the foot of a very steep hill, the great town of Halifax, or 'the holy hair', from a legendary tale not worth mentioning. It is seated in a very deep bottom, and concealed from view on every side, till approached very nearly. The streets are narrow; the houses mostly built and covered with stone, and the streets have been lately paved in the manner of those at Edinburgh. The town extends far in length, but not in breadth. Here is only one church, spacious, supported by two rows of octagonal pillars, and supplied with a handsome organ. The Conqueror bestowed the lordship of Wakefield,[40] of which this place is part, on his relation, William, Earl of Warren and Surry, who gave the church and manor to the Abbot of Lewes; and his successors constantly held courts here from that time to the dissolution.[41] The parish is of vast extent, contains above one and forty thousand inhabitants, and is supplied with twelve chapels. In the town are

[38] Camden II, 857, who says, that the Araris, the modern Saone, takes its name for the same reason. The Swiss Aar is very rapid.
[39] Camden II, 859.
[40] Wright's *Halifax*, 202.
[41] Wright, 8.

several meeting-houses; one, called the chapel, is a neat and elegant building, erected by the independents, and even stuccoed.

Halifax rose on the decline of the woollen trade at Rippon; which was brought from that town in the time of Mr John Waterhouse, of this place, who was born in 1443, and lived near a century. In the beginning of his time, here were only thirteen houses, but in 1556 above a hundred and forty householders paid dues to the vicar;[42] and in 1738, says Mr Wright, there were not fewer than eleven hundred families. The woollen manufactures flourish here greatly; such as that of the narrow cloth, bath-coatings, shaloons, everlastings, a sort of coarse broadcloth, with black hairlifts for Portugal, and with blue for Turkey, Sayes, of a deep blue colour, for Guinea: the last are packed in pieces of twelve yards and a half, wrapped in an oil-cloth, painted with Negroes, elephants, etc., in order to captivate those poor people; and perhaps one of these bundles and a bottle of rum may be the price of a man in the infamous traffic. Many blood-red clothes are exported to Italy, from whence they are supposed to be sent to Turkey. The blues are sold to Norway. The manufacture is far from being confined to the neighbourhood, for its influence extends as far as Settle, near thirty miles distant, either in the spinning or weaving branches. The great manufacturers give out a stock of wool to the artificers, who return it again in yarn or cloth; but many taking in a larger quantity of work than they can finish, are obliged to advance farther into the country in search of more hands, which causes the trade to spread from place to place, which has now happily extended its influence; but not all ways alike, for it is bounded by the kerseys at Soyland, and by the bays at Rochdale.

In passing through the end of Halifax, observe a square spot, about four feet high and thirteen broad, made of neat ashler stone, accessible on one side by four or five steps. On this was placed the maiden, or instrument for beheading of criminals; a privilege of great antiquity in this place. It seems to have been confined to the limits of the forest of Hardwick, or the eighteen towns and hamlets within its precincts. The time when this custom took place

[42] Ibid.

is unknown; whether Earl Warren, lord of this forest, might have established it among the sanguinary laws then in use against the invaders of the hunting rights, or whether it might not take place after the woollen manufactures at Halifax began to gain strength, is uncertain. The last is very probable; for the wild country around the town was inhabited by a lawless set, whose depredations on the cloth-tenters might soon stifle the efforts of infant industry. For the protection of trade, and for the greater terror of offenders, by speedy execution, this custom seems to have been established, so as at last to receive the force of law, which was, that 'if a felon be taken within the liberty of the forest of Hardwick, with goods stolen out, or within the said precincts, either hand-habend, back-berand, or confession'd, to the value of thirteen pence half-penny, he shall, after three market-days or meeting-days within the town of Halifax, next after such his apprehension, and being condemned, be taken to the gibbet, and there have his head cut from its body'.[43]

The offender had always a fair trial; for as soon as he was taken, he was brought to the lord's bailiff at Halifax: he was then exposed on the three markets (which here were held thrice in a week) placed in a stocks, with the goods stolen on his back, or, if the theft was of the cattle kind, they were placed by him; and this was done both to strike terror into others, and to produce new informations against him.[44] The bailiff then summoned four freeholders of each town within the forest to form a jury. The felon and prosecutors were brought face to face; the goods, the cow, or horse, or whatsoever was stolen, produced. If he was found guilty, he was remanded to prison, had a week's time allowed for preparation, and then was conveyed to this spot, where his head was struck off, by this machine. I should have premised, that if the criminal, either after apprehension, or in the way to execution, could escape out of the limits of the forest (part being close to the town) the bailiff had no farther power over him; but if he should be caught within the precincts at any time after, he was immediately executed on his former sentence.

---

[43] Wright 84, and *Halifax and its Gibbet Law*, etc. 18.
[44] Gibbet law says that he is exposed after conviction.

This privilege was very freely used during the reign of Elizabeth: the records before that time were lost. Twenty-five suffered in her reign, and at least twelve from 1623 to 1650; after which I believe the privilege was no more exerted.

This machine of death is now destroyed; but I saw one of the same kind in a room under the parliament house at Edinburgh, where it was introduced by the regent Morton, who took a model of it as he passed through Halifax, and at length suffered by it himself. It is in form of a painter's easel, and about ten feet high: at four feet from the bottom is a cross bar, on which the felon lays his head, which is kept down by another placed above. In the inner edges of the frame are grooves; in these is placed a sharp axe, with a vast weight of lead, supported at the very summit with a peg; to that peg is fastened a cord, which the executioner cutting, the axe falls, and does the affair effectually, without suffering the unhappy criminal to undergo a repetition of strokes, as has been the case in the common method. I must add, that if the suffer is condemned for stealing a horse, or a cow, the string is tied to the beast, which on being whipped, pulls out the peg, and becomes the executioner.

On descending a hill, have a fine view of a vale, with the Calder meandering through it. Towards the upper end are two other little vales, whose sides are filled with small houses, and bottoms with fulling mills. Here are several good houses, the property of wealthy clothiers, with warehouses in a superb and elegant style; the fair ostentation of industrious riches. Dine at a neat alehouse, at the foot of the hill, at the head of the canal, which conveys the manufactures to the Trent. Call here on my old correspondent Mr Thomas Bolton, and am surprised with his vast collection of natural history, got together to amuse and improve his mind after the fatigues of business.

Cross the Calder at Lowerby Bridge; after a steep ascent arrive in a wild and moory country, pass by the village of Loyland; reach Blackstone Edge, so called from the colour of certain great stones that appear on the summit. The view is unbounded of Lancashire, Cheshire, and Wales. The ancient road down this hill was formerly tremendous; at present a new one winds down the sides for two miles excellently planned. The parish of Halifax reaches to this hill.

It is my misfortune that the Reverend Mr Watson's full account of this parish did not fall into my hands till this sheet was going to the press; for my account would have received from it considerable improvements. That gentleman has closely attended to antiquities of every kind, but his discovery and figures of those attributed to the Druids are uncommonly curious. A little before our arrival on the top of this hill, enter the county of Lancashire. Reach Rochdale; a town irregularly built, noted for its manufactory of bays. The church is on an adjacent eminence, to be reached by an ascent of about a hundred and seventeen steps. The Roche, a small stream, runs near the town.

After six miles ride, pass by Middleton. In a pretty vale, on an eminence is Alkrington, the seat of Ashton Lever, Esq., where I continue the whole day, attracted by his civility, and the elegance of his museum.

Wearied with the length of my journey, hasten through Manchester and Warrington, and find at home the same satisfactory conclusion as that of my former tour.

APPENDIX I

CONCERNING THE CONSTITUTION OF THE CHURCH OF SCOTLAND

PRESBYTERIAN government in Scotland took place after the reformation of popery, as being the form of ecclesiastical government most agreeable to the genius and inclinations of the people of Scotland. When James VI succeeded to the crown of England, it is well known that, during his reign and that of his successors of the family of Stewart, designs were formed of altering the constitution of our civil government, and rendering our kings more absolute. The establishment of Episcopacy in Scotland was thought to be one point proper in order to facilitate the execution of these designs. Episcopacy was accordingly established at length, and continued to be the government of the church till the revolution, when such designs subsisting no longer, Presbyterian government was restored to Scotland. It was established by Act of Parliament in 1690, and was afterwards secured by an express article in the Treaty of Union between the two kingdoms of England and Scotland. Among the ministers of Scotland, there subsists a perfect equality; that is, no minister, considered as an individual, has an authoritative jurisdiction over another. Jurisdiction is competent for them only when they act in a collective body, or as a court of judicature: and then there is a subordination of one court to another, or inferior and superior courts.

The courts established by law are the four following, viz. church sessions, presbyteries, provincial synods, and above all a national or general assembly.

A church session is composed of the minister of the parish and certain discreet laymen, who are chosen and ordained for the exercise of discipline, and are called elders. The number of those elders varies according to the extent of the parish. Two of them, together with the minister, are necessary, in order to their holding a legal meeting. The minister always presides in these meetings, and is called moderator; but has no other authority but what belongs to the praeses of any other court. The church session is appointed for inspecting the morals of the parishioners, and managing the funds that are appropriated for the maintenance of the poor within their bounds. When a person is convicted of any instance of immoral conduct, or of what is inconsistent with his Christian profession, the church session inflicts some ecclesiastical censure, such as giving him an admonition or rebuke: or if the crime be of a gross and public nature, they appoint him to profess his repentance in the face of the whole congregation, in order to make satisfaction for the public offence. The highest Church censure is excommunication, which is seldom inflicted but for contumacy, or for some very atrocious crime obstinately persisted in. In former times there were certain civil pains and penalties which followed upon a sentence of excommunication; but by a British statute, these are happily abolished. The Church of Scotland addresses its censures only to the consciences of men; and if they cannot reclaim offenders by the methods of persuasion, they think it inconsistent with the spirit of true religion, to have recourse to compulsive ones, such as temporal pains and penalties.

If the person thinks himself aggrieved by the church session, it is competent for him to seek redress, by entering an appeal to the presbytery, which is the next superior court. In like manner he may appeal from the presbytery to the provincial synod, and from the synod to the assembly, whose sentence is final in all ecclesiastical matters.

A presbytery consists of the ministers within a certain district, and also of one ruling elder from each church session within the district. In settling the boundaries of a presbytery, a regard was paid to the situation of the country. Where the country is populous and champaign, there are instances of thirty ministers and as many elders being joined in one presbytery. In mountainous countries where travelling is more difficult, there are only seven or eight ministers, in some places fewer, in a presbytery. The number of presbyteries is computed to be about seventy. Presbyteries review the procedure of church sessions, and judge in references and appeals that are brought before them. They take trials of candidates for the ministry: and if upon such trial they find them duly qualified, they licence them to preach, but not to dispense the sacraments. Such licentiates are called probationers. It is not common for the Church of Scotland to ordain or confer holy orders on such licentiates till they be presented to some vacant kirk, and thereby acquire a right to a benefice.

It is the privilege of presbyteries to judge their own members, at least in the first instance. They may be judged for heresy, that is, for preaching or publishing doctrines that are contrary to the public standard imposed by Act of Parliament and assembly; or for any instance of immoral conduct. Prosecutions for heresy were formerly more frequent than they are at present; but happily a more liberal spirit has gained ground among the clergy of Scotland. They think more freely than they did of old, and consequently a spirit of inquiry and moderation seems to be on the growing hand; so that prosecutions for heresy are become more rare, and are generally looked upon as invidious. Some sensible men among the clergy of Scotland look upon subscriptions to certain articles and creeds of human composition as a grievance, from which they would willingly be delivered.

Presbyteries are more severe in their censures upon their own members for any instance of immoral conduct. If the person be convicted, they suspend him from the exercise of his ministerial office for a limited time: but if the crime be of a heinous nature, they depose or deprive him of his clerical character; so that he is no longer a minister of the Church of Scotland, but forfeits his title to his benefice, and other privileges of the established church. However, if the person thinks himself injured by the sentence of the presbytery, it is lawful for him to appeal to the provincial synod, within whose bounds his presbytery lies: and from the synod he may appeal to the national assembly. Presbyteries hold their meetings generally every month, except in remote countries, and have a power of adjourning themselves to whatever time or place within their district they shall think proper. They choose their own praeses or moderator, who must be a minister of their own presbytery. The ruling elders, who sit in presbyteries, must be changed every half-year, or else chosen again by their respective church session.

Provincial synods are the next superior courts to presbyteries, and are composed of the several Presbyteries within the province and of a ruling elder from each church session. The ancient dioceses of the bishops are for the most part the boundaries of a synod. Most of the synods in Scotland meet twice every year, in the months of April and October, and at every meeting they choose their praeses or moderator, who must be a clergyman of their own number. They review the procedure of presbyteries, and judge in appeal, references and complaints, that are brought before them from the inferior courts. And if a presbytery shall be found negligent in executing the ecclesiastical laws against any of their members, or any other person within their jurisdiction, the synod can call them to account, and censure them as they shall see cause.

The general assembly is the supreme court in ecclesiastical matters, and from which there lies no appeal. As they have a power of making laws and canons, concerning the discipline and government of the Church, and the public service of religion, the king sends always a commissioner to represent his royal person, that nothing may be enacted inconsistent with the laws of the state. The person who represents the king is generally some Scots nobleman, whom his Majesty nominates annually some time before the meeting of the assembly, and is allowed a suitable salary for defraying the expense of this honourable office. He is present at all the meetings of the assembly, and at all their debates and deliberations. After the assembly is constituted, he presents his commission and delivers a speech; and when they have finished their business, which they commonly do in twelve days, he adjourns the assembly, and appoints the time and place of their next annual meeting, which is generally at Edinburgh, in the month of May.

The assembly is composed of ministers and ruling elders chosen annually from each presbytery in Scotland. As the number of ministers and elders in a presbytery varies, so the number of their representatives must hold a proportion to the number of ministers and elders, that are in the presbytery. The proportion is fixed by laws and regulations for that purpose. Each royal burgh and university in Scotland has likewise the privilege of choosing a ruling elder to the assembly. All elections must at least be made forty days before the meeting of the assembly. Their jurisdiction is either constitutive or judicial. By the first they have authority to make laws in ecclesiastical matters: by the other they judge in references and appeals brought before them from the subordinate courts, and their sentences are decisive and final. One point which greatly employs their attention is the settlement of vacant parishes. The common people of Scotland are greatly prejudiced against the law of patronage. Hence when a patron presents a candidate to a vacant parish, the parishioners frequently make great opposition to the settlement of the presentee, and appeal from the inferior courts to the assembly. The assembly nowadays are not disposed to indulge the parishioners in unreasonable opposition to presentees. On the other hand, they are unwilling to settle the presentee in opposition tot he whole people, who refuse to submit to his ministry, because in this case his ministrations among them must be useless and without effect. The assembly therefore for the most part delay giving sentence in such cases, till once they have used their endeavours to reconcile the parishioners to the presentee. But if their attempts this way prove unsuccessful, they proceed to settle the presentee in obedience to the Act of Parliament concerning patronages. Upon the whole it appears that in the judicatories of the Church of Scotland, there is an equal representation of the laity as of the clergy, which is a great security to the laity against the usurpations of the clergy.

The business of every minister in a parish is to perform religious worship, and to preach in the language of the country to his congregation every Sunday, and likewise on other extraordinary occasions appointed by the laws and regulations of the church. The tendency of their preaching is to instruct their hearers in the essential doctrines of natural and revealed religion, and improve these instructions in order to promote the practice of piety and social virtue. Of old, it was customary to preach upon controverted and mysterious points of divinity, but it is now hoped that the generality of the clergy confine the subject of their preaching to what has a tendency to promote virtue and good morals, and to make the people peaceable and useful members of society.

Ministers likewise examine their parishioners annually. They go to different towns and villages of the parish,[1] and in an easy and familiar manner converse with them upon the essential doctrines of religion. They make trial of their knowledge by putting questions to them on these heads. The adult as well as children are catechised. They likewise visit their parishes and inquire into the behaviour of their several parishioners, and admonish them for whatever they find blameable in their conduct. At these visitations the minister inculcates the practice of the relative and social duties, and insists upon the necessity of the practice of them. And if there happen to be any quarrels among neighbours, the minister endeavours by the power of persuasion to bring about a reconciliation. But in this part of their conduct much depends upon the temper, prudence, and discretion of ministers, who are clothed with the same passions, prejudices, and infirmities, that other men are.

To this sensible account of the church of North Britain, I beg leave to add another, which may be considered as a sort of supplement,

---

[1] I must observe, that Bishop Burnet (by birth a Scotchman) adopted in his diocese the zeal of the church of his native country, and its attention to the morals and good conduct of the clergy and their flocks. Not content with the usual triennial visitations, he every summer, during six weeks, made a progress through some district of diocese, preaching and confirming from church to church, so that before the return of the triennial visitation, he became well acquainted with the behaviour of every incumbent. He preached every Sunday in some church of the city of Salisbury; catechised, and instructed its youth for confirmation; was most vigilant, and strict in his examination of candidates for holy orders; was an invincible enemy to pluralities, and of course to non-residents; filled his office with worth and dignity, and by his episcopal merits, it is to be hoped, may have atoned for the acknowledged blemishes in his biographical character.

and may serve to fling light on some points untouched in the preceding: it is the extract from an answer to some queries I sent a worthy correspondent in the Highlands, to whom I am indebted for many sensible communications:

> *To apprehend well the present state of our church patronage and mode of settlement, we must briefly view this matter from the Reformation. At that remarkable period the whole temporalities of the church were resumed by the Crown and Parliament; and soon after a new maintenance was settled for ministers in about 960 parishes. The patrons of the old, splendid Popish livings, still claimed a patronage in the new-modelled poor stipends for parish ministers. The Lords, or Gentlemen, who got from the Crown grants of the superiorities and lands of old abbies, claimed also the patronage of all the churches which were in the gift of those abbies during popery. The King too claimed the old patronage of the Crown, and those of any ecclesiastic corporations not granted away.*
>
> *Lay-patronages were reckoned always a great grievance by the Church of Scotland; and accordingly from the beginning of the reformation the church declared against lay-patronage and presentations. The ecclesiastic laws, or acts of assembly, confirmed at last by parliament, required, in order to the settlement of a minister, some concurrence of the congregation, of the gentlemen who had property within the cure, and of the Elders of the parish.*
>
> *The Elders, or Kirk Session, are a number of persons, who, for their wisdom, piety, and knowledge, are elected from the body of the people in every parish, and continue for life, sese bene gerentibus, to assist the parish minister in suppressing immoralities and regulating the affairs of the parish. Three of these men and a minister make a quorum, and form the lowest of our church courts.*
>
> *Thus matters continued to the year 1649, when by act of parliament patronages were abolished entirely, and the election or nomination of ministers was committed to the Kirk Session or Elders; who, in those days of universal sobriety and outward appearance at least of religion among the Presbyterians, were generally the gentlemen of best condition in the parish who were in communion with the church. After the restoration of King Charles II along with episcopacy patronages returned, yet under the old laws;*

and all debates were finally determinable by the General Assembly, which even under episcopacy in Scotland was the supreme ecclesiastic court. Thus they continued till the Revolution, when the Presbyterian model was restored by Act of Parliament.

The people chose their own ministers, and matters continued in this form till the year 1711, when Queen Anne's ministry intending to defeat the Hanover succession, took all methods to harass such as were firmly attached to it, which the Presbyterian Gentry and Clergy ever were, both from principle and interest. An act therefore was obtained, and which is still in force, restoring patrons to their power of electing ministers.

By this act the King is now in possession of the patronage of above 500 churches out of 950, having not only the old rights of the crown, but many patronages acquired at the Reformation not yet alienated; all the patronages of the 14 Scots Bishops, and all the patronages of the Lords and Gentlemen forfeited in the years 1715 and 1745. Lords, Gentlemen, and Magistrates of Boroughs, are the patrons of the remaining churches. A patron must present a qualified person to a charge within six months of the last incumbent's removal or death, otherwise his right falls to the Presbytery.

A Presbytery consists of several Ministers and Elders. All parishes are annexed to some Presbytery. The Presbytery is the second church court, and they revise the acts of the Kirk Session, which is the lowest. Above the Presbytery is the Synod, which is a court consisting of several Presbyteries, and from all these there lies an appeal to the General Assembly, which is the supreme church court in Scotland. This supreme court consists of the King represented by his Commissioner, Ministers from the different Presbyteries, and ruling Elders. They meet annually at Edinburgh, enact laws for the good of the church, finally determine all controverted elections of ministers. They can prevent a clergyman's transportation from one charge to another. They can find a presentee qualified or unqualified, and consequently oblige the patron to present another. They can depose from the ministry, and every intrant into holy orders becomes bound to submit to the decisions of this court; which, from the days of our reformer John Knox, has appropriated to itself the titles of The Very Venerable and Very Reverend Assembly of the Church of Scotland.

All clergymen of our communion are upon a par as to authority. We can enjoy no pluralities. Non-residence is not known. We are bound to regular discharge of the several duties of our office. The different cures are frequently visited by the Presbytery of the bounds; and at these visitations strict enquiry is made into the life, doctrine, and diligence of the incumbent. And for default in any of these, he may be suspended from preaching: or if any gross immorality is proved against him, he can be immediately deposed and rendered incapable of officiating as a minister of the gospel. Appeal indeed lies, as I said before, from the decision of the inferior to the supreme court.

Great care is taken in preparing young men for the ministry. After going through a course of philosophy in one of our four Universities, they must attend at least for four years the Divinity Hall, where they hear the prelections of the professors, and perform the different exercises prescribed them: they must attend the Greek, the Hebrew, and Rhetoric classes; and before ever they are admitted to tryals for the ministry before a Presbytery, they must lay testimonials from the different professors of their morals, their attendance, their progress, before them: and if upon tryal they are found unqualified, they are either set aside as unfit for the office, or enjoined to apply to their studies a year or two more.

Our livings are in general from £60 to £120 sterling. Some few livings are richer, and a few poorer. Every minister besides is entitled to a mansion-house, barn and stable; to four acres of arable and three of pasturage land. Our livings are exempted from all public duties; as are also our persons from all public statute works. As schools are erected in all our parishes, and that education is cheap, our young generation is beginning to imbibe some degree of taste and liberal sentiment unknown to their illiterate rude forefathers. The English langauge is cultivated even here amongst these bleak and dreary mountains. Your Divines, your Philosophers, your Historians, your Poets, have found their way to our sequestrated vales, and are perused with pleasure even by our lowly swains; and the names of Tillotson, of Atterbury, of Clarke, of Secker, of Newton, of Locke, of Bacon, of Lyttleton, of Dryden, of Pope, of Gay, and of Gray, are not unknown in our distant land.

APPENDIX II

OF THE
FAMA CLAMOSA
by
The Rev Mr Rutherford

Sir,

WHEN I had the pleasure of seeing you last, you desired me to give you some account of the proceedings of the Church of Scotland against a minister in case of a *Fama Clamosa*. I would think myself happy, if I could in the least contribute to assist you in your laudable design of diffusing knowledge, and of making one part of the kingdom acquainted with the manners and customs of the other. You are well acquainted with the Church Courts, and the method of proceeding in ordinary cases, as I find from your Tour. An appeal can be made from a Session to Presbytery, from a Presbytery to a Synod, from a Synod to the General Assembly, which is the supreme court, and from its decision there lies no appeal. Any person who is of a good character, may give to the Presbytery a complaint against one of their members; but the Presbytery is not to proceed to the citation of the person accused, or, as we term it, to begin the process, until the accuser under his hand gives in the complaint, with some account of its probability, and undertakes to make out the libel, under the pain of being considered as a slanderer. When such an accusation is brought before them, they are obliged candidly to examine the affair. But, besides this, the Presbytery considers itself to proceed against any of its members, if a *Fama Clamosa* of the scandal is so great that they cannot be vindicated, unless they begin the process. This they can do without any particular accuser, after they have inquired into the rise, occasion, and authors of this report. It is a maxim in the Kirk of Scotland, that religion must suffer, if the scandalous or immoral actions of a minister are not corrected. And wherever a minister is reputed guilty of any immorality, (although before the most popular preacher in the kingdom) none almost will attend upon his ministry. Therefore the Presbytery for the sake of religion is obliged to proceed against a minister in case of a *Fama Clamosa*. This however is generally done with great tenderness. After they have considered the report raised against him, then they order him to be cited, draw out a full copy of what is reported, with a list of the witnesses names to be led for proving this allegation. He is now to be formally summoned to appear before them; and he has warning given him, at least ten days before the time of his compearance, to give in his answers to what is termed the libel; and the names of the witnesses ought also to be sent him. If at the time appointed the minister appear, the libel is to be read to him, and his answers are also to be read. If the libel be found relevant, then the Presbytery is to endeavour to bring him to a confession. If the matter confessed be of a scandalous nature, such as uncleanness, the Presbytery generally depose him from his office, and appoint him in due time to appear before the congregation, where the scandal was given, and to make public confession of his crime and repentance.

If a minister absent himself by leaving the place, and be contumacious, without making any relevant excuse, a new citation is given him, and intimation is made at his own church, when the congregation is met, that he is to be holden as confessed, since he refused to appear before them; and accordingly he is deposed from his office. When I was in Caithness, an instance of this took place. A certain minister of that county was reported to have a stronger affection for his maid than his wife. He made frequent excursions with this girl; and although no proof of criminal conversation could be brought, yet there was great cause for censure, as all the country took notice of the affair. Upon meeting of the Presbytery, his brethren candidly advised him to remove from his house a servant with whom the public report had scandalized him; that her longer continuance would increase the suspicion; and as it gave offence to his parishioners, if he would not immediately dismiss her, they must consider him as an enemy to his own interest, if not as guilty of the crime laid to his charge. They remonstrated with him in the gentlest terms; but he was still refractory, left the country, and carried his favourite maid in his train. The Presbytery considered this as a confession of his guilt, and deposed him from his office.

APPENDIX III

GAELIC PROVERBS

1   *Leaghaidh a Chòir am bèul an Ammbuinn.*
    Justice itself melts away in the mouth of the feeble.
2   *'S làidir a thèid, 's anmbunn a thìg.*
    The strong shall fall, and oft the weak escape unhurt.
3   *'S fàda Làmh an Fhèumanaich.*
    Long is the hand of the needy.
4   *'S làidir an t' Anmhunn an Uchd Treòir.*
    Strong is the feeble in the bosom of might.
5   *'S maith an Sgàthan Sùil Càrraid.*
    The eye of a friend is an unerring mirror.
6   *Cha bhi 'm Bochd sògh-ar Saibhir.*
    The luxurious poor shall ne'er be rich.
7   *Far an tàin' an Abhuin, 's ànn as mùgha a fùaim.*
    Most shallow — most noisy.
8   *Cha neil Clèith air an Olc, ach gun a dhèanamh.*
    There is no concealment of evil, but not to commit it.
9   *Gìbht na Cloinne-bìge, bhi 'ga tòirt 's ga gràdiarraidh.*
    The gift of a child, oft granted — oft recalled.
10 *Cha neil Saoi gun a choi-meas.*
    None so brave without his equal.
11 *'S mìnic a thainig Comhairle ghlìc a Bèul Amadain.*
    Oft has the wisest advice proceeded from the mouth of Folly.
12 *Tuishlichid an t' Each ceithir-chasach.*
    The four-footed horse doth often stumble; so may the strong
      and mighty fall.

13   *Mar a chaimheas Duin' a Bheatha, bheir e Brèith air a Choim-*
     hearsnach.
     As is a man's own life, so is his judgment of the lives of others.
14   *Fànaidh Duine s òna' re Sìth, 's bheir Duine dòna duì-leum.*
     The fortunate man awaits, and he shall arrive in peace: the
        unlucky bastens, and evil shall be his fate.
15   *Cha do chùir a Ghuala ris, nach do chuir Tuar haris.*
     Success must attend the man who bravely struggles.
16   *Cha Ghlòir a dhearabbas ach Gnìomh.*
     Triumph never gained the sounding words of boast.
17   *'S tric a dh' fhàs am Fuigheal-fochaid, 's a mheith am Fuigheal-*
     faramaid.
     Oft has the object of causeless scorn arrived at honour, and
        the once mighty scorner fallen down to contempt.
18   *Cha do deìobair Feann Rìgh nan Làoch riamh Fear a làimhe-*
     deise.
     The friend of his right hand was never deserted by Fingal, the
        king of heroes.
19   *Thìg Dia re h' Airc, 's cha 'n Airc nar thig.*
     God cometh in the time of distress, and it is no longer distress
        when He comes.

EPITAPH
by Ben Johnson

Underneath this marble hearse
Lies the subject of all verse;
Sidney's sister, Pembroke's mother:
Death, ere thou hast kill'd another,
Fair and learn'd, and good as she,
Time shall throw a dart at thee.

Translated into Gaelic

An sho na luighe fo Lìc-lìghe
   Ha adh-bheann nan uille-bhuadh,
Mathair Phembroke, Piuthar Phillip:
   Ans gach Daan bith' orra luadh.

A Bhais man gearr thu fios a coi-meas,
   Beann a dreach, sa h' Juil, sa Fiach,
Briftidh do Bhogh, gun Fhave do shaighid:
   Bithi'– mar nach bith' tu riamh.

A Sailor's Epitaph
In the churchyard of Great Yarmouth, Norfolk

Tho' Boreas' blow and Neptune's waves
   Have tost me to and fro,
By God's decree, you plainly see,
   I'm harboured here below:
Where I must at anchor lye
   With many of our fleet;
But once again we must set sail,
   Our Admiral Christ to meet.

Translated into Gaelic

Le Uddal-cuain, 's le sheide Gaoidh
   'S lionmhor Amhra thuair mi riamh;
Gam luasga a nùl agus a nàl,
   Gu tric gun Fhois, gun Deoch, gun Bhiadh.
Ach thanig mi gu Calla taimh,
   'S leg mi m' Achdair ans an Uir,
Far an caidil mi mo Phramh,
   Gus arisd an tog na Sùill.
Le Guth na Troimp' as airde fùaim
   Dus gidh mi, 's na bheil am choir
Coinnich' shin Ard-Admhiral a Chuain
   Bhon faith shin Fois, is Duais, is Lònn.

Sappho's Ode

Blest as the immortal Gods is he,
The youth who fondly sits by thee, etc.

Translated into Gaelic

1   *'A Dhmhur mar Dhia neo bhasmhor 'ta*
  'N t'Oglach gu caidreach a shuis re d'sqa:
  Sa chluin, sa chìth re faad na hùin
  Do Bhriara droigheal, 's do fhrea gradh cùin.

2   *Och! 's turr a d' fhogair thu mo Chloss*
  'Sa dhuisg thu 'm Croidh' gach Buaireas bochd:
  'N tra dhearc mi ort, s' mi goint le 't Aadh
  Bhuail reachd am uchd, ghrad mheath mo Chail:

3   *Theogh 'm Aigne arìs, is shruth gu dian*
  Teasghradh air feadh gach Baal am Bhiann:
  Ghrad chaoch mo shuil le Ceodhan Uain
  'S tac aoidh mo Chluas le bothar-fhuaim.

4   *Chuer Fallas 'tlàth mo Bhuil gun Lùth*
  Rith Eal-ghris chuin tre m' fhuil gu dlu.
  Ghrad thug am Plosg a bheannachd leom
  Is shnìomh mi sheach gun' Diog am Chòmm.

Epitaph on a Lady
in the parish church of Glenorchy, in North Britain

1   *An sho na luigh ta san Innis*
  Bean bu duilich leom bhi ann
  Beul a cheuil, is Lamh a Ghrinnis,
  Ha iad 'nioshe sho nan tamh.

2   *Tuill' cha toir am Bochd dhuit beannachd:*
    An lom-nochd cha chluthaich thu nis mo'
    Cha tiormaich Dèur bho shùil na h'Ainnis:
    Co tuill' O Lagg! a bheir dhuit treoir?
3   *Chan fhaic shin tuille thu sa choinni:*
    Cha suidh shin tuille air do Bhòrd:
    D'fhàlabh uain sùairceas, seirc is mòdhan
    Ha Bròn 's bì-mhulad air teachd oiru.

In English

1   Low she lies here in the dust, and here memory fills me with grief: silent is the tongue of melody, and the hand of elegance is now at rest.

2   No more shall the poor give thee his blessing: nor shall the naked be warmed with the fleece of thy flock. The tear shalt thou not wipe away from the eye of the wretched. Where now, O Feeble, is thy wonted help!

3   No more, my Fair, shall we meet thee in the social hall: no more shall we sit at thy hospitable board. Gone for ever is the sound of mirth: the kind, the candid, the meek is now no more. Who can express our grief! Flow ye tears of Woe!

A Young Lady's Lamentation on the Death of her Lover
Translated from Gaelic

Gloomy indeed is the night and dark, and heavy also is my troubled soul: around me all is silent and still: but sleep has forsaken my eyes, and my bosom knoweth not the balm of peace. I mourn for the loss of the dead – the young, the beauteous, the brave, alas lies low – Lovely was thy form, O youth! Lovely and fair was thy open soul! – Why did I know thy worth? – Oh! Why must I now that worth deplore?

Length of years seemed to be the lot of my love, yet few and fleeting were his days of joy – Strong he stood as the tree of the vale, but untimely he fell into the silent house. The morning sun saw thee flourish as the lovely rose – before the noontide heat low thou droop'st as the withered plant.

What then availed thy bloom of youth, and what thy arm of strength? Ghastly is the face of Love – dim and dark the soul-expressing eye – The mighty fell to arise no more!

Whom now shall I call my friend, or from whom can I hear the sound of joy? In thee the friend has fallen – in thy grave my joy is laid. We lived – we grew together. O why together did we not also fall!

Death – thou cruel spoiler! How oft has thou caused the tear to flow! Many are the miserable thou hast made, and who can escape thy dart of woe?

Kind Fate, come lay me low, and bring me to my house of rest. In yonder grave, beneath the leafy plane, my love and I shall dwell in peace. Sacred be the place of our repose.

O seek not to disturb the ashes of the dead!

APPENDIX IV

ACCOUNT OF THE FASTING WOMAN OF ROSS-SHIRE

Dunrobin, Aug. 24, 1769
The Information of Mr Rainy, Missionary Minister, in Kincardine,
anent Katharine McLeod

KATHARINE McLeod, daughter to Donald McLeod, farmer, in Croig, in the parish of Kincardine, Ross-shire, an unmarried woman, aged about thirty-five years, sixteen years ago contracted a fever, after which she became blind. Her father carried her to several physicians and surgeons to cure her blindness. Their prescriptions proved of no effect. He carried her also to a lady skilled in physic, in the neighbourhood, who, doubtful whether her blindness was occasioned by the weakness of her eyelids, or a defect in her eyes, found by the use of some medicines that the blindness was occasioned by a weakness in her eyelids, which being strengthened, she recovered her sight in some measure, and discharged as usual every kind of work about her father's farm; but tied a garter right round her forehead to keep up her eyelids. In this condition she continued for four or five years, enjoying good state of health, and working as usual. She contracted another lingering fever, of which she never recovered perfectly.

Some time after her fever her jaws fell, her eyelids closed, and she lost her appetite. Her parents declare that for the space of a year and three-quarters they could not say that any meat or liquid went down her throat. Being interrogated on this point, they owned they very frequently put something into her mouth: but they concluded that nothing went down her throat, because she had no evacuation; and when they forced open her jaws at one time, and kept them open for some time by putting in a stick between her teeth, and pulled forward her tongue, and forced something down her throat, she coughed and strained, as if in danger to be choked. One thing, during the time she ate and drink nothing, is remarkable, that her jaws were unlocked, and she recovered her speech, and retained it for several days, without any apparent cause for the same; she was quite sensible, repeated several questions of the shorter catechisms; told them that it was to no purpose to put anything into her mouth, for that nothing went down her throat; as also that sometimes she understood them when they spoke to her. By degrees her jaws thereafter fell, and she lost her speech.

Sometime before I saw her she received some sustenance, whey, water-gruel, etc., but threw it up, at least for the most part, immediately. When they put the stick between her teeth, mentioned above, two or three of her teeth were broken. It was at this breach they put in anything into her mouth. I caused them to bring her out of bed, and give her something to drink. They gave her whey. Her neck was contracted, her chin fixed on her breast, nor could by any force be pulled back: she put her chin and mouth into the dish with the whey, and I perceived she sucked it at the above-mentioned breach as a child would suck the breast, and immediately threw it up again, as her parents told me she used to do, and she endeavoured with her hand to dry her mouth and chin. Her forehead was contracted and wrinkled, her cheeks full, red, and blooming. Her parents told me that she slept a great deal, and soundly, perspired sometimes, and now and then emitted pretty large quantities of blood at her mouth.

For about two years past they have been wont to carry her to the door once every day, and she would show signs of uneasiness when they neglected it at the usual time. Last summer, after giving her to drink of the water of the well of Strathconnen, she crawled to the door on her hands and feet without any help. She is at present in a very languid way, and still throws up what she drinks.

APPENDIX V

PARALLEL ROADS
IN GLEN ROY

———⟶⊷●⊶⟵———

A LL the description that can be given of the parallel roads, or terraces, is, that the glen of itself is extremely narrow, and the hills on each side very high, and generally not rocky. In the face of these hills, both sides of the glen, there are three roads at small distances from each other, and directly opposite on each side. These roads have been measured in the completest parts of them, and found to be 26 paces of a man five feet ten inches high. The two highest are pretty near each other, about 50 yards, and the lowest double that distance from the nearest to it. They are carried along the sides of the glen with the utmost regularity, nearly as exact as drawn with a line of rule and compass.

Where deep burns or gullies of water cross these roads, they avoid both the descent and ascent in a very curious manner; so that on the side where the road enters those hollows, they rather ascend along the slope, and descend the opposite side until they come to the level, without the traveller being sensible of ascent or descent. There are other smaller glens falling into this Glen Roy. The parallel roads surround all these smaller ones; but where Glen Roy ends in the open country, there are not the smallest vestiges of them to be seen. The length of these roads in Glen Roy are about seven miles. There are other two glens in that neighbourhood, where these roads are equally visible, called Glen Gluy, and Glen Spean, the former running north-west and the latter south from Glen Roy. Both these roads are much about the same length as Glen Roy.

It is to be observed that these roads are not causeway, but levelled out of the earth. There are some small rocks, though few, in the course of these roads. People have examined in what manner they made this passage through the rocks, and find no vestige of roads in the rock; but they begin on each side, and keep the regular line as formerly. So far I am indebted to Mr Trapaud, Governor of Fort Augustus.

I cannot learn to what nation the inhabitants of the country attribute these roads: I was informed they were inaccessible at the east end, open at the west, or that nearest to the sea, and that there were no traces of buildings, or Druidical remains, in any part, that could lead us to suspect that they were designed for economical or religious purposes. The country people think they were designed for the chase, and that these terraces were made after the spots were cleared in lines from wood, in order to tempt the animals into the open paths after they were roused, in order that they might come within reach of the bowmen, who might conceal themselves in the woods above and below. Ridings for the sportsmen are still common in all great forests in France, and other countries on the continent, either that they might pursue the game without interruption of trees, or shoot at it in its passage.

Mr Gordon, p. 114 of his itinerary, mentions such terraces, to the number of seventeen or eighteen, raised one above the other in the most regular manner, for the space of a mile, on the side of a hill, in the county of Tweeddale, near a village called Romana, and also near two small Roman camps. They are from fifteen to twenty feet broad, and appear at four or five miles distance not unlike a great amphitheatre. The same gentleman also has observed similar terraces near other camps of the same nation, from whence he suspects them to be works of the Romans, and to have been thrown up by their armies for itinerary encampments. Such may have been their use in those places: but what could have been the object of the contrivers of the terraces of Glen Roy, where it is more than probable those conquerors never came, remains a mystery, except the conjecture above given should prove satisfactory.

APPENDIX VI

OF SLOUGH DOGS

———➤●◄———

S IR Wilfrid Lawson, and Sir William Hutton, Knights, two of his
Majesties Commissioners for the Middleshires of Great
Britain. To John Musgrave the Provost Marshall, and the rest
of his Majesties Garrison, send salutations. Whereas, upon due
consideration of the increase of stealths daily growing both in deed
and reporte among you on the borders. We formerly concluded
and agreed, that, for reforming thereof, Watches should be sett,
and Slough Doggs provyded and kept, according to the contents
of his Majesties directions to us in that behalf prescribed. And for
that, according to our said agreement, Sir William Hutton, at his
last being in the country, did appoynt how the Watches should be
kept, when and where they should begin, and how they might best
and most fitly continue. And withall for the bettering his Majesties
servyce, and preventing further danger that might ensure by the
Outlaws, in restoringe to the houses of Thomas Routledge, alias
Baylihead, being neere and next adoyninge to the waysts, he himselfe
beinge fled amongst them, (as it is reported) Order and Direction
was lykewise, that some of the Garryson should keepe and resyde
in his the said Thomas Routledge's houses, and there to remaine till
further directions be given them, unlesse he the said Tho: Routledge
shall come in and enter himselfe answerable to his Majesty's Lawes,
as is convenient. Further, by virtue of our authority from his
Majesty to us directed, touching the border servyce. We command
you that the said Watches be duely searched as was appointed,
and presentment to us, or th' one of us, be mad of every default,

726

either in constables for their neglect in not settinge yt fourth, or in any persons slyppinge or neglectinge their dutyes therein. And that you likewyse see that Slough Doggs be provyded accordinge to our former directions, and as this Note to this Warrant annexed particularly setts down. Faile yee not hereof, as you will answer the contrarye at your perrills. Given under our hands and seals this 29 of November 1661

A NOTE how the SLOUGH DOGGS was agreed upon to be provyded and kept at the Charge of the Inhabitants, as followeth:

Imprimis, beyond Esk, by the inhabitants there, to be kept above the foot of Sarks	1 Dogg.
Itm. by the inhabitts. of the insyde of Eske, to Richmond Clugh, to be kept at the Moot	1 D.
Itm. by the inhabitants of the parish of Arthuret above Richmdclugh, to be kept at the Bailyhead	1 D.
Itm. Bewcastle parish, besides the Baylye and Blackquarters, to be kept at Kinkerhill	1 D.
Itm. the parish of Stapilton	1 D.
Itm. the parish of Irdington	1 D.
Itm. the parish of Lanecrost and Walton	1 D.
Itm.	1 D.
Itm.	1 D.
	Total 9 Dogs.

It was appointed and commanded that the chiefe officers, bayliffes, and constables, within everye circutt and cumpasse wherein the Slough Dogs are appointed to be kept, should take charge for taskeing the inhabitants towards the charge thereof, and collect the same, and for provydinge the Slough Doggs, and to inform the commissioners, if any refused to pay their contribution, whereby such as refused should be committed to the gaole till they paid the same.

N.B. Bishop Nicolson has published the orders of the Watches, 6. Ed. 6. in his *Border Laws*, p. 215, etc., but as I have met with nothing concerning the Slough Dogs till the time of James I, am inclined to think it was a new institution in that king's reign, when they were also appointed in the Scotch borders.

APPENDIX VII

A LETTER FROM MR GEORGE MALCOLM
concerning
SHEEPFARMS, etc.

Communicated by John Maxwell, Esq. of Broomholme

———◦◦◦———

THESE grounds are not in common as in England, but are all separate properties, and divided into extensive farms, with distinct marches, from three to four thousand acres. They are mostly pastured with sheep; that is to say, the farmer depends upon his sheep for paying the rent and yielding him profit. The cows which he keeps, and the corn which he sows, seldom do more than maintain his family. Farms of this large extent become necessary; for as they are not enclosed, the sheep could not be pastured with ease and convenience within narrow marches. Though the country was in a complete state of improvement, it is probable the hills will never be enclosed, as nature seems to have intended them for breeding cattle to supply the cultivated pastures in the low lands which fatten. So long as they are applied to that purpose, and I think they never can be made fit for any other, they cannot pay the expense of enclosing. Every flock has a shepherd to take care of them, whose business it is to make them eat the ground equally, and in bad weather to keep them on such parts of the farm, where they are most sheltered from the storms. He can do nothing without his dog, which, you know, he learns to do wonderful things; but it would be wrong to mention them to strangers, as they would think we bordered on the marvellous. It is sufficient to inform them, that he can command all or any part of his flock, at the distance of more than a mile. As the kinds of sheep, and the methods of managing them, vary so much in different parts of the country, it will be difficult to give your friend any clear idea of them. There is a gradual decline of soil from the east to the west coast. This fact is put beyond a doubt, from the size of both sheep and black cattle turning smaller and smaller as you advance from the east to the west. The large sheep of the east border have often been brought here, but they did not thrive, but turned smaller; and I have known our sheep sent to them, which you would not have known for largeness in a year or two. This shows that the alteration of the size is not owing to the fancy of the farmer, but to a real difference of soil. There are different kinds of soil required for different kinds of sheep, and at different ages. The hogs, which is the name they go by before they are a year old, should have dry pasture, well mixed with heaths, and not much exposed to storms of snow, which breeds them firm and sound. The ewe, which is the female, should have much grass, and not very high land, on account of the lambs which they bring forth in the spring, and the wedder, which is the gelded male sheep, is fittest for the very high grounds, as being strongest and most hardy. This accounts for most farmers having more farms than one, as one seldom contains all these different soils and situations. Through Tiviotdale, the product which most of the farmers sell is wedders above three years old, and about a seventh or eighth part of the oldest of their ewe stock, which are commonly about six years old. They sell the wethers in June, and the ewes about Michelmas. They are mostly bought by the English for feeding. It is impossible to give you an account of prices, as they vary almost every season. Within these twelve years, I have known the Tiviotdale wethers sell from ten to fifteen shillings, and the ewes from six to ten shillings. We shear or clip the wool in the months of June and July. The price of the wool varies as much as the price of the sheep, from three shillings and six pence to six shillings and six pence per stone English, 16 lb. to the stone. From five to between six and seven fleeces go to the stone. The market for wool is sometimes at Edinburgh, and sometimes in England. In some parts of the east of Tiviotdale, they do not salve their sheep; but they do it in most places. It is thought tar warms the sheep and destroys a kind of vermin called a cade, which infests them much. The method of salving is very different, with regard to the quantity of butter mixed with the tar, and also with regard to the quantity of both laid on the sheep. The mixture is from twenty-four pounds English to above three stones of butter to sixteen quarts of tar; and with this quantity they will salve from forty to one hundred and twenty sheep. The greater proportion of butter, the better the wool is; not in point of fineness, but it washes whiter, and consequently takes a better dye. The colder the ground is, the more salve is laid on. It costs from two pence halfpenny to three pence halfpenny each sheep. In Tiviotdale, they have got much into the practice of giving their sheep hay in the snows of winter, which is of much service to them. I cannot pretend to give you my opinion positively with regard to the rents paid, and how many sheep are kept by the acre: they vary with the soil of the ground, and often according to the opinion the different landlords entertain of the value of their estates. More grounds keep below a sheep to the acre than above it; and the rent stands from two shillings to three shillings and six pence for each sheep. The rents of most farms have advanced within these twelve or fourteen years, from a third to double; which great advance has made Highland farming very uncertain; as no improvements which meliorate the farms can be made; but they entirely depend upon the rise and fall of the markets, besides running a great risk from bad seasons. In Eskdale, where we live, we sell no wedders, because we cannot afford to breed wether hogs, on account of a disease, which kills great numbers of that age in our grounds. Our product is lambs and ewes at the age already mentioned. Within these twelve years, we have sold our lambs from two shillings to four shillings and six pence; and our ewes from five shillings and six pence to nine shillings. Our markets are the same as in Tiviotdale: our wool sells lower. Many of us have a practice of milking our ewes; though it is going fast into disuse, because it is generally thought to be hurtful. It renders the ewe less fit to bear the storms in winter; it makes her have less wool; and she will sell at a much higher price at Michaelmas, if not milked, being fatter. The great temptation to milk ewes is to provide butter for salving, which of late years has been very dear. As perhaps Mr P. may have a curiosity to see a calculation of how much is made by milking, I shall give you an account of what I made this year out of three hundred and eighty ewes at Burnfoot; for I milk at no other of my farms:

			£	s
I made 75 stones English of cheese in six weeks at 4s 4d per stone			16	5
12 stones of butter, at 5s 6d per stone English			3	6
			9	11
	£	s		
Wages of four women	2	8		
Wages of eweherd	0	18	3	6
			16	5

N.B. The whey made from the milk is more than equal to the maintenance of the above five servants.
This comes to about 9 $\frac{1}{2}$d each sheep.

To the north-west of us, in Tweddale, Clydesdale, the head of Annandale and in Galloway, the farmers sell for their product wether hogs, and some of them lambs, as we do. For the most part the English buy them to lay on their commons. They are a short coarse-woolled sheep, and esteemed very hardy. In these parts they are free of that disease which kills the young sheep in our country, and which is the reason for their keeping all their male lambs on most of the farms. These hogs have sold within these twelve years, from five shillings to eight shillings and six pence. The diseases to which sheep are liable are many. I shall only mention three of them, which are most mortal. That which we esteem the worst is called the rot. They contract it by pasturing in wet marshy ground, when it happens to be a rainy season in the months of August and September. The only remedy is draining. A bad season will even bring on a rot in dry grounds, where there is much grass. If they suffer much hunger, either from an overstock in summer, or from the snows in winter, it will occasion this disease. We call another disease the sickness, it appears to be a kind of colic, as it swells them much in the body: it mostly attacks young sheep from before Martinmas until the spring. We have no remedy for it. The third disease is called the louping ill, which rages mostly from the 1st of April to the 1st of June. It deprives them of the use of their limbs. We likewise know no remedy for it.

P.S. In reading over my letter, I think it right to explain that part of it, where I say, that there are farms of four thousand acres. I do not mean, that these large farms are all pastured by one flock of sheep, for one flock has seldom above seven or eight hundred acres to go on.

APPENDIX VIII

OF THE ANTIQUITIES FOUND AT THE STATION AT BURRENS

—◦►●◄◦—

No. I This altar was found in the great Station at Burrens, the Blatum Bulgium of Antonine. It is dedicated to a local goddess, whose name has not yet occurred in history. The nation, she was worshipped by, or that of the devotee that erected it is unknown. The reading may be thus:

DEAE HARIMEL
LAE. SACGA
MIDIAHVS
ARCXVSLL^M.

Deae Harimellae, Sacgamidiabus Architectus X. Votum Solvit L. Libentissima mente.

XLV

ANTIQUITIES AT HODDAM CASTLE

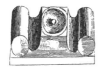

Moses Griffiths del.   P. Mazell sculp.

I did not fail consulting the learned on this occasion; but they rung such a number of changes on the words, that I content myself with giving the plainest reading.

No. II   is an altar addressed to another unknown goddess; for we know no more of Virndesthis or Viratis, (as one of my learned friends will have it) than we do of Harimella:

> DEAE VIRADES
> THI. PAGVS CON
> DRVSTIS MILItavit
> IN COHorte II. TVN
> GRorum SVB SIVO
> AVSPICE PR
> AFEcto

All we can say of this goddess is that she was worshipped by the Tungri, or the people of Liège, who served in the Roman army in Britain.

No. III   is designed for the figure of Fortune; with the following dedication inscribed beneath her feet:

> FORTVNAE Reduci pro
> SALVTE P. CAMmii
> ITALICI PRAEFecti COh. II.
> TUNgrorum CELER LIBERtus
> LL M.

This is a complimentary address to Fortune, by Celer, a freed-man probably of Cammius, in gratitude for having brought his master safely back from some journey.

No. IV   is a sepulchral stone, with a rude head on it.

These four are engraven in plate. The following are preserved with them in the same place.

1.   Part of the figure of Victory, with one foot on a globe. Her vest and part of her wings only are to be seen.

2. A sepulchral stone, with this inscription:
   Diis manibus Asutiano Bassi ordinato
   Tribuno Coh. II. Tungrorum Flavia Baetica
   Conjunx faciendum curavit.

By the frequent mention of the Tungri, it appears they were stationed here for some time.

3. A very plain altar, addressed also to Fortune:
   FORTUNAE Cohortis primae Nerviorum
   Mille Germanorum Equitum.

4. A fragment of an earthen vessel, with a naked female leaning on a column.

5. Another, with part of a boar beneath a tree. This perhaps alludes to the Caledonian forest. The fragment of the inscription above the boar is only *II. TVN*. I suppose done by an officer of the Tungrian cohort, and after the defeat of the Caledonians at the battle of the Mons Grampius, where two cohorts of that body were distinguished greatly.

6. An inscription:
   C.L.
   PED. BR. P.

Collegium ligniferorum peditatus Briganticae posuit.
This is a conjecture collected from the following, which gives some light into the letters C. L:

7. *Numini Augusti Deo Mercurio*
   Signum posuerunt Cultores Collegii Ligniferi
   Ejusdem Dei curatore Ingenno Ruso. V.S.L.M.

8. An altar, with an inscription similar: *DEO. MERCURIO. JUL.*
   CEREALIS Censor Sigillorum Collegii Ligniferorum Cultorum
   ejus de suo dedit votum solvit libens merito.[1]

---

[1] Numbers 7, 8, and 14, were purchased by the late Sir John Clerk, of Penycuick, near Edinburgh.

9. A piece of an ornamental stone, inscribed Legio XX. Vict.

10. An inscription: *Imperatori CaesARI TRAJANO HADRIANO Legio secunda Augusta.*

11. Another piece of a vessel, inscribed *Sac. EROR.*

11. An inscription: *IMP. CAES. FLAVIO VALERIO CONSTANTINO PUBLII FILIO INVICTO AUGUSTO.*
This was found on the Roman road, in the parish of Hesket, between Carlisle and Penrith.

12. An inscription in memory of one Pervica, by her mother Julia: *Dis Manibus Sacrum JULIA PERVICAE Filiae.* Mr Horsely, no. LXIV, *Northumberland*, preserves one of the same kind.

13. A fragment, containing
                    AXAN
                    CONIS.

14. A stone, with the figure of the goddess Minerva. It is engraven no. XXXXIV *Scotl.* by Mr Horsely, but not explained. On her breast is the aegis; beneath on one side of her shield; in right hand a spear; her hair long; on her head a helmet surrounded with a mural coronet, denoting, according to Lucian, that she was the inventress of the art of building; the summit is crowned with olive, another concomitant of this deity. She is styled Brigantia from her delight in war. This is indeed a new epithet; but as the stone was carved in Britain, the inscriber gave her the appellation of the most warlike of our tribes. That such was the derivation of the name of the Brigantes appears from Camden. He does not give the true British etymology, which is from *brig*, 'choice' or 'chief men'. This tribe was famous for its plundering excursions, which hardened them to war, and gave them a superiority over their neighbours. This sculpture perhaps belonged to a temple dedicated to Minerva, founded in the country of the Brigantes, whose limits, in all probability,

extended beyond Burrens, the place it was found at. By the inscription, it appears to have been done by order of Julian, in honour of his favourite goddess, to whom he constantly paid his devotions in secret before his apostasy:

Brigantiae Sacrum Amandus Architectus ex Imperio Imperatoris Juliani posuit.

APPENDIX IX

LIST OF BARONS SUMMONED TO THE SIEGE OF CAERLAVEROC

Ellis de Aubigni
Aimar de St. Amand
Brian fitz Alan
Hugh de Bardolf
John de Beauchamp
John de Bar
John de la Brecte
Walter de Beauchamp
John Botetorte
Anth. Beke, Bp. of Durrham
Maurice de Barkley
Alexr de Bailioll
Barth. Badlesmeri
Barth. Barkley
Barth Basset.
John de Clavering
Robt. de Cliffort
Hugh de Courtenay

Wm. de Cantelo
Wm. de Cromwelle
John de Cretingnes
Hugh le Dispenser
Patric de Dunbar
Edm. Daincourt
John Daincourt
Earl of Lincoln
Earl of Hereford
Earl of Warwick
Earl of Bretaigne
Earl of Oxford
Earl de Laonis
Earl of Gloucester
John de Engaine
John le Estrang
Simo Frefill
Thomas de Furnival

Hugh de Couches
Adam de la Ford
Henry de Graye
Wm. de Grantson
John de Graye
Gerard de Grondonvile
Henry de Graham
Ralf de Gorges
Eustace de Hache
John de Hastings
Simo de Hastings
Robt. Haunsert
Robt. de Hontercomb
Nich. de Karrn
Philip de Kime
Tho. de Lankaster
Wm. de Latimer
Wm. de Layburn
Wm. le Marshall
Walterus Money
John de Moun
Roger de Mortaign
John de la Mare
Hugh de Mortimer
Simo de Montagu
Roger de Mortimer
Ralf de Monthermer
Bertrand Mountboucher
John de Warron
Rich. fil. Wmi.
Adam de Welles
Rob. de la Ward
Rob. de Willeby
Alvin de la Zouch

Wm. de Ferrers
Robert de Montealto
Thomas de Multon
Johes. de Odeston
Henry do Pery
Rob. fitz Payne
Hugh Poinz
Johes. Paignell
Rob. fil. Rogeri
Wm. de Ros
John de Rivers
Wm. de Ridre
Tho. de Richmond
Richard de Rokele
Nich. de Segrave
Nich. de Segrave
John de Seagrave
Robt. de Scales
Rich. Sieuart
John de St. John
John de St. John
John de Tatersall
Rob. de Tony
Henry le Tieis
John fitz Marmad. Thweng
John de Vavasours
Aimar de Valence
Rob. fil. Walteri
Edvardus Rex
Ed. fil. Regis
Tho. fil. Regis.
Baro de Wigneton
Baro de Kirkbride

APPENDIX X

OF THE GOLD MINES OF SCOTLAND

From a MS of Col. Borthwick of Scotland and others

⬤

MR Cornelius Devossec, a lapidary in London, was the first who discovered gold in Scotland. In the valleys of Wanlockhead (near Leadhills), Abraham Grey, a Dutchman, who lived some time in London, got a good quantity of natural gold. He payed his workmen weekly, and lent to diverse men beforehand, as it is written in that parchment book, saying, with this natural gold, gotten in Greatbeard's time (for so he was called, because of his great long beard, which he could have bound about his middle) was made a very fair deep basin, without any addition of any other gold, at Edinburgh, in the Canongate street. It was made by a Scotsman, and contained by estimation, within the brims thereof, an English gallon of liquor; the same basin was of clean neat natural gold. It was then filled up to the brim with coined pieces of gold, called unicorns (which appear to have been only coined in James II's and James IV's time. For this, vide Anders. *Diplom. et Numismata Scotiae*) which basin and pieces both were presented to the French king by the regent Earl of Morton, who signified upon his honour to the king, saying, 'My lord, behold this basin and all that therein is; it is natural gold got within this kingdom of Scotland, by a Dutchman, named Abraham Grey.' Abraham was standing by and affirmed it upon a solemn oath, but he said unto the said king, that

742

he thought it did ingender and increase within the earth; and that he observed it so to do by the influence of the heavens: then Earl Morton stood up, saying, 'I also believe that it engenders within the earth, but only of these two elements, viz. water and earth; and that it was made perfect malleable gold from the beginning by God; and am certain that this cup, and all the pieces therein, are of natural Scots gold, without any other compound or addition.'

Mr Atkinson and Mr George Bowes, both Englishmen, procured a commission into Scotland unto the gold mines; and I happened on a book of his making in England: I compared the same (having carried it with me into Scotland) with the report of the country: and the countrymen at Wanlockhead said it was so, and most true, that Mr Bowes discovered a small vein of gold upon Wanlockhead. He swore all his workmen to keep it secret from the King of Scotland and his council; and so he promised, before his departure from England, to the Queen Elizabeth; and by her letters to the council of Scotland, got a new warrant; so was suffered to dig and delve as he would, after another fashion than Mr Bulmer or his men did. He digged sundry shafts; found oftimes good feeling gold, and much small gold, of which he gave ten or twelve ounces, to make friends in England and Scotland. He had both English and Scots workmen, and paid them with the same gold. Mr Bulmer's men found little or none. And when he and his men filled their purses, then he caused the shaft to be filled up again, swearing his men to secrecy, and keep it close, from the King of Scotland and his council. This was confessed by some of Mr Bowes's chief servants, since his death. On his return to England, he showed the Queen a long purse full of the gold found in the vein he had discovered, and it was valued to be worth sevenscore pounds. He told her majesty he had made it very sure, and hid it up till next going there. She liked well thereof, promising him a triple reward, and to prepare himself next spring to go there at her majesty's charge alone, to seek for a greater vein: he went home reit to his own country in the north of England, where he dwelt; but unfortunately riding to see the copper works and mines in Cumberland, at Keswell, as he was going down into the deep, the ladder broke, the earth fell in, and he was bruised to death.

Then Mr Atkinson succeeded Mr Bowes, and found gold which was presented to King James. Cornelius Devossec, painter to Queen Elizabeth, excellent in the trial of minerals and mineral stones, and acquainted with Nicholas Hilliard,[1] goldsmith and miniature painter to her majesty, engaged in the adventure with him in search of gold in Scotland. Both made an assignment to Arthur van Brownchurst to operate for them. They being informed by travellers of good experience, how that as sand and gravel have their several beds in England, even so as there beds of gold and silver in foreign countrys they had travelled; rocks and craigs having veins and beds of iron, copper, and tin mine, even so gold and silver have their veins amongst rocks and in the ground; so they hoped to find out a bed or vein of gold in Scotland. In consequence Brownchurst searched, and found gold in sundry places; but was forced to leave all in the mint-house by command of the King, being a minor; and Earl Morton, Regent, refused Brownchurst the liberty of search, without paying full value for all such natural gold as should be gotten by him in Scotland; and though a suitor four months, never obtained it, but became one of his majesty's sworn servants in Scotland, to draw small and great pictures to the King. Mr Bulmer, in Queen Elizabeth's time, searched and found gold, etc. in these places in Scotland, viz. 1. Upon Mannock Moor in Niddesdale. 2. Wenlock Water, on Robert Moor, in Niddesdale. 3. Frier Moor, or Glengonnar Water in Clydesdall. 4. Short-Cleugh Water in Crawford Moor. 5. Long-Cleuch Braes or Long-Cleuch Head. He presented to the Queen a gold porringer, upon which were engraven the following lines:

> *I dare not give, nor yet present,*
> *But render part of that's thy own:*
> *My mind and heart shall still invent*
> *To seek out treasures yet unknown.*

But having lost his living by his own and others prodigality, he recalled himself, and penned a book of all his acts, works, and devices, named *Bulmer's Skill*, and another great book on silver

---

[1] Mr Walpole's *Anecdotes of Painting* I, 148.

mines, minerals, mineral stones, tin-mines, coal-mines, and salt-works, etc. It was proposed in council for him to procure twenty-four gentlemen of land, etc. rent £10,000 value, or £500 yearly, who were to disburse £300 sterling each man, in money or victuals, for maintenance of gold-mines in Scotland; for which each was to be knighted, and called the Knight of the Golden Mines, or the Golden Knight; but it did not take place, for the Earl of Salisbury crossed his views: only one knight was made, Sir John Claypool, with Sir Bewes Bulmer. Mr Bulmer writeth of the variety of stones and metals found by him in Scotland, viz. 1. Natural gold great and small. 2. Natural silver. 3. Copperstone. 4. Lead ore. 5. Iron stone. 6. Marble. 7. Stone-coal. 8. Beds of Alabaster. 9. Amethyst. 10. Pearls.

Memorandum of the minerals found in Scotland by Colonel Borthwick. 1. A silver-mine on the north side of the hill S. Jordin in the parish of Foveran. 2. Gold found about Dunidur beyond Aberdeen. 3. Silver called golden bank, at Menzies, in the parish of Foveran. 4. Silver, at the back of a park, where there is a well that serves Disblair's household, parish of Fintra, eight miles north by Aberdeen. 5. Gold in the boggs of new Leslie, at Drumgarran, two miles from Dunidur. 6. Iron at the well of Sipa, west side of Woman Hill, near Gilkomstone miln, quarter of a mile from Aberdeen. 7. Gold, very rich, in a town called Overhill, parish Bechelvie, belongs to L. Glames, fourteen fathoms below the kiln. 8. Lead, at the head of Loughlieburn, north side of Selkirk. 9. Copper, in a place called Elphon, in a hill beside Allen, Laird of Hilltown's lands. 10. Silver, in the hill of Skrill, Galloway. 11. Silver, in Windyncil, Tweedale. 12. Gold, in Glenclought, near Kirkhill. 13. Copper, in Locklaw, Fife. 14. Silver, in the hill south side Lochenhill. 15. Lead, in L. Brotherstone's land. 16. Several metals near Kirkcudbright. 17. Copper, north side Borthwickhill, Hawick, and Branxome. 18. Silver, in Kylesmoor, Sorn, and Machlin, Airshire. 19. Several ores in Orkney.

APPENDIX XI

A DISSERTATION ON THE GOVERNMENT OF THE PEOPLE IN THE WESTERN ISLES

Written November 17th 1774, By the Rev Mr Donald
MacQueen, of Kilmuir, in the Isle of Skie

<hr/>

T HE distance of these isles from the centre of the state, secured
as they were from the awe of supreme power, by high
mountains, extensive moors, and impetuous seas, while their
sovereigns were employed in quelling more dangerous insurrections
at home, or in repelling the frequent incursions of their southern
neighbours, left them in a kind of independency on the crown of
Scotland, especially while, for some centuries, they continued to
be governed by Norwegian viceroys, who coming from a wild and
barbarous country, cannot be expected to have brought order or
civilisation along with them; nor was the matter much mended
when Somerlade, the famous Thane of Argyle, upon being married

to a daughter of Olave, depute King of Man, got a footing in the isles, all of which to the north of the Mull of Kintire, together with Kintire itself, he possessed by himself or his descendants, or those having right from them, until about the beginning of the 15th century. All this while whatever reformation was made in the heart of the kingdom on the manners and prejudices of barbarous times, could have made but a very slow progress in the Isles: though, as islands, they must be supposed to have yielded to the arts of peace and good order earlier than their neighbours upon the continent. Islands, on account of the goodness of the soil, and the additional subsistence they draw from the sea, are generally closer inhabited; crimes could not then lie so long concealed among them as in distant unhospitable glens and mountains. They are also more frequented by strangers; and therefore by a sort of collision the men would polish one another into good manners. They had a Sheriff of the Isles under the Norwegian dynasty; but when the lands were parcelled out afterwards by the Lords of the Isles, the descendants of Somerlade, among barons of different ranks and sizes, each of these barons, assisted by the chief men of the community, held his court on the top of a hill called Cnock an Eric, i.e. 'the hill of pleas', where the disputes they had among themselves were determined, where the encroachments of their neighbours were considered, and the manner of repelling force by force, or the necessary alliances they were to enter into, resolved on. In this period, when agriculture, trade, and manufactures were at a very low pitch, the laws were few and general; their little contracts were authenticated by being transacted in the presence of witnesses; the marches of the different barons were fixed before a croud by two or more sagacious men, and two or more young lads were scourged with thongs of leather, that they might the better remember the transaction. The last who was thus used is now an old man, and a pensioner to the family of MacDonald. Nor were the people in their purchases so diffident of one another, as to insist upon a cautioner, that the beast or subject exposed to open sale was fairly come by or would not be reclaimed by another, which was once a common practice over the kingdom called in plain Gaulic, Ra-disneah. The penal laws were more numerous, severe, and particular; for when restraints are put upon natural liberty, and the customs to which men were habituated in a state of barbarity were to be reduced or abolished, men must have very alarming examples painted before their eyes. The laws of the first legislators in all countries are very severe, and are softened and moderated according to the progress of civilization. The legislator of the Jews, though a very meek man, punishes several crimes with the most cruel kinds of death, stoning and burning. Of Draco's laws, one of the first Athenian legislators, it is said that they were written with blood; and it is well known, that the laws of the twelve tables were very severe. Traitors were put to death in the isles, being, according to a custom that prevailed among the Norwegians, first gelded and both their eyes pulled out. Incestuous persons were buried in marshes alive, and bankrupts, without entering into a consideration of the nature of their misfortunes, were stripped of their all, clad in a party-coloured clouted garment, with stockings of different sets and had their hips dashed against a stone in presence of the people by four men, each taking hold of an arm or a thigh. This punishment they called *ton cruaigh*: and cowardice, when not capitally punished, was accompanied with perpetual infamy. The prisons were dark vaults, without beds, or the smallest crevice to introduce light, where no friend was permitted to comfort the criminal, who, after a long fast, was often killed with a surfeit. This was the case of Heitchen, the son of Archibald Clerich, a traitor against the family of Macdonald, who died in the vault of Duntulm, of a surfeit of salt beef, being refused any kind of drink. The severity of justice laid hold but on a few; for the protection of the tribe or clan was generally resorted to, who did all in their power to save their own man from distress, or to pursue with vengeance the person who had offended any of their number. It often happened in this case, that among powerful tribes, the voice of the judge was too weak to be heard: then religion stepped in as a necessary supplement to his power. Sanctuaries, called girths, were consecrated in every district, to which the criminal fled; where the superstition of the times, countenanced by the political institutions, secured him from every act of violence, until he was brought to a judicial trial. To this day we say of a man who flies to a place of security, *Hug e an girt Er*: and whatever party violated the sanctuary, which very seldom happened, brought the terrible vengeance of the church upon their back. Such a bridle as this became absolutely necessary to restrain the anger and impetuosity of a lawless tribe when provoked. Again, when the criminal got in among his own people, they did all in their power to justify his conduct and save his person. In this case the resentment turned on the clan, and any one of them who fell into the hands of the offended was sure to suffer distress, or to be kept in durance, until the criminal was delivered over to justice, which practice was at last found expedient to be turned into a law in the kingdom, to prevent the clans from coming buckled in all their armour to the field, to determine their own quarrels.

In process of time, they learned from their neighbours, as well as from their own experience, that to perpetuate strife and disorder among tribes who were almost in full possession of their natural liberty, excepting when the local custom stood in their way, was dangerous to the public, and ruinous to themselves. To stop the progress of resentment, they cancelled the injury by satisfaction with their cattle, by a mutual agreement betwixt the parties, which therefore was called a composition, to be divided betwixt the injured person and his clan. But as the composition was not always easily accepted, the principals of the different tribes fixed the value of it for every injury, and estimated the life of a man according to his rank; here a people void of refinement made little distinction betwixt voluntary and involuntary trespasses, for fear that impunity in any case should give a scope to wicked persons to abuse the indulgence of custom or law. The greatness of the composition in this case brought not only honour along with it, but greater security in a rude and barbarous neighbourhood. This ransom was called Eric. The clan was then obliged to give up the defender, or become liable for the penalty proportioned to the injury committed. Thus the clans became mutual pledges for the good behaviour of the individuals who composed them. When specie found its way in among them, a price was put upon the cattle, and by the necessary decrease in the value of money, which they were not aware of, the Eric came at length to be very trifling; but by this time the laws of the kingdom had made near approaches to them, which were far from being welcome to men closely attached to their own customs and connections, being deaf to the voice of parties, and to the distinctions of clans and individuals. 'The law hath come the length of Ross-shire,' saith one neighbour by way of news to another. 'O ho!' replies he, 'if God doth not stop it, you will soon have it nearer home.' Much after this manner hath the progress of civilization been carried on in all the countries of Europe; for similar causes produce similar effects.

All the time preceding the beginning of the fifteenth century, and somewhat later, the government of the Isles and of the neighbouring continent was of the military kind. The people were made up of different clans, each of which was under the direction of a chief or leader of their own, and as their security and honour consisted in the number and strength of the clan, no political engine was neglected, that could be thought of, to increase their numbers or inflame their courage. The children of the principal people were given out to nurses: the foster-brothers, or 'coalts', as they called them, with their children and connections for many generations, were firmly attached to their will and interest. This sort of relation was esteemed a stronger bond of friendship than blood or alliance. It was to increase their numbers that bastardy was under no sort of dishonour: besides that the children got out of wedlock, to remove the uncertainty of their birth, expressed more love, and underwent more hazards on account of the clan, than the lawful children, by which they generally acquired a higher degree of strength both of mind and body, and therefore were sometimes called to the succession by a heroical tribe, in preference of those who by the present laws should enjoy it. Such a breach in the lineage of a family is disavowed as being a dishonourable blot by the present race, though the several branches are apt to charge it upon one another, when debating upon the ideal chieftainry of a clan. It was however reckoned no discredit in the days of military prowess. Abimelech, King of Sichem, was begot by Gideon, on a concubine, and preferred to the seventy children he had by his married wives. William the Conqueror was not ashamed to call himself the Bastard of Normandy; as little was Ulysses to acknowledge that he was the son of a concubine. The safety of the community is the supreme law, to which every political consideration must occasionally yield.

It would be astonishing to hear that theft and plundering, instead of being infamous, were reckoned the most wholesome exercise of youth, when they went without the limits of their own community, and were not taken in the fact, if it were not commonly known to have been the case every where. From this source, the chieftains derived rewards for their numerous followers, and dowries sometimes for their daughters. It is known that one of them engaged in a contract of marriage to give his son-in-law the purchase of three Michaelmas moons, at a season of the year when the nights were long, and the cattle strong enough to bear hard driving. This transaction happened on the mainland, where dark woods, extensive wastes, high-forked mountains, and a coast indented with long winding branches of the sea, favoured the trade. These were strongholds, little frequented by strangers, where the ancient practices and prejudices might be preserved to the last periods of time, without some such violent shock as that of the year of 1745. The islanders yielded much earlier to the arts of peace and civility, for the Dean in the year 1549 mentions only some petty piracies from a few of the smaller islands which were divided from a well-peopled neighbourhood.

In the military days, the chieftain drew little or no rent from his people: he had some of the best farms in his own hands, to which there was a causal accession by forfeitures; he had his proportion of the fines laid upon the trespassers of the law; he had the herezield horse when any of his farmers died; he had a benevolence or voluntary contributions sent him, according to the power and good intentions of every man; he and his coshir, or retinue, could lodge upon them when he pleased; and they were obliged to support him and his baron-like train, when he was employed in dispensing justice among them. This allowance was called 'a cutting for the court', or *gearrigh moid*. When rents began to be levied, which were at first but a moderate part of the produce of each farm, the former revenues gave way gradually, though some branches of them were preserved till within the memory of men now living. Nor was it necessary to use distress for levying these accustomed taxes or servitudes; an attachment to the chief was the first principle of the people's education; a defect on that head was judged a renunciation of all virtue; their thoughts and words were much employed about him; it was the usual acclamation on a surprise from any unexpected misfortune, 'God be with the chief! – May the chief be uppermost!' and swearing by his hand was a common form of asseveration; on every such occasion giving him his proper title. Further, on the side of the chieftain, no art of affability, generosity, or friendship, which could inspire love and esteem, was left untried to secure a full and willing obedience, which strengthened the impressions of education, while they were not yet abused by the chief, at the instigation of luxury, and the ambition of cutting an unmeaning figure in the low country, where numbers were more respected, and his usefulness could very well be spared.

All this while the people preserved a good deal of their liberty and independence; the dispensation of justice, such as it was, kept them however in order within the limits of their own country; but there was a law of another kind planted in the human breast by the friendly hand of our Maker, which bridled their natural impetuosity much more; that was, a quick sense of honour and shame, which was nourished by their education, being all bred to the use of arms, to hunting, to the exertion of their strength in several amusements, games, and feats of activity. The bard celebrated the praises of him who distinguished himself on any of these occasions, and dealt out his satire, but with a very sparing hand, for fear of rousing up the ferocity of men, who were in use to judge in their own cause, when they appealed to the sword, and either retrieved their honour, or died; valour was the virtue most in repute; according to their progress in it were they distinguished by their chieftain and friends. Every one of the superior clans thought himself a gentleman, as deriving his pedigree from an honourable stock, and proposed to do nothing unworthy of his descent or connections; and the inferior clans, the 'boddacks', as they called them, tread at an humble distance in the steps of their patrons, whose esteem and applause they courted with passionate keenness. The love, affection, and esteem of the community all aimed to procure by a disinterested practice of the social duties, truth, generosity, friendship, hospitality, gratitude, decency of manners, for which there are no rewards decreed in any country, but were amply paid among the Highlanders by that honour and respect of which they had a very delicate taste. Avarice, debauchery, churlishness, deceit, ingratitude, which can scarcely be punished by the magistrate, were banished by the dreadful fear of shame. These two provisions, which kind Nature hath made for directing the conduct of man, were so incorporated with the hearts and manners of the people, that the influence of them came down to our days, and continued a good supplement to the want of law, and to the lame execution of what law they had. Men of lively open tempers are generally sincere, faithful, and religious observers of their words. Men used to terminate their disputes by the sword will detest fraud and duplicity as the true ensigns of cowardice. Yet it must be owned, that their virtues were too much confined to their own community, whose friendships and enmities every individual espoused, and were therefore more animated by the spirit of faction, than by their regard to reason and common justice, which led them often in a wrong way. Of all virtues their hospitality was the most extensive; every door and every heart was open to the stranger and to the fugitive; to these they were particularly humane and generous, vied with one another who would use them best, and looked on the person who sought their protection as a sacred depositum, which on no consideration they were to give up. Men of narrow principles are disposed to attribute the uncommon hospitality of the Highlanders not so much to generosity as to self-love, the absolute want of inns making it necessary to receive the stranger, in hopes of being repaid in their own persons, or in that of their friends. Hospitality was founded on immemorial custom, before the thoughts of men were contracted by the use of weights and measures, and reckoned so far a sacred obligation as to think themselves bound to entertain the man who from a principle of ill-will and resentment, sorned upon them a numerous retinue, which went under the name of 'the Odious Visitor', *Coinimh Dhuimigh*. Of this there have been instances within a century back; which kind of hospitality would scarce be supposed self-interested.

To return from this digression (if it be one) about the favourite virtues of the islanders and their neighbours on the opposite coast: Let us recollect, that when our sovereigns had any respite from foreign and domestic troubles, they did not neglect to try all means to assimilate these distant skirts of their dominions to their other more peaceable and industrious subjects. The most of the proprietors, instead of holding of the Lords of the Isles, were, on the fall of that great family, directed by their best friends to get their charters confirmed by King James IV. King James V made an expedition among them, to quell their insurrections; and King James VI seriously proposed to introduce the comforts of civilization among them, when, in his 15th parliament, he erected the three burghs of Kilkerran or Campbeltown, Inverlochy, and Stornoway, which, though among a people impatient of foreign intruders, they did not produce the full effect intended by government, yet made way for beating and distressing the renegadoes into good manners, by means of the Campbels and Mackenzies, loyal subjects supported by public authority, as could not miss to determine the Islanders and others to submit to good order.

At length the local customs, and such new statutes as occasion required, enacted by the proprietor, his bailey, and some of the better sort of people, were reduced into writing, not above a century ago, in the isle of Sky, and proclaimed annually at the church-doors. Some of these regulations are surprizingly regular and distinct; and under the administration of a humane master and a judicious bailey, the people found themselves happy enough. While the spirit of clanship preserved any of its warmth, the chieftain seldom intended an injury; and when any was offered, by him or by another, it was soon demolished by the weight of a multitude; but when this balance of power was weakened and dissolved, the people lay much at mercy. In time of a long minority, or when the proprietor took it into his head to visit London or Edinburgh, the estate being left under the management of this bailey, who generally was the steward or factor, the rights of mankind were often trampled underfoot: being his master's eyes, ears, and almost his very soul, by whom he saw, heard, and understood every thing, any obnoxious person was easily misrepresented. In time of a minority his powers of doing mischief were more unrestrained, tutors being less attentive than any men to their own interest. Scarce an imperial procurator sent to one of the distant provinces, clad in all the authority of the sovereign city, was more dreadful than he, when a judge, executor of the laws, raiser of the rents, a drover, and entrusted with keeping the lands. The seats of justice were at too great a distance; the law a slow, uncertain, expensive redresser of grievances; the factor like to be supported by his constituent, while the general voice of a servile neighbourhood went along with the man in power. These were discouragements which the feeble efforts of a farmer could not easily surmount. In proportion as the old military spirit decayed, all the natural and artificial connections of the clans dissolved apace; every man was then left single, to combat a force too strong for him to manage. In a very seasonable hour the heritable jurisdictions were abolished, and sheriffs depending upon the sovereign alone appointed to dispense justice, which was surely a great relief to the leidges, where their sphere of action was not too extensive for themselves or the substitutes they were able or willing to employ in eccentric corners; even in that case the people mustered up more spirit, and acquired some knowledge of the rights they were born to.

The proprietors had still a hold which the laws could not even moderate; for they could set what value they pleased on their freehold; and some among them who had run themselves in debt by high living; some who had a passion for money, and did not sufficiently consider the state of their people, the greater number mistaking the high prices of cattle and of the other produce of their lands, for the true standard by which to estimate their rent-roll, without making the necessary allowance for the greater disbursement of the farmers in servants wages, implements of tillage, and in every article of living and family-keeping; and others, a few I believe, unwilling to see any part of their former authority taken away without a suitable compensation for it, loaded their people with heavier rents than the advanced price of their cattle, etc. could bear; and rather than sink under this burden, crowds of them made their way to the wilds of America; though the rage of emigration, like a contagious distemper, seized upon several who had little cause to complain.

P.S. The hand-fisting of the southern part of Scotland has put me in mind of an omission in the above. It was an ancient practice, among the men of rank especially, to take an year's trial of a wife, and if they were mutually satisfied with one another in that time, the marriage was declared good and lawful at the expiration of it. But when either of the parties insisted upon a separation, and that a child was begotten in the year of probation, it was to be taken care of by the father only, and to be ranked among his lawful children, next after his heirs. He was not considered as a bastard, because the cohabitation was justified by custom, and introduced with a view of making way for a happy and peaceable marriage. One of the great Lords of the Isles took such a trial of a nobleman's daughter upon the continent, got a son by her, and after separation settled an extensive fortune upon him in lands *tenendus de me, et heredibus meus*, the greater part of which his honourable posterity possess to this day. Such was also the power of custom, that this apprenticeship for matrimony brought no reproach on the separated lady; and if her character was good, she was entitled to an equal match as if nothing had ever happened.

Adultery was punished here by dipping the guilty in a pond, or by making him or her stand in a barrel of cold water at the church door: and when the rigour of judicial discipline was a little softened, the delinquent clad in a wet canvas shirt was made to stand before the congregation; and at the close of service, the minister explained to him the nature of his offence, and exhorted him to repentance.

All civil professions were anciently hereditary in the isles. The bards, the *sheanchies* or genealogists, the physicians, the pipers, and even the cooks, all of whom had appointments in lands settled on them, according to the munificent temper of the feudal government. It was only in the time of our fathers, that MacDonald of clan Ronald's Scheanchy and Bard, MacMhurach, began to pay rent for his heretable farm. The other hereditary professions have long been come to a close, except the MacKarters and MacKrumens, the pipers of the family of MacDonald and MacLeod, who still preserve their appointments. I shall also except Doctor John Maclean, whose ancestors have been physicians to the family of Macdonald for time immemorial, educated at the expense, and preferred to the farm of Shulista, near the gates of Duntulm. The late Sir James MacDonald, for the farther encouragement of the above gentleman, settled upon him a considerable pension during life, to raise also the emulation of any of his sons who might be bred to his business, when they observe a distinction made according to the merit of the these hereditary professors of medicine.

Though the professions were confined to one family, which might naturally be supposed to quench emulation, yet the frequent occasion these artists had of intermixing with the neighbouring chieftains, determined them to support the pride of their superiors, by exerting their whole powers to excel every other professor of their own art; because their love and attachment to their chief was the first principle of their education.

Neither have I heard that any of these families ever failed, though, according to the course of things, that sometimes might have happened; but they had the choice of the women among their own rank, the superior often giving directions in this momentous affair: and among a number of children, some one or other would be bound to fit to follow his father's, or, in case of an accident, his uncle's calling. It would be strange indeed, if among ten or twelve sons, Dr MacLean could not find one with a genius for physic.

OF THE GRUAGICH
by the same.

Before the arts of carving, ingraving, or statuary work were invented, or in the countries, into which they were not introduced, the representations of the divinity, whether high or subordinate, were no other than the trunks of trees, or rude unformed stones. The emblem of the supreme god at Dodona, consecrated by the Hyperboreans, was the trunk of an oak, and so it was in the Massilian grove:

> Simulacrque mista Deorum
> Arte carent, caesisque extant informia truncis

The emblem of Apollo at Delphi, set up by the Pelas-Gi, the primitive inhabitants of Greece, was no other than a pillar of stone. Several examples of this kind are mentioned by Clemens Alexandrinus and Eusebius.

As the Celtic tribes worshipped spiritual gods, whether the supreme, or subordinate ones; they well knew that material representations could not be expressive of them, though the trunk of a tree or a stone could very well mark out the place of worship, in a grove or on the summit of a mountain, where the small societies in the neighbourhood might convene on solemn occasions, or as the necessity of the community might seem to require, in order to conciliate the favour and assistance of the divinity whom they resorted to. Men of different religious principles have often been unjust to one another in common charge of idolatry; the Protestants lay it to the account of the Catholics, the Catholics to the account of pagans of all denominations, which all deny, who know best what they are employed about. They surely pray, such at least of them as can think, not to a stock or a stone, whether in the state of nature or formed by art into a statue, but to the divinity, of which one or the other is an emblem. Among the variety of subaltern divinities, which the Celtic tribes worshipped, the spirit of the sun was in the foremost rank, the sun being the most cheerful, and the most universally beneficent of all created and visible beings. It brought joy and gladness along with it to all the animal creation, to groves, to fields, and meadows. The day of its return was celebrated in every district by a *feu de joye*; whence May Day was called in the Gaulic, *la beltein*, 'the day of Bel's fire', Belis being one of the names of the sun in Gaul. Herodian, lib. 8. The worship of the sun was so frequent, that several mistook it for the principal object of adoration. The enclosures called *grianan*, or *grianham*, 'the house of the sun', are to be met with everywhere, in which they offered their sacrifices, commonly horses, burnt betwixt two large fires; whence the proverb, 'He is betwixt two beltein fires', which is applied to one in the hands of two artful persons, whose intrigues he is not able to escape. From these enclosures they also received oracular responses. When the elegant arts were invented, the Celtic deities appeared carved, engraved, or painted, in such forms as the imagination of the workman suggested to him as the most emblematical and expressive of the common conceit they entertained of the divinities they meant to point out. Then they changed the rude lamps into figures resembling, living creatures, generally into men, as being the most honourable forms. The spirit of the sun, or the god who, according to the ancient creed, guided it in its course, was figured as a young lively man, with long, yellow, dishevelled hair: under this appearance Apollo hath the epithet of χευσοχομος", 'the goldenhaired', given him by Euripides; and of αχειριεχομος", 'the unshaven', by Homer, alluding to beams of the sun, which are long and yellow. This imaginary conceit of the Hyperborean Apollo made its way to the Highlands of Scotland, where to this day he is called by the name of Gruagich, 'the fair-haired'. The superstition or warm imagination of ignorant people introduced him as a sportive salutary guest into several families, in which he played many entertaining tricks, and then disappeared. It is a little more than a century ago, since he hath been supposed to have got an honest man's daughter with child, at Shulista, near to Duntulme, the seat of the family of MacDonald: though it is more probable, that one of the great man's retinue did that business for him. But though the Gruagich offers himself to every one's fancy as a young handsome man, with fair tresses, his emblems, which are in almost every village, are no other than rude unpolished stones of different figures just as they seemed cast up to the hand of the Druid who consecrated them. Carving was not introduced into the

Hebrides; and though it had, such of the unformed images as were preserved would for their antiquity be reverenced, in preference of any attempts in the modern arts.

The Gruagich stones, as far as tradition can inform us, were only honoured with libations of milk, from the hands of the dairy maid, which were offered to Gruagich upon the Sunday, for the preservation of the cattle on the ensuing week. From this custom Apollo seems to have derived the epithet Galaxius. This was one of the sober offerings that well became a poor or frugal people, who had neither wine nor oil to bestow; by which they recommended their only stock and subsistence to their favourite divinity, whom they had always in their eye, and whose blessings they enjoyed every day. – The inscription *Apollini Granno* ('Grianich the sunny') was on a stone of this kind, dug up from the ruins of the Roman pretenture, in King James VI's time. – The inscription in Gruter, *Apollini Besino,* seems to have been on such another. – The rock idols of Cornwal, in Dr Borlase, seem to be of the same kind, though of different forms; for it was not the shape, but the consecration, that pointed out their uses. Notwithstanding they are numerous in this island, you will scarce meet with any two of them of the same cast. The idol stones besides that remain with us are oblong square altars of rough stone, that lie within the Druids' houses, as we call them. Observe also, that the worship of the sun seems to have continued in England until King Canute's time, by a law of his, which prohibits that, with other idolatrous practices.

APPENDIX XII

OF THE NUMBERS IN THE HEBRIDES AND THE WESTERN HIGHLANDS

———◆———

Counties	Parishes			Protestants catechisable	Roman Catholics
Argyle	Toracy Ross } Isle of Mull Kilmore			893 1,200 1,800	7
Argyle	Cannay			16	276
	Muck			80	9
Inverness	Rum			271	13
	Egg			44	390
	Slate			1,400	1
	Strath			900	
	Portree	Isle		1,100	
	Brakadel	of		2,500	
	Diurnish and Waternish	Skye		2,500	
	Kilmuir			1,300	2
	Snizort			800	

Counties	Parishes		Protestants catechisable	Roman Catholics
Ross	Loch Broom		2,000	
	Assynt		1,600	
	Gairloch		3,000	
	Applecross		1,200	
	Loch Carran		{ 1,774 souls	
	Kintail		600	
Inverness	Glenelg, Bernera		660	
	Knodyant and North Morrar }			950
	All in the Parish of	South Morrar		300
		Arisaig	4	500
		Moydart	10	500
Argyle		Sunart	439	4
	Ardnamurchan		957	
	Morvern		1,100	
	Lismore and Appin		2,860	

These are the parishes mentioned in the report, which I either visited or sailed by. The reader may be probably desirous of a view of the numbers contained in the other islands; which shall be given from the same authority, except when otherwise mentioned.

Counties	Parishes	Protestants catechisable	Roman Catholics
Inverness	Isle of Lewis[1]		
	Stornaway	2,000	
	Lochs	800	
	Elig	1,000	
	Barvas	1,000	
	Isle of Harris		
	with Bernera		
	Pabbay		
	Killegray	2,000	
	Ensay		
	Toronsay		
	Scaop		
	North Wist		
	with Heyskir	1,700	1
	Barra		
	South Wist		
	with Benbecula	250	1,850
	Erisca		
	Barra[2]	80	1,020
	St Kilda[3]	88	
Argyle	Tir-I	1,240	
	Col.	900	3

[1] According to the account communicated to me by Mr Gillander, agent of the island, the number of souls, in 1763, amounted to between eight and nine thousand.

[2] Barra was a Protestant isle till the reign of Charles II, when some Catholic missionaries, taking advantage of the neglect and ill conduct of the minister, brought the inhabitants over to their religion.

[3] From Mr Macaulay's history of that island.

APPENDIX XIII

COPY OF
A WRIT OF
FIRE AND SWORD

CHARLES, by the Grace of God, King of Great Britain, France, and Ireland, Defender of the Faith, to our Lovites:

Messengers, our Sheriffes in that part, conjunctly and severally, specially constitut; And to all and sundry our Leidges whom it effeirs, Greitting. Forasmuchas Wee and the Lords of our Privy Councell being informed, that upon the 23rd day of June last bypast, the Persons underwritten, viz. Lauchlan McLaine of Broloies, Hector Oig McLaine his Brother, etc. were orderly denounced Rebels and put to the horn by vertue of Letters of Denounciation direct at the instance of Duncan Fisher, Procurator Fiscal of the Justiciar Court of Argyle for our interest, against them, for their not compearing personally within the Tolbuith of the Burgh of Innerrary, upon the said 23d day of June last, before Mr John Campbell of Moy, Sheriffe Depute of the Sheriffedome of Argyle, to our right trusty and well beloved Cousine and Councellor Archbald Earle of Argyle, Heretable Justiciar General of the said Shyre of Argyle and the Isles thereof, as they who were lawfully cited upon the 24th and 25th days of May last, by Duncan Clarke, Messenger, to have compeared the said day and place, to have found

764

caution acted in the bookes of adjournall for their compearance the said day, to have answered and underlyen the law for their convocating the number of three or four hundredth men in Aprile last, by sending of Fyre proces thro' the Isle of Mull, Moveran, and other places, and remaining and abydeing upon the lands of Knokersmartin in ane warlyke posture, from the 22d of the said month to the last thereof; as also convocating one hundreth men, and keeping them in arms the space foresaid at Gadderly and Glenforsay; and sicklike for garrisoning the house and fort of Cairnbulg upon the — day of the said month, or ane or other of them, with the number of — armed persons, and appointing a captain and other officers for keeping the same, and securing the country against the execution of our laws; for their violent away carrying several corns, bear, horse, and swyne, arrested upon the lands of Crosschoill and Sulanavaig, by Duncan Clarke Messenger, notwithstanding of a lawful intimation made by the said Messenger of the said arrestment: and likewise for the said Lauchlan McLaine of Broloies, and David Ramsay Commissary of the Isles, and their followers, being in Tirie in Aprile last, and oppressing the tennants there, by quartering and sorning upon them, and causing bring meal and provision frae the tenants and possessors of Kendway in Tirie, and others, to Lauchlan McLaine Baillie, in Tirie, his house in Kilsaile; and lastly, for the forsaid persons and their followers, in the months of March or Aprile last, their entering into a league and bond, and obligeing themselves by oath to join and adhere one to another, and immediately thereafter garrisoned the house and fort of Cairnbulg in manner of forsaid, contrar to and in contempt of our laws and acts of parliament made against these crymes in manner at length specified in the Criminal Letters raised against them thereanent, as the said Letters of Denunciation, duly execute and registrate in the books of adjournal of the Justice Court of the Shyre of Argyle, conform to the act of parliament, produced in the presence of the Lords of our Privy Councel bears. At the process of the which horn the forenamed persons most proudely and contemptuously lye and remain taking no reguard thereof nor of our authority and laws; bot in contempt of the same haunts, frequents, and repairs to all places within this our realm, as if they were our free Leidges. Wee therefore, with the advice of the Lords of our Privy Council, have made and constitute, and hereby make and constitute, the Lord Neill Campbell, John Campbell younger of Glenorchy, Sir James Campbell of Lawers, John McLeod of Dunvegan, Sir Norman McLeod, — Campbell of Ardfinglas, — McDonald Captain of Clanronald, Alexander Campbell, uncle to Auchinbreck, — McAlaster of Loop, and Duncan Stewart of Appin, our Commissioners in that part, to the effect after specified Givand, Grantand, and Committand to them conjunctly and severally our full power and commission, express, bidding, and charge to convocat our leidges in armes, and to pass, search, seek, take, and apprehend, and in case of resistance or hostile opposition to pursue to the death the saids Lauchlan Maclaine of Broloeis and remnant persons foresaids rebells, for the causes above-written. And if for their defence they shall happen to flee to strengthes or houses, in that case, Wee, with advice foresaid, give full power and authority in our saids Commissioners conjunctly and severally as said, is, to pass, persue, and assedge the saids strengths and houses, raise fyre and all kynd of force and warlyke engynes that can be had, for winning and recovering thereof, and apprehending the saids Rebells and their Complices being thereintill; and if in pursute of the saids Rebells and their Complices, they resisting to be taken, or in assedging the saids strengths and houses, there shall happen to be fyre raising, mutilation, slaughter, destruction of corns or goods, or other inconveniences to follow, Wee, with advyce foresaid, Will and Grant, and for us and our Successors, Decern and Ordain, that the same shall not be imputed as cryme or offence to our said Commissioners, nor to the persons assisting them in the execution of this our commission; with power to our saids Commissioners, or such as shall be convocat be them, to bear, wear, and make use of hagbutts and pistolls in the execution of this our commission, notwithstanding of any law in the contrary. And farder, We do hereby take our saids Commissioners and such persons as shall assist them in the execution of this our commission, under our special protection and safeguard. And this our commission to continow and endure for the space of ane year after the date hereof; Provyded that our saids Commissioners give and account to us of their diligence and procedure herein betwixt and the first day of January next.

Our will is therefore, and We charge you strictly and command, that, incontinent thir our Letters seen, ye pass to the market crosses of — and other places needful, and thereat in our name and authority command and charge all and sundry our good and loving subjects, in their most substantial and warlyke manner, to ryse, concurr with, fortify and assist our saids Commissioners in the Execution of this our commission under all highest paynes and charges that after may follow. Given at, etc.

The above is copied from the Records of the Privy Council of Scotland, on the 22nd July, 1675.

APPENDIX XIV

OF THE SIVVENS

———⟶✦⟵———

A loathsome and very infectious disease of the venereal kind, called 'the sivvens', has long afflicted the inhabitants of the Highlands, and from thence some parts of the Lowlands in Scotland, even as far as the borders of England. Tradition says that it was introduced by the soldiers of Cromwell garrisoned in the Highlands. It occasions foul ulcers in the throat, mouth, and skin, and sometimes deep boils, which, when ulcerated, put on a cancerous appearance. It sometimes destroys the nose, or causes the teeth to drop out of their sockets; sometimes a fungus appears in various parts of the body, resembling a raspberry, in the Erse language called *sivven*. This disorder chiefly attacks children, and the lowest class of people, who communicate it to each other by their dirty habit of living. It is propagated not only by sleeping with, sucking, or saluting the infected, but even by using the same spoon, knife, glass, cup, pipe, cloth, etc. before they have been washed and cleaned. This, like other species of the venereal disease, is cured by mercury; and the only means of preventing so dreadful a malady is by the strictest attention to every circumstance of cleanliness.

APPENDIX XV

REPOSITORY OF ASHES, ETC.

—————⇒⊃●⊂⇐—————

Two miles north of Coupar Angus, near a small village called Coupargrange, on a gentle eminence, was lately discovered a repository of ashes of sacrifices, which our ancestors were wont to offer up, in honour of their deities. It is a large space, of a circular form, fenced with a wall on either side, and paved at bottom with flags. The walls are about 5 feet in height, and built with coarse stone. They form an outer and inner circle, distant from each other 9 feet. The diameter of the inner circle is 60 feet; and the area of it is of a piece with the circumjacent soil. But the space between the walls is filled with the ashes of wood, particularly oak, and with the bones of various species of animals. I could plainly distinguish the extremities of several bones of sheep; and was informed that teeth of oxen and sheep had been found. The top of the walls and ashes is near two feet below the surface of the field. The entry is from the north-west and about 10 or 12 feet in breadth. From it a pathway, 6 feet broad, and paved with small stones, leads eastward to a large freestone, standing erect between the walls, and reaching 5 feet above the pavement, supported by other stones at bottom. It is flat on the upper part, and 2 feet square. Another repository of the same kind and dimensions was some months ago discovered at the distance of 300 paces from the former. From the numbers of oak trees that have been digged out of the neighbouring grounds it would appear that this was anciently a grove.

Description of Craighall

Craighall, a gentleman's seat, two miles north of Blairgowrie. The situation of it is romantic beyond the power of description. It is placed in the midst of a deep glen, surrounded on all sides with wide-extended dreary heaths; where are still to be seen the rude monuments of thousands of our ancestors, who here fought and fell. The house itself stands on the brow of a vast precipice, at the foot of which the River Erecht runs deep and sullen along. It commands a prospect for the space of half a mile northward, the most pleasant and most awful that can be conceived. About twice the distance now mentioned, the river, that had for many miles glided along beautifully-sloping banks, covered with trees of various kinds planted by the hand of nature, feels itself confined in a narrow channel, by rocks of an astonishing height, through the chinks of which the oaks shoot forth and embrace each other from opposite sides, so as to exclude the kindly influences of the sun, and to occasion almost a total darkness below. The stream concealed from our view makes a tremendous noise, as if affrighted by the horrors of its confinement. The echoing of the caves on every side render the scene still more dreadful. At length the river is diverted in its course by a promontory of a great height, vulgarly called Lady Lindsay's Castle. Near the summit this rock is separated into two divisions, each of which rises to a considerable height, opposite one to another, and appear like walls hewn out of solid stone. In the intermediate space, fame says, this adventurous heroine fixed her residence. After a few more windings, the river directs its course to Craighall, having saluted several impending precipices as it rushed along; particularly one of enormous size and smooth in front, at the base of which, in a hollow cavern, is heard a continual dropping of water at regular intervals.

Reeky Linn

Reeky Linn, three miles north of Alyth, and two from the famous hill of Barry, is one of the largest and most beautiful cascades of water in Scotland. The River Islay here darts over a precipice 60 feet in height. Through the violence of the fall, the vapour is forced upward in the air like smoke, or, as the Scotch term it, 'reek', from whence it has its name. For a considerable space along the course of the river, the rocks on each side rise 100 feet, and the river itself in several places, has been found 30 fathoms deep.

Of Certain Antiquities in the Neighbourhood of Perth communicated by Mr Thomas Marshall

On the eastern banks of the Tay, about a mile and quarter above Perth, is a place called Rome, to which the Roman road, traced from Ardoch to Innerpeffery and Dupplin, points, and is continued on the other side of the Tay, in the manner that shall be presently observed.

At Rome is supposed to have been a bridge made of wood; for, in very dry season large beams of oak, placed up and down the stream, are seen. These were the foundations, fixed exactly in a spot where the tide never flows; and is only immediately out of its reach. This bridge was much frequented: strongly guarded; perhaps often attacked, for in the ground on the western side are frequently found urns.

About half a mile east of Rome, at a place called Sherifftown, are the vestiges of a fort but much defaced by agriculture The causeway or Roman road is continued from Rome, turns north at the fields of Sherifftown, and passes through a noted Roman camp at Grassywall.

In its course, it goes by a Druidical temple consisting of nine large stones, surrounding an area of twenty-five feet diameter, placed on a summit commanding a great view. The road then passes Berry-hile, and through the village of Dirigemoor, where it is very complete. From thence it is continued by the house of Byres, Stobhall, and Gallowmoor, near which are two other Druidical temples, of nine stones each. The road afterwards passes near East Hutton, and from thence runs to the banks of the Illa or Ilay. Its whole course from Rome to this place is nine miles, visible in many places, lest so near to the villages as the stones have been removed for building.

At the spot where the road touches on the Illa, a bridge is supposed once to have stood: the necessity is evident; for on the opposite side was a considerable Roman post. The Romans profited of the commodious accident of the two rivers, the Tay and the Illa, which unite at a certain distance below. These formed two secure fences: the Romans made a third by a wall of great thickness, defended again by a ditch both on the inside and the outside. These extend three miles in a line from the Tay to the Illa, leaving within a vast space, in form of a delta. Near the head of the bridge is a large mount exploratory, and probably once protected by a tower on a summit. On a line with this are two others; one about the middle of the area; the other nearer the Tay. These are round; but Mr Marshall doubts whether they are the work of art. But close to the junction of the Tay and Illa is a fourth, artificial, which is styled Carrackknow, or the 'boat hill', and seems designed to cover a landing-place. I must note that the wall is styled the Cleaving Wall. It merits further disquisition, as it will probably be found to be subservient to the uses of the camps at Hiethic and other places in the neighbourhood, which some native antiquary may have ample time to explore.

Not far from Blairgown is a vast rectangular enclosure, encompassed with a lofty rampart and a deep ditch; the length is an English mile and a quarter; the breadth half a mile. Three rising grounds run parallel to each other the whole length of it. Two rivulets and Lornty Water take likewise parallel courses at the bottom between these risings. In certain parts within are multitudes of tumuli. The same are observed in greater numbers on the south exterior sides, and some on the east. With them are mixed several circular buildings, with an entrance on one part. Of these little more than the foundations are left, which are six feet thick. Some include an area of forty-eight feet; but the greater number only twenty-seven. The ditch is on the inside; by which this inclosure appears to have been designed for a different purpose than a camp. It probably was an *oppidum* of the ancient inhabitants of the country: the circular foundations, the relics of their habitations, which, when entire, might have been of the form of the Danish Dunes, so frequent in the Hebrides; as the tumuli are certainly the places of interment.

APPENDIX XVI

AN ABRIDGED ACCOUNT OF THE EFFECTS OF THE LIGHTNING,

which broke on Melvill House in Fifeshire, the seat of the Earl of Leven, on the 27th October, 1733:

being extracts of a Letter from Mr Colin Maclaurin, Professor of Mathematics, at Edinburgh, to Sir Hans Sloan

————⟶∞⟵————

Sir,   Edinburgh, Dec. 3, 1733.

At the desire of the Earl of Leven, I went to Melvill House, and took a particular survey of the effects of the lightning, which broke upon the house on the 27th of October last. As some of them were very surprising, I thought it might be worth while to send you the following relation, not doubting of your thinking it worthy the attention of the Royal Society. The house stands about 20 miles north from Edinburgh, on the north side of a plain, which extends far from east to west and towards three miles broad, fronts to the eastward of south, and near it are great plantations, which almost surround it, and in some places extend to the distance of three miles.

We had fine weather in this country from the 9th to the 25th of October, when the mercury fell very considerably, and the weather changed. The 26th was a very bad day, having heavy rain, and in some places snow and hail. On the 27th, the wind was west, the morning cloudy, and we had thunder and lightning in many places very remote from Melvill.

It was on the 27th, betwixt six and seven in the morning, that the lightning broke upon the house, attended with loud peals of thunder. I could only meet with one man who was in the fields at that time, who was so much terrified that I could gather but little from him. He said the storm came from the north-east towards the south-west, felt it very hot, and a strong sulphurious smell as the lightning passed over him, saw it break, as he imagined, with all the colours of the rainbow among the trees near the house, filling all the country round with an extraordinary light.

The house is covered with lead, and has four chimneytops on each side of the cupola. Of the four on the east end of the house, one of them, in which was one of the kitchen vents, and where there only was fire at that time of the morning, was beat down level with the lead roof: some of the stones were carried above one 100 feet into the garden. The scates which covered the sloping part of the roof on the west end were broke off for a considerable space. There was one breach appearing in the outside of the wall, which we were sure pierced through it. This was in the attic storey, towards the west end of the north front. A stone was drove 20 feet from the breach upon a level, broke a splinter off a stone step of a back staircase, and rebounded 12 feet. That part of the lightning which produced the most considerable effects came down the chimney-head which is the most northerly of the four on the east of the cupola, where there is a vent of another chimney in the kitchen. In its descent it made several breaches in the vent; it is plain that two proceeded from it, because the smoke from that chimney proceeded from both: one of them in the great staircase, from which a stone of 32 lb heavy weight, was beat out, so as to strike the marble floor at 26 feet distance, measured on a level, and after that rebounded on the adjoining wall. All the windows were entire in this staircase; nor did any other effects appear there. The other breach in this vent was in the opposite direction, and pierced into a bedchamber on the east side, where was a noisome, sulphureous smell for a considerable time after, and a great heat. It made in the bedchamber a large breach in the plaister cornice, and carried plaister and lath quite across the room. Many panes of glass were broke in both windows. I apprehend there must have been another breach from the same vent with a south direction, because of the wonderful effect in the corner of the great dining room, where a small splinter of wood, about 13 inches long, and not heavier than two quills, was beat with so much force against the floor, as to leave a mark equal to the depth and length of its own body. On taking down the panel belonging to this bit of moulding, there was a crevice found; and this is very near opposite to the great breach in the staircase, only about 4 feet higher; but divided by the solid mid-wall of the house. In this dining-room many of the picture frames were scorched, and paintings defaced and spoiled, but the canvas entire. Panes broke here in all the windows; and the window-curtains so much singed as to blacken our hands, on rubbing the side next the windows. In the drawing-room at the east end of the great dining-room, the cornice plaister was broke in many places, and panes broke. The bedchamber next it was already mentioned.

In the drawing-room on the west end of this dining-room, the windows were entire, the shutters close, the doors locked, and no soot came down the chimney; yet there is a large deep splinter tore out of a strong oak panel. Before the panel stands a japaned cabinet, greatly tarnished at one end. A peir glass betwixt the windows, in a glass frame, has two breaches in the frame, and the rest entire. In the bedchamber next to this drawing-room nothing was observed. In the corner of the dressing-room belonging to this apartment, there stood a barometer, which was broke in pieces. The mercury disappeared, and we could find no remains of it. I must mention in this place, that his Lordship would not allow a servant to clean any part of this principal floor till I should see the effects of the lightning. In this dressing-room the panels were much broke and shattered; and of 30 panes 15 were broke.

Below these apartments, in the first floor, is the bedchamber where my Lord and Lady lay, being the centre room in the west front. Two panes of one of the windows were broke, and the glass found sticking on the curtains of the bed. Many pieces of the mouldings of the panels were broke and tore off. The mirror of a dressing-glass broke to pieces; the quicksilver melted off; but the frame entire, and stood in its place; it smelt of sulphur for some hours after. Two small pictures beat from one side of the room to the other. A peir glass betwixt the windows entire, but the panel below it beat out; and a chest of drawers before the panel received no harm. The frames of two pictures, which hung at the side of the bed, were much broke; and one of the panels fell out lately, when a servant was dusting it.

My Lord's account of what he observed is, that he was awaked with the noise of a great gust of wind; that, upon looking up, and drawing the curtain, he perceived the lightning enter the room with great brightness, appearing of a bluish colour. It made him cover his eyes for a moment; and on looking up, the light seemed to be abated, and the bluish colour had disappeared; at the same time he heard the thunder, which made an uncommon noise; he felt at the same time the bed and the whole room shake, much in the same manner one feels a horse when he rouses; and was like to be choked with the sulphur. When the maid opened the door, she was scarcely able to breath from the sulphureous steams which filled the room; happily the room was large, being 22 feet square, and 16 feet high.

In an adjoining bedchamber a gilded screen was quite spoiled, and though folded up, the gilding is burnt off every leaf.

In the parlour the gilding was melted off the leather hangings nearly of this form >; and in the window directly opposite, at the distance of 24 feet, in one of the panes, there is a rent exactly of the same form with the melted place of the gilding, which does not reach to either end of the pane, about 2 inches long, each line, the length of the lines of the melted hangings, being above 2 feet each. This room is the south front.

In the drawing-room on this floor there were many effects of the lightning. It has two windows to the south, and two to the east. A panel was loose, but kept from falling by a half-length picture which hung before it, upon a nail in the wall above the top of the panel: on removing the picture the panel came down, and a piece of stone in the wall fell in, which probably had beat the panel out of its place. On the outside of the house we discovered two breaches opposite to the panel; but they did not seem to go deep. Several other panels were beat out, and particularly one of 9 feet high, and 3 feet broad, was beat out so as to have the inside turned outward, and was found resting with the end upon a chair. Betwixt the two south windows stood a pier glass, which has a piece taken out of it of a semicircular figure, nearly 3 inches long and 2 inches deep, and no crack or flaw in the rest of the glass; the gilded frame much singed above and below: the piece was found broken, and one part had the quicksilver melted: above the glass we perceived a hole in the panel, as if burnt through. There was only one pane broke in this room, which was in one of the east windows. The hole in the pane was of the size and shape of a weaver's shuttle. A glass (like the other) which stood betwixt the two east windows was broke in pieces: the chimney-glass not touched. The vent of this room goes to the chimney-top, which was beat down.

In the adjoining bedchamber, there were several panels beat out, and some parts of them appeared to be burnt. A piece of stone was found in the floor, which was evidently beat from behind one of the panels, from a large hard stone, which appeared to be much shattered.

In the Attick storey is the billiard room, above the two east drawing-rooms: here the floor is tore up in two places, and large splinters are carried off from the middle of the planks. A picture was driven out of its frame towards the other side of the room. The leather hangings torn, and the gilding melted in many places. Of 40 panes in this room, 34 were broke.

Above the dressing-room where the barometer was broke, is an intersole, where there is a considerable breach in the inside of the wall, from which lime and rubbish were beat over the room. On a shelf several glasses were broke, as were some bottles, and a china bowl, four large bottles full of gunpowder on the same shelf escaped untouched.

In the under story, in the kitchen, one of the windows looking east was beat to pieces; one of the iron bands beat to the opposite wall; the other was driven out of a door, in a direction at right angles to the former; the plaster below the window torn up; and a lead cistern which stood near it received some damage.

No person in the house received any harm, except that my Lord complained much of his eyes for some days.

APPENDIX XVII

COPY OF KING MALCOLM'S CHARTER TO THE TOWN OF SAINT ANDREWS

MALCOLMUS, *Rex Scottorum, omnibus suis probis hominibus salutem. Sciatis me concessisse hac Carta confirmasse Burgensibus Episcopi Sancti Andreae omnes libertates et consuetudines, quas mei Burgenses communes habent per totam terram meam, et quibuscunque portibus applicuerint. Qua de re volo et firmiter super meum plenarium foris factum prohibeo ne quis ab illis aliquid injuste exigat. Testibus, Waltero Cancellario, Hugone de Moriville, Waltero filio Alani, Waltero de Lyndysay, Roberto Avenel. Apud Sanctum Andream.*

APPENDIX XVIII

COMPARISION OF MEASURES

———❧———

$\mathbf{T}$HE Roman measures, whereof Vespasian's *congius* was their standard, compared with the measures used at present (*anno* 1775) in Annandale, where, as in all other parts of Scotland, the Stirling jug, or Scots pint, continues to be the standard.

Roman measures	English cubic inches	Annandale measures	English cubic inches	Difference
3 Sextarius ½ Congius	$103.\frac{53}{100}$	1 Scots Pint or Jugg	$103.\frac{40}{100}$	$00.\frac{13}{100}$ Cub. Inch.
6 Ditto 1 Congius	$207.\frac{06}{}$	2 Pints 1 Annandale Cap	$206.\frac{8}{}$	$.\frac{26}{}$ D°. D°.
4 Congius 1 Urna	$828.\frac{26}{}$	4 Ditto Caps ½ Firlot	$827.\frac{23}{}$	$1.\frac{03}{}$ D°. D°.
8 Congius 1 Amphora	$1656.\frac{53}{}$	8 Ditto Caps 1 Firlot	$1654.\frac{46}{}$	$2.\frac{07}{}$ D°. D°.
3 Modius 1 Amphora	— —	4 Firlots 1 Boll —	$6617.\frac{85}{}$	— — —
20 Amphora 1 Culeus	$33130.\frac{72}{100}$	20 Firlots 5 Bolls —	$33089.\frac{28}{100}$	$41.\frac{44}{100} = 6.\frac{4}{10}$ Scots Gills

John Leslie

APPENDIX XIX

LIST OF SCOTS MANUFACTURES, WHICH ARE EXPORTED; AND WHERE MADE, ETC.

————◆————

CORDAGE, ropes, and all sorts of twine; Leith, Greenock, Port Glasgow.

Earthen, Delft, and stonewares; Prestonpans, Glasgow.

Green glass bottles; Alloa, Leith, etc.

Cast and wrought iron work; Carron.

The finest chimney grates, made and polished at Edinburgh, cutlery ware of different kinds.

Leather manufactures of all kinds; Edinburgh, Kilmarnock, etc.

Linens plain, diaper, damask, lawns and gauzes; printed, chequered, and striped linen, etc. Edinburgh, Glasgow, Paisley, etc.

Stuffs of silk only, silk and cotton, silk and worsted; silk gauzes, ribbons, etc., at same places.

Woollen manufactures, viz. Edinburgh, Haddington, Musselburgh;

781

friezes, serges, Stirling; tartans, blankets, Stirling, Kilmarnock, etc. Worsted, thread, silk stockings, Aberdeen; the finest worsted stockings from Schetland; stocking-pieces, Edinburgh, Stirling, Glasgow, etc. Blue bonnets, caps, etc. Kilmarnock; carpets, carpeting, etc. Edinburgh, Kilmarnock, etc.

Painted cloths and callicoes; many factories near Edinburgh.

Copper, tin and pewter manufactured; printing-types, greatly improved.

Cotton manufactures, fustians, etc.

Refined sugars; Edinburgh, Glasgow, Dundee, etc.

Hats nearly equal to the English; Edinburgh.

Thread and yarn of all kinds.

Thread lace; Dalkeith, Hamilton, Leith.

Paper, both for printing and writing.

Candles.

Soap, hard and soft; Leith.

Snuff.

Salt; Alloa, Kirkcaldy, Prestonpans, etc. Vitriol and sal-ammoniac.

Bricks and tiles.

Considerable breweries for exportation at Edinburgh and Glasgow.

Among the arts not essentially necessary for human life may be reckoned the curious manufactures of leather snuff-boxes. The artists Messrs. Wilson and Clerk have extended it even to musical instruments, and made a violin entirely out of leather, which, I hear, gives as melodious a sound as the best of wood: and that they have lately made a German flute of the same materials. Paper has been lately made of the weeds taken out of Duddingston Loch; I do not know with what success. Perhaps this was attempted after the example of the Germans, who have of late made a sort of nettle, and other vegetables.

Woollen Manufacture

Woollen manufactures are mentioned in 1424, in the second parliament of James I, where it is discouraged by a tax. 'Item, It is ordained, that of ilk poundes worth of woollen claith had out of the realme, the King fall have of the out-haver for custom twa shillinges.'

After this, several regulations were prescribed by legislature, and the wool prohibited from being sent into England. A law of James II in 1457, (perhaps for the purpose of peopling the boroughs, and civilizing his people, by drawing them out of the woods into civil society) prohibits any but burgesses to buy wool, 'to lit, nor mak claith, nor cut claith'. Yet, not to leave the majority of his people naked, adds, 'Bot it is to be otherwise said, gif ane man hes woll of his awin sheip'.

James VI, who (notwithstanding some of us English may think otherwise) had frequent intervals of wisdom, prohibited the wearing of any cloth in Scotland but what was the manufacture of the country.

I imagine, that in defiance of all the laws against smuggling of wool out of the kingdom, it was carried to Flanders. Old Hackluyt mentions it among the few exports of Scotland:

> *Moreover of Scotland the commodities*
> *Are felles, hides, and of wooll the fleese.*
> *And all these must passe by us away*
> *Into Flanders by England, sooth to say,*
> *And all her woolle was draped for to sell*
> *In the townes of Poperinge and Bell.*[1]

At length a woollen manufacture arose in some degree. There was an exportation of it into Holland till 1720: it was a coarse kind, such as is made in the Highlands: much of it was sold to Glasgow, and sent into America, for blankets for the Indians. It is in Scotland a clothing for the country people, and is worth about 10d or 12d a yard. The only broad cloth worth mentioning is that made at Paul's work in Edinburgh, which is brought to great perfection.

Linen Manufacture

I cannot ascertain the time when the linen manufactures arose. There could not be a great call for the commodity, a century and

---

[1] Hollinshead mentions these towns, p. 614.

half ago, when people of fashion scarcely changed their shirts above once the week in England. But, thanks to the luxury, or rather the neatness, of the times, this article has become a most national advantage. The following table will show the flourishing state of it in this kingdom; and its great advance in forty three years. At the foot of it is an account of the imports of flax into England and Scotland; and of the exports of coal from the last.

Accompt. of Linen Cloth stamped in Scotland, from 1st Nov. 1727 to 1st Nov. 1728; and from 1st Nov. 1770 to 1st Nov. 1771										
Shires	Yards	Value			Price per yard at a medium	Yards	Value			Price per yard at a medium
Aberdeen	41,040 $^2/_8$	1,539	0	$2^3/_{12}$		198,177	14,716	1	$4^3/_4$	1 $5^9/_{12}$
Air	26,699 $^4/_8$	2,086	17	2		193,413	10,530	1	8	1 1
Argyle	432	32	8	0						
Banff	101,618	3,810	13	6		54, 385	3,132	9	0	1 $1^{10}/$
Berwick	9,293	365	16	1		56,129	5,645	4	$5^1/_2$	1 $7^{10}/$
Bute										
Caithness										
Clackmannan	2,895	240	10	2						
Cromarty						5,591	187	7	0	0 8
Dumbarton	66,027	2,356	8	6		173,892	11,618	17	$1^1/_2$	1 4
Dumfries	3,002	152	13	8		43,167	2,134	8	$3^1/_2$	0 11^{10}
Edinburgh	747	198	17	0		214,834	19,487	12	0	1 $9^2/$
Elgin	1,254	47	12	6		63, 676	2,344	8	$4^1/_2$	0 $8^{11}/$
Fyffe	361,985 $^6/_8$	30,175	10	$9^6/$		1,885,622	72,138	3	$2^1/_2$	0 $9^2/$
Forfar	595,821 $^4/_8$	14,733	13	$0^6/$		5,700,851$^1/_2$	147,456	19	3	0 $6^2/$
Hadinton	363	18	3	0		111,835	10,838	6	$11^1/_2$	1 $11^3/$
Inverness	10,696	401	2	0		223,798	6,425	5	2	0 $6^{10}/$
Kincardine	27,885 $^6/_8$	1,045	14	$3^9/$		118, 628	4,030	3	2	0 $8^6/$
Kinross	53,921	2,906	19	0		79,450	2,852	3	$1^1/_2$	0 $8^7/$
Kirkcudbright						1,302	114	19	10	1 $9^2/$
Lanerk	272,658 $^6/_8$	9,968	0	3		2,019,782	172,347	12	9	1 $8^5/$
Linlithgow	6,353	476	9	6		2,204	188	4	1	1 $8^5/$
Nairne						14,734	852	12	8	1 $1^{10}/$
Orkney						21,088	2,257	12	5	1 $9^3/$
Peebles										
Perth	477,743 $^6/_8$	23,955	0	$4^6/$		1,674,717	66,153	6	3	0 $9^5/$
Renfrew	85,527 $^2/_8$	6,852	14	9		684,557	70,177	9	6	2 $0^7/$
Ross	10,844	402	6	6		10,145	410	9	4	0 $9^7/$
Roxburgh	15,822 $^6/_8$	914	16	$8^6/$		55,625	3,379	10	$11^1/_2$	1 $2^6/$
Selkirk	8,732 $^4/_8$	436	12	6						
Stirling	2,548 $^4/_8$	191	2	9		47,956	2,278	15	0	0 $11^4/$
Sutherland										
Wigton	67	3	7	0		16,996	691	0	5	0 $9^9/_{12}$
Total	2,183,978	103,312	9	3	0 $11^4/_{12}$	13,672,548$^1/_2$	632,389	3	$5^1/_4$	

An Account of the Total Quantities of Flax, Hemp, Flax-seed, and Linen yarn, imported in England and Scotland, from 5th January 1764 to 5th Ditto 1772:

together with

The Total Quantities of Coals exported from Scotland to Foreign Parts, from 5th January 1765 to 5th January 1772.

	From 5th January 1764 to 5th January 1772						
	Flax Rough			Hemp Rough			Linseed	Yarn Linen Raw
	Cwts.	qrs.	lb.	Cwts.	qrs.	lb.	Bushels	lb.
Total of Flax, etc., imported in England	1,130,719	0	3	2,639,236	2	22	1,792,465$\frac{1}{2}$	55,006,029
Total of Flax, etc., imported in Scotland	533,749	3	11	112,980	3	4	455,243$\frac{1}{4}$	954,972$\frac{1}{4}$

	From 5th January 1765 to 5th January 1772		
	Great Coals	Great Coals	Pitforan Coals Duty Free
	Tons Cwts qrs	Chalders. Bush.	Chalders
Total of Coals exported from Scotland	86.050 14 0	27.797 7$\frac{1}{4}$	4681

APPENDIX XX

ITINERARY

Part One

England

	Miles
Downing to	
Lancaster	95
Hess Bank	4
Cartmel sands	11
Cartmel	3
Ulverstone	6
Whitrig iron-mines, and back to Ulverston	8
Hawkshead	16
Graithwaite	5
Boulness	4
Ambleside	7
Keswick 16, Ormathwaite 2	18
Cockermouth (by Bridekirk)	15
Whitehaven	13
Workington	8
Maryport	7
Allanby	5
Wigton	11
Carlile	10
Warwick, Corbie, and back to Carlile	12
Netherby	12

Scotland

Langholme, and back to Netherby	
Annan	14
Ruthwel, and back to Annan	12
Springkeld	7
Burnswork Hill	4
Hoddam 3, Murraythwaite I	4
Comlongan	4
Caerlaveroc	6
Dumfries	8
Lincluden, and back to Dumfries	3
Drumlanrig	
Morton Castle 4, Durisdeer 2, Drumlanrig 3	9
Leadhills	13
Douglas	12
Lanerk	8
Hamilton	14
Glasgow	12
Greenock, and back to Glasgow	44
Cruikston Castle	4
Paisley 2, Renfrew 2, Glasgow 5	9
Drummond	17
Loch Lomond	4
Buchannan	3
Glasgow	20
Greenock, by land	21
Mount Stuart, in the isle of Bute	16
Cilchattan Hill	5
Kingarth manse 2, Rothesay 5	7
St. Ninian's Point	$3^{1}/_{2}$
Inchmarnoc	$1^{1}/_{2}$
Loch Tarbat	12
Loch Ranza	14
Brodic Castle	12
Fin MacCoul's cave, and back to Brodic	22
Kirkmichel, Dunsion, and again to Brodic	10

Lamlash isle	6
Crag of Ailsa	24
Campbeltown	22
Kilkerran caves, and back	6
Bar	12
Gigha isle	6
Small isles of Jura	15
Ardfin	4
Paps of Jura	10
Port Freebairn, in the isle of Ilay	7
Brorarag	3
Killarow	9
Sunderland	9
Sanneg cove, and back to Sunderland	10
Port Freebairn	18
Oransay	15
Killoran, in Colonsay	9
Port Olamsay	1
Iona	18
Cannay	63
Loch Sgriorsart, in Rum	12
Point of Slate, in Skie	18
Sconser	24
Talyskir	10
Loch Bracadale	18
Cross the loch	4
Dunvegan	4
Kingsburgh	6
Duntuilm	12
Loch Broom	15
Little Loch Broom	51
Dundonnel	15
Loch Maree, the east end	18
Loch Maree, the west end	18
Polewe 1, Gairloch, 6	7
MacKinnon's Castle	42
Glenbeg, and back to Glenelg	6

Loch Iurn, extremity of	24
Arnisdale	10
Isle Oransay	12
Ardnamurchan Point	40
Tobirmoire bay, in Mull	9
Aros	8
Castle Duart	12
Dunstaffage	10
Beregonium	4
Ardmuchnage	2
Dunstaffage	6
Lismore	4
Armadie	12
Circuit round Suil, etc.	15

Part Two

Scotland

	Miles
Armady to Port Sonnachan	18
Inveraray	11
Cladich	10
Tiendrum	12
Killin	20
Taymouth	16
Logierait	12
Blair	12
Dunkeld	20
Delvin	7
Perth	15
Dupplin	5
Innerpeffery	10
Crief, by Fintillick	5
Comerie	6
To Loch Earn, and 3 miles along its side	9
Back to Fintillick	18
Castle Drummond	1
Kaymes Castle	4
Ardoch	3
By Tullibardine to Dupplin	20
Tibbimoor, Huntingtower, and again to Dupplin	10
Perth	5
Errol	10
Dundee	15
Panmure	10
Aberbrothic	7
Ferriden, Montrose	12
North Bridge	5
Lawrencekirk	6

Stonehive	15
Urie	2
Fettercairn	18
Catterthun	9
Brechin	3
Careston	5
Forfar	6
Glames	5
Belmont	6
Dunsinane	10
Perth	7
Dupplin, by the Sterling road	3
Earnbridge	4
Abernethy	4
Falkland	8
Melville	4
St Andrew's	14
Levin	15
Kirkaldie	9
By Kinghorn to Aberdour	8
Dunferline	8
Limekilns near Broomhall	4
Culross	4
Clackmannan	4
Alloa	1
Sterling	7
Falkirk	11
Linlithgow	8
Kirkliston	8
Edinburgh	8
Hawthornden, Roslin, and back to Edinburgh	14
Dalkeith, and again to Edinburgh	14
Cranston	10
Crichton and Borthwick Castle, and back to Cranston	10
Blackshields	4
Lauder	11
Galashields	10

Melros	3
Dryburgh	3
Kelso	10

England

Carham	5
Palinsburne	8
Wooler	8
Woolerhaugh Head	2
Chillingham Castle	3
Percy's Cross	5
Whittingham	5
Halfway House	4
Rothbury	5
Cambo	11
Hexham	18
Corbridge	4
Newcastle	17
Durham	15
Bishops Aukland	10
Peirce Bridge	12
Richmond	10
Wensley	10
Kettlewell	16
Skipton	18
Keighly	10
Halifax	12
Alkrington	6
Manchester	6
Barton Bridge	5
Warrington	15
Chester	20
Downing	22

.

.